PRAISE FOR CATHY GLASS

'Poignant and revealing ... real-life stories such as these have helped to move and inspire a generation'   *Sunday Mirror*

'A true tale of hope'   *OK!* Magazine

'Heartbreaking'   *Mirror*

'A life-affirming read ... that proves sometimes a little hope is all you need'   *Heat* Magazine

'A hugely touching and emotional true tale'   *Star* Magazine

'Foster carers rarely get the praise they deserve, but Cathy Glass's book should change all that'   *First* Magazine

'Cannot fail to move those who read it'   *Adoption-net*

'Once again, Cathy Glass has blown me away with a poignant story'   The Writing Garnet, book blogger

'Brilliant book. I'd expect nothing less from Cathy ... I cried, of course'   Goodreads review

'... gripping page-turner from start to finish ... emotive and heart-wrenching ...'   Kate Hall, book blogger

Finding Stevie

THE MILLION COPY BESTSELLING AUTHOR

CATHY GLASS

Finding Stevie

A dark secret. A child in crisis

HARPER
element

Certain details in this story, including names, places and dates, have been changed to protect the family's privacy.

HarperElement
An imprint of HarperCollins*Publishers*
1 London Bridge Street
London SE1 9GF

www.harpercollins.co.uk

First published by HarperElement 2019

7 9 10 8 6

© Cathy Glass 2019

Cathy Glass asserts the moral right to be
identified as the author of this work

A catalogue record of this book is
available from the British Library

ISBN 978-0-00-832429-2

Printed and bound in Great Britain by
CPI Group (UK) Ltd, Croydon

MIX
Paper from
responsible sources
FSC™ C007454

This book is produced from independently certified FSC paper
to ensure responsible forest management.

For more information visit: www.harpercollins.co.uk/green

ACKNOWLEDGEMENTS

A big thank you to my family; my editors, Carolyn and Holly; my literary agent, Andrew; my UK publishers HarperCollins, and my overseas publishers who are now too numerous to list by name. Last, but definitely not least, a big thank you to my readers for your unfailing support and kind words. They are much appreciated.

CHAPTER ONE

STRUGGLING TO COPE

'… and he's gender-fluid,' Edith continued. 'So together with all his behavioural problems his grandparents don't feel they can look after him any longer.'

'No, quite, I can see that's rather a lot to cope with,' I sympathised. 'His grandparents must be stretched to the limit, looking after his younger brother and sister too.'

'So you'll take him?' Edith asked. She was my supervising social worker, employed by the local authority to supervise and support their foster carers, of which I was one. She'd just been telling me about Steven, who liked to be known as Stevie. Aged fourteen, he needed a foster home as – according to his grandparents – he was confrontational, moody, withdrawn, stayed out late, didn't do as they told him, wasn't going to school and was generally making their lives a complete misery.

'So I'll tell his social worker you'll take him,' Edith said, slightly impatient at my hesitation.

'Yes, but I have a question.'

'Go on.'

'What does gender-fluid mean?' I asked reluctantly, not wanting to appear ignorant and make a fool of myself. 'Is he gay?'

1

'Not sure,' she said. 'I think it's mainly to do with whether he is male or female, but his social worker will be able to tell you more. It's not a problem for you, is it?'

'No.'

'Good. I'll tell his social worker to phone you. They want to move Stevie as quickly as possible.'

'How quickly?'

'Within the next few days.'

'All right.'

'And you had a good Christmas?' Edith asked. It was 27 December and the first day back at work for many.

'Yes, thank you, and you?'

'Busy.'

We said goodbye and I replaced the handset on its base in the hall. Our Christmas had been a good one, although it was the first since my father had passed away and, as anyone who has lost a loved one knows, the first Christmas and their birthday can be rather emotional. But my family and I had enjoyed ourselves for Dad's sake; a child at heart, he always loved Christmas.

'Was that Edith?' Paula, my youngest daughter, aged nineteen, asked as I returned to the living room. I'd left the room to take the call in the hall so I wouldn't disturb her. We'd been watching a box set of a detective series, although she'd paused it anyway.

'Yes, it was,' I said, returning to sit next to her on the sofa. 'The social services are bringing a fourteen-year-old boy into care as soon as they can and would like him to come here.' She nodded. 'Paula, do you know what gender-fluid means?' At her age and attending college, I thought she might.

She shrugged. 'Not really. I've heard of it, but I don't really know exactly what it means.'

'Me neither. You continue watching the programme while I check online.'

'It's OK, I'll wait for you,' she said, and kept the programme on pause.

I picked up my mobile phone and entered *gender-fluid* into the search engine. As a foster carer I attended regular training, but so far the training on sexual matters had centred around keeping children in care safe – paedophiles, STDs (sexually transmitted diseases), birth control and so on. Gender-fluidity hadn't been covered, but I knew how important it was to keep abreast of such matters, as well as acquiring the correct terminology. In the twenty-five years I'd been fostering, children in care had variously been known as FC (foster child), CiC (child in care), LAC (looked-after child), and the foster parents as Mum and Dad, foster mum and dad, and foster carers. This was the tip of the iceberg; beneath that lay a mass of acronyms ready to catch out any unsuspecting foster carer: SSW (supervising social worker), CPP (child-protection plan), CIN (child in need) and IEP (individual education plan), to name a few.

'Gender-fluid', I read out from my phone, 'is someone who does not see themselves as having a fixed gender – that is, male or female.'

'Oh,' said Paula.

I read on: 'It's not about the sex they were born, but about how they see themselves. A gender-fluid person may identify as male or female or a combination of both. Their gender can vary with their circumstance. Gender-fluid people may be known as multigender, non-binary or transgender.' See what I mean about terminology! 'They may also be known as genderqueer.'

'That doesn't sound a very nice term,' Paula said, and I agreed. But at least I now had an understanding of what gender-fluid meant, which was just as well, for as Paula pressed play for us to continue watching the television series the landline phone rang again. Paula sighed and pressed pause as I reached over to answer the handset in the living room.

'Is that Cathy Glass?' a female voice asked.

'Yes, speaking.'

'I'm Verity Meldrew, Stevie's social worker. I believe Edith has spoken to you about Stevie and you've agreed to take him?'

'Yes.'

'Good. I'll give you some background information then.'

'That would be helpful.'

'The social services have been involved with the family since Steven – or rather Stevie – was born. His mother has a long history of alcohol and drug dependency and has been diagnosed with alcohol psychosis, resulting in her having hallucinations and delusions. She has spent time in a psychiatric unit, but at present is in prison. She has no face-to-face contact with Stevie, although in the past they may have been in contact through social media. As far as we are aware Stevie has no contact with his father. Stevie's maternal grandparents have brought him up and are working with us, so he will be coming into care under a Section 20.' This is also known as 'accommodated' and means that no court order is required, as the parents or guardians of the child (in this case the grandparents) have agreed to the child going into care voluntarily.

'Stevie's grandparents have guardianship of the two younger siblings,' Verity continued. 'There are no issues with their care, so they will be staying with them. However, the grandparents have been under huge pressure and have reached the point where they feel they can no longer cope with Stevie's challenging behaviour. It came to a head when they received notice threatening court action in respect of Stevie not attending school.'

'I see. Do we know why he hasn't been going to school?' I asked.

'He says it's not relevant to him. He's a nice kid but is struggling with a number of issues. He's got into trouble at school, although the school has been supportive, especially in respect of his gender identity. He sees himself as gender-fluid – you know what that means?'

'Yes,' I was able to say.

'Good. His grandparents can't deal with it and feel he is a bad influence on his younger siblings.'

'How old are they?'

'Six and eight. I think Stevie's been winding up his grandparents, but I'm sure he'll settle once he's in care.' How often had I heard that? I thought. 'I'd like to bring him for a pre-placement visit, and his grandparents would like to meet you before the move too, but they will need to arrange child care for the younger two.'

'OK. When were you thinking of?'

'I'll bring Stevie for a pre-placement visit tomorrow, the twenty-eighth, then set up a meeting with the grandparents for the following morning, the twenty-ninth, and move him in the afternoon'

'That's fine with me,' I said, making a mental note of the arrangements.

'I'll be in touch with the times and to confirm the dates.'

'Thank you.' We said goodbye and Paula and I continued watching the detective series. However, my thoughts were not on the programme but with Stevie. Many young people his age are moody, withdrawn and confrontational at times –

it's part of the teenage years – but what was worrying was that he wasn't attending school. Not only because he was missing out on an important part of his education, but school offers socialisation – a place to meet and make friends. Children who are not in school can become very isolated. It also leaves them unoccupied for large parts of the day. I'd fostered young people before who weren't in school and had found there were only so many activities I could provide at home before they grew bored and went off, hanging around the streets with the potential for getting up to all sorts of mischief. School gives structure to the day. Edith had said that Stevie's school was being supportive, so I hoped it wouldn't be long before I had him attending school again. Although I sympathised with his grandparents, as I knew from experience just how difficult it was to persuade a fourteen-year-old out of bed and into school.

A short while later a key went in the front door and Lucy, my twenty-one-year-old daughter, let herself in. She'd been visiting a friend. 'Hi!' she called from the hall, kicking off her shoes.

'We're in here!' I returned.

Sammy, our (rescue) cat, raised his head at the sound of her voice and then returned to sleep.

'You're never watching daytime television, surely!' Lucy exclaimed with a laugh as she came into the living room. I didn't normally watch daytime television and discouraged others from doing so, feeling they could be engaged in a more productive activity, but it was the Christmas holidays.

'It's catch-up,' Paula said.

'Are you going to join us?' I asked Lucy.

'No. I've got a few things to sort out ready for work tomorrow.'

'All right, love. Edith phoned while you were out about a fourteen-year-old lad who will very likely be coming to stay,' I told her. 'She's planning on bringing him for a visit tomorrow and then moving him the day after.'

'OK, cool. See you guys later then.' Lucy disappeared off to her room.

Lucy had come to me as a foster child nearly ten years before and I'd adopted her. She couldn't be more loved and cherished, and was as easy with fostering as Paula and my son Adrian were. Lucy had studied child care and was now working in a local nursery, while Adrian, twenty-three, had returned home to live after completing his degree. He was now working at his temporary job in a supermarket until he found a trainee position in a firm of accountants. As a single parent (my husband had left when the children were little), juggling fostering and part-time clerical work (mainly from home), I was kept busy – pleasantly so – and I felt very happy with the life I'd been given.

Paula and I had just finished the episode in the series we were watching when the phone rang again. She pressed pause and I picked up the handset in the living room.

'Cathy, it's Verity, getting back to you.'

'Hello.'

'Slight change of plan. I've spoken to Stevie's gran and she's asked me to explain to him why he has to move. She's worried he might kick off and blame her if she tells him. So I'll visit them tomorrow morning and then bring Stevie to you straight after for a short visit. We should arrive around one o'clock. I've set up a meeting at eleven o'clock for the following morning when you will be able to meet his grandparents. It's here at the council offices. Stevie will be coming, and a friend of the gran's will be looking after the younger two siblings. If all goes to plan, Stevie will go home with his grandparents after the meeting and then I'll move him to you that afternoon. We should arrive around three o'clock, but I'll phone you before we set off.'

'Thank you,' I said, scribbling the dates and times on a notepad by the phone. 'That works for me.'

'See you tomorrow then.'

'Yes. Goodbye.'

I told Paula and then Lucy the arrangements, and Adrian when he came home, so we were all prepared. Fostering involves the whole family, so it's important everyone knows what is going on. I should have realised from twenty-five years of fostering that situations in social care can and do change quickly. The following afternoon Stevie didn't arrive.

CHAPTER TWO

DIFFICULT MEETING

The house was tidy, Stevie's room was ready, so all we needed was Stevie and his social worker, Verity. Adrian and Lucy were both at work, so there was just Paula, me and Sammy, our cat, at home. I hadn't been expecting Verity to arrive with Stevie at exactly 1 p.m., but when it got to 1.30 I started to feel something might be amiss. I'd kept the afternoon free, so it wasn't as though I had an appointment to go to, but it was unsettling just waiting. Even after years of fostering, I'm still a little anxious before meeting a new child, especially if they are older, hoping they will like me and that I will be able to help them. I didn't have Verity's mobile number so at 1.45, when there was still no sign of her and Stevie, I telephoned her office.

'She's out seeing a client,' a colleague told me.

'Yes, that would be Stevie Jones,' I said. 'She was going to bring him to me for a pre-placement visit at one o'clock. I'm Cathy Glass, the foster carer he's going to be living with.'

'Oh, OK. She must have got held up.'

'Would it be possible for you to phone her and ask what time she'll be coming, please?' I knew she wouldn't give out a social worker's telephone number without her permission.

'Yes, I can, but if she's with a client her phone will be on voicemail. I'll leave a message asking her to phone you.'

'Thank you.'

Half an hour later the landline rang and it was Verity. 'Stevie is missing and hasn't been since ten o'clock this morning.'

'Oh dear, I see.'

'There was an incident at home,' Verity explained. 'Stevie was planning on going out for the day and his gran asked him to stay in, as I was coming to see him. He got angry and said he didn't want to see his effing social worker and stormed off out. Gran hasn't seen him since.'

'That's worrying.'

'Yes. Gran thinks he'll be back before long – when he's hungry – but I can't wait here indefinitely. I've told her I'll give it another fifteen minutes and then we'll have to reschedule.'

'All right, you'll let me know?'

'Yes, of course.'

While I was concerned that Stevie had disappeared, he wasn't my responsibility yet, and his gran seemed to think he'd return soon. If a young person regularly runs away, as Stevie had been doing, there often isn't the same sense of urgency as there would be if a child or young person with no history of running away suddenly went missing. Complacency can be dangerous, as it might be the one time they need help. Foster carers follow a set procedure if a child or young person in their care goes missing, which includes informing the social services and the police.

By three o'clock when I'd heard nothing further from Verity I guessed they wouldn't be coming, and Paula and I continued our day as normal. Just after four o'clock Edith phoned asking how Stevie's visit had gone. I explained what had happened and that I was waiting to hear from Verity with the new arrangements. She wished me luck and we said goodbye. Edith had been my supervising social worker (SSW) for nearly a year and was different from my previous SSW, Jill, whom I'd worked with for many years. She'd retired when the Independent Fostering Agency (IFA) she worked for had closed its local office, so I'd begun fostering for the local authority (LA). Jill was always very well informed and would offer hands-on support if necessary, whereas Edith tended to concentrate on the administrative side of her role, but we jogged along together OK.

Adrian and Lucy came home from work expecting to hear how Stevie's visit had gone, and I explained over dinner that he hadn't arrived and why, then listened to their news. 'I hope you haven't been watching television all day,' Lucy teased me.

'As if!'

I went to bed that night assuming the meeting the following morning at 11 a.m., when I was to meet Stevie and his grandparents, wouldn't be going ahead. However, just after 9 a.m. Verity phoned and said that Stevie had returned home late the previous evening and she'd see me at the meeting as planned at the council offices.

'OK,' I said, gulping down the last of my coffee. 'What about the pre-placement visit?'

'We'll have to skip that, there isn't time. After the meeting I'll go back with Stevie and his grandparents and then bring Stevie to you. I've asked his gran to pack a bag ready for him.'

'So Stevie knows he's coming to live with us?'

'Yes. When he finally returned home late last night his grandfather, Fred, was angry he'd caused them so much worry and blurted it out. It wasn't the best way to tell him, but at least he knows.'

'And Stevie's OK with it?'

'Apparently. His gran told him he'll get more pocket money with you and he can visit them whenever he likes, but we'll have to look at contact arrangements.'

'Thank you.' Verity knew as I did that while it was important Stevie had regular contact with his grandparents and siblings, it would stop him from settling with me if he felt he could pop home whenever he wished. It would also be difficult to keep an eye on him and know where he was.

Although I had showered, I was dressed casually, and I quickly changed into a smarter outfit – navy trousers and pale blue jersey. I was going to meet Stevie, his grandparents and Verity for the first time, so I wanted to create a good impression. As a foster carer I viewed myself as a professional and felt it was appropriate to dress smartly for all meetings. I also put a notepad and pen into my bag together with a small photograph album that showed pictures of my house, my family and me, which I would show to Stevie and his grandparents. It would mean that it wasn't all strange for Stevie when he arrived and would hopefully reassure his grandparents.

Paula was up but in her dressing gown, as college didn't start again until the following week, so I told her where I was going and that I'd see her later.

I arrived at the council offices with ten minutes to spare and parked in a side road. I signed in at reception, hung the security pass around my neck and made my way up to the room where the meeting was to be held. I wasn't expecting to see Edith at the meeting. When I'd worked for Homefinders – the IFA I'd fostered for – Jill had attended most meetings with me, but the local authority's supervising social workers didn't.

The room was empty and I sat in one of the chairs arranged around the table in the centre, and took out my notepad, pen and photograph album, hoping I'd been given the right room number. It was exactly eleven o'clock. I'd wait five minutes, then go down to reception and check. The time ticked by and I could hear movement in the corridor outside. Presently a woman came in carrying a large file and a mobile phone. 'Cathy Glass, the foster carer?' she asked.

'Yes, that's me.' I smiled.

'I'm Verity Meldrew, Stevie's social worker. Nice to meet you.'

'You too.' She sat opposite me.

'Stevie and his grandparents are on their way,' she said.

'Good.'

Of average height and build, I guessed Verity was in her late thirties. Her manner came across as confident but approachable. 'How are you? All set to go?' she asked.

'Yes, indeed. My family and I are looking forward to meeting Stevie.' Although in truth I was feeling anxious again and the delay wasn't helping.

'Sorry about yesterday,' she said.

'At least Stevie returned home. Does he run off like that often?'

'He has been doing recently,' she said, and was about to add more when her mobile phone started ringing. 'Sorry, I need to take this call.' She stood and left the room.

I was left gazing around and twiddling my pen as her muted voice floated in from outside. A few minutes later it stopped and the door opened. Verity came in followed by an elderly couple and a young lad I took to be Stevie. Tall for his age, slim, with styled blond hair flopping over his forehead, he was clearly dressed to impress. Straight-legged, pink-sheen jeans, with a white jersey under a zip-up black leather jacket. I stood and went over to greet them.

'This is the foster carer, Cathy Glass,' Verity said, introducing me.

Stevie threw me a small nod and rearranged his fringe, while his grandmother said hello and his grandfather shook my hand. First meetings between the child's family and the foster carer are always a little difficult and I sensed their reservations. Although I had the best intentions, I was, after all, usurping their role by looking after their grandchild.

'Mr and Mrs Jones,' Verity added.

'Peggy and Fred,' his grandfather said, and I smiled.

We settled around the table. Verity moved to the end so the three of them could sit together, opposite me, but Stevie sat at the far end of the table, putting as much space as possible between him and his grandparents. Despite this and his flamboyant clothes suggesting confidence, I could see he was nervous. 'It's good to meet you,' I said to him.

He gave a small smile and flicked back his fringe. I saw then he was wearing eye make-up – not a lot, just mascara and eyeliner.

'So,' Verity began, 'this is a short meeting to give us a chance to get to know each other. I'll make a few notes as we go, but I won't produce minutes. Let's start by introducing ourselves.' Fred sighed, but all social services meetings start with the formality of introductions, even if those present know each other. 'I'm Verity Meldrew, Stevie's social worker,' she said, then looked to Peggy sitting on her left.

'I'm Peggy Jones, Steven's grandma, and I apologise for the state he's in. I told him to change his clothes and take off that make-up, but he refused.' Stevie responded with a dismissive, overstated shrug.

'Cheeky bugger!' his grandfather fumed. It was instantly clear how easily Stevie could wind up his grandparents.

Verity threw me a glance, then said, 'Let's continue with the introductions. Mr Jones, you're next.'

He huffed and said, 'Fred Jones. And unlike my wife I'm not apologising for the state of him. We brought him up proper, as best we could, and at our age it hasn't been easy.'

'Thank you,' Verity said, then looked to Stevie to introduce himself. My heart went out to him; although it was his choice to sit at the far end of the table, he now looked very alone. I felt I wanted to reach out and give him a hug, as big as he was.

'*Stevie* Jones,' he said, emphasising 'Stevie' as he wanted to be known, rather than Steven as his grandmother had called him. 'It's not my fault. They won't accept me for who I am.'

Verity smiled at him reassuringly and then looked to me to introduce myself.

'Cathy Glass, foster carer,' I said.

'Thank you,' Verity said, making a note of those present. 'Cathy, would you like to start by telling Stevie and his grandparents a bit about you and your family?'

'Certainly.' I'd done this many times before; it's standard at meetings like this. Looking at Stevie and his grandparents as I spoke, I told them I was a single parent and had been fostering for twenty-five years; that I had three adult children at home. I said Adrian and Lucy worked, while Paula was at a local college. I described an average day and what we liked to do in our leisure time in the evenings and at weekends. I finished by passing them the photograph album to look at. I'd written a caption beneath each picture, so they were self-explanatory. Verity thanked me and we were silent as first Peggy and Fred looked at the album and then passed it to Stevie. I couldn't tell from his expression what he thought.

'What do you think?' Verity asked him as he closed the album and pushed it across the table to me.

'I'll have my own room then?' he asked.

'Yes,' Verity confirmed.

'There's a photo in here,' I said, opening the album. 'I've written your room beneath it.' I showed him.

He nodded and seemed pleased.

'He has to share with Liam, his younger brother, at home,' Peggy said. 'Kiri, his sister, needs her own room.'

'I have a question,' Fred said. 'Are you going to stop him dressing like a tart? It's embarrassing.'

So was his comment, although of course Peggy and Fred were of a different generation and probably didn't realise that such comments were unacceptable. The short answer was no, I wouldn't be stopping him from dressing as he wished in the evenings and weekends. I looked at Stevie and said, 'I assume you wear your school uniform for school?'

'He doesn't go to school,' Peggy said.

'Cathy will be liaising with the school to help Stevie return,' Verity said.

'I'll give you a bloody medal if you succeed!' Fred said. 'We've both tried and got nowhere.'

'He has a mentor,' Peggy said. 'That's who we see.'

'And a fat lot of good she is!' Fred said. 'Lots of talk, but is she willing to come round and get him out of bed? No!'

I looked at Stevie, who'd lost some of his previous nervousness and was now looking rather smug at having antagonised his grandfather. 'Is there a reason you haven't been going to school?' I asked him.

Tilting his head to one side, he gave an exaggerated shrug. 'It doesn't suit me,' he said.

'Doesn't suit you!' Fred thundered. 'You cheeky bugger! It didn't suit us to bring up you lot after we'd brought up our own kids, but we got on with it so you'd all have a proper home.'

'And you've done a good job,' Verity said pacifyingly.

Fred scoffed, while Stevie provokingly took a small compact from his jacket pocket and checked his face in the mirror.

'Look at him!' Fred fumed.

Clearly Stevie knew exactly which buttons to press to annoy his grandparents perfectly!

The only positive part of the meeting, I thought as I drove home, was the photograph album. Stevie and his grandparents had asked to look through it a second time, and his gran said she was less worried now she knew he would be living in a nice house and had met me, as she'd heard some bad things about foster carers not treating kids right. Verity reassured her that I was well thought of and gave the children I looked after a high standard of care. Stevie didn't say much other than asking how much pocket money he would be getting.

'You won't get any if you don't go to school,' Fred had seethed. They'd stopped his pocket money when he'd refused to attend school, but as a foster carer I had to give the child or young person their allowance regardless of their behaviour, which of course limited the options available to sanction negative behaviour. Many parents withhold their children's pocket money if they misbehave and some children are expected to do household chores to earn the money. Young people in care receive an above-average pocket money allowance for their age, plus an amount set aside in a savings account and a clothing allowance, which, at Stevie's age, he would expect to have in his hand. He would also very likely have a pay-as-you-go mobile phone, which I would be expected to top up, but I didn't explain all this at the time to Peggy and Fred, and neither did Verity.

It was one o'clock when I arrived home. Paula had left a note saying she'd gone shopping with a friend and would be back around 4 p.m. I had a sandwich lunch and then did some clerical work while I waited for Verity to arrive with Stevie – at around three o'clock. However, just before three the landline went and when I heard Verity's voice I knew something had changed or gone wrong.

'Cathy, I've just left Mr and Mrs Jones. Stevie won't be coming to you this afternoon. His grandparents want to give him another chance. They felt bad after the meeting and they think the threat of going into care might give him the shock he needs. I'll be monitoring the situation and we'll have to see how it goes.'

'OK. Thanks for letting me know,' I said.

While I wasn't happy at being seen as a 'threat', I hoped it all worked out for them. Obviously it's better for a child or young person if they are able to live with their family, although something told me (from years of fostering) that wasn't going to happen here, and I was right.

CHAPTER THREE

TROUBLE

It was midday on 2 January. Lucy and Adrian were at work and Paula was in her room reading in preparation for returning to college the following day. I hadn't heard anything further from Verity, and I assumed Edith would phone before long with details of another child in need of a foster home. There was never much of a gap between one child leaving and the next arriving. I'd spent the morning taking down the Christmas decorations while I had the time and was thinking of making Paula and me some lunch when the front doorbell rang. I wasn't expecting anyone, but sometimes a friend or neighbour dropped by, and we also had regular deliveries as we all shopped online.

But it wasn't a parcel, friend or neighbour. To my utter amazement, as I opened the front door I saw Stevie standing there, a large holdall at his side.

'Sorry to turn up like this,' he said, seeing my expression of surprise. 'But I will be staying with you after all.'

'Oh, I see. I'm afraid it's not that simple, but come in,' I flustered, trying to clear my thoughts. 'What's happened? Does anyone know you're here? How did you know where I live?'

'I found your address on some papers Gran had,' he said, stepping into the hall.

'Does your gran know you are here?'

'Yes.' If she hadn't, I would have phoned her straight away to let her know Stevie was safe.

Paula was still upstairs in her room and must have heard the doorbell and our voices but decided to stay put for now.

'Shall I slip off my shoes and leave them here with yours?' he asked, referring to the place beneath the coat stand where our outdoor shoes were.

'Yes, please,' I said absently.

'And hang my coat here?'

'Yes.' I usually told my new arrivals where to leave their shoes and coat, but I was still recovering from the shock of finding Stevie on my doorstep.

I waited while he paired his shoes precisely next to ours, then hung his tweed coat on the hall stand, a multitude of questions running through my head. He was well dressed again, but the colour scheme had been toned down a little from the meeting and he was now wearing blue jeans with a yellow sweater.

'Come through to the living room so we can have a chat,' I said, leading the way down the hall.

'It's just like in your photographs,' he said, looking around as we went. 'Very nice.'

'Thank you.'

'Oh! You've got a cat, how delightful!' he cried as we entered the living room. Sammy, who was still nervous of strangers, shot off the sofa and out of the room. 'Oh, he's gone.' Stevie looked hurt.

'Don't worry. He'll be back. Sit down.'

He settled on the sofa while I took one of the easy chairs.

'Does Verity know you're here?'

'Gran phoned her,' he said, flicking back his fringe and crossing one leg over the other. He didn't appear particularly anxious; in fact, he looked quite at home on the sofa.

'OK, I'll need to talk to Verity. If she doesn't phone soon, I'll call her. Do you want anything to eat or drink?' I always ask new arrivals this, as some of them haven't eaten properly for days if they've come from homes where they've been neglected.

'I'm good, thanks,' he said. 'Gran cooked me breakfast before I left. I can stay here, can't I? I mean, for now.'

'I don't see why not, the room is free, but it's not my decision. Verity will need to decide. It's a foster placement. It's not like a hotel where you can check in and out.'

'She'll be fine with it,' he said confidently, smoothing his jeans.

'So what happened at home? I thought you and your grandparents were going to give it another go.'

'We did.' He sighed theatrically. 'It was cool for a day, everyone was on their best behaviour, until I got ready to go out on New Year's Eve. Well, I mean, you get dressed up to go clubbing, don't you?' He pursed his lips indignantly.

'Clubbing! A nightclub?' I asked, shocked.

'Yes. I've been before,' he said defensively.

'But you're only fourteen. You're not allowed into nightclubs.'

'Nearly fifteen,' he corrected. 'I look older.' Which was true.

'Don't the clubs ask for proof of age?'

He smiled. 'Of course. Don't tell anyone, but I've got a fake ID off the internet.' I should have guessed – I'd heard this before. But I would be telling his social worker. It was unsafe behaviour for a boy of fourteen to be in a nightclub, and if I was going to be his foster carer I had a duty to pass this on, but I'd explain all that later.

'It's a straight and gay club where I can be myself,' he added, and watched me for my reaction.

'That's irrelevant,' I said. 'A lad of your age shouldn't be in a nightclub at all, which I'm guessing is what your grandparents said.'

'I didn't tell them where I was going. It was when Grandpa saw me all dressed up ready to go out with my eye glitter on that he blew his top. He said if I went out looking like that I needn't come back. So I didn't. I just went home this morning for some of my things.'

'So you were missing from New Year's Eve?'

'Yes,' he said almost proudly. 'Gran kept leaving messages on my voicemail. The last one said the police were out looking for me.' His eyes lit up at the drama of it all.

'I would think they were worried sick. Where were you all that time?'

'After the club closed I went back to a friend's pad to crash.'

'If you are going to live with me, there will be rules and boundaries.' Best say it now, I thought, for I was concerned by his attitude.

'Not too many rules, I hope,' he said, flicking back his fringe again.

'No, just enough to keep you and everyone here safe. What did your grandfather say when you returned this morning?'

'He wasn't there, just Gran. He'd taken Liam and Kiri to the park with their bikes. They both had new bikes for Christmas.'

I nodded. 'And what did you get for Christmas?'

'Money for clothes. Can I see my room now?'

'In a minute. I'll phone Verity first and make sure you can stay. She may have other plans for you.'

'I'm not going back home,' he said, his face setting. 'She can't make me.'

'Let's see what she has to say.' I picked up the handset from the corner unit and pressed the social services' number.

Verity was now at her desk. 'I was about to phone you,' she said. 'Has Stevie arrived?'

'Yes. About ten minutes ago.'

'He can stay, but I'll need to place him. I'm in a meeting soon so I'll come over later, around three. Can you keep him in until I arrive?'

'Yes.'

We said goodbye. 'She said you can stay,' I said to Stevie. 'I'll show you around the house.'

'Thank you so much,' he said, and came over and kissed my cheek.

Usually when a new child arrives it is with their social worker, so I show them around the house together, as the social worker needs to see where the child is living, but Stevie was keen to look now, so I'd show Verity around later when she arrived. I began with the room we were in, pointing out the television, and explained how we tended to relax in here in the evenings and weekends.

'Do you have wi-fi?' Stevie asked, taking his phone from the pocket of his jeans.

'Yes.'

'Can I have the password?'

'I don't know the code off by heart, it'll be on the router in the front room. I'll give it to you in a moment when we go in there.'

'You know about the internet and stuff?' he asked.

'A reasonable amount, yes,' I said.

'Gran and Grandpa don't. I had to use my phone credit to get online cos he kept switching off the router at night. He thought it would catch fire.' He raised his eyebrows in exasperation.

'We all have different ways of doing things,' I said, and led the way into our kitchen-diner. To a younger person who'd grown up with computers, routers and mobile phones, switching off the wi-fi at night would seem ludicrous, but not to someone of Fred and Peggy's generation.

While we were in the kitchen I took the opportunity to ask Stevie if he had any special dietary needs or was allergic to anything. It's something the social worker would tell me in respect of a younger child.

'No, I eat most things,' he said easily.

'Excellent,' I smiled.

We left the kitchen-diner and went down the hall and into the front room. 'I call it a quiet room,' I said. 'You can read and do your homework in here or in your room, whatever you prefer. The computer and printer are here too,' I said, pointing. These were now considered essential items in a foster carer's home.

'And there's the router,' Stevie said, spotting the hub on the bookshelf. I didn't have to read out the passcode, as he beat me to it. Going over, he entered the code and began tapping away at the keypad on his phone as if his life depended on it. I watched him for a while as his fingers flew over the letters. Completely absorbed, I think he almost forgot I was there.

'Stevie, what do you do on the internet?' I asked.

He looked up. 'Chat to friends, you know, the usual stuff,' he said, and returned his attention to the screen.

At his age, of course, he would need internet access; teenagers are all computer savvy and online now. But whereas a younger child would use my computer, which had parental-control software to protect them while online by limiting the websites they could access and filtering out inappropriate content, I guessed his phone did not. Internet safety is part of foster-carer training now and foster carers are expected to include it in their safer-caring policy. The older the child, the more difficult it becomes to monitor their activity on the internet.

'You are careful who you talk to online, aren't you?' I asked. 'I mean, you wouldn't give out your personal details to a stranger.'

He looked slightly startled. 'No. Why do you ask?'

'There are some nasty people out there who can hide behind the anonymity of the internet. They can be very devious in getting what they want. I'm not trying to frighten you, but you do need to be aware.'

He nodded and continued with whatever he was doing on his phone. I'd talk to him more about internet safety another time, just as I had with Adrian, Lucy and Paula. They were of an age now to appreciate the dangers, but Stevie wasn't. Despite the image he liked to portray, he was a vulnerable young person who was undecided about his gender identity – just the sort of person who could be preyed upon. 'Come on, I'll show you upstairs,' I said. 'Bring your bag with you.'

Still tapping his phone with one hand, he collected his bag from the hall with the other, and we went upstairs and into his room. He dropped his bag on the floor and looked up from his phone long enough to glance around and say, 'Cool.' He followed me out and as we continued round the landing Paula came out of her room.

'Oh my!' Stevie cried, clapping his hand to his chest. 'You gave me such a fright. I didn't know anyone else was in.'

'Sorry, I should have told you,' I said. 'This is Paula, my youngest daughter. Adrian and Lucy are at work.'

'Hello, Paula, lovely to meet you,' he gushed. 'But don't go jumping out on me like that again, will you? You scared me half to death.' His manner was effusive, over the top and completely unnecessary. It was as if he was acting a part.

'Nice to meet you,' Paula said, ignoring his theatricals.

I threw her an appreciative smile and then showed Stevie where the bathroom was as Paula disappeared back into her room. I didn't take Stevie into our bedrooms, I just pointed them out and explained that all of them, including his, were private and we didn't go into each other's. 'If you want Adrian, Lucy or Paula, you knock on their door and wait until they answer,' I said. 'They will do the same to you. OK?'

'OK,' he said absently, concentrating on his phone. 'I'll go to my room now.'

'If that's what you want to do,' I said. 'Unpack your bag and you will feel more at home. Do you need any help with your unpacking?' He shook his head. 'Are you sure you don't want a drink and a snack to see you through till dinner?'

But, lost in his phone, he was already on his way to his room, and I heard the door close. I looked in on Paula, who was reading, and then went downstairs. I tidied away the work I'd been doing before Stevie had arrived, and then texted Adrian and Lucy to let them know that he was here so they didn't just come back to find a stranger in their home.

Half an hour later I went up to check if Stevie was all right. Despite his age and apparent confident manner, he was away from his family and in an unfamiliar house. His door was closed so I knocked. 'It's Cathy,' I called.

It was a few moments before he replied. 'Yes?'

'Is everything OK?'

Silence, so I knocked again. 'Are you all right?' More silence. 'Can I come in?'

Giving another knock, I slowly opened the door and poked my head round. He was sitting on his bed, completely engrossed in his phone, the bag, not yet unpacked, on the floor. 'Are you OK?' I asked.

'Yes,' he said, but some of his charisma had gone and he seemed worried.

'Sure?' I asked. He nodded. 'OK, but don't sit up here by yourself. Unpack your bag and come down if you want some company.'

He nodded again and I left him with his phone. Little wonder his grandfather had turned off the wi-fi, I thought. But I had some house rules about mobile phones, which I would explain later when his social worker was present.

I checked on Stevie again half an hour later: his bag still hadn't been unpacked, his phone was on charge and he was gazing out of his bedroom window. His room was at the rear of the house and overlooked the garden, although there wasn't much to see in winter.

'Gran phoned me,' he said quietly, turning from the window. 'I told her I was OK.'

'Good. And are you?'

'What?'

'Are you OK?'

'Yeah, I guess.' He shrugged.

'You don't seem very sure,' I said gently, taking another step into his room. 'You know if there's anything worrying you, you can talk to me.'

'I doubt it,' he said under his breath.

'Stevie, I have three adult children of my own and have fostered a lot of young people. I'm pretty good at listening and I won't make judgements or be shocked by anything you have to tell me.'

He looked at me, his face serious. There was no sign of the flamboyant lad I'd seen previously. Indeed, he looked as though he had the weight of the world on his shoulders.

'Well?' I asked. 'Is there something you'd like to share? It often helps to talk.'

He hesitated as if he might be considering this, then said, 'No.'

'All right, but if you change your mind, you know where I am. If I'm busy, or with Adrian, Lucy or Paula, just say, "Cathy, can I talk to you?" and we'll find somewhere quiet to go for a chat.' I didn't want to labour the point, but I knew from fostering and bringing up my own children just how much young people can bottle up their problems so that they escalate and get out of all proportion. The teenage years can be challenging and confusing for children living at home with loving parents, even more so for a young person in care.

'There is something,' Stevie said as I was about to leave his room.

'Yes?' I stopped and turned.

'Can I have my pocket money? I have to go out later,' he said anxiously.

'Where to?'

'Just out.'

'I usually give pocket money on a Saturday,' I said, 'but you can have yours early this week. However, I don't want you going out tonight. Verity is coming soon and then I want you to meet Adrian and Lucy, settle in and get ready for tomorrow.'

'Why? What's happening tomorrow?' he asked.

'I'm hoping you will be going to school. And one of the things I want to discuss with Verity is when you will be going out. Of course you will want to see your friends, but it won't be every night. We can decide on days and the times you have to be back when we see your social worker.'

'But I have to go out today,' he said, growing more anxious.

'Why?' He couldn't meet my gaze. 'Stevie, are you in some sort of trouble?'

'No,' he said far too quickly. I knew then he was, but he wouldn't be telling me yet.

CHAPTER FOUR

STRAIGHT TALKING

Verity arrived as planned shortly after three o'clock. 'Is Stevie still here?' she asked, as if he might not be.

'Yes. He's in his room. Shall I fetch him?'

'Please.'

'The living room is through there,' I said, pointing, and went upstairs to fetch Stevie. 'Verity is here,' I said, knocking on his door.

'I'll be down later,' he returned.

'No, now, please. She needs to see you.'

No response. 'Can I come in?' I knocked again and gently eased open the door. He had taken some of his clothes from his bag and dumped them on the bed. I could see what looked like a school uniform, which I thought was hopeful.

'Gran packed this,' he said, scowling. 'She's left out most of my good stuff.'

'Don't worry, we'll sort it out later. Come down now, Verity is here.' I've found before that children of all ages sometimes need things repeating, and often.

Clearly not happy with the clothes his gran had packed – image appeared to be very important to Stevie, more so than the average teenager – he came with me downstairs and into the living room. 'Hello, how are you settling in?' Verity asked him brightly, taking a wad of paperwork from her bag-style briefcase.

Stevie shrugged and flopped into one of the easy chairs. 'I have to go out later, but Cathy won't let me,' he said.

'I've asked him to stay in tonight,' I explained. 'I think that going out, and coming-home times, is something we need to discuss.'

'Let's deal with that first then, shall we?' Verity said positively and, taking a pen from her bag, she opened a notepad on her lap.

'At my gran's I went out whenever I wanted,' Stevie said ruefully.

'But that didn't work, love, did it?' I said to him.

Stevie and I both looked at Verity for her view, but she didn't immediately reply. I've found before that social workers are sometimes reluctant to talk straight to the teenagers in their care in case it jeopardises their relationship. I didn't have the same reservations, for ultimately the young person I was fostering was my responsibility and I needed to keep them safe.

'What do you suggest?' Verity asked me after a moment.

'I think it's reasonable that Stevie sees his friends at the weekends. If he wants to go out then I suggest Friday and/or Saturday evening.' Stevie was glaring at me, but I continued anyway. 'During the week he'll have homework to do, and I am assuming he'll want to see his grandparents and brother and sister.'

'That won't work,' Stevie said. 'I need to be able to go out when I want, not when she says.'

I was now seeing a different side to him. Gone was his previous charm and charisma, and here was a belligerent teenager, which, to be honest, I found more natural and quite reassuring.

Verity was waiting for my response. 'Why won't it work?' I asked Stevie. 'I'm sure your friends have similar arrangements at their homes. We'll also need to set the time you are to be back, and I'll need to know where you are going and how you will get home.'

'That's fucking ridiculous!' Stevie stormed. 'I'm not a kid!'

'No, but you are still a minor,' I said.

'Cathy and I have a duty to protect you and keep you safe,' Verity added.

'Bollocks!' Stevie fumed. 'You're like my bleeding grandparents,' he said to me, and I don't think he meant it as a compliment.

'OK,' Verity said, drawing a breath and addressing Stevie. 'What if we say you can go out Friday and Saturday, plus one day in the week. Does that help?'

'A bit,' he conceded.

'Good.'

This was far more than Adrian, Lucy and Paula had ever been allowed out at his age, but then going out hadn't been an issue for them as the boundaries had been in place from the start. It's far more difficult to change behaviour once it's set. Stevie, like many teenagers who come into care because of behavioural issues, had been used to his freedom and didn't want to relinquish it. I had to be realistic and accept a compromise. 'OK. Coming-home times,' I said, moving on. 'I would like Stevie to be back by nine o'clock at the latest on a weekday and nine-thirty at the weekend. I will also need to know where he is and how he will get home.'

'I won't know what time I'll be back,' he said disparagingly.

'You will,' I said, 'by leaving wherever you are on time.'

'But what if I can't? I might not be able to leave and come home when you say.' Which seemed an odd thing to say, but he was looking worried and that wasn't my intention at all.

'You'll have your phone with you,' I said. 'So on the rare occasion you can't help being late, you can phone or text me. Remember, this isn't about me wanting to stop you having fun, but about keeping you safe.'

'Like Gran,' he said, with less hostility.

So I thought that maybe he was starting to realise his grandparents' boundaries were not so unreasonable after all.

'We'll say nine o'clock on a weekday and ten at the weekend,' Verity said, making a note. 'And you'll let Cathy know where you are and how you are going to get home?'

Stevie shrugged and took his phone from his pocket to check it.

'Do you have credit on your phone?' Verity asked him.

'No,' he said, without looking up.

'Can you top it up?' she said to me.

'Yes. How much a month?' The guidelines change in line with inflation and telephone call charges.

'How much phone credit was your gran giving you?' Verity asked him.

'Twenty pounds a month.'

'We'll keep to that then,' Verity said.

I made a note. Stevie nodded and continued scrolling down his phone. This seemed a good time to say what I wanted to in respect of his phone.

'I understand it is now possible to restrict internet access on mobile phones,' I said to Verity. She nodded. 'I was wondering if Stevie's grandparents had done that when they bought his phone?'

'No,' Stevie sneered, 'of course they didn't. They wouldn't know how. But I'm not downloading porn if that's what you think.'

'It's not,' I said. 'It's just seems a sensible precaution.' But I knew there was no use in pursuing this. Had the internet access been restricted on his phone from the start he would have accepted it, but not now at his age. Looking after teenagers is give-and-take and this was something I had to let go, like the number of times he was allowed out in the evening, and hope he was sensible. 'While we're talking about mobiles,' I continued, 'I have a couple of small house rules.' Stevie sighed. 'I like all mobiles switched off at night so everyone gets a good night's sleep, and I ask that no mobiles are used at the dinner table.'

'That seems reasonable,' Verity said. Stevie didn't object, but whether he would comply or not remained to be seen. 'School,' Verity said as she finished writing, moving on.

'Cathy says I have to go tomorrow,' Stevie said moodily.

'I'm not sure that will happen,' Verity said to me. 'His mentor wants to see him first. She arranged a meeting last week with his grandparents, but Stevie didn't show.'

'I wasn't well,' he said, looking at his phone.

'Oh dear, but you're better now,' I said. 'If Stevie and I could meet with his mentor tomorrow perhaps he could be in school the following day?' I suggested to Verity.

'I don't see why not,' she replied. 'The mentor's contact details are on the Essential Information form. I'll leave a copy for you. Have you got your school uniform here with you?' she now asked Stevie.

He nodded glumly without taking his eyes from his phone. 'It's my other stuff I haven't got.'

'Casual clothes?' Verity asked.

'Yes.'

'You can collect what you need from your grandparents, but give them a ring before you go to make sure someone is in.'

'I've got a key,' Stevie said.

'Yes, but your grandparents would still like to know when you're going, which brings me to contact.'

'What is contact?' Stevie asked, finally looking up from his phone.

'It's when you see your family – your grandparents, Liam and Kiri.'

'I can go and see them any time,' he said with attitude. 'My gran said I could.'

'Yes, so when are you thinking of going?' Verity asked.

'I dunno, when I want to. After school maybe, or at the weekend.' He shrugged.

'OK, but phone Gran first and tell her. Also let Cathy know, otherwise she will be expecting you home here.'

I would have liked some more precise contact arrangements – days and times – but Stevie was in care under a Section 20 so there was no court order setting out specifics, and teenagers in care are notorious for popping home when the mood takes them.

'Perhaps you could liaise with Mr and Mrs Jones?' Verity suggested to me. 'They have your details, and theirs are on the Essential Information sheet.' All of which was quite normal under a Section 20.

'Can I go now?' Stevie said, tucking his phone into his pocket.

'Is there anything else you want to talk to me about?' Verity asked.

'No.'

'OK, I'll say goodbye to you when I leave.' Stevie nodded and left the room. Verity wasn't just being polite; as Stevie's social worker she would want to see his bedroom as well as the rest of the house.

I waited until he was out of earshot before I said, 'I am worried about Stevie's safety. Did you know he's been going to nightclubs?'

'I didn't until his grandparents told me,' Verity said. 'The boundaries have been a bit lax at home, but you can understand why. At their age it's been a struggle bringing up three grandchildren.'

'They've done well.'

'It started going pear-shaped with Stevie about a year ago. Puberty, and not feeling comfortable in his body. His grandparents haven't been able to support him with his gender identity. It might help him to have a referral to a clinic that offers a gender-identity development service for young people. They can prescribe hormone treatment if necessary.'

'Really? Isn't he a bit young for that?'

'They're not the hormones taken by a person who is transitioning – wanting to change sex – but they stop puberty to give the young person a chance to think about their gender identity.'

'I see, I've got a lot to learn,' I said.

'So did I, but more young people are questioning their gender, so the social services, schools, health care and society in general is having to catch up. I'm not saying the treatment is necessarily right for Stevie, but it could be an option. It would need his grandparents' consent, as they are his legal guardians, so we'll have to see.'

Verity then ran through the Essential Information Form, which included brief details of Stevie's family, ethnicity,

religion, education, health, any behavioural problems and
other basic information I would need to look after him. This
came with the Placement Agreement Form that I had to sign.
Verity gave me a copy of both sets of forms, which I clipped
into my fostering folder. I started a new folder for each child.
I then showed Verity around the downstairs of the house first
and then upstairs, ending with Stevie's room. 'Verity is here,'
I said, tapping on his door. 'Can she come in?' Privacy is so
important to young people.

'Yes,' came his reply.

I left Verity with Stevie. It's usual for the social worker to
spend some time alone with the child or young person in case
there are any issues they want to discuss that they might find
uncomfortable with the foster carer present. I looked in on
Paula, who was still in her room. 'Verity is going soon,' I said.
'She's just saying goodbye to Stevie.'

'OK, I'll come down when she's gone.'

Paula knew she could go downstairs any time, although it
wasn't appropriate for her to sit in on some of the meetings
that took place in our living room, including Verity placing
Stevie. Fostering is intrusive and disruptive to the foster
family and it's often this that puts off prospective carers.
Foster carers have regular visits from the child's social
worker and the carer's supervising social worker – both of
whom look around the house at each visit. There are also
visits from many other professions involved in the case,
including the educational psychologist, the Guardian ad
Litem and the child's solicitor if the case is going to court,
the health visitor, LAC nurse and sometimes the child's
family. In addition, the child's reviews are often held in the
carer's home. It can seem like a never-ending procession of
visitors, and of course it's disruptive for the child in care as

well, who just wants to be loved and to lead a normal family life.

Verity was with Stevie for about ten minutes and then I saw her out. Paula came down for a snack and drink to see her through to dinnertime, and I persuaded Stevie to come down too. He and Paula sat at the table in the kitchen-diner while I was in the kitchen. I could see and hear them from where I worked and Stevie was talking really nicely to Paula, asking her about college, what she wanted to do when she left and whether she minded fostering. Although aged fourteen, Stevie could pass for much older. He was tall and there was a sophistication about him, which Paula didn't have.

'You'll meet my brother Adrian and my sister Lucy later,' I heard Paula tell him.

'Do all the family have dinner together?' he asked. 'We did at Gran's.'

'Yes, if everyone is in.'

'I'd better get ready then,' he said. Having finished his snack, he stood.

'Stevie,' I said, going into the dining area, 'we usually have dinner around six o'clock, and you're fine as you are.' For I didn't really know what he meant by 'get ready'.

'Oh no, I need to look my best for when I meet Adrian and Lucy – first impressions and all that.' With a flick of his wrist he left. Clearly, looking after Stevie was going to be a whole new experience for us all.

CHAPTER FIVE

SECRETS

Stevie stayed in his room until I called everyone for dinner. Adrian, Lucy and Paula were already seated at the table when Stevie (having been called twice) arrived. I think he'd waited until everyone was there so he could stage an entrance. Although he was wearing the same clothes – blue jeans and a yellow sweater – he now had a light blue silk scarf tied loosely around his neck, had painted his nails bright red and was wearing a lot more make-up.

'This is Adrian,' I said, introducing him to Stevie.

Adrian had never experienced any doubts about his gender and had a long-standing girlfriend, Kirsty. He could also be a bit conservative, which was no bad thing, but to his credit he just said, 'Hello, Stevie, nice to meet you.'

'And you.' Stevie smiled charmingly.

Lucy on the other hand didn't have the same reservations as Adrian, and sometimes there was no filter on her thoughts. 'You're never called Stevie!' she cried, horrified, staring at him.

His face fell. Clearly he had wanted to be noticed, but in a positive way, and it was clear from his expression this wasn't the reaction he'd anticipated. I must say I'd expected better from Lucy. I've tried to bring up my children to be non-judgemental and accepting of differences whether they are race, religion, physical or – as with Stevie – gender related.

I threw her a warning glance, which she either didn't see or ignored.

'You're not really called Stevie, are you?' Lucy persisted dramatically. 'Please tell me it's not true!'

The poor lad looked mortified and I was about to tell Lucy off when I realised what she meant. 'Oh, Lucy. Stop it. Shall I tell him or will you?'

'You can.' She laughed.

Stevie was looking at me, worried and confused, as well he might. 'Many years ago Lucy came to me as a foster child and stayed,' I explained to him. 'I wanted to adopt her, but her social worker at that time was against it. She felt she should live with a family that reflected her ethnicity.' (Lucy has dual heritage, and I tell her story in *Will You Love Me?*). 'Thankfully we had a change of social worker and the adoption went ahead. That first social worker was called Stevie. I had forgotten. It's no criticism of you – Lucy just didn't get on with her.'

Stevie gasped with relief and managed a smile. 'My grandparents call me Steven, but I prefer Stevie.'

'That's fine,' I said.

'Can we eat now, Mum?' Adrian asked patiently. 'I'm starving.'

'Yes, of course.'

I served dinner and everyone tucked in so all that could be heard for some minutes was the chink of cutlery on china. Lucy was sitting directly opposite Stevie and I saw her keep looking up at him. I had a good idea what she was thinking even before she said it.

'Stevie, why are you wearing all that make-up?' she asked at length, not rudely, but it was a forthright question, and probably one he'd heard before.

He didn't take offence but, setting down his cutlery, he said, 'It's a statement about who I am. I see myself as gender-fluid, which means I haven't got a fixed gender. That's not to say I'm gay, although it's possible, I haven't decided yet. I'm trying to find out if I want to live my life as male or female, so at present I'm gender-fluid.' I thought that, for a fourteen-year-old, he was very articulate in matters that deeply affected him.

'So you're making up your mind, right?' Lucy asked him.

'Yes, although I could stay gender-fluid all my life and not identify with either sex. Some days I feel more female than male, then it can change. Sometimes it can change during a day depending on who I'm with and what I'm doing.'

'That must be confusing,' Adrian remarked.

Stevie shrugged. 'It would be more confusing for me if I pretended to be male all the time, like my grandparents want me to.'

'Do you get bullied at school?' Paula asked sensitively.

'I used to,' Stevie said, picking up his knife and fork again, 'so I stopped going.'

I looked at him carefully. 'Stevie, is that the reason you haven't been attending school – because you were being bullied?'

'Sort of,' he admitted.

'Did you tell anyone you were being bullied?'

'My grandparents, but Grandpa said I needed to man up, and if I stopped behaving like a pansy I wouldn't attract the bullies.'

Having met Fred, I could hear him say that – a flippant, simplistic solution – but his intolerance and lack of sensitivity obviously hadn't helped Stevie, who was looking for support.

'Did you tell your social worker you were being bullied?' I asked.

'No. I thought she would side with Grandpa and say I had to go to school.'

'I'll explain to Verity, and when we see your mentor tomorrow we'll talk to her about what the school can do to help, all right?'

He shrugged and continued eating while I thought, Well done, Paula, for spotting that. Bullying was such an obvious reason for a child or young person refusing to go to school, especially for someone who stood out as being different, like Stevie. Bullying can make a child's life a misery and all schools in the UK have an anti-bullying policy. But of course for it to be effective the school needs to be aware the bullying is taking place, and children often don't want to admit they're being bullied, feeling it is their fault. Unfortunately, Fred's bigoted remarks had compounded that, but I was pleased that Stevie had been able to share it with us so I could help him.

'OK,' Lucy said, 'I understand what you're saying about the gender stuff, but why are you wearing so much make-up?' Let it go, Lucy, I thought, you've made your point. 'I mean, it's too much,' she continued. 'It's like you think that's how girls should look. Most of us don't. It's so stereotypical, and as Mum tells us – when it comes to make-up, less is more.'

So she had been listening to me, I thought! I waited tentatively for Stevie's reaction. I hoped he didn't feel Lucy was getting at him, although what she'd said was true.

'So you think I'm wearing too much make-up?' he asked, as though it was a revelation.

'Yes, I do, far too much. Don't you think so, Paula?'

'A little,' she said diplomatically.

'What about you, Adrian?'

'I don't know the first thing about make-up,' he replied.

'But Kirsty doesn't wear a lot of slap, does she?' Lucy persisted.

'No,' Adrian conceded.

Lucy returned her attention to Stevie. 'If you like, I'll show you how to apply make-up,' Lucy offered. 'I wanted to be a beautician once.'

'Really? That would be wonderful!' Stevie cried passionately.

'I wouldn't wear it for school, though,' Adrian said.

'No,' Paula agreed. 'Girls aren't allowed to wear make-up in school, so that rule should apply to everyone.'

I felt rather proud of my family. Here they were, discussing this sensitive and unusual topic constructively and being supportive of Stevie. None of us had faced the challenges he had, so it was a learning curve for us all. The conversation now changed to other things, and once we'd finished eating everyone helped clear the table. Then Stevie asked Lucy, 'Can you come up to my room now to show me how do my make-up?'

'Yep, I can give you half an hour, then I have to watch *EastEnders*,' she said.

'I love that programme,' Stevie enthused, clasping his hands together.

'Stevie, can you bring your make-up down here and do it at the table?' I said. Lucy knew why. It's part of our safer-caring policy that young people aren't alone in one of the bedrooms. Not because I didn't trust them or imagined they'd get up to anything inappropriate, but safer caring is about avoiding situations that could be misinterpreted so that all family members feel safe and secure.

Stevie fetched his make-up, which he kept in a silky floral patterned cosmetic bag, and sat at the table with a mirror in front of him while Lucy gave him a lesson in applying make-up. Paula and Adrian had gone up to their rooms and I was in the kitchen clearing up. Lucy and Stevie had quite a laugh, but by the time Lucy had finished, Stevie's make-up looked much better – subtle. She also got him to take off the bright red nail varnish, ready for school. They then went up to their respective rooms, which left Sammy and me in the living room.

I took the opportunity to go through the Essential Information Form and then wrote up my log notes. All foster carers in the UK are required to keep a daily record of the child or children they are looking after. This includes appointments, the child's health and wellbeing, education, significant events and any disclosures they may make about their past. When the child leaves this record is placed on file at the social services. I'd begun my log for Stevie when I'd attended the pre-placement meeting, and now I wrote a short paragraph detailing his arrival, what he'd disclosed about being bullied and how he was settling in.

Adrian, Paula, Lucy and I are not night owls during the week, as we all have to be up in the morning for work or college. I needed to get Stevie into the same routine, so at nine o'clock I asked him if he wanted a hot drink and a snack before he went to bed. 'Can I have an Ovaltine, please?' he asked. 'My gran always makes me one.' It's little details like this that help a child or young person to settle and feel at home.

I didn't have any Ovaltine so I said I'd buy some the next day and he had a hot chocolate instead. I then gave him a set of towels and checked he had everything he needed for the night; his gran had packed his nightclothes and a wash bag with a toothbrush and so on. I suggested he had his shower first, as we all had to use the bathroom. I expect all the children I foster as well as my own to have a daily shower or bath. Some children who have come from neglected homes aren't used to this, but Stevie was – it was part of his grandparents' routine.

By ten o'clock we were all upstairs in bed or getting ready for bed. Before I went to bed I looked in on Stevie to say goodnight and remind him to switch off his phone. 'You know where I am if you need anything in the night?' I said. Despite his age, he was in a strange house, and had been used to sharing a bedroom with his younger brother.

'What time do I have to get up?' he asked.

'Nine tomorrow, but it will be earlier when you are back in school.'

I never sleep particularly well when there is a new child or young person in the house. I worry about them and listen out in case they wake with a start, upset and not knowing where they are, when I go round and reassure them. It didn't matter that Stevie was nearly fifteen; I still listened out for him. As it was, he seemed to sleep well and only surfaced when he heard the rest of us getting up in the morning.

I find it takes a few days for a new arrival to fit into the family. At the start everyone is a little self-conscious as my family adapts their routine to include another family member and they adapt to fit in with us. Then usually we all chug along without too much trouble. We all need to use the bathroom in the morning and sometimes a queue forms, although this morning Stevie didn't have to be out the door at any set time. I made him breakfast – cereal and toast as his gran did

– and saw Adrian, Paula and Lucy off at the door. Just after nine o'clock I telephoned Stevie's school and asked to speak to his mentor, Carolyn. It took a few minutes before she came to the phone and was confused when I introduced myself – 'Cathy Glass, Stevie Jones's foster carer.'

'I didn't know Stevie had gone into care,' she said. 'Although there was some talk about it at the end of last term.'

I explained it had all happened quickly the day before and said Stevie was fine and settling in, and that his social worker was aware I was phoning her to arrange a meeting to get Stevie back into school as quickly as possible.

'Yes, of course. Could you make one o'clock today?' she asked.

'Perfect.'

'Will Stevie's grandparents be coming too?'

'I don't think so.'

'OK. When you arrive, come in the main entrance and give your name at the office and the school secretary will buzz me.'

'Thank you.'

I said goodbye and then wondered if Stevie's grandparents would want to attend the meeting as they had before. Stevie was in care voluntarily and there were no child-protection issues to prevent them from attending. It's always better for the child to see their family working with the foster carer, although in many cases it's very difficult, even impossible, if the parents are angry that their child has been taken from them as a result of abuse or neglect. But that wasn't so with Stevie's grandparents. The problem I could foresee was that Fred could easily do more harm than good with an outspoken, thoughtless comment. Even so, I felt I should mention the meeting to them. I had their contact details on the Essential Information Form, and sometimes it's the way a question is phrased that directs the outcome.

'Peggy, it's Cathy Glass. Stevie is fine,' I said straight away to reassure her. 'But I wanted to ask you something?'

'Yes?'

'I've just spoken to Stevie's mentor, Carolyn, and I'm going to see her at one o'clock today. Are you happy for me to take Stevie? I'm guessing you're very busy with Liam and Kiri.'

'You can say that again!' Peggy said. 'They've been playing me up a treat with all Steven's comings and goings. I was relieved that school started again today. Fred has taken them. I'm exhausted. Yes, you go to the meeting with Steven, if it does any good.'

'OK.' I wasn't going to mention at this point that Stevie had disclosed he was being bullied, as it could have made Peggy feel bad for not acting on it.

'Verity said that Steven wants more of his clothes,' Peggy said. 'He can come and get them later if he likes. It's only a short bus ride from school.'

I didn't really want Stevie jumping on a bus and going back to his grandparents by himself until he was more settled with us and in the routine of school. So many young people are placed with a foster carer one day and then leg it home the next, then go back and forth between their home and the carers like a yo-yo, which is unsettling for everyone involved.

'I could bring him in the car after we've seen Carolyn,' I suggested. 'It will give me a chance to tell you how the meeting went, and he can bring as much of his stuff with him as he wants.'

'That would be good,' Peggy said. 'Liam and Kiri won't be here, but Steven can see them another time.' She paused. 'Cathy, has Steven said anything to you about a secret?'

'No, why?'

'It's probably nothing, but when he was missing over the New Year Liam and Kiri kept messing around and saying, "We've got a secret and we're not going to tell you." It's not my birthday, so I thought it was just one of their pranks and they would tell me in time. Those two are always up to mischief. Then yesterday after Steven had gone off they went very serious and Liam said, "We still can't tell you our secret, Stevie said we mustn't, not ever." So I'm wondering what exactly they've done this time. Last year the pair of them hid Fred's false teeth.'

'Oh no!'

'They were missing for three days and they wouldn't tell where they were. Eventually I spotted them in the goldfish bowl among the weeds.'

I laughed as Peggy was doing.

'I'll ask Stevie if he knows what they have been up to,' I said.

'Thank you. See you later then, and good luck with the meeting.'

I was still smiling at the image of Fred's false teeth in the goldfish bowl as I went upstairs to find Stevie. He was just on his way out of his room. I told him about the appointment with Carolyn at one o'clock and that I'd spoken to his gran and would take him home after the meeting for some more clothes. Then I said, 'Your gran has asked me to find out if you know what Kiri and Liam have been up to?'

'What do you mean?' Stevie asked, suddenly growing serious.

'Don't look so worried. She thinks they might have played another joke like they did with your grandpa's false teeth. They keep telling her they have a secret and you've told them not to tell.'

'Is that all they said?' he asked, really concerned.

'Yes, as far as I know.' I looked at him. 'Stevie, is there something your grandparents need to know? If so, I think you should tell me now.'

There was a moment's hesitation before he said, 'No.'

'Are you sure?' He nodded, and I was almost certain he was lying – a sixth sense from years of raising children.

CHAPTER SIX

INAPPROPRIATE

The morning was free, so I suggested to Stevie we went into town shopping and had some lunch out. I had to get a few things and I didn't want to leave him alone in the house just yet. Also, I find that a trip out, whether it is shopping or visiting a place of interest, is a good way of bonding with a young person. Stevie liked the idea of shopping and I gave him his clothing allowance for the month, credit for his phone and his pocket money. I also asked him not to wear make-up, as we would go straight to the meeting with his mentor, Carolyn, at school once we'd finished shopping. He accepted my wishes about make-up as easily as he had accepted Lucy's. I thought now as I had then that what he needed was guidance on matters associated with gender identity, rather than someone ignoring or dismissing them – as Fred was doing.

I parked in the multi-storey car park in the shopping centre and went with Stevie to the stores he liked. Once we had his clothes from home I would have a better idea of what he needed and could advise him on what to buy, otherwise teenagers often end up with a wardrobe full of jeans and no socks or winter coat. But for now I let him spend his money as he wished, and within half an hour he'd spent most of his clothing allowance on a pair of light grey jeans he said he'd been wanting for ages. They were tasteful and fitted him well. Most clothes would. Tall and slender, he had a model's physique and I saw young people – male and female – glance at him admiringly as they passed.

While we shopped we talked, and I learnt that his gran used to buy his clothes – what she and Fred thought he should wear – but it had obviously caused arguments, so for the last year he'd been buying what *he* wanted, and then the arguments had taken place when he'd worn the clothes and they'd seen them for the first time. He also told me he had been given clothes for Christmas and birthday presents, but he'd chosen them. He liked his clothes and he liked to shop. I learnt that he had two good friends at school, a lad of the same age who thought he might be gay, and a girl in his class whom he said was just a friend but was kind and understanding. Most of the other lads in his class had little to do with him, he said, and some teased and bullied him. I reassured him that we'd address that when we saw Carolyn later, and I suggested he might like to invite his friends home for dinner one time. He'd said he'd think about it. He wasn't sure he'd tell them he was in care, which is true for many children and young people. They prefer to say the person waiting for them in the playground is a friend of their mother's or an aunty, rather than admit it's their foster carer. Although of course at Stevie's age he wouldn't even have to say that, as I wouldn't be in the playground at the start and end of school as I was with younger children.

Stevie only checked his phone a couple of times while we were shopping, but once we sat down with our lunch, chosen from a hot buffet, he suddenly cried, 'Shit!' And pulled his phone from his pocket as if his life depended on it.

'Is everything all right?' I asked him a few moments later, as, food untouched, he was still staring at the screen.

He nodded absently.

'Are you sure?'

'Yes.' But I wasn't convinced, and it crossed my mind that perhaps he was being bullied online too. There was a time when bullying stopped at the school gates, but now it can follow the victim home through text messages, social networking websites, photos and video clips. It's vicious, insidious, relentless and has in extreme cases caused a young person to commit suicide. Also, I remembered Verity had mentioned that Stevie might be in contact with his mother online and I wondered if this was causing a problem.

'Are you on Facebook?' I asked him casually as he finally picked up a chip and began eating.

'Yes.'

'So am I. I could send you a friendship request.' If he accepted it then I should be able to see quite a lot of his online activity on that website and who he was in contact with. It's for this reason it's a good idea for parents and foster carers to have social networking accounts; it allows them to keep an eye on their young person as well as keeping them up to speed with technology. A friend of mine only discovered that her daughter had traced her father (my friend's long-time ex) through social media. She was then able to broach the subject with her daughter and reassure her that she didn't mind. Adrian, Lucy and Paula had Facebook accounts, although only Lucy used hers regularly.

Stevie hadn't responded to my suggestion, but I'd send the friendship request anyway. He could accept or decline it, it was his choice.

'Do you chat to your parents at all online?' I asked. Many young people do without their carer's or guardian's knowledge.

'Sometimes Mum, when she's not in prison. They don't have the internet in prison.'

So I guessed that wasn't the reason he was often anxiously checking his phone.

'The kids at school who bully you, do they target you online? Or message you at all?' I asked outright. It was no good hedging the matter and then regretting it later.

'No. They haven't got my phone number,' he said. 'Only my friends have.'

'Good.'

It was the school's lunch break when Stevie and I arrived and there were students milling around outside, some standing in small groups, others sitting on benches, coats on and huddled over phones as they ate from lunch boxes and packets of crisps.

'What's the school's policy on mobile phones?' I asked Stevie as we made our way to the main entrance.

'They have to be switched off while on school premises,' he replied.

'Is yours off?'

'I'll turn it off now.'

We went to the reception desk, separated from the school office by a low counter, and the secretary recognised Stevie and knew we were expected. 'I'll give Carolyn a ring and let her know you're here,' she said. 'Please sign in the visitors' book and then take a seat.'

I thanked her and, having signed in, we sat in the chairs arranged on the far side of the reception area, and Stevie powered off his phone. I looked around. The walls were adorned with framed photographs of school achievements – winning sports teams, successful examination results, students who'd become distinguished in a particular field, dignitaries and famous people who'd visited the school, and so on, much as you'd find in many secondary schools.

Stevie was clearly anxious and, with no phone to occupy him, was tapping his foot nervously.

'There's nothing to worry about,' I told him. 'You know Carolyn, and she and I want to help you get back into school.'

He gave a curt nod, but his foot kept tapping. I felt as though we were waiting to see the dentist rather than his mentor.

'There she is,' he said as a young woman entered reception.

We both stood. 'Hello, Stevie,' Carolyn said, then, 'Nice to meet you, Cathy.'

'And you,' I replied. Carolyn was fashionably dressed in black leggings and a long, baggy top. In her mid to late twenties, she didn't look much older than Stevie or many of the other senior pupils.

'I have a small office at the top of the building,' she said brightly. 'This way.'

We followed her out of reception and up two flights of stairs, passing students coming down. None of them seemed to know Stevie. 'My classroom is at the other end of the building,' he told me, so I guessed that's where most of his classmates gathered.

Carolyn showed us into her office, just big enough to hold a small desk, a filing cabinet and three steel-framed chairs. She pulled her chair out from behind the desk, so we sat in a small circle.

'This is where I see students if they want to talk in private,' she explained to me. 'Some of my job is counselling, and I spend time in the classroom supporting those who need extra help.'

'Thank you for seeing us at such short notice,' I said. 'Do you have my contact details?' She didn't. I gave them to her and she said she'd advise the secretary, so she could update the school's records.

'So, Stevie,' she said, smiling reassuringly at him, 'a lot of change for you. How do you like it at Cathy's?'

'It's all right,' he said with a shrug. You could hardly expect him to be jumping for joy given he'd had to leave home the day before.

'It must be strange,' Carolyn commiserated. 'Are you seeing your grandparents and your brother and sister?'

'Yes,' Stevie replied tightly.

'Good. You're a bright student, but you have missed a lot of school. The last time I saw you, you told me you didn't feel you fitted in and school seemed irrelevant. We talked about ways I could help you. How do you feel now about school?'

He shrugged.

'There is another reason Stevie hasn't been in school,' I said. 'Apparently he's being bullied.'

'Not all the time,' he put in, embarrassed. 'Just some days.'

'You shouldn't be bullied at all,' I said.

'Why didn't you tell me?' Carolyn asked, concerned. 'We talked about how you were getting on with other students. Didn't you feel able to tell me?'

He shrugged again and looked uncomfortable.

'Is it one person who's doing the bullying or a group?' Carolyn asked.

'One mainly, and the others follow.'

'What have they been doing?' she asked, leaning in to invite confidence. 'Can you tell me? You know we have a firm anti-bullying policy here in school.'

My heart went out to him, he looked so self-conscious. 'They call me names and push me in the corridor,' he admitted. 'Sometimes they put things in my bag and follow me into the toilet, that type of stuff.' I guessed this was probably only part of it – the bit he felt able to tell.

'What is the name of the ringleader?' Carolyn asked.

'What will you do?' Stevie replied, clearly worried about reprisals.

'The headmaster and I will talk to the person and make it clear his or her behaviour is unacceptable and if it doesn't stop they will be suspended.'

'It's ——,' he said, and gave a boy's name.

'I know who you mean,' Carolyn said seriously. 'We'll speak to him this afternoon so you can return to school tomorrow morning. But in future, Stevie, please come and see me if you have any problems.'

He gave a half-hearted nod, and Carolyn then went on to talk about his school work. He was behind in most subjects, partly from missing school, but also because he hadn't been handing in his homework.

'I haven't got anywhere quiet to study at my gran's,' he said, which may have been true.

'That won't be a problem now,' I said. 'You have your own bedroom, which has bookshelves and a small table for studying. Also, I showed you the front room you can use, which has a computer.' So there won't be any excuses, I could have added but didn't.

Carolyn told Stevie – I guessed not for the first time – that it was an important year for him academically, as they had started the syllabi for examinations the following year. Stevie promised to do better in future, and Carolyn then talked easily and at length about gender identity. She said that schools were having to address how best to accommodate LGBT+ – lesbian, gay, bisexual, transgender and other – students. In line with other schools they were considering installing gender-neutral toilets and changing rooms for PE. She said there was no provision for this at present and asked Stevie if he had any particular concerns about using the boys' toilets and changing rooms. If so, she'd look into what other arrangements could be made.

'No, I'm OK with that,' he said, a little embarrassed.

Carolyn added that at present Stevie would be expected to wear the boys' school uniform, which wasn't so different from the girls' (although they had a choice of trousers or a skirt), but that could change in the future.

I thought that the school was being very sensitive and proactive in addressing the issues surrounding LGBT+ students. To be honest, I hadn't given it much thought until Stevie had been placed with me.

Carolyn finished by asking Stevie if there was anything else he wanted to discuss or that she could help him with, and he said there wasn't.

'See you tomorrow in school then,' she said positively as we stood.

I thanked her again, and she saw us down to reception where we signed out.

As soon as we were outside Stevie took his phone from his pocket, and it instantly sprang into life.

'That wasn't switched off,' I said. 'It was on silent.'

'I'll switch it off properly when I'm in school.'

'You must. Don't start tomorrow by breaking one of the rules,' I said. He shrugged. 'Anyway, it will be a nice short week. Friday tomorrow and then the weekend.'

'Yes, and I can go out.'

'If you want to.'

Stevie was quiet in the car as I drove to his grandparents'. He checked his phone every so often, but otherwise just stared out of his side window. I sensed he was worrying about something, but it could have been any number of things: returning to school, facing his grandparents, wishing he was still living with them and hadn't stormed off, or something completely different. The teenage years are difficult with all the changes in the body and mind; problems that might not affect adults can play havoc with a young person.

'A penny for your thoughts,' I said, glancing at him as I drove. He looked at me, puzzled. 'It's an expression my father used to use,' I explained. 'It means you seem deep in thought.'

'Oh, right, yeah,' he said, but that was all.

A few moments later I said, 'Stevie, I know I've told you this before, but you can talk to me if there is something bothering you. It's not a good idea to keep worries to yourself. If you've got a problem, I'm sure we can sort it out.'

He threw me a cursory nod and continued to gaze through his side window.

Five minutes later I pulled in to the housing estate where his grandparents lived and Stevie directed me to their house. It was a 1960s semi-detached with an integral garage and small open-plan front garden similar to the other houses in the street.

'I've forgotten my keys,' Stevie said as we got out.

'It doesn't matter. Your gran will be in. She's expecting us.'

We went up to their front door and he pressed the door-bell. The door was opened by his grandfather with a rather gruff, 'Oh, it's you. Come in, but don't make a noise. Your gran isn't so good.'

'I'm sorry,' I said, hesitating on the doorstep. 'Shall we come back another time?'

'No, you're here now. He can get his clothes.'

Stevie went past him and disappeared upstairs as Fred closed the front door.

'I'm here,' Peggy said, appearing in the hall. 'I've just got a migraine. It came on all of a sudden. I've taken some tablets. Come through while Steven gets his things.'

I went with Peggy into their sitting room as Fred went upstairs. The room was at the back of the house and cosy with floral carpet and curtains, three armchairs and lots of china ornaments on display shelves. 'Do you want a cup of tea?' Peggy asked, sinking into a chair.

'No, thank you. I'm fine.' She looked pale and drawn. While I've never suffered from migraine headaches, I have a friend who does and I appreciated what sufferers go through. When migraines strike they are debilitating until the medication takes effect. 'We've just come from seeing Carolyn,' I said. 'Steven's going to school tomorrow.'

'Good. What did Carolyn say?'

I told Peggy more or less what we'd discussed with Carolyn, leaving out Stevie's excuse of not having anywhere quiet to study as the reason he hadn't been doing his homework. She didn't need to know that with a headache.

'I didn't realise the bullying was that bad,' she said wearily.

'No. In my experience teenagers try to deal with it themselves first. It slipped out when he was talking to my children.'

Peggy nodded thoughtfully and her face clouded. 'You know, Cathy, I feel so bad about him going into care.' Her eyes filled.

'Don't upset yourself,' I said, touching her arm. 'I'm sure you did the right thing. It will give you all a chance to have a breather, and you'll be seeing him regularly.'

She took a tissue from the sleeve of her cardigan and dabbed her eyes. My heart went out to her. She looked defeated – as if she'd tried her best and failed. 'I would have him back now and make it work,' she said. 'It's Fred. He's told Steven he needs to sort himself out first. You know, all that stuff about if he's a girl or a boy. I can't stand any more arguments, not with looking after the younger two as well. I'm worn out.'

'I think you've done a fantastic job,' I said. 'I really do. Three young children is a lot to cope with.' I hope I didn't sound patronising, but I meant it.

'Fred thinks Steven is doing this on purpose to wind us up and get attention.'

This was difficult. 'I think Stevie is confused about his gender identity,' I said carefully. 'I know it's difficult for us to understand; we've never been in that position. But I think he is genuinely struggling to sort out how he sees himself.'

'Do you?' she asked. 'You never heard of that sort of thing when I was young. You were either male or female. Some people were homosexual, but they knew that. There was never any of this "I might be a girl or I might be a boy or maybe I'm both".' She looked sad, confused and out of her depth. 'Is it something I've done wrong?'

'No, Peggy, of course not. You haven't done anything wrong. You've done a good job of bringing him up. He's a nice lad. You can be proud of him.'

'He should be living here with me,' she said mournfully. 'Not with a foster carer. I don't mean to be rude, but that's how I feel.' She'd obviously been thinking about this a lot.

'I understand,' I said. 'Try to look upon it as me helping you out for now. We all need help sometimes, don't we?' I was about to say more when Fred came in.

'Is he wearing your knickers yet?' he quipped, sitting in the largest armchair, which I took to be his.

He was joking, but it was an entirely inappropriate comment. I thought it was probably his way of coping with a situation he didn't understand and perhaps found embarrassing. Maybe he felt his masculinity was under threat, or maybe he recognised something in Stevie he didn't want to acknowledge in himself. Who knows? But making Stevie the butt of his jokes wasn't going to help – quite the opposite. Since I'd first been told I would be fostering Stevie, I'd researched gender online and I'd come to realise that it isn't always clear cut, but a spectrum, with male and female either end and degrees of gender in between. Fred needed to be more aware, to stop teasing his grandson and help him if there was any chance of healing their damaged relationship. I thought Fred was a man who would appreciate straight talking.

'Fred, do you ever use the internet?' I asked him.

'What would I want with that?' he scorned.

'There's a lot of information on the internet, like all the books, newspapers and magazines in the world put together. I go online if I need to know something. Have a look on the internet for the term "gender-fluid". I think you may be surprised by what you find. There are other families facing the same issues you are, and online support groups have been set up. The library has computers you can use for free.'

'You mean there's others like him!' he jeered.

'Yes.'

'Thank you, Cathy,' Peggy said quietly. 'I've seen the computers in the library, but I don't know how to use them.'

'An assistant should be able to show you,' I said. 'Otherwise give me a ring and I'll meet you there. Once you know how to use the internet, it's easy.'

She managed a small smile and tucked away her tissue. 'Steven is going to school tomorrow,' she told Fred positively.

'About bloody time too!' he snapped. I was sure Fred loved Stevie as he did Liam and Kiri, but he could be abrupt and scathing, which children don't need. It undermines their self-confidence if they're put down when they speak. It's not good for adults either.

Peggy changed the conversation and began talking about the weather, and we continued making polite conversation until Stevie appeared at the door carrying bin liners full of his belongings. 'I'm ready to go,' he said, apparently not wanting to come into the living room and spend time with his grandparents.

Peggy and I stood, I said goodbye to Fred and Peggy saw us to the front door. 'Bye, Gran,' Stevie said, kissing her cheek. 'See you soon.'

'Yes, you take care.' Her eyes filled again.

CHAPTER SEVEN

QUIET AND WITHDRAWN

Once home I asked Stevie to unpack the bags he'd brought from his gran's and get out his school uniform, so he was ready for school the next day. Paula returned home from college – her first day back after the Christmas break. She was studying business studies, which she hoped would allow her a career in a company, though exactly what type of company she wasn't sure yet. She was quieter than Lucy and tended to give matters a lot of thought, sometimes overthinking. But she could be assertive and stand up for herself if necessary. She and Adrian saw their father every six weeks or so, and made their own arrangements now they were older. Lucy saw her birth mother once or twice a year.

Adrian was working a late shift, so I plated up his dinner for when he came home, and called Lucy, Stevie and Paula to the table. Stevie arrived wearing make-up – but not too much – and had changed clothes and was now wearing dusty pink skinny trousers and matching shirt.

'Wow!' Lucy said admiringly. 'You look good.'

'You like it?' Stevie asked, pleased and doing a turn.

'Yes, it suits you.'

It did. Although I could see how his grandparents might struggle with their grandson in pink when it was a colour traditionally associated with girls. An outfit like this would also draw attention to him, possibly unwanted attention, I thought protectively. But you can't keep young people wrapped up in cotton wool; sometimes they have to learn for themselves.

Stevie took his place at the table and we all began eating.

'How did you get into all this tranny stuff?' Lucy asked after a moment.

'Online, I guess,' Stevie replied with a shrug. 'Although it's not really tranny. I googled how I was feeling and up came all these websites. I couldn't believe it – young people discussing exactly how I felt! It was such a relief.'

I nodded. I could imagine the comfort he'd found in discovering other like-minded people. Although there is a dark side to the internet, there are many positives too: easy access to information and learning, shopping, up-to-the-minute news and the ability to connect people all over the world for business and socialising, support and reassurance, to name a few.

'I've made a lot of friends online,' Stevie added. 'I can share stuff with them that I can't with others because they understand. They know how I feel.'

'That's good,' I said, 'but just remember that online friends aren't the same as those you know in person – at school or in the area. The only thing you know for sure about the person you are talking to online is that they can type.'

Stevie looked at me for a moment, puzzled, then said, 'Oh yes, I see what you mean.'

'Mum says that a lot when she lectures us about staying safe online,' Lucy said.

Stevie had paused from eating and appeared deep in thought.

'Are you going to school tomorrow?' Paula asked him presently.

'Yes,' he replied, and continued eating.

The conversation ran on as we ate, with talk about school and college. I offered to take Stevie to school in the car the following morning for his first day back, but he didn't want me to, saying he would use the bus. He knew the bus stop was a short walk away at the top of our road and that the bus would take him right to his school.

'I *will* go,' he said to me, as if the reason I'd offered him a lift was because I doubted he'd get there.

'I know, I trust you,' I said. 'I just thought you might prefer a lift on your first day back. A bit of support.'

I did trust him. I always trust people until they give me a reason not to. At Stevie's age, of course, he should be allowed to go to school and come home by bus. I told him what time he'd need to be up in the morning to leave the house on time. 'And I'll expect you home by four-thirty,' I said. 'Text me if you're going to be late.'

One of the first things I do when I'm fostering a young person is to exchange mobile phone numbers, so I can get in touch with them and they with me. My number was now in Stevie's phone and his was in mine.

That evening, while everyone was occupied in their rooms, I wrote up my log notes, then went online and found Stevie's Facebook page. His security was set to high strength so none of his details or photographs were public; only 'friends' could see them. I clicked on the box to send him a friendship request.

* * *

Stevie slept well again, very well, and it took a bit of persuading to get him up the following morning so he had time for breakfast. I gave him money for his school dinner and checked he had his bus pass with him, then saw him off at the door. 'Good luck. Text me if you want a lift home, otherwise I'll see you at four-thirty,' I said.

He nodded and, slipping in the earbuds he'd brought from home, went up the front path. He looked very smart in his school uniform, although I noticed his trousers were a fraction too short. At his age he would be having growth spurts and continually need new clothes. But of course he'd spent all his clothing allowance for the month on a new pair of jeans, so I would buy what he needed. Foster carers receive an allowance, but it rarely covers everything a young person needs and they dig into their own pockets as they would for their own children.

Lucy had already left for work, and Paula left for college soon after Stevie. Adrian, having worked a late shift the night before, was just getting up as he didn't have to be in until ten. I cooked him breakfast, cleared up, said goodbye to him as he left and then the day slipped by. Housework, laundry, I phoned Verity and left a message with her colleague to say Stevie was in school today, did some clerical work, phoned my mother for a chat, and before long it was time to start thinking about what to give everyone for dinner.

Four-thirty came and went and there was no sign of Stevie. At five o'clock, when he still wasn't home and hadn't texted, I began to worry. I didn't want him to think I didn't trust him or to appear overprotective, but when it got to five-thirty I was really worried and texted. *Are you OK? Had expected you home by now. Cathy x*

Paula was now home from college and was trying to talk to me about her day, but I was only half listening. Having texted Stevie, I gave her my full attention for all of two minutes until my phone bleeped with an incoming text. It was from Stevie and I immediately read it. *On the bus now. Went to see Kiri and Liam.* Which was fine, but he should have told me before that he was going to see his sister and brother, not after the event. I'd remind him when he got home. 'Sorry, love,' I said to Paula. 'Thanks for your patience. Let's go and sit in the living room and have a chat.' Which we did. It's so important to make time for your own children when you foster.

Stevie arrived home twenty minutes later, just after Paula and I had finished our chat. As I let him in I asked him how Liam (aged eight) and Kiri (aged six) were. He said they were 'fine, same as usual'. He took off his shoes and coat and I asked him how his day had been at school, and he said, 'Fine.' Then he added that he'd seen Carolyn and she and the Head had spoken to the boy who'd been leading the bullying and he'd been made to apologise.

'Did that help?' I asked.

'I think so,' Stevie said.

'Good.' I then reminded him to text me if he wasn't coming straight home from school. 'And the same applies for tonight,' I said. 'You said you wanted to go out, so I'll expect you home by nine-thirty. I'd like to know where you're going and how you are getting home.'

'I'm not going out now,' he said.

'Oh, OK.'

He went up to his room and stayed there until dinner was ready. I assumed he was changing out of his school uniform, but when he came down he was still in his school jersey and trousers, and seemed subdued. 'Everything OK?' I asked him. He nodded and joined us at the table.

It was just Paula, Stevie and me for dinner, as Adrian and Lucy were both still working – Adrian until eight o'clock and Lucy on the late shift at the nursery, which finished at seven. As we ate I tried to make conversation, but only Paula responded. Stevie was clearly preoccupied and, once finished, he stood, took his plate and cutlery to the kitchen and went upstairs. Usually I like us all to stay at the table until everyone has finished eating (as he had the previous night) – it's polite – but it was only a small matter and he obviously had things on his mind. Stevie remained in his room all evening, despite me going up a couple of times and suggesting he come down. I wasn't unduly worried; many young people like to spend time in their rooms, and he'd had a pretty emotional week and been to school that day.

I try to see my mother every two weeks, usually at the weekend, when we all go if possible. She lives about an hour's drive away. However, Mum understood I wouldn't be going this weekend, as I wanted Stevie settled in first. I'd phone her again over the weekend and my brother would visit. On Saturday morning, when Stevie surfaced, I asked him if he had any plans for the weekend. He said he didn't and wouldn't be going out that night even though it was Saturday. I knew young people's plans often changed and didn't read anything untoward into it. I suggested he might like to see his grandparents and Liam and Kiri, as there was more time at the weekend, rather than after school. But he didn't want to do that either; he said he'd seen them the day before.

Adrian was working Saturday, and Lucy and Paula were thinking of going shopping after lunch, and they asked Stevie if he wanted to join them. I was expecting him to jump at the chance, given his enthusiasm for shopping when I'd taken him, but he said he wasn't in the mood for shopping and was going to chill in his room. That afternoon there was just him and me in the house and I suggested he might like to come down rather than sit in his room, where he'd been all day.

'I'm good here,' he said. He was propped up on his bed, texting.

'OK. Have you got any homework to do?'

'Yes, I'll do it later.'

I assumed that, having shared a bedroom with his younger brother, he was enjoying having his own space. In respect of his homework, it was reasonable that he should take responsibility for it at his age, although I would remind him again to make sure it was done. With younger children I often sat with them downstairs while they did their homework, giving them help as and when necessary. Of course I would help Stevie too, if he asked. He remained in his room for the whole afternoon and only came down for dinner when Adrian, Lucy and Paula were back. There was no trace of make-up and he was still subdued. I asked him if he was OK and he said he was, but he didn't join in any of our conversation at all.

Sunday was bitterly cold, but having not been out the day before I felt in need of a breath of fresh air. I asked if anyone would like to join me for a walk, but there weren't any takers, so I went alone. I wouldn't have left a teenager alone in the house when they'd only recently arrived, but Adrian, Paula and Lucy were in. Paula and Lucy were my nominated carers. Foster carers can nominate family members or close friends to help out and babysit when necessary. They are assessed by the carer's supervising social worker for suitability, and sometimes police checked (now called a DBS check – Disclosure and Barring Service). Lucy had qualifications in childcare, experience of being fostered and of course lived with the looked-after child, so knew them well. I would never have them solely responsible for a lad of fourteen in case he kicked off, but with Adrian there too I felt comfortable going for a short walk. I was home again in under half an hour.

Adrian went out shortly after I returned and was spending the rest of the day with Kirsty. After lunch, Lucy, Paula and I were in the living room, reading: Paula on her laptop for college, Lucy a true story on her Kindle and I was reading a paperback thriller. I asked Stevie if he would join us, but he said he hadn't finished his homework yet. He finally joined us for dinner and then in the evening came to watch a television programme, but only for fifteen minutes and was very quiet. After he'd left the room Lucy said exactly what I'd been thinking: 'What's the matter with him?'

'I don't know,' I said. 'I keep asking if there is anything wrong, but he says there isn't. If he says anything to you, please let me know.'

'Yes, of course.'

I've found before that children and young people some-times confide in one of my children before they tell me. It used to happen when my family were little too, and they knew they had to tell me so I could help sort out the problem. Obviously we hadn't known Stevie long and it was possible he often had mood swings as his grandparents claimed – flamboyant and extrovert one day and quiet and introspective the next – but I had the feeling it was more than that.

On Monday morning we all fell into the routine of the work-ing week. Stevie left for school on time, assuring me he had done his homework and he would see me at 4.30. By 9 a.m.

the house was empty save for me and Sammy, who was curled in front of the radiator in the living room. Verity telephoned just after nine and asked how Stevie had been over the weekend. I said he had spent most of it in his bedroom with his phone, and when he had joined us he had been very quiet. I said that I'd asked him a number of times if anything was worrying him and he'd said there wasn't. 'OK, I'll speak to him,' Verity said. 'I need to see him this week. I'm thinking of Wednesday after school. What time does he get in?'

'Four-thirty.'

'Please tell Stevie I'll see him then, but he knows he can phone me before if he needs to.'

'Yes, will do.'

Social workers are obliged to visit a child placed with foster carers within the first week, then every six weeks after that – more if necessary. I wrote Verity's visit in my diary, and when Stevie arrived home (on time) I told him, and asked him if he'd had a good day. He nodded and disappeared upstairs. Apart from coming down for dinner he spent the rest of the evening in his room, saying he had homework to do.

That night I was late going to bed and it was nearly midnight before I went up. I saw a light coming from under Stevie's bedroom door; everyone else had been asleep for some time. I gently tapped on the door. 'Stevie, are you awake?' I asked quietly. There was no reply. I tapped again and then slowly opened the door. He was propped up in bed, earbuds in and with his phone in his hand. He started when he saw me and quickly pulled out his earbuds. 'I'm switching my phone off now,' he said.

'Yes, please. It's very late. You need to get to sleep. Is everything all right?'

He nodded and lay down, his back to me.

'Goodnight,' I said, but there was no reply.

I came out and quietly closed his bedroom door. The guilt on his face when I'd opened his door had been out of all proportion to being caught using his phone when he should have been asleep. I started to think that whatever was worrying Stevie could be the result of something he'd done, and it might be serious. But until he wanted to share it, there was nothing I could do to help.

On Tuesday Stevie decided to visit his gran after school and remembered to text me to tell me he'd be late. He was home in time for dinner, ate with us, hardly said a word, and then spent the rest of the evening in his room – 'doing homework', he said. I thought at this rate he was going to be top of his class! However, the following morning, after everyone had left, Peggy telephoned me. 'Is Stevie all right?' she asked. 'He's not sickening for something? He was very quiet yesterday.'

I said he didn't appear to be unwell and wasn't off his food but agreed that he was very quiet and had been all weekend. I told her that when I asked him if anything was worrying him he said there wasn't. 'I've told Verity and she is coming to see him this evening,' I said. 'What did Stevie do while he was with you yesterday?'

'He kept out of Fred's way,' Peggy said with a humourless laugh. 'He spent most of his time with Kiri and Liam. I think that's why he came – to see them.'

'Have they said any more about their secret?'

'No, and nothing seems to be missing. Fred's still got his teeth.'

I smiled. 'OK, I'll let you know what Verity says.'

'It's probably just teenage angst,' Peggy said. 'Stevie seems to get a lot of that.'

Quite possibly she was right, although I wasn't convinced.

That Peggy was able to phone me so we could discuss our concerns allowed us to work together in Stevie's best interest. Sometimes parents or guardians are so angry that their child is in care that the foster carer's contact details are withheld to protect the carer, and sometimes they are withheld to protect the children if the parents have been abusing them. But now my relationship with Peggy was textbook good and I hoped it would continue.

I messaged Stevie at 3.30 to remind him that he had to come straight home as Verity was coming to see him at 4.30. He'd see the message when he switched on his phone at the end of school. Apart from once when he'd first arrived, he'd been getting home on time, and hadn't wanted to go out, so I'd seen very little of the behaviour his grandparents had struggled with when he'd disappeared off and stayed out all night. However, it was early days yet and we were in what foster carers often refer to as the honeymoon period. The child is on their best behaviour to begin with, then they start to relax and test the boundaries. Boundaries are a sign of caring and the child or young person tests the boundaries to see if the carer loves them enough to forgive them – anything. But foster carers are only human and sometimes the child's behaviour is so extreme that the carer has to ask for the placement to end and the child to be moved. As well as making the carer feel guilty, this rejection compounds the child's feelings of being unwanted, and their challenging behaviour escalates, when a bit of extra support for the carer might have been able to save the placement and keep the child where they were.

Stevie arrived with Verity. She'd seen him walking down the road and had given him a lift in her car. Having taken off their coats and shoes, they went into the living room while I made Verity a coffee and poured Stevie the glass of juice he wanted.

'Shall I leave you to it?' I asked Verity as I set the drinks on the table within their reach.

'Yes, please,' Verity said. 'I'll see you before I go.'

I came out, closing the door behind me, and went into the kitchen to start preparing dinner. Paula, Lucy and Adrian knew that Verity was coming, and Paula arrived home first. She came into the kitchen and we chatted for a while about her day, then she took a drink up to her room. Just after five o'clock I heard the living-room door open and then Verity called, 'Stevie is going to show me his room.'

'OK,' I returned.

Five minutes later she came down into the kitchen to find me. I stopped what I was doing to talk to her. 'Stevie's staying in his room,' she said. 'He likes having his own room but misses his brother and sister.' I nodded. 'I asked him if there was anything in particular worrying him and he said there wasn't. He says he's not depressed. Actually, he was quite talkative – as much as any young person his age talks to their social worker.' She gave a rueful smile. 'I've told him I'll apply for a laptop for him, as he hasn't got one at present.'

'He can always use the computer in the front room,' I said. 'I've shown him where it is.'

'Yes, but we like all our looked-after young people to have their own laptops,' Verity said. 'I'll have a chat with his mentor tomorrow and see what he's been like in school. I think if he is quieter than usual it's because he's adjusting to living here, plus the issues surrounding his gender. Was there anything else you wanted to raise?'

'Not really.'

'I've said goodbye to Stevie so I won't disturb him again,' Verity said, and collected her bag from the living room. I saw her out.

Verity obviously knew Stevie better than I did, as she'd been working with the family for a while, so I was relieved she felt it was just a matter of him settling in with us, and I assumed Carolyn would phone me if there was a problem at school. Hopefully, Stevie would return to his bright and bubbly self before long. However, it was a hope that was short-lived.

CHAPTER EIGHT

ERROR OF JUDGEMENT

After Verity had left I finished preparing the evening meal and then once Adrian and Lucy were home I called everyone for dinner. Stevie didn't appear, so I called him again, served dinner and then, leaving mine untouched, went upstairs. His bedroom door was closed and I assumed he had his earbuds in and hadn't heard me calling him. 'Stevie,' I said, knocking on his door. 'Dinner's ready.' There was no reply. 'Stevie,' I said, knocking more firmly this time. 'Dinner.' Nothing. 'Stevie!' I knocked again and then slowly opened the door. He was sitting on the edge of his bed, not with his earbuds in, but bent forward, with his head in his hands. 'Are you OK?' I asked, going further in.

He shook his head and looked up. His cheeks were stained with tears; his face crumpled. 'Whatever is the matter?' I asked, going to him. He shook his head in despair, as if the problem was too big to share.

I'm always moved when I see someone crying, especially if it is a child, as I'm sure most people are, but there was something particularly upsetting in seeing Stevie, aged fourteen, and outwardly mature for his age, crying like a baby. I sat beside him on the edge of the bed, with the door open.

'What is it, love? What's upset you so much?' I asked him gently.

He shook his head again. 'I can't tell you,' he murmured.

'Please try,' I said, and wondered what could possibly have reduced him to this state. 'Are you being bullied at school?' I asked. It seemed the most likely reason.

'No,' he said, his voice breaking.

'Well, what is it, love? I've had a feeling something is worrying you.' As old as he was, he was clearly in need of some TLC and I placed my hand on his arm and lightly rubbed it. 'I'm sure I can help if you'll let me.'

'You can't,' he said. Fresh tears formed and I passed him a tissue from the box open on his bed. He wiped his eyes.

'Mum!' Paula called from the foot of the stairs. 'What are you doing? Your dinner is getting cold.'

'I'm with Stevie,' I returned. 'I'll have it later, thanks.'

'You go,' Stevie said. 'I'll be OK.'

'No, I'm not leaving you like this.' I slipped my arm around his shoulders and gave him a hug. 'Can you please try to tell me what is upsetting you?' I asked after a moment.

Taking a deep breath, as if summoning the courage, he said, 'I've been dumped.'

I must admit I found some relief in this, although I appreciated just how painful breaking up with a loved one can be, especially at his age.

'I am sorry,' I said. 'I didn't know you had a girlfriend.'

'Boyfriend,' he corrected.

'Sorry,' I said again, and thought, Come on, Cathy, get up to speed! 'Was it someone you met at school?' I asked, feeling it would help if he could talk about it.

'No. Online,' he said.

'Oh, I see, so you met online. Does he live locally then?'

'No, over a hundred miles away, which is why we never met. We were going to meet, then he dumped me.'

'I understand,' I sympathised.

'No reason, he just dumped me,' Stevie repeated. 'He won't answer my calls or reply to my messages. He said he loved me, and I loved him. I'm gutted. I'll never trust anyone again.' He took another tissue from the box.

To anyone who has never tried online dating, Stevie's distress must seem out of all proportion; he'd never even met the guy! But he was fourteen and this was probably his first love, and I was aware of just how much information was swapped online during the build-up to actually meeting – like a courtship. I'd tried online dating once. Having been alone for many years and finding it difficult to meet single, like-minded people of my age, I joined an online dating website for a couple of months. That had been enough for me. In my opinion, all the emails, texts and instant messages are no substitute for getting to know someone in person over a coffee. But that wouldn't help Stevie.

'How old was he?' I asked.

'Fifteen.'

'Had you known him for long?'

Stevie nodded. 'Four months.'

'Which website was it?' For I knew that most dating websites have a minimum age of eighteen to register, but of course it's easy to lie.

'It was on one for young people like me,' Stevie said.

'So not a dating website?'

'No. Just somewhere to meet, chat and hangout. He was on Facebook too.'

'What's his name?' I asked after a moment. 'Do you want to tell me?'

'Joey. We got on so well. He was easy to talk to and we had everything in common. He lives with his grandparents and has a younger brother and sister just like me. We shared everything.'

It was no good telling Stevie he would get over it and that his broken heart would heal. What he needed now was a sympathetic ear; one that would appreciate his suffering.

'I feel betrayed,' he said. 'He seemed so nice and understood me. He was very good-looking too.'

'Do you have a photo?' I asked.

'Yes, loads.' He reached under his pillow for his phone. As he touched the screen it sprang into life with a photo, so I guessed he'd been looking at Joey's photo before I'd come in, torturing himself with what might have been. 'That's his profile picture,' he said, tilting the phone towards me so I could see.

I looked at the head-and-shoulders photograph of a young man with fashionable styled hair like Stevie's and dark, warm, smiling eyes, who was indeed good-looking. He looked older than fifteen, but then so did Stevie.

'I am sorry,' I said. 'You must be feeling very rejected.'

He nodded. 'I feel violated.' Which I thought was a bit strong for an online relationship when they'd never even met. 'We told each other so much and we swapped photos. I wish I hadn't now. I don't like the thought of him having all those photos of me. He betrayed me.'

'I can appreciate that,' I said, and I did. When my husband had run off with a younger woman it had taken some time for me to get over the betrayal and to trust again.

'Cathy,' Stevie said awkwardly after moment, putting the phone on the bed, 'I'm really worried because some of the photos I sent him were private photos.' He looked embarrassed. 'You know, I took selfies, some without my clothes on.'

'I see.' As a foster carer and parent, I knew that if a child or young person began to disclose, it was important to remain calm and not throw up my arms in horror. It will have taken a lot of courage and they'll be looking for reassurance. 'How revealing were the photographs?' I asked, my voice steady.

'Very,' he said, embarrassed. 'I sent him one of my —' He hesitated. 'You know what.'

'Your private parts?'

He nodded self-consciously. 'He sent me one of his, but please don't tell my gran. She'll be furious.' Understandably, I thought, and I dreaded to think what Fred would say. Not only that, I knew from foster-carer training that in the UK it is an offence to take, distribute, possess or show any indecent images of anyone under eighteen, even if they were taken by the young person or with their consent. I didn't want to panic Stevie, but this was serious.

'No, I don't have to tell your grandparents,' I said, 'but I will have to tell your social worker and she will decide what to do for the best. You are a minor and your grandparents are your guardians and therefore responsible for you.' Then a horrendous thought occurred to me. All that time Stevie had spent in his room on his phone, had he taken the photos while he'd been in my care? As his foster carer I was acting in loco parentis and would have been responsible had they been taken here, although of course it's impossible to supervise young people all the time. 'When did you take the photographs and send them?' I asked.

'When I was at my gran's,' Stevie said. 'I've deleted the photos from my phone and Joey promised to do the same. But I feel bad he saw me like that, and what if he shows them to someone or puts them online?'

'That's exactly why it's not a good idea to send intimate photos of yourself,' I said.

'I know,' Stevie said dejectedly.

Sexting is the term used to describe the exchange of sexually explicit messages, photos and videos by text, app or online. The problem is that once you press send you have no control over where that photo will end up, as Stevie had now realised – too late. 'Did you know it's illegal to send photos like this at your age?' I asked him.

He looked horrified. 'No! But I'm not the only one who does it. What will happen to me?'

'First and foremost, it's important that you learn a lesson from this,' I said. 'From what I understand Verity will need to inform the police.' He gasped. 'They may want to see you and it will be their decision if you are charged.' This piece of UK law was relatively new, but the guidelines were that while the police had to record incidents of sexting involving minors, what action they took was at their discretion and the crime should be viewed proportionately and as a safeguarding issue. However, had one of them been an adult it would have been viewed differently and fallen into paedophile activity. I hoped the police would view this as an error of judgement between two young people, but that would be their decision.

Stevie looked as though he'd learnt his lesson already; the colour had drained from his face. 'I'm glad you felt able to tell me,' I said. 'Try not to worry. I'll speak to Verity first thing tomorrow. You've deleted all the indecent photos from your phone and Joey has said he has done the same, but if any of you do appear online, you need to tell me straight away. OK?'

'Yes, I will,' Stevie said glumly.

* * *

By the time Stevie and I went down to dinner Paula, Lucy and Adrian had finished theirs but were still at the table, talking. They obviously knew something significant and upsetting that involved Stevie had taken place but were sensitive enough not to ask. It would be up to Stevie if he told them. I pinged my and Stevie's dinner in the microwave and we ate together, then instead of disappearing up to his room he stayed at the table chatting to the girls for a while, then joined me in the living room and watched some television. While he was still clearly worried – this would be hanging over him for some time while the police made their decision on what action to take – he'd stopped frantically checking his phone and did seem more relaxed and talkative. He had an early night and after he'd gone to bed I took the opportunity to write up my log notes, detailing what Stevie had told me. I hadn't telephoned Peggy as I said I would after Verity's visit as I needed to update Verity first about this disclosure, and I knew she'd want to speak to Peggy and Fred.

I didn't sleep well and I don't think Stevie did either as I heard him get up twice to go to the bathroom. What Stevie had told me played on my mind – despite all the warnings, he'd put himself in an unsafe position online. Peggy and Fred weren't tech savvy and as far as I knew didn't own mobile phones, but warnings about staying safe online were everywhere, and the school would have warned its students too. But like other young people Stevie and Joey hadn't heeded the warnings, probably feeling they didn't apply to them and, caught up in the excitement of their romance, had not only compromised their safety, but unwittingly committed a crime. I wondered if Paula, Lucy or Adrian could ever do similar and hoped not, after all my warnings. As far as I knew all their friends had been made in person and not online – from school, college, university, work, our neighbourhood and so on. I trusted them to do the sensible thing, but of course you can never be sure, even though they were young adults now.

In the morning, once the house had emptied, I telephoned Verity and told her exactly what Stevie had told me. She wasn't shocked – as a social worker she would have had to deal with matters far more shocking than sexting – but she was concerned and immediately appreciated the implications. The social services had been involved with the family for some time and Stevie was a looked-after child in care, so we all bore some responsibility for him. 'Joey is fifteen and the website where they met is for young LGBT people,' Verity clarified, I guessed making notes.

'Yes, that's what Stevie said, and that he was on Facebook too.'

'And Stevie's already deleted all the indecent images he had on his phone?'

'Yes, although I didn't check.'

'OK. I'll need to see him again, but I'll speak to his grandparents first. Wish me luck.'

I didn't envy Verity having to tell Peggy and Fred what Stevie had done, but when Peggy telephoned me two hours later she appeared to have taken the news very well. 'The silly sod,' she said lightly, referring to Stevie. 'Fancy him sending photos to that other lad when he didn't even know him.' So I guessed she understood what was involved.

'I think Stevie has learnt his lesson now,' I said. 'He was very remorseful. Does Fred know?'

'Yes. He thought it was funny to begin with until Verity told him she would have to report it to the police. I mean, we took some saucy photos of each other on our Polaroid camera when we were courting. But of course back then if you split up, you just handed the photo back. They faded anyway after a while.' Polaroid cameras were fashionable in the 1970s and allowed you to print a photograph instantly, but the photos then, when the technology was just out, were small, lacked detail and, as Peggy said, could fade with time. Very unlike the clarity and detail in the digital photographs we have now, that can be taken on a phone and have the potential to be shared with thousands around the world in minutes.

'Anyway, at least it's out in the open,' Peggy said. 'Hopefully Stevie will be in a better mood now. Fred was more concerned it was a bloke he'd sent the photo to. I won't tell you what he said.'

'No, best not.'

That afternoon, when Stevie arrived home from school, he said that Verity had seen him while he'd been at school and had asked him about Joey and the photographs. That was all he said and I didn't press him for more details. What took place between him and his social worker was private and Verity would hopefully tell me what – if anything – I needed to know. I guessed Stevie had told her pretty much what he'd told me. They'd used Carolyn's office and Verity had spoken to her after she'd finished talking to Stevie.

By Friday I thought Stevie would probably want to go out, given that he was in a better frame of mind now and had pushed to be allowed out more when he was first placed. But when I asked if he had any plans for the weekend, he said he didn't.

'Is everything OK?' I asked. 'You used to go out a lot when you lived with your grandparents.' Indeed, his going out and staying out had been one of the problems.

'It was different at my gran's,' Stevie said. 'I didn't have any privacy and Grandpa kept going on at me. He was doing my head in, I had to get out. And the longer I stayed out the better.'

'I understand,' I said.

'Also, the guy I used to spend time with has just been sent to live with his father abroad. He got into trouble with the police and his mum decided it was best for him. We still message.'

'How old is he?' I asked.

'Fifteen.'

'What sort of trouble was he in?'

'Not sure, drugs, I think,' Stevie hedged. 'And before you ask, no, I don't do drugs. I wouldn't. I've seen what they've done to my mum, drugs and drink. They make you look like shit and screw up your brains.'

'Yes, they do,' I said, pleased Stevie could share this with me. 'Most of the children I've fostered were from homes where one or both parents were drug or drink dependent.'

'I don't have to go out, do I?' he then asked. 'I mean, you don't want to get rid of me?'

'No, of course not.' I smiled. 'I'm glad you're spending time with us.'

'I'm glad too. I like living here,' he said a little self-consciously.

'And we're all very pleased to have you,' I replied. I was really touched.

On Saturday Stevie went to see his grandparents in the afternoon for a couple of hours. It was the first time he'd seen them since the sexting had become known and I wondered what they'd say to him, especially his grandfather. Fred wasn't renowned for his subtle, sensitive approach. However, when Stevie returned he said his grandpa had been out, and his gran had told him he'd been stupid sending sexy photos to a stranger, and not to do it again, but that was all she'd said. He'd then spent a nice afternoon playing with Liam and Kiri.

On Sunday we all piled into my car and went to my mother's for the day. We were dressed smart-casual, including Stevie, who hadn't gone over the top. I hadn't told Mum that Stevie saw himself as gender-fluid; I doubted she'd know what I was talking about and Mum took everyone at face value anyway. She was always pleased to see us and was supportive of my fostering, as Dad had been, welcoming the children into her home and heart. If she noticed that Stevie was wearing make-up, she didn't say as she greeted us and made us feel at home. I thought Stevie would take to her, and he did. She's just like a nana should be – kind, loving, attentive, non-judgemental and always has lots of time for her family.

Since Dad had died Adrian did odd jobs for Mum and she kept a list of what needed doing. Top of her list today was that the lock on the shed had rusted or broken, and she couldn't get in to the bird seed to refill the feeders. She was concerned the birds were hungry in the middle of winter, as the feeders had been empty for a week. Stevie went with Adrian to fix the lock. We could see them through the patio windows. They chatted and laughed as they worked together, doing this job and others. It's little moments like this that bond a family, and I hoped Fred spent time with Stevie – making him feel useful and wanted.

Mum had insisted on cooking us dinner (sometimes we took her out for a meal), so the girls and I helped prepare the food – a full Sunday roast, followed by apple pie and custard. Adrian and Stevie washed up and I dried, while Lucy and Paula sat in the living room chatting to Mum. It was a lovely day and I found it helped put what had been a troubled week into better perspective. As we came away, Stevie cheek-kissed and hugged Mum as we were doing as if he'd always been part of the family. 'You're in a good family,' she said to him, and embarrassingly I teared up.

'I know,' he said.

CHAPTER NINE

FIRST REVIEW

Although we still had the decision of the police hanging over us, Stevie was more like his old self – the Stevie who'd arrived, charismatic, flamboyant and sometimes theatrical; indeed, I thought he could do well on the stage. Sometimes he dressed femininely and wore make-up, and sometimes he wore gender-neutral clothes like jeans and jerseys. He was starting to grow facial hair and if he left it for a few days a faint stubble appeared around his chin and over his top lip. I knew from raising Adrian that this was the age many boys began to shave and Stevie had an electric shaver his grandfather had bought for him. I heard it going in his bedroom sometimes.

'Do you think I should grow a beard?' Stevie asked us one Sunday evening when he hadn't shaved all the weekend. To be honest there wasn't really enough to make much of a beard, but I knew that wasn't what you said to a lad of his age.

'You could,' Lucy said, 'but not with make-up. That would look weird.'

'No, of course not,' Stevie said. 'But some days it feels good being a guy. There are advantages.'

'You're telling me!' Paula exclaimed. 'Gender pay gap, for

one. Why should a guy be paid more than a woman for doing the same job?'

'Well said!' Lucy applauded.

'Because we're better than you,' Adrian teased.

'In your dreams!' Lucy retorted.

There followed a rather heated discussion not only about the gender pay gap, but other areas where women and men were discriminated against because of their gender – maternity leave, for example. I sat back and enjoyed listening to their lively debate. It's so rejuvenating being among young people.

Eventually I said to Stevie, 'If you are going to grow a beard, you'll have to do so at weekends and school holidays. I think I'm right in saying that schools don't allow beards.'

'Yes, you're right,' Stevie agreed. 'A guy in my class had to shave his off in the medical room at school.'

Verity arranged Stevie's first LAC (looked-after child) review for the last Thursday in January, at 4.30 p.m. at my house. All children in care have regular reviews and the child's parent(s) or guardians, social worker, teacher, foster carer, the foster carer's support social worker and any other adults closely connected with the child meet to ensure that everything is being done to help them, and that the care plan (drawn up by the social services) is up to date. Very young children don't usually attend their reviews, while older children are expected to.

Verity sent out the invitations to the review to all parties. Stevie's and mine came with a review form each for us to complete and return to the Reviewing Officer. Stevie was obviously of an age where he could complete his form without my help; young children and those with learning difficulties often require the foster carer's assistance. The questions on the forms are designed to give a picture of how the foster carer(s) and the child feel the placement is going. They include the child's health and general wellbeing, school, cultural, religious and linguistic needs, friends, contact and hobbies. Stevie completed his form in the privacy of his bedroom and posted it on his way to school the following morning. My responses were all positive and I hoped Stevie's were too, and that he was happy living with me. These forms would be part of the review and would then be filed at the social services.

Edith telephoned the day before the review and asked for an update on how Stevie was doing and said she would be attending the review. Peggy also phoned and asked for instructions on how to get to my house, and she wrote them down. She said she'd made arrangements for Liam and Kiri to stay at after-school club that day so both she and Fred could attend the review – usually they went straight home at the end of school. She asked me a few questions about what she could expect at the review, having never attended one before, and then said, 'We'll have to leave at five-thirty to collect Liam and Kiri from the after-school club; it closes at six o'clock.'

'That should be fine,' I reassured her. 'Reviews usually only last for about an hour.'

I told Lucy, Paula and Adrian that Stevie's review would be taking place at our house the following day so they wouldn't just walk in and find a room full of strangers. Sometimes reviews are held at the social services' offices or the child's school, but there was no reason why Stevie's review couldn't be held at my house and it's usually considered best – less stressful – for the child to be in the comfort of their (foster) home than in a stark, impersonal office.

On Thursday morning as Stevie left for school I reminded him to come straight home at the end of school for his review and said again there was nothing for him to worry about. Reviews can be daunting for a child or young person, with so many adults gathered formally together to discuss them. But Stevie seemed unfazed at the prospect and appeared to be taking it in his stride. That morning I put the hoover around the house, took my fostering folder from the locked drawer where I kept it, and our surviving set of matching cups and saucers from the cupboard ready for later. Carolyn telephoned early afternoon to say she would be representing the school at Stevie's review and had got updates from his class and subject teachers, which she would bring with her.

At 3.30 I texted Stevie to remind him to come straight home and he texted back, *On the bus now x*, which was a very quick exit from school. He'd been good with his time keeping, remembering to text me if he was going to his grandparents, and not wanting to go out in the evening meant that I'd had none of the worry and stress his grandparents had. If it crossed my mind that perhaps the dramatic change in Stevie's behaviour was too good to be true, I put it down to him being relieved of carrying the burden of Joey's photographs; that the friend whom he'd stayed out all night with had been sent abroad to live; and Stevie now had the privacy of his own room and was away from his grandfather's criticism.

Stevie arrived home at four o'clock and went straight up to his room, saying he had to get ready.

'You're fine like that,' I called after him, but he'd gone.

Verity arrived at 4.20 and I told her Stevie was already here.

'Excellent,' she said.

I made her a cup of coffee and took it together with a plate of biscuits into the living room. Next to arrive was the IRO (Independent Reviewing Officer), and I recognised him, although I couldn't remember his name.

'You look familiar,' I said as he came in.

'Yes, I thought I recognised your name. I was the IRO at Zeena's review – Richard,' he said, shaking my hand.

'Yes, of course. Nice to meet you again.' It wasn't appropriate for us to start discussing another child now; that was confidential, and this review was about Stevie. (I tell Zeena's story in *The Child Bride*.)

I showed him through to the living room and then went into the kitchen to pour him a coffee. Edith arrived, followed shortly by Carolyn and, having shown them into the living room and made them a drink, I went up to Stevie's room. 'Can you come down now?' I called through his bedroom door.

'Are my grandparents here?' he asked.

'Not yet.'

'I'll come down when they are,' he said. I assumed he wasn't as unfazed by the review as he had appeared and was waiting for his grandparents before coming down for support.

Peggy and Fred arrived five minutes later, rather flustered and blaming each other for having got lost. 'I told you to turn right,' Peggy said.

'But which right!' Fred wisecracked.

'At least you're here now,' I said. I took their coats and showed them through to the living room where the IRO, Carolyn, Verity and Edith sat with notepads and files on their laps.

'Where's Steven?' Peggy asked, glancing around the room.

'Upstairs. I'll call him down now,' I said. 'Would you like a drink?'

Fred didn't want anything and Peggy asked for a cup of tea. Before I made her tea I went halfway up the stairs so Stevie could hear me and called, 'Your grandparents are here now, Stevie. Come down, please.'

I took Peggy's tea into the living room and then sat on one of the dining chairs I'd brought in. I wasn't sure how many were coming to the review – it can vary depending on the number of professionals involved – so I'd brought in some extra chairs.

'Who are you?' Fred bluntly asked Richard.

'I'm the Independent Reviewing Officer, but we'll do introductions once Stevie is with us.'

'Are you a social worker?' Fred asked, a little suspiciously I thought.

'I am a qualified social worker, yes, with extra training. But I'm independent and unconnected with the social services for this review.'

'Why are you here then?' Fred persisted. Peggy looked a bit uncomfortable by his forthrightness.

'To make sure the care plan is in Stevie's best interest and the review goes as it should. All looked-after children reviews have an Independent Reviewing Officer to chair and minute the meeting.'

We heard a bedroom door open and then footsteps coming downstairs. 'That'll be Stevie,' I said.

'Late as usual! He's too slow to catch a cold, that one,' Fred chortled.

Verity smiled politely while the rest of us looked away. I hoped Fred found something positive to say about Stevie at his review.

When Stevie came into the room I knew exactly why he'd spent so long getting ready and why he'd waited until his grandparents had arrived: not for support, but to stage an entrance. He was now dressed in purple trousers and a lilac shirt, had painted his nails purple and was wearing light blue eyeshadow and black mascara.

'What the fuck!' Fred exclaimed, sitting forward with a jerk. For a moment I thought he was going to get up and confront Stevie.

'Ssh,' Peggy told him. Stevie sat on the dining chair adjacent to me and facing them.

'No, I won't ssh,' Fred said. 'Look at the state of him!' Then he turned to me. 'You want to be ashamed of yourself, allowing him to dress like that. I bet you don't let your own kids go around looking like the dog's dinner.'

'Fred!' Peggy said, embarrassed. 'Be quiet.'

'No, it's time someone said it. He's supposed to be getting help in care, getting himself sorted out, but he's worse now than he was with us. She', he said, glaring at me, 'is pandering to his silly ways, encouraging him!' I felt my heart start to race. Fred was so agitated and wound up. Meanwhile Stevie, I'm sorry to say, was looking quite pleased with himself. He'd calmly crossed one leg over the over and lightly cupped his hands over his knee.

'Well?' Fred demanded, looking at the others. 'Am I the only one who feels this way?'

There was an awkward silence. I could see Carolyn and Edith looking at Stevie. They were aware of his gender-identity issues, but this was the first time Edith had met Stevie, and presumably Carolyn had only ever seen him in school uniform before. I wondered again why Stevie took such delight in winding up his grandfather. He could have easily stayed in his school uniform. Perhaps it was just teenage rebellion and he was using his gender to wind up Fred. It was the perfect tool.

'Mr Jones, perhaps this is something you'd like to bring up during the review?' Verity suggested diplomatically. 'Or another time.'

Fred huffed and the IRO took control. 'Are we expecting anyone else? If not, I'll open the meeting.'

'We're all here,' Verity confirmed.

'Welcome everyone to Stevie's first review,' Richard said evenly. I'm sure he'd witnessed worse outbursts than Fred's during reviews. 'Let's start by introducing ourselves.'

Fred whispered something to Peggy and she said, 'I'm not staying by myself.' So I guessed Fred was threatening to leave. I felt bad that the review had got off to such a poor start and Fred was blaming me for not helping Stevie as he thought he should be helped.

'Are we good to begin the introductions then?' Richard asked Fred and Peggy. She nodded while Fred, beside her on the sofa and red in the face, looked fit to burst.

The IRO began the introductions by stating his name and position, and then passed to Verity on his left, and so we went around the room, stating our names and roles – Cathy Glass, Stevie's foster carer, and so on. When it got to Fred and Peggy, she spoke for them both. 'I'm Mrs Peggy Jones and this is my husband, Fred Jones. We are Steven's grandparents and his legal guardians. We have brought him up.'

'Thank you,' the IRO said, making a note of those present.

'And we didn't bring him up to look like that,' Fred said, glaring at me.

'You'll have your turn to speak shortly,' the IRO said in a conciliatory tone, then he looked at Stevie. 'This is your review, it is about you, and I'm pleased you felt able to attend. I've read your review form, thank you for returning it. Would you like to start and tell us a bit about yourself, and how you feel you are doing, living here with Cathy?'

Placed on the spot, like many young people, Stevie's confidence vanished. Uncrossing his legs, he pushed himself back into his chair as though trying to get away. 'I'm good,' he said self-consciously.

'You're healthy?' the IRO asked, trying to draw him out.

'Yes.'

'And you're settling in with Cathy and her family?'

'Yes.'

'How are you getting along with the other young people who live here?' The IRO would have been given the basic details of the placement prior to the review.

'Fine. I like them,' Stevie said.

'How old are they?' the IRO asked.

Stevie wasn't sure and looked at me. 'Twenty-three, twenty-one and nineteen. A boy and two girls,' I said.

'Thank you.' The IRO wrote and then looked again at Stevie. 'And you're attending the same school. How is that going?'

'Fine,' Stevie said with a nervous shrug.

'What are your favourite subjects?'

'Not sure.'

The IRO smiled encouragingly. 'I'm sure you are doing well. Do you have friends at school?'

'Yes.'

'Do you see them out of school?'

'No.'

The IRO glanced at me for further explanation.

'Stevie tells me he has two good friends in his class and I've suggested he might like to invite them here for dinner.'

'Good,' the IRO said, making a note. Out of the corner of my eye I could see Fred and Peggy. Fred was still agitated and perched on the edge of the sofa like a vulture waiting to swoop.

'I believe there was a problem with bullying?' the IRO said to Stevie.

'Little wonder, dressed like that!' Fred put in.

'I wear my school uniform for school,' Stevie returned curtly.

'The bully was spoken to,' Carolyn said. 'There haven't been any further incidents, have there, Stevie?'

He shook his head.

'Good. You know who to tell if there is?' the IRO asked him.

'Yes,' Stevie said, and nodded towards Carolyn.

'You could also tell Verity and Cathy,' the IRO said. 'And the problem with the online friend, where are we with that?' he asked. Stevie shrugged.

'It's been reported and I'm waiting to hear if any action will be taken,' Verity clarified.

The IRO thanked her, made a note and then asked Stevie, 'How is contact going with your grandparents and siblings?'

'OK, I guess,' he said, then, keeping his gaze down and away from his grandparents, he added pointedly, 'I like seeing Liam and Kiri.'

'Good. And hobbies? What do you like doing in your spare time?' The IRO was going through a checklist; the questions were similar at most reviews.

'Watching television, listening to music and doing my homework,' Stevie said.

'Any out-of-school activities like football or rugby?' he asked.

Fred scoffed. 'You must be joking with him looking like that!'

Peggy nudged him, while Stevie shook his head.

'And you're receiving your allowance from Cathy?' the IRO asked. It was another standard question.

'Yes.'

'Good. Is there anything else you'd like to tell this review? Any complaints? Or anything we can help you with?'

'No, I'm good,' Stevie said, and he visibly relaxed.

'Thank you. Cathy, perhaps you'd like to go next? Then we'll pass to you,' he said to Fred and Peggy.

'I've got plenty to say, if anyone is listening,' Fred snapped at me.

CHAPTER TEN

CONTROLLING

I tried to ignore the hostility flying at me from Fred as I glanced at my notes and began to talk about Stevie, but it wasn't easy. I concentrated on the IRO, Verity, Carolyn and Peggy, aware that Fred was sitting to my right looking daggers at me.

'Stevie is a very likeable and sociable young person,' I said, 'who gets on with all my family, including my elderly mother, whom he met recently. He has settled in well, seems relaxed here, and is going to school and coming home on time by bus. If he is going to be late, he texts me. I met Carolyn, his mentor at school, when Stevie first arrived. He wasn't in school then, largely due to being bullied. The school dealt with it straight away. I was pleased Stevie felt he could tell me about the bullying and also the trouble he was having online. I think that incident has reinforced for Stevie just how important it is to be aware and stay safe while using social media. He is healthy and I have registered him at our doctor's.'

'Why?' Peggy asked. 'He sees our doctor.'

'It's usual to register a child in care with a doctor in the area where the carer lives,' the IRO said. Peggy nodded and I continued.

'Stevie tells me he is up to date with his dental check-ups,' I said. 'But he can't remember when his last check-up was. He doesn't wear glasses, but I understand he did have his eyes tested last year.' The review would expect to be told this. Fred huffed impatiently, and I nearly didn't say what I was about to, but it was important – a part of who Stevie was, and this review was about him. 'Stevie sees himself as gender-fluid,' I continued, 'and I am trying to give him the space here to allow him to explore this and be himself.'

'Is that what you call it!' Fred snapped.

'Thank you, Cathy,' the IRO said. 'So, no behavioural issues?' He glanced at Stevie.

'No,' I said. 'He's doing very well.'

'And no accidents or injuries?' It was a standard question, also asked on the review form.

'No,' I confirmed.

'Thank you,' the IRO said as he wrote.

When I foster younger children I say more and speak on their behalf, but Stevie could speak for himself, so this was a résumé of how I saw his progress so far.

'Mr Jones,' the IRO said, turning to Fred, 'would you like to go next? Perhaps you could start by telling us when Stevie had his last dental check-up for our records?' The question took Fred by surprise and he opened and closed his mouth like a fish.

'I don't know, you'd have to ask her that,' he said, referring to Peggy.

'Half-term holiday, October last year,' Peggy said. 'I take all three children to the dentist regularly.' I wondered just how much Fred really knew about his grandson. All he seemed to see was a rebellious teenager who flouted his rules and expectations, not the sensitive, vulnerable young person beneath who was struggling to come to terms with, and feel comfortable in, his rapidly changing body.

The IRO looked to Fred to continue, and he was more than ready to vent his anger and frustration. 'That's typical of you lot!' he seethed. 'Sitting in a meeting, talking about his teeth, while he's poncing around looking like a twat. I'm a laughing stock at my local pub and she –' he said, pointing at me, '– is making him worse.'

'Mr Jones,' the IRO said, 'I won't tolerate homophobic language in this review.'

'Homophobic? What the hell are you talking about? He's my grandson! A few years in the army would sort him out.'

'Even the armed forces are looking at ways to accommodate LGBT recruits,' Verity said calmly. I knew Fred wouldn't know what LGBT stood for.

'What the hell is that?' he asked.

'It's short for lesbian, gay, bisexual and transgender,' Stevie said quietly.

Peggy lay a restraining hand on Fred's arm, trying to calm him down.

'I appreciate this may be difficult for you,' the IRO said placatingly to Fred. 'But this review is about Stevie and looking at ways in which we can help and support him in the decisions he is facing.'

'Dress him proper; get all that make-up and nail polish off!' Fred said, seething. 'That's what you can do to help him, instead of pandering to him.' He glared at me accusingly.

'When you say help him, what sort of help?' Peggy asked Verity quietly.

'We could make a referral to CAMHS,' she said. 'That's the NHS Child and Adolescent Mental Health Service. They offer support and therapy for young people. We could also look at starting a referral to a clinic that specialises in gender-identity development. If necessary, they can prescribe hormone treatment to stop puberty. I'm not saying we should, but it's an option.'

I knew that wouldn't go down well with Fred.

'I don't believe I'm hearing this!' he stormed incredulously. 'Hormone treatment to turn him into a girl! Come on, we're going. I've heard enough.' He tugged at Peggy's arm. 'I'm not listening to this nonsense any more.'

'It's not nonsense,' Stevie said plaintively. 'And the treatment doesn't turn you into a girl, it just stops puberty.' So I guessed he'd given this some thought.

'I think it would be better if you could stay,' the IRO said to his grandparents.

Peggy hesitated and looked at Stevie. I saw the pain and confusion in her eyes – torn between staying for Stevie's sake or leaving and remaining loyal to her husband.

'Are you coming or what?' Fred said to her and, standing, he began towards the door.

'Bye, love,' Peggy said to Stevie and, also standing, she followed Fred.

'I'd better see them out,' I said. Placing my notes and fostering folder on the floor, I went into the hall. Fred had grabbed both their coats from the hall stand and was opening the front door.

'Sorry,' Peggy said to me. 'Tell Stevie we love him.'

'I will. Take care.' I tried to raise a reassuring smile.

She turned and followed Fred down the front path.

Disappointed that they hadn't stayed, I closed the door and returned to the living room. Stevie had lost the smugness he'd had earlier and was now looking quite remorseful. The IRO was talking to him, saying it wasn't his fault.

'Your grandfather is finding this very difficult,' Verity added. 'I'll phone him tomorrow when he's calmed down. Don't take it personally.'

Stevie gave a half-hearted nod and the review continued – uneventfully. Verity spoke next and at some length, covering the matter of the indecent photographs Stevie had taken and she'd reported to the police – she was waiting to hear the outcome. She went over the care plan: Stevie would remain in care under a Section 20 until he was eighteen when (technically an adult) he would leave care. I was asked if he could stay with me for the duration and I said he could. Verity then said she had asked Stevie if he wanted to see a counsellor at CAMHS. He didn't at present but knew if he changed his mind he should tell her and she'd arrange a referral. She also said she'd spoken to Stevie about the possibility of referring him to a gender-identity clinic and he was thinking about it. However, as there weren't many clinics offering this service and there was a waiting list, she felt it was worth starting a referral now in case he wanted an appointment in the future, and he'd agreed. She added that it wasn't a foregone conclusion he would be prescribed hormone treatment, as there would be an assessment first with other options like talking therapy.

I thought it was a pity that Stevie's grandparents hadn't stayed to hear all of this; they might have learnt something and perhaps been reassured. Although you have to be open and receptive in order to learn and change your view, and I didn't think Fred was ready yet, though Peggy might have been.

Verity confirmed she had visited Stevie in placement and was happy with the level of care he was receiving with me. She said contact with his grandparents seemed to be working and Stevie agreed, so she saw no need to formalise the arrangements. She also said she'd speak to Mr and Mrs Jones and tell them what happened in the review after they'd left – as Stevie's guardians they had a right to know – and they'd be sent a copy of the minutes once they were available. She finished by saying she had applied for a laptop for Stevie.

The IRO thanked Verity for her report and asked Carolyn to go next. She began by explaining her role as mentor, then said she'd spoken to Stevie's form teacher who was also his maths teacher, and his other subject teachers, and they all spoke highly of him. They said he was an intelligent and pleasant student. I saw Stevie glow from the praise. However, she did say that he mustn't miss any more school as the work they were doing now would form part of his GCSE examinations the following year. She said he was handing in his homework on time, which I was pleased about. She covered the matter of bullying and said Stevie knew he must tell her, his form tutor or me if there were any repeat incidents. Stevie said there hadn't been, which again was good news. She finished by telling the review – as she had told me – that in line with other schools they were considering installing gender-neutral toilets and changing rooms for PE, but for the present Stevie used the boys' facilities and said he didn't have a problem with that.

The IRO thanked her and asked Edith to speak.

'I am the foster carer's supervising social worker,' she said. 'I have no complaints.' And that was all. When I thought back to the glowing praise I'd received from Jill – my lovely SSW for many years when I'd worked for Homefinders – I felt sad. I gave so much to fostering, as most carers do, and Edith's bland comment seemed dismissive of my efforts and hard work. We all benefit from praise and it doesn't take much – just a positive comment.

The IRO finished by asking Stevie whether he saw his social worker enough and if he felt she listened to him – a standard question – and he said it was fine. The IRO made a note and set the date for the next review, then thanked us all for coming and closed the meeting.

'Can I go to my room now?' Stevie asked.

'Yes,' the IRO smiled. 'Thank you for attending.'

Stevie quickly left and went upstairs to his bedroom while I saw everyone to the front door. I felt shattered, emotionally drained and concerned that Fred clearly didn't think I was looking after Stevie in the right way by allowing him the space to explore his gender identity. His criticism had made me doubt if I was doing the right thing, but I wasn't sure what else I could do. This is when a good SSW is invaluable – a professional to discuss issues like this with and who can give advice. I could have asked Edith, but I felt that Verity was more in tune with Stevie's needs, and of course knew him better. I made a mental note to speak to her about the issue; the review hadn't been the place for that discussion.

It was nearly six o'clock now and I'd heard Paula come in while I'd been in the review and go up to her room. I now went up, knocked on her door and told her everyone had gone. She said she'd come down. I knocked on Stevie's door and asked him if he was OK, and he called back that he was. I'd talk to him later about the review, but for now I needed to get some dinner on the table.

Lucy arrived home just as dinner was ready, but Adrian wasn't expected back for dinner as he was seeing Kirsty. As we ate there was the usual chatter, although Stevie was quieter than usual. Lucy, who knew all about reviews, having attended them herself when she'd been in care, asked him how his had gone. He shrugged. 'All right, I guess,' he said as he ate. 'But my grandparents didn't stay. Fred threw a wobbler.'

I noticed Stevie had used Fred's name rather than Grandpa, as if he was distancing himself from him. If Fred didn't change has attitude soon, I thought, he was going to irreparably damage his relationship with Stevie.

Lucy commiserated on the 'cringing awfulness' of reviews and how she was so pleased when she didn't have to attend them any more. After I'd adopted her and she was no longer in care, they'd stopped. Which wasn't necessarily what Stevie needed to hear right now as he would be having regular reviews for the next three years.

Once we'd finished dinner and left the table, I said quietly to Stevie, 'I think we need to have a chat about your grandfather.'

'Not now,' he said. 'I've got schoolwork to do.'

'OK, another time then.'

He, Lucy and Paula disappeared up to their rooms; Lucy to chill and message her friends, and Stevie and Paula hopefully to do their homework. All three of them reappeared downstairs every so often for drinks, snacks and a quick chat, just as many young adults do.

At nine o'clock I was in the living room when the landline rang. I was slightly surprised to hear Peggy's voice. 'I'm sorry Fred was so rude to you,' she said.

'Don't worry, I've heard worse,' I replied lightly.

'Please don't hold it against him. He feels bad for being rude. He loves all his grandchildren, but he can't accept what Stevie is doing.'

'I understand,' I said, 'but I don't think Stevie has a choice. I believe he has real problems in identifying with being the young man Fred wants.'

'Fred thinks you are encouraging him.'

'I don't think I am, more giving Stevie the space to explore who he wants to be. Gender is a big part of who we are and something most of us take for granted. I think Stevie is genuinely confused right now.'

'Yes, he is confused,' Peggy said. 'But Fred thinks a lot of it is to annoy him.'

'Why would Stevie want to annoy his grandfather?' I asked. Although it had crossed my mind that Stevie liked to provoke him for a reaction.

'I don't know. We've done our best. Perhaps he's angry he can't live with his mother and father.'

It was certainly possible, and had Stevie been going to CAMHS it was something they could have explored. 'Peggy, when Stevie came into the living room for his review, having got dressed up, it occurred to me he could more easily have stayed in his school uniform or worn more sombre casual clothes, and not put on make-up and nail polish. But what would I have achieved by making an issue of it? I give him guidance, but I don't want to stifle how he feels. I will discuss all of this with Verity the next time I see her to make sure I'm handling it the right way. It's new for me too. If I'm doing something wrong I will change my fostering. Perhaps you could tell Fred that? It might help to reassure him.'

'I'll tell him, although I'm not sure how much good it will do. He and Stevie seemed to be locked in a battle since all this started.'

'It must be difficult for you both. It has made me think about how I would have reacted had one of my children faced gender issues.'

'And?' Peggy prompted.

'I would have done exactly the same as I'm doing for Stevie. Give them the time, space and support they need, and get some professional help if necessary. Also reassure them that they are loved, whatever their decision.'

Peggy fell silent.

'Anyway, tell Fred I will discuss all this with Verity.'

We said goodbye and I sat for a moment staring into space, deep in thought. What I'd just told Peggy was true. Had one of my children questioned their gender identity, I would have supported them in the same way I was Stevie. Fostering Stevie had forced me to consider a number of issues, and although having to accept Adrian, Lucy or Paula in a different gender would have taken quite a bit of getting used to, I would have valued, loved and cherished them just the same. Male, female, heterosexual, gay, trans or bi, they were still the same person, and that's what Fred needed to understand, difficult though it was for him.

I went upstairs and knocked on Stevie's bedroom door. 'Come in,' he called. He was listening to music on his phone. I could hear the faint buzz coming from his earbuds as he took them out.

'Your gran just telephoned,' I said, going further into his room. 'She wanted to apologise for your grandfather's behaviour at the review.'

'So why didn't Fred phone me?' he asked, already on the defensive.

'I think that would have been asking rather a lot of him right now, don't you?'

He shrugged. 'I guess.'

'Stevie, he was rude, but I think you could help the situation.' I paused and chose my words carefully. 'This isn't a criticism and you're probably not aware you're doing it, but sometimes it seems you could be goading your grandfather – you know, winding him up.'

I expected him to deny it, but he said, 'So? He deserves it.'

'Why?'

'Because he's controlling and always has to be right. With him it's do, think and say as I do or you are wrong. His opinion is always the right one and he never backs down.'

'Does he ever hit you?' I asked.

'No – well, he walloped my backside once when I was a kid because I'd done something wrong, but Gran told him off and he hasn't touched any of us since.'

'Good.'

'He wants me to be like him,' Stevie lamented. 'A man's man. But I'll never be that, even if I'm not gay. I don't want to be like him.'

'There's no reason why you should be like him, we're all different, although he has done a good job of bringing up you, Kiri and Liam.'

Stevie shrugged.

'Peggy wondered if you were angry with them because you couldn't live with your parents.'

'No. They're like my mum and dad.'

I nodded. 'You know that CAMHS could help you to explore some of these issues?'

'I don't want to talk to them now.'

'OK, fair enough.'

He picked up his earbuds ready to put in, signalling our conversation was at an end.

'All right, love, I'll leave you to it. But remember, your grandparents love you, and no one gets it right all the time.'

With a reassuring smile, I left the room and went to spend time with the other members of my family.

CHAPTER ELEVEN

MISSING

The following day Stevie's laptop was delivered and he was very pleased. Adrian, Lucy and Paula had their own laptops, and there was the PC with a printer in the front room for us all to use. As Stevie disappeared upstairs clutching his new laptop, it crossed my mind that he hadn't ever responded to my Facebook friendship request, but I didn't read anything into it. The need to see who he was in touch with online had lessened since he'd confessed about Joey, and his behaviour had settled down.

February arrived and we woke up one Sunday morning to find a thick blanket of snow, and everyone became a child again. Because it was Sunday we were all at home and could make the most of it. Adrian had arranged to see Kirsty, but they cancelled as the roads hadn't been cleared and were unsafe to drive on. Big as my family were, when I suggested we got the toboggan out of the shed and took it to our local park, there were cheers of delight. Stevie said he'd been tobogganing when he'd lived with his grandparents and would have liked to have played in the snow with Liam and Kiri, but he understood that I couldn't take him there in my car because of the snow and there weren't any buses running.

The park is only a short walk from our house and is known in the area for the hill that makes a good toboggan run in the snow. It was late morning when we arrived and we saw some of our friends and neighbours there. Stevie saw a boy from his class and they chatted for a few minutes, then we dragged our toboggan to the top of the hill and took turns coming down. It was great fun and the air was alive with laughter and screams as children of all ages, and adults, hurtled down the slope on toboggans, trays, sheets of plastic and cardboard – anything that would slide. We were there for a couple of hours and then, with our cheeks glowing from the cold, we returned home for hot drinks and lunch.

While I love summer, I think winter has a special quality in bringing families closer together. With the curtains closed against a cold night sky, no one is in any rush to go out and everyone is more content to spend time with each other in the warmth of the house. Winter seems to cocoon the family and strengthen family bonds, although perhaps that's just me being sentimental. At the weekends we group around board games – Scrabble, Monopoly, Cluedo and so on – and play with a real competitive spirit. Stevie said nostalgically that he used to play board games with just him and his grandparents when Kiri and Liam had been little. 'That's a nice memory,' I said. 'Why not suggest playing next time you're there? Kiri and Liam are old enough to join in now.' I thought again what a good job of parenting Peggy and Fred had done and how committed they'd been to raising Stevie and then later Kiri and Liam. They'd had no retirement in which they could slow the pace and take things easy, and I hoped Stevie appreciated that.

The whole of February was bitterly cold, although we didn't get any more snow. Then March arrived and the first green buds of spring started to appear. Stevie had been with us for two months and I felt everything was going well. I'd had a chat with Verity and she'd confirmed the way I was fostering Stevie was fine, and she'd spoken to Fred and Peggy about this. Stevie was attending school, seeing his grandparents and Liam and Kiri a couple of times a week, and getting along with my family. Indeed, it was difficult to remember a time before he'd arrived, although of course I'd never forget the other children I'd fostered.

Then suddenly and dramatically, almost overnight, Stevie changed. He became withdrawn, moody and snapped if anyone asked him what was the matter. It was difficult to get him to shower and he spent most of the time in his room. He wanted his meals there too, although I insisted he come down to eat with us, as I thought the last thing he needed was to spend more time alone. When I asked him what was worrying him – which I did often – he said, 'Nothing.' If I pressed him, he just got annoyed.

Stevie's behaviour continued for a week. I noted the change in my log and also telephoned Verity. She said she'd talk to Stevie to see if he would tell her what was wrong, but it wouldn't be for a few days, as she was in court on another case for most of the week. She added that Stevie should really see a therapist at CAMHS and she'd suggest it to him again.

Stevie had stopped visiting his grandparents and when I asked him why he said sulkily, 'Don't want to go.'

'Have you and your grandfather been arguing?' I asked.

'No more than usual,' came his terse response.

Peggy naturally telephoned to find out why Stevie hadn't been to see them. I said he seemed down again and anxious, and that I'd informed Verity. While Peggy was concerned, she said, 'Probably best Stevie doesn't come here while he's like that. Fred doesn't have time for the sulks.' Which I could imagine.

I hadn't telephoned the school, as I hoped Stevie's behaviour wasn't impacting there but was confined to home. I assumed if there was anything wrong Carolyn would phone me. She did, the following Tuesday. She said that during the last lesson Stevie had been caught in class checking his phone, which should have been switched off and in his bag. In keeping with school policy, the teacher had asked him to hand over his phone, as it would be confiscated until the end of the school day. Stevie had refused, then shouted at her to fuck off and had stormed out of school. I wasn't wholly surprised. I'd guessed something had been building inside Stevie, I just wished he could have told me what. I apologised for Stevie's behaviour, told Carolyn I'd speak to him as soon as he came home and admitted that his behaviour with me had been giving me some cause for concern, although he'd been quiet rather than aggressive. Carolyn said Stevie could return to school the following morning, but he would need to see the Head first and apologise to the teacher before he was allowed to rejoin his class. I thanked her and said again I would talk to Stevie as soon as he came home.

But he didn't come home. Four-thirty came and went, and when it got to five o'clock I called his mobile. It went through to voicemail. I left a message and also texted him: *Can you text or phone me, please. I'm worried about you. Carolyn phoned. You're not suspended but we need to talk*. It was possible he'd gone to his grandparents, but I hesitated in calling them because if he wasn't there it would worry them, perhaps unnecessarily. However, foster carers have to follow a set procedure for reporting a child or young person missing, and I knew I'd have to call the duty social worker before long, then the police. They'd want to know I'd checked all the possible places he might be. I tried Stevie's phone again and it went through to voicemail, so at 5.45, with the daylight failing and no word from Stevie, I called his grandparents. A child answered.

'Hello. Is that Liam?' I guessed it was him rather than his younger sister.

'Yes.'

'Can I speak to your gran or grandpa, please?'

'Grandpa is here.'

'Thank you.' I would rather have spoken to Peggy, but I couldn't really say that.

Fred came on the line with a gruff 'Hello?'

'Fred, it's Cathy, Stevie's carer. Is Stevie with you?'

'So he's up to his old tricks again. No. Haven't seen him for over a week.'

'I'm sure there's nothing to worry about, but there was a bit of an incident at school this afternoon and he hasn't come home yet. I've tried phoning him, but it goes through to voicemail.'

'Just like what happened to us,' he said with a certain satisfaction.

'Can you think of anywhere he might have gone?'

'He's probably with one of his nancy friends.'

Ignoring his derogatory terminology, I said, 'As far as I know, the only friend Stevie used to see out of school has gone to live abroad.'

'Wouldn't know about that,' Fred said, which of course was part of the problem. Fred had been so dismissive of Stevie's friendships and lifestyle choices that he had no idea who his grandson had been associating with or what he'd been doing.

'So you can't think of anywhere he might be?' I asked. 'The police are sure to ask me.'

'Police? Why are you telling them? It's only six o'clock.'

'Yes, but Stevie should have been here at four-thirty, he's not been in touch, so technically he's been missing for an hour and a half. As his foster carer I have a duty to contact the social services and then report him missing to the police.'

'And then he'll breeze in, pleased with himself and enjoying all the attention,' Fred said.

'Possibly, but better that than the alternative – that something dreadful has happened to him.' I didn't want to alarm Fred, but his blasé attitude was not only annoying me, it was dangerous. Young people, especially those struggling with issues such as Stevie, are vulnerable and need protecting. All Fred saw was a stroppy teenager hell bent on antagonising him. 'If he gets in touch or arrives there, will you let me know, please?'

'Yes,' he said bluntly. 'But I doubt he'll come here if he's in trouble.' Which, sadly, was probably true.

I tried Stevie's mobile phone again, but it went through to voicemail. I told Adrian, Lucy and Paula to help themselves to dinner – there was a casserole in the oven – and I'd join them when I'd phoned the social services. They knew Stevie hadn't come home and were aware of the procedure I had to follow, as I'd had to report other young people I'd fostered missing. At this point they weren't unduly worried, more concerned – as I was – but as the evening wore on that would change.

Following procedure, I telephoned the call operator at the social services and briefly explained why I needed to speak to the emergency duty social worker. She took my details and said the emergency duty social worker would return my call as soon as possible and certainly within an hour. That was standard; had it been an emergency I would have phoned the emergency services directly – fire brigade, police or ambulance. I quickly went through to the kitchen, where I gobbled down some dinner and plated up some for Stevie. While part of me thought that Stevie was just cooling off somewhere after the incident at school and would come home soon, there was always the chance that something bad had happened – something connected to whatever had been worrying him for the past week.

The landline rang just as I'd finished eating. It was Peggy, wanting to know if I'd heard from Stevie. I said I hadn't, and that I was waiting to hear back from the duty social worker and would phone her as soon as I had any news.

Twenty minutes later the duty social worker returned my call. The duty social worker doesn't usually know the child, so I had to give him Stevie's background information, which he noted, including Stevie's date of birth, the reason he was in care, the type of care order and the circumstances leading up to him going missing. I explained what had happened at school and that he hadn't been in touch since – either with me or with his grandparents. He advised me to leave another message on Stevie's mobile saying that I had spoken to him, and that if he didn't return home or contact me by 7 p.m. then I would have to report him missing to the police. The mention of the police sometimes prompted the young person to get in touch, then, with the barrier they'd erected around themselves lowered, it usually became easier to open the line of communication and for them to return home. He said I should telephone him to let him know the outcome.

Increasingly concerned for Stevie, I followed the duty social worker's instructions and called Stevie's mobile again. It went through to voicemail, so I left a message: 'Stevie, it's Cathy. I'm worried about you, love. Can you phone or text me, please, to say you're OK? Whatever the problem is, I am sure we can sort it out. I've just called the duty social worker and he told me that if you haven't got in touch by seven o'clock I should report you missing to the police. Come home, love, please, we miss you.' I ended the call. It was dark outside now and bitterly cold, and I was worried Stevie was out there somewhere alone and, for whatever reason, too scared to come home.

Adrian came downstairs. 'Shall we go out and look for him, Mum?' he asked.

I was touched. 'That's nice of you, but I wouldn't know where to start looking.' I'd done similar before when a young person had gone missing, but then I'd had an idea of where they might be as I knew who they associated with and what their favourite haunts were (for example, Joss in *Girl Alone*). Now I had no idea where Stevie might be, and neither did his grandparents.

Adrian nodded. 'Try not to worry. I'm sure he'll be back soon.'

I smiled weakly, for, as Adrian knew, with every passing minute our concerns would grow.

At seven o'clock, with no word from Stevie and following the duty social worker's advice, I telephoned the police – not 999 (the emergency services number) as I would have done if a small child had gone missing, but our local police station. Once connected, I explained to the officer that Stevie, aged fourteen, was a looked-after child, that I was his foster carer and the circumstances surrounding him going missing. Of course he wanted to know if he'd gone missing before and I explained that he had when he'd lived with his grandparents, but not since he'd been with me. He asked for a description and what Stevie was wearing – his school uniform – if he had any health issues or if he was depressed or suicidal. I said he'd been quiet the previous week, which had made me think something was worrying him, but I didn't think he was suicidal, although of course you can never be sure. The officer wanted the name and contact details of Stevie's social worker and his grandparents. I had them ready. He said he'd send an officer to my house as soon as one became available, and in the meantime Stevie's details would be circulated through the police computer. He told me to have a recent photograph of Stevie ready to give to the police, which I also knew. I always made sure I had at least one good photo of the child I was fostering for official use, in addition to family photographs of the child's time with us, a copy of which the child kept to remember us by.

I thanked the officer and felt some relief that the police were now looking for Stevie.

A few minutes later Adrian came into the living room with his coat on. 'I'm going to walk around the block and up to the High Street to make sure Stevie's not in the area and worried about coming back.'

'Thanks, love, that is kind of you.'

'It's better than doing nothing,' he said.

Then Lucy and Paula appeared, slipping on their coats. 'We're going too.'

Tears sprung to my eyes; I was so moved by their thoughtfulness. 'Thank you. Don't be too long, though. I don't want you getting cold.' Although it was early March, the temperature at night was dropping to freezing. 'I'll wait here for the police to arrive. I'll call you if Stevie comes home.'

Yet while I appreciated their concern, the fact that they were going out to look for Stevie seemed to heighten the seriousness of what was unfolding. I still hoped that Stevie would breeze in shortly as Fred said he'd done when he'd gone missing before, but as time passed I thought it less and less likely.

By 8.30 I was starting to worry where my three children were, and was about to phone one of their mobiles when Adrian texted to say they'd got delayed and were now on their way back, although they hadn't seen Stevie. As soon as I heard the front door open I was in the hall to meet them.

'You must be freezing,' I said. 'You've been gone ages.' They looked cold.

'We helped a guy in the High Street,' Adrian explained as they took off their coats.

'Mum, did you know there's a man sleeping rough in the High Street?' Paula asked, shocked.

'No, I didn't.' Although I was aware the number of rough sleepers in the country was increasing.

'He's in a doorway in an old sleeping bag,' Paula said. 'We bought him sausage and chips and a cup of tea.'

'That was kind of you.'

'He wasn't very old,' Lucy added. 'I'd guess mid-twenties. I asked him why he was there and not with his family, but he wouldn't talk to us.'

'I'm sure he appreciated the food and drink,' I said.

I feel it's a disgrace and a dreadful indictment of our society that anyone has to sleep rough. It's a sad fact that a sizeable proportion of those sleeping rough are care leavers. Looked-after children leave care at eighteen and then receive some support until they are twenty-one (longer if they are in education or training). During the transition to independence they are usually put in a hostel, lodgings or a small council flat, then they are on their own. With little or no family support, they often struggle to pay their bills. They fall behind with their rent and are eventually evicted. One recent study showed that 25 per cent of homeless people in the UK have been in care, and 20 per cent of care leavers become homeless within five years of leaving care. Shocking statistics.

Peggy telephoned and I told her I'd reported Stevie missing and was waiting for the police to arrive, and that Adrian, Lucy and Paula had checked the local area. She thanked me and began to tell me all about what had happened when Stevie had been living with them and gone missing, reliving it, when the front doorbell rang – two firm rings.

'Peggy, I have to go,' I said, interrupting her. 'I think the police have arrived.'

'Tell them if they want to search my home they need to wait until morning – the kids are in bed. Last time they woke them.'

Saying a quick goodbye, I went into the hall just as Adrian was opening the front door.

CHAPTER TWELVE

SOMETHING MUCH WORSE

Adrian and I showed the two male police officers into the living room and we all sat down. Lucy joined us, but Paula stayed in her room. The lead officer asked me questions as the other officer took notes: about his background, the reasons for him coming into care, how long he'd been living with us, the events leading up to his disappearance and so forth, much as I'd already given when I'd reported Stevie missing. I appreciated Adrian and Lucy being present. When they were young, as a single-parent foster carer I'd had to face situations like this alone. Now they were older it was reassuring to have them by my side for moral support and also to supplement details I might have missed. I told the officers what steps we'd taken to find Stevie, including leaving messages on his mobile, contacting his grandparents and that Adrian, Lucy and Paula had looked for him in the area.

'Do the police know there's a man sleeping rough in the High Street?' Lucy asked the officers.

'Yes, he should be on his way to a hostel now,' the lead officer said. 'We spotted him on our way here. They make room at the hostel in really cold weather, even though they're full.'

'Good,' said Lucy. Although I remained concerned that anyone should be sleeping on the streets in the first place.

The officers asked if Stevie kept a diary or had left a note and I said I didn't think so. They asked if he took drugs or drank alcohol, and I said I was sure he didn't because he'd seen what they'd done to his mother. They asked about his usual hangouts, and if he had a laptop or tablet, and I confirmed that he had a laptop but had taken it to school that day. A call came through on the second officer's phone and they both paused to listen to it. It was in respect of another young person who'd gone missing but had just been found at the home of her boyfriend. 'We usually find runaways within twenty-four hours,' the lead officer said, which was reassuring.

'But what if they're not found?' Lucy asked, worried.

'Then we keep looking until they are,' he said with a positive smile.

As I expected, they wanted to search the house. As well as confirming that Stevie wasn't here, they'd be looking for any clues that might suggest where he could be. I showed them into our kitchen-diner first and they had a look around, opened and closed a few cupboard doors and looked out the back door. As we returned into the hall we passed the walk-in cupboard under the stairs and the lead officer paused and asked, 'What's in there?'

'A mess,' Lucy quipped. I opened the door so they could see in. It held the vacuum cleaner, broom, dustpan and brush, a no-longer-used gerbil cage, shopping bags, bric-à-brac and anything we didn't use but didn't want to throw out.

Satisfied, the officers followed us into the front room.

'Does Stevie use that computer?' the second officer asked, referring to the PC.

'He hasn't done,' I said.

They looked around and then Adrian headed our little procession upstairs to Stevie's room. 'It's very tidy for a fourteen-year-old lad,' the lead officer commented as we went in.

'Yes, Stevie keeps his room neat,' I agreed.

They gave this room a more thorough search and looked under the bed, pulled back the duvet, checked inside the pillowcase, drew back the curtains, and opened and closed the drawers. Stevie's make-up, nail varnish and floral cosmetics bag were in the top drawer, but they didn't comment. Only when they opened the wardrobe door did their expressions change and I saw them do a double-take. 'They're bright,' the lead officer said, glancing at me. 'Does Stevie wear these?'

'Yes, sometimes,' I said.

'And the make-up in the drawer?'

'Yes, but not for school. He's in his school uniform.' I felt Stevie's privacy was being invaded, but then again, if he hadn't gone missing the police wouldn't be here rummaging through his private belongings. Until now I hadn't mentioned gender, as it hadn't seemed necessary, but as they examined his clothes and checked the pockets I thought I should say something. Lucy got in first.

'Stevie is gender-fluid,' she said proudly. 'That means he doesn't have a fixed gender and likes to dress femininely sometimes. I've helped him with his make-up.'

'He's gay?' the lead officer asked me.

'No, he's undecided,' I said. 'Although he did go to an LGBT nightclub before he came to live with us.'

'At fourteen?'

'Yes.'

He tutted. 'Do you know which one?'

'No, sorry. I don't.'

They checked down the side of his wardrobe, looked in a carrier bag hanging on the back of the door and the pockets of his dressing gown, then, with a final glance around, the second officer said, 'There's nothing in here.'

We all came out and I showed them round the landing to our bedrooms. When we came to Paula's room I knocked on her door and stuck my head round. She was propped up on her bed, reading. 'The police need to have a look in here,' I said. She got off her bed and stood beside it, clearly embarrassed, as both officers came in and looked around. Although it was necessary, it was an imposition. They thanked her on their way out and I showed them my bedroom and finally the bathroom.

'There's nowhere he can hide in there,' Lucy said pointedly.

The junior officer smiled at her. 'You can never be sure.'

Downstairs again, we stood in the hall as the officers prepared to leave. They confirmed that Stevie's details had already been circulated, and we should contact them if he got in touch or returned home, which they felt sure he would do before long. They said they would visit his grandparents; I didn't tell them what Peggy had said about not going there until morning. It seemed rude and I doubted that waking Kiri and Liam would be a factor in timetabling their visit, with their busy work schedule.

It was after 10.30 by the time the officers had left. Sammy came out from his hiding place behind the sofa and curled up in his basket, and by eleven o'clock we were all upstairs getting ready for bed. I left my mobile phone switched on and within reach on my bedside cabinet in case Stevie phoned, then lay in the dark running through the day's events and wondering where on earth he could be. Suddenly I was startled by the landline ringing. I quickly grabbed the handset. 'Cathy?' It was Peggy wanting to know what had happened when the police had visited. I told her, said I'd phone her when there was any news and wound up the conversation. I think she would have liked to talk for longer, but it was nearly midnight and I was shattered.

I lay in the dark again with my thoughts buzzing like trapped flies, and tried to imagine where Stevie might be. My bedside clock clicked away the time: 12.30, 1.07, 1.43. Then I must have dropped off, for suddenly I was awake again, and aware my mobile was ringing.

'Yes?' I said immediately, answering it.

'Is that Cathy Glass, Stevie's foster carer?' a male voice asked.

'Yes.' My heart began thumping wildly as I sat bolt upright and switched on the bedside lamp.

'It's one of the officers who visited you earlier. We've found Stevie. He's in the car with us.'

'Thank goodness.' I breathed a huge sigh of relief. 'Is he all right?'

'Just a bit cold. But there is a problem.' My stomach churned.

'What?'

'He doesn't want to come back to you.'

'Why not?'

'He's not saying. He just says he can't.'

'I don't understand. Can I speak to him?'

'No, he doesn't want to talk to you.'

Not only was I hurt, but it seemed to reflect badly on me as a foster carer that Stevie didn't want to come home or even talk to me.

'Has he given you any idea why he ran away?' I asked.

'No. We're going to contact the social services now. They'll have to find him a bed for the night.'

'What about his grandparents? Can't he stay there for tonight?'

'He says he doesn't want to go there either.'

'You've spoken to them?'

'Yes. They know he's safe.'

'Where did you find Stevie?' I asked.

'At the bus terminus.'

'Was he going to catch a bus?'

'No, it was just somewhere to shelter. But the heating goes off in the waiting room at midnight when the last bus leaves, so it was cold. I need to phone the social services now, but at least you know he's safe,' the officer said.

'Yes, thank you. Please tell Stevie I would like him to come home. He's not in any trouble.'

'Will do.'

I dropped my phone beside me on the bed and leant back on the headboard with a very heavy heart. I'd failed Stevie. What had started off so positively, with him quickly settling in, being able to work with his grandparents and the likelihood of him staying with us for at least three years, was ending in failure, and for reasons I didn't know. I wasn't being dramatic: a young person running away and then refusing to return to their foster carer was a failure; it couldn't be looked upon any other way. I was the adult, Stevie was the minor, so it was my responsibility to make it work. That Stevie had refused to go to his grandparents didn't lessen my feelings of failure; indeed, I had even more concerns now. Stevie would be placed with an emergency foster carer for the night and then be moved to a more suitable placement within the next couple of days. That would mean he would have had four homes and three foster carers in the last three months. And there was no guarantee he would settle with the next carers, resulting in yet another move. I thought I'd established a bond with Stevie, as had Paula, Lucy and Adrian, so why didn't he feel he could come home? I was upset and bitterly disappointed, as I knew my children would be. It was one of the worst endings imaginable for a foster family.

With my thoughts in turmoil, I wondered if I should telephone Peggy but decided against it. It was 2.30 a.m. She'd been told Stevie was safe and would have probably gone back to sleep now. I needed to try to get some sleep too so that I was in a better frame of mind to deal with whatever tomorrow brought. I'd phone Peggy in the morning. However, fifteen minutes later, when I was still wide awake, torturing myself with what more I could have done to help Stevie, the landline rang. It was Peggy. 'Well, at least he's been found safe,' she said. 'Strange that he doesn't want to return to you, though. That makes two of us.' I heard the self-exoneration in her voice, because I had failed as she had done.

'Yes,' I said wearily.

'What about all his belongings at your place? How will he get them?' she asked.

'His social worker will make arrangements to collect them. Don't worry, he'll get them.'

'You'll take them?' she asked. I really didn't need this conversation now.

'I don't know yet,' I said.

'Fred said that the social worker will have to get it sorted.'

'Yes, she will.' Peggy seemed to see me as a kindred spirit, a confidante, and I think she would have talked all night. 'Peggy, I'll phone you tomorrow when I know more, OK?' I wound up the conversation and replaced the handset.

I lay on my back, staring at the bedroom ceiling. The shade of my bedside lamp was casting a round shadow on the ceiling, infilled with irregular patterns that seemed to resemble a map of the world. A big lonely world if you didn't have anyone, I thought. Why was Stevie cutting himself off from the only homes he knew – mine and his grandparents'? What had been going through his mind as he'd sat alone in that cold and draughty waiting room at the bus terminus, and then in the back of the police car, telling them he didn't want to return to me or his grandparents? I thought I'd understood Stevie and what he needed, but apparently I'd got it just as wrong as his grandparents, only in a different way. It's at times like this that foster carers doubt themselves and wonder if it's time to quit.

Gazing up at the ceiling, my eyes gradually grew heavy and finally closed. I was woken again by my mobile ringing. The lamp was still on and my clock showed 3.21 a.m.

'Yes?' I asked groggily, answering.

'Cathy Glass?'

'Speaking.'

'It's the duty social worker. We spoke earlier.'

'Yes.'

'The police have been in touch, but we've nowhere suitable to place Stevie, so he's agreed to come back to you for tonight rather than be placed out of the area. He's at — police station. Can you collect him from there?'

'Now?' I asked, struggling upright in the bed and trying to clear my thoughts.

'Yes, as soon as possible.'

'I'll have to get dressed first.'

I'll tell them you're on your way. How long do you think you'll be?'

'Half an hour.'

'I'll let them know, and please don't tell Stevie off. Wait until his social worker sees him to discuss his absence.'

'Of course, I'm an experienced foster carer,' I retorted. I was tired, stressed and now expected to get out of bed on a cold night to collect a teenager who thought staying with me for a night was the lesser of two evils. I didn't need the duty social worker telling me how to behave. 'I'll be there as soon as I can,' I confirmed.

He didn't even say thank you.

But once out of bed and on the move, my ill-humour evaporated, the adrenaline kicked in and I became more positive. That Stevie had agreed to come back to me even for one night gave me some hope. Tomorrow we would talk and try to get to the bottom of what had been worrying him so much to make him run away, and what I could do to help.

I threw on my clothes, splashed cold water on my face, and was about to leave a note for Adrian, Lucy and Paula to say where I was in case they woke to find me gone when Adrian's bedroom door opened. 'I heard you on the phone,' he said, coming round the landing. 'Have they found Stevie?'

'Yes, I've got to collect him from the police station.'

'I'll come with you.'

'No, you have work tomorrow.'

'I'm coming, Mum. I won't sleep,' he said firmly. 'I'll get dressed and de-ice the car.'

'Thanks, love. I'll leave a note for Lucy and Paula.'

I took a sheet of writing paper from a drawer downstairs and wrote in black marker pen: *Adrian and Mum have gone to collect Stevie xx*. I propped it on the landing where the girls would see it if they came out of their rooms. They were sure to text or phone if they did.

Adrian appeared from his room, having thrown on jeans

and a jumper, and was smoothing his hair flat. Downstairs we put on our coats and braced ourselves for the cold night air. We made as little noise as possible as we scraped the frost from the windows of the car, trying not to disturb the neighbours. Once the windscreen was clear, I started the engine and drove quietly from the house. The police station where Stevie had been taken was about a ten-minute drive away. The roads were virtually empty and as I drove I told Adrian where Stevie had been found and that to begin with he hadn't wanted to return to us, but the only other option had been to go to a carer out of the county.

'So what have we done wrong?' Adrian asked in a dead-pan voice.

'No idea, love. But I'm sure it will come out in time.' When a placement ends abruptly like this was going to, there is usually a placement disruption meeting to try to see if any lessons can be learnt. Sometimes carers feel it's a witch-hunt, with the carer being targeted.

'Perhaps it's not us,' Adrian said presently. 'Perhaps Stevie's got a guilty conscience, like he had before with those photographs.' Stevie had told Adrian, Paula and Lucy what had happened with Joey.

'It crossed my mind,' I said, 'but I would have hoped he could have told me as he did before.'

'Unless it's something much worse.'

I shivered, but not from the cold. 'Like what?' I asked, glancing at him. 'Stevie never goes out apart from going to school and seeing his grandparents. And I'm sure he wouldn't make the same mistake twice online.'

Adrian shrugged. 'Unless it was something he did before he came to us and he's only just been found out.'

How true those words would turn out to be.

CHAPTER THIRTEEN

CONFESSION

The police station I had to collect Stevie from was open twenty-four hours, and even at 4 a.m. there were two people in the waiting area. Adrian and I went up to the counter where the duty officer was standing behind a computer screen. Adrian gave our names and said we were here to collect Stevie.

'I'm his foster carer and this is my son,' I added.

The duty officer tapped the keyboard of his computer and then told us to take a seat and that an officer would bring Stevie to us. The other two waiting looked as though they'd been there a while, but we'd only just sat down when a door opened and Stevie appeared with a female police officer. Dressed in his school uniform and with his head hung low, he looked guilty and remorseful. Adrian and I stood and went over.

'Cathy Glass?' the officer asked.

'Yes.'

She confirmed my address and then said, 'I've had a chat with Stevie and either I or another officer will visit you both during the next couple of days to check all is well.'

I thanked her. She said 'Good luck' to Stevie, and we left.

'You OK?' Adrian asked as he pressed the button to release the outer doors.

Stevie gave a small nod. Shoulders sagging, he looked dejected and was clearly tired, as were we. He walked beside Adrian to the car and I opened the rear door for him to get in.

'You'll be ready for bed,' I said lightly to Stevie as I started the engine. He didn't reply. As I drove I occasionally glanced at him in the rear-view mirror and saw his eyes gradually close as he began to nod off, only opening when I had to suddenly brake to avoid a cat that had shot across my path. 'Sorry,' I said.

A few minutes later I was parking outside our house, relieved that Stevie was safely back with us. Whatever had happened would wait until tomorrow. What we all needed now was sleep. Adrian used his key to let us in and Stevie went straight upstairs.

'Do you want anything to eat or drink?' I called after him.

'A glass of water, please,' he said quietly.

'I'll bring it up.'

Adrian poured himself a glass of water too, and I thanked him for his help. He said he'd set his alarm for the morning as he was on an early shift, and would try not to wake me when he left. He'd only get two hours' sleep at the most. I took Stevie's glass of water up and saw that my note on the landing to Paula and Lucy hadn't been moved. Given neither of them had phoned or texted, I assumed they'd slept through our absence.

Stevie had left his bedroom door ajar, so I knocked on it and went in. He was sitting on his bed, still in his school clothes and looking sad. 'Do I have to go to school tomorrow?' he asked as I handed him the glass of water.

'Probably not. Get some sleep. I'm guessing Verity will want to see you tomorrow. And if you are leaving, we will have to pack your things.'

He took a sip of water and I left him to change and get into bed. Did I hope he could be persuaded to stay? Yes. But that would depend on a number of issues, including what Stevie wanted and what the social services considered best for him. Without any real idea of what had made Stevie run away and then refuse to return to us, I couldn't really say how Verity would view this placement, although it is generally considered better for the child or young person to be kept with the same foster carer if possible.

I climbed into bed and, utterly exhausted, slept. I was woken by my alarm at 7 a.m. Adrian had already left for work and I could hear the girls on the move. Music was coming from Lucy's room and Paula was downstairs playing with Sammy and hopefully getting herself some breakfast. I slipped on my dressing gown and went round the landing where I knocked lightly on Lucy's door. 'Can you keep the music down?' I said, opening it slightly. 'Stevie's in bed. I collected him in the early hours.'

She turned down her music and continued getting ready for work. Downstairs I found Paula in the kitchen and I told her what had happened during the night.

'I'm glad Stevie's safe,' she said, and carried her breakfast to the table. I made a cup of coffee and took it upstairs to drink while I showered and dressed. I guessed Stevie would sleep for some time, but I needed to be up and ready for whatever the day had in store.

It was only when I went downstairs again that I found Stevie's dinner from the night before plated up and in the stone-cold oven. I scraped it into the bin, saw the girls off at the door and then poured myself another coffee, which I took with my fostering folder into the living room. Social services, police and fostering practices have changed over time, but based on my experience I was expecting Verity and the police to call at some point today and probably visit. I brought my log notes up to date and then at 9 a.m. I telephoned Stevie's school and told the secretary that Stevie had been found safe but wouldn't be in school today. I asked her to tell Carolyn. I assumed the police had contacted the school as his class teacher had been the last one to see him before he went missing. Just as I returned the phone to its base, Peggy rang.

'Sorry I couldn't talk last night,' I said straight away. 'I was shattered.' On reflection, I felt I'd been a bit curt with her.

'Join the club,' she said wearily. 'We were up too. So what's Stevie been saying about why he ran off?'

'Nothing at present. He's still in bed. I didn't press him last night. I'll talk to him today once he's up.'

'Hold on a minute. Fred's just let himself in from taking the kids to school.' I waited while Peggy relayed what I'd said to Fred. She came back on the line. 'Fred says Steven needs a good talking to, not his beauty sleep.'

I sighed. 'Please reassure Fred that I will be talking to Stevie once he's awake.'

'Don't you ever get angry with him?' she asked.

'More frustrated,' I admitted. 'Peggy, do you have any idea what could be worrying him now?'

'No, we haven't seen him for over a week and he didn't return my call.'

'All right. I'll talk to him and try to find out. I'm expecting Verity to speak to him too, so I'll phone you when I have any news.'

'Thanks.' She paused. 'We do love him, you know. But we can't cope when he's like this, what with Kiri and Liam as well. We're not young and it's very stressful. Fred was so wound up again last night. I worry who would look after Kiri and Liam if anything happened to us.' I sympathised. Even though Stevie wasn't living with them, they were still suffering the fallout from his behaviour.

'I'll give Stevie your love and tell him to phone you once he's up,' I said.

'Thank you.'

Having said goodbye to Peggy, I telephoned Verity. It went through to her voicemail so I left a message saying that Stevie had been found safe and well, and was with me, but hadn't gone to school today. The duty social worker should have updated her, but I thought it best to make sure.

With the house quiet and warm, I rested my head back on the sofa, and despite the caffeine from two coffees I began to doze. I was awoken by the sound of the landline ringing, and automatically reached out to take it from my bedside cabinet before I realised I was in the living room. I took the handset from the corner unit. 'Hello?' The clock on the mantelpiece showed it was 9.45 a.m.

'Cathy, it's Verity. I got your message. How is Stevie?'

I shook off the sleep and tried to gather my thoughts. 'He seems unharmed, just quiet. He's still in bed. I've told the school he won't be in today.' I then went over the details of him being found at the bus terminus and collecting him from the police station.

'Did Stevie say where he'd been, or why he'd run away?'

'No. There was an incident at school yesterday in last lesson. He was caught using his mobile phone and the teacher wanted to confiscate it until the end of the day. He swore at her and ran off. But I'm sure there's more to it. He's been quiet and withdrawn all week and hasn't seen or spoken to his grandparents or Liam or Kiri.'

'I'll need to talk to him, but it won't be until after one o'clock.'

'We'll be here,' I said.

I replaced the handset and stared, unseeing, into space – that zoned-out feeling that comes from lack of sleep. Five minutes later the front doorbell rang, startling Sammy who shot behind the sofa. I answered it to find the woman police officer I'd seen earlier at the police station. 'I was passing so I thought I'd pay Stevie a quick visit now so we can sign him off,' she said. 'Is he in?'

'Yes, but he's still in bed. Shall I get him up?'

'Yes, please.'

I showed her through to the living room, then went upstairs to fetch Stevie. He took some waking and I had to tell him three times that a police officer was here and needed to see him. 'Why?' he mumbled.

'To make sure you're OK. It's standard when a young person goes missing.'

'But I'm still tired.'

'So am I, love. Put on your dressing gown and come down. You can come back to bed once she's seen you.'

Groaning and still half asleep, he did as I said and staggered down in his dressing gown, his hair all over the place. Usually immaculate, if he hadn't been so tired he'd never have been seen like that.

'Don't worry, I won't keep you long,' the police officer said, smiling, when she saw him. 'How are you?'

He flopped onto the sofa and yawned. 'Tired.'

'Yes, I can imagine,' she said. 'We had a good chat yesterday at the police station while we were waiting so I'm not going over all that again. You understand why it's dangerous to run away? As well as causing your foster carer and grandparents a lot of worry?' He nodded. 'Is he allowed to stay here permanently then?' she asked me as Stevie yawned again.

'I'm not sure yet. His social worker will be seeing us later.'

'And you're happy to stay here?' she asked Stevie, not fully understanding how the fostering system worked.

Stevie shrugged.

'You said you were when you were at the police station.'

'Yes,' he said. 'I guess.'

'That's it really then,' she said to me. 'I just needed to check he was safe and well.' She stood ready to leave. 'Don't run away again,' she said to him.

He gave a half-hearted nod. 'Can I go back to bed now?' he asked me.

'Yes, but only for a couple of hours. We have Verity coming later.'

He heaved himself off the sofa and went upstairs as I saw the police officer to the front door.

'Did Stevie tell you why he'd run away?' I asked her once Stevie's bedroom door had closed.

'He said he thought he'd be in trouble if he came back.'

'Trouble. What for?'

'He wouldn't say any more. But he certainly didn't want to go back to his grandparents. He thought he'd be in more trouble there. He seems to trust you, so try talking to him.' Which niggled me, given all the time I had spent talking to Stevie, trying to find out what was wrong.

'I will,' I said. 'But I hope Stevie already knows he can confide in me.'

'At his age problems can get out of proportion, especially if they can't live at home, poor kid.' I nodded. 'Hopefully he won't come to our attention again.'

'I hope not,' I agreed, then I thanked her, and we said goodbye.

While Stevie slept, I got on with the housework and had a tidy-up. Then just after midday I woke him and told him he needed to shower and dress as his social worker would be coming before long and he also needed to telephone his grandparents. He moaned, turned over and said he was very tired. I told him he could have an early night as Adrian and I would be doing, and pointed out that we'd had less sleep than him. He moaned some more.

'I expect you're hungry,' I said. 'When did you last eat?'

'I got chips and had them in the bus shelter,' came his mumbled reply from beneath the duvet.

'Do you want a cooked breakfast?'

He nodded. In my experience, growing lads can usually be persuaded from their beds with a fry-up.

'Up you get then. I'll cook it while you shower and dress.'

Downstairs, I waited until I heard Stevie in the shower before I started cooking his breakfast. When he appeared he looked quite rejuvenated, clean and with conditioned and towel-dried hair. He was dressed in freshly laundered jeans and a pale blue jersey, and I noticed he was wearing a delicate silver necklace that I hadn't seen before.

'That's nice,' I said, pointing to it as I set his breakfast on the table in front of him.

'It was Gran's,' he said. 'I always liked it when I was little and she gave it to me on my thirteenth birthday.'

'That was kind of her. I expect you treasure it.'

'I do.' He touched it reflectively, then picked up his knife and fork.

'Once you've finished you need to phone your gran,' I said.

'She and your grandfather were very worried about you last night.'

He nodded.

I busied myself in the kitchen while Stevie ate, then once he'd finished I went to the table and sat opposite him. 'Stevie, now I need you to tell me what has been bothering you lately and made you behave as you did yesterday – swearing at your teacher and then running away.'

He shrugged, couldn't meet my gaze and then said, 'I had my phone on in lessons.'

'Yes, I know that. Carolyn told me. You know you're not supposed to, so why didn't you hand your phone to the teacher as she asked, instead of swearing and running off? She would have given it back to you at the end of the day.' I was struggling to believe this was the only reason for his behaviour.

He shifted uncomfortably. 'I didn't want her to see some of the stuff on my phone.' I went cold. Surely he hadn't made the same mistake twice? We were still waiting to hear the outcome of the police investigation into the indecent images he and Joey had swapped.

'What stuff?' I asked.

'Text messages about her,' he said, still unable to meet my gaze. 'Most of the class are in a WhatsApp group and sometimes we keep our phones on silent and text.'

'During lessons?'

He nodded. I thought that schools must fight a continuous battle with the use of mobile phones. It was bad enough at home, but what Stevie had said did seem plausible.

'What did your text message say about her?' I asked.

'That she was a useless teacher.' He finally met my gaze.

'Is there anything else on your phone you didn't want her to see?' I asked.

He shook his head and looked away. 'I just didn't want her to see my texts about her. I would have been in trouble and so would all the others in the group. They're being OK to me now, you know, accepting who I am. I wasn't going to drop them in it.'

Which sounded like the truth to me. 'All right, thank you for telling me. In future, if you can't trust yourself to keep your phone switched off while you're in school, it would be better to leave it here so you're not tempted.' I knew there was as much chance of that happening as pigs flying. Most teenagers are glued to their phones.

'I'll keep it off at school,' he promised.

'Good, make sure you do.' But of course if all the others in the class were texting during a lesson, I doubted Stevie would be left out. 'Now you need to phone your grandparents. Verity will be coming later, but I don't know the exact time.'

'Can't you phone them?' he asked. I would have done with a much younger child, but he needed to speak to them.

'No, they need to hear from you,' I said. 'They were very worried. Use the landline in the living room if you like. If your granddad answers the phone then apologise for worrying him and ask to speak to your gran.' Stevie didn't need a dose of Fred's caustic comments right now.

He did as I asked and went into the living room while I stayed in the kitchen. I heard the relief in his voice when Peggy answered. 'Hi, Gran, sorry for upsetting you,' he began, and then told her what he'd just told me. She must have warned him – as I had – about following school rules, for I heard him promise he wouldn't get into trouble again. He also said he'd see them at the weekend, then he fell silent for some time as she spoke. I heard him say a subdued 'I love you too' and then 'goodbye'. When he came through he looked relieved but sad. 'Well done. Is everything all right?' I asked.

'Gran was crying. She said how much she and Grandpa love me.'

'Of course they do, very much.'

'And I love them.'

CHAPTER FOURTEEN

DISCLOSURE

When a young person has been missing, or 'absent' or 'away from placement' as it's also known, the local authority – usually the child's social worker – has to interview them on their return to establish why they ran away, where they were while absent and what can be done to resolve the issues that led to them running away. Stevie was sitting at the table in our kitchen-diner finishing off his homework when Verity arrived, and she was suitably impressed.

'I wish my kids did their school work on a day off,' she said.

'It's a school day, really,' I pointed out, and offered her a drink.

'I'm fine, thanks. I won't stay for long, but I did need to see Stevie today.' She sat beside him at the table.

'Shall I leave you to it?' I asked.

'Yes, please. I'll see you before I leave.'

I went out, closing the door behind me to give them some privacy, and went into the front room where I logged on to my PC. I continued working on the Excel spreadsheet I was updating for work. Fifteen minutes or so later I heard the door to the kitchen-diner open, and then Stevie came into the front room. 'She wants to see you now,' he said.

I clicked the mouse to save the spreadsheet and followed him into the kitchen-diner. He returned to sit next to Verity and I sat opposite.

'We've had a good chat,' Verity said, closing the diary she'd had open in front of her. 'It seems Stevie ran away because of the incident at school involving him using his mobile phone. Stevie says the reason he didn't want to return to you or go to his grandparents was because he knew he'd be in trouble.'

'We were obviously worried,' I said, for it sounded as though I was an ogre. 'And before then? Have you talked about what was worrying Stevie in the week before the incident?' I glanced at him.

'Nothing,' he said. 'It's doesn't matter.' Which Verity accepted.

'Stevie feels he can remain in placement with you.'

'Good. I'm pleased you feel you can stay with us,' I said to him, 'but I don't want a repeat of last night.' Then, looking at Verity, I said, 'Not only did Stevie put himself in danger by running away, but he caused his grandparents, my family and me a lot of unnecessary worry. My son, Adrian, came with me to the police station and didn't get to bed until four-thirty. He had to be up at six o'clock to go to work. If Stevie has a problem, he needs to discuss it like the young adult he is, not run off.'

'I think he knows that,' Verity said a little curtly.

'Excellent.' But it needed to be said with his social worker present.

'He'll be in school tomorrow,' Verity said, winding up. 'I'll phone Mr and Mrs Jones and let them know he's staying here. OK, Stevie, I'll leave you to finish your homework.' She stood and I saw her to the front door.

'Carry on as you were before,' she said to me. 'Don't hold a post-mortem.'

'I don't intend to,' I replied, which I would have hoped she'd know. We said goodbye and she left.

It would have been helpful if she'd lectured Stevie a bit more, as I had, but I'd seen far worse behaviour in a child or young person go unchecked by their social worker for fear of jeopardising their relationship. I appreciated it must be difficult to get the balance right, but then it is for parents and foster carers too. Of course I wouldn't dwell on Stevie running away; we would carry on as normal and hope there wasn't a repetition.

Adrian was home at four o'clock, having worked an early shift, and went up to his room for a sleep before dinner. We all ate together, the subject of Stevie's absence forgotten. Stevie joined in the conversation more like his old self. The following day he went to school, had the meeting with the Head, apologised to the teacher he'd sworn at and rejoined his class. The weekend arrived, and not a moment too soon. Stevie visited his grandparents on Sunday while Adrian and Paula went out with their father for lunch, and Lucy went ice-skating with a friend. The few hours I had alone gave me a chance to finish the spreadsheets I'd been working on and then sit quietly and do nothing. But while it was relaxing to have the house to myself for a while, I was pleased when everyone returned and the house was again filled with the sounds of my family.

I hadn't given Stevie a front door key yet and he hadn't asked for one. Giving a young person their own key can be a matter of contention. Some young people ask for a key as soon as they arrive, but I'd learnt from experience to wait and let them prove themselves first. Once I knew I could trust them to act responsibly with a front door key and not party, steal or truant from school if I wasn't in – as had happened to me before – then I gave them a key. I was planning on waiting another couple of weeks and then, if everything settled down, I'd give Stevie his own key as a sign I trusted him to act responsibly.

A few days passed when Stevie seemed perfectly normal, then abruptly his behaviour deteriorated again. He became silent, withdrawn and spent a lot of time in his room, snapping at anyone if they asked if he was all right. It could simply be teenage angst, and had I raised Stevie from a baby or young child I would have felt more confident in just giving him the space and time he needed to work through it. But as similar behaviour from him previously had been symptomatic that something was brewing, I kept asking him if he was OK. Finally he exploded. It was at the end of dinner. Just he, the girls and I were in and he'd sat sullen and silent throughout the meal, head down, hunched over his plate and hardly eating a thing. As we cleared away I asked him if he was feeling all right.

'Will you please shut the fuck up and just leave me alone!' he snapped. Throwing his plate on the floor, he stormed off upstairs, into his bedroom, and slammed the door. I was shocked, Paula looked close to tears and Lucy was angry.

'He's not talking to you like that!' she said and went up after him.

'Lucy!' I called. 'Come here! Let him cool off first, then I'll talk to him.'

I went after her. As I arrived on the landing she was at his bedroom door. Giving it a good thud, she didn't wait for a reply but flung it open. Then she stopped. 'Oh,' she said. I joined her. Stevie was sitting on the edge of his bed, head in his hands and sobbing.

'What is the matter, love?' I said, going into his room. Lucy returned downstairs.

I sat beside him on the bed and waited for him to calm down enough to talk. His anger had been replaced by tears, and seeing him cry so openly broke my heart. 'What is it?' I asked gently. I slipped my arm around his waist and waited some more. His tears kept falling. He was so distraught he was beyond speaking. I passed him tissues from the box and, keeping his head down, he dabbed at his eyes. I could hear Lucy and Paula downstairs in the kitchen beneath and I guessed they were clearing up the mess Stevie had made, which was kind of them.

'It can't be that bad,' I said presently.

'It is,' he sobbed.

'Is it to do with school?' I asked. He shook his head. Then I wondered if perhaps it wasn't a specific problem, but he was generally feeling low, even depressed, and should see a doctor. 'Are you feeling very sad and maybe missing your family?' I asked.

'Sometimes.'

'Can you talk to me about how you are feeling?' I tried.

He shook his head and fresh tears fell. I passed him another tissue. He wiped his eyes again and then the sobbing gradually eased, and we sat quietly side by side for some time. Just as I thought he was starting to recover, his face clouded and silent tears fell. I was really worried. I was unable to reach him. 'Stevie, you need to tell me what's wrong,' I tried again.

He shook his head in despair. 'I've been so stupid,' he said at last. 'If I tell you, you'll hate me forever.' So I knew it was something specific that was upsetting him rather than generally feeling low. I didn't believe it could be anything so bad that I would hate him. I needed to try to coax it out of him.

'Of course I won't hate you,' I said. 'I'll try to help you.'

'My grandparents will hate me.'

'They might be annoyed with you, but they won't hate you, they love you.'

'Not after this they won't. They'll never forgive me.' I was now feeling uneasy at the enormity of whatever it was Stevie perceived he'd done.

I looked at him as he sat with his head in his hands in complete despair. I couldn't begin to guess what the problem was, although part of me still felt he was probably overreacting and had blown it out of proportion, but of course I couldn't be sure. 'Stevie,' I said after a while, 'you are going to have to share this with someone sooner or later, otherwise it's going to eat away at you just like when you had the problem with Joey and the photographs you sent him of yourself.' I saw him flinch.

'It's worse than that,' he said. I felt another stab of unease.

'Go on,' I prompted.

He raised his head slightly and stared at a place on the floor a little way in front of him. Taking a deep breath, he said, 'You know my gran asked you about a secret Liam and Kiri had?'

'Yes, I remember. It wasn't long after you moved in.'

'It's about that secret,' he said.

'OK.' I felt another stab of unease. I hadn't got a clue where this was leading. Peggy hadn't mentioned it again.

'I didn't tell you the whole truth. There were more photos.'

'You mean the photos you sent to Joey of you naked?'

He shook his head. 'No, there were some others. Of Kiri and Liam.'

I stared at him, hoping I'd misunderstood. 'Not like the ones you sent of yourself?' He nodded. 'Without their clothes on?'

He nodded again, and I felt physically sick.

'You took photos of Kiri and Liam naked?' I asked, unable to believe what I'd heard. 'Oh Stevie. Why? Whatever made you do that? Are they still on your phone?'

'No, I deleted them after I sent them.'

'Sent them where?' I asked, my stomach contracting with fear.

'To Joey.'

'Oh no.' His eyes filled again. I continued to stare at him. This had taken a new and horrifying turn, as Stevie knew. 'Why?'

'Joey told me to. He said if I didn't he would send the pictures of me to my grandparents, all my friends, the school and post them online. What else could I do?' There was plenty Stevie could and should have done, but he'd panicked. 'So I took the photos and told Kiri and Liam not to tell anyone – that was our secret.'

'But you must have known it was wrong?' I said, struggling to take it in.

He nodded and his tears fell again. 'I did, but I hoped it would put a stop to it and Joey would go away. I couldn't tell my grandparents, they would have killed me.'

'So it's been on your conscience all this time,' I said, though I'm afraid to say that my sympathy was waning. Kiri and Liam were six and eight years old, and Stevie had taken indecent images of them and sent them to a stranger. Where were those photos now? What pervert was drooling over them? This was no longer two teenagers making an error of judgement and sexting, but paedophile activity in which Stevie had been complicit. For a moment I wished he'd never set foot in my house. Then I knew I had to pull myself together and act professionally. Thankfully my own children were older, otherwise I would have asked for Stevie to be moved. Harsh though that may seem, I would never have put my own family at risk. 'Why didn't you tell me about those photos when you told me about the ones you'd taken of yourself?' I asked after a moment.

'I knew it was bad and I hoped that once I'd sent the photos to Joey he would just go away and leave me alone. He did for a while. Then he contacted me again and said he wanted more photos or he would send the photos of Liam and Kiri to my grandparents and post them online with my name on them.'

'You didn't take any more, did you?' I asked, a cold chill running up my spine.

'No.'

I sat for a moment, taking it all in. Never in my wildest imagination would I have guessed Stevie's secret. It wasn't for me to question him about the details of the photographs – where and when he'd taken them. That was for the police. The less I knew about them the better, for once something is seen or heard it cannot be undone. I knew that what I'd learnt so far would plague me for ever. I'd fostered enough abused children to know what paedophiles are capable of, and reluctantly I now had to admit I had one in my home – a fourteen-year-old boy. Yes, it might have been a grave error of judgement on Stevie's part, but I was struggling to understand why, having been well brought up by his grandparents – who as far as I knew had sound moral principles – Stevie had actually done this. I hoped he was telling me the truth about the circumstances in which he'd taken the photographs of Liam and Kiri – that he'd been blackmailed. For the alternative – that he had taken them of his own free will through some perverse pleasure and then shared them with Joey online – was too awful to contemplate.

'I'll need to phone your social worker,' I said, and left the room.

Shaking and with my stomach churning, I went into my bedroom and closed the door. I felt hot and queasy as I perched on the bed and picked up the phone. I tried Verity first, but it was after six o'clock and her work voicemail clicked in, inviting me to leave a message or, if it was urgent, to contact the emergency duty social worker. I did both. 'Verity, it's Cathy, Stevie's carer,' I said, unable to keep the tremor from my voice. 'I'm afraid that Stevie has just disclosed. He has taken indecent photographs of his siblings, Kiri and Liam, and sent them to Joey – the same lad he sent the indecent images of himself to. I'll phone the duty social worker now.'

I cut the call, phoned the social services' out-of-hours number and explained to the call operator why I needed to speak to either Verity or the emergency duty social worker as soon as possible. She took my details, asked if Kiri and Liam were in any immediate danger, which as far as I knew they weren't, and said the emergency duty social worker would call me back. I replaced the handset and continued sitting on my bed, my thoughts all over the place. A knock sounded on the door. 'Mum, are you OK?' It was Paula.

'Yes, I'm waiting to speak to the duty social worker. I'll be down shortly.'

'We've cleared up,' she said.

'Thank you, love.' She stayed outside my door. 'I'll be with you soon,' I called. She'd be looking for an explanation and reassurance after Stevie's outburst. Goodness knows what I was going to tell her, Lucy and Adrian. 'I'll see you when I've finished on the phone,' I said. I heard her go round the landing to her bedroom.

The landline rang and it was the duty social worker, but not the one I'd spoken to before when Stevie had gone missing. I explained in more detail Stevie's disclosure, gave him Stevie's details again, how long he'd been with me and why he'd originally come into care. He asked where Stevie was now and I said in his bedroom at my house. 'And the photos were taken when he lived with his grandparents and siblings last year?' he confirmed.

'Yes.' The duty social worker said he'd try to speak to Verity, and in the meantime Stevie wasn't to contact Liam and Kiri, which I knew. He or Verity would phone me back this evening. There would now be safeguarding issues around Stevie's two younger siblings, and indeed any other young children he had been in contact with. The consequences of Stevie's actions would be more far-reaching than Stevie could have ever imagined. Having ended the call, I sat for a moment and then went to Stevie's room. His door was closed so I knocked on it. 'Come in,' he called, subdued.

He was sitting on his bed as I'd left him, but now had his phone in his hands. 'What are you doing?' I asked suspiciously.

'Messaging the WhatsApp group from my class,' he replied.

'About what?'

'School stuff.'

Would I ever trust him again? I had no idea. 'I'm waiting to hear back from the duty social worker or Verity,' I said.

He put his phone to one side. 'What's going to happen to me? Will she tell the police?'

'Yes, she will have to. Joey needs to be caught and stopped,' was all I said, not wanting to go into all the procedure that awaited Stevie. That was for Verity and the police to explain to him. He looked at me, naively surprised, still not grasping what he and Joey had done. 'If Joey has done this to you, he will be doing it to others,' I said. 'Are you still in contact with him?'

'He's just messaged me again.'

'Saying what? Show me, please.' My heart was thumping wildly as I went over. Stevie turned the phone so I could see the screen. The message from Joey was threatening: *Where are the photos, Stevie boy? Don't keep me waiting.* I felt sick at the thought of that pervert at the other end of this message, still out there and free to perpetrate more evil.

'Don't reply,' I said. 'And don't tell him you've told me. Hopefully the police will be able to trace him, so don't make him suspicious by deleting your account. Just leave everything as it is for now.' As I continued to look at Joey's profile picture my anger and disgust rose, but also I thought he looked slightly familiar, although I didn't know where from.

'Is that a recent photo of him, do you know?' I asked, returning the phone to Stevie.

'He said it was, but perhaps he was lying about that too.'

'I want you to take a screenshot of his page and send it to my phone, please. Do you know how to do that?'

'Yes. Why?'

'He looks familiar,' I said. 'I want to check something.' Also, I thought, if Joey deleted his account I'd have something to show Verity and the police.

Stevie did as I asked and sent the screenshot to my mobile phone, which I would collect presently. 'Are you OK?' I asked him. It was a daft question and he shrugged despondently. 'I'll let you know when I hear from Verity or the duty social worker.'

I pulled his door to and was about to look in on Paula when the house phone rang. I continued round the landing to take the call in my bedroom, where I closed the door. It was Verity. I told her exactly what Stevie had told me about taking the indecent images of Kiri and Liam. I could hear the gravity in her voice as she replied, 'I'll contact the child protection officer [from the police] first thing tomorrow morning. I'll see Stevie just after nine.'

'I'll keep him off school then?'

'Yes. And he's not to go to his grandparents' house or have any contact with Liam or Kiri for now.'

'I'll keep him at home with me.'

'How is he coping?' she asked. For despite what Stevie had done, he was a minor and a looked-after child. Hopefully one who'd acted foolishly and had been taken advantage of, rather than the more sinister option that he'd willingly engaged in paedophile activity.

'Shocked, worried and upset,' I said.

'Keep an eye on him and I'll see him first thing tomorrow.'

I went round to Stevie's room and told him that Verity had phoned and would be visiting us at nine o'clock the next morning. He was lying on his bed, staring up at the ceiling. 'Is there anything else you want to tell me?' He shook his head. 'I'll be downstairs if you want to talk.'

'I don't,' he replied.

I stopped off at Paula's room, but she was in the middle of a telephone conversation with a friend, so I went downstairs. Lucy was on her way up. Unaware of what Stevie had told me, she was still annoyed with him. 'Did he apologise to you?' she asked.

'Not yet, but don't push it, love. I'll explain later.'

'Well, he needs to,' she said, and went into her room.

While I was touched by her support, Stevie apologising was the last thing on my mind. I took my mobile phone into the front room, logged on to my computer and then sent the screenshot of Joey's profile page to it. The image was clearer and bigger. He still looked familiar and I now had a vague idea where I'd seen him before. Five minutes later I had the answer and had identified 'Joey'. Only of course the photo wasn't of 'Joey', but a little-known actor called Robin. I found the exact same photograph online, which is where 'Joey' would have stolen it from. Paedophiles often steal photos from online to disguise their true identity. It was pure chance I recognised it. Robin had had a few small parts in repertory theatre, but had toured with a company the year before in a show I'd gone to see. It was a fluke, and although it wouldn't help identify who Joey really was it showed he was a fraud. I made a note of the website address where I'd found the photo in case Verity or the police wanted it, and then I went upstairs and told Stevie. He was obviously shocked.

'Why did he do that?' he asked naively. 'I sent him my real photo.'

'I know you did, love. You're honest, but this person, whoever he is, is a liar, a pervert and a paedophile.'

'So he's not gender-fluid like me?' Stevie asked innocently.

'No, and I don't suppose he's fifteen, or has a younger brother or sister, or lives with his grandparents or any of the other things he told you. He's lied to get what he wants – it's too easy online.'

CHAPTER FIFTEEN

EXCLUDED

Stevie stayed in his room for the rest of the evening and I checked on him regularly. He seemed to be coping, although at present he was unaware of the wider implications of what he'd done. Apart from the effect his abuse would have had on Liam and Kiri, teenagers younger than Stevie had been put on the sex offenders' register for being in possession of child pornography, and Stevie had actually taken the indecent images. Stevie knew what he'd done was wrong, but never in a million years would he have classified it as paedophile activity. If found guilty, he could be given a custodial sentence and, once released, placed on the sex offenders' register, which he'd have to disclose on any college or job application, as well as it affecting his future relationships.

Just before 9 p.m. Stevie came down for a drink before going to bed and I asked him for his phone.

'Why? Don't you trust me?' he asked moodily. The short answer was no, not right now. Although this was for his own good, as I didn't want him to keep checking his phone while 'Joey' was issuing threats. 'I always switch it off at night,' he added.

'Good, but I think it would be better if it was down here tonight. I won't look at it. You can switch it off first and I'll put it in my drawer in the front room. Has Joey been in touch again?' I asked. He nodded. 'Saying what?'

'That if I didn't do as he said and take more photos he'd post the pictures of Liam and Kiri online with my name.'

'So why didn't you tell me?'

'He only just messaged.'

'Have you replied?'

'No.'

'I want you to bring your phone down and I'll put it away until Verity comes tomorrow. It's likely the police will want to see it too, so bring it down now, please.'

'But I won't be able to WhatsApp my class.'

'No, you won't for now.'

He sighed and reluctantly went off to do as I'd asked. This was all new territory for me, so I was running on common sense in dealing with it and learning as I went. Stevie was vulnerable and frightened, and I knew it wouldn't take much for Joey to push him into doing something else. I thought it was a pity that the police weren't involved now while Joey was active online, but then again, I knew that police digital forensics would be able to trace Joey from his IP address. IP stands for Internet Protocol and is the unique number that identifies each of us online.

A few minutes later Stevie came down and handed me his phone. 'There's no credit on it,' he said, as if I was going to use it.

'It doesn't matter. I'm going to put it safely away until we see Verity tomorrow.' He hesitated. 'Yes?'

'Can you tell Adrian, Lucy and Paula what I've done?' he asked quietly.

'If you want me to.'

'I can't face telling them.' His eyes filled, and at that point I felt sorry for him. 'Please tell my grandparents too.'

'Verity will need to tell them,' I said.

He went into the kitchen, poured himself a glass of water and went to bed. While I felt sorry for Stevie, I also had deep sympathy for his grandparents, who had yet to be told, and little Kiri and Liam, who'd been abused by the older brother they'd trusted, for this was abuse. Whether they'd been threatened, coerced or tricked into taking off their clothes and posing for the photographs was for Verity and the police to discover. I thought Kiri and Liam would probably need counselling to get over what had happened.

At 9.15 Adrian let himself in the front door, having worked a late shift. I went into the hall. 'Have you eaten?' I asked him.

'Yes, thanks. I had something in my break at work.'

'Good.' I tried to raise a smile.

'What's the matter, Mum?' he asked, seeing through me straight away. 'Is Nana ill?'

'No, she's fine. Something has happened in connection with Stevie. He's in bed, but I need to speak to you, Lucy and Paula. Can you wait for me in the living room while I fetch the girls?'

'What is it?' he asked, worried.

'Please wait until I've got Lucy and Paula. I don't want to go through it all twice.'

Upstairs, I went first to Paula's room and then Lucy's and asked them to come down, as I needed to talk to them. Paula was already in her dressing gown, and Lucy was about to shower, but they came down as I asked, guessing it was serious.

I closed the living-room door and we sat down. They looked at me, their expressions full of questions and concern.

'As you know, Stevie hasn't been himself for some days,' I began.

'Tell me about it!' Lucy put in.

I nodded. 'He clearly had something worrying him and this evening he told me what it was.' I took a breath and steeled myself. 'It seems that Stevie not only took indecent photographs of himself and sent them to "Joey" – the guy he met online – but he also took some of his younger brother and sister.' I paused. There was silence as they continued to look at me and the enormity of what I'd said hit them.

'He sent indecent photos of Kiri and Liam to his friend Joey?' Paula asked incredulously.

'Yes, except Joey isn't his friend. I'm almost certain he's a paedophile, and Joey isn't his real name. I've informed Verity and she will be coming here tomorrow to see Stevie. The police will be involved.'

'Stevie took photos of his brother and sister without their clothes on?' Lucy asked, still struggling to take it in. I nodded. 'That's really sick. Why?'

'Joey threatened to send the photos of Stevie to his friends and post them online if he didn't.'

'Blackmail,' Adrian said.

'Yes, and now he wants more indecent photographs of children.'

Paula's hand shot to her mouth. 'That's awful, Mum,' she cried, shocked.

'Stevie's such an idiot!' Lucy exclaimed.

'I think he knows that now,' I replied.

'I can't believe he'd do something like that,' Paula said. 'He seems so nice.'

'I think he panicked and made a bad decision,' I said. 'But that's for the police to investigate.' I looked at their shocked and saddened faces. It wasn't the first time since we'd begun fostering that I'd had to tell them something I would rather have protected them from. When they'd been little it had been even more difficult, and at times I'd loathed myself for taking away their innocence by explaining something the average child wouldn't have heard about but they had.

'What will happen to Stevie?' Adrian asked.

'I don't know yet, but for the time being I think the social services will want him to stay here. Long-term will depend on the outcome of the police investigation.'

'Will he go to prison?' Paula asked.

'I honestly don't know.'

'But he didn't actually abuse them?' Lucy said. 'You know, do stuff to them?'

'Not as far as I know, but making two children take off their clothes to photograph them is an abuse as well as illegal. Stevie is still being investigated for sexting, but this is a lot more serious.'

'What did his grandparents say?' Paula asked anxiously. 'I bet they were upset.'

'They don't know yet, but yes, they will be very upset when they're told.'

Adrian shook his head sadly.

'I know this is a huge shock,' I said. 'Stevie knows what he's done is wrong. He asked me to tell you because he couldn't bear to tell you himself. Don't raise it with him unless he wants to talk about it, but obviously if he tells you any more about the images he's taken or that he's taken others then you need to tell me.' They nodded solemnly. 'Don't demonise him. From what he's told me, he made a huge error of judgement and will need our support.'

Lucy grimaced. 'Not sure I can do that, Mum. I mean, who goes around taking photos of their little brother and sister without their clothes on, and sends them to a paedo?'

I nodded. 'Although Stevie didn't realise he was a paedophile.'

'Why else would a guy online want photos of naked kids?' Lucy asked, amazed. 'I mean, it doesn't take much to make the connection.'

'That's maybe true for young people like you,' I said. 'I've brought you up to be aware of the dangers online. But while Stevie was at home I don't think he was. His grandparents don't even own mobile phones. They've no idea about computers or the internet. I think Stevie was naïve and was taken advantage of by someone he thought he could trust. I would hope that you'd have had alarm bells ringing, but he didn't. He thought he was in a relationship when he sent the photos of himself, then it all changed and he found himself being blackmailed and panicked. To be honest, it was probably easier for him to take the photos than to admit to his grandparents what he'd done.'

'I thought Facebook had better controls now for keeping paedophiles out,' Adrian said.

'It wasn't Facebook but a much smaller website for young gender-fluid teenagers. I think Joey probably targets websites and forums like these because he knows that's where he can find vulnerable young people confused about their gender. They are easy targets.'

'So the website administrators need to do more,' Adrian said.

'Yes,' I agreed.

'Joey could be a woman,' Lucy added.

'It's possible,' I said.

'Will you tell Nana?' Paula asked.

'I don't think so. She'll only worry, and it's not like we have young children in the family who need protecting.'

'You don't think he would do it again?' Lucy asked, horrified.

'No, I don't, but the police and social services will investigate all possibilities. To be honest, I'm still struggling to believe he's done this at all.'

'So am I,' Adrian said, and Lucy and Paula agreed.

It was a conversation I would rather not have had.

Needless to say, I didn't get much sleep that night and I don't think anyone else did. At some point I heard everyone get out of bed, and at 2 a.m. I went to check on Stevie. He was in bed, staring at the ceiling. 'Are you OK?' I asked quietly so as not to disturb the others.

'Yes, I guess.'

He wasn't distraught or in tears, so I said, 'Try to get some sleep. You know where I am if you need to talk,' and left him.

I then lay in the darkness of my room thinking not so much about Stevie, but little Kiri and Liam. Whatever had been going through their minds when the abuse had happened? The fact they'd told their gran they had a secret a number of times showed they wanted to tell her and had got close to doing so. What had stopped them? I wondered. Had Stevie bribed them with treats or threatened them not to tell? Or perhaps, aware they'd done wrong, they thought that if they told they'd be in trouble. Doubtless the truth would come out. Pity the poor grandparents, I thought again. I knew that if Stevie was staying with us then I would need to support him, for I doubted Peggy and Fred would be able to. They'd be too shocked, and their main concern would be for Liam and Kiri. I also knew that for the foreseeable future Stevie wouldn't be allowed home to see his brother and sister until the police and social services were satisfied he no longer posed a threat to them or any other children he might come into contact with. People like 'Joey' ruin lives.

Having not slept well, it was an effort for everyone to get up, and for Adrian, Lucy and Paula to leave the house on time, so there was little said beyond 'hi' and 'goodbye, see you later'. I woke Stevie at eight, but he didn't come down until after Adrian, Lucy and Paula had left. His eyes were bloodshot and puffy from lack of sleep, and he was wearing old joggers and a jersey. He just wanted a bowl of cereal and juice for breakfast.

'Did you tell them?' he asked, sliding into his chair at the table.

'Yes.'

'What did they say?'

I took my mug of coffee and joined him. 'They were shocked, obviously.'

'Do they hate me?'

'No. But it may take them a while to come to terms with it.'

'I bet they think I'm a right dick,' he said, unenthusiastically scooping up a spoonful of cereal.

'They think you acted foolishly, but you know that now.'

Stevie nodded solemnly, ate another spoonful and then pushed the bowl away. 'I don't want any more,' he said. 'I'm not hungry. Do you think I should phone my gran and try to explain.'

'No, not now.'

'Can I have my phone back?' he asked.

'I need to wait and see what Verity says. She shouldn't be long. If you want to make a phone call then use the landline in the living room.'

'I don't,' he said sulkily. 'But I'm lost without my phone.'

As most of us would be.

'I know. Have you got any homework you could finish? Or a book to read until Verity arrives?'

'I'll find something,' he said dejectedly. 'Will I be going to school this afternoon?'

'I don't know yet.'

Hauling himself from the chair, Stevie shuffled into the kitchen, put his uneaten bowl of cereal on the worktop and then went upstairs to his room. I realised I should telephone his school to tell them he wouldn't be in, as they asked parents and carers to do. Using the handset in the living room, I dialled the school and told the secretary only that Stevie wouldn't be in school this morning. She was clearly expecting a reason, but I didn't want to lie and say he was ill, neither did I feel it necessary to tell her the truth at present. 'I'll phone if he's coming in this afternoon,' I said. 'Otherwise he'll be in tomorrow.'

Five minutes later Verity arrived, dressed sombrely in a dark-grey skirt and jacket, her expression serious. She had a business-like efficiency about her and I thought that, as a social worker, she would have to play many roles, but this must be one of the worst – questioning a young person about child sexual abuse.

'Is he in the living room?' she asked, going down the hall.

'No, in his room. Shall I fetch him?' I wondered if she'd want to talk to me first, but she didn't.

'Tell him to come straight away as I'm pushed for time.'

As I went upstairs I heard her mobile go off and knew this emergency would be adding even more to a workload that was probably already stretching her to the limit. I knocked on Stevie's door. 'Verity is here. She needs to see you straight away.' He appeared immediately and came with me downstairs and into the living room. Verity had put away her phone and was now sitting upright on the sofa with a large notebook open on her lap. 'I'll need to speak to Stevie alone,' she said. I nodded and went out.

Sometimes it's obvious to a foster carer why they aren't included in a meeting; for example, the meeting isn't directly relevant to their role, or in the case of the social worker's six-weekly visit it gives the child a chance to talk in private. But sometimes, like now, being excluded or not invited to a meeting makes no sense at all. Stevie had disclosed to me about what had happened; the social services were expecting me to continue to foster him, so what he told Verity could impact on me and my family. I felt I should have been included and hoped that Verity – as busy as she was – remembered to tell me what I needed to know. Had I still been fostering for Homefinders Jill, as my supervising social worker, would have made sure I was informed. Edith wasn't as efficient or proactive and it was often left to me to update her.

I went into the front room, logged on to my computer and tried to do some work, but it was difficult to concentrate, and my thoughts were all over the place. I could hear the low hum of Verity's and Stevie's voices coming from the living room with silences in between. At one point I thought I heard Stevie crying – another reason for being present would have been to support him. It was over an hour before the living-room door opened and Stevie appeared. 'You can go in now,' he said, and disappeared up to his room.

In the living room I found that Verity had put away her notebook and pen and was slipping on her jacket, ready to leave. 'Stevie is very remorseful about what he's done,' she said, now checking her phone. 'I've explained the procedure: that he will be interviewed by the police and an officer will also see Kiri and Liam. The police will look at the evidence and then decide if they are going to prosecute. It's likely Stevie will be interviewed by the police later today. I'm waiting to hear, so I'll let you both know.' She stood.

'Verity, there are a few things I need to discuss.'

'Yes?'

'Joey is still trying to contact Stevie, and that's not his real name.'

'Stevie told me, and we'll pass all this on to the police.'

'I've got Stevie's phone. I thought it best. He wants it back.'

'I've told him he can't have it until we've seen the police. In fact, I can take it with me now.'

'I'll fetch it. And what about his grandparents? I'm assuming he can't go there at present.'

'No, I've told him that he mustn't try to contact or see Liam and Kiri.'

'Shall I keep him off school for the rest of the day?'

'Yes.'

'I'll get his phone.'

I went through to the front room and took Stevie's phone from the drawer. I also took out the piece of paper on which I'd written the website address where I'd found details of the actor, Robin, whose photograph Joey had stolen. Verity was now in the hall by the front door and listening to voicemail messages. She took the paper and phone with a nod. I opened the front door and she mouthed 'speak later' and went. Not a word about how my family should cope with all of this, or any acknowledgement that it must be difficult for us. I hadn't expected it, and Verity was very busy, but it would only have taken a few minutes.

CHAPTER SIXTEEN

ANOTHER POLICE SEARCH

S tevie couldn't find anything to occupy himself, and so he didn't spend all day moping around I found him some jobs to do: oiling a squeaky door hinge – I showed him what to do – and vacuuming his bedroom carpet and round the landing. He went about the tasks apathetic and in silence, but at least he was occupied. At midday Verity telephoned and said the police would interview him at 2.30 that afternoon. She would be present but asked that I take him to the police station – the same one I'd collected him from when he'd gone missing – and she would drop him off after.

Stevie had come down and was trying to wind up the vacuum-cleaner flex as I took the call. I told him what Verity had said, at the same time showing him which button to press on the cleaner to make the flex retract automatically. 'Will I get my phone back?' he asked as I finished.

'I don't know.'

I stowed the cleaner in the cupboard under the stairs, and then made us a sandwich lunch. We sat either side of the table in the kitchen-diner, awkward and mainly silent as we ate unenthusiastically. Stevie clearly didn't want to talk and I didn't feel like making conversation; I was too worried by what was unfolding. When I looked at his pale, dispirited face I felt sorry for him. He'd had enough to cope with before all this, yet at the same time what he'd done to Liam and Kiri couldn't be minimised. He should have refused to take the photos. The only thing Stevie said during lunch was, 'Do you think Verity has told my gran yet?'

'I would think so,' I said. It seemed Stevie was more worried about letting her down than his grandfather, which was understandable given the friction between him and Fred, and that Peggy had been his and Liam and Kiri's main caregiver. I wondered where her sympathy would lie.

After lunch I suggested to Stevie that he change from his joggers into something smarter for the police interview. 'Do you have some dark trousers? Black or navy?' I asked. He shook his head. 'OK. Wear your school uniform then.' As far as I knew, it was the only conservative outfit he possessed.

'Why?' he asked. 'Am I going to school later?'

'No, there won't be time, but I want you to look smart for the police interview. I think something dark rather than yellow or pink is more appropriate, and don't wear any make-up or nail varnish.' I doubted in his present mood he would consider getting dressed up, but I thought I should say it to make sure. Appearances are important, and looking smart would give the impression he was taking the matter seriously, which is why lawyers always advise their clients to wear a suit for court.

Stevie did as I said and went upstairs to change and then stayed in his bedroom until I called him at two o'clock to say it was time to leave. He came down looking smart in his school uniform and younger – less sophisticated and streetwise.

'Thanks for your help this morning,' I said as we left the house.

He shrugged despondently. 'I used to help my gran with the housework. There's a lot with the three of us, and Fred thinks it's women's work.'

'Fred has a lot to learn,' I said lightly as we got into the car. 'Although I expect he helps your gran in other ways.'

'He cuts the grass and clears out the gutters,' Stevie said. I nodded. Now we were on our way he was more talkative, probably from nerves. 'Verity said the police will want to see Kiri and Liam,' he said as I drove. 'But I don't understand why. They didn't do anything wrong. It was me.'

'I know, but it's usual practice to interview all those involved,' I said. 'What reason did Verity give?'

'She said the police would need to hear their version of events, but I've told the truth. They shouldn't be involved.'

'The police will handle it sensitively,' I said. Of course the police would need to speak to Liam and Kiri to make sure that Stevie's account was true and that he hadn't assaulted them in any other way. Thankfully, I wouldn't be present at that interview when Kiri and Liam were asked the details of what happened, as I had been before when I'd fostered children who'd been abused.

As we approached the police station Stevie became very anxious and fell quiet again. He began tapping his foot and nervously smoothing his hair. The road outside the police station was a lot busier than when I'd collected Stevie the night he'd run away, and I had to go down a side road to find a place to park. 'I'll see you in,' I said, 'then I'll go home.'

He took a deep breath, bracing himself, and got out of the car. We walked without speaking round to the front of the building where we saw Verity crossing the road. She waited for us. 'Hello, Stevie,' she said, then to me, 'I'll drop him off once we've finished.' I said goodbye and retraced my footsteps to my car. It didn't seem appropriate to wish Stevie good luck. I just hoped he told the truth.

An afternoon of conjecture and worry loomed ahead of me. Once home, I couldn't settle to anything and with one eye on the clock I continuously thought of Stevie and how he was faring at the police station. During my years of fostering I'd taken a number of children to various police stations to be interviewed, and the officers had treated them sensitively when questioning them. However, they'd been the victims; Stevie was older and the perpetrator – not a welcome thought. I assumed that Verity, there in the capacity of Stevie's social worker and what's known as an appropriate adult, would support him as necessary.

I opened the freezer door to see what I could take out for dinner later, rummaged inside for a while and then closed the door again without making a decision. In the front room I logged on to my computer and tried to do some work but made so many mistakes that I logged off again. Going into the living room, I stared through the patio windows; the garden was in need of a good tidy-up after the winter, but I couldn't raise the enthusiasm to do it now.

Paula arrived home at four o'clock and I asked her about her day, then I told her what had happened since she'd left for college that morning: that Verity had come to see Stevie and he was now being interviewed at the police station.

'Hope he's all right,' Paula said, concerned.

'Yes, so do I,' I replied.

She poured herself a glass of water and went up to her room. I opened the freezer door and tried again. I'd no idea how long the interview would take – until the police were satisfied, I supposed. When would they see Kiri and Liam? I wondered. I assumed quite soon, or perhaps they'd already seen them.

Shortly after five o'clock, as I was preparing dinner – lasagne – I heard the front doorbell ring. I immediately went to answer it. Stevie stood before me, and behind him I could see Verity in her car with the engine running. Seeing me, she gave a little wave of acknowledgement and pulled away. Some feedback would have been useful, I thought, but she'd be busy, and having spent most of the afternoon at the police station would have a lot of catching up to do.

'How did it go?' I asked Stevie as he slipped off his shoes.

'They're keeping my phone,' he grumbled. 'And they want my laptop.'

'Do we take it to the police station?' I asked.

'Not sure. I think the copper said they'd collect it.'

'From here?' It was in his bedroom.

'Dunno,' he said moodily. He looked exhausted.

'OK. But everything seemed to go all right?'

'Suppose,' he said, and went upstairs to his room.

With no idea what had been said during the interview, I didn't know what, if anything, I could say to reassure Stevie, so I gave him some time alone and returned to the kitchen. As I finished making the lasagne I wondered what Stevie had told the police. Was it the same as he'd told me? Or had he – heaven forbid – admitted to something worse? I shuddered at the prospect. Not knowing how worried I should be was a horrible situation to be in and I hoped Verity would phone before long – if not this evening then tomorrow – to update me. I didn't think it was appropriate for me to press Stevie for details.

Lucy and Adrian arrived home within ten minutes of each other just before six o'clock, and I told them briefly that

Verity had taken Stevie to the police station to be interviewed that afternoon, but I didn't know the outcome. We all ate together shortly after six, but dinner wasn't the usual chatty occasion. The atmosphere was leaden with the unspoken, and Stevie kept his eyes down as he ate. Eventually Lucy said to him, 'So how did it go?'

He shrugged dejectedly, and the gloom continued.

'I have some good news,' Adrian said after a moment.

I looked at him hopefully. 'Yes?'

'That letter that arrived for me today, it's a job interview.'

'Fantastic, well done,' I said.

'It's a large firm of accountants in town. They're looking for a graduate trainee, but they advertised in the national press, so they'll be a lot of competition.'

'You did well to get shortlisted,' I said.

'Yes, well done you,' Paula added.

'You'll get offered it,' Lucy said.

'We'll see,' Adrian said with a smile. 'It would be nice if I did. The interview is next Wednesday. I'll ask work tomorrow for the time off.'

'And don't forget to tell the firm that you will be attending the interview,' I reminded him.

'Already done, Mum,' he said with an indulgent smile. 'I emailed them straight away.'

'Good.' I was so pleased for Adrian; competition in the job market is very fierce, especially for young people just starting their career. I glanced at Stevie, who was still looking morose and hadn't joined in congratulating Adrian. I hadn't expected him to with everything that was going on in his life, but on the other hand, neither was I going to marginalise the achievements of other members of my family because of

Stevie's problems. 'Well done,' I said again to Adrian. I could see it had given his confidence a real boost.

We'd just finished eating when the doorbell rang. 'I wonder who that is,' I said, standing.

'You won't know until you answer it,' Lucy joked. It was our standard repartee for when the doorbell or telephone rang.

Two police officers stood on my doorstep, one male and one female. 'Cathy Glass?' the female officer asked as they both flashed their ID cards.

'Yes.'

'Stevie Jones lives here?'

'Yes.'

'He should have told you we'd be calling to collect his laptop.'

'Oh, I see,' I said. 'He wasn't sure. Come in.' Although I wondered why it took two officers to collect a laptop. 'We're through here,' I said, leading the way down the hall and into the kitchen-diner where Paula, Stevie, Lucy and Adrian were clearing the dinner dishes from the table.

'Sorry for interrupting your meal,' the female officer said.

'It's OK, we'd finished,' I said.

'Stevie,' the male officer said, nodding to him. Stevie flushed, embarrassed.

'Are these all foster kids?' the male officer asked me.

'No, this is my son, Adrian, and my daughters, Lucy and Paula,' I said, introducing them. Adrian said hello, Paula looked worried, while Lucy's eyes had lit up with excitement. It's not every dinnertime that ends with the arrival of two police officers – thank goodness.

'You're not going to arrest anyone and drag them off in handcuffs, are you?' Lucy asked dramatically.

'I hope not,' the male officer replied with a polite smile. Yet I saw his gaze and that of the female officer sweep the room. I supposed they were trained to be observant.

'My laptop is in my room,' Stevie offered self-consciously.

'OK, we'll come up with you to get it,' the male officer replied.

Lucy's eyes widened theatrically as Stevie went out of the room. The two officers followed him and I went too. As we passed the living room both officers looked in, giving the room the same scrutinising gaze as they had the kitchen-diner.

'Have you been fostering long?' the female officer asked as we went upstairs.

'Yes, for many years.'

'My aunt used to foster,' she said. 'I played with the kids when I was a child.'

'That was nice.'

Stevie led the way round the landing and into his room. I remained by the door as the officers went in. His laptop was on his table and, closing the lid, he handed it to the male officer. 'Thanks, we'll send you a receipt,' he said. They didn't immediately leave the room but continued to look around and out of the window. 'You'll have the laptop back once forensics has finished with it,' the male officer confirmed to Stevie, and he nodded.

They left his room and began along the landing. 'Whose is this room?' the male officer asked, pausing outside Adrian's open bedroom door.

'My son's,' I said. He pushed the door further open and looked in, before continuing round. 'That's Paula's room,' I said as the female officer paused outside her room.

'Is that her laptop?' she asked. It was open on her bed.

'Yes.'

'I told you, I never used anyone else's laptop,' Stevie said.

'He didn't,' I confirmed. Had Stevie used our laptops, I guessed they would have wanted to take them as well, which would have been very disruptive for us all.

I thought I may as well show them Lucy's room, where we had a similar conversation about her laptop, then I showed them my bedroom. It didn't escape my notice that this was the second time the police were searching my house in under a month. 'I don't have a laptop,' I said. 'I use the desktop computer in the front room.'

Downstairs we went into the front room. 'That one?' the male officer asked, going over to the computer. It was in sleep-mode, the screen blank, with some of my printed spreadsheets beside it.

'I use it for work,' I said. 'Stevie hasn't been on it at all.' He stood beside me awkwardly.

'Not even when you were out, maybe?' the female officer asked us both.

'No,' I said. 'Stevie has never been alone in the house.'

'That's right,' Stevie said.

They glanced around the front room and, apparently satisfied, returned to the hall. 'I assume your adult children all have their own smartphones?' the male officer now asked. I knew what was coming.

'Yes, and so have I, but Stevie has never had access to any of them.'

'I told you that at the police station,' he said.

They hesitated, exchanged a glance and then thanked me for my time, apologised for disrupting my evening and left. Relieved, I closed the front door.

'What am I supposed to do without any phone or laptop?' Stevie bemoaned.

I could have snapped at him and told him it was the least of his worries, and his own fault for being so stupid, but I took a deep breath and tried to calm myself.

'Did they tell you how long they'd keep them for?' I asked.

'Weeks,' he said despondently.

I knew it was asking too much for a lad of his age to be without means of personal communication in this day and age for weeks on end, despite what he'd done, so I said, 'I've got an old phone you can borrow for now.'

'Is it a smart phone?' he asked.

'No, you can text and make calls on it. It will connect to the internet but very slowly. You won't be able to use WhatsApp or similar websites.' He pulled a face. 'It's up to you, Stevie. I'd have thought it was better than nothing.' I began to walk away. He was really testing my patience.

'Yes, please,' he called after me.

'OK, I'll find it later.'

Stevie went up to his room as I returned to the kitchen-diner where Adrian, Lucy and Paula were still gathered. I wasn't sure that even now Stevie fully appreciated the seriousness of what he'd got himself into. 'They had a good snoop around,' Lucy said, referring to the police. 'Are they allowed to do that without a search warrant?'

'It doesn't hurt to cooperate with the police,' I said, filling the kettle.

'Why were they asking about the computer and our phones?' Paula asked innocently.

'Because if Stevie had used any of them, they'd have to check them for illegal activity. I am right in saying that he hasn't ever used your laptops or phones?'

'No, he hasn't,' Adrian said. Paula and Lucy nodded in agreement.

'Even if he had, I wouldn't let the police take my phone or laptop,' Lucy said defiantly.

'You wouldn't have any choice if they came back with a search warrant,' I said, filling the kettle to make tea. 'They could take the lot, but I'm sure that won't be necessary.'

'Can you imagine no phones or laptops?' Lucy asked, horrified.

'Yes, I can actually,' I replied. 'I remember when there was just the landline and no internet.'

They looked at me with great pity.

'And Nana remembers when they had their first television, and central heating installed,' I added.

'Yes, but she's old,' Lucy said.

'Which by inference suggests I'm not. Thank you, Lucy. Anyone want a cup of tea?'

CHAPTER SEVENTEEN

DISAPPOINTING NEWS

The following day Stevie went to school as usual and before he left I reminded him to come straight home and not to visit his grandparents for the time being, which Verity had also told him. I assumed that Verity would inform the school of what they needed to know; it wasn't for me to tell them that Stevie had been interviewed by the police. However, a little after nine o'clock, when there was just Sammy and me at home and he was meowing at me for more food even though he'd only recently had breakfast, the house phone rang and it was Carolyn, Stevie's mentor.

'Stevie wasn't in school yesterday,' she said. 'I'm due to see him this afternoon. I wanted to speak to you first to make sure he's all right and not being bullied again.'

'Thank you. That's kind of you. No, he's not being bullied again,' I said.

'Was he ill yesterday?' she asked.

I hesitated. 'No. He had an important meeting with his social worker, but I'll leave it to her to update you.'

'OK,' Carolyn said easily. 'As long as Stevie is all right.'

'Thanks again,' I said, and we said goodbye. I hadn't lied; Stevie had met with Verity. I thought that Verity would probably tell the school that Stevie had been questioned by the police and why, as social services try to work closely with other agencies involved with a child. I was also expecting Verity to update me at some point, but it didn't happen that week.

The weekend arrived. Adrian worked Saturday, Lucy went out with a friend, and Paula and Stevie did their homework, then watched some television. I arranged to go to Mum's on Sunday and booked a table for lunch at a nice pub restaurant a short walk from her house. Stevie didn't want to go at first and said he'd be OK staying behind by himself, but I wasn't convinced. Not only did I not want him left alone with large tracks of time to worry about what was happening in his life, but also, to be honest, I didn't completely trust him. Although I'd lent him my old phone, I knew he'd struggle to access the internet on it – that had been one of the reasons I'd upgraded – but with us out all day he'd have plenty of opportunity to use the laptops or my PC. They weren't password protected – until now there'd been no reason for them to be, as we trusted each other. If the police revisited I wanted to be in a position to tell them that Stevie hadn't had access to any of our computers. I told Stevie we wouldn't be late back, and that I wanted him to come with us, and if he really didn't want to I'd make arrangements for him to spend the time with another foster carer. Not overly happy, he agreed to come.

Mum's always pleased to see us and today she had her best coat ready to go to the pub restaurant. She linked arms with Adrian and we took a slow stroll there, with the spring sun shining. We had a leisurely lunch, which Stevie ate, although he was quiet. On returning to Mum's, Adrian took Stevie off to do the little jobs that helped her so much, including cutting the lawn. Mum then remarked to me that Stevie hadn't seemed himself over lunch.

'He's got a lot on his mind,' I said.

'Oh dear, I hope things improve soon.' That was all she said. She knew there were issues in fostering that I couldn't discuss with her because of confidentiality. Also, she would have worried about this.

We had a cup of tea and a slice of Mum's homemade sponge cake mid-afternoon and then left around five o'clock. I put the radio on in the car as I drove for my and Stevie's benefit, as everyone else had their earbuds in and were listening to music on their phones. The phone I'd lent Stevie didn't have the technology to download and save music. Once home, Adrian went out to see Kirsty, Lucy phoned a friend – the laughter coming from her room reverberated around the house – and Paula and Stevie watched television in their rooms. All the bedrooms except mine had a small portable television, as most young people's rooms do now, but I also liked them to come and sit in the living room sometimes so we could watch a programme or download a film together. This happened less and less frequently and I had to accept that my family were young adults now and had their own lives to lead. Sometimes I welled up at the many happy memories of when they were little and we did everything together: playing in the garden or indoors, days out, reading them bedtime stories and so on. Now I was grateful for the times when we were all together as a family, and that they still wanted to come with me when I visited Mum, but I doubted that would ever change. They loved and cared for her so much.

I had half expected Peggy to telephone after Stevie had confessed and the police had visited her, but she hadn't. However, that Sunday evening, at nine o'clock, she phoned, having settled Kiri and Liam in bed first. When I'd imagined this conversation taking place I'd pictured her very angry with Stevie for what he'd done to Kiri and Liam, but now her voice was flat and emotionless, more defeated than furious. I'd taken the call in the living room, and now pushed the door to so I couldn't be overheard.

'What a ruddy mess,' she said with a long sigh.

'Yes,' I agreed. 'It is.'

'Fred and I can't believe Stevie could have been so stupid, but he's no pervert, and we told the police that.' I was relieved they thought that, for clearly they knew Stevie a lot better than I did. They could have turned right against him. 'Liam and Kiri knew it was wrong,' she continued, 'that's why they kept telling me they had a secret. I just wished they'd told me what it was.'

'I know,' I sympathised. 'I suppose they felt they'd be letting Stevie down and they'd be in trouble.'

'You know he's not allowed to come anywhere near them at present?' she said. 'If we want to see him it's got to be without Kiri and Liam. Verity went on about safeguarding concerns and supervised contact.'

'Yes, that would be usual in a situation like this,' I said. 'I expect Verity will arrange some supervised contact so Stevie can see his brother and sister.'

'The police searched our home from top to bottom. Fred had to go out, he was so angry. I know it's their job, but goodness knows what they thought they'd find here. Did they search your place?'

'They had a look around and took Stevie's laptop,' I said.

'You got off lightly then. They questioned Fred and me too.' I knew this was because the crime had been committed while he'd been living with his grandparents. The police would need to satisfy themselves that Fred and Peggy weren't involved in taking those indecent photographs, nor that they participated in any other paedophile activity.

'What did Kiri and Liam tell the police, do you know?' I asked.

'No, we weren't allowed to stay in the room while the police officer talked to them. But Liam had already told us that the reason they'd done it was because Stevie had said he'd be in a lot of trouble if they didn't and might never be able to see them again. That guy Joey was blackmailing Stevie. I hope they catch him.'

'So do I,' I said. 'How are Liam and Kiri?'

'Not too bad. At the time it happened I don't think they really understood the seriousness of what they'd been asked to do, but all the fuss since has been upsetting for them. In some ways it's a pity it's all come out. As Fred said, lots of kids take their clothes off and show each other their privates. It's part of growing up.'

'But that's different, Peggy,' I said. 'Kiri and Liam were coerced into taking off their clothes by a much older boy – their brother – who knew what he was doing was wrong.'

'I know, I told Fred that. Fred's a funny old sod. He made Stevie's life hell while he was here because he wanted to be like a girl, so much so that Stevie avoided coming home and then had to live with you. But now this has happened and it's more serious, Fred's standing up for Stevie – you know, supporting him, as you lot say. Of course he doesn't agree with what Stevie did, but he thinks Verity and the police are making too much of it, treating us all like criminals, and not allowing Stevie to see Kiri and Liam.'

'It's very difficult, I know, but the police and social services have to be certain that Stevie doesn't pose a danger to Kiri,

Liam or any other children he may come into contact with. That's why they've taken those steps.'

'They aren't in danger. He won't do it again,' she said defensively.

'You know that, but they have to make sure. Anyway, I'm glad Fred is now able to support Stevie,' I said. I noticed Peggy was using Stevie instead of Steven, which I felt was also positive – that she at least was more accepting of the person he wanted to be.

'When something like this happens,' she continued, 'it sets you thinking about the past. I've been thinking that if Fred had had a better relationship with Stevie then the lad might have been able to tell us about Joey and the photographs he'd taken of himself when he first started to blackmail him. Before it all got out of control and Stevie took the pictures of Liam and Kiri. I always felt Fred was too hard on him and I've told him so.'

'I think it's very difficult to get the balance right when you parent teenagers,' I said. 'You need rules for good behaviour and to keep them safe, but at the same time they need to feel they can come to you with any problems. I find it a continuous juggling act.'

'Yes,' she agreed thoughtfully. 'You see, we don't feel we were firm enough with our daughter – you know, Stevie, Liam and Kiri's mother. She got in with a bad lot and started taking drugs, then went right off the rails. We learnt our lesson and were much stricter with Stevie, so when he started all that nonsense about not wanting to be a boy Fred thought he could stamp it out of him.' She sighed. 'We thought we were doing the right thing. The last time we were at a police station was when our daughter was in trouble.' She let out a heartfelt sigh. 'It seems history has repeated itself.'

'For what it's worth, Peggy, I think you've done a good job of bringing up your grandchildren. I've fostered a lot of children over the years and it's obvious which of them have had some good parenting. Stevie has, trust me, and that's down to you and Fred.'

There was a short pause when I heard Peggy sniff before she said, 'Thanks, love. That's nice of you to say. I'll tell Fred. And while you're on the phone, Stevie's got a birthday coming up. Can you ask him what he wants from us? I'm guessing money for clothes, but I wanted to make sure.'

'Yes, of course, I'll ask him.'

We said goodbye and I replaced the handset, pleased that Peggy and Fred were now able to support Stevie. If Stevie was charged and this went to court, he was going to need all the support he could get. While Peggy had told me what she and Fred thought about what Stevie had done and the way the police and social services were handling it, she hadn't asked me for my opinion or if I considered him a danger to other children, and I was relieved. At this point I simply didn't know, and neither, to be honest, did Fred and Peggy. They hadn't been in the room when Liam and Kiri had been questioned by the police, so they didn't know if their story matched Stevie's. It was possible that they'd said something quite different, which could mean that Stevie did pose a threat to other children, horrendous though that possibility might be.

When Stevie came down for a glass of water before going to bed I told him his gran had telephoned and that she wanted to know what he'd like for his birthday. His mouth dropped open in astonishment. 'She wants to buy me a present after all I've done?' he asked.

'Yes, Stevie, they still love you.'

'Do they?'

I stood and went to him. 'Of course they do. That won't change. They think you acted foolishly but your granddad is going to stand by you.' He looked even more astonished. 'There's another side to him,' I said. 'He and your gran are having to think about the way they've treated you on some matters.' I smiled. 'So let me know what you'd like from them for your birthday and also from us.'

'Will I be able to see Kiri and Liam on my birthday?'

'I don't know. I'll need to speak to Verity and ask her.'

'If I could that would be the best birthday present ever,' he said. I saw the look on his face and at that point I was 99 per cent certain that Stevie's version of events was true, and he'd had no other motive for taking those indecent photos of Liam and Kiri beyond getting Joey off his back.

On Monday I had a full day's foster-carer training – 9 a.m. to 4.30 p.m. – which left little time to do anything else. Sitting in a warm room and just having to listen, my thoughts drifted again and again to Stevie. I wondered how long it would be before Verity gave me some feedback on the interview he'd had with the police, and what Liam and Kiri had told them. I knew how busy Verity must be, so I didn't want to keep phoning or emailing her, but I decided that if I hadn't heard from her in the next couple of days I'd contact her. Foster carers need to be kept up to date so they can meet the needs of the child or children they are looking after and provide the best possible level of care, as well as keep everyone in the household safe.

As it turned out I didn't have to contact Verity; the next day Edith telephoned me. 'I'm due to visit you, so can we set a date?' she said. Actually she was overdue to visit me, but I didn't say so.

'Yes, of course. I'll fetch my diary. Also, can you give me some feedback on Stevie's police interview?'

'Stevie's been interviewed by the police? Why?'

I told her and then said, 'I haven't heard anything further from Verity.'

'I expect she'll tell you when there is any news,' she replied, and her dismissive attitude irritated me. Jill would have been straight onto it, finding out, if she didn't already know.

'Also, I'd like some feedback on what Stevie's brother and sister told the police,' I said. 'And when Stevie can see them again. He's asking.'

'Let me write this down,' she said.

I waited before continuing. 'I am very concerned that it was felt necessary to stop Stevie from seeing his brother and sister, but I haven't been told if I should be taking extra precautions. I have young children coming into my house; children of friends and other foster carers – we help each other out. Should I be worried? Extra vigilant?'

'You practise safer caring anyway, don't you?' she said.

'Yes, but I'd put in place more safeguarding measures if I knew Stevie posed any threat to children.' I'd had to do this with Jodie, whose story I told in *Damaged*, to keep her and all those who came into contact with her feeling safe. 'It's not that I personally believe children need protecting from Stevie,' I said, 'but nobody has told me to the contrary. I am concerned and I need some advice.'

'Shall I try to speak to Verity?' Edith asked.

'Yes, please. Any feedback would be useful.'

'I'll see what I can find out,' she said, and without arranging her next visit she said goodbye.

* * *

It was towards the end of the week before Edith telephoned again and she had the news I wanted. She said that Verity had apologised for not being in touch, but she could confirm that Stevie had told the police what he'd told me, and that the police would now make a decision on whether to prosecute him.

'How long will that take?' I asked, aware this would be hanging over us until a decision was made.

'She didn't say, but I'm guessing weeks.'

'And Liam and Kiri?' I prompted. 'What did they say?'

'The same as Stevie, that it was the one time he told them to take off their clothes so he could photograph them, and if they didn't he would be in very big trouble. Poor little mites,' she added.

'And contact? When can Stevie see them?'

'Contact has been suspended for now.'

'I know. I was wondering if Verity would set up some supervised contact.'

'I could ask her.'

'Thank you.'

We arranged the date for her visit and Edith said she'd be in touch if she had any news about contact.

So while I was relieved that Stevie seemed to have told me the truth, and the incident with Liam and Kiri appeared to be a one-off, what he had done was still an offence with the possibility of a police prosecution and a custodial sentence if he was found guilty.

Edith didn't call me back about supervised contact between Stevie, Kiri and Liam, so the following week I emailed Verity and asked her if it would be possible to set up contact on Stevie's birthday, and also if it was all right for him to phone his grandparents as long as he didn't speak to Kiri and Liam.

She replied: *Please explain to Stevie that it is not possible for him to see his siblings while the police investigation is ongoing. I will ask Mr and Mrs Jones to telephone him on the understanding that he must not speak to Kiri and Liam.*

I felt Stevie's disappointment, as I appreciated how much he wanted to see Kiri and Liam, and I knew he would take this news badly. However, we did have some good news that day: the firm of accountants where Adrian had gone for an interview phoned and offered him a post – one of two trainee positions. He would start in one month, so he could work out his notice at the supermarket. We were all delighted, as was my mother when he phoned her. Even Stevie, who clearly had a lot on his mind, said, 'Well done.'

CHAPTER EIGHTEEN

DEJECTED AND MOODY

I found a quiet time after dinner to explain to Stevie what Verity had said about him not being allowed to see Kiri and Liam. As I thought might happen, he quickly became angry and upset.

'She's treating me like a bloody pervert!' he said. 'I only did what I did because I had to.'

'I know, but you do understand why Verity can't allow you to see Liam and Kiri until the police have finished their investigation?' I asked, having already explained.

'I told the police what happened. There isn't anything else,' Stevie persisted, annoyed.

'Yes, I believe you, but until the police are satisfied the social services can't let you see or speak to Kiri or Liam. I know it's difficult.'

'Supposing I just go to my gran's? I still have a key,' he said confrontationally.

'That would be very unwise. It would place your grandparents in a difficult position, and could be upsetting for Kiri and Liam if there was a scene.'

'So I'll go to their school instead and see them in the playground,' he retorted belligerently.

I looked at him carefully. I knew that Kiri and Liam's

school would most likely have been told that Stevie was under police investigation in connection with child pornography. They would have him removed if he showed up there, but I didn't think it wise to tell Stevie that and make him even more angry. 'That would be very unsettling for Kiri and Liam,' I said. 'I'm sure you wouldn't want to do anything else to upset them.'

'I haven't upset them!' he snapped back.

We were in the front room with the door pulled to, so no one else could hear. I looked at him carefully, thinking he still didn't understand the full implications of what he'd done. 'Stevie, taking those photographs of Kiri and Liam was upsetting for them. I know they might not have burst into tears at the time, but they knew it was wrong, which was why you had to tell them you'd be in a lot of trouble if they didn't do as you said. Afterwards, they must have felt very guilty and were clearly worried about what they'd done, which was why they kept trying to tell your gran they had a secret. They needed to share it. What you did upset them, just as it must have upset you.'

He looked away and I could see he'd identified with what I'd said.

'So, difficult though it is,' I continued, 'you have to do what Verity says, and stay away from Kiri and Liam until the police investigation is finished. But your grandparents can phone you.'

'They don't have my new number,' he said, referring to the mobile phone I'd lent him.

'I gave it to Peggy and she also has the house phone number. She said she will phone within the next couple of days. You can ask her how Liam and Kiri are, but you won't be able to speak to them for the time being.'

He shrugged despondently, almost as if he didn't care, but I knew he did. 'I'm sorry, love, but that's all I can offer for now, so please don't do anything that could make matters worse.'

'What would happen if I did see them?' he asked, glaring at me.

'The social services would be informed and if you persisted in doing so you'd probably be found somewhere to live right out of the area.'

'They can't force me to go anywhere!' he snapped defiantly.

'Stevie, they can. At present, as far as the police and social services are concerned, you pose a threat to Kiri and Liam, and until you are cleared you mustn't go near them, do you understand?' I said firmly.

His anger flared. 'Oh fuck off!' he said. Pushing past me, he stormed up to his bedroom and slammed the door.

Shaken, but not wholly surprised by Stevie's outburst, I stayed where I was in the living room and took a few deep breaths to calm myself. Once I'd recovered I went to reassure Paula and Lucy, who had heard Stevie's bedroom door slam and had come out onto the landing.

Having spoken to them, I gave Stevie fifteen minutes to calm down and then knocked on his door. 'Stevie, it's Cathy. Can we talk?'

'Go away.'

'I know you're upset, but –'

'Go away!' he shouted, angrier than ever. So I did.

I checked on him a couple of times during the evening and was met with a similar response. 'If you want to talk you know where I am,' I said.

'I don't,' he returned from the other side of the door. 'I'm in bed.'

'OK. See you in the morning.'

I thought that after a night's sleep he'd probably be in a better frame of mind and more accepting of what I'd said. The following morning I heard him get up at his usual time, but instead of coming down to breakfast when I called him he just went straight out the front door. I was in the kitchen and by the time I was outside he had disappeared up the road. I returned indoors and went up to his room where I checked in his wardrobe and saw that a set of school uniform was missing, and his school bag had gone. However, at 9.30 the school secretary telephoned to say Stevie wasn't in school. I tried his mobile but it went through to voicemail, so I left a message asking him to phone me. I heard nothing from him, but an hour later Peggy called. 'I thought you should know that Stevie is here with me.'

'And after everything I said to him! Are Liam and Kiri at school?'

'Yes. Stevie came here after Fred had taken them. I've given him some breakfast. He's not saying much but I thought you should know where he is.'

'Yes, thank you. What are you going to do?'

'I've told him he can stay here for a while, but he'll need to go back to you before Fred brings Kiri and Liam home from school, otherwise we'll all be in trouble.'

'Is Fred there now?' I asked.

'Yes, he and Stevie are in the sitting room watching a football replay on the television.'

'Really?' I asked, surprised. 'I didn't know Stevie was interested in football.'

'He's not, but when he was younger he used to spend hours with his grandpa watching the footie. Stevie was in the sitting room when Fred came back and Fred put the television on.

193

He does that when he doesn't know what to say. He used to when Verity visited and she asked him to turn it off, but that's Fred for you.'

'Well, at least Stevie is safe,' I said.

'Yes, and maybe he and Fred will start talking soon. I'll give Stevie lunch, then when Fred leaves at three o'clock to collect Liam and Kiri from school I'll send Stevie back to you.'

'Thank you, or shall I come and collect him to make sure he does come back?'

'If you like.'

'I'll see you at three then, and Peggy, I'll have to let Verity know. If I don't, the school will flag it up as an unauthorised absence.'

'Do as you see fit,' she said.

I thanked her for letting me know that Stevie was there and we said goodbye. Although Stevie wasn't where he should have been, I knew where he was so technically he wasn't a missing person. I therefore saw no urgency in notifying Verity, so rather than phoning her I sent her an email explaining what had happened. I hoped she would take the same view as I had: that Stevie could stay at his grandparents' for a few hours. However, when I saw him later I'd make it clear to him that this was a one-off and going to his grandparents' when he was supposed to be at school couldn't become a habit.

As I went about the housework I tried to picture Fred and Stevie in their sitting room using the television as a displacement for what must have been a very awkward meeting. Perhaps some good would come of it, I thought; maybe it would remind them both of happier times when Stevie had been little and – as Peggy had said – they'd sat together watching football, and begin to heal the rift between them.

However, when I rang their doorbell at three o'clock Stevie answered, school bag over his shoulder, ready to leave and clearly in a bad mood. 'Silly old bugger!' he cursed under his breath. He came out and strutted off down the path.

Peggy appeared in the hall. 'Don't ask,' she said, raising her eyes in exasperation.

I glanced at my car where Stevie was now agitatedly pulling the door handle to get in. 'I'd better go,' I said, pressing the fob to open the car doors.

'Yes. Good luck.' With a heavy sigh, she closed their front door.

In the car Stevie angrily jabbed the metal tongue of his seatbelt into the buckle. 'He always has to open his big mouth!' he fumed. 'He just won't let it go!'

'I assume you mean your grandfather,' I said. 'What did he say?'

'He started going on about the other stuff.'

'What other stuff?'

'You know, about my gender. He said if I hadn't got into all that queer stuff and met Joey online, none of this would have happened. I know it's my fucking fault! I don't need him to keep telling me.'

'I can see that. But don't swear. He has a habit of saying the wrong thing.'

Stevie huffed. 'Come on, let's go.'

I started the car engine and headed for home. 'Stevie, I'm here to support and help you through this, but I can't do it if you keep running away. If your gran hadn't phoned me, I would have had to report you missing again.'

'Whatever,' he said, and stared moodily out of his side window. I concentrated on driving and gave him the time he needed to calm down.

Once home, Stevie went up to his room where he spent the rest of the evening, although he did come down for dinner. My family were getting used to his mood swings and, aware that he had a lot to cope with, didn't press him to join in our conversation.

As Stevie's birthday was approaching I asked him what he'd like to do by way of a celebration. Despite the police investigation hanging over us, I wanted to do something to mark the day. Clearly he wouldn't be celebrating with his brother and sister, so I asked him if he'd like a few friends round. He didn't, so I suggested we went bowling and had a meal out.

'Don't mind,' he shrugged. Which was better than 'don't care', which I was getting a lot of lately.

I went ahead and booked bowling at our local leisure centre and a table at a nearby Italian restaurant. Stevie's birthday fell in the Easter holidays, so he, Paula and Lucy already had the day off and Adrian took a day's leave so he could join us. We made a fuss of Stevie on his birthday and called him 'the Birthday Boy', which made him smile. I think he enjoyed it, especially when he won at bowling. Once home, I produced the birthday cake I'd ordered from our local bakery. A rainbow cake with an arc of different colours – vibrant, as Stevie had been and I hoped would be again one day. I'd had *Happy Birthday Stevie – 15 Today* piped on top of the cake in icing, and I'd arranged fifteen birthday candles around the edge. We sang 'Happy Birthday' and as he blew out the candles I wondered where he'd be this time next year. With us, or serving time in a young offenders' institution? It was a chilling thought.

His gran telephoned once Kiri and Liam were in bed to wish him a happy birthday, and they chatted for ten minutes or so. Fred didn't come to the phone.

Stevie had wanted money from me for his birthday as well as from his grandparents. Adrian had also put some money in a card for him, as had my mother, while Lucy and Paula had clubbed together and bought him a jersey from one of his favourite stores. Stevie was pleased with his presents, and in total had £200. 'Spend it wisely,' I told him.

'I will,' he replied, then thanked me for a nice day and went quietly to his room. I felt we'd done the best we could in difficult circumstances.

While Stevie had dressed smartly when we'd gone out on his birthday – as of course we had – there'd been none of the flamboyant dressing up we'd previously seen, and he'd only worn a little mascara. Since all this had started, his gender-identity issues had been put on hold. The police investigation was weighing him down, stamping out his natural exuberance, and I hated 'Joey' even more for what he was doing to Stevie. I hoped it didn't put Stevie off forming relationships in the future with genuine young people – male or female.

Stevie had asked me a few times when I thought he'd get his laptop and phone back. I'd had to say I didn't know, but I was sure that the police or Verity would let us know once the police had finished with them. The morning after his birthday Stevie said he was going into town shopping to spend his birthday money, I assumed on clothes. He returned around midday with a new smartphone, on which he'd spent all his birthday money. We all admired it. I could see how pleased he was with it, and I didn't point out that at some point he would be getting his old phone back and could have spent his money on something else. I supposed at his age it was asking too much to wait indefinitely, and like many young people he couldn't bear to be without a decent phone. He immediately entered our wi-fi code and spent the rest of the afternoon adjusting the phone settings and ring tones to suit him and downloading WhatsApp and so forth. He was like a kid with a new toy and kept coming to show us. I was pleased for him, but also worried.

'You will be careful online,' I said, for while my old phone hadn't had the software to support most of these websites, clearly his new phone did.

He nodded as he fiddled with his phone. I watched him for a moment.

'Stevie, out of interest, why didn't you accept my Facebook friendship request?' I asked. 'It doesn't matter, I was just curious.'

He glanced up, puzzled, as if he was trying to remember, then he looked embarrassed. 'Joey told me not to. He knew the grief I was getting from my grandpa, and he said I should put my security settings on high and not accept Facebook friends from any of my family or adults who knew me, so I wasn't hurt any more.'

Clever, I thought. Under the guise of caring for Stevie's feelings, 'Joey' had effectively stopped the possibility of any adult monitoring Stevie's activity on Facebook where they might have become suspicious of 'Joey'. 'Did you do that on the other website too – the one where you met Joey?'

'Yes.'

I explained my concerns and why I thought 'Joey' had given him that advice. 'I'm not saying you have to accept my friendship request,' I said, 'but don't shut everyone you know out again, will you? Think of these websites as a room you are in and there are people outside wanting to get in. You'd allow in those you knew and could trust, wouldn't you? And be more wary about the strangers. I doubt you would have shut the door in my face if it had been a real room, or let Joey in.'

'No,' he agreed. 'I wouldn't.'

I'd said what I wanted to, and I hoped again that Stevie now appreciated the dangers of meeting strangers online. That evening he accepted my Facebook friendship request, which allowed me to have a look at his friends and some of the conversations they'd been having on his timeline. There was no sign of Joey or anyone suspicious, but I would check every so often, just as I had when my children had been Stevie's age. How different it was now, protecting young people, to when I'd first begun fostering. I'm not sure it was easier then, just different.

Stevie's second review was held at the end of April, three months after the first, and he refused to attend. 'I'm not sitting there while they all have a go at me,' he said. 'I know what I did was wrong.'

'Stevie, that's not the purpose of the review – just the opposite, in fact,' I said. 'It's about making sure you have everything you need, you're safe and well, and being properly looked after. What's happened might be mentioned, but no one is going to question you. It's not an interview. It gives you the chance to ask any questions you might have.'

'Will my grandparents be there?'

'They will be invited, yes.'

'If *he* comes, I'm definitely not going.'

'There is no reason for Verity to exclude your grandfather,' I said. There has to be a very good reason to exclude parents or guardians from their child's review.

'I'll fill in the form they've sent, but I'm not coming,' Stevie said adamantly.

I tried to persuade him to attend and told him it was the adult thing to do, but he still refused. Although Peggy had said that Fred was being supportive of Stevie in the matter of the police investigation, clearly the argument they'd had when he'd visited had set back any chances of healing their relationship. I informed Verity by email that Stevie wouldn't be attending his review, and she replied that she'd try to speak to him before the review. I completed my questionnaire and returned it in the post. Two days later Verity saw Stevie in school, but he wouldn't change his mind about attending his review. On the morning of the review, before he left for school, I told him it wasn't too late and if he decided to attend to just join us. He should be home around the time it started anyway, as the review had been set for 4.30 at my house.

'I won't,' he said, and left looking downcast and moody, which was how he usually looked now.

At 4.30, all those attending the review gathered in my living room and the IRO – the same one as last time – opened the review, without Stevie. The IRO, Richard, was now using a small laptop to take the minutes rather than pen and paper. He typed as he, then Verity, myself, Edith, Peggy, Fred and Carolyn introduced ourselves. Carolyn added that she'd seen Stevie in school and he'd told her he wouldn't be coming to the review.

'Do we know why?' the IRO asked, glancing up at us.

'I've spoken to Stevie,' Verity said, 'and he doesn't feel comfortable attending.'

Peggy nudged Fred. 'It's probably because of me,' Fred said. Which seemed to suggest he was becoming more sensitive to Stevie's needs, until he added, 'He needs to man up. Little wonder he's been taken advantage of!'

The IRO noted Stevie's absence and said, 'It's a pity Stevie didn't feel able to attend. I understand quite a lot has happened since his last review. I'll try to see him another time. When is he expected home?'

'Now, if not before,' I said.

'If he does return while the review is on, I can see him in another room, or I'll arrange to see him another day,' the IRO said. I nodded. 'So, would you like to begin by telling us how Stevie is doing now?' he asked me. 'Are we all aware of what has happened since the last review?'

Everyone nodded and Fred said, 'Too bloody right! You'd have thought the police had better things to do than go after Stevie. It wasn't his fault. He was blackmailed into doing what he did. They need to catch that Joey, or whatever his real name is.'

'I'm sure the police are doing all they can,' the IRO said in a conciliatory tone.

'Well, they need to try harder and leave my boy alone. He made a mistake, that's all,' Fred said.

While it was positive to hear Fred standing up for Stevie and referring to him as 'my boy', his comment rather undermined what Liam and Kiri had been through, which Verity picked up on.

'I'm sure we all appreciate the anxiety and stress this is causing you all,' Verity said. 'But we shouldn't forget that taking photographs of children without their clothes on is a form of sexual abuse.'

'Stevie wouldn't harm them,' Fred retaliated angrily.

'Sshh, be quiet, we know that,' Peggy hissed at him. 'You're making it worse.' And for the time being, Fred was quiet.

CHAPTER NINETEEN

MESSED UP

'Cathy,' the IRO said, turning to me. 'Let's start with Stevie's health.'

'Stevie hasn't had any illnesses or accidents since his last review,' I said, beginning with the easy bit. 'He had a routine dental check-up during the Easter holidays and his teeth are good. No fillings. His next optician's appointment isn't due for six months. His eating and sleeping are problematic now. If he's worried, they both suffer.' I paused to allow the IRO time to type. 'Physically, Stevie is in good health, but he is struggling to cope with what is going on. He's often very quiet and withdrawn, and spends a lot of time in his room.'

'Has he been referred to CAMHS for counselling?' the IRO asked.

'No. Both Verity and I have talked to him about it, but he doesn't want to go. I asked him if he'd like to see his doctor, but he said he didn't.'

The IRO nodded. 'But there was a referral to a gender-identity clinic?'

'I haven't heard anything yet,' I said.

'I made the referral,' Verity confirmed. 'But there is a long waiting list.'

'I'm not sure it's the best time for Stevie to go anyway,' I said. 'He's got so much on his mind.'

The IRO nodded. 'And behavioural issues?' he asked, glancing up from his laptop. 'Staying out late, not doing as he's asked or going missing?'

'I had to report him missing once.' I gave the date. 'It was after an incident in school, but at the time Joey was threatening to expose him and Stevie hadn't told anyone. He couldn't cope and disappeared. He was found in the early hours of the following morning by the police and was eventually brought back to me.'

'Eventually?' the IRO queried.

'Yes, he didn't want to come to begin with, as he thought he'd be in trouble.'

'Has he gone missing any other times?' the IRO asked.

'Not while he's been with me, but he took a day off school to visit his grandparents.'

'Does he go out in the evenings? Do we know who he's associating with?'

'He hasn't been going out in the evenings. He goes to school, and now contact has stopped he comes straight home. He has been shopping a few times by himself, but otherwise he's here with us.'

'So no late nights as he had when he was living with his grandparents?' the IRO asked, throwing Peggy and Fred an acknowledging look in recognition of what they'd been through.

'No late nights,' I said. 'I don't think Stevie is in the mood for partying right now. I should mention that he has bought himself a new smartphone with his birthday money.' Fred sighed. 'The police still have his old phone and laptop. I've talked to him about staying safe online.'

The IRO nodded as he typed. 'So I'm right in saying there are now two outstanding police matters? Sexting and the indecent images of his siblings.'

'Yes,' Verity said. 'But the police are treating it as one investigation because it appears to be the same person involved – Joey.'

'And bullying?' the IRO asked, glancing at me. 'Any more incidents of bullying at school?'

'No, not as far as I'm aware.'

'No, there haven't been,' Carolyn confirmed.

'Good. Does Stevie have any hobbies or out-of-school activities?' he asked me. 'Or is that a daft question with so much going on in his life?'

'He doesn't attend any clubs or out-of-school activities,' I said. 'Although he does come with us on family outings. We all went bowling for his birthday and he comes with us when I visit my mother.'

'What interests did Stevie have before he came into care?' the IRO asked his grandparents.

Peggy shook her head. 'None, really. He used to play with Liam and Kiri a lot and take them to the park, but that has stopped now.'

'He liked to dress up and go out,' Fred said dryly. 'If you can call that an activity.'

'I was thinking more of football, tennis, swimming, that type of thing,' the IRO said, ignoring Fred's chagrin.

'Not really,' Peggy said. 'To be honest, we didn't have the time or money for all those things, what with having to look after the three of them.'

'It's a lot,' the IRO agreed. Then, looking at me, 'Anything else you'd like to add.'

'I'm trying to support Stevie through this. Sometimes he

opens up and talks, but other times he can't be bothered with any of us. Once the police have made a decision on whether they are going to prosecute, we'll know where we stand. At present I feel we are in limbo – especially Stevie, who seems to have put his life on hold.'

The IRO nodded sympathetically, finished typing and then asked Verity to give her report. She began by saying that Stevie could have his laptop and phone back, as the police had finished with them. She said he could collect them from the police station.

'Does that mean they are getting close to making a decision on whether they are going to prosecute?' the IRO asked.

'I don't think so, just that forensics have finished with his laptop and phone.'

'I'll tell Stevie,' I said.

For the sake of the review, Verity then said that contact between Stevie and his siblings had been suspended pending the police investigation. She said she'd explained to Stevie why he wasn't to visit his grandparents' house when Liam and Kiri were there or approach them at school or in the street. I saw Fred sit forward and take a breath, as if he was about to say something, but Peggy placed a restraining hand on his arm and he kept quiet.

'It must be difficult for you,' the IRO said, having also seen this.

'Yes, it is,' Peggy agreed, while Fred rubbed his forehead agitatedly, clearly struggling to contain himself.

'Supervised contact isn't an option then?' the IRO asked Verity.

'No, it's not appropriate while Stevie is being investigated.'

'But Stevie can still see his grandparents?' the IRO confirmed.

'Yes, as long as Kiri and Liam aren't present. Stevie did see his grandparents quite recently when he went there when he was supposed to be in school. He's allowed phone contact with them.'

The IRO noted all of this. 'Presumably Stevie could see his grandparents here?'

'Yes, if that works for everyone,' she said. I nodded, and she continued with her report. 'The care plan remains the same for now, but if Stevie is prosecuted and found guilty then that could affect where he lives.'

'Why?' Peggy asked.

'It might be that the court rules he should spend time in a young offenders' institution.'

'You're fucking joking me!' Fred exclaimed, finally giving vent to his feelings. 'I don't believe it! For one photograph!' So I thought he still hadn't grasped the seriousness of what Stevie had done – that it was child abuse.

'It was more than one photograph, Mr Jones,' Verity said evenly. 'On the instructions of "Joey", Stevie took a number of indecent images of his brother and sister.'

I saw Peggy's eyes fill and I felt so sorry for her. She took a tissue from her bag and blew her nose.

Verity continued by giving the date on which she'd made the referral to the gender-identity clinic and repeated that it was likely to be many months before an appointment was issued.

'Over my dead body,' Fred exclaimed.

'You and your wife will be consulted,' the IRO said. Fred huffed and Peggy shushed him to be quiet again.

'Is there anything else you wish to say?' the IRO asked Verity.

'Not at this point,' Verity said, checking her notes.

'And you're satisfied with the standard of care Stevie is receiving here?'

'Yes.'

The IRO now asked Peggy and Fred to speak. I could see how difficult it was going to be for them both. Fred was clearly struggling to contain his anger and frustration, while Peggy teared up again. 'Stevie's a good boy,' she began. 'I blame myself for the mess he's in. If he'd been able to come to us with his problems – when that Joey first started threatening him, he wouldn't have taken those photos.'

'You've got nothing to blame yourself for,' Fred said vehemently. 'You worked yourself into the ground bringing up the three of them, on top of all the problems we had with their mother. It's not your fault. As I told the police, they need to get off their bleeding arses and find that pervert rather than going after Stevie.' At that moment the front doorbell rang and there was no one else at home to answer it.

'I'm sorry,' I said. 'I'd better get that.' Standing, I quickly left the living room. To my delight, Stevie was standing there. 'Oh, you've come for the review,' I said. 'Well done.'

'Are they still here?' he asked, slipping off his shoes.

'Yes, in the living room.'

'I need a glass of water first,' he said.

He disappeared into the kitchen while I returned to the living room. 'It's Stevie,' I said.

'Is he going to join us?' the IRO asked.

'I hope so. He's just getting a drink.'

'We'll wait for him then,' the IRO said.

A few moments later Stevie came in, carrying a glass of water.

'Welcome,' the IRO said.

Verity and I made room for Stevie on the sofa.

'Hello, love,' Peggy said.

'Steven,' Fred said stiffly by way of acknowledgement.

Stevie threw them a small nod. I could see he was nervous.

'I'm glad you were able to make it,' the IRO said warmly. 'We've heard from Cathy and Verity. We were just hearing from your grandparents, and then perhaps you'd like to speak next?'

'Don't mind,' Stevie said with a shrug and took a sip of his water.

The IRO threw him a reassuring smile and then looked at Peggy and Fred to continue. Clearly it was different now Stevie was present. They could no longer speak uninhibited. 'Would you like to continue?' the IRO prompted.

They looked uncomfortable and then looked at Stevie. Peggy said, 'Like I told you when you bunked school to see us, we're your family and we'll stand by you no matter what.'

'Thank you,' Stevie said quietly, and set his glass on the table.

'Mr Jones, would you like to add anything to this review?' the IRO asked.

'No, my wife's said it.'

The IRO finished typing and looked at Stevie. 'What would you like your review to know?' I glanced at him sitting next to me and saw him flush. He took a couple of short breaths as he prepared to speak. I knew then that whatever he was about to say he'd thought long and hard about, probably for most of the day. I looked down and waited as the others did.

'I know I've made a complete mess of my life,' Stevie began, his voice trembling. 'But I really didn't mean to hurt Kiri and Liam in any way. They are my little brother and sister and I love them. I have protected them in the past. I can't believe I allowed myself to take those photos and then send them to that man Joey. At the time I really didn't know what else to do. Now I realise I should have told an adult. I thought that once I'd given Joey the photos he'd leave me alone. I didn't know he was a paedophile and would share the pictures.' He paused and swallowed hard. 'The police don't believe me, but it's true, I promise you,' he said, his voice catching. 'I didn't stop and think why Joey wanted the photos, I just did it so he'd leave me alone. The police kept asking me if I'd taken more pictures of Kiri and Liam or other children, but I haven't, honestly. I'm not a pervert. I know I've upset those who love me and I'm truly sorry for letting everyone down. I've messed up and I know I'm not the grandson Nana and Grandpa wanted. Sorry.' He stopped and the room fell silent. Even the IRO had stopped typing and was looking at Stevie.

Stevie was concentrating on the floor, unable to meet our gaze. I touched his arm reassuringly. Peggy's eyes had filled and both she and Fred were looking very serious. It was impossible to know what Fred was thinking or feeling. Suddenly Fred stood and came towards us. It was such an abrupt movement that for a second I wondered if he was going to hit Stevie. Then he said, 'Can I sit beside him?'

Verity and I both moved so that Fred could sit next to Stevie. He put his arm around Stevie's shoulder and drew him close. 'You've messed up big time, lad,' he said, 'but we still love you. That won't change. No matter what the outcome, we will be here for you.' Fred's eyes glistened with tears and a lump rose to my throat. The others in the room were looking emotionally at Fred too. Usually so forthright, unyielding and set in his ways, he was now showing Stevie his unreserved affection and the support he needed. Stevie's face crumpled and he began to cry.

'Shall we take a short break?' the IRO asked.

'I think that would be a good idea,' Verity agreed.

We stood and, leaving Stevie with his grandparents, went into the kitchen-diner where I made some drinks. The IRO allowed ten minutes, during which time we made small talk, then he said, 'I'll see if they're ready to continue.' He went into the hall and knocked on the living-room door. 'Are you ready to resume?' he asked. They must have said yes for he called to us to return.

Peggy and Fred were sitting on the sofa either side of Stevie, together but not touching, their expressions sombre. I asked them if they wanted a drink and Peggy said she'd like a glass of water. I refilled Stevie's glass at the same time. Once resettled in the living room, the IRO asked Carolyn to give her report and as she talked – saying that Stevie was a very pleasant student who was a good average academically – I stole glances at Peggy, Stevie and Fred, now sitting opposite me. While they appeared united and had put their differences behind them to stand up for Stevie, I wondered how long it would last before Fred said something insensitive again. I doubted he had radically changed his views on Stevie's gender-identity issues, which caused much of the friction between them and had been the main reason for Stevie coming into care in the first place.

Sadly, it wasn't long before my concerns were proved correct. Carolyn finished her report and then Edith said her bit about her role and me. The IRO set the date for the next review, thanked us all for coming and we stood. Peggy kissed Stevie goodbye, while Fred, having now recovered from his display of emotion, clapped Stevie on the shoulder and said, 'Well, I guess some good has come out of all this then, lad.'

Stevie looked at him questioningly. 'What?'

'You've come to your senses and stopped all that silly nonsense about wanting to be a girl.'

'No, I haven't,' Stevie replied, affronted, and taking a step back.

'Well, you're wearing normal clothes and not prancing around in frillies with make-up and nail varnish on.'

'That's because I've come straight from school!' Stevie said, mortified. Turning, he fled the room.

CHAPTER TWENTY

A DREADFUL MISTAKE

I checked on Stevie after everyone had left his review. He was in his bedroom, more angry than upset. There wasn't much I could say to him about Fred beyond what I'd already said – that he loved him, but he didn't think before he spoke. Stevie knew his grandfather far better than I did. Having made sure Stevie was OK, I told him not to sit alone brooding and to come down when he was ready. He didn't come down until I called everyone for dinner. He was very subdued at the table, didn't contribute to the conversation and just shrugged when Lucy asked him how his review had gone.

After dinner, as we were clearing away the dishes, I suggested to him again that he might like to invite a couple of his friends back from his class at the weekend, or go out with them – bowling, swimming, cinema or similar. Some months ago he'd mentioned he had two good friends in his class and I thought he needed to socialise, which would give him something to think about other than the police investigation. I did see the irony in what I was doing – trying to persuade Stevie to go out. When he'd first arrived, going out, staying out and ignoring his grandparents' boundaries had been an issue, but now he wasn't going out socially at all. He didn't seem keen on my idea, but agreed to think about it, then spent the rest of the evening in his room. I kept a close eye on him, for while Stevie maintained he didn't need to see a counsellor or doctor, I was worried his anxiety was building, which could spiral into a deep depression or worse. I think it is easy for teenagers to allow problems to escalate and dominate their thoughts so they can't see a way forward. But there is always a way forward, hope and a solution, whatever the problem, which is why I wrote *Happy Adults*.

It was no great surprise that once Peggy had put Kiri and Liam to bed that night, she telephoned me. I took the call in the living room where – not unusually – I was alone.

'Fred just can't keep his mouth shut,' she began. 'But he doesn't mean any harm by what he says. He loves the kids.'

I felt that excusing Fred like this was starting to wear a bit thin now and that he needed to channel some of that love he felt into accepting Stevie for who he was, and stop making snide remarks, or he'd never have a positive relationship with his grandson. I thought Fred would benefit from a self-awareness or emotional-intelligence workshop, but I didn't say so.

'You see, Cathy,' Peggy continued, 'Fred can get his head round supporting Stevie in the police investigation, but not the other stuff. His dad did something similar for Fred when he was a lad and got caught trying to hotwire a car him and his mates were going to steal. But a boy wanting to be a girl he can't hack.'

'I realise that, Peggy, but Fred might have to get his head round it if he wants to be part of Stevie's life in the future. It can't be so difficult if he loves him, can it? I know this is all new territory for you, as it was for me, but there's a lot of information on the internet about gender identity with details of support groups. Did you ever try researching on a computer in the library?'

'I went there but it was busy and the computers were being used, so I came out again.' This, of course, was the problem with using the computers in the library, you sometimes had to wait for a turn.

'It might be worth giving it another go,' I suggested. 'There is a lot of information online that could help. Sometimes just knowing that other families are going through similar difficulties can make you feel better.'

'Yes,' she said unenthusiastically. 'I'll take Fred with me, then I won't feel such an ass not knowing what to do. He doesn't mind asking daft questions. Anyway, the main reason I'm phoning is that I think it would be best if just I saw Stevie for now. Fred has offered to look after Liam and Kiri for an hour or so after school. I could come to your place or Stevie and I could go to a café as he can't come here. What do you think?'

'I think that's a very good idea, Peggy. Do you want me to tell Stevie or will you?'

'I'll phone him,' she said. As Stevie was in care voluntarily under a Section 20, Peggy was free to make these arrangements, although Verity would be informed.

Peggy must have telephoned Stevie straight away, for a short while later, when I went upstairs to shower and start getting ready for bed, Stevie came out of his room to find me.

'I'm going to meet Gran tomorrow after school,' he said. 'Just to let you know I'll be back late.'

'Thanks for telling me. Have a nice time.' He seemed a bit brighter.

'It should be OK without *him* there,' he said, referring to Fred. Which was a pity but true. It might be that Fred never accepted Stevie for who he was and it would always be the case that he had to see his gran without Fred there. It crossed my mind that if Stevie was sent to a young offenders' institution, would Peggy be able to make the journey alone to see him on a regular basis or would that be completely impractical? There aren't many of these institutions and our nearest was about seventy miles away, and even then it would depend if they had a vacancy. I wasn't sure how often I'd be able to visit him if I was fostering other children, and I forced myself to think of something else. I believed what Stevie had told me about the reasons he'd taken the indecent images of Kiri and Liam, but would the police?

The following day Adrian asked me if I'd go shopping with him to help him choose two new suits for when he started work the next day. He often went shopping with Kirsty now and would have asked her, but she was working. I was a bit concerned that he'd left it rather late to decide he needed new work clothes, but thankfully, although Adrian is tall, he is of average build, so we didn't have a problem. He quickly found two suits, then bought half a dozen shirts and ties and some grey socks. It occurred to me how easy it is for a guy to buy clothes for work compared to what the average woman needs: a selection of skirts, trousers, coordinating tops, dresses, jackets and so on. Perhaps gender-neutral clothes were the answer. I guessed we were heading that way compared to a generation ago, with girls now routinely wearing trousers at school and in the workplace.

Stevie didn't arrive home from seeing his gran until nearly seven o'clock – later than I'd expected. As I let him in the front door I asked him if he'd had a nice time.

'We went to the police station to get my phone and laptop,' he said.

'Oh, I see.'

He took his laptop from his school bag to show me. 'I gave Gran my old phone, as I've got a new one.'

'That was nice of you. Dinner's ready. Does she know how to use it?'

'No!' He laughed. 'We went to a coffee shop and I've been trying to teach her. I think she can phone now, but I'm not sure about texting or using the camera. She's going to practise this evening and try to phone and text me.'

I smiled. 'That sounds good, but you know you mustn't speak to Kiri or Liam even on her mobile?' I'd said it before, but it was important.

'Yes, I know,' Stevie said amicably. 'I'll teach her a bit each time we meet and in between she can practise.' I was pleased that seeing his gran had been such a positive experience.

Dinner the next day was livelier than it had been recently. Adrian told us about his first day in his new job and Stevie entertained us with snippets from the mobile-phone lesson he'd given his grandmother. 'She still doesn't understand why it's possible to use the phone outside the house,' he said, and the others laughed loudly.

'It's all right for you lot,' I said. 'You've grown up with all this technology, but for some of us it has been a sharp learning curve.'

'And you're doing very well, Mum,' Lucy said patronisingly.

'Good, so this evening I'll give you all a lesson on how to work the washing machine.'

A light-hearted groan went up. I'd recently had to replace the washer-dryer and the new one had so many function programmes only I had mastered it. But I was pleased that we were all able to joke and laugh again; a feeling of normality had returned.

Stevie met his grandmother after school for a second time that week and then again at the start of the following week. These meetings seemed to be having a positive effect on him. He was brighter when he returned, and once he'd eaten he set about doing his homework with little prompting from me. I didn't ask what he and his gran talked about, it was really none of my business. I assumed they were continuing with their mobile-phone lessons, and they chatted generally, probably with Stevie telling her about school and life with us, and Peggy telling him about Kiri and Liam, which was fine as long as they didn't have any contact. If I had asked more questions, would I have become suspicious? I wondered later. I doubted it. All I saw was the positive effect their meetings were having on Stevie. I wrote as much in my log notes. *Stevie saw his gran again today after school. He arrived home at 7 p.m. and had clearly enjoyed his one-to-one time with her.* How naïve those words seemed a few days later when I was asked to check my log notes for the details of the days and times they'd met.

On Tuesday evening of the second week in May, when Stevie had seen his grandmother three times and had a fourth meeting arranged for after school the following day, the house phone rang. I answered it in the living room where I was alone. It was eight o'clock, and having eaten dinner together the rest of my family were doing their own thing in other parts of the house.

'Hello?' I said, but no one spoke, although the line was open. I thought it might be a nuisance call. Our landline number was ex-directory, but we still received nuisance calls from time to time.

'Hello?' I said again, and was about to hang up when I heard a small noise on the other end of the phone, like a stifled sob. 'Is someone there?'

Another sob, then, 'It's Peggy. Oh Cathy, I've been so stupid. I don't know what to do.' She could barely get her words out, she was so distraught.

'Peggy, whatever is it? What's the matter? Is Fred with you?'

'Yes,' she faltered. 'He's seeing to Kiri and Liam. I can't deal with them right now.'

'Why? Is someone hurt?' I asked, my anxiety growing.

'No,' she sobbed. I waited until she was able to speak. 'Cathy, you know I've been seeing Stevie after school?' Her voice trembled.

'Yes. You saw him last night. He really enjoys his time with you.'

'I've been so stupid. I took Kiri and Liam with me to see Stevie.'

I went cold and my heart began thumping loudly. 'Oh Peggy, you didn't.'

'I know it was wrong, but they missed Stevie so much. They couldn't understand why they weren't allowed to see him. I didn't think it would hurt. I was with them the whole time.'

'Where was this? In the coffee shop?'

'That's where we met, then we went on to the park.'

'Yesterday?'

'Yes, and the time before. It was Stevie's idea – not that I'm blaming him; I should have said no. Fred thought it would be OK, and they did have a nice time.' Her voice broke. 'But someone saw us all together.'

'Who?'

'A colleague of Verity's.'

'Oh Peggy.' Immediately I could see the implications.

'Verity phoned this afternoon,' Peggy continued between sobs. 'The social services are having a meeting tomorrow morning that Fred and me aren't allowed to attend. After that she and another social worker are coming to see us. They may take Kiri and Liam into care.' She broke down and sobbed. My heart went out to her.

Peggy had every right to be distressed, for there was a real chance that Kiri and Liam would now be taken into care. Stevie was being investigated for paedophile activity and Peggy (and Fred) had allowed contact between him – the abuser – and his victims, Kiri and Liam. Of course, that was on top of already failing to protect Kiri and Liam when they'd all lived together and Stevie had taken the indecent images of them. I knew Peggy and Fred wouldn't see it that way, but the social services would. They had to. They had a duty of care to Kiri and Liam and needed to protect them.

'Oh Peggy,' I said again.

'I know. I can't believe how stupid I've been.'

'Does Stevie know?'

'No. Can you tell him? I can't speak to him now. Tell him what's happened and that I won't be able to meet him tomorrow.'

'I will. What time are Verity and her colleague visiting you?'

'Two o'clock. She wants to speak to Fred and me before he collects Kiri and Liam from school.' Her voice broke again. 'Cathy, do you think they'll take Kiri and Liam into care?'

'I don't know, Peggy, but I think you need to be prepared for that possibility.'

'I couldn't bear to lose them.' She cried openly. 'I've lost my daughter and Stevie. If I lose the little ones too, my life won't be worth living.'

My eyes filled. What could I say? Like other families who faced having their children taken into care, Peggy was devastated, as I knew Fred would be. Although I'd never met Liam and Kiri, I'd heard so much about them from Stevie and Peggy I felt I did know them. I could imagine the heart-breaking scene in their house if they were taken away, with all of them in tears and begging that Kiri and Liam be allowed to stay. How would they cope in the aftermath? I had no idea. As upsetting as that scene would be, worse was the knowledge that it could all have been avoided. If Stevie had felt able to talk to his grandparents when Joey had first asked him to take the indecent images of Liam and Kiri, and Peggy hadn't now broken the contact rules, none of this would have happened.

'I'll tell Stevie,' I said.

'Yes, please, and tell him I'm sorry and we love him.'

'I will. Phone me if you need to,' I said.

She said a small 'thanks' and put the phone down.

With a very heavy heart, I went slowly upstairs to Stevie's room, dreading what I had to say. I paused outside his door, summoning the courage to knock. 'Stevie, it's Cathy. I need to speak to you.'

'Come in,' he called.

I went in, leaving the door slightly ajar. Stevie was sprawled on his bed, watching a video on his laptop. Seeing my sombre expression, he immediately sat upright. I took the chair by the small desk.

'What's the matter?' he asked.

'Your gran just phoned me. You haven't spoken to her this evening, have you?'

'No. I sent a text, but she hasn't replied. I'm seeing her tomorrow anyway.'

'I'm afraid you won't be seeing her tomorrow, Stevie.' There was no easy way to say this. 'The four of you – you, your gran, Kiri and Liam – were seen together yesterday by a social worker.'

'No, I never –' he began, immediately going on the defensive.

'Stevie, there is no point in lying. Your gran has just told me she's been taking Liam and Kiri to see you. A colleague of Verity's spotted you all together yesterday. This is very serious, Stevie. And after everything that was said to you about not having any contact with Liam and Kiri!'

'I'm sorry,' he said with a small, dismissive shrug.

I looked at him carefully and thought he had no idea of the implications of this. 'Stevie, Verity has told your grandparents that there is a possibility Kiri and Liam will be taken into care.'

The colour drained from his face. 'They can't do that! They haven't done anything wrong.'

'No, Liam and Kiri haven't, but your grandparents have, in allowing you to see them.'

'We won't do it again, I promise,' Stevie said, panicking. 'I'll tell Verity. I'll phone her now.' He grabbed his phone from the bed.

'She won't be there now,' I said. 'It's after eight.'

'I'll phone her tomorrow morning then. I'll tell her it was my fault. I asked Gran, and I'm sorry, and it won't happen again.'

I supposed there was a slim chance this might help, but I didn't want to give him false hope.

'There's no harm in phoning Verity tomorrow if you want,' I said. 'But I honestly don't know how much good it will do.'

'I'll make her understand,' he said. 'I'll phone Gran now and tell her I'll make it OK.' He had the phone to his ear.

'I'll be downstairs if you need me,' I said, and left his room.

Five minutes later Stevie came down. 'Gran's mobile is off, so I tried the house phone. Grandpa answered and said Gran was too upset to talk. One of them will phone when they know what's happening. Grandpa sounded like he was crying.' Finally, the enormity of what was happening hit him.

CHAPTER TWENTY-ONE

WAITING FOR NEWS

Stevie looked dreadful the following morning – pale, tired and drawn – so I guessed he hadn't had much sleep either. He didn't want any breakfast, just a glass of juice.

'If you're still going to phone Verity, make sure it's not while your phone is supposed to be switched off in school,' I said. 'We don't want any more trouble. If she's not there, leave a message on her voicemail.'

He nodded dejectedly.

'And please make sure you go to school,' I added later as I saw him off at the door. 'There's nothing you can do, and we'll be told when there is any news. Take care and phone me at lunchtime if you want to.' Head down, with his shoulders slumped and school bag hanging desultorily from one arm, he went down the front path and out onto the pavement. A shadow of his former self. I closed the front door.

Before I did anything, I made myself another coffee. I felt shattered from worry and little sleep. Problems that affect the looked-after child affect everyone else in the family. As far as I knew, Stevie hadn't told Adrian, Lucy or Paula about this new upset – that he'd been seen with Kiri and Liam – and there'd been no time this morning. I didn't mention it to them. They were all busy getting ready to go to work or college. If necessary, we could talk about it this evening.

I was expecting Verity to phone at some point and she did at midday, her voice business-like, formal and efficient. 'I've just come from a meeting,' she said. 'Stevie's left me a voice-mail message, saying he is sorry. I assume you know that Mrs Jones has been taking Liam and Kiri to see Stevie?'

'I found out last night,' I said. 'Peggy telephoned me to tell me what had happened. She was very upset and asked me to tell Stevie. I had no idea prior to last night that Stevie had been seeing Kiri and Liam. I thought he understood he wasn't to see them while the police investigation was ongoing.' I felt I should make that clear in case Verity was under the impression I had colluded with them in seeing each other, which would have probably resulted in me being barred from fostering.

'I'll see Stevie tomorrow,' Verity continued. 'I won't have time today. Can you send me the dates and times of when Stevie saw his grandmother? Also, any relevant information surrounding those meetings. What he said and so forth.'

'Yes.' This is one of the reasons why foster carers are expected to keep accurate log notes.

'Email them to me, please, as soon as you can.'

'I'll do it now,' I said. 'Peggy and Stevie are very sorry for what they've done.'

'I know. I understand that Stevie gave his grandmother his old phone and they have been in touch that way.'

'Yes. Peggy told me you were thinking of taking Kiri and Liam into care.'

'We will be. That's what the meeting was about. They've given us no choice. If you could send through the details of when they saw each other as soon as possible that would be good. Sorry to rush, I'm really pushed for time.'

I replaced the handset and went into the front room where I sat at the computer, tears welling in my eyes. The decision had been made: Kiri and Liam were being taken into care. I tried to focus on the job in hand. I opened my log notes and did as Verity had asked, and typed the details of when Stevie had seen Kiri and Liam with his gran into an email, then sent it to Verity. I knew why she'd asked about Peggy having Stevie's old mobile phone – in colluding in the deception of contact, it raised the possibility that she may have colluded with him in other matters. Now under suspicion, it was likely her phone would be examined by the police, and she and Fred interviewed. It was a shocking mess, and what had once been a stable, loving family was now being torn apart.

There wasn't much else I could do now but wait, and then be ready to support Stevie when he returned from school or phoned during the day. I felt I needed to be active to escape from my troubled thoughts, so having cleared up the house I went into the garden and set about some gardening, my mobile phone close by. At 12.30 Stevie phoned during his lunch break (when they were allowed to turn on their phones). 'Have you heard anything?' he asked, his voice tight.

I went indoors to take the call so that any neighbours in their gardens couldn't overhear. 'Verity phoned,' I said. 'She's listened to your voicemail message.'

'Will it be OK then?' he asked naively, believing his admittance of guilt and apology were enough to keep Liam and Kiri out of care.

I didn't want to tell him now and have him upset at school where I couldn't comfort him, so I said, 'Verity was in a hurry and couldn't talk. We'll know more later.'

'But she listened to my message?'

'Yes, she did.'

'Shall I phone her again and see if she's there now?'

'It's up to you, Stevie, but I doubt it will make any difference to the outcome.' A young person in care has the right to talk to their social worker whenever they want; it's not for the foster carer to dictate.

'Yes, I'll do that now,' he said. 'I'll phone her.'

'All right, but make sure you have some lunch too. You didn't have any breakfast.'

'Yes,' he said unenthusiastically, and ended the call.

I returned to the gardening and channelled my mounting anxiety and worry on the weeding and snipping. An hour later Edith telephoned and again I stepped indoors to take the call. 'I understand Stevie's siblings are coming into care later,' she said.

'That's right.'

'We are thinking of placing them with Terry and Bridget.' I knew the couple, who, like me, were local-authority carers. 'I've been looking on the map and they live about a mile and a half from you,' Edith continued. 'That should be far enough. You're not likely to bump into them, are you? Stevie isn't to have contact with his siblings.'

'That should work,' I said. 'I'll be vigilant.' I knew carers were in short supply so there wouldn't be much choice, but it was prudent of Edith to check. In the past I'd had a child placed with me whose mother had lived in the next street and we were forever bumping into each other, which was upsetting for her and the child.

'Can you tell me a bit about Kiri and Liam so I can pass it on to the carers?' Edith asked. 'It will help Terry and Bridget to settle the children in.'

Clearly Edith had forgotten what I'd told her when I'd updated her. 'I've never met them,' I said. 'But I'm sure Terry and Bridget will know what to do. They're experienced carers, although Liam and Kiri are likely to be very upset.'

'Yes,' she said. 'So you don't know the children's routines, likes and dislikes?'

'No.'

'Why can't they see Stevie?'

'Because he is under investigation for taking and distributing indecent images of them,' I said, reminding her of what I'd previously told her. Each supervising social worker is responsible for at least twelve foster carers, so perhaps it was asking a lot of her to remember all this information, although Jill would have, I thought churlishly.

'Will they be seeing their grandparents?' she asked.

'I assume so, but you'll have to ask Verity.'

'I'm calling her shortly to confirm the placement. Verity is hoping to place the children at Terry and Bridget's between five and six this evening, so they will be there for dinner.'

My heart clenched as the details brought the reality that much closer.

'All right,' I said. 'Will you keep me updated? I need to tell Stevie what's happening when he comes home.'

'Yes.'

I returned to the garden but was unable to take any pleasure from the warm May sunshine, pretty flowers, birdsong or the effects of my gardening. At 3.30 Stevie phoned again, having just come out of school.

'Any news?' he asked.

'Edith, my supervising social worker, called. I'll tell you what she said once you're home. If you get on the bus now, I'll see you in half an hour.'

'Can't you tell me now?' he asked. I could hear street noise in the background.

'No, I'd rather wait until you're home.'

He cut the call. I quickly cleared away the gardening tools, dumped the weeds in the green bin and went indoors, where I washed and changed out of my dirty clothes. At just gone four o'clock the doorbell rang and I immediately answered it, my mouth dry and my pulse raising.

'What's going on?' Stevie demanded, his face set.

'Come and sit down.'

He dumped his school bag in the hall, kicked off his shoes and, throwing his jacket over the hall stand, followed me into the living room. We were the only ones home. I sat beside him on the sofa and turned slightly towards him as I spoke.

'Stevie, I'm sorry, but Liam and Kiri will be going into care today.'

'Why?' he said, his eyes filling. 'I told Verity it was my fault and it won't happen again. I left her two messages. They've done nothing wrong.'

'I know.' I went to touch his arm, but he pulled it away. 'You see, the social services have a duty to protect Kiri and Liam.'

'What, from me?' he asked angrily.

'While you are being investigated by the police, yes,' I replied honestly.

'But they're just kids. Why punish them?'

'Going into foster care isn't a punishment,' I said. Although I knew it could feel like that to the child. 'The social services will have decided that there are what's called safeguarding issues. Your grandparents were in a position of trust and responsibility, and unfortunately they made a decision that could have jeopardised the children's safety.' I was trying to say this nicely while telling Stevie the truth.

'It's not fair,' he said angrily. 'It's not right.' Then he suddenly looked at me with hope in his eyes. 'Can you foster them? They can have my room and I'll sleep on the sofa. I don't mind.'

'Stevie, love, the reason why Kiri and Liam are going into care is because you're not allowed to see them for the time being. There is no way the social services would consider placing them here so you are all under one roof.'

'OK, so they can come here and I'll go somewhere else.' I suppose he thought it was better they went somewhere he knew.

'What purpose would that serve?' I asked him gently. 'You need somewhere to live and you're settled here. I know the carers Liam and Kiri are going to and they are really nice. They're a little older than me and from what I remember their own children are adults and have left home, so they will have lots of time to look after Liam and Kiri and play with them. I promise you, love, they will be well cared for.'

'They'll be so upset,' he said, all hope going and his face creasing. 'They've never been away from Gran and Grandpa before.'

'I expect they will be upset to begin with, but they will settle, just as you did. The carers will keep them occupied and make sure they're all right.'

'Can I phone my gran?' he asked.

'Not just yet. They'll be a lot going on and your grandfather told you when you spoke to him yesterday that they'll phone us when they are able.'

Leaning forward, he dropped his head into his hands. I couldn't tell if he was crying – I couldn't see his face – but I thought he was pretty close to it. I touched his shoulder and this time he didn't pull away.

'I know it's difficult, love, but at some point all this will be over and you'll all be able to get on with your lives.'

'Then can we all go home to Gran's to live?' he asked, his head still in his hands.

'I don't know.' Clearly this depended on a number of factors, including the outcome of the police investigation, but I'd noticed he'd said "can we *all* go home to Gran's to live" – including himself. Sometimes a crisis can reunite a family, although I couldn't see how that was going to happen here – at least, not in the near future.

'I'm going to my room,' he said suddenly, standing. 'Will you tell me when you hear anything?'

'Yes, of course.'

I watched him go, blaming himself and his spirit broken, as though he hadn't a hope in the world. I checked on him regularly, every twenty minutes or so. I knocked on his bedroom door and asked, 'Are you OK, Stevie?' A couple of times he didn't reply so I opened the door to check. Each time he had his earbuds in, so I nodded to him and closed the door again. He came down for dinner, still in his school uniform, and was obviously very low.

'What's the matter with you?' Lucy asked as soon as she saw him. I hadn't had a chance to tell them. When they'd come in they'd gone to their rooms to unwind before dinner, and I was still deciding if they needed to know at all and whether I could avoid sharing yet another of Stevie's burdens.

'Kiri and Liam have to go into foster care,' Stevie replied.

'Why?' Lucy asked, shocked. Adrian and Paula were looking at Stevie, as concerned as Lucy was.

'Because I saw them when I wasn't supposed to,' Stevie said bluntly, not meeting their gaze.

They looked at me for confirmation and I nodded.

'For how long?' Paula asked.

'I don't know,' Stevie said miserably.

Little more was said after that and Stevie ate his meal in silence, then left the table to go to his room.

'It all seems a bit sudden, taking Liam and Kiri into care,' Adrian said. 'I thought they were being well looked after.'

'They were,' I said. 'It's not the level of care.' I explained what had happened. They felt sorry for Stevie, but having been involved in fostering for a long time they understood why the action taken by the social services was necessary.

I didn't hear from Verity or Edith that evening – I hadn't expected to. By the time Verity had finished placing Liam and Kiri it would be quite late. I guessed Peggy and Fred wouldn't be in any fit state to phone either. My heart went out to them as I pictured them at home, surrounded by their children's belongings – toys, clothes, books and so on, but with the children gone. It would be dreadful. How were they coping? I couldn't begin to imagine. I wondered if they'd tell their daughter – the children's mother. I supposed at some point she would be told. Although she was in prison and Peggy and Fred had guardianship of the children, she had a right to know. My heart went out to her too. Locked in a cell, she had all the time in the world to think, worry and regret.

Emotionally drained, and physically exhausted from gardening, I did sleep that night. The following morning, when Stevie came down, I asked him if he'd managed to get some sleep and he said yes, but he'd had nightmares. 'Little wonder with all this going on,' I said.

'Will I find out about Kiri and Liam today?' he asked as I passed him the slice of toast he wanted.

'Verity said she's going to see you at some point,' I said. 'I expect she'll phone me or you to say when.' Sometimes social workers phone young people of Stevie's age directly to make arrangements, which is fine as long as they remember to tell the foster carer.

'Stevie, just one thing I need to say. If you do see Kiri and Liam out in the street with their carers, just walk away. I know it's asking a lot, but until this is all sorted you need to stay away from them. Don't approach them, will you?'

'Where do they live?' he asked.

'I'm not telling you. You mustn't go there. Do you understand?' He nodded. Of course, there were ways he could find out where Liam and Kiri were living – go to their school and follow them home with their carers. It's happened before: children are placed with a foster carer and the parents are not given the address for good reason, then a family member or friend goes to the school and follows them home.

'What would happen if I did?' he asked.

'Kiri and Liam would probably be moved to another carer out of the area, which would result in them having to change schools. That would be very unsettling for them. I am sure you wouldn't want that to happen.'

He shook his head and seemed to accept what I was saying.

I saw him off at the door, and at eight-thirty Verity telephoned from her mobile. 'Kiri and Liam were placed yesterday evening,' she said. 'I'll see Stevie after school this afternoon. Remind me again what time he gets home.'

'Between four and four-thirty.'

'OK. I'll see you both then. Can you tell Stevie I'm coming, please?'

'Yes. How were Liam and Kiri last night?' I asked.

'The move went smoothly. I'll talk to you more about it tonight.'

Having said goodbye, I texted Stevie to tell him to come straight home, as Verity would be visiting us. I added Verity had said that Kiri and Liam's move to the carers had gone smoothly, which I thought might reassure him.

CHAPTER TWENTY-TWO

ANGRY AND UPSET

S tevie arrived home at exactly 4 p.m. I asked him what sort of day he'd had and he just shrugged. He had time for a glass of water before Verity arrived, briefcase-style bag in her hand, and went into the living room where Stevie was already waiting. She wanted to see him alone first and said she'd speak to me afterwards, so I went into the kitchen and began peeling vegetables for dinner. I could hear the low hum of their voices and a few times I heard Stevie raise his voice.

Paula came home twenty minutes later and shouted, 'Hi, Mum!' as she let herself in. I quickly went into the hall and told her that Verity was with Stevie in the living room, and asked her if she'd had a good day.

'Yes, but I need to use the printer,' she said. 'I've got to print out some worksheets our tutor has emailed to us.'

'Do it now while it's all quiet,' I suggested. Although everyone had their own laptop, we shared a printer, which was by the computer in the front room.

Paula poured herself a drink and, taking a piece of fruit for a snack, went into the front room. The door to the living room opened and Stevie came into the kitchen. 'She wants you now,' he said moodily. He had red flushes of colour on his cheeks, which I'd noticed before when he got angry, emotional or upset.

'Thank you.' I headed for the living room.

As Stevie passed the front room on his way upstairs I heard Paula call out, 'Hi, Stevie, how are you?'

'Hello,' he managed, his voice flat, and continued up to his room.

Verity was sitting on the sofa, her briefcase closed and at her feet. I sat in one of the easy chairs.

'Stevie is angry with me for taking Liam and Kiri into care,' she began. 'Although I've explained why it was necessary.'

'So have I,' I said.

She nodded. 'Mr and Mrs Jones are angry with me too, but the move went reasonably smoothly. I managed to persuade them that it would be better if Liam and Kiri came into care voluntarily under a Section 20 – the same as Stevie – rather than the social services applying to court for a care order. I also explained to them that it would be less upsetting for the children if they could try to be positive, but I knew it was asking a lot. Mrs Jones was very upset. I stayed with her while my colleague went with Fred to collect Liam and Kiri from school, then I explained to the children about coming into care while their grandparents were present. Seeing their grandmother in tears upset Kiri and Liam, but I have to say Fred was excellent. He did a good job of calming everyone down and then took Liam and Kiri upstairs to pack a bag, including their favourite soft toys.'

'Good,' I said. I knew how important those familiar things would be in helping the children to settle.

'I asked Mr and Mrs Jones not to tell Kiri and Liam that the reason they were going into care was because Stevie had been seeing them when he wasn't supposed to, as it could make them feel guilty. Fred told them that he and their gran were having a short break, as they were getting older and needed a rest, but that they would still see them after school some days and then eventually they could come home to live.'

'Well done, Fred,' I said, and I meant it. The reassurance from their grandfather would be invaluable. I was also pleased that Verity was giving me some detailed feedback.

'It was after six o'clock by the time we got to the carers,' she continued. 'Once my colleague and I had placed Kiri and Liam, we left them to have their dinner. I've spoken to the carers this morning and the children are in school.'

I nodded.

'I've set up supervised contact at the Family Centre for Liam and Kiri to see their grandparents tonight, then every Monday, Wednesday and Friday. I've told Stevie this, as he asked. He also asked how long they'd be in care and I said I hoped it would be short-term. It will largely depend on the outcome of the police investigation and any prosecution that may follow.'

'How long before the investigation is complete?' I asked. 'It seems we've been waiting for ages.'

'It's difficult to say. I'm in touch with CAIT [Child Abuse Investigation Team] and made them aware of the effect this is having on Stevie and the wider family. They are still gathering evidence but should know before long if there is a case to take to the Crown Prosecution Service.'

'Have they caught Joey?' I asked.

'Not as far as I know, but I understand he might have popped up online with a different identity. Someone using the same patter has been busy on the websites that Stevie accessed. He has a different name and photo, but there are similarities. The police are monitoring his online activity.'

'I hope they catch him and others like him, preying on vulnerable young people,' I said passionately.

'Yes. Last month one of our fourteen-year-old girls went to meet someone she'd been chatting to online, thinking he was the same age as her. Thankfully, the foster carer was clued up and became suspicious, and followed her to their meeting place. The guy waiting in his car to pick her up was middle-aged. He saw the foster carer and drove off at speed. Unfortunately, he couldn't get the registration number, but we're sure she had a lucky escape. If it hadn't been for the vigilance of the foster carer, the outcome doesn't bear thinking about.'

We fell silent for a moment as the enormity of Verity's words hung in the air, then after a moment she said, 'I need to be going now. Is there anything else you want to ask me?'

'Is Stevie seeing his grandparents?' I asked.

'He can see them, but I'll talk to them about the arrangements in a few days when Mrs Jones is less upset.'

'Presumably he could go to their home now Kiri and Liam aren't there.'

'I don't see why not. There is no need for supervised contact, but I'll have a chat with them and let you know. Liam and Kiri's carers are aware of the restrictions on contact – that the children aren't to see Stevie at present.' Standing, Verity picked up her briefcase. 'Say goodbye to Stevie for me, please, and reassure him that Kiri and Liam are being well looked after. He was very concerned about them.'

'I will.'

I saw her out, then went straight upstairs to Stevie. Paula had finished in the front room and was in her bedroom. Stevie's door was shut, so I knocked. 'Stevie, it's Cathy. Can I come in?' There was no reply, so I knocked again and then went in, expecting to find him propped on his pillows with his earbuds in. However, he was just slipping on a pair of shoes, having changed out of his school uniform and into casual clothes. 'I'm going out,' he said bluntly.

'What, now? Before dinner?' I asked.

'I don't want dinner.'

'Where are you going? I'd like to know how you're getting home. It's a school night, so you mustn't be late.'

'I'll come back when I'm ready,' he said and, pushing past me, went downstairs and out the front door, slamming it behind him.

I knew not to try to stop him – he was angry – but I was taken aback. Verity had decided when he'd first arrived that he could go out one evening during the week as well as at the weekend, but I just wished he hadn't left like this, angry and upset, as I knew it could lead to trouble.

Paula had heard the front door slam and came out of her room. 'It was Stevie,' I said. 'He's angry because Liam and Kiri have been taken into care.'

'I'm sure he'll come back later, once he's calmed down,' she said, trying to reassure me. 'He's got nowhere else to go apart from his grandparents' house and he won't go there.'

But of course that in itself was worrying. I wasn't aware of any good friends where Stevie might have gone. Despite suggesting that he invited friends home or did something with them at the weekends, it hadn't happened.

It was now 5.15. I gave Stevie a cooling-off period, during which time I continued to prepare dinner, and then at six o'clock, before I served dinner, I phoned his mobile. It went through to his voicemail, so I left a message: 'Stevie, it's Cathy. Can you phone or text me, please, to let me know you're OK, and what time you will be back, so I don't worry? Thanks, love.'

Adrian, Paula and I sat down to eat. Lucy was on a late shift at the nursery and wouldn't be back until seven o'clock, so I plated up hers and Stevie's dinner. I told Adrian why Stevie wasn't with us and he was worried, given what had happened the last time Stevie had gone missing, and hoped, as Paula did, that he would be back before long once he'd calmed down.

After we'd eaten I cleared away the dishes and tried Stevie's phone again. It went straight through to voicemail, so I left another message: 'Hi, Stevie, Cathy again, could you let me know you're safe, please? Thank you.'

Over the next hour I grew increasingly worried, but I was also annoyed with Stevie for causing me all this extra anxiety on top of everything else. Lucy arrived home just after seven o'clock and I sat with her at the table while she ate her dinner and told her what had happened.

'Do you remember when I used to storm off and you would come and find me?' she asked.

'Yes, but I always had a good idea of where you'd be.'

'It was so embarrassing – the scene you used to make in front of my friends in the high street.'

'But it worked, didn't it? You stopped storming off.'

Lucy smiled. 'I did.'

Lucy, like some other young people I'd fostered, had bolted after a disagreement rather than staying to talk about the issue like an adult. If I felt it was the right course of action, I went after them, either on foot or in the car, and made such a fuss in public about loving them and them needing to come home now so we could talk, that they were so embarrassed they did as I asked. It wasn't long before they stopped bolting, which made life easier for us all. Stevie had been angry when he'd pushed past me, so I'd felt he'd needed a cooling-off period, but now I wasn't so sure. Perhaps I should have gone after him; there was no point now – too much time had elapsed; he could be anywhere. When he'd gone missing before Adrian, Lucy and Paula had looked for him and he hadn't been in the area. I knew that before long I'd have to phone the social services and report him missing. I also knew the social services and the police would ask if I'd checked to see if he was at his grandparents', but I was reluctant to telephone them now with everything they were going through. They didn't need the additional stress of knowing Stevie had gone missing. Unless, of course, he was there.

At 7.30 I texted his phone: *Stevie, I will have to report you missing if you don't come home or get in touch soon.*

I waited for half an hour and then telephoned the call operator at the social services and explained that I needed to speak to the emergency duty social worker to report the young person I was fostering missing. She took my details and said the emergency duty social worker would return my call as soon as possible. As I waited, I pictured being up all night again and the police searching my home. The level of disruption caused by some young people in care cannot be overstated. In cases like this, all the carer can do is give them love, support, understanding and firm boundaries and hope they turn a corner before long. Most of them do.

When the duty social worker telephoned, he recognised Stevie's name from the last time I'd reported him missing, although I still had to give him Stevie's details again, his background information and the circumstances leading to him going missing. I said I'd tried to contact him by phone and gave him the times I'd called and texted him during the evening. I said I hadn't contacted his grandparents – the only place I knew of where he might possibly be – and explained why. The duty social worker told me to leave another message on Stevie's mobile, saying I'd reported him missing to the social services and if he didn't make contact straight away I would have to report him missing to the police as well. He also told me – as I thought he would – to phone Stevie's grandparents. He finished by saying to call him again if I needed any more assistance and to let him know if Stevie returned.

I stayed where I was in the living room and tried Stevie's mobile again, hoping he would pick up so I could persuade him to come home and end all of this, but it went through to voicemail. I left the message as the duty social worker had advised me to and also added that I was about to phone his grandparents, which I hoped might give him an added incentive to get in touch. I waited ten minutes and then reluctantly picked up the phone again and dialled Mr and Mrs Jones's landline number. It crossed my mind to text Peggy's mobile instead; it would have been less painful – *Stevie is missing. Is he with you?* – but that didn't seem appropriate. It was cold and unfeeling, and possibly the police had her mobile now anyway.

I was slightly relieved that it was Fred who answered, as Verity had said he was coping better than Peggy. Even so, I was anxious speaking to him.

'Fred, I'm sorry to disturb you, it's Cathy.'

'Yes, what do you want?' he asked gruffly.

'I wondered if Stevie was with you?'

'No, he's not. And neither are Liam and Kiri thanks to him!' He hung up and the line went dead.

Damn, I thought. I'd been worried that Fred might blame Stevie for Liam and Kiri being taken into care, and it seemed he did. Gone was any sign of the support Peggy had said Fred was giving Stevie about the police investigation; instead he was holding Stevie responsible for Liam and Kiri going into care. Of course Fred was angry and needed to blame someone, I appreciated that, although Peggy – as the adult – held more responsibility for what had happened than Stevie. She was the one who should have refused his requests to see Liam and Kiri, and explain why, regardless of how much Stevie asked. It was unfair to blame him for the consequences of her decision. She was the adult and Stevie was the child.

With the information I now needed – that Stevie wasn't with his grandparents – I telephoned the police and went through the procedure for reporting him missing. I gave the officer Stevie's details, emphasised he was a child in care, gave a description of him and what he was wearing when he'd left the house. When the officer asked if he was depressed or suicidal, I said he was upset and had stormed off angrily. He asked if I'd tried to contact him and I said I'd phoned and texted him a number of times during the evening but without any reply. Of course he wanted to know if Stevie had gone missing before and I said he had and gave the date, and also that it had happened when he'd been living with his grandparents. The officer asked for the contact details of Stevie's social worker and his grandparents. I gave them but said I'd just phoned Mr and Mrs Jones and Stevie wasn't there. He said he'd send an officer to my house as soon as one became available and to have a recent photograph ready. I said the police still had the photograph I'd given them when Stevie had gone missing before, as it had never been returned. He said it should be on file but to have another one ready in case it wasn't.

I stayed in the living room with my mobile on the sofa beside me, willing it to spring into life with a call or text from Stevie. At various times over the next half an hour or so, Lucy, Paula and Adrian came into the living room to find out if there was any news. I told them that Stevie hadn't been in touch and wasn't at his grandparents', so I'd reported him missing and was waiting for the police to arrive. While they were sympathetic and worried, it was only natural that, like me, they were a bit put out at the anxiety and disruption Stevie was causing everyone.

At 9.15, about forty minutes after I'd reported Stevie missing, the front doorbell rang and I assumed it was the police. I was pleased they had arrived so quickly. The sun had just set so it was dark outside, which seemed to make Stevie being missing even more worrying. Flicking on the hall and porch lights, I answered the front door and was surprised and relieved to find Stevie. 'Good, you're home,' I said.

'Hello, Cathy. I've come back,' he slurred. His eyes were glazed, he was unsteady on his feet and I could smell alcohol on his breath.

'Oh Stevie.' I helped him over the doorstep and he flopped into the chair by the telephone table. Bending forward, he tried to take off his shoes but couldn't quite coordinate the movement. Adrian, having heard the door, appeared on the landing, saw the state Stevie was in and came down to help.

'You're not going to be sick, are you?' he asked him.

'Don't think so,' Stevie slurred.

'I'll get a bucket anyway,' Adrian said.

'What have you had to drink?' I asked Stevie, helping him take off his shoes. Knowing what he'd drunk and how much would be important in deciding what I should do next. Young people can become intoxicated quite quickly, but if he'd had a lot to drink, especially spirits, I'd take him to the hospital, or call an ambulance if he passed out.

'Beer,' he said, and hiccupped. 'Pardon me.' He pressed his fingers to his lips and grinned.

'How much beer?'

'Four bottles, but I gave most of the last one to a guy sleeping rough.'

'And that's it?' He nodded. 'Have you taken any pills?'

'No. I'm a good boy.'

'Where have you been?' I asked, removing his second shoe.

'In the park.'

'Our local park?' I asked. Adrian returned with the bucket and placed it beside Stevie.

'No, the big park near my gran's. It's where I used to take Liam and Kiri. I sat on the bench and drank, then got talking to a guy sleeping rough.'

Stevie was able to answer my questions and, although he was intoxicated, he hadn't had a huge amount to drink and hadn't taken any drugs, so I didn't think it necessary to take him to the hospital or call an ambulance, but I would monitor him.

'How did you buy the alcohol?' Adrian asked. 'Didn't they ask for your ID?'

'I have fake ID,' Stevie said, and hiccupped again.

I nodded. Stevie had told me shortly after he'd arrived that he'd used fake ID he'd bought from the internet to get into nightclubs.

'Let's get you up to bed so you can sleep it off,' I said to him.

'Good idea, Cathy,' he replied, grinning inanely.

Adrian sighed and helped him off the chair and then upstairs, while I followed a couple of steps behind, carrying the bucket. Stevie was tall but slightly built, whereas Adrian was tall and more sturdily built, so he was easily able to give Stevie the support he needed to get him safely upstairs and into his bedroom. I placed the bucket beside his bed.

'Get changed and into bed,' I told Stevie. 'I'll check on you in a few minutes.'

'Thanks, guys,' he said affably. We came out and left him to it. Alcohol affects people in different ways: some become loud and aggressive when they've had too much to drink, while others, like Stevie, just go soppy. Although, of course, at his age he shouldn't have been drinking at all.

Lucy and Paula, having heard Stevie, had come out of their bedrooms and were now on the landing. 'Stevie is drunk,' I said, 'but at least he's back safely. I need to phone the police and social services and tell them.'

I left the girls talking to Adrian and went into my bedroom, where I used the handset there to make the calls. Ten minutes later, when I'd finished, I checked on Stevie. He was lying flat on his back on top of the duvet, with only his underpants and socks on, and snoring like an old drunk. I'm sure he would have been acutely embarrassed had he seen himself like that. I know some parents teach their teenagers a lesson by taking photos of them when they're the worse for drink and showing them afterwards, but as a foster carer that wouldn't have been appropriate or professional, even though shaming Stevie might have stopped him from doing it again.

I called to Adrian to help me and together we put Stevie on his side in the recovery position in case he was sick in his sleep. I didn't think he would be; it was a precautionary measure. I drew the duvet over him, dimmed his bedroom light and, leaving the bucket by his bed and the door open, we came out. I thanked Adrian for his help and went downstairs. I knew I should phone Peggy and Fred to let them know Stevie was back, for, despite Fred's harsh words, he and Peggy loved Stevie and were sure to be worrying about him.

In the living room I dialled their landline number, but it went to answerphone so I left a message. 'It's Cathy. Stevie has returned safely. He's had a few drinks but is OK, and is now in bed sleeping it off.' I paused, trying to think of something encouraging to say about Liam and Kiri being in care, but all the platitudes – like 'try not to worry' and 'they are being well looked after' – seemed inadequate, so I just hung up. I doubted any words of mine could ease the pain they must be feeling at having lost all their grandchildren into care.

CHAPTER TWENTY-THREE

PROSECUTE

I checked on Stevie before I went to bed and again in the early hours. He was still on his side, but no longer snoring, and in a more natural sleep. The following morning it took a while to wake him and he told me to go away and he wasn't going to school. I said he was and that he'd feel better once he was up and showered. I then gave him a glass of ice-cold water to drink, which did help his hangover. Now wasn't the time to lecture him about the dangers of storming off angrily and drinking to excess. I'd talk to him this evening.

Once showered and dressed, he came downstairs. He looked pale but otherwise all right. He didn't want anything to eat but, craving something sweet, he had two glasses of orange juice.

As usual on a weekday everyone was busy getting ready to leave the house. When Adrian saw Stevie he asked him how he was and Stevie had the decency to look embarrassed and replied, 'OK, thanks for asking.'

Paula said, 'Hi,' when she saw him.

But when Lucy passed him in the hall on her way out she said, 'It ain't big and it ain't clever, Stevie. You need to grow up.'

I didn't say anything, but that night I'd remind her that Stevie was only just fifteen and had a lot to cope with. I thought that going off like that and getting drunk was probably a one-off and a reaction to Liam and Kiri going into care, and that once I'd had a good chat with him he'd settle down again. However, I didn't get the chance to talk to him that afternoon or evening as he didn't come home from school.

'Not again!' Paula sighed when she came home from college to find me on the phone to the duty social worker – not the same one as the night before.

I nodded and continued giving the details leading up to Stevie's disappearance: that he'd been upset the day before because his younger siblings had been taken into care and had stormed off; that I'd reported him missing but he'd returned home drunk at 9.15. I said he'd gone to school this morning but hadn't returned. I'd phoned and texted his mobile, but there'd been no reply. The duty social worker asked if I'd checked with the school to make sure he had arrived and I said yes, he had been to school, and that I'd called his grandparents to see if he was there, but their answerphone was on so I'd left a message. He asked if there was anywhere else Stevie could be and I said the only other place I knew was the park he'd gone to yesterday. He told me to check the park first, and if Stevie wasn't there and still wasn't answering my calls to report him missing to the police. Although it was only 5.30, he was supposed to be home from school between 4 and 4.30, so he'd been missing an hour.

I knew the park Stevie had referred to near where his grandparents lived, and I told Paula that I was going there now. She said she'd come with me, and I was grateful for her company. As I drove she asked, 'Do you ever think about giving up fostering, Mum?'

I glanced at her. 'At moments like this, yes,' I said truthfully. 'It's a lovely evening and I'd rather be in our garden than chasing around after Stevie. But then again, fostering is very rewarding. What made you ask? Do you think we should stop?'

'Sometimes,' she replied honestly. 'I worry about you.'

'Why?'

'The stress it puts you under. I know we've been doing it a long time – forever, really – but you're not as young as you used to be.'

'Thanks, love!' I laughed.

'You know what I mean.'

'Yes, I do.' I smiled at her, touched by her thoughtfulness.

'Not having a father makes you even more special to me.'

'You have a father, he just doesn't live with us,' I said as I'd said before.

'He never has,' she replied reproachfully.

'Yes, he did, but he left when you were very young.'

'I know, and I used to worry who'd take care of us if anything happened to you.'

'And I always told you that Nana and Grandpa would. You are all young adults now and I'm not going anywhere for a long time, I've too much to do. But if something unexpected did happen, I'm assuming you'd all look after each other, wouldn't you?'

'Yes, of course.'

'Good, but what brought this up? The worry Stevie is causing us?'

'Partly,' Paula admitted. 'Also, a girl I'm friends with at college lost her mum to cancer at Christmas. She talks to me about her sometimes, and how much she misses her.'

'Poor girl. She must miss her a lot.'

'She does. She lives with her older brother and his partner.'

'How is that working out?' I asked, glancing at her and pleased we'd found the chance to have this chat.

'She gets on well with them both. She couldn't afford to stay in the house where she lived with her mother.'

'No, and to be honest she would probably have been lonely. It's better she is with family if they are all getting along. She lost her mother young and it does happen. But I'm fit and well, and if ever I feel that fostering is causing me too much stress, I'll stop.'

'I believe you,' she said with a smile.

'But Paula, do you want to continue fostering?' It was a question I'd asked all three of them before, although not recently. Fostering affects the whole family and while one parent may be the main care-giver, all family members need to be committed for it to work.

'Yes,' Paula said. 'Mostly it's fine.'

'What about Adrian and Lucy?'

'I think they're happy with it too, but we haven't talked about it in a long while.'

'OK, I'll ask them later. And please don't worry about me. I'm made of strong stuff.'

She smiled again. It was the reassurance she needed to hear.

We arrived at the park and I pulled in to a side road, cut the engine and gave her a big kiss on her cheek. 'Love you.'

'Love you too.'

We got out, entered the park and, arm in arm, did a complete circuit, checking benches, the children's play area, the tennis courts, pavilion and the old bandstand where some children were roller skating, but there was no sign of Stevie. It was a warm evening and parents had brought their children here after school to play — ball and Frisbee, or riding their bikes. I could picture Stevie with Liam and Kiri playing here in happier times. As Paula and I made our way back towards the park entrance we passed two girls who looked about thirteen, furtively smoking behind a tree. 'It's not big and it's not clever,' I said, using Lucy's phrase, much to Paula's embarrassment.

'Mum!' she said, drawing me on, while the girls looked surprised.

'It's stupid to start smoking,' I said loud enough for them to hear.

'Mum,' Paula hissed again, 'you're so embarrassing.'

'Sorry, love.'

But maybe the girls would heed my words and think twice about lighting up next time. Smoking is a killer and, as an ex-smoker, I knew how difficult it was to quit, so it makes sense never to start in the first place. Lecture over.

Once in the car I tried Stevie's mobile again. It went through to voicemail, so I left a message saying I was about to report him missing to the police. Paula, having forgiven me for embarrassing her in the park, began talking about her college work and our summer holiday, which I had yet to book.

As soon as we were home I put the dinner in the oven, checked my mobile, then reluctantly telephoned the police and reported Stevie missing again. Adrian and Lucy arrived home in time for dinner and as we sat at the table to eat I told them Stevie hadn't returned from school and to expect another visit from the police.

'It's so disruptive,' Lucy said vehemently, while Adrian nodded.

It was Friday and Lucy and Adrian said they were going out later, but before they left, and while it was on my mind, I asked them separately if they were happy to continue fostering. 'Yes, of course,' Lucy said, 'but I need to get ready, Mum.'

Adrian said, 'Yes, for as long as you want to. It's something Kirsty and I have talked about doing in the future once we're settled in our own place and have our own family.'

'That sounds promising,' I said, smiling. Kirsty and Adrian had been seeing each other for some years, and while I'd always thought they would end up together, it hadn't been stated so clearly. I was also pleased he and Lucy wanted to continue fostering.

Two police officers arrived shortly after Adrian and Lucy had left. One of them had attended the last time I'd reported Stevie missing and I apologised that they'd had to come here again. 'We're just doing our job,' he said. They took a few details, said they had a photo of Stevie on file and gave the house a perfunctory search. I apologised again as I saw them out and then added, 'As Stevie's foster carer I have to report him missing each time he doesn't come home when he is supposed to.' They hadn't said as much, but I could tell they thought this was a waste of police time, as I was starting to.

At eight o'clock Paula joined me in the living room to watch a television series we were both enjoying, but my mind wasn't on it. I was listening for the doorbell – willing it to ring – and wondering what Stevie was doing. An hour later, when the episode had finished, Paula said she was going to shower and get ready for bed. 'Where do you think Stevie is?' she asked, worried.

'I've no idea, but hopefully he'll be back soon.'

She kissed me goodnight and I told her not to worry and said again I was sure he'd be back before long. Indeed, I was half expecting him to return drunk at any moment as he had before. I made a cup of tea and then sat in the living room with the television on low, my mobile phone on the sofa beside me, and deep in thought. Lucy arrived home from seeing her friend at around ten-thirty and Adrian an hour later. He was surprised to see me still up as I was usually in bed when he got home from seeing Kirsty. 'Is Stevie back?' he asked.

'No. I'll wait up a bit longer, don't worry.'

'Wake me if you need any help,' he said thoughtfully.

Tired, anxious and increasingly annoyed with Stevie for causing me all this worry, as the minutes ticked by I began to imagine all sorts of dreadful scenarios: Stevie lying some-where drunk and unconscious, hurt and in hospital, or alone and depressed and thinking of taking his life. Like many young people who go missing, he would have little idea of the upset he was causing his family. I'm sure Peggy would have told him how worried she and Fred had been when he'd been living with them and had gone missing, but I don't think young people appreciate the extent of our anguish. The protective love of a parent or carer knows no bounds and can send you to hell and back when something like this happens.

At midnight I made another cup of tea and wondered if I should try to get some sleep on the sofa or go to bed. If I went to bed then it would take me longer to get dressed if Stevie phoned and I had to collect him as I'd done before with other missing teenagers I'd fostered. Sammy, his routine disrupted, put himself to bed, while I drank my tea in the living room. Then I dimmed the lights and lay on the sofa, my mobile at my side. I dozed a little but couldn't sleep as I tried to think where on earth Stevie could be. As far as I knew, he hadn't taken a change of clothes with him – it was something the police had asked – so he would still be in his school uniform and therefore unlikely to have got into a bar or club using his fake ID.

At 3 a.m., with no word from Stevie, I knew I needed to try to get some sleep if I was going to function the next day, so I went upstairs, undressed and got into bed, leaving the volume turned up on my mobile. I'd just dropped off when it rang, startlingly loud in the stillness of the night. The illuminated screen showed it was 4.05 a.m. and the call was from a private number. Normally I wouldn't have answered a private number as they were often nuisance calls, but Stevie was missing so I immediately accepted the call.

'Yes?' I said, sitting upright and switching on the bedside lamp.

'Mrs Cathy Glass?' a male voice asked.

'Yes, speaking.'

'I'm the duty sergeant at —.' He named a police station in an area over 100 miles away. 'I have Stevie Jones with me.'

'What's he doing there?' I gasped. 'Is he all right?'

'Yes, he's come to no harm. He's been with us since nine o'clock yesterday evening when we brought him in, but he's only just given us his real name and your telephone number.'

'But what's he doing there?' I asked again.

'He was caught on a train without a ticket, which is an offence. When the inspector asked for his name and address he refused to give them, so the police were called.'

'Oh. But it's miles from where we live. You know I reported him missing earlier?'

254

'Yes, we do now, and I've taken him off the system. Once he'd given us his real name and contact details he came up on the police computer.' It crossed my mind that the officer would probably have also seen Stevie was being investigated for sexting and taking and sending indecent images of minors. I wondered what he thought of Stevie.

'Where was Stevie going?' I asked.

'He says he was lost. I will need you to come to the police station to collect him.'

I sighed. 'All right, but it will take me at least two hours to get there.' Foster carers are expected to collect – or make suitable arrangements to have collected – the young person they are fostering, from the police station or anywhere they might be stranded or couldn't reasonably be expected to make their own way home.

'That's fine,' the officer said. 'He'll be safe here until you arrive.' I wondered if he was in a cell, but I didn't ask. 'Do you know where we are or do you need the postcode?' the officer asked.

'Postcode, please. Just a moment.' I reached for the pad and pen on my bedside cabinet, then wrote the postcode he gave me. 'Thank you. I'll be there as soon as I can.'

As I got out of bed I felt sick and dizzy, I assumed from worry and lack of sleep. I took a deep breath and began to dress. Had Stevie really got lost as he'd told the police? I doubted it. But where had he been going on the train without a ticket? I couldn't begin to imagine. It was 4.20 a.m. as I went quietly downstairs. In the kitchen Sammy looked at me from his bed but sensibly stayed put. I poured a glass of water, drank half of it, and with the queasiness subsiding I sent a group text on WhatsApp to Adrian, Lucy and Paula: *Stevie's been found. Going to collect him in the car. Should be back by midday xxx*. They would read the message when they checked their phones in the morning.

I finished the glass of water and then slipped on my shoes and jacket and quietly left the house. It was 4.30 a.m. and in May the sky was already growing light and birdsong could be heard coming from the trees and shrubbery. In my car I switched on the satnav and entered the postcode of the police station. The route showed it was mainly motorway and I started the engine, hoping I wouldn't wake my family or the neighbours. Tiredness had left me now and adrenaline had kicked in. I was greatly relieved that Stevie had been found safe and well; I wasn't angry with him, but I was very concerned. I wouldn't tell him off; however, I would make sure he understood the worry he'd caused all of us, including his grandparents, who would have been informed he was missing again and had possibly been visited by the police. Also, and importantly, I needed to try to find out why Stevie had been on that train to stop it happening again. The officer hadn't said Stevie was drunk or under the influence of drugs, so I assumed he wasn't, but Stevie was in enough trouble without all this. It was set to get much worse.

The traffic was light at this time on a Saturday morning, and with no hold-ups I arrived outside the police station at 6.45 a.m. It was a modern two-storey building with a flat roof and lots of tinted glass windows. I went up the steps and pressed the buzzer as the CCTV overhead watched. The doors released and I stepped into the waiting area where a woman I guessed to be in her early twenties was sitting on one of the chairs, texting. She glanced up as I came in and then returned to her phone. Dressed up for a night out, she looked worse for wear with a shoe missing, dishevelled hair and smudged black mascara around her eyes.

I crossed to the officer at the desk. 'Good morning,' she said brightly.

I felt like replying, 'Is it?' But I managed a weak smile. 'Cathy Glass. I've come to collect Stevie Jones. The duty sergeant telephoned a couple of hours ago.'

'Yes, that would be my colleague,' she said, tapping the keyboard and checking the screen. 'You're his foster carer?'

'Yes.'

'Take a seat and I'll have someone fetch him.'

As I sat down opposite the woman her phone rang with a loud rap ringtone. 'Where were you?' she demanded as she answered. 'I've been here ages.' She fell silent as the caller spoke, then she said, 'No, of course I can't come on the bus, Mum, get real. I've lost me shoe.' Another pause, then, 'I haven't got any money for a cab,' she snapped rudely. She listened again and said, 'OK,' and cut the call. I then heard her ordering a cab, so I guessed her mum was picking up the bill.

Stevie appeared with a police officer, still in his school uniform and with his school bag over his shoulder. He looked pale and tired and there was a haunted look in his eyes. I went to them. 'Are you OK?' I asked, touching his arm. He managed a small nod.

'Cathy Glass?' the officer asked me.

'Yes.'

'Stevie is free to go now. The railway company will write in respect of him travelling without a valid ticket.'

Naively I asked, 'Can we pay the fare and any fine now?'

'No. We don't deal with it,' she said. 'It's a matter for the railway company. And I should warn you that this railway company have a policy of prosecuting fare evaders.'

'Prosecuting!' I said, horrified. 'For not having a ticket?'
'I'm afraid so.' She nodded solemnly. 'It's theft.'

CHAPTER TWENTY-FOUR

LOST

'Whatever were you doing on that train without a ticket?' I asked Stevie once we were outside the police station, unable to hide my annoyance.

He shrugged. 'Don't know.'

I opened the car doors and we got in. I looked at him sitting in the passenger seat. He turned on his phone.

'Stevie, I'm talking to you,' I said.

'I know,' he replied moodily.

'Well, can you please answer me? I've been up all night worried sick. Then I have to drive over a hundred miles to collect you from a police station to be told you are likely to be prosecuted for fare evasion. Whatever made you do that?'

'If you have a go at me, I'm off and this time for good,' he threatened. He put his hand on the door as if about to get out.

'OK, calm down. I'm worried that's all. Fasten your seat-belt and we'll go home.' I started the engine, pressed *Home* on the satnav and pulled away. After a few minutes I said evenly, 'Stevie, we need to find a way for you to deal with your feel-ings so you don't have to run away.'

He shrugged and looked at his phone. As I drove all I could think about was that Stevie could be facing an additional prosecution – for not having a ticket. It would be another blot on his character, and one that could so easily have been avoided. Whatever had made him risk travelling on a train without a ticket? Where had he been going? Neither of us spoke for about ten minutes as I concentrated on driving and Stevie fiddled with his phone. Then, in an unthreatening manner, I asked, 'Stevie, why were you on that train?'

He shrugged.

'You must know, love. You're not daft.'

'I must be daft,' he snapped, 'getting into all this mess!'

'No, you're not, but we do need to talk about it. Where did you go after you left school yesterday? You couldn't have been on the train all that time.'

'I wandered around for a bit,' he said, his voice flat, and still looking at his phone.

'Have you been drinking?' I couldn't smell alcohol.

'No.'

'And you haven't taken any drugs?' Although Stevie had said he'd never take drugs because he'd seen what they'd done to his mother, he'd also said the same about alcohol, but had come home drunk.

'No.'

'So why did you get on that train?' I asked.

'Dunno.'

'Stevie, I'm trying to understand so I can help you, but you're not making it easy for me.'

'So don't try,' he said bad-temperedly.

I glanced at him; head down, he was looking at his phone, although he didn't appear to be doing anything with it – a distraction rather than talking to me. The police officer had said that the railway company would write, I assumed to

Stevie. Verity would need to know, and probably so too would his grandparents.

'Stevie, when the letter from the railway company arrives, make sure you show it to me. Don't just ignore it, tempting though that might be. It won't go away. We will need to deal with it.'

He didn't reply for some time, then suddenly said, 'I was lost. I didn't know where I was.'

'How did you get lost?' I asked.

There was another long pause, then he looked up and, staring straight ahead, began to tell me. 'I was really pissed off when I came out of school yesterday. It was Friday and I always used to play with Kiri and Liam on a Friday after school, and take them out over the weekend. It hurt, remembering. I wandered around the town, then caught a bus to the city train station. It was busy and I sat there watching people – some of them were families going away. The trains kept leaving and I thought how good it would be to just get on a train and keep going and never stop. Leave the mess I'd made of my life behind. It was easy getting on the train without a ticket, but then the inspector got on at one of the stations we stopped at and asked to see tickets, and of course I didn't have one.'

I nodded.

'I *was* lost, Cathy. I didn't know where I was and wanted to stay lost. Away from everything for ever.'

'I think I understand,' I said.

'The ticket inspector was really nasty. Everyone was looking. He took me off the train and because I refused to give him my name and address, he called the police. I gave them a name but not my real one.'

'Surely you must have known they'd check the details you gave them on their computer and see they were false?'

'I didn't really think about it. I knew I was in trouble, so giving them a false name delayed it.'

'Delayed me finding out?'

'Yes, and Gran and Grandpa, and everyone else I've let down. Kiri and Liam used to look up to me. What a shit brother I turned out to be!'

'Stevie, I'm sure they don't think like that,' I said gently.

'What else can they think? I'm the reason they're in care.'

I glanced at him. He looked close to tears. Despite everything I'd said, he was still blaming himself. I needed to stay constructive to try to help. 'Stevie, I know you've made some mistakes, but it's not all your fault and it's not the end of the world. This dark time will pass, I promise you. But there are some things we can do to help.'

'Like what?' he asked gloomily.

'Verity has talked to you about seeing a counsellor at CAMHS and I think that would be useful now. Also, I'm going to ask her if she can speak to the police to find out when their investigation will be complete. It's dreadful having it hanging over you all this time at your age.'

'I know,' he agreed. 'But supposing the police decide to prosecute me? I could be found guilty and go to prison.'

'That is the worst that could happen, but it's not inevitable. If the police do prosecute, you will have a good lawyer to speak up for you. And Stevie, whatever happens, I will still support you.'

'Thanks,' he said, his voice trembling.

When we were halfway home I stopped at a service station for something to eat and drink. Neither of us had eaten since yesterday and I needed a coffee to help me concentrate. Stevie said very little as we ate and he looked shattered. It was 8.30

a.m. as we finished our breakfasts and a WhatsApp message arrived on my phone from Paula, first awake. *Are you OK, Mum?*

I messaged back: *Yes. Stevie is with me. Stopped off for something to eat. Will be home in an hour or so. Love you xxx.*

Love you too xxx.

In the car again, Stevie soon fell asleep and I continued the journey with only my thoughts for company. They weren't good. I found myself thinking back to when Stevie had first arrived and had settled in so well. How long ago and far away that time seemed. Now we appeared be on a downward spiral, going from bad to worse. I had formed the impression in talking to Stevie that he felt he had nothing left to lose, which is a dangerous place to be. Having lost everything he valued and held dear, he had no reason to behave, conform, cooperate, do his school work, socialise or see a future. He'd be at the mercy of dark, impulsive and irrational behaviour. I'm a glass-half-full type of person, but I needed to know what we were facing so I could meet the challenge and help him. I thought that even if the worst-case scenario happened and Stevie was sent to a young offenders' institution, it wouldn't be forever. With support he would come through it, but we needed to know what we were dealing with. The uncertainty was crippling me, as I was sure it was him.

Stevie only woke when I drew up outside my house and cut the engine. It was 10 a.m. He yawned and stretched as he got out of the car. I let us in and he said he was going to bed and went straight upstairs to his room. Paula was up and dressed and eating toast in the living room. She was relieved to see me and wanted to know what had happened in the night. She was as surprised as I had been that the railway company prosecuted fare evaders rather than simply fining them. When Adrian and Lucy came downstairs, they too wanted to know what had been going on. 'You should have woken me,' Adrian said, 'rather than drive all that way by yourself.'

'I'm OK. At least Stevie is back safely.'

'But for how long?' Lucy sighed.

We talked for a while and then I made a coffee and phoned the social services to advise them that Stevie had been found and was now at home with me. The duty social worker took brief details of where and when, and I said the police had taken him off their missing persons' register. Once we'd finished, and while it was still fresh in my mind, I went into the front room and emailed Verity with an update so she would have it first thing on Monday morning. I included that Stevie was now willing to see a counsellor at CAMHS, and also asked her if she could find out from the police the outcome of their investigation as I felt Stevie's behaviour was in part due to all the uncertainty.

Stevie slept most of Saturday. I dozed on the sofa for about twenty minutes. Around five o'clock I heard him get up and shower, and he came down and joined Paula, Lucy and me for dinner. Adrian was having dinner with Kirsty. Stevie was quiet, sullen and withdrawn, despite the girls trying to include him in the conversation. Straight after dinner he returned to his room, and I checked on him periodically during the evening. He didn't want to talk or join us downstairs but said he was OK. I told him I'd emailed Verity and I hoped he would be able to see a therapist before too long. The last time I checked on him was around 9.30 when I went up to bed. He had his earbuds in and was listening to music and said he'd be getting into bed soon too. I'd left Paula and Lucy downstairs watching a film. Exhausted, I quickly fell into a deep sleep and didn't wake until just before eight the next morning.

I was the first one up, not unusual for a Sunday morning, so I went quietly downstairs and fed Sammy and made myself a coffee. About an hour later I heard Stevie moving around in his room and then he came down and had some breakfast. I asked him if he'd like to do something today, maybe go to the cinema, ice-skating or swimming at the leisure centre. I said I was sure that Lucy and Paula would join us. He said he wasn't in the mood and, having finished his breakfast, returned to his bedroom. Ten minutes later I heard him come downstairs again. I was in the kitchen and before I realised what he was doing he'd let himself out of the front door. I rushed out and onto the pavement in time to see him running up the street. I'd need my car to try to catch up with him and I returned indoors for my car keys. As I did my mobile sounded with a text message. I quickly checked it. It was from Stevie: *Don't try to find me, I need to be alone.* After everything I'd said about talking about his feelings rather than running away!

I took my car to the top of the road and into the high street, then drove around the area, but Stevie was nowhere to be seen, so I returned home. Given how low Stevie was feeling, I was even more worried now than when he'd previously run away. I tried his phone but it went through to voicemail, so I left a message asking him to call me so we could talk. I doubted he would. I then sat in the living room and phoned the social services and explained I needed to speak to the duty social worker as a matter of urgency. There'd been another change of shift and a woman social worker unfamiliar with Stevie's case was on duty and returned my call. I explained what had happened, and when I said I thought Stevie could harm himself, she told me to phone the police and report him missing straight away.

As I ended the call, Lucy, who'd been listening to music in her bedroom, came into the living room. 'Stevie's not in his room,' she said.

'I know. He's gone again.'

'Idiot!' she snapped.

'Lucy, that's not helping.'

She flounced off. I took a deep breath and phoned the police. By the time I'd finished reporting Stevie missing, Lucy had calmed down and returned to the living room to apologise. 'Sorry,' she said, kissing my cheek. 'Love you.'

'Love you too. I know this is worrying for us all, especially Stevie.'

Adrian and Paula appeared and offered to go out to look for him. 'We could try that park near his gran's again,' Paula suggested.

I looked at their worried faces and was deeply touched by their concern. Here were three young adults willing to give up their Sunday to search for someone they'd only known for five months and who was causing them so much anxiety and disruption. But that's the nature of fostering. Bonds quickly form between the foster family and the child and can remain in place for years, sometimes forever. 'That's kind of you,' I said, 'but it's your day off, and I've done all I can. The police will be looking for him. Do what you were planning to do.'

But, of course, with the worry of Stevie hanging over us, none of us could settle to much or enjoy what should have been a relaxing day. If it crossed my mind that Stevie was acting selfishly by causing us all this upset, I dismissed it. He was in a very dark place and I was sure in normal circumstances he wouldn't have knowingly upset us. His troubles had begun when his grandfather had refused to accept his gender identity and had gone on from there, with Stevie becoming increasingly lost as a person.

During the course of the morning I tried his mobile every hour or so, but it always went through to voicemail. I left two messages: 'Stevie, can you get in touch, please, to let me know you're OK?' And, 'Stevie, it's Cathy again. Please call or text.' He didn't.

Mid-afternoon, Mum phoned for a chat. I didn't tell her that Stevie was missing, nor about the trouble he was in. There was nothing she could do but worry. Thankfully she didn't ask specifically how he was, just, 'How are you all?' Which allowed me to say, 'We're fine, Mum. How are you?'

The afternoon ticked by. Outside the weather was sunny – a complete contrast to our feelings. Lucy and Paula decided to go for a walk, as they'd been in all day. I would have joined them, but I had to wait for the police. They finally arrived at 4 p.m. Just one female officer whom I hadn't met before. She knew Stevie was in care and that he had a history of running away. We sat in the living room as she took down some details, although I assumed she would have seen much of this on the police computer, including the ongoing investigation, and that Stevie had spent most of Friday night in a police station 100 miles away. She was with us for about an hour, during which time Paula and Lucy returned home and came to join us. The officer concluded her visit by searching the house. Lucy and Paula stayed in the living room, but Adrian was in his room, working on his laptop. She apologised for disturbing him. 'No worries,' he said amicably. 'We're used to it here.'

I smiled grimly. 'Some of the other young people we've fostered have gone missing,' I explained, although I'm not sure that made it sound any better.

We returned downstairs and the officer said goodbye to Lucy and Paula. I showed her to the door and she was just about to leave when her phone rang. She paused to answer it and I thought I heard the call operator say Stevie's name. She listened and then looked at me as she replied. 'Yes, I'm still with his foster carer.' I couldn't hear what the operator said, but the officer then said, 'OK, thanks, I will.' Ending the call, she said to me, 'Stevie is at his grandparents' house. Mr Jones has just phoned.'

'Thank you,' I said, utterly relieved.

'I suggest you call them to make arrangements to bring him back if this is where he's supposed to be.'

'Yes, I will,' I said. I thanked her again and she left.

I told Adrian, Lucy and Paula that Stevie had been found with his grandparents and they were obviously pleased. The atmosphere lifted, although they felt that he could have texted to say he was there, or at least that he was OK, to stop us all from worrying.

'I know,' I said, 'but Stevie isn't thinking straight at present. We have to make allowances for him.'

But I wondered how long he'd been at his grandparents' house and felt that Peggy or Fred could have phoned me to say he was safe and well. That Stevie was there at all seemed to suggest Fred had in part stopped blaming him for Liam and Kiri going into care. I wasn't wholly surprised he'd gone there. They were his family and they'd been close for many years, and he was in crisis. I supposed I could have phoned them to see if Stevie was there as I had before, but I'd assumed he wouldn't be or they'd have contacted me. Perhaps they were holding me responsible for the mess Stevie was in – and to be honest, I did feel responsible. Although I really didn't know what else I could be doing to help him.

It was therefore with some trepidation that I picked up the phone in the living room and called Mr and Mrs Jones. Fred answered with a very brusque 'Hello?'

'Fred, it's Cathy. The police tell me Stevie is with you. How is he?'

'He'll live,' he said curtly.

'Shall I come to collect him now?'

'No. Peggy is doing him some dinner. I'll drop him off later.'

'OK, thanks. Do you know roughly what time?'

'When I'm good and ready,' he said. 'Goodbye, Cathy.' He hung up.

Although I wouldn't take offence, again I could see how Fred's manner would have affected Stevie. Young people are often more sensitive to harsh words, as they haven't built up the protective armour that adults have. For Stevie to be on the receiving end of Fred's curt and abrasive comments would have undermined his confidence and feelings of self-worth. I half expected that by the time Fred returned Stevie they would have had another argument and Stevie would be in an even worse place. However, I was pleased to be proved wrong. When Stevie returned home shortly after 8 o'clock, he looked a lot less stressed and began by apologising. 'I'm sorry I cleared off like that. Grandpa said it was wrong of me. I won't do it again.'

CHAPTER TWENTY-FIVE

LIFE'S NOT WORTH LIVING

'Good, I'm pleased to hear that,' I said as Stevie came in. I closed the front door. 'Did Fred bring you home?' He was nowhere to be seen.

'Yes. He said to say good evening to you.'

I watched as Stevie slipped off his shoes and hung his jacket on the coat stand. 'Do you want anything to eat?'

'No, I've had dinner, but I'll get a drink of water.'

'Do you want to talk?'

'Not really. I've been talking to Gran. She said she'll phone you next week.' I nodded. 'I'm going to my room to do my homework,' he said. 'I've got school tomorrow.'

'All right. I'll be in the living room if you want me.'

He went into the kitchen and I heard him run the tap for a glass of water, then, as he passed the living room, he looked in and said, 'Thanks.'

'What for?'

'Everything. I'll try not to bolt again.'

'Good.' I smiled, and he managed a small smile in return.

I heard him go upstairs where he said a pleasant hello to Paula, who was just coming out of her room, before continuing to his room. Whatever had happened today – I assumed at his grandparents' – had clearly had a positive effect. I wouldn't press him to talk if he didn't want to. I'd learnt that with teenagers – my own and those I'd fostered – there's a time to talk and a time to stay quiet and let them have their space, just as there is with adults.

Stevie stayed in his room, I assumed doing his homework, for the next hour and then watched a film on his laptop, and the evening continued for us all as normal. No one stayed up late, as we all had to be up in the morning. Before I went to bed I wrote up my log notes and sent Verity another email, updating her on what had happened since the one I'd sent the day before. I slept reasonably well; so too did Stevie, and he took some waking in the morning.

There was the usual Monday-morning bustle to leave the house on time with everyone passing each other on the landing, stairs or in the hall and then calling goodbye as they left. I had a tidy-up after they'd gone and then sat at the computer in the front room, doing some admin work. An email arrived from Verity in response to mine saying she'd referred Stevie to CAMHS and would ask the police when their investigation was likely to be completed, although she felt they would contact her as soon as it was finished. She also said she'd spoken to Mr and Mrs Jones, but that was all. She didn't say what had passed between them, so I assumed it didn't affect my fostering of Stevie.

Stevie came home from school on time, ate with us and then did his homework. While he wasn't his old self, he was still significantly better than he had been recently, and I thought again that whatever had happened while he'd been at his grandparents' had done him some good. On Tuesday morning he went to school as usual and then texted in the afternoon to say he was going to see his grandparents straight after school and would have dinner there, and then come home. I didn't see a problem with that. Kiri and Liam weren't there and clearly Peggy and Fred were happy with Stevie going, so I texted back: *OK, thanks for telling me. Have a nice time.*

Stevie returned around 7.30 and I asked him how things were.

'It was very quiet without Kiri and Liam,' he said.

'I can imagine. How are your grandparents?'

'Not happy. Gran says she'll phone you.'

That was all he said, and again I didn't press him further. He went upstairs to his room to do his homework, and then later chatted to Lucy and Paula, mainly about popular bands and music.

I didn't hear anything further from Verity, but on Thursday afternoon Peggy telephoned.

'How are you?' I asked her straight away.

'Coping,' she sighed. 'Now we're doing something. Fred arranged for us to see a solicitor and we're fighting to get Liam and Kiri back. The solicitor is reviewing our case now and is very hopeful. He says taking Liam and Kiri into care was an overreaction by the social services, so we should be able to get them back soon.'

'That's sounds promising,' I said.

'Yes. We also discussed Stevie's problems with the police.'

'Good. How are Liam and Kiri?' I asked. 'I believe you see them Monday, Wednesday and Friday at the Family Centre.'

'The first time was dreadful. They were so upset – we all were – but now we only get upset when we have to say goodbye at the end of contact.'

'It's very difficult,' I agreed. 'Have you met their foster carers?'

'Oh yes, we see them at the start and end of contact and they tell me what Kiri and Liam have been doing. They're a nice couple and have helped to put our minds at rest. I know Kiri and Liam are being well looked after, although we obviously miss them dreadfully. But it's manageable now we know it won't be for long. We've told the children they'll be coming home soon.'

'Has Verity told you they'll be home soon?' I asked.

'No, but the solicitor is optimistic.'

My heart sank. It's very unwise to tell children in care that they will be going home until it is 100 per cent certain and a date has been set. It could take many weeks, even months, for their solicitor to obtain records and review their case, and it wasn't his decision whether Kiri and Liam returned to their grandparents, but the social services', and ultimately the court's. At present Liam and Kiri were in care under a Section 20 – voluntarily – as was Stevie, so technically Peggy and Fred could remove them from care and take them home whenever they wanted to. However, that would be unwise because if the social services thought there were still safeguarding issues they would immediately apply for a court order – within hours – to keep them in care. If the order was granted, Peggy and Fred would lose their parental rights and it would need another, more lengthy court case in the future to have them returned. I assumed their solicitor had explained all this to them. Peggy and Fred had made a promise to their grandchildren they couldn't fulfil, and it was likely to make them very unsettled and anxious. But I didn't think it was for me to tell Peggy.

'Stevie seems to be coping better now he's seeing you both,' I said.

'Yes, he understands that Fred is on his side and no longer blames him for Liam and Kiri being taken into care. He also told Stevie he's put in a complaint to the police about the way they've handled the investigation and how long it's taking. Fred is fighting on all fronts! I've never seen him so animated.' She gave a small laugh.

'Good. Well, thanks for phoning and letting me know what's going on,' I said.

'You're welcome.'

Peggy said she'd phone again when she had any more news, which she hoped to do soon, and we said goodbye.

While all this was positive, I knew that if Kiri and Liam weren't returned home as Peggy and Fred were expecting, they were all – including Stevie – going to be bitterly disappointed and very likely angry. Stevie's behaviour would suffer and I was sure Kiri's and Liam's would too. But it was positive that Peggy and Fred were now able to support Stevie.

Stevie came home from school on time that afternoon and again on Friday, talked to us and did his homework. He spent most of Saturday on a sun lounger under the tree in the garden with his earbuds in listening to music, and then on Sunday he went to see his grandparents while the rest of us visited my mother. Outwardly, therefore, Stevie appeared far more relaxed and less anxious than he had done for some time, although I knew the matter of the police investigation and now the fare evasion must be playing on his mind, as it was on mine.

It was only ever going to be a matter of time before we heard from the railway company, and on Monday morning when the mail arrived there was an official-looking letter addressed to Stevie. Having seen his grandparents the day before, Stevie came straight home from school that afternoon and was in good spirits. I waited until he'd poured himself a glass of juice before I handed him the letter, which I'd kept with my mail on a countertop in the kitchen.

'What's this?' he asked, looking at it, puzzled.

'I think it's the letter from the railway company.'

'Oh,' he said. He was going to take it up to his room to read but I asked him to open it with me, so we could decide what needed to be done.

He set down his glass of juice and opened the letter. There were two sheets of closely printed paper. He began reading the top sheet and then sighed and passed it to me. 'You read it.'

The letter was on the railway company's headed paper; it appeared to be a standard letter but with Stevie's details inserted. It began with the date of the offence. I read it out loud.

'On 20 May you were spoken to by an authorised member of staff with regard to an incident of the non-payment of a rail fare. Before the company proceeds further with its investigations, we would like to give you the opportunity of responding with your explanation concerning it. Please complete the second page and return it to us immediately. Do not delay. This is a serious incident and failure to respond to this letter or provide a satisfactory explanation with regards to this incident will result in legal action being taken.

'I must inform you that should legal proceedings be invoked, in addition to any fines imposed by the court there will be an application for £150 as a contribution to our costs. Offences are recordable, and should you be convicted you will receive a criminal record.

'Criminal record', I read again, and, trying to hide my shock, I looked up. Stevie was watching me, waiting for my response. 'You need to fill in this form with your account of the events,' I said evenly, referring to the second page. 'But I want to speak to Verity first and let her see this letter. She

needs to know, and it's possible she may be able to add something to help.'

'Like what?' Stevie asked.

'That there were mitigating circumstances surrounding what you did. You had some problems and didn't intentionally get on the train without a ticket and set out to defraud the company, as they are suggesting here.'

'But I did,' he said. 'I knew I didn't have a ticket when I sneaked on.'

I looked at him, so honest and naïve. 'Yes, I know, Stevie, and you're not going to lie, but you told me the reason you did that was because you wanted to get lost. You were feeling low and confused. You wouldn't have done that if you'd been your normal self, would you?'

'No, I guess not,' he agreed.

'Perhaps Verity as your social worker can add something and say she has made a referral to CAMHS. I'm not saying it will have any effect on the outcome, but she needs to know anyway. Shall I phone her or do you want to?'

'You can,' he said gloomily and, taking his glass of juice, went up to his room.

I'd have done the same for my own children. I'm sure most parents and carers would. Stevie had made an error of judgement in getting on that train without a ticket, but he hadn't been himself, and to receive a criminal record for something so relatively minor seemed preposterous to me. Surely a hefty fine would have been more appropriate? It also seemed a massive waste of the court's time. If someone is repeatedly found travelling on a train without a ticket then it's probably apt to prosecute them, but surely not for a first-time offender?

I telephoned Verity straight away, but she wasn't at her desk. A colleague checked her diary and said she wouldn't be in the office again until the following afternoon, as she had a home visit to make in the morning. Thanking her, I decided to email Verity so that she would know about the letter from the railway company as soon as she logged on to her computer. I scanned the letter and attached it to the email, and suggested that a report from her might help Stevie's defence. I asked her if she wanted me to help Stevie complete his statement or if she did. Aware of how busy she was, I pointed out that the railway company had stated our response had to be made without delay. I sent the email, filed the letter in my fostering folder and then went upstairs to Stevie. He was lying on his bed, not doing much. I told him I'd emailed Verity, and that the letter from the railway company was in my folder for safe keeping, but he could have it if he wanted it.

'I don't,' he said grumpily.

I could tell from his expression and general demeanour that receiving this letter had set him back, although we'd been expecting it. 'Don't let it get you down, love,' I said. 'Verity and I will help you deal with it.'

He shrugged despondently.

I went over to him. 'Stevie, worse things than this happen in life. I know you've had a lot to cope with recently, but just learn from it.'

'I'll tell Grandpa,' he said, suddenly meeting my gaze. 'He'll go and see them and complain like he did to the police and social services.'

'Tell him by all means, but I don't think he will be able to do any more.'

'Yes, he will,' Stevie said confrontationally. 'You don't know. He'll see a solicitor.'

'OK, fine. I'll be downstairs making dinner if you need me.' I came out of his room.

I thought Stevie had an inflated view of what his grand-father was capable of, probably as a result of Fred expounding his achievements. I could picture Fred as he told Stevie and Peggy of his battle with the police and social services. Peggy regarded his authority with some reverence, just as Stevie was now doing. However, if this did go to court, having his grand-parents there supporting him would be positive for Stevie, providing Fred didn't try to tell the magistrates how to do their job! They would expect humbleness and remorse from the accused.

Stevie was quiet and sullen at the dinner table, and when Lucy asked him what the matter was, he replied, 'If you *must* know, that fucking railway company are going to prosecute me.'

'Sorry I asked,' Lucy said with attitude, while Adrian and Paula kept their heads down and concentrated on their food.

'Please don't swear, Stevie,' I said. 'We don't know for certain you will be prosecuted.'

'There's a bloody good chance!' he returned.

The rest of the meal continued in an uncomfortable silence, and as soon as Stevie had finished he pushed back his chair and went up to his room.

'He can be so rude sometimes,' Lucy said. 'He needs to grow up.'

'He's got a lot on his mind,' I replied, 'and we all have our moments.'

Stevie spent the rest of the evening in his room and I checked on him a few times. He was always propped on his bed with his laptop open, which he closed when I went in. I asked him if he wanted to talk, but he shook his head.

In the morning Stevie seemed a bit brighter. 'I'm going to Gran's straight after school,' he told me.

'Are you having dinner there?'

'Probably. I need to take the letter to show Grandpa so he can deal with it.'

I didn't want the original letter leaving the house in case it got lost, so I quickly went downstairs and into the front room where I photocopied it, and then gave the copy to Stevie.

'Have a good day,' I said as he left to go to school. 'See you around seven-thirty.' Which was the time he usually returned from his grandparents'.

That afternoon Verity replied to my email and said she would write a short report to accompany Stevie's statement for the railway company and asked me to send the letter to her, as she would take care of it. I put it in an envelope straight away and posted it that afternoon.

Adrian, Lucy, Paula and I had just sat down to dinner that evening when the doorbell rang. Not expecting Stevie until much later, I was surprised to see him standing there, his face set like thunder.

'He's a fucking wanker!' he said as he came in, and then stormed up to his room. At the same time the house phone rang. I answered it in the hall. 'Is Stevie with you?' Peggy asked anxiously.

'Yes, he's just this second arrived, and not in the best of moods by the look of it.'

'That's because Fred told him he was an idiot for getting on that train without a ticket.'

'Oh, I see.'

'He said he'd stuck up for him about the photos of Liam and Kiri, as he knew he hadn't meant any harm, but getting on a train without a ticket was plain stupidity and he could sort out his own mess.'

Clearly this wasn't the reaction Stevie had expected. 'OK, Peggy, thanks for letting me know. I've sent the letter from the railway company to Verity and she is going to deal with it, so don't worry. I'd better go and make sure Stevie is all right.'

'Thanks. He hasn't had any dinner either. Sorry.'

'Don't worry. I'll give him some. At least he came back and didn't go missing again.'

'I suppose that's something. Dear me, it's one upset after another. I'm at my wit's end.'

'I can imagine. Look after yourself.'

We said goodbye, and as I began upstairs Paula called from the kitchen-diner, 'Mum! Your dinner is getting cold!'

'Don't worry, I'll reheat it.'

I knocked on Stevie's bedroom door. 'Can I come in?'

There was no reply, so I knocked again and then eased open the door and went in. Stevie was sitting on the floor, his back against the wall and his head in his hands, crying. He looked up as I entered. 'Everyone hates me,' he said through his tears. 'My life isn't worth living.'

CHAPTER TWENTY-SIX

THE LETTER

I sat on the floor beside Stevie and held him as he cried his heart out. I felt so sorry for him. The railway company threatening to prosecute and his grandfather's rejection had been the final blow. When his tears began to subside, I passed him a tissue. As he dried his eyes I tried to reassure him and put what had happened in some perspective. I said we were all on his side, that Verity would write a report for the railway company and help him with his statement. I said his grandfather had reacted angrily because he was worried, but he loved him just the same. Stevie nodded, wiped away his tears, and did seem less distressed, but I wasn't sure how much I had truly helped him, for nothing had really changed. I hoped the referral to CAMHS came through quickly so he could talk to a trained therapist about his feelings at this difficult time. Half an hour later I had managed to persuade him to come downstairs for some dinner.

I reheated the two plates of casserole in the microwave while Stevie sat at the dining table. Adrian, Lucy and Paula had finished eating and had gone. I sat opposite Stevie. He didn't want to talk as we ate, and neither of us wanted pudding. He carried his plate and cutlery into the kitchen and then said he was going to his room to do his homework.

'All right, love, but don't sit alone and fret, please. Come and talk to me.' How many times had I said that? I thought.

Of course I checked on him every so often, and at various points during the evening Adrian, Lucy and Paula knocked on his door and spoke to him too. It wasn't just about letting Stevie know we were concerned for his well-being; I was also checking that he wasn't doing anything to harm himself. When I'd first started fostering, I'd looked after a teenage girl who'd sat in her bedroom and self-harmed. It was only after she'd gone out and I saw the blood that I realised to my horror what she'd been doing. I've never forgotten that experience and still blame myself for not realising sooner that she was self-harming.

The following day Stevie went to school but didn't return home. I called his mobile and left a message to phone or text me. He didn't. At six o'clock, when I knew his grandparents would have returned home from seeing Kiri and Liam at the Family Centre, I telephoned them. Peggy answered and I asked her if she'd heard from Stevie, as he hadn't returned home from school. She said she hadn't and wouldn't really expect Stevie to go there after the argument he'd had with Fred. I hadn't expected him to either, but I thought I should check. I asked her how Kiri and Liam were and then said goodbye and phoned the social services. The duty social worker told me to wait until 7.30, three hours after Stevie should have been home, to report him missing to the police.

I served dinner and another mealtime passed with the atmosphere heavy from Stevie's disappearance. At 7.30, following the duty social worker's instructions, I reported Stevie missing to the police. We all then spent yet another very unsettled evening, worried about Stevie and waiting for the police to arrive to search the house. Eventually at 10 o'clock, with no sign of the police or Stevie, Lucy said she was knackered and was going to bed and that the police had better not come into her room and wake her, which of course they would.

'I'm sorry,' I said.

'It's not your fault, Mum,' Adrian said.

'Stevie needs help,' Paula added.

'I know,' I agreed.

I sat in the living room with my mobile on the sofa beside me, staring unseeing at the television with the sound on low, tired and wretched and at a loss to know how I could help Stevie. At around 11.30 the doorbell rang. It was pitch dark outside and I went down the hall and peered through the security spyhole in the door. By the light of the porch I could see Stevie with two police officers, both of whom I recognised from before.

'Thank goodness you're safe,' I said to Stevie as I let them in.

'We've been here before,' one of the officers remarked.

'Yes,' I said wearily, and led the way into the living room, hoping their arrival hadn't woken Paula, Lucy or Adrian.

'I've had a good chat with Stevie in the car,' the female officer said as we sat down. 'He now appreciates he mustn't keep running away but needs to talk to his social worker.'

'Good,' I said, thinking, if only it was that simple! 'Where did you find him?' I glanced at Stevie, who couldn't meet my gaze.

'At the mill pond,' the male officer replied. I knew where he meant: it was a local beauty spot, but over two miles away, and not on a bus route.

'How did you get there?' I asked Stevie.

'Walked,' he said sullenly, without looking up.

'Why did you go there?' I asked.

'Because I wanted to. It's peaceful. My gran used to take us there when we were little.'

'But not late at night.'

'A local resident saw him and phoned the police,' the male officer said. 'He reported that a lad had been sitting by the pond all evening and he was concerned for his safety.'

'That was kind of him,' I replied. 'Have you had anything to eat and drink?' I now asked Stevie. He nodded.

'We'll send a report to the social services,' the male officer added and, satisfied, they stood to leave. They both said goodnight to Stevie and I saw them out as Stevie went up to his room.

Once the officers had gone I went up to make sure Stevie was all right and say goodnight.

'I don't want to talk about it,' he said moodily.

'No, OK. You know where I am if you need me.' I came out.

I made a mental note to ask Verity to speed up the referral to CAMHS and mark it as urgent. It worried me that Stevie had been by that mill pond all evening. It was deep, and some years ago a young man had taken his life there by drowning.

That night I lay awake for a long time thinking about Stevie and where this would all end. It seemed we kept taking one step forward and two back. Just as we emerged from one crisis, the next hit.

The following morning Stevie left for school at the usual time but didn't arrive. The school secretary telephoned at 9.30 to check if there was a reason for his absence and my heart fell. I told her there wasn't. I tried Stevie's mobile and it went through to voicemail. I left a message asking him to contact me to let me know he was safe. I telephoned Verity, who was at her desk, and brought her up to date. She said I should wait until 4.30 (the time Stevie should be home from school) before reporting him missing to the police. She was concerned for Stevie's safety and agreed he needed to see a therapist as a matter of urgency and said she'd contact CAMHS. She also said she'd try Stevie's mobile and leave a message on his voicemail.

Just when I thought things couldn't get any worse, mid-morning the mail arrived and included another official-looking letter for Stevie – not from the railway company this time; the envelope bore the stamp of the county police. I assumed this was notifying Stevie of the outcome of the police investigation into the offences of sexting and taking and distributing the indecent images of Liam and Kiri. But surely Verity would have been informed, and I'd just finished speaking to her. Wouldn't she have told me?

I held the envelope up to the window but couldn't read the print on the letter inside. I turned it over and thought about picking it open and resealing it, but it was stuck fast. I wondered if I should phone Verity, but what would I say? That a letter had arrived from the police and did she know what it contained? It sounded like a waste of her time, and I was sure she would have told me if she'd known. Unless this was unrelated and Stevie was in even more trouble with the police.

I couldn't settle to anything and over the course of the morning convinced myself that Stevie was indeed in more trouble. He was missing and the unopened letter on the kitchen worktop loomed at me. Around 12.30 I got in my car and drove to the mill pond to see if he was there. He wasn't, just a retired couple sitting on a bench and watching the baby ducklings. It was a lovely, tranquil spot, with waterlilies and the scent of flower blossom during the day, but at night I could imagine the deep water became dark and menacing. I returned to my car and drove to the park near his grandparents' house, where Stevie had been before when he'd gone missing. It was largely empty now during the school day, with just a few dog walkers. I walked around the perimeter, checked the children's play area, the pavilion, bandstand, benches and tennis courts, just as Paula and I had done, but there was no sign of Stevie. Increasingly anxious for his safety, I returned to my car and drove home.

An hour later the landline rang and I answered it in the kitchen where I was staring through the window, wondering where Stevie could be. 'Cathy, it's Verity. Is Stevie back yet?' she asked.

'No, and he hasn't been in touch. But a letter from the police has arrived for him today.'

'It'll be the outcome of the police investigation. I've just opened one too.'

My heart began to race and my mouth went dry. I leant against the work cabinet for support, dreading what was to come next.

'I've left a voicemail message for Stevie, two actually,' Verity continued, 'but I thought you'd want to know. The police have accepted Stevie's version of events and won't be prosecuting him on either the sexting charge or that of taking and sending indecent images.'

'Thank goodness,' I breathed. I could hardly believe it. Relief flooded through me.

'Yes, it is a relief,' Verity said. 'Although I've left Stevie a message, I will need to speak to him. On another matter, I've written to CAMHS, and I'll write to the railway company once I've seen Stevie.'

'Thank you so much. I'll tell him.'

'Hopefully he'll be able to settle down now and get on with his life.'

'Yes, I hope so. Do Peggy and Fred know?'

'Yes, I've just spoken to them. I'm in a meeting soon, so I'll phone or email you with a date and time when I'll visit Stevie.'

I was trembling with relief as I returned the phone to its base, and said a silent prayer of thanks. Although Stevie had done wrong in taking and sending those photos, I knew there'd been no evil intent on his part and he wouldn't do it again. It appeared that the police thought so too. Verity had said she'd left Stevie a voicemail message telling him, but I wanted to make sure he understood. I called his mobile and it went through to voicemail. 'Stevie, it's Cathy. The police are not going to prosecute you for taking the photos of Liam and Kiri, nor for the sexting. Come home. I know you weren't in school today, but you're not in any trouble.'

I'd just put the phone down when it rang again and I snatched it up. 'Peggy here,' she said, her voice brighter than I'd heard it in a long while. 'Has Verity told you the good news?'

'Yes, just now. I am so relieved.'

'So are we. Does Stevie know yet?'

'I'm not sure. He hasn't come back yet. Verity and I have both left him messages on his voicemail, but I don't know if he's listened to them.'

'I've left a message too,' Peggy said, clearly elated. 'As you can imagine, Fred is cock-a-hoop. He said we'd still be waiting on the police if he hadn't made a fuss and complained.'

What effect Fred's intervention had had in speeding up the police investigation wouldn't be known, and it didn't matter. The main thing was that Stevie was not facing serious charges in court with the possibility of a custodial sentence. It was the right decision.

'Fred has told Verity we'll be collecting Liam and Kiri from school and bringing them home this afternoon,' Peggy continued. 'She wanted us to wait until she or the foster carers had spoken to the children and prepared them for returning home. Fred told her bollocks, they were our kids and didn't need preparing, and they should never have left home in the first place. The carer is going to pack their belongings and drop them off later, but we're having our kids home as soon as school finishes.'

'I am pleased.'

Although it was advisable, as Verity had said, for Liam and Kiri to be prepared for the move rather than Fred and Peggy suddenly arriving at school, I fully appreciated they wanted them home as quickly as possible. To be honest, had they been my children, I think I would have done the same.

'Verity is going to tell the school we will be collecting them,' Peggy added. 'Their teacher will tell Liam and Kiri.'

'Good.'

'But what isn't so good,' Peggy continued, 'is that Verity has told us if Stevie visits us he shouldn't be left alone with Kiri and Liam. That although he won't be prosecuted, there are still safeguarding issues because he took the indecent images. He's never denied that.'

'I can see why she said that,' I said.

'Fred couldn't. I won't tell you his exact words, it would turn the air blue. But I agree with him that Stevie isn't a threat to them or any other children, and never has been. He knew what he was doing was wrong at the time but was blackmailed into doing what he did by that Joey. I told Stevie in my voicemail message that we're looking forward to having him home again as soon as possible. Must fly now, we're leaving soon to collect Liam and Kiri from school.'

'Have a good evening.'

'We shall!'

I put the phone down, happy but wondering about what Peggy had just told me. Verity hadn't said anything to me about Stevie returning to live with his grandparents. I assumed that, if he did, it would be when she was satisfied there were no further safeguarding issues, and that it would be a planned move, so I would be told in advance. Also, I had concerns that it might not be in Stevie's best interests at present. One of the main issues that had brought Stevie into care in the first place had been Fred's inability to accept Stevie's gender identity. As far as I knew, Fred hadn't changed his views on that. However, I didn't let that dampen my spirits. I was looking forward to seeing Stevie and sharing in his good news.

It was half an hour before the doorbell rang and I rushed to answer it. It was Stevie, but, far from looking happy, he appeared very sullen.

'Are you all right?' I asked, wondering if he was ill.

'Sorry I haven't been to school,' he said gloomily as he came in.

'OK, but have you listened to your voicemail messages?'

'Yes.' He began taking off his shoes.

'Aren't you pleased? The police won't be prosecuting you.'

'I know, but do I have to live with my grandparents again?'

I looked at him. 'Not if you don't want to. At your age you will be asked your view on where you want to live.'

'I feel bad,' he said, taking off his second shoe. 'Gran phoned all excited and is looking forward to me going home. But I really can't live with my grandfather. It would do my head in. Can I stay here?'

'Yes, although you'll need to discuss it with Verity. But please cheer up, Stevie. We can sort that out. You don't have to worry about the police investigation any more. There's a letter for you.'

He followed me into the kitchen, where he opened the letter and we read it together. It was formal and cloaked in legal jargon, but the message was clear. The police wouldn't be prosecuting him.

'There is still the chance the railway company will prosecute me,' he said.

'I know, and Verity is going to talk to you about that. But it's minor compared to this. You could have been facing very serious charges.'

'I know, I can't believe it's over.'

'Well, it is, so stop worrying, and no more going missing.'

Finally, he smiled.

As Paula, Lucy and Adrian came home Stevie told each of them in turn his good news and they of course were delighted. The girls gave him a hug.

'I'm pleased for you,' Paula said.

'Learn from my mistakes,' Stevie said to both of them.

Paula smiled, while Lucy retorted, 'No need, Stevie. I wouldn't have been so stupid in the first place.' Stevie didn't take offence. He was used to Lucy and knew she could be outspoken. I think he respected her for that, and that she'd overcome a very unsettled and unhappy early life to do well.

* * *

I made dinner and called everyone to the table. Adrian, always hungry, came first. Paula and Lucy followed, but Stevie didn't appear and remained in his bedroom. I served dinner and then called to him again from the foot of the stairs. 'Stevie! Your dinner is ready.'

'I'm coming,' he replied.

I joined the others at the table and we began to eat. 'What's he doing up there?' I grumbled as Stevie still failed to appear. 'His dinner is getting cold.' Then I heard his bedroom door open and his footsteps on the stairs. 'At last.'

I had my back to the door so didn't immediately see Stevie when he came in. Adrian, Lucy and Paula did, and suddenly they'd all stopped eating and were smiling at him. I turned to look. Stevie had staged his entrance and was looking good. He'd styled his hair, applied a little make-up and was dressed beautifully in deep-pink trousers and a light-pink shirt. I smiled too. 'Look at you,' I said. The old Stevie – the one we'd first welcomed into our home – was back. Thank goodness.

He didn't immediately take his place at the table but instead stood at the end where he could see us all. 'I'd like to say something,' he said. We were all looking at him. 'Thank you – Cathy, Paula, Lucy and Adrian – for standing by me and seeing me through this shit. I know my behaviour has caused you all a lot of worry and I acted selfishly. I'm sorry. I hope you can forgive me. I really appreciate you guys being there for me. Not many would have done what you did, so thank you. I'll never forget what you did for me. My life is worth living again, thanks to you all.'

His eyes glistened, and he wasn't the only one who was moved. I swallowed hard and the girls were looking emotional too. Adrian nodded and said, 'You're welcome.'

Stevie smiled and then went to each of us in turn and kissed our cheeks, even Adrian. His face was a picture!

'Good to have you back, Stevie,' I said as he finally sat down.

'It's good to be back. Thanks.' And he blew me an extra kiss.

CHAPTER TWENTY-SEVEN

MOVING ON

Life with Stevie finally settled down. He saw Liam and Kiri the following evening after school at his grandparents' house and stayed for dinner. Thereafter, he got into the routine of visiting his grandparents twice a week after school, when he'd stay for the evening and return to us by bus at around 7.30. He also began going there either on Saturday or Sunday. I always asked him if he'd had a nice time, but I didn't enquire closely if his grandparents had been present the whole time he'd been with Kiri and Liam. To be honest, I didn't want to know. If they hadn't, then I would have been duty bound to inform Verity. I knew Stevie well enough to feel confident he didn't pose a threat to his siblings or any other children. Had I had any doubts, I would have told Verity. Also, I thought that if she had serious concerns for the children's safety, they would have stayed in care and not been allowed home. By asking Peggy and Fred to be present, she was sending them a message to be more vigilant in the future. Had they been more vigilant in the past, it's unlikely Stevie would have taken the indecent photographs in the first place. Sometimes, when Stevie returned from his grandparents' house, he had a grumble about Fred, but generally he seemed more tolerant and forgiving of his grandfather. I think he now appreciated that he loved him and had stood up for him in the matter of the police investigation. And perhaps Fred had mellowed and was more tolerant, I didn't know.

Verity visited Stevie at my house and, among other things, helped him write his statement for the railway company, which she said she would send off with her report. She agreed with Stevie that it was better if he remained with me, at least for now. She told him he could stay until he was eighteen, when he would be found semi-independent accommodation. The referral to CAMHS came through and Stevie began seeing a therapist after school for an hour once a week. When he returned, I never pried into what had taken place. Those sessions were private and between him and his therapist. He knew he could tell me if he wanted to. I asked him once if he was finding the sessions useful and he shrugged and said, 'I guess.'

One Saturday evening towards the end of June Stevie telephoned from his grandparents' and said he wanted to stay the night. I said I didn't see why not, but I thought we should clear it with Verity first and suggested making it the following weekend instead. 'Grandpa says he wants to talk to you,' Stevie said, and passed the phone to Fred.

'Good evening, Cathy. How are you all?' Fred said, clearly in good spirits.

'Very well, thank you, and you?'

'Well. There's no need for you to worry about Verity. I will tell her on Monday. Stevie would like to spend the weekend here, so that is what will happen. He will return to you on Sunday evening.'

'OK,' I said. 'Thank you for telling me. Have a nice weekend.'

I made a note of the arrangements in my log and emailed

them to Verity. The following week Verity emailed a reply to say she had spoken to Mr and Mrs Jones and approved the new arrangements for contact. After that, Stevie began staying at his grandparents' house every weekend, going on Saturday morning and arriving home Sunday evening. With Stevie spending so long with Fred, I was half expecting it to go pear-shaped and for the two of them to clash and have an argument. Stevie was becoming more and more confident in expressing his gender identity. He was in school uniform when he visited his grandparents during the week, but at the weekends he dressed up. He wore eye-catching clothes, make-up, jewellery and nail varnish. He had grown his hair longer and, while he wore it unobtrusively tucked behind his ears for school, at the weekend he curled and styled it – sometimes with Lucy's help. I wondered how Fred was coping with all of this.

Now Stevie's behaviour had settled down and he could be trusted, I gave him a front-door key so he could let himself in like the rest of us. One Sunday evening I was sitting in the living room, reading, when I heard him return. 'Hi, Stevie!' I called. 'I'm in here!'

He came into the living room, smiling.

'You look very pleased with yourself,' I said. He sat in one of the armchairs.

'You're not going to believe this, but Grandpa has bought himself a laptop! I've spent most of the weekend showing him how to work it. He's like a kid with a new toy.'

'Well done, Fred,' I said.

'He told me that what happened to me online had taught him a lesson. It had made him realise he needed to learn to use a computer and go online, so he could keep an eye on Liam and Kiri, and stop them getting into trouble.'

'Very sensible,' I said. 'So you two are getting along much better?'

Stevie nodded. 'I showed him some of the websites for people like me that offer advice and support for friends and relatives, and he was interested. But what has really helped is that a guy he knows at the pub he goes to told him his son has come out as gay. Grandpa said it made him see that worse things can happen.' Stevie smiled. 'He said now he knew someone with a queer son, he didn't feel so bad.'

I smiled too. 'That sounds like Fred.'

In July the schools broke up for the long summer holiday and Stevie began spending more time at his grandparents', sometimes staying there for three days at a time, returning to us for one night, then going again. As a foster carer I was starting to feel redundant and that my work with Stevie was largely done, although of course he could have his home with us for as long as he and the social services wanted. But I knew this situation wouldn't be allowed to continue indefinitely. There is always a shortage of foster carers and now I had an empty bedroom for most of the week. Also, Fred was upping the pressure on the social services to have Stevie home again.

Towards the end of August, Edith arranged to see me for one of her supervisory visits, and, once settled in the living room, she got straight to the point.

'Verity has met with Stevie and Mr and Mrs Jones with a view to him returning to live with them permanently.'

It wasn't a great shock, it had crossed my mind, but I knew there'd be a number of issues to deal with first. It seemed they'd done that now. One of them was that Stevie had previously shared a bedroom with Liam before coming into care and had complained about a lack of privacy, and he hadn't had anywhere quiet to do his homework. I now learnt that some time ago Mr and Mrs Jones had converted their garage into a small bedsit for their adult daughter, but it hadn't been used for many years, except for storage. Fred and Stevie had been clearing it out and it had become Stevie's room. Another, more pressing issue was that of Stevie's gender identity, and Verity had made it a condition of Stevie returning home that Mr and Mrs Jones would support him in the referral to the gender-identity clinic – Stevie was still waiting for a first appointment. In addition, Verity had told them that Stevie should continue to see the therapist at CAMHS once a week for as long as it was needed.

'Verity wants Stevie to move next week, so he will have time to settle in before the start of the new school term in September,' Edith said.

'Oh, as soon as that,' I said, and immediately teared up. Although I'd been half expecting this to happen, it's never easy when a child or young person you've looked after and cared for, and who's been part of your family, leaves. The loss is like a small bereavement. Despite, or maybe because of, all the worry he'd caused me, I felt very close to Stevie; we'd been through so much together. His journey had become my journey too, as it had Paula, Adrian and Lucy's.

I put the date of his move in my diary and Edith completed the rest of her supervisory visit. I told Adrian, Lucy and Paula that Stevie was going over for dinner that evening. Stevie was with his grandparents again for the night.

'I hope it works out for him,' Adrian said.

I nodded. 'So do I.'

'He should be with his family if he can,' Lucy said.

'Is his mother still in prison?' Paula asked.

'As far as I know,' I replied.

Our mood was sombre and bittersweet. It was good for Stevie that he was able to go home, although of course in so doing he was leaving our home, and we'd be a family member short.

When Stevie returned to us the next day, I could tell he was finding it difficult now we all knew he was leaving. He was in transition, with a foot in each house, and was feeling disloyal to me. 'You do understand why I have to go?' he asked for the second time.

'Yes, of course, love. That's your home. My job is done. We'll miss you, but I'm sure you'll stay in touch.'

He gave me another big hug. 'My new room is great,' he said, brightening. 'Do you want to see some photos?'

'Yes, please.'

He took his phone from his pocket and showed me photographs of the garage conversion. The bedsit was comfortable, with magnolia-painted walls and a deep-blue carpet. There was a single bed, wardrobe, chair and television, and a kettle stood on a small cabinet at one end. At the other end, in a specially built cubicle, was a toilet, shower and washbasin.

'I can't cook in my room, so I'll be having my meals with everyone else,' he explained.

'It looks fantastic,' I said. 'But why didn't your grand-parents think of you using the room when you lived there before?'

'It was full of Mum's stuff. They were keeping it for her in case she came back, but that won't happen now.'

The weekend before Stevie was due to move, he asked if he could phone my mother to say goodbye, for he was unlikely to see her again.

'Yes, of course, love. Let me speak to her first,' I said.

We went into the living room, where I used the landline to phone Mum. She already knew Stevie was leaving and I now said he wanted to say goodbye, and then passed the phone to him.

'You've been really nice to me,' Stevie said. 'Thank you for helping to make my stay here a good one, and for accepting me for who I am. You made me feel like one of your family. I'll miss you.'

I couldn't hear Mum's reply, but when Stevie passed the phone back to me she was clearly moved. Over the years, she'd said goodbye to many children I'd fostered, but it's not something you ever get used to. Goodbyes are important, difficult though they may be, as they offer some closure and allow everyone to move on with their lives.

'He's a good lad,' Mum said, her voice unsteady. 'I'm sure he'll do well. You'll miss him.'

'Yes, we all will.'

I told Stevie I'd like him to spend the evening before he moved with us, and we ordered his favourite takeaway. Once we'd eaten, we gave him a leaving card signed by us all and a present. It was a silver bracelet similar to the necklace his grandmother had given him on his thirteenth birthday. It was the right gift. Stevie was delighted and immediately put it on. The delicate silver links looked good on his slender wrist and sparkled in the light as he turned it. He thanked us all again for looking after him and I felt a lump rise in my throat.

The following morning Lucy and Adrian said an emotional goodbye before they left for work and, after breakfast, Paula – on college holiday – helped Stevie and me load the car with his belongings. His grandparents were expecting us around eleven o'clock. Paula wasn't coming, as she was meeting a friend for lunch. I checked that Stevie's room was clear and went downstairs, where Stevie was stroking Sammy, who'd come to see what was going on. He then hugged Paula goodbye.

'Don't forget to message me,' he said.

'I won't.'

They gave each other another hug and I could see Stevie was reluctant to leave, and I had welled up again, so I ushered him outside and into the car. Paula stood in the porch and waved him off.

'I'm going to miss you guys,' he said, his voice breaking.

'We'll miss you too, but you'll be OK. And you know where we are if you want to visit.'

He nodded and wiped his eyes.

He was quiet as I drove and just gazed straight ahead. I was quiet too, and thought back over the time Stevie had spent with us. As we neared his grandparents' house he perked up. 'I could make you a cup of tea in my room,' he said.

'Sounds good to me.' I glanced at him and smiled. 'I'm pleased you came to stay with us, Stevie.'

'Thanks, so am I.'

As soon as we drew up outside his house, the front door burst open and Liam and Kiri rushed out, followed more slowly by Peggy and Fred.

'Stevie's home!' the children shouted as we got out. 'Stevie's home for good!'

I'd never met Liam and Kiri before, but they were cute kids with mischievous smiles. 'Is this the woman who looked after you?' Liam asked Stevie.

'Yes, this is Cathy.'

'Hi,' I said, smiling at them both. 'I can see you're pleased to have your brother back.'

'Don't you want him any more then?' Kiri asked, and we all laughed.

Everyone helped unload the car and we carried Stevie's bags straight into his room, which I admired. Stevie was then so busy trying to contain Kiri and Liam, who were eager to help him unpack, that he forgot about the cup of tea. I decided it was best to leave them to it and not prolong the goodbye.

'I'll be off then, Stevie,' I said, touching his arm to gain his attention. 'You take care.' He turned from the suitcase Kiri and Liam were unpacking and hugged me goodbye. I then said goodbye to everyone else.

'I'll see you out,' Fred said.

With a final goodbye, I went with Fred into the hall, where he gave me a box of chocolates. 'Thanks for all you did,' he said.

'You're welcome, and thanks for these. My favourites. I'm so pleased it's all worked out for you.'

'So am I,' he said, and opened the front door. 'Strange old world, isn't it? As they say, there's nowt so queer as folk.' He burst into laughter at his own joke.

'You can say that again, Fred,' I said with a smile, and went down the path to my car.

CHAPTER TWENTY-EIGHT

PROUD

We missed Stevie, of course we did, but that's the nature of fostering. Heart-breaking though it is, you welcome the child or young person into your home and hearts, do the best you can for them, and then say goodbye, hoping you've helped them to a better future. Stevie texted us all every day for the first week and then his messages tailed off, although he still kept in touch with the girls to chat about music and fashion. A new child arrived, or rather two, a few days after Stevie left, but that's another story.

In November, three months after Stevie had moved out, an official-looking letter arrived for him bearing the stamp of the railway company that had been pursuing him for non-payment of fare. When he'd left the matter had still been outstanding and I hadn't heard anything in the interim. It had obviously slipped everyone's minds to notify the company of Stevie's change of address. I hoped the letter contained good news – I thought it would – and that the company had decided there'd been mitigating circumstances when Stevie had got on the train without a ticket, wanting to get lost, and that they wouldn't take any further action. I readdressed the envelope straight away and reposted it. But two days later, to my horror, Stevie texted: *The railway company are prosecuting me. I've got to go to court.* :)

I couldn't believe it. What a waste of court time! I texted back: *Sorry to hear that. Let me know if there's anything I can do x.*

I was worried how this would affect Stevie and it played on my mind for the rest of the week. On Friday morning, once I knew Stevie, Liam and Kiri would be at school, I telephoned Stevie's grandparents. Peggy answered. She was pleased to hear from me but guessed why I was phoning. 'Did Stevie tell you about that bloody railway company, excuse my language?'

'Yes, he texted. I was horrified. How is he coping?'

'He was shocked when he opened the letter. We all were. To be honest, I'd forgotten about it, and Fred had assumed they weren't pursuing it. We've been to see the solicitor. You don't have to have a solicitor to represent you in the magistrates' court, but we thought it wise. It'll stop Fred giving his all to the magistrates, and the solicitor will speak for Stevie in court.'

'That sounds wise, but I'm so sorry you've had all this extra worry. Will you let me know the outcome?'

'Yes, of course. The hearing is in ten days' time. I've told Stevie not to worry, but of course we're all worried. If he's found guilty, he could have a criminal record just for not buying a ticket!'

'Yes, I know. It's appalling.'

Two weeks later Peggy phoned, relieved. On the advice of their solicitor Stevie had pleaded guilty, said how sorry he was that he'd forgotten to buy a ticket and promised never to do it again. He was fined but didn't have a criminal record, as the railway company and magistrates accepted there were extenuating circumstances. Peggy wasn't sure what exactly had taken place in court, as their solicitor had told them to wait outside and just he and Stevie had gone into court. I was relieved and pleased by the outcome, although Peggy, like me, wondered what all this had cost the railway company and taxpayer. Wouldn't it have made more sense to have issued a fine on the spot? It would certainly have saved a lot of time and worry.

I asked Peggy if she knew if 'Joey', or whatever his real name was, had been caught and she said she didn't think so, as they hadn't heard anything further from the police. We chatted for a while longer and then said goodbye. It would be up to her and Stevie to keep in touch now. Some families of the children I've fostered do keep in touch, while others want to forget that difficult time and don't.

Christmas came and went, and I was very busy with the two children I was fostering. In February, Stevie texted me saying he'd finally received the appointment at the gender-identity clinic. It was a year after he'd first been referred by Verity, but it was an NHS service, so free to the user. He said his gran was going with him. I messaged back saying I hoped the appointment went well. I knew that first appointment would be lengthy and involve discussion and assessment.

I didn't hear any more, but two months later, during the Easter holidays, while I was in town with the two young children I was fostering, I suddenly heard a cry of 'Cathy!' from across the road. I looked over and saw Stevie on the other side, waving at me. I waited for him to come over. He was as pleased to see me as I was him, and we hugged, then I introduced him to the children.

'You're looking very well,' I said to him. 'How are you doing?'

'Good. What do you think of the pink, then?' He had a bright-pink flash running through his hair.

'You certainly won't get lost in a crowd,' I joked.

He laughed. 'I had it done last week. Grandpa went spare.'

'I hope you're not trying to wind him up again,' I said.

'As if I would. No, I did it because I wanted to.'

'Very eye-catching.'

As flamboyant as ever, Stevie was dressed strikingly in turquoise trousers and jumper beneath a camel-coloured coat. Tasteful and stylish. I knew from when he'd lived with me that, as well as asking for clothes for his birthday and at Christmas, he eked out his allowance by shopping in second-hand shops, where he found great bargains. As we talked he asked after my mother, Adrian, Paula and Lucy.

'How did the appointment at the clinic go?' I eventually asked. 'I've been thinking about you since you texted saying you were going.'

'Good, but I've decided not to take the tablets to stop puberty. Having talked to the doctor and the therapist, I've come to see that there are masculine and feminine traits in us all. It's not like I want to be a girl all the time. I know some kids feel they've been born in the wrong body and they're so unhappy they have to change gender, but I don't. I feel comfortable as a boy or a girl – gender-fluid, that's me.'

'As long as you're happy,' I said.

'I am.'

He looked it. 'You've come a long way, Stevie.'

'Thanks to you. I was in a really bad way when I first arrived at your place. I had all that stuff going on with Joey. I didn't know who I was or what I wanted. And I had Grandpa going on at me. You and your family treated me with respect and gave me the space and confidence I needed to find myself and make proper friends.'

I was really touched that he still felt this way and, ridiculously, in the middle of the high street, I felt my eyes fill. He gave me another big hug. 'Softy,' he said.

'How is it going with your grandpa?' I asked.

Stevie rolled his eyes indulgently. 'You know Grandpa. I have to walk away sometimes so I don't say something I'll regret. Having my own room helps. I can go in there and be alone. But he's OK, and it can't have been easy for him and Gran.'

I smiled. 'His heart's in the right place.'

'Yes, that's what Gran says. Anyway, I'd better be going, I'm meeting up with some friends soon, but I saw you and wanted to say hi.'

'I'm glad you did. Take care, and give my love to your family.'

We hugged goodbye and I watched him go, a confident young person at peace with himself. My heart swelled with pride and I was really touched that Stevie felt I had helped him to become the person he was.

For the latest on Stevie and the other children in my books, please visit www.cathyglass.co.uk.

SUGGESTED TOPICS FOR
READING-GROUP DISCUSSION

At the start of the book Stevie's grandparents, Peggy and Fred, are struggling to understand Stevie's gender identity. What, if anything, could Stevie have done or not done to ease the tension?

At Stevie's first review Fred accuses Cathy of encouraging Stevie. What does he mean by this? Do you think Cathy's approach to looking after Stevie is correct? If not, what would you have done differently?

Cathy describes Stevie as vulnerable and an easy target for someone like Joey. What do you think she means? How was Stevie more vulnerable than the average fourteen-year-old?

Peggy feels she and Fred have been stricter with Stevie because of their experiences bringing up their daughter. How else might this have affected their parenting of Stevie?

What emotional damage might Liam and Kiri have suffered as a result of Stevie taking photographs of them naked?

What do you think parents, guardians and carers can do to keep children and young people safe online?

Despite Fred's abrasive manner, 'his heart's in the right place'. Discuss.

Fred comes to realise that he needs to be computer savvy and learn how to use the Internet in order to protect Kiri and Liam. How do you think he can achieve this?

What are your views on prosecuting first-time offenders for fare evasion?

Our society is having to change its attitude to gender. Discuss.

Cathy Glass

One remarkable woman, more than **150** foster children cared for.

Cathy Glass has been a foster carer for twenty-five years, during which time she has looked after more than 150 children, as well as raising three children of her own. She was awarded a degree in education and psychology as a mature student, and writes under a pseudonym. To find out more about Cathy and her story visit **www.cathyglass.co.uk**.

Where Has Mummy Gone?

When eight-year-old Melody is taken into care, she worries obsessively about how her mother will cope alone

It is only when Melody's mother vanishes that what has really been going on at home comes to light.

A Long Way from Home

Abandoned in a run-down orphanage, little Anna's future looks bleak – until Elaine and Ian adopt her

Anna's new parents love and cherish her, so why does she end up in foster care?

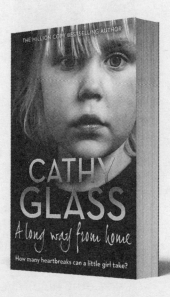

Cruel to be Kind

Max is shockingly overweight. Not only is his health suffering, but he struggles to make friends ...

With Max's mother and social worker opposing her at every turn, Cathy faces a challenge to help this unhappy boy.

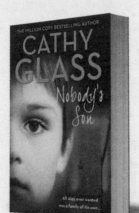

Nobody's Son

Born in prison and brought up in care, Alex has only ever known rejection

He is longing for a family of his own, but again the system fails him.

Can I Let You Go?

Faye is 24, pregnant and has learning difficulties as a result of her mother's alcoholism

Can Cathy help Faye learn enough to parent her child?

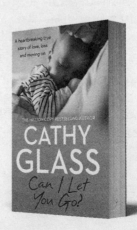

The Silent Cry

A mother battling depression. A family in denial

Cathy is desperate to help before something terrible happens.

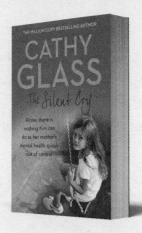

Girl Alone

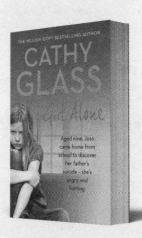

An angry, traumatized young girl on a path to self-destruction

Can Cathy discover the truth behind Joss's dangerous behaviour before it's too late?

Saving Danny

Danny's parents can no longer cope with his challenging behaviour

Calling on all her expertise, Cathy discovers a frightened little boy who just wants to be loved.

The Child Bride

A girl blamed and abused for dishonouring her community

Cathy discovers the devastating truth.

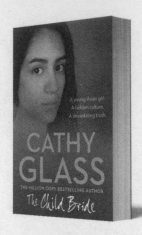

Daddy's Little Princess

A sweet-natured girl with a complicated past

Cathy picks up the pieces after events take a dramatic turn.

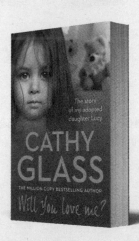

Will You Love Me?

A broken child desperate for a loving home

The true story of Cathy's adopted daughter Lucy.

Please Don't Take My Baby

Seventeen-year-old Jade is pregnant, homeless and alone

Cathy has room in her heart for two.

Another Forgotten Child

Eight-year-old Aimee was on the child-protection register at birth

Cathy is determined to give her the happy home she deserves.

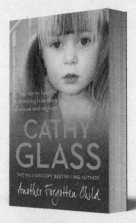

A Baby's Cry

A newborn, only hours old, taken into care

Cathy protects tiny Harrison from the potentially fatal secrets that surround his existence.

The Night the Angels Came

A little boy on the brink of bereavement

Cathy and her family make sure Michael is never alone.

Mummy Told Me Not to Tell

A troubled boy sworn to secrecy

After his dark past has been revealed, Cathy helps Reece to rebuild his life.

I Miss Mummy

Four-year-old Alice doesn't understand why she's in care

Cathy fights for her to have the happy home she deserves.

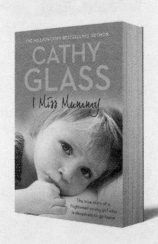

The Saddest Girl in the World

A haunted child who refuses to speak

Do Donna's scars run too deep for Cathy to help?

Cut

Dawn is desperate to be loved

Abused and abandoned, this vulnerable child pushes Cathy and her family to their limits.

Hidden

The boy with no past

Can Cathy help Tayo to feel like he belongs again?

Damaged

A forgotten child

Cathy is Jodie's last hope. For the first time, this abused young girl has found someone she can trust.

Inspired by Cathy's own experiences...

Run, Mummy, Run

The gripping story of a woman caught in a horrific cycle of abuse, and the desperate measures she must take to escape.

My Dad's a Policeman

The dramatic short story about a young boy's desperate bid to keep his family together.

The Girl in the Mirror

Trying to piece together her past, Mandy uncovers a dreadful family secret that has been blanked from her memory for years.

Sharing her expertise...

About Writing and How to Publish

A clear and concise, practical guide on writing and the best ways to get published.

Happy Mealtimes for Kids

A guide to healthy eating with simple recipes that children love.

Happy Adults

A practical guide to achieving lasting happiness, contentment and success. The essential manual for getting the best out of life.

Happy Kids

A clear and concise guide to raising confident, well-behaved and happy children.

THE DARKNESS WITHIN

You know your son
better than anyone.
Don't you?

Be amazed
Be moved
Be inspired

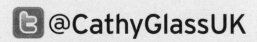

About Island Press

Island Press, a nonprofit organization, publishes, markets, and distributes the most advanced thinking on the conservation of our natural resources—books about soil, land, water, forests, wildlife, and hazardous and toxic wastes. These books are practical tools used by public officials, business and industry leaders, natural resource managers, and concerned citizens working to solve both local and global resource problems.

Founded in 1978, Island Press reorganized in 1984 to meet the increasing demand for substantive books on all resource-related issues. Island Press publishes and distributes under its own imprint and offers these services to other nonprofit organizations.

Support for Island Press is provided by Geraldine R. Dodge Foundation, The Energy Foundation, The Charles Engelhard Foundation, The Ford Foundation, Glen Eagles Foundation, The George Gund Foundation, William and Flora Hewlett Foundation, The Joyce Foundation, The John D. and Catherine T. MacArthur Foundation, The Andrew W. Mellon Foundation, The Joyce Mertz-Gilmore Foundation, The New-Land Foundation, The J. N. Pew, Jr. Charitable Trust, Alida Rockefeller, The Rockefeller Brothers Fund, The Rockefeller Foundation, The Florence and John Schumann Foundation, The Tides Foundation, and individual donors.

ENERGY *and the* Ecological Economics *of* Sustainability

E NERGY *and the* Ecological Economics *of* Sustainability

John Peet

ISLAND PRESS

Washington, D.C. ☐ *Covelo, California*

Library of Congress Cataloging-in-Publication Data

Peet, John.
    Energy and the ecological economics of sustainability / John Peet.
      p. cm.
    Includes bibliographical references and index.
    ISBN 1-55963-161-9 (cloth).—ISBN 1-55963-160-0 (paper)
    1. Environmental policy—Economic aspects.   2. Human ecology.
3. Thermodynamics.   4. Paradigms (Social sciences)   I. Title.
HC79.E5P42 1992
333.7—dc20   91-41207
                                                      CIP

Printed on recycled, acid-free paper

Manufactured in the United States of America

10 9 8 7 6 5 4 3 2 1

To my parents and your parents
To my children and your children
To their children, and their children's children

Contents

PART II: Limits: The Dark Side   97

PART III: Choices: Toward the World as It Could Be 177

Preface

Many people feel that humankind is on the verge of major changes; it seems to be the end of one age and the beginning of another. To many, it seems planet Earth and all living things on it are being treated by societies as if there were a new planet parked alongside, ready to step onto.

In order to look at ourselves and our planet more clearly, I believe it is important to learn to use some important, yet little-understood, tools of science to enable us to gain insight into the events that face us. These tools, especially the part energy plays in the world as seen through physics and ecology, enable us to look at what is happening from viewpoints very different from those that are normally available. What we *want* to do is always, and always will be, limited by what we *can* do. If we can be guided in our decisions by what we can do, we will choose those options that we think we can work toward, rather than always assuming that technology will come to the rescue.

In writing this book, I have attempted to clarify a number of policy issues that face us, as people and as societies, as we move toward the end of the twentieth century. To do so, I have set out my case in three main parts.

In part one, I describe some important tools that are available from physics and ecology. Most of them have been available for a long time—more than a century in some cases—but are still only dimly understood by most decision makers. The tools I describe lead us to a biophysical systems understanding, which explains some very important aspects of what is happening in the world. The understanding we gain from use of these tools differs markedly from an understanding built on scientific and economic understanding, which was part of the schooling of most of those currently in positions of power in government and commerce. In particular, the tools I describe help us understand that *the environment is the playing field on which all other social concerns compete.*

In part two, I turn to areas influenced by misconceptions and conflicts of opinion—for example, whether there are limits to the growth of an economy. The common view is that all things are possible, but in fact there are laws of nature, such as the second law of thermodynamics, that give us precise statements of processes that are absolutely impossible. Classical physics, even after Einstein, could conceive of a "supreme mathematician" who would possess the "super formula" to describe all of nature. Modern physics, on the other hand, suggests that in the long term, nature actually works via random, irreversible processes, not deterministic, reversible ones. Nature is generally not predictable, nor are the development paths of human societies.

In part three, I have attempted, so far as is possible, to reflect my feelings about answers to important questions gained from more than twenty years of working on energy, environmental, and related public policy matters in industry, at a university, and in citizens' groups. I am convinced that the problems that face us as we move through the closing decade of the twentieth century are not being adequately solved by methods derived either from political economics or from the natural and physical sciences, used alone. A new way of looking at the world—a new image—must be constructed, from tools that may be beaten out of the old tools but that have a shape and function quite unlike the old. I and others use the term "ecological economics" for the approach that we believe is needed.

We do have the choice to invent our own future, but if we do not take up that choice, the future will be shaped for us, with tools that were made in the past and that are largely irrelevant today.

The question "What sort of future do we want?" should be answered by everyone, but this will be possible only if people are empowered to do so, by having access to as comprehensive a picture as possible. We need the wisdom of everyone in society, especially people who have been alienated from normal decision-making processes by institutional structures that support the status quo and the powerful. We will not be able to use that wisdom unless we have a society in which experts accept that it is their function to assist people to gain the power to make their own decisions rather than to help the powerful make decisions for everyone else.

Why did I write this book? My aim was to promote the ideal of a just, peaceful, compassionate, and sustainable society that recognizes that there will be approximately 6 billion people in the world by the year 2000. The means was to describe perspectives and tools that might assist people to make choices consistent with the transition toward such a society, in preference to alternatives that promise destruction or degradation for humanity and for nature.

Acknowledgments

I have had an enormous amount of help from many people over the years, and I would like to thank them.

Five in particular have guided me through some of the mine fields. Over the years, I have met and learned directly from Herman Daly, Kenneth Denbigh, Howard Odum, and Malcolm Slesser. I have learned a great deal indirectly from the writings of Nicholas Georgescu-Roegen.

Of my friends and colleagues in Aotearoa–New Zealand, I must make special mention of James Baines, with whom I have worked for several years. Valuable contributions to my understanding have been made by Louis Arnoux, Geoff Bertram, Graeme Britton, Garth Cant, Paul Dalziel, Kelly Duncan, Brian Earl, Brian Easton, Murray Ellis, Bob Entwistle, Evelyn Entwistle, Jeanette Fitzsimons, Chris Harris, John Hayward, Charles Hendtlass, Molly Melhuish, Martin O'Connor, Gordon Rodley, Basil Sharp, Jim Stott, Cath Wallace, Arthur Williamson, and Janice Wright.

Friends in the international Balaton Group have also given me a great deal of help, and their insights have expanded my horizons considerably. Bert de Vries, Dennis Meadows, Donella Meadows, Richard England, Neva Goodwin, Thomas Johansson, Jane King, Ulrich Loening, Niels Meyer, Jorgen Norgard, Aromar Revi, Chirapol Sintunawa, John Sterman, and Qi Wenhu are members whom I would specifically mention as sources of material used in this book, but all have helped me enormously.

Support from the New Zealand Energy Research and Development Committee was valuable in giving me the resources to develop some of the data sources used as background. My friends in the Sustainable Energy Group, in Engineers for Social Responsibility, and in American Engineers for Social Responsibility also gave me valuable support when I needed it. The many

xviii   *Acknowledgments

students who carried out projects under my guidance often taught me more than I taught them, and I am very grateful to them.

students who carried out projects under my guidance often taught me more than I taught them, and I am very grateful to them.

If I have inadvertently reproduced too many of the views and/or expressive writings of these (and any other) good people, I apologize and hope they accept it as a compliment!

My partner, Katherine, and our children, Amanda, William, and Ben, have given me a great deal of encouragement, support, and love during a time when it often appeared that I was with them in body but not in spirit. Katherine's help in several areas, especially in chapter 17, has been of key importance.

Part I

NATURE

The World as We See It

1

Energy in Nature

THE WORD "ENERGY" is used widely, but often in ways that inadequately reflect its deeper scientific meaning. For the moment, let us regard it as a property of matter that enables us to describe why physical and chemical transformations occur. (I discuss its meaning in more detail in chapter 3.)

The word "nature" has a number of meanings, but most people see nature as that which is living: soil, plants, trees, animals, birds, fishes, and so on. In the Western tradition, the word's connotations derive from the idea that "man" is separate from the rest of the environment.[1] Nature is that which is alive, but not human, and of no "value" until man takes hold of its resources and transforms them into usable things. This ideology has been a powerful force behind the dominance of the Western tradition over the past few centuries. Most other cultures see humans as an integral, inseparable part of the natural environment.

In this book, I use "nature" to encompass everything in the environment of planet Earth, but with particular reference to the domain of living organisms in the sea, land, and air. In this perception, humankind is obviously *part of* nature, not *apart from* her.

EARTH AND SUN

The sun is the source of energy for almost everything that happens on earth. The nonrenewable stocks of fossil fuels, coal, oil, and gas in most economies come from the remains of plants and animals that lived millions of years ago, absorbing solar energy as they grew and reproduced. Renewable energy sources, such as water in mountain lakes and rivers, wind, and waves, result directly from the action of the sun on the earth's atmosphere.

To put the sun and the earth into their wider context—the physical universe—let us look briefly at current ideas of how they came into being.

HOW IT ALL BEGAN

Theories as to the origin of the universe—like many scientific theories—have gone through major changes over the past hundred years. The main impetus for the changes has been the realization that creation accounts, common to many cultural and religious traditions, need to be reinterpreted in the light of the scientific discoveries of this century. The reason why the biblical accounts of creation (Genesis 1 and 2, for example) have been reinterpreted is not that these ideas are wrong. Rather, they were written as part of a cultural-historical framework of belief, expressed in the language of imagery. They should not be seen as scientific explanations of a cosmic physical process. Thus, the truth of accounts of creation, from no matter which great religious tradition, should not be judged by the methodology of science; they are *myths* with spiritual and religious meaning. As such, they stand separate from scientific theories and should not be compared with them.

Currently, the most widely accepted scientific theory is that the physical universe originated in a cataclysmic event (the "big bang") some 10 to 20 billion years ago.[2] The primeval building blocks of all the matter-energy of the universe started off concentrated into an unbelievably small, super-hot "fireball." This then exploded, flinging its contents out into space.

In the sense in which the terms are used here, matter and energy are not really distinguishable from each other. This is why we use the term "matter-energy." Under the extreme conditions of a big bang, temperatures would be of the order of a million million degrees: so hot that even electrons, protons, and other elementary particles could not exist independently. Although that initial state lasted for only a small fraction of a second, these conditions indicate that in the beginning the universe could be regarded, in a sense, as pure energy, much of which subsequently changed into matter.[3]

Subsequent cooling then produced gases, which over billions of years aggregated into condensed masses and eventually formed the first stars. Many of these stars generated so much heat (from gravitational collapse and their own radioactivity) that they exploded again. This process may have occurred several times and may be going on today in some distant part of the universe. It is believed, for example, that our sun is probably a fourth-generation star.

The physical universe owes its nature and structure to that initial process. The theory tells us nothing, however, about what happened before the big bang. Indeed, the question of whether even time and space existed before that event cannot be answered unequivocally.

Stars are usually too hot for simple molecules to form in them—their high energy levels ensure that atoms that come together to form molecules are immediately flung apart again. Formation of a variety of stable molecules results from cooler conditions that may be found in regions some distance away from the stars. Our solar system was probably formed around 4.5 to 5 billion years ago from a huge cloud of interstellar dust that came together as a result of gravitational attraction. The earth is thought to have condensed out of a part of the cloud that contained a diversity of elements, especially those necessary for the development of life.

LIFE ON EARTH

It is not known how life began on earth. One hypothesis is that spontaneous generation of simple life forms occurred in a "primeval soup" of hydrogen, ammonia, methane, carbon dioxide, hydrogen sulfide, water vapor, and other simple gases formed from combinations of the lighter atoms. These could have been present soon after the earth cooled enough for them to be formed. Lightning discharges could have provided the energy needed to trigger chemical combinations, giving rise to elementary life forms.

Another hypothesis is that on the tiny dust grains in interstellar clouds, conditions may have been conducive to the formation of the building blocks of life. These grains, diffused over the universe and aggregated into meteorites and comets, may have served as "seeds" for the generation of life here. If correct, this theory also suggests that such a process may have occurred elsewhere in this galaxy and others.

Yet another hypothesis suggests that in some situations, there were minerals (probably clays) with complex surfaces to which simple molecules may have become attached. Under certain circumstances, the attached molecules could undergo reactions with adjacent ones to form larger, more complex molecules, which could have been precursors of the first simple organisms.

Whichever hypothesis eventually turns out to be correct, the important thing is that life has apparently existed on earth for several billion years and that over this time there has been a process of evolution, with more and more complex forms of life coming into existence.[4]

The initial life forms came into being around 3.5 billion years ago. They were probably one-celled bacteria existing in water, perhaps close to seashores. Single-celled algae came on the scene about 2 billion years ago. These organisms did not "breathe" oxygen, because free oxygen was not present in the atmosphere in those early days. However, they produced oxygen as a result of their activities, excreting it as a waste product into the water in which they lived. Over millions of years, oxygen built up in the seas and in the atmosphere until, about 1 to 2 billion years ago, it reached today's level of 21 percent, at which it has stayed reasonably constant.[5]

After the oxygen level settled down, evolution quickened. Simple cells gave rise to more complex cells and multicellular organisms. Sexual reproduction introduced a vastly greater range of genetic combinations, in turn increasing the likelihood of successful development of new organisms. In time, life forms came into existence that were able to feed off other life forms. Instead of having to make their nutrients from minerals and gases via the photosynthesis process driven by light energy, these more advanced forms could obtain them ready-formed into the amino acids, carbohydrates, and so on manufactured by simpler organisms. They then had a competitive edge and were able to develop faster as species.

Over time, more and more specialization occurred. Plants developed from simple organisms and in turn provided a food source for animals. About 450 million years ago, plants began to colonize the land. Animals followed them about 50 million years later.

The processes of evolution did not take place in a continuous manner. Evolution apparently occurred in jumps, with long periods of relative stability in between. Sudden transitions after long periods of stability may have occurred due to changes in the environment, perhaps from climatic factors (ice ages, for example), volcanic activity, or meteorite impact.

The awesome complexity of life on earth is the result of hundreds of millions of years of development. How the process started is a matter of great interest, but in some respects it is largely irrelevant to the questions that face us today. The most important group of questions relates to the power of humanity to make choices (especially about survival), not only for itself as a species but for virtually all other life forms as well.[6] In order to understand more about where we humans are going, we need to know not only where we have come from but also where we are now. We do this by looking first at the place of energy in the natural environment.

ENERGY FLOWS TO EARTH

In the general sense, life on earth (including virtually all activities of human societies) stems, directly or indirectly, from the sun. The sun is the source of effectively all of the energy available to the solar system. The earth is a "consumer" of some of the sun's energy in that energy absorbed from the sun is used to drive atmospheric and life processes before being rejected to the cosmic "heat sink" of outer space. The radiant energy received from the sun supplies heat to the earth's surface and light for the processes of photosynthesis in plants. The complex hierarchy of animal life depends on these flows of energy, from the simplest organisms to the giants of the forest, from bacteria to humans.

Energy from the sun heats the sea and the land, thereby creating convection currents in the atmosphere that result in air movements, evaporation of water from the sea, and rain. Table 1.1 gives data on some of the paths taken by incident solar radiation in the earth's atmosphere. It also shows the approximate percentages of the total incident solar energy traveling along each path.[7]

From these data, for each solar constant joule (SCJ) (units of energy are described in chapter 3) of solar radiation that reaches the outer atmosphere, 53 percent never reaches the earth's surface. Of the remaining 48 percent, 34 percent falls on the oceans and 14 percent falls on the land.[8]

When energy takes part in activities at the earth's surface, some of it is always degraded into low-temperature heat. This heat is ultimately lost from the earth's system by long-wavelength (infrared) radiation into space. A small part of that energy may be stored for a time, either as plants and animals or as fossil fuels. Eventually, even these will be degraded into low-grade heat, but modern societies are accelerating the process by using the reserves at a

TABLE 1.1 *Paths Taken by Incident Solar Radiation*

	In the Atmosphere
Reflected back into space	
From upper atmosphere	30%
From earth's surface	6%
Absorbed by clouds	3%
Absorbed by the atmosphere	14%
Total	53%

	At the Earth's Surface	
	Ocean Area	Land Area
Evaporation of water	17%	6%
Heating of surface	17%	8%

rate vastly greater than their formation by natural and geological processes. In this context, accelerated global warming, forest death, and damage to the ozone layer testify to the limited ability of the earth's ecosystem to absorb wastes.

ENERGY AS THE BASIS FOR LIFE

The main energy pathways shown in table 1.1 are the energy supply for the environment within which life exists, but they do not directly involve living things as such. To incorporate the activities of living organisms into our picture, we need to look in more detail at solar radiation as the energy source for biological photosynthesis in plants.

The majority of plants obtain most of their energy from the sun in the form of light. Together with chlorophyll, light energy enables the manufacture of food and other materials needed for plant maintenance and growth,

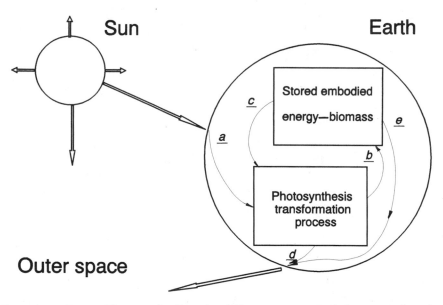

FIGURE 1.1 Energy Flows in the Growth of Plants. a, *incoming solar energy flow;* b, *embodied energy of the new biomass (plant matter) created as a result of the photosynthesis transformation process;* c, *embodied energy in the biomass (e.g., leaves) used to intercept incoming solar energy;* d, *heat energy dissipated in the photosynthesis process;* e, *heat energy dissipated from the plant in other metabolic processes (e.g., growth and maintenance).*

from the carbon dioxide in the air and from other nutrients obtained from the soil via root structures. In a sense, energy is "embodied" in plant tissue as it grows, in that energy and matter combine to create more complex structures than those of the food taken in. Figure 1.1 shows this process in diagrammatic "systems" form, with a store of plant matter (biomass) being built up as a result of interaction between incoming energy from the sun and existing plant matter, such as leaves. Energy is continually being degraded to low-temperature heat.

Figure 1.1, which shows only the energy flows involved in overall plant growth, is, of course, heavily simplified. Nevertheless, energy flow is a critical element in such systems, and a great deal of important information and deep insight may be gained by consideration of flows of direct and embodied energy. Embodied energy flows provide a unique means of following processes and systems in nature and in society.

The growth process depicted in figure 1.1 may also be represented on a graph to show how the size of the embodied energy store (the biomass) changes with time. Figure 1.2 shows how the size of a plant increases slowly at first, then at an accelerating rate. Known as exponential growth, this pattern is typical of the early stages of growth in many systems (see chapter 7). It is an example of a *positive feedback system*, in which growth reinforces itself (see also chapter 5). Such processes cannot go on forever, of course, since they will in time be limited by the rate of energy flow available (usually

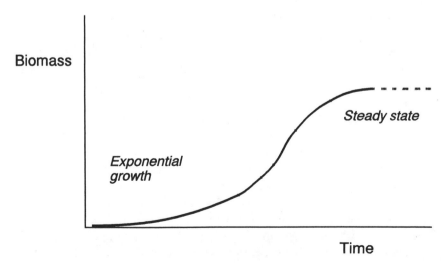

FIGURE 1.2 The Growth of Stored Plant Biomass

from the sun). Eventually, after the plant's essential needs for its own main-tenance have been met, a stage is reached at which no surplus energy is avail-able for growth. The system then settles down to a more or less constant level (represented by the dashed section of the growth curve). The growth curve as a whole, known as a *logistic curve,* is typical of the long-term behavior of all ecosystems and many other systems.[9]

FOOD CHAINS

Plants, on land and in the sea, are food for many animals (herbivores) and small fish, which in turn are food for flesh-eating animals and larger fish (car-nivores). The energy flows that enable plants to grow are the basis for the whole web of life.[10] Although a large quantity of plant matter is needed to feed one herbivore and a large quantity of herbivores is needed to feed each carnivore, only part of the solar energy embodied in each kilogram of plant matter eventually ends up in the carnivore as tissue (muscle, bone, etc.). This is because energy is always "lost" at each stage in the process (more correctly, it is degraded into an unavailable form—see chapter 3) and is re-jected into the surrounding environment. When animals die, their remains decompose and fertilize the growth of biomass. Animal dung has a similar function.

In such a chain, embodied sunlight is progressively "concentrated" through each successive transformation process. At each step in the chain, the output can be described as being of energetically higher quality, because it has more embodied energy per unit of organism. In short, more embodied energy is required to keep a carnivore alive than to keep an herbivore alive. This is not surprising, since a consequence of this increase in embodied en-ergy is that the total quantity of organisms in each stage is very much less than in the previous one. Thus, a very large quantity of soil is required to support a large quantity of plants, which in turn support a much smaller number of insects, a yet smaller number of birds and rodents, and so on, up to the level of the higher carnivores. This way of looking at things uses the image of the pyramid.[11] Lines of dependence for food and other services within the pyramid are what we have already referred to as food chains. The pyramid as a whole is a tangle of food chains—the higher and more complex the pyramid, the more evolved is the ecosystem that it models.[12]

An example is a food chain comprising grass, grasshoppers, frogs, trout, and humans.[13] At each stage of the chain—when the grasshopper eats the grass, the frog eats the grasshopper, and so on—there is a "loss" of energy. In the process of consuming food, most animals lose about 90 percent of the food energy to their surrounding environment as low-temperature heat and as dung. Only around 10 percent of the food energy remains embodied in the tissue of the eater, for transfer to the next stage of the food chain. In our example, the pyramid involves around 1,000 tons of grass to feed 27 million grasshoppers, which feed 90,000 frogs, which feed 300 trout, all to sustain 1 human for a year.

Every living thing maintains its structure at the expense of an enormous dissipation of energy into the surrounding environment. The biologist A. J. Lotka pointed out that organisms are designed to be collectors and transformers of energy. If they do not do so, they will not survive. That they do so more often in cooperation with other members of the ecosystem than in competition with them is well known to most ecologists.[14] Regrettably, it is becoming very clear that humans, at the apex of the pyramid, demand so much of the earth's production (about 40 percent)[15] that other life forms are in jeopardy.

THE MAXIMUM POWER PRINCIPLE

In the context of evolution, Lotka argues that *those systems that survive in the competition among alternative choices are those that develop more power inflow and use it best to meet the needs of survival.*[16] This statement, often referred to as the maximum power principle (MPP), means that natural selection tends to favor organisms that maximize the flow of energy. The rate of flow of energy (the energy flow per unit of time—for example, joules per second) is what we call *power*.

If an organism can maximize its flows of energy, it will grow faster than competitors that do not. Once it is larger than they, it commands greater resources, can use yet more power, and can grow even faster. The importance of using that energy inflow efficiently (in order to satisfy the MPP's requirement to ". . . use it best to meet the needs of survival") is illustrated by the example of a plant that grows fast but does not put down good roots in case of a drought. Alternatively, if it devotes its energy to putting down deep roots, it risks being cast in the shade by a competitor.[17] The need to achieve a balance is part of the process of "survival of the most fitting" that characterizes nature. Most importantly, that process often is one not so much of ruthless competition as of cooperation, with organisms maximizing power jointly rather than individually.[18]

ENERGY AND GROWTH

In the early stages of biological growth (figure 1.2), most energy goes into growth and little goes into maintenance. With maturity, the balance changes, until most inputs are required just to maintain the system. At maturity, there is what appears to be nonproductive growth, although this is needed to maintain and renew the fabric of the system and ensure its health.

The MPP is quite a good model for describing the early stages of an ecological system's development when there is a surplus of energy. In such a system, organisms (initially plants) must compete ruthlessly and grow fast in order to gain a toehold. After the initial, colonizing, stage of habitat occupation, there is an increased quantity of organisms, so they have to adapt to the limited energy flow available to them by using it more efficiently. Sooner or later, all ecosystems stop growing because of inescapable physical limitations to the flow of energy, whether this be in the form of sunshine or of stored food reserves within organisms.[19]

In nature, the fast-growing species that dominate the growth phase tend to be overtaken by more adaptable species that can survive shortages or changes in availability of food and energy and can maximize their own flows when energy is difficult to find. This later stage generally results in greater complexity and range of organisms than in the colonizing stage. Often, many of the initial colonizers are replaced by later, more specialized arrivals.

Energy is used by an organism primarily as the means whereby the processes of life are fueled. Without energy, life could not exist. Nutrients are important both for their matter and for their energy content. Matter can be recycled in an ecosystem, but energy is always degraded in use and can never be reused in the same form without expenditure of more energy (see chapter 3). The use and recycling of matter are part of the natural life system, with energy needed at all times to drive these processes. This is why the concept of embodied energy is such a valuable means of studying complex systems in the living environment.

POPULATION GROWTH DYNAMICS—R- AND K-SELECTIONISTS

The growth dynamics of populations of organisms are of great importance in helping us understand some of the characteristics of ecological systems. The growth dynamics of some animal species—insects especially—are such that their populations boom during good times and collapse rapidly when conditions are not so good.[20] These *r-selectionists* have short breeding cycles; parent animals produce large numbers of offspring (e.g., in the millions); and the young are given no parental care. Such species rapidly populate an area where food, climate, and so forth are favorable, but they may be unable to maintain their numbers after only small changes in their environment.

The other main type of population growth is that of the *k-selectionist*, in which the population grows slowly, parental care is given, and the animals are generally more versatile in their ability to survive in times of change in their surrounding ecosystem. The larger mammals, including humans, are in this category; they tend to grow until they are in a steady state with their surroundings. At that time, their population is more or less constant, reflecting the logistic type of relationship in figure 1.2.

Many natural systems adopt a dynamic characterized by *pulsing*, in which populations of one type of organism may grow at some times and decline at others, allowing their surrounding ecosystems to recover in the meantime.[21] Pulsing is one possible explanation why both *r-* and *k-*selectionist mechanisms appear to be successful in their separate ways. It may also, in the social context, be a possible explanation for business cycles.

Conventional economies, capitalist and socialist, encourage *r-*selectionist behavior in that their socioeconomic messages encourage a maximum growth rate as the primary criterion of success. As we will see in later chapters, this type of behavior is unstable. As yet, few politicians, economists, and technologists have learned that the social structures they promote are inherently unstable and can be expected to bring our species (and many others) to collapse before long. It is not clear whether that collapse will be severe (as can be expected for *r-*selectionist behavior) or whether it can be moderated by socially adaptive *k-*selectionist behavior by the human population of the planet.

OPEN, CLOSED, AND ISOLATED SYSTEMS

In modern science, complex systems are seen in three different ways, depending on how they relate to their surroundings:

- An *open system* exchanges both energy and matter with its environment. Thus, all living organisms, ecosystems, and economies are open systems, since they consume food, reject wastes, and take heat from or give it to their environment.

- A *closed system* exchanges only energy with its surrounding environment. The earth is a closed system, since only solar energy comes in and only heat is rejected to outer space.[22]
- An *isolated system* exchanges neither energy nor matter with its environment. So far as we know, there is no such system on earth; even a good vacuum flask will not keep tea hot for more than a few hours. For some purposes, the solar system can be considered to be isolated, although even that is an approximation, since the sun's energy eventually goes to outer space.

NATURE AS A SYSTEM, NOT A MACHINE

Processes and systems in nature depend on continuing inflows of energy to build and maintain their structures. It can be valuable to study natural processes by using insights gained from the study of simple machines. As I hope will become clear later, however, the complexity of nature (with systems inside larger systems) is such that her characteristics go far beyond those of machines. Many people believe that given the advances of science, all that is needed to gain understanding is more, and more detailed, study. One of my purposes in this book is to attempt to explain why more and better microscopes will not enable us to understand nature better; they will only enable us to understand some parts of her better. To understand more about nature as a whole, new perspectives are needed.

Thus, in no sense should the natural environment be seen as some form of "grand machine." The behavior of nature is not predictable other than in the most general sense, and not always even then. Her responses to changes in significant environmental factors often are small and tend to correct for the changes. In other cases, her response can be rapid, unpredictable, and highly unstable, leading to new structures (see chapter 5). Change, not stability, is the basic process of nature. Stability may exist for a while, in the absence of disturbance, but not forever. Any part of nature is thus normally in a dynamically unstable, or *metastable*, state.

In a sense, nature must be regarded as too complex for her behavior to be predictable. Study of her structure and her responses to change is nevertheless of great value in understanding some of her complexity. If that study also helps us to understand where she is strong and where she is fragile, so much the better.

THE GAIA HYPOTHESIS

A few years ago, James Lovelock introduced the concept of Gaia to describe the complex, self-regulating characteristics of the earth's atmosphere.[23] The Gaia hypothesis is really a way of thinking about our planet in which the activities of the biosphere are intimately and inextricably linked with the complex processes of geology, climatology, and atmospheric physics. In this concept, the chemical conditions for life on earth are created and maintained by life itself in a self-sustaining process of feedback.[24] Thus, in this model, the entire biosphere is treated as a single living thing.

NATURE AND HUMANITY

All social systems are derived from and entirely dependent on the natural environment for their sustenance. An understanding of how that environment functions, therefore, is not only of great value in assisting in better social policymaking but also is actually a prerequisite. Knowledge of what humankind can and cannot get away with provides salutory information for decision makers and their advisers.

Nature can be, and has been, very forgiving of misuse and insults over very long periods. But when pushed too far, she can—and does—respond with a violence that renders technology impotent. Erosion and desertification of overused land and flooding of plains after removal of upland forests are examples that come readily to mind. This is why it is so important to understand something of the way nature behaves, in order to help avoid some of the technological arrogance that humankind has demonstrated all too often in the past and that, regrettably, is still central to much of our present-day policymaking.

2

The Scientific World View

THE GREAT AIM of science is to make the world intelligible. Science is often described as organized knowledge, but this is not an adequate description. After all, there is a well-organized body of knowledge about the writings of Shakespeare, but few would confuse the study of his art with science. Science is really a search for "law and order" in the universe, for explanations of why things happen. It is an active process of acquiring new knowledge while critically examining existing knowledge. As a consequence of these basic aims, "our knowledge can only be finite, while our ignorance must necessarily be infinite."[1]

Perhaps a better description of science is *the body of knowledge obtained by methods based on observation, including careful experimentation.* Thus, science ultimately depends on accurate observation, along with experimentation, for its validity.

A PRIORI AND EMPIRICAL SCIENCES

There are two main kinds of science, often not clearly distinguished from each other.[2] *A priori sciences* are concerned with abstract items that cannot be perceived by means of the senses. These include mathematics and other forms of logic. In many ways, the a priori sciences can be seen as interesting academic exercises involving exploration of ideas and their consequences. Although often based on observation and experimentation, much a priori scientific research is also exploratory and only tenuously related to the real world. Much of economic theory belongs in this area.

The *empirical sciences*, on the other hand, are concerned with concrete things that are observable by means of the senses. Physics, chemistry, biology, and so on are empirical sciences. For most people, "science" means empirical science; in this book, I use the word in that everyday sense.

PURE AND APPLIED SCIENCES

Within the empirical sciences, there is a further distinction between pure science and applied science. *Pure science* is theoretical in the sense that it aims to explain or predict real-world events. *Applied science* is mainly practical in that it may use the findings of pure science to help in the construction of useful things. Much of what is often termed applied science is, in practice, more of an art. Engineering, for example, is widely believed to involve application of the findings of physics and chemistry. In reality, although engineering is powerfully assisted in many areas by those sciences, it is often ahead of them. There is a long history of successful engineering achievements occurring long before scientific understanding of the underlying processes was developed.

FACTS AND VALUES

In the classical scientific method, science is concerned with facts. In this positivist approach, it is believed possible to distinguish between facts and values and be confident about the distinction.

A *fact* can be roughly described as something that is known to be true and a *value* as something that is good or something that ought to be the case. Moral values express how we, as humans, feel people should interact, on the assumption that we all share certain basic wants, needs, and interests. Facts are primary; they come before values. There can be facts without values, but there can never be values without facts. Values are always attached to facts in that it is facts that we value (or not). In using the positivist approach, before we try to develop our value systems (whether we express them in religious, political, or economic terms), it is important that we are clear about our facts. If our facts are wrong—or misunderstood—our values and the judgments that depend on them cannot be relied on.

Recently, the positivist approach has had to be modified to take account of complicating factors. For many people, it is impossible to distinguish between facts and beliefs: what they "know" to be true is the same as what they "believe" to be true. What we "see" and how we interpret what we see depends to a large extent on what we expect or want to see. There are also quite a few areas of scientific study in which it may not be at all clear what is or is not a fact. "Hard facts" and "soft values" are not as clearly distinct as we once thought. This occurs frequently in the study of complex systems and in the social sciences; some of what we might think is a sharp distinction between fact and value blurs into uncertainty. In many respects, it means that positivism itself must nowadays be seen as a myth—partly true and partly untrue.[3]

In the context of this book, however, there are some very important facts whose existence we can acknowledge without recourse to belief. It is a fact, for example, that a boiling pot cools down when removed from a hot plate and placed on a cool surface. This meaning is highly specific. It is a cornerstone of the arguments I use in this book that facts such as these, when interpreted from a modern biophysical systems understanding, provide us with a firm factual base for clarifying some of the values of our social and economic systems.

If a general cause-and-effect relationship is claimed to exist—for example, when such-and-such a cause gives rise to such-and-such an effect—that too is often called a fact. In terms of the logic of the scientific method, however, it is a *hypothesis*. Only when the hypothesis has been subjected to scientific test can it be interpreted as factual, and even then it is provisional.

It is when the word "fact" is applied to human behavior that the main misunderstandings arise. This is because the study of human behavior is strongly influenced by ideology and beliefs. What is considered factual is closely bound up with what the proponents of the ideology or belief believe to be "normal" behavior. In situations such as this, science usually goes out the window, to be replaced by assertions. Such is the basis of most political-economic theories, in both capitalist and socialist camps.

There are few, if any, facts of human behavior. People are not machines. Their behavior is not reproducible, even in large groups, unless they are forced to behave in specific ways by externally applied pressures or inducements. It is a fact, for example, that most people will obey orders at the point of a gun. The existence of martyrs in every age and civilization, however, demonstrates that this fact is not universal. In the strict scientific sense, then, the observation that many people do obey such orders does not support any scientific hypothesis of relevance.

Science is always provisional. In its applications, therefore, one must be on guard not to ascribe to any scientific theory validity beyond that which can clearly be demonstrated. Where scientific theories are claimed to have applications in social decision-making processes, caution is necessary. Michael Rutter gives a valuable reminder that "science does not deal in certainties; rather it provides evidence on probabilities, and it is on these probabilities that political decisions have to be made."[4]

THE SCIENTIFIC METHOD

Science is a process, a method of studying reality in order to gain knowledge. The scientific method usually involves *reductionism*—the breaking down of problems into small parts to be studied separately. Thus, a large single problem is separated into a number of smaller, more manageable problems. The scientific method also requires that observations or measurements be repeatable (i.e., that the same conditions give rise to the same results); otherwise, other factors that were not under full control would have to be involved in the occurrence. Interim ideas (hypotheses) of why things happen are tested against experimental data to support or disprove the ideas.

The scientific method has made it possible for humanity to make enormous strides in understanding the world and in learning to control and change it. But in some contexts, the scientific method has also taken on the connotation of being the best or even the only valid way of doing things, thus excluding other methods of study that could be regarded as equally valid.

In the social sciences, it is often difficult to know how far to go in the reductionist process before losing sight of the whole. For example, how do we know whether an individual is typical of the community in which she or he lives? It is a related issue that in physics, the question of the nature of elementary particles has become largely theoretical.[5] Taken to excess, reductionism encourages concentration on detail to the exclusion of the whole and can be seriously misleading.

Induction

Scientists base their actions on carefully controlled and measured observation. From the results of observation, they formulate a hypothesis to fit the facts and explain the relationships among them. They then try to obtain evidence to support the hypothesis, and if they are successful they have established another *theory* (or a *law*, if enough supporting evidence is available). Science thus appears to be based on the accumulation of certainties based on observation and experimental evidence. This method of basing laws on accumulated observations, known as the process of *induction*, was for centuries seen as the hallmark of science.

It has been known for some time, however, that no matter how many observations appear to confirm a hypothesis, we can never be absolutely certain that the next observation will also confirm it. The solution to this problem was offered by the philosopher Sir Karl Popper, who pointed out that only one valid counterobservation is needed to falsify a hypothesis completely.

The logic of scientific discovery thus starts with a problem, to which is offered a tentative theory or hypothesis or even a conjecture. The theory is then criticized to try to eliminate errors, whereupon the theory and its critical revision give rise to new problems. Problem formulation is a highly creative activity; theory testing is sometimes more of a mechanical activity, which is where the scientific method comes in.

Falsifiability

At each stage in the scientific method, the investigator is required to suggest a hypothesis as to why the event being studied occurs and then to construct an experiment to test the suggested explanation. It is an essential part of the method that the test must always be done in such a way as to enable the hypothesis to be refuted, or falsified, if wrong. Popper pointed out that it is not the verifiability but the falsifiability of a theory that is the important criterion. It must be possible for an empirical scientific system to be refuted by experience.[6] In other words, the investigator must be scrupulously honest and at all times prepared to let a treasured hypothesis go if it does not adequately explain the occurrence at all times and under all circumstances.

Hypothesis selection is an evolutionary process. Sometimes it proceeds steadily and sometimes by jumps, as old ways of thinking about major issues are superseded by new, richer methods. When one way of seeing the world— a *paradigm*, according to Thomas Kuhn—is superseded, a *paradigm shift* occurs.[7] Such a shift occurred in the replacement of the biblical story of creation by the big bang theory and the theory of evolution.

Paradigm competition often takes a long time and may not result in a clear-cut distinction for many years. The problem is that the Popperian test of falsifiability is in some cases not directly usable; different paradigms use different sets of concepts, and it is often difficult to develop a clear test of one over the other.[8]

The accumulation of anomalies in a long-dominant paradigm is often the key to its replacement by a better one. In some situations, we cannot be clear-cut about our preferences for one theory over another, but we can aim to subject both theories to strong criticism, including applying the test of falsifiability wherever possible. The important thing is that in complex situations (such as the behavior of ecosystems and economies), we cannot always expect science to provide us with unambiguous answers to all of the important questions that face us.

THE USE OF MODELS

When we use the scientific method to help us grasp the complexity of systems (for example, the environment and the way in which life goes on), we use the reductionist approach to create *models*, which we then try to understand. Although a model can never be as good as the original, it may help us study and identify issues of importance. Its limitation is that it gives only partial information about the functioning of the whole of the original, whether it is an organism, an animal, a society, or an ecosystem.

The conflict between the model and the original—or, to put it another way, between reductionist and holistic approaches to the study of an occurrence—may be illustrated by the simple example of a model car. No matter how detailed it is, it is not and never will be the real thing. But to someone who had never seen anything but the model, the temptation to put it under a magnifying glass in order to learn more about the real thing could be irresistible. Such is the case with many of the models used in engineering and economics.

The value of a model lies in its ability to aid in the development of understanding and insight; no model can ever explain more than a small part of the whole. Models are also used by people in everyday speech, but then they are called *metaphors*—used to illustrate an idea more vividly than is possible with simpler words. Models cease to be useful when they are so much a part of our lives that they become straitjackets, limiting our ability to look at the world about us in an open-minded way. Many such straitjackets exist in our societies.

THE FALLACY OF MISPLACED CONCRETENESS

When users of models become convinced that the reality the model purports to describe is described better by the model than by observation of the reality itself, the scientific method is brought into disrepute. This process was described by the philosopher Alfred North Whitehead half a century ago as the *fallacy of misplaced concreteness:* "neglecting the degree of abstraction involved when an actual entity is considered merely so far as it exemplifies certain categories of thought."[9]

Regrettably, this process is widespread, as the economist Nicholas Georgescu-Roegen points out: "It is . . . beyond dispute that the sin of standard economics is the fallacy of misplaced concreteness."[10] The most common example of the fallacy is known to economists as *money fetishism,* in which the characteristics of the abstract symbol—money—are applied to the concrete use value, the commodity itself. Thus, if money can grow at compound interest, so too can real gross national product—and so can the number of pigs and cars and haircuts.[11] I address this fallacy in more detail in later chapters and show that it is at the center of some serious misrepresentations of the importance of environmental and other resources in economic activity.

WHAT IS *NOT* SCIENCE?

The requirement for rigorous testing of theories as an integral part of the scientific method is not generally understood. Many people (including many scientists) feel that any test that gives evidence in favor of a hypothesis must support it. In practice, it is very easy to construct a hypothesis that is so general that it is all things to all people—not capable of meaningful testing yet so superficially attractive that people are persuaded by it. This has happened often in science, and it still happens. Some social sciences are particularly susceptible to this type of pseudoscientific activity, often because of a slavish reliance on the results of statistical analysis (usually by computer) of vast arrays of data.[12]

Another example of the misuse of science is that of not carefully distinguishing between *correlation* and *causation.* It is common for apparently unrelated events to occur at the same time; for example, certain planetary arrangements may occur at the same time as human activities. People often come to the conclusion that one causes the other. The social sciences are, unfortunately, full of relationships based on comprehensive studies of correlations, but few good causative relationships have been unequivocally confirmed.[13] Many economic measures (GNP, fixed capital formation, balance of payments, etc.) are subject to significant, and often substantial, errors of measurement and also to ambiguities in definition. The errors are often in excess of what is acceptable in scientific measures; thus, the hypotheses cannot be properly tested.

Lack of evidence of causality does not prove its absence any more than it disproves its presence. It simply indicates that judgment in favor of a causal relationship must be suspended until evidence is obtained one way or the other to strengthen or weaken the hypothesis. In social activities, one must also remember the basically indeterminate nature of human behavior. Even though such-and-such an event may indeed have been caused by such-and-such an action in the past, this provides no scientific evidence whatsoever that the same action will have the same consequence in the future.

A common problem (especially in advertising and public relations) arises when the claim is made that a study is "scientific," with the implication that its results must be accepted as reliable. Simply saying that something is scientific does not make it so. It is always necessary to examine such claims, whether made by scientists or not, to determine whether they stand up to critical investigation. [14]

WHAT SCIENCE IS NOT

Science is often pictured as driven by its own internal logic and dynamics, existing in splendid isolation from the world around it. Science is, in practice, an intensely human activity. [15] Despite its apparent (and often claimed) objectivity, science is powerfully influenced by its external environment and is also shaped by cultural receptivity to its dominant ideas. It does not exist apart from society and culture, and it never has.

Nevertheless, those towering figures of early science Sir Isaac Newton and Pierre-Simon de Laplace envisaged the universe as a machine, with every part of its operation completely predictable, if only we had all the facts. Here are Newton, in 1687, and Laplace, in 1814, respectively:

> I wish I could derive all phenomena of nature, by some kind of reasoning, from mechanical principles: for I have many reasons to suspect that they all depend upon certain forces by which the particles of bodies are either mutually attracted and cohere in regular figures or are repelled and recede from each other.

> We should regard the present state of the universe as the effect of its antecedent state and the cause of its subsequent state. An intelligence acquainted with all the forces of nature, and with the positions at any given instant of all the parts thereof, would include in one and the same formula the movements of the largest bodies and those of the lightest atoms.

Ideas such as these were powerful forces for development of theories of society and government, and some of them contributed to the framing of the U.S. Constitution as a machine to take over government of the people. Later developments gave rise to the Marxist ideal of science as a superstructure mounted atop a socioeconomic base.[16] In various forms, these ideas are still central to major political and economic theories.

The idea that everything can be envisaged as part of a mechanical universe began to be challenged scientifically in the later part of the nineteenth century. The challenge came about largely as a result of discoveries of thermodynamics and quantum physics that demonstrated that some things were absolutely impossible. These discoveries gave rise to a revolution in scientific thinking that is still going on. The physicist Paul Dirac wrote, in 1933:

> The classical tradition had been to consider the world to be an association of observable objects moving according to definite laws of force, so that one could form a mental picture of the whole scheme. . . . It has become increasingly evident, however, that nature works on a different plan. Her fundamental laws do not govern the world as it appears in our picture in any direct way, but instead they control a substratum of which we cannot form a mental picture without introducing irrelevancies.

Unfortunately, some of the changes in thinking that this revolution has brought about have yet to be understood by many of the professions. Consider, for example, the following quotation: "The only reason we have not yet succeeded in formalizing every aspect of the real world is that we have been lacking a sufficiently powerful calculus."[17]

Because the behavior of some physical phenomena can be approximated by mathematical expressions, that writer made the assumption that the activities of the real world are underlain by one powerful formula. I will argue in later chapters that the world is in reality so complex that it cannot adequately be described according to any mechanistic calculus. But many scientists still cling to the belief that better microscopes are all that is needed to gain a more complete understanding of reality. This is the main danger of reductionism taken out of context.

As another example, workers in the field of artificial intelligence attempt to redefine humans in terms of machines. The result is the symbolic representation (often in the form of a computer program) of what is in reality a dynamic, ever-changing, thinking person. In such a context, the richness of the person's humanity is lost and all that remains is the caricature, whose behavior is described largely in terms of analogies gained from laboratory experiments on pigeons, rats, and monkeys.

As Einstein pointed out, "We should be on our guard not to overestimate science and scientific methods when it is a question of human problems; and we should not assume that experts are the only ones who have a right to express themselves on questions affecting the organization of society."[18]

EMERGENT PROPERTIES AND THE SYSTEMS APPROACH

The classical scientific method has a major drawback: it is easy to forget that the sum of the parts is not the same as the whole. Reductionism works on the assumption that by taking something to pieces and putting it back together, it is possible to gain a good understanding of the thing. The inadequacy of the approach can be illustrated by the ease with which a blossom may be reduced to botany or a beautiful sunset to meteorology. Such a view is a parody of understanding, but it is firmly adhered to as "objective" and "value free" by many scientists.[19]

In the case of simple machines, it is not at all difficult to relate the parts to the whole. A clock can be put together in only one way that will enable it to tell the time. But more complex systems, and organisms, cannot adequately be studied in this way. The systems approach (see chapter 5) has helped us understand that most complex systems show emergent properties, properties that may be studied directly but are not predictable from their separate parts.

In the case of a living animal, it is not sensible to assume that by separating certain critical parts and learning more about them, the understanding of the whole organism will in some way be ensured. This is not to suggest that by doing so we do not learn more about the parts, of course. There is something about the whole animal, however, that is much more than its legs, head, and body or its cells, enzymes, and biochemistry.

Classical science gets around this problem by a useful trick. We hedge our conclusions by saying that they are valid ceteris paribus—"all other things being equal." In this way we can, at least temporarily, ignore the complexity of the real system.

Recent advances in the scientific method have concentrated on looking at whole systems using the systems approach. This is really a way of thinking about the set of interconnected parts that makes up the whole in such a way as to bring out the properties of the whole rather than those of the parts. "Systems thinking" implies thinking about the world outside ourselves in order to order our thoughts and initiate and guide our actions.[20]

Wherever possible, I use the systems approach in this book when examining the wider implications of the place of energy in the physical and social environment. Thus, instead of looking only at a single plant or animal or at one process in an economy, I try to place the subject in its wider context. By this means, I hope to avoid some of the more crass distortions of reality produced by a slavish application of the scientific method. I emphasize, however, that no scientific inquiry can be pursued free of consequences for the basic needs, wants, and interests of people. Science is not—and never will be—value free. It is a human activity, and we scientists should be proud of the fact instead of so often denying it or avoiding the question.

3

Energy—A Scientific Perspective

IN EVERYDAY LANGUAGE, the term "energy" is commonly applied to electricity, coal, gasoline, and natural gas. The last three should more specifically be termed "fuels"; all are forms of "consumer energy" in that they are bought by people for use in everyday life. We also use the word in less obvious ways, with terms such as "energetic" and "nervous energy" used to describe personal characteristics.

WHAT IS ENERGY?

In a strict scientific sense, *energy* is the ability to do work. This apparently obscure statement means that energy has the ability to cause changes in the physical or chemical nature, structure, or location of matter or things. In this context, "work" has a very specific meaning only vaguely related to the social meaning of the term, with which it should not be confused.

Energy is not a thing that can be seen or touched; it is a concept used to explain changes in the state of matter under certain circumstances. Heating, cooling, chemical change, motion, and so on result from changes in the nature or location of the energetic state of matter. Some such changes alter the structure of matter, as when dough is (chemically) converted into bread by baking (heat energy). Other examples, involving less obvious structural changes, arise when a speeding vehicle (kinetic energy) is slowed by the use of its brakes (heat energy) or when elevated water (high gravitational potential energy) falling to a lower level (low gravitational potential energy) is used to turn turbines (rotating mechanical energy) in a hydroelectric power station to generate electricity (electrical energy).

Energy is thus a generalized attribute of physical transformation and change, not a commodity.

Energy may be seen to be *flowing,* as in the case of sunshine, where radiated energy is the basis for the flows of water vapor and air in the atmosphere and for the whole complex system of life on earth. When clouds come between a person and the sun, that person's skin and eyes respond immediately to the change in energy flow.

Energy may be *stored,* in the energy of elevated water in lakes and rivers, in chemical form in plants and animals, or as the highly concentrated stocks of carbon and hydrogen chemically combined in coal, oil, or gas in underground reservoirs.

STOCKS AND FLOWS

The distinction between stock and flow resources is of vital importance. Only human societies have learned to use large quantities of stock resources to supplement the natural energy flows from the sun. Stock and flow resources are often described, respectively, as *nonrenewable* and *renewable,* since stock resources required millions of years for their formation and cannot be replaced within a time period of relevance to humankind. Flow energy may be stored for relatively short periods in vegetable and animal tissue, and many animals (including, of course, humans) store food for winter use. The flow energy in the water cycle may also be stored for long periods in lakes, glaciers, or aquifers.

ENERGY POTENTIAL

All energy has the potential ability to do work. The potential of a form of energy to do work varies according to its nature. Stored energy's potential to do work cannot be exploited, however, until a transformation pathway exists for it to be released. Examples of types of potential energy are as follows:

- *Gravitational.* The height of a lake determines the amount of work that can be done by its water in descending to a lower level.
- *Mechanical.* The energy of motion of a flowing river, the energy stored in a wound-up spring, a rotating flywheel, or a moving object such as a truck can all do work in unwinding or slowing down.

- *Chemical.* Fossil fuels (coal, oil, and gas) contain high concentrations of carbon and hydrogen arranged in structures that bind large quantities of potential energy. The same amounts of carbon and hydrogen bound in carbon dioxide and water (the main products of burning fuels in air) contain much less potential energy.
- *Nuclear.* Uranium and plutonium store energy in their atomic structures. In these atoms, among the largest known, the atomic building blocks (neutrons and protons) are packed tightly into the nucleus of the atom. When such atoms are "split," fragments are produced, with the release of very large quantities of energy.[1]
- *Electrical.* Lightning is a well-known example of the release of stored electrical energy. The processes inside thunderclouds generate high electrical charges (millions of volts). These build up until the air between the cloud and the earth's surface is able to conduct electricity, whereupon the charge is released and lightning energy "flows."
- *Thermal.* Thermal energy (heat) is available from direct or focused solar radiation, from geothermal sources, and from the burning of fossil fuels, wood, and so on. Its potential depends on the extent to which the temperature achieved is higher than that of its surroundings. Heat may be "stored"; familiar examples are vacuum flasks and hot water bottles. The length of time for which it can be stored depends on the level of insulation; the better the insulation, the slower the rate of cooling. Things do not stay hot indefinitely unless supplied with "new" heat energy.

TRANSFORMATION PATHWAYS

Flows and transformations of energy into work occur spontaneously only when both the potential and an appropriate pathway exist. If a pathway does not exist, the energy remains at its original potential, either flowing or stored. Water in a lake can turn the turbines of a hydroelectric power station only when it flows (via penstocks) down a gravitational potential to a lower level. Similarly, other forms of stored energy cannot perform work unless they are also released from their stored form and move down an appropriate transformation pathway to a lower potential energy state. The pathway may be a power station or a fire in which coal or wood is burned.

Having done that work, the energy is at a lower level (a lower potential), and experience tells us that *it cannot be used to do the same work again without expenditure of additional energy from outside the system.* In the case of the hydroelectric power station, the only way the water could be used to generate power again at the same station would be for it to be pumped back from the downstream river into the lake above the dam. In practice, this pumping always requires more energy than is obtained by running the water back down through the turbines.

In figure 1.1, photosynthesis was shown as providing a transformation pathway that enabled sunlight to do work in the building of plant tissue (biomass) from simpler molecules. In a related manner, figure 3.1 shows how a power station provides a transformation pathway for the conversion of coal (a stock resource) into electricity, which can then be delivered to an economy. Note that *feedback energy* is required from the economy to build, operate, and maintain the power station.

As well as depending on the difference in potential between the stored energy and its surrounding environment, the energy released in a process also depends on the amount of energy in the store. For example, the energy released by a lake depends not only on the difference in height between the lake and the turbine outlet but also on the quantity of water that flows out of the lake through the turbines. The energy available from a tank of gasoline depends on the difference in chemical potentials of the fuel and of the carbon dioxide and water in the exhaust and also on the size of the tank. The "usefulness" of any energy resource depends on its size as well as its potential relative to the baseline energy potential in its local or global environment.

Sunlight performs work in heating the atmosphere and in driving photosynthesis because it comes from a source that is at a temperature of about 6,000 degress Kelvin (on the Kelvin scale, 0 degrees Kelvin is approximately the temperature of outer space).[2] Since the average temperature of the earth's surface is around 285 degrees Kelvin (about 12 degrees Celsius), solar energy flows "down" a radiation pathway from the sun to outer space, with the earth temporarily intercepting a little of that energy.

Nuclear energy is so highly concentrated that it cannot normally be used

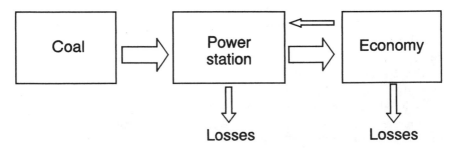

FIGURE 3.1 Transformation Pathway from Coal to Electricity

directly; it must first be converted in a nuclear reactor into heat, which is then used to raise steam and drive turbines.

Electrical energy is a very useful, high-grade energy source because it is almost entirely capable of conversion into mechanical work through the pathway provided by an electric motor.

Heat is the least useful form of energy in terms of the ability to do work, and low-temperature heat is less useful than high-temperature heat. Water in the oceans of the world is not a useful source of stored energy for ordinary work processes, despite its vast quantity. The difference in temperature (potential) between ocean water and its surroundings is in most cases too small for a useful amount of work to be obtained from it.[3]

ENERGY BASIS FOR ACTIVITY

Without expenditure of potential energy, there can be no activity in the natural environment. In nature, interaction of sunlight with matter over hundreds of millions of years has enabled the evolution of plants, animals, and ecosystems that provide a multitude of mechanisms for energy transformation and use. These systems exist as the result of prior energy inflows and interactions. Even in ecosystems, development of "natural technologies" depends on the recycling of energy stored from previous inflows.

Early human societies simply "plugged in" to stores of energy that were provided via natural mechanisms from the sun. These provided food and essential materials for clothing and so on. Modern societies have gained access to sources that enable much greater quantities of energy to be harnessed in one place than are available directly from the sun. Because these sources—coal, oil, and gas—are much more concentrated than sunlight, they can be used to supply the large quantities of energy needed to build yet larger systems.

Work done in societies to construct structures (buildings, factories, etc.) depends totally on prior energy inflows to the natural and socioeconomic systems. Structures can be built only if energy is expended in their construction. Energy must be used in manufacturing the tools and factories that make and shape the cement, bricks, steel, timber, and so on that make up the new structure.

All systems and structures, including social ones, also depend on continuing energy inflows for their maintenance and renewal. Dependence on fuels often blinds us to the fact that inflows from the sun (which dominate food production, for example) remain the principal energy source for all earthly systems. Hence the concern many people feel about the facts that industrialized countries are using up nonrenewable resources much faster than they can be created and that the pollution effects of using these resources cause massive destruction of the natural environment.

The basis for all physical activity, on earth as elsewhere in the universe, is the existence of sources of potential energy. This is sometimes more usefully described as *availability*, in that only some forms of energy are, in practice, available for work processes. One form of energy can often be substituted for another; trains can be pulled by locomotives using coal, oil, or electricity, and homes can be heated by many different fuels. Nevertheless, *there is no substitute for energy.* Available energy is an absolutely unsubstitutable input to any physical process. That statement may seem extreme, but it is based on fundamental laws of physics for which no counterevidence has ever been produced.

THERMODYNAMICS—THE SCIENCE OF ENERGY

Many processes, both in nature and in technology, involve one form of energy being changed into another. Radiation from the sun is changed into heat at the earth's surface; into chemical energy (via photosynthesis) in plants; and into latent heat of vaporization when water evaporates from the sea or from puddles on a road. The science of thermodynamics is a set of bookkeeping principles that enable us to understand and follow energy as it is transformed from one form, or state, to another. As mentioned in chapter 1, all forms of energy eventually end up as low-temperature radiation into outer space.

The most important accounting principles are the first and second laws of thermodynamics. The zeroth and third laws of thermodynamics are included here for completeness, but they are less important for our purposes.

THE ZEROTH LAW OF THERMODYNAMICS

The zeroth law was enunciated after the first law, hence its curious number! The zeroth law of thermodynamics states: *If two bodies are each in thermal equilibrium with a third, they must also be in thermal equilibrium with each other.*

In this context, equilibrium implies the existence of a situation in which the system undergoes no net change—that is, there is no net transfer of heat between the bodies. A hot saucepan is not in equilibrium with its surroundings in the kitchen when it is taken off the stove; but if left for long enough, it will lose heat to the surroundings and eventually end up at the same temperature. When that state is reached, there is no transfer of heat from the pan to the surroundings or in the reverse direction; the pan and its surroundings are in equilibrium. The zeroth law of thermodynamics gives the basis for the concept of temperature in a closed system. Its main use is in formalization of the logic behind the other laws, and we need not refer to it again.

THE FIRST LAW OF THERMODYNAMICS

The first law of thermodynamics, the law of conservation of energy, states: *Energy can be neither created nor destroyed, only converted from one form to another.*

When one energy form is converted into another, the total amount of energy remains constant. When gasoline is burned in an engine, the chemical energy in the fuel is converted into various forms: kinetic energy of motion; potential energy (if the car has been driven up a hill); chemical energy in the carbon dioxide and water of the exhaust gas; heat energy in the exhaust and cooling systems, transmission, brakes, and so on. All of the energy in the fuel can be accounted for, using appropriate measurements. The accounts always balance; no exception has ever been identified.

Units of Energy

The first law of thermodynamics is basically a means whereby different forms of energy may be equated with one another. Common units for energy are the British thermal unit (Btu), the calorie (cal), the kilowatt-hour (kwh), and the joule (J). In the SI (*Système international d'unités*) system of units, the joule is the standard unit of energy, but the others are easily related to it.

The joule in this context is the amount of energy needed to heat 1 cubic centimeter of water by about a quarter (actually 0.239) of a degree Celsius. Alternatively, it is the energy needed to lift a weight of 1 kilogram about 10 centimeters. Table 3.1 summarizes the relationship between the joule and a number of common energy units. Note that the food calorie is a thousand times larger than the thermal calorie. This is the result of a historical accident: "kilocalorie" was shortened to "calorie" for use in food and dietetic matters, and the "kilo" part of the name was forgotten.

Since the joule is a very small unit, multiples are generally used for practical purposes. A kilojoule (kJ) is a thousand (10^3) joules; a megajoule (MJ)

TABLE 3.1 *Energy and Work Equivalents*

Energy Unit	Number of Joules
Calorie (thermal) (cal)	4.187
Calorie (food) (Cal)	4,187
British thermal unit (Btu)	1,055
Horsepower-hour (hp-hr)	26,800
Kilowatt-hour (kwh)	3,600,000

is a million (10^6) joules; a gigajoule (GJ) is a billion (10^9) joules; and a tera-joule (TJ) is a trillion (10^{12}) joules. The largest common multiple unit is the petajoule (PJ), a thousand million million (10^{15}) joules, although the exa-joule (EJ) (10^{18}) joules, is sometimes used.[4]

A petajoule can be visualized as the energy contained in the contents of a coastal oil tanker, the gasoline in a million small cars, a million bags of coal, a year's natural gas for 25,000 households, or a year's electricity for a small city. Similarly, a small car's gasoline tank holds about 1 gigajoule, a bag of coal also contains 1 gigajoule, and a 2-kilowatt electric heater uses a little more than 7 megajoules of electricity per hour. The solar constant joule unit mentioned in chapter 1 refers to a joule of solar radiation reaching the earth's outer atmosphere.

A quad (a unit used mainly in the United States) is 10^{15} British thermal units (Btu).

Power

The consumption of energy can usually be measured by the size of a "packet" that we buy, such as a tank of gasoline or a bag of coal. With electricity, however, this is not normally the case, since we usually pay for the rate at which we use it (the power) and the time for which it is used. The unit of power in SI units is the watt. One watt is the *rate of supply of energy* of 1 joule per second. Thus, a 100-watt light bulb used for 10 hours uses 1,000 watt-hours, or 1 kilowatt-hour (kwh) of electricity, which is what the meter measures. A 2,000-watt heater used for 1 hour uses 2,000 watt-hours, or 2 kwh. What is paid for is energy, not power, but since energy equals power multiplied by time ($E = P \times t$), power is obviously important. Turning lights off when they are not needed obviously saves some money, but at noth-ing like the rate at which savings are made by turning off heaters.

Calorific Values

Table 3.2 summarizes typical values of the energy contents (as net calorific value)[5] of a number of common fuels relative to the unit of weight or volume in which they are usually measured.[6]

Energy Quality

The first law of thermodynamics is of only limited use. It does not help us understand why, if energy cannot be destroyed, we cannot reuse the energy in a tank of gasoline. The answer is that although the total energy remains constant, the potential of each subsequent form to do work is not the same as at the start of the process. One cannot pipe exhaust back into the tank

TABLE 3.2 *Typical Net Calorific Values of Some Common Fuels*

Fuel	Net Calorific Value
Liquid fuels	
"Super" gasoline	32.4 MJ/l
"Regular" gasoline	31.6 MJ/l
Diesel fuel	36.0 MJ/l
Fuel oil	39.0 MJ/l
Kerosene	34.4 MJ/l
Methanol	15.8 MJ/l
Ethanol	21.3 MJ/l
Liquefied petroleum gas (LPG)	24.1 MJ/l
Natural gas	34–39 MJ/m^3
Coal	
Bituminous	27.8 MJ/kg
Subbituminous	21.9 MJ/kg
Lignite	16.0 MJ/kg
Wood	
Dry	15–20 MJ/kg
Wet	5–10 MJ/kg
Electricity	3.6 J/kwh

and run the car on it.[7] The spent energy is not available for further work to the same extent as was the energy in the original fuel because it has been degraded into lower-temperature and lower-chemical-potential forms. The high temperature of combustion of the gasoline (more than 1,000 degrees Celsius) enables much more of it to be converted into work than do the lower-temperature heat energy (about 100 degrees Celsius) and the minimal quantity of chemical energy in the exhaust gas. We need to formalize this fact, which is where the second law of thermodynamics comes in.

THE SECOND LAW OF THERMODYNAMICS

The second law of thermodynamics—the entropy law—can be stated as follows: *All physical processes proceed in such a way that the availability of the energy involved decreases.*

What this statement means is that no transformation of energy resources can ever be 100 percent efficient. All processes irrevocably degrade available energy to an unavailable state. In any closed system, whether natural or technological, the total energy available to do work must decrease. Eventually, any system runs out of available energy and comes to a stop.

Many books have been written about this apparently simple law. Equivalent statements (which tell us more about specific topics within thermodynamics) are as follows:

- In any transformation of energy, some of it is always degraded.
- It is not possible to convert a given quantity of heat (thermal energy) into an equal amount of useful work (mechanical energy).
- Heat will not of itself flow from a colder body to a hotter body.
- The availability of a quantity of energy can be used only once.[8]

These four statements follow from the previous discussion and also from everyday experience. Nobody has ever built a car that converts all of its gasoline into motion, with no heat release through the radiator or exhaust. A saucepan of water placed on a hot stove does not get colder while the stove gets hotter; nor does it get hotter when removed from the stove altogether. A stone may spontaneously roll down a hill, but it always has to be pushed back up again. The second law of thermodynamics merely formalizes situations that people have known about since the dawn of consciousness.

The second law declares that the material economy *necessarily and unavoidably* degrades the resources that sustain it. Increasing resource scarcity on the one hand and pollution on the other are the results of this unvarying one-way sequence of material consumption and depletion.[9] Even though many natural resources (timber, plants, etc.) can grow again, the rate of natural renewal of resources is, on the world scale, generally smaller than the rate of use. Where stock resources (e.g., fossil fuels and high-quality mineral deposits) are concerned, the renewal process takes place over eons of geological time and is therefore irrelevant compared with the rate at which humans are presently using them.

Conversion of Heat into Work

A powerful consequence of the second law of thermodynamics is that it can be used to predict the maximum possible performance of certain types of machines, even without knowing in advance the design of the machine. We may also determine the minimum amount of energy needed for such processes as the separation of salt from seawater, metals from their ores, and pollutants from vehicle exhausts, to give three examples. This may be done without knowing anything about future inventions that might be devised for these purposes. Similarly, if we can find the temperature and extent of a source of thermal energy—such as geothermal heat—we can easily evaluate the maximum possible amount—of, say, electricity—we can obtain from it, regardless of the cleverness of future inventors.

Temperature difference (potential) determines the ability of thermal energy sources to do work. Even under "ideal" circumstances, an amount of heat energy at a given temperature above that of the surrounding environment can yield only a fixed amount of mechanical work. The fraction of heat energy Q that is convertible into work W at any temperature difference (potential) is given in Table 3.3.

At a temperature of 1,000 degrees Kelvin above that of the environment, which is roughly what is obtained from burning a fuel such as oil or gas in an engine, table 3.3 shows that an absolute maximum of only 0.77 (i.e., 77 percent) of the heat energy can ever be convertible into mechanical energy. In practice, less than half of this is generally available, even under laboratory test-bed conditions. On the road, and particularly in city traffic, most motor vehicle engines are probably at best 10 percent efficient in converting fuel energy into motion. All of the fuel energy and mechanical energy is eventually converted to heat, at 100 percent efficiency.

TABLE 3.3 *Heat Energy and Work*

Temperature Difference (Degrees Kelvin)	Fraction of Heat Energy Convertible into Work (W/Q)
100	0.25
300	0.51
1,000	0.77
5,000	0.94
10,000	0.97

NOTE: The work W obtained from a quantity of heat Q absorbed by a Carnot engine at temperature T_2 and rejected at T_1 is $W/Q = (T_2 - T_1)/T_2$. The data in this table were calculated assuming $T_2 = 20\ °C = 293\ K$. Note that Kelvin (absolute) units must be used for such calculations.

Efficiency and Speed

These "ideal" processes are largely of academic interest, since the figures in table 3.3 are attainable *only if the machine runs infinitely slowly*. In such a process, inefficiencies such as friction losses would be at a minimum. Such a machine does not exist, and if it did, it would not do anything, since no one would be willing to wait around long enough for it to complete its infinitely slow job! But this fact also shows us that real machines, which convert heat into work at a rate useful to humankind, must always work at a considerably lower efficiency than ideal machines.

In a very generalized way, figure 3.2 shows the power (the rate of doing work, or the work done in a given space of time) available from an energy source for a range of machines of different efficiencies. The "best possible" machine, one that achieves close to the maximum second-law efficiency, is so slow that it delivers little or no power. The poorest-performing machine wastes so much energy due to its low efficiency that it also delivers relatively little. Intermediate machines achieve a "reasonable" power output at a "reasonable" level of efficiency. In practice, most people are willing to sacrifice some efficiency for reasonable speed. What is important to most people and societies is power, the rate at which work is done.

Thermodynamic analysis shows that for most practical purposes, the efficiency of real machines is unlikely ever to exceed half to two-thirds that of the ideal second-law machine. Nevertheless, many current machines are far from achieving even that figure, so there is plenty of room for improvement. Improvements will be subject to diminishing-returns effects, however; each stage of innovation gives rise to a smaller improvement than the one before.

Limits to Technological Innovation

From these and other arguments, it can be seen that there are some absolutely fixed limits to technological developments, limits that humanity has no power to circumvent. This is a hard fact; no evidence exists that it is not totally true. It obviously has far-reaching consequences for the ways in which humanity can develop in the future, and it points to some ways in which we cannot develop.

The statements and examples of the second law of thermodynamics illustrate why nobody has managed to produce a perpetual-motion machine—one that runs forever without a fuel supply. Since the conversion of any source of energy into, say, motion, is always less than 100 percent effective, even the best possible machine that can be imagined will, slowly but surely, slow down and eventually stop. Similar arguments tell us that no one will ever be able to make an automobile run using water as fuel. This is because water is a degraded product of combustion (with oxygen) of a fuel containing hydrogen; it cannot be reused without supplying additional energy. This is the same argument as the one stating that exhaust fumes cannot be used again in an engine.

Other powers of the second law go beyond the simple area of accounting for the relationship between energy and work—for example, in explaining how refrigeration works.[10]

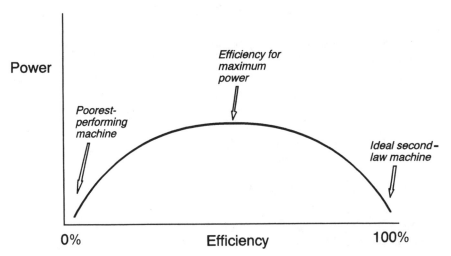

FIGURE 3.2 Power and Efficiency

Primary, Secondary, and Consumer Energy

Some forms of energy exist as such in nature, whereas some must be produced from other forms. Electricity cannot be made available in a controlled form for an economy without its being produced from another form of energy, such as geothermal or nuclear heat, coal, oil, or gas in a power station or elevated water in a hydroelectric station. Those forms of energy that are obtained or extracted without requiring the transformation of significant proportions of other forms of energy are termed *primary energy;* other forms, such as electricity, are *secondary energy.*

All forms of energy are subject to losses in distribution to the consumer. Electricity distribution systems typically "lose" some 10 to 15 percent of the electricity produced by the power stations in transmission along lines to the consumer. Crude oil is subject to refining losses of 5 to 8 percent, representing the oil consumed to drive processes in the refinery. The energy actually delivered to consumers is termed *consumer energy.*

The Accessibility of Energy Resources

Extraction of an energy resource (from a coal mine or an oil or gas well) is followed by conversion (coal washing, oil refining, gas treatment, or thermal power station) and then delivery (via train, truck, pipeline, or transmission lines) before reaching the consumer. This raises the seldom-recognized but very important question of the accessibility of energy resources. We will look at accessibility in more detail in chapter 6, but the general principle is illustrated in figure 3.3.

This type of energy study is often termed *net energy analysis,* since its aim is to determine how much net energy is actually delivered to the economy. Obviously, if more energy is delivered to the economy (flow E) than is required from it in flow F, there is a net energy flow into the economy. But if the reverse applies, more energy is needed to run the energy industry than the economy gets from it. That would be a rather pointless activity! However, in times of strong pressure to expand growth in the energy sector, it is not impossible to envisage such an occurrence.

Reversibility

An important benefit of thermodynamics is that unlike classical physics or neoclassical economics, it does not assume that processes are perfectly reversible. *Reversibility* would mean that any action could always be reversed, and the original state always perfectly restored, after any displacement. If this were so, machines could go on forever; perpetual motion would be possible. Thermodynamics shows us why this is not so and why real processes and machines are, and always will be, irreversible. Although hydrogen and oxygen can combine to form water (and in doing so release energy—e.g., as heat of combustion), and it is also possible to decompose that water back into hydrogen and oxygen (e.g., by electrolysis), more energy is always required for the reverse process than is released in the first process.[11]

The Direction of Time

Another valuable attribute of the second law of thermodynamics is its ability to enlarge our understanding of the meaning of time. This has applications in many areas of science and will, in time, affect a number of areas of economics.

Consider the distinction between the past and the future. Taking a movie film and running it backward is always good fun. The swimmer who jumps backward out of the water, landing dry on the diving board, and the broken pieces of a plate on the floor that reassemble themselves before rising to the table next to the elbow of the person who knocked it over, are well-known jokes, but they have important things to say about energy.

Since perfect reversibility is impossible, thermodynamics provides us with a means of showing why time goes in one direction only—why it cannot be

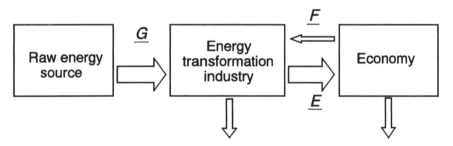

FIGURE 3.3 Energy Supply Industry. *An energy-refining industry (e.g., a thermal power station) takes a quantity G of raw resource (e.g., coal) and converts it, with the aid of a quantity F of a feedback flow of embodied energy from the economy, into a quantity E of a form suitable for delivery to the economy (e.g., electricity).*

turned back, like the hands of a clock. The broken plate provides us with a good illustration of the point. Ignoring, for the moment, the fact that the plate is broken, let us concentrate on the fact that it is on the floor, having fallen from the table. We know from experience that no matter how long we wait, the plate will not spontaneously rise from the floor and reposition itself on the table. To achieve that increase in potential energy, someone has to pick it up. In other words, energy has to be supplied from an external source—the person who picks it up. In falling to the floor, the plate first converted its potential energy (a function of the height of the table above the floor) into the kinetic energy it gained as a result of falling from the table to the floor. What happened to this energy? It was converted, when the plate hit the floor, into the energy required to break it into pieces and into heat energy. After the fall, the pieces and the floor would have been just a little warmer than before. (In the same way, the water at the bottom of Niagara Falls has been measured as being just a little warmer—about a quarter of a degree—than that leaving the top of the Falls.)

We know that it is not possible to capture all of the energy released in the plate's fall in order to restore it to its position on the table. Equally, it is not possible to restore the broken plate to complete wholeness again, even though the pieces may be stuck together into an approximation of their former shape by the application of care, concentration, and glue. The breakage is irreversible. This illustration points out that things always happen irreversibly in real life; divers have to get out of the pool and climb back up to the diving platform; machines always wear out; squashed hedgehogs on a road do not spontaneously reassemble themselves, get up, and amble away; nothing lasts forever. Time rolls on, in one direction only.

It is important to remember, however, that the phenomenon of "running down" applies only to isolated systems. Thus, provided one winds a clock regularly, one is supplying it with the energy it needs to keep going; if forgotten, the clock soon stops. Open and closed systems, which receive energy (and, for open systems, matter) from their surroundings, can in theory go on forever provided energy keeps coming in. The earth is a closed system in that it exchanges only energy with its surroundings, outer space.[12] But the earth-sun system is approximately isolated, since so far as we know it does not receive significant amounts of energy from elsewhere in space.[13] Thus, life on earth can go on for a long time to come using the constant supply of energy available from the sun. Such processes are energetically sustainable, whereas life-styles typical of present-day Western nations, which depend on exploitation of limited stock resources, are not.

Entropy

A fifth statement of the second law of thermodynamics is not so obvious as the previous ones, but it brings in some of the points just discussed: *In spontaneous processes, concentrations tend to disperse, structure tends to disappear, and order becomes disorder.*

In thermodynamics, there is a concept called *entropy* that is a measure of the amount of energy no longer capable of conversion into work after a transformation process has taken place. It is thus a measure of the unavailability of energy. Entropy can also be shown to be a measure of the level of disorder of a system. Thus, the pile of broken pieces of china on the floor has a greater entropy than would the same plate, unbroken, on the floor, and the plate on the floor has a greater entropy than did the same plate on the table. If the second law is restated in yet another way, still equivalent to the others, in order to bring in the concept of entropy, it becomes this: *All physical processes proceed in such a way that the entropy of the universe increases.*

Order and Probability

The meaning of the term "disorder" is bound up with the concept of probability. *Disorder* is represented by a situation in which the outward appearance of an object is consistent with a large number of different possible internal arrangements. *Order* represents a situation in which there are relatively few possible arrangements. The overall structure of a hay barn, for example, represents order, since very few of the multitude of possible arrangements of lengths of timber and boxes of nails can be interpreted as being those of a barn. A heap of that same timber and nails, on the other hand, can be arranged in an enormous number of ways, while still recognizable as nothing but a heap. It thus represents disorder.

Order signifies that the whole of any assembly is not just the sum of its parts. The whole is strongly affected by the relationships among the parts and how these relationships are organized. The whole is therefore a *system*, the behavior of which is strongly affected by its design. The barn is a system whose form and function are strongly affected by its structure and whose characteristics go far beyond those of the heap of nails and timber used to build it.

Similar arguments can be applied to a society. Order in a society implies structure, and structure implies that some combinations of the people in it have properties different from those of people in other structures. That brings in the issue of politics and the ways in which society orders its activities and processes, and structures its political and administrative systems, to benefit its members (or otherwise).[14]

THE THIRD LAW OF THERMODYNAMICS

The third law of thermodynamics—the law of unattainability of absolute zero temperature—states: *The entropy of an ideal crystal at 0 degrees Kelvin is zero.*

This law provides an absolute benchmark—the temperature 0 degrees Kelvin, or −273.15 degrees Celsius. This is unattainable because it is the lowest temperature that can possibly exist, and it can be only approached, never actually reached. The third law is not needed for most thermodynamic work, but it is a reminder that like the maximum efficiency of an ideal engine, there are a number of absolute limits—impossibilities—in physics. No matter how ingenious humans may become in the future, they can never beat these limits.

NATURE, NONEQUILIBRIUM PROCESSES, AND THERMODYNAMICS

Natural processes do not constitute a violation of the laws of thermodynamics, despite the fact that order appears to have come out of disorder. The development of complex living organisms and ecosystems was achieved by the interaction of earthly matter and solar energy; the flow of energy from the sun is the central feature of that interaction.

Animals and plants use energy inflow to build order and structure out of disorder—raw materials in their environment. In doing so, they operate far from equilibrium with their surroundings. For this reason, the ordered structures must also, according to the second law, dissipate into their surroundings as low-temperature heat a significant proportion of the energy that they take in. Living systems are *dissipative structures;* they not only obtain available energy from their surroundings but also use that availability to reduce their own entropy. They take *negentropy* (negative entropy, or order) from their surroundings. At the same time, they increase the entropy (disorder) of those surroundings by a greater amount.

The process that enables living systems to maintain and reproduce themselves is known as *autopoiesis.* It is a product of the complex, interdependent relationships of energy and material flows that link an ecosystem's components. The structure and integrity of these relationships not only define the system but also are essential for the production and maintenance of the participating components in it. Autopoiesis is possible only because ecosystems, unlike economic systems, are driven by an external source of available energy, the sun. That stream of solar energy sustains essentially all biological activity and makes possible the diversity of life on earth. Through photosynthesis, living systems concentrate simple chemicals and use them to synthesize complex and energy-rich compounds. In thermophysical terms, photosynthesis is the most important truly productive process on earth. In strong contrast to economic systems, ecosystems accumulate energy, matter, and order.[15]

The fact that evolution occurs in the natural world is a direct consequence of the irreversibility of real-world processes. As I pointed out earlier, if everything were perfectly reversible, every disturbance would eventually be canceled out, and the original state would be restored. In real life, this is not possible; the result is a new state. The reversible world of classical physics (and of neoclassical economics) is limited to a state of "being." The real world of nature (and of complex systems) allows for the state of "becoming," in which the new is created irreversibly and spontaneously from the old, and opportunities exist for radical change. Ecosystems are inherently self-organizing and self-sustaining and contribute to reduction of global entropy. In doing so, they do not grow beyond a dynamic *steady state*, characterized by the presence of limiting factors and feedback flows that constrain the system to a scale that is sustainable from the resources available to it. I draw the reader's attention to the fact that conventional economics acknowledges no such limits, nor any form of steady state, as the long-term outcome of social evolution. Since every economy exists physically within its surrounding ecosystem, this raises serious doubts about the fundamental assumptions of mainstream economic theories.[16] I address these issues in detail in later chapters.

An important conclusion we reach from the biophysical systems viewpoint of nature is that all life is characterized by processes that are far from equilibrium. Anything that is in equilibrium with its surroundings is inanimate or dead. Life exists only in the absence of equilibrium.

As I pointed out earlier, the earth is not an isolated system—it receives a vast flow of energy from the sun. Any decrease in entropy on the earth due to the development of natural and technological structures is more than counterbalanced by the increase in entropy of the sun itself. The earth-sun system's entropy is therefore increasing in accordance with the second law of thermodynamics. We expect the sun to keep on shining for another few bil-

lion years, but on present indications, the fossil fuel resources on which recent technological developments have been based are likely to become less
accessible, and therefore more costly, sometime in the next few decades—
long before they are in any sense exhausted. This is another subject to which
we will return later.

ENERGY AND THE ECONOMIC PROCESS

The central physical fact about the economic processes of production and
consumption is that matter is rearranged. Matter cannot be created or destroyed by an economy, only changed in form. This is the case when ores are
processed into motor vehicles and the matter (steel, etc.) in those same vehicles is eventually dissipated as waste by being dumped or recycled as scrap.
Some wastes are recyclable, but many have to be assimilated by nature. We
know that nature's capacity to absorb waste is limited—often severely—and
in such cases, wastes accumulate.

All such processes are associated with the transformation of high-quality
available energy into low-quality waste energy. Entropy provides us with a
useful index for measuring the accumulation of useless and/or harmful wastes
from human economic activity.[17] The entropy concept applies as much to
materials (in which energy is a measure of structural order) as to heat flows.

SCIENTIFIC DEVELOPMENT AND THE
LAWS OF THERMODYNAMICS

Some people argue that it is stupid to accept the laws of thermodynamics
slavishly. After all, Einstein overturned much of what was known in physics
by his work on relativity. Once thermodynamics has its Einstein, humanity
will be free to find ways around the problems of limits to technological innovation.

This type of argument results from a fundamental misunderstanding of the
ways in which scientific knowledge develops over time. Einstein's theories did
not change the ways in which the planets move, nor the direction in which
an apple falls from a tree; his theories were better models of physical phenomena than Newton's but nothing more. In the same way, we can be confident
that the laws of thermodynamics will someday be developed and refined, but
a hot saucepan will still cool when removed from a stove, and stones will not
spontaneously roll uphill. Reality itself will not change one iota, even though
our explanations for it will evolve from time to time.

4

The Political-Economic World View

IN THIS BOOK, I contrast two very different world views, the political-economic and biophysical systems views. From the political-economic viewpoint, the world is a place where people make all decisions of importance and human ingenuity is the main determinant of options for the future. An economy is seen as a system of production, organized according to a social system of signals.[1] In market economies, these signals are in the form of prices paid by consumer to producer for goods and services. In centrally planned economies, the signals are often expressed in monetary units, but they may be determined by criteria other than markets.

ECONOMICS

The word "economics" is derived from the Greek word *oikonomia*, which means "management of the household." It has come to apply to the whole range of households, from the person to the nation-state or group of states. Its original ("household") meaning actually spans the range from cost accounting to loving care of everyone and everything.

In the classical economic tradition, land and resources were the base on which economic activity was built.[2] The scientific discoveries of the eighteenth and nineteenth centuries encouraged many economists and technologists to believe that humanity could free itself from the limitations of resource scarcity and that anything was possible, virtually without limit (see chapters 9 and 12). The classical tradition then separated into three main lines, the neoclassical, the neo-Marxist, and the neo-Malthusian.[3]

Standard neoclassical economics (in the Western tradition) directs its attention to the study of how best to allocate scarce means among given ends. That being so, it is not surprising that theories of human behavior are at the very center of the subject. The methods of neoclassical economics are based on ideas about the behavior of people as individuals, which are then used to develop hypotheses about the behavior of whole societies.

In the Marxist economic tradition (and in its successor, the neo-Marxist), the main concern is not allocation but distribution of the fruits of production. In that tradition, individuals are less important than the collective, and (in theory, at least) the function of the state is to ensure that everyone in the working class obtains a share of the goods and services available.

Over the past hundred years, as is well known, these dominant views have been in conflict economically, politically, and militarily. The recent collapse of the Soviet Union system appears, however, to have come about more through the inefficiency and corruption of entrenched state planning bureaucracies than through any demonstrated fundamental defect in the underlying theory.

In neither view is the environment important; it is no more than the source of raw materials and the sink to which wastes may be sent.

The assumptions on which both of these systems of economics depend are, I would point out, neither proved nor (in most cases) provable, and they are still subject to a great deal of contention. They are more ideologies than scientific theories, despite widely held views to the contrary.

The biophysical systems concern that is the main topic of this book can be seen in some respects as a modern reflection of the views of Thomas Malthus (1766–1834), who suggested that since unchecked human populations tend to increase at an accelerating rate, food and other resources will in the long term not be adequate.[4] That Malthus's projections were not correct in the short term has not in any way demonstrated that they may not be correct in principle in the long term. Hence, those who view the question of scale as a dominant long-term issue for societies are sometimes termed neo-Malthusians.

TWO WORLD VIEWS

Standard economic theory (both neoclassical and neo-Marxist) rests on the assumption that resources obtained from nature are "free goods" that have no value other than that given by the economy. Both the resources and the waste-absorbing capacity of the environment are assumed to be either infinite or directly controllable such that in neither case is there any real limit to total economic activity. In market economies, commodities (goods and services) have prices that measure their value.

From the biophysical systems viewpoint, however, society is part of a world where physical factors are often important and sometimes dominant, where some things are physically impossible, and where people have limited (albeit still considerable) freedom to choose their futures.

The political-economic view is dominant in the Western, "developed" one-third of the world and affects much of what goes on in the "developing" two-thirds. The biophysical systems view is commonly ignored by people holding to the political-economic view because humankind has apparently overcome resource shortages in the past and is believed capable of doing so in the future. From the point of view of its protagonists, however, the biophysical systems world view describes the framework within which the political-economic view has its existence.

SOCIAL AND ECONOMIC SYSTEMS

Human beings always have needs, for material sustenance and for social and personal security. Society is the vehicle within which these needs can be met. For most of human history, the two types of need existed together and were supplied together, in communities. As populations grew, ideas about society evolved. At least three main approaches to the organization of society have been devised—the informal economy, the formal economy, and the mixed economy—and these will undoubtedly evolve further.

The *informal economy* has probably existed since humanity evolved. Examples of present-day structures are the migratory bands of Australian Aboriginals and the settled villages of the Polynesians. From birth to death, members' essential needs are met in the context of the group. The size and nature of the group may change with seasons and availability of food supplies or as the result of other activities. Items of property may be shared or privately owned, according to custom and negotiation.

Formal economies are more recent. As populations grew and as technology (especially agriculture) improved, societies were organized on a larger scale. Two types of formal social organization are the state redistributive economy and the market economy. In a *state redistributive economy*, the tools and fruits of production are controlled by state rulers and bureaucrats. Ancient Egypt under the pharaohs functioned for around 3,000 years. The former Soviet Union and China are more recent examples.

Some degree of trading is probably as old as humanity itself. For the necessities of life, however, people depended on their local resources, families, and kin groups, trading only surpluses with others to obtain goods not available within their own groups. As surpluses and wealth increased, those who had them devoted a greater fraction of available resources to maintaining social order and protecting the accumulated wealth. The cost of maintaining law and order and protecting wealth (and privilege for those who "owned" it) increased rapidly, until nowadays a very large proportion of most countries' production of goods and services is devoted to the armaments and social structures that "ensure" security.

A full-fledged *market system* probably came into operation around the Mediterranean a few centuries before Christ.[5] In such systems, together with the much more recent emergence of cheap energy and modern technology, lie the roots of modern capitalist society. Although not needed in informal economies, money soon came to be the generally accepted and culturally conditioned means of exchange among large, diverse groups and societies, for which a barter system was no longer adequate. Money has developed to provide economies with a criterion with which to measure social activities.

Most countries now employ some kind of *mixed economy*, in which the market system operates for much of the exchange of goods and services and of labor and capital, but central government provides such services as defense and justice. In many countries, the government also redistributes some wealth to meet people's needs for essentials, including education, health, and financial security. This in turn provides the market sector with able-bodied and trained workers.

In the conventional political-economic perspective, work is engaged in for the purpose of earning money, which in turn is necessary to ensure survival. Not often appreciated is the fact that formal economies are entirely dependent on (informal) household or kin groups as their basic units. "Nonworking" women usually provide the social infrastructure that holds society together and without which it could not function. This work (sometimes termed *shadow work*) may involve a wife's support of her husband in paid employment—support without which he would be unable to carry out that employment—and the bearing and care of children. Another type of women's work is *gift work*, characterized by the free giving of time and effort to others in the community. Responsibility for care of the elderly and sick, and support of other activities that ensure cohesion and stability of society, are tasks that are normally accepted by women. These types of work—and they are as physically and mentally demanding as paid work in the labor market— form the foundation of a stable society and a healthy economy, but they are neither directly rewarded nor included in aggregated national economic accounts. They are therefore invisible to conventional economic and political theorists.[6]

Over the past two hundred years, economists have advanced our understanding of economic behavior as an important part of the general area of decision making in society.[7] Because of its intimate involvement in many areas of government, especially those that involve advising politicians on matters relevant to social decision making, economics is also profoundly (and properly, although seldom acknowledged as such) political. Hence the title of this chapter.

POLITICAL-ECONOMIC BELIEFS

Those who hold to the political-economic world view take for granted, among other things, that

- people exist as individual, independent entities;
- nature and societies have an order to them;
- scientific observation is objective;
- people have always desired private property;
- competition between individuals has always occurred.

These beliefs are considered to be part of human nature, common to all societies and therefore unchanging. (In the remainder of this book, I concentrate my attention on conventional market economies of the Western tradition, since it is those with which I am generally familiar.)

The two most basic "laws" of conventional economics are as follows:

- The *law of diminishing marginal utility* states that people satisfy their most pressing wants first. Each additional dollar, pound, or franc of income or unit of resource is used to satisfy a less pressing want than the previous one.
- The *law of increasing marginal cost* states that producers first use the best-quality inputs (most experienced workers, most fertile land, cheapest resources, etc.) in their best combination. They use the poorer-quality (more costly or less productive) inputs only when they run out of the better ones or when an input (e.g., land) becomes fixed in size.[8]

The basic beliefs of conventional economics stem largely from eighteenth- and nineteenth-century scientific ideas. Many of these ideas have since been modified, and others rejected, by sociologists, anthoropologists, and psychologists who study human behavior. That they are still firmly held by many economists and politicians of the Western tradition is a good reason to be careful in interpreting some of the findings of conventional economics. Whereas hypotheses in the physical sciences are tested according to the criteria listed in chapter 2 (especially the criterion of refutability), it is difficult to subject hypotheses in the social sciences to such tests. Thus, many have not been tested according to strict scientific principles. This is one reason for the disagreement between the social scientists and the economists and politicians.

Welfare

Economics studies how to make choices among scarce means that satisfy human wants. A good is scarce whenever something else we want has to be sacrificed in order to get it. The satisfaction of wants that results from dealing with scarce means is called *welfare*. Conventionally, the level of welfare is measured in terms of the monetary value of the basket of goods and services produced by society and by virtually nothing else. However, although goods and services are of considerable importance, we also know that welfare depends on such things as

- scarce environmental goods (in the broad sense, including space, energy, natural resources, plants, and animals);
- time, including leisure time;
- income distribution;
- working conditions;
- employment;
- the safety of the future, insofar as this depends on our behavior in relation to the use of scarce goods.[9]

All seven factors play a role in our dealings with scarce goods, and in everyday life there is a sense in which we or our decision makers constantly weigh them against one another. Many of us would hesitate to measure any but the first—goods and services—in monetary terms—they are too complex for money to measure.

THE ECONOMIC VIEW OF HUMAN BEHAVIOR

Traditional economics rests on several important assumptions about the way humans behave in society.[10] More particularly, these assumptions relate to the way in which a simplified model of humanity, *Homo oeconomicus* ("economic man"), behaves in the marketplace, for that is where most important social decisions are believed to be made. The assumptions reflect a belief that some basic types of human behavior are inherent in all people:

- Individuals always act rationally in the pursuit of their self-interest; that is, people act in such a way as to maximize their satisfaction, or utility. Similarly, firms seek to maximize a criterion such as profit.
- Each individual has personal preferences (desires and tastes) that are independent of everyone else's.
- The information required to maximize utility is freely available, accurate, and timely. Another way of putting this assumption is that everyone in a market has perfect information.
- Markets are efficient.
- The pursuit of maximal individual gain often produces optimal social welfare.
- Departures from the ideal of the free market usually reduce efficiency and social welfare, though markets are often regulated to meet political and social ends.

There is also the implicit assumption that there is no clear limit to people's wants. In other words, acquisitiveness is unlimited.

There is a philosophical distinction in economics between the *positive* (or descriptive) branch, which attempts to study questions of "why things happen," and the *normative* (prescriptive) branch, which examines questions of "what ought to be." The normative branch depends on prior definition of a social objective. Ethical and political theories thus provide the underpinnings of normative economics, together with assumptions about the meaning of utility, welfare, and so on. The distinction between the branches is often not clear, and in any case it is usually forgotten or ignored in practice, particularly by politicians.

The Marketplace

These assumptions, together with the associated assumption of *property rights*—that everything that can be treated as individual property is tradable—are the basis of what is known as the *marketplace,* or equilibrium price auction, in which willing buyers interact with willing sellers. In such an auction, people ("actors in the marketplace") bid for goods and services; the highest bidder gets them. If there are a lot of bidders for a small quantity of goods, the bids will be high; the converse holds if there are only a few bidders for a lot of goods. Bids soon settle down to an equilibrium level, or *price,* at which the supply of goods is in balance with customers' willingness to pay. Free markets are self-controlling in that they automatically *clear.* This means that excess supply is mopped up by low prices, which induce greater purchasing, whereas lack of supply encourages higher bids, which cut out demand from people who are unwilling (or unable) to pay the higher prices.

With such assumptions about property rights and the behavior of individuals in a marketplace, economics has come up with many powerful hypotheses. These attempt to explain not only what happens in certain social situations but also, more significantly, what *should* happen in those situations for the social systems to operate at maximum "efficiency." The theories help us understand much of importance in society, but they can also be used as tools (and as blueprints) for control of people by the governments that set the economic mechanisms in place.

This description of people as actors in the marketplace derives from the eighteenth-century ideas of Adam Smith (who in turn was influenced by the seventeenth-century philosophers Thomas Hobbes and John Locke—see chapter 12). According to Milton and Rose Friedman:

> Adam Smith's key insight was that both parties to an exchange can benefit and that, so long as cooperation is strictly voluntary, no exchange will take place unless both parties do benefit. No external force, no coercion, no violation of freedom is necessary to produce cooperation among individuals all of whom can benefit. That is why, as Adam Smith put it, an individual who "intends only his own gain" is "led by an invisible hand to promote an end which was no part of his intention. Nor is it always the worse for the society that it was no part of it. By pursuing his own interest he frequently promotes that of the society more effectually than when he really intends to promote it. I have never known much good done by those who affected to trade for the public good."[11]

As observed by Smith, the market was a place where buyers and sellers came together in one place to sell food, clothing, domestic animals, and so on. Although such markets still exist, the term is now more of an abstraction. A reference to the marketplace is now a reference to the general process of buying and selling of some product, service, or token. It is as likely to take place via telephone or computer terminal as between people in one place. The cooperative spirit and personal relationships of a village or community market are thus often excluded. For many people, nevertheless, even such a mundane task as shopping involves much more (e.g., social contacts) than a simple trading opportunity.

BRANCHES OF ECONOMICS

Figure 4.1 illustrates the distinctions among different branches of economics relevant to the topics discussed here.[12] Standard economics generally addresses itself only to human-human situations. Environmental economics deals with issues relating to the effect of human economic activities on nature—for example, "externalities" such as pollution. Resource economics concentrates on the flow of resources from nature to humanity. Ecology studies the nature-nature system.

Ecological economics is a modern development that attempts to address the whole humanity-nature system in a nonreductionist, scientific "systems" way. It looks at transformation of resources into goods and services for the human system, including the inevitable waste and pollution returned to nature. Throughput of energy and matter is the central concept in ecological economics. I discuss it in chapters 15 and 16.

EFFICIENCY AND OPTIMAL RESOURCE ALLOCATION

The concept of *economic efficiency* arises from the aim of economics to study the allocation of scarce resources among competing ends. "Resources" in this

	To human society	To nature
From human society	Standard economics	Environmental economics
From nature	Resource economics	Ecology

Ecological economics

FIGURE 4.1 Branches of Economics Included within Ecological Economics

context means anything desired by a potential buyer. Conventional economic theory focuses on the question of how to allocate resources (labor, capital, etc.) in such a way as to achieve optimum production or distribution. An efficient allocation is known as a Pareto optimum. In the context of distribution, a *Pareto optimum* is that allocation of resources such that no other allocation would make any consumer better off without making another consumer worse off. In the context of production, the situation is optimal if it is not possible for one producer to increase the production of economic goods without diminishing that of another by a greater amount. Efficiency is a characteristic of the whole economy.

The Pareto optimum should be determined using entirely general concepts of socioeconomic value, but in practice all that is available is prices in the marketplace. Markets are never ideal; hence, prices are never more than an approximation of the nebulous concept of socioeconomic value. For that reason, economic efficiency should be regarded as a concept, not a number. It is never unequivocally clear that an optimum allocation has been achieved in any situation; all that can be said is that a certain policy or decision appears likely to give rise to an increase or a decrease in efficiency. In practice, any such conclusion is more likely to reflect beliefs of the analyst than objective measurement.

There is a clear distinction between the aggregate economic advantage gained by society as a whole and the relative advantages gained by particular groups within that society. If a person benefits from an activity by, say, $10,000 and a hundred others gain nothing, their aggregate economy has benefited by a total of $10,000. If each of the hundred has a small benefit of, say, $10 and the individual has nothing, the economy benefits by only $1,000. The first of the two activities is clearly much better for the economy as a whole, but the fabric of society may benefit more from the second. Thus, the "efficient" allocation may be manifestly unfair to those with no economic power. A common response is that the person with $10,000 can be expected to spend it, with results that provide employment and income to others. This is the trickle-down theory, which undoubtedly has some validity. But the fact remains that in one case, a hundred people have some power over their lives; in the other, they depend on another person. Justice, equity, and freedom involve more than aggregate monetary income.

Economic efficiency has nothing to do with *equity*, which is the fairness of, or absence of discrimination in, allocation of resources. Pareto efficiency is an individual-directed criterion that excludes any ethic of collective values, especially those involving future generations. [13]

PRODUCTION

Production is the creation of a good or service that people will buy. Materials of low value are transformed by the production process into something of higher value, where value is determined by the price that people will pay in the marketplace. Coal in the ground or water in a mountain lake is of no "value" until potentially or actually transformed into something (coal delivered to a factory or electricity transmitted to a meter) that people are willing to pay for. The theory of production explains how producers combine inputs to provide a given output.

The whole point of production is that value is embodied in the product at each stage of production. There is no point in producing something unless it can be sold at a price higher than the cost of making it. The selling price is measured by social means via the marketplace and is independent of the physical inputs to the production process (the cost).

Production is often represented by an output, which is a good or service produced from inputs. In the most general case, the inputs are of labor and capital, according to some relationship (governed by technology) that is specific to the process involved. All of these are expressed in monetary terms in that the important things are the costs of the factors of production (labor and capital) determined in appropriate markets in a consistent monetary unit, such as the dollar or pound. The good or service itself may be produced from various combinations of labor and capital, and the mix of these (and/or other) factor inputs can be varied (assuming that they are substitutable) to minimize the cost of production. This is an important point because in an ideal marketplace, a customer is willing to pay only up to a certain maximum price for the item. For a given price, the lower the cost of production, the higher will be the profit taken by the producer.

If one input to production becomes more expensive than an alternative, substitution can be expected to take place in order to minimize the total cost of production and thereby maximize profit.[14] Thus, when wage costs (labor) increase, producers tend to install labor-saving equipment (capital). Many transnational producers shift production from one country to another to take advantage of low labor rates (and other inducements negotiated with the host country, such as tax breaks).

The Marginal Cost of Production

The marginal cost of production is the cost of producing one more item over and above that which is currently produced. In most industries, new investment enables an organization to reduce the marginal cost of production, perhaps because of better technology. The lower cost of marginal production means that the product either gives a better profit figure or can be sold for a lower price in the market. In this way, competition in the marketplace ensures that efficient producers supersede others.

In the energy field, however, the opposite is beginning to occur. Until relatively recently, each new power station generated electricity at a lower cost than the one before it. Over the past decade or so, the situation has changed in that current average production costs are (relatively) low but further increments of production are often achieved only at a higher cost. This has been observed in many industrialized countries. Competition in the marketplace does not easily occur in this type of situation. New power station construction is in one sense encouraged; people paying current (usually averaged) prices do not receive signals from the marketplace to limit the increases in consumption that will collectively give rise to the need for new capacity. However, the generating authority can afford new power stations only if it charges higher prices than necessary to cover current costs or borrows heavily. Although most people are prepared to buy electricity at current prices, many would be unable to maintain their present level of consumption if prices were much higher.

The point needs to be emphasized that efficient allocation of resources cannot easily occur when the cost of extra production is rising and extra consumption is charged for at the average cost of production. Thus, the electricity supply industry will never be economically efficient if its tariffs are based on average production costs. The same general argument applies to the coal industry, in which most new mines will produce coal at a higher cost than in the past. In the long term, it will happen to the gas industry; when the gas fields now in use are exhausted, gas will be available from coal but at a much higher cost, especially if environmental pollution costs are included.

One theory of economics suggests that the answer to this problem is to charge for *all* present-day supply at the long-run marginal cost—that is, the cost of supply from new power stations. [15] By this means, a surplus is generated, which may be used by the supplier for investment in the new capacity and/or by government to recompense consumers who are disadvantaged by the high prices, such as those on low incomes. Of course, prices of that size would rapidly discourage most forms of consumption to the extent that the "need" for new generating capacity would soon decline.

CONSUMPTION

Given a limited income, the consumer is faced with the decision as to how to spend it. Consumption of goods and services gives rise to utility, or satisfaction. It is assumed that consumers always attempt to maximize their utility by rational decision making in the marketplace and to increase it if possible. When the price for one good or service is low compared with a related one, that fact will encourage purchase and thereby give satisfaction to the consumer. The principal economic determinants of consumer behavior relative to a given commodity are believed to be monetary income, consumer tastes, and the prices of related commodities.

THE ECONOMIC MODEL OF SOCIETY

The conventional economist's model of society (figure 4.2) is that of a place in which consumers sell their labor and capital to producers, who in turn sell

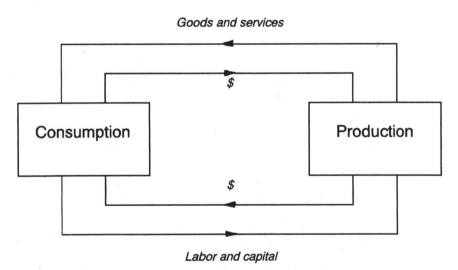

FIGURE 4.2 The Economist's Model of Society

goods and services for consumers to buy. Each depends on the other; the economy is essentially a perpetual-motion machine that runs according to its own internal rules. Resources are obtained from the environment and wastes are rejected back to it, but everything of real importance is internal to the economy.

EQUILIBRIUM AND GROWTH

In economics, the term "equilibrium" refers to a configuration of the economy in which there is no tendency toward relative change. The most straightforward example is when demand and supply are in balance; the forces of the marketplace will always move the system back to equilibrium if it departs from it.

An economic system is generally regarded as normal and healthy if it is steadily growing, with all of its components in market equilibrium. Standard economic theories generally assume that once equilibrium is reached, any change or evolution in the internal structure of the system will take place in a steady, progressive manner. It will do so in response to changes in production and consumption brought about by technological developments and to changes in prices of imports and exports.

THE ECONOMIC VIEW OF NATURAL RESOURCES

The environmental strategy of mainstream economics is to use markets to solve environmental problems. The strategy stands on three legs—the sovereignty of the individual, the sanctity of private property, and the domination of present-day interests over those of the future.[16]

In most countries, resources start off as common property, usually controlled by the government. For a value to be attached to them, they must be put into the marketplace by assigning property rights for their exploitation. This is usually done by putting blocks of a resource out to tender or by assigning ownership to some individual or organization, who then obtains the best price possible in the marketplace. It is an implicit assumption in all of this that participants in the marketplace are in a position to evaluate the present and future demand-price relationship for the resource. They then act in such a way as to maximize their own commercial benefit and, through it, that of the economy as a whole. Prices are the most efficient means of controlling flows of resources from the environment to the economy, as well as flows of goods and services within the economy.

In standard economics, the economy interacts with its environment to obtain resources and reject wastes. Nature is a munificent source of free resources and an unlimited sink for free disposal of wastes. Only the economic effort required to extract resources and reject wastes is measured directly. The value of resources is set by the marketplace in that the "owner" of a resource can put it up for auction and the highest bidder will obtain it. Wastes can be treated similarly, with the "owner" (if there is one) of a sink inviting bids from producers of wastes for their disposal.

Standard economic theory thus stands on the questionable assumption that nature is effectively inert to humanity until human labor and capital are expended in her domain, whereupon she yields free gifts and free waste disposal. Thus, man (again, I use the term "man" deliberately, to draw attention to the context of this model) is the only active participant. Damage to nature is acknowledged only when man judges that damage to have affected his use or enjoyment of life. Nature exists only to service man. This picture is common to capitalist and socialist traditions alike.

In the standard economic viewpoint, resources, both now and in the future, are "worth" what people will pay for them today. It is a short step further to see resources in the generalized sense, as dollars or pounds, not as trees or tonnes of coal. Thus, the market functions much as a food processor—it reduces a rich, complex mixture to a uniform mush. If all one needs is mush, that is no disadvantage, but many resources are needed for characteristics that are highly specific and not necessarily substitutable by another.

If one gets into the habit of thinking of resources in monetary terms, the information ("informational mush") one obtains is much less ordered than the reality it purports to value.[17] This way of thinking can also give rise to *money fetishism*, a condition in which the pursuit of money in its own right comes to take precedence over the physical realities of production and consumption of material goods and services. I discuss this in more detail in chapter 9.

EXTERNALITIES—THE ECONOMIC VIEW OF POLLUTION

The market's inability to assign a value to everything that a society judges to be of importance is summed up under the term "externalities." This term represents components of importance to society that are outside the marketplace. Although their existence is readily accepted by economists, externalities are almost impossible to evaluate and are usually ignored.

Externalities can, in theory, be internalized when the costs are immediately imposed elsewhere—for example, when taxes, cleanup costs, or damages can be demanded as compensation from those responsible. But such internalization at best applies only to other economic actors, such as people affected by pollution; it never applies to nature herself. Externalities to be borne by future generations are also excluded from current economic decisions because the interests of the present generation are seen as overwhelmingly greater than those of future generations. (See chapter 8 for a more detailed discussion of externalities.)

THE TIME VALUE OF MONEY

Most economic concepts relate to structures (or models) of society that are seen as more or less static, but economics does recognize the need to allocate resources over time as well as among consumers in a marketplace at a given point in time. Capital theory purports to enable the question to be asked: "How should a market resolve the problem of allocating resources over time in order to maximize welfare?"

The social valuation of time depends heavily on the historical and cultural background of a society. It is observed that societies that do not value time highly do not use large amounts of resources, whereas societies that consider time very important attempt to "save" time by using large quantities of resources, such as fuels. The social value of time should reflect social factors, but in practice it is usually evaluated via the activities of financially powerful groups operating in large-scale money (capital) markets.

The economic treatment of time is bound up with the idea that a dollar in the hand today is worth more than a dollar in the hand in, say, a year's time. One can use today's dollar now to create additional wealth. If one invests the dollar, it will earn interest and will be larger after a year than a dollar kept under the mattress. The converse of this argument is, of course, that next year's dollar is less valuable (in present-day terms) than today's, a dollar in two years' time is worth less again, and so on. The process of addition of interest to money is known as *compounding*. Thus, a dollar invested at 10 percent per annum compounds to $1.10 after one year. Conversely, a dollar that one expects to receive in a year's time is worth only $0.909 in today's monetary terms. This reverse process is known as *discounting*. The higher the discount rate, the less a dollar in the future is worth in today's terms. At high discount rates, even in two years' time, a dollar will have lost a lot of value. At a rate of 10 percent, anything of an economic nature that happens more than ten years into the future is of little value at all and hence takes a relatively small place in today's decision making. (See chapter 7 for more information on compound interest.)

The concept of the time value of money is quite separate from the general effects of inflation. Inflation will reduce the value of money too, but it is usually possible to put money in a reasonably safe bank to retain its purchasing power—its value before inflation. Thus, if inflation is running at, say, 5 percent, all that is necessary to retain the value of money is to get 5 percent interest on it. By careful selection, it is usually possible to get more than 5 percent—say, 8 percent. By this means, the money will increase by around 3 percent net of inflation or, in economic jargon, by 3 percent in real terms. Money kept in a lower-interest deposit or under the mattress will decline in value in real terms, even though the notes or coins themselves may not change.

When individuals decide to save money, they sacrifice the opportunity to spend today in order to enjoy a higher rate of consumption in the future. The time preference of the market as a whole (the interest rate) thus measures the gain required by savers to persuade them to delay consumption.[18] *Social time preference* reflects the idea that most private decisions are believed to neglect the need to take account of future generations. In other words, individuals are seen as always acting in such a way as to maximize their *current* personal utility.

As a result of examination of factors involved in the long-term allocation of resources (mainly of money in capital markets), many economists are of the opinion that the social value of time, known as the *social opportunity cost,* is around 5 to 7 percent in real terms[19] and sometimes is as high as 10 percent.[20] This rate is commonly the basis for decisions about resource allocation by governments. Many economists disagree with these figures; for some, 3 percent is believed to be more realistic. The debate has a long way to go before the viewpoints of the main protagonists are reconciled, but economic advisers who support high rates tend to dominate political decisions.

The problem of allocating resources over time in economics thus comes down to maximizing benefits over the time period of interest. Consider a situation in which a government has two options before it, one that returns a large amount of money toward the end of the project and another that returns less money but does so immediately. By discounting future benefits by, say, 10 percent per year, one can determine the *present value,* the amount of money (in present-day terms) each project will return. The option with largest present value is the better one, economically. When the discount rate is large, quick returns are valued more highly than slow ones, even though the latter may last longer. Hence the advantage of a "quick buck" over a "slow buck."

Economic methods of analysis that use this technique, usually termed *cost-benefit analysis* (CBA), require that future monetary flows (costs and benefits) be known, which obviously is not possible, although they can often be approximately estimated.

In all of this, it is worth remembering that although money is commonly discounted, the idea that resources themselves can or should be discountable is not so clear-cut. Money itself is a socially determined measure of exchange value, expressed as a token. It is not something that has distinct meaning of itself, like cheese or toothpaste, earth, water, or air. Only money slavishly follows the "laws" of compound interest, so only money can be discounted. Many environmental resources may well be worth more in the future than at present, so arguably they should be assigned a *negative* discount rate. Thus, it may be better not to use them now and to keep them for the future.

COST-BENEFIT ANALYSIS

Cost-benefit analysis requires that costs and benefits be reduced to single numbers—present value or a similar measure. Benefits are defined by the extent to which they contribute to achievement of a society's objectives. Costs are defined in terms of the benefits forgone by not using the resources in their next best alternative use. In this manner, we ensure that an alternative way of using the resources would not secure a better result in terms of the society's objectives. By carrying out a CBA, a government determines whether scarce resources, such as capital, should be transferred from the private sector (where they are the property of individuals) to the government (which is supposed to act on behalf of everyone). Such a transfer should be made whenever the net benefits to the whole of society exceed the opportunities forgone by the private sector.

According to this philosophy, the public sector should adopt a lower discount rate than the private sector to give a higher value (resulting from less discounting of future value) to options that lie in the future. In practice, however, the government rate (often about 10 percent) may be as high as that in the private sector. This has important consequences for long-term valuation of resources and means that their value to future generations may be set at a significantly lower level than many people think appropriate. Oil or gas still in the ground in twenty years' time is discounted into insignificance in a CBA, meaning that according to conventional (economic) wisdom, there is no point in not using it now, even if today's uses are far less beneficial than they might be in twenty years.

Environmental and other pollution consequences of a project (externalities) should also be included in a CBA. Even though these factors are external to the economist's abstract world of commodities, they are very much internal to the world in which we live, move, and have our being and our future. That externalities are often difficult to quantify is often used as an excuse for not including them in a CBA, but in such cases (the majority, I suspect), the results will be inherently biased and therefore untrustworthy.[21]

CBA as a technique is not a means of determining what is "best" for society. It is one of a number of crude empirical tools that can be used to illuminate certain perspectives of an area in which a political choice is to be made that is likely to have economic consequences. A project judged to be feasible according to a CBA is in no way certain to ensure that everybody will be better off as a result of the decision.

Sunk Costs

It often happens that capital investments are made before their output is needed by the economy. Well-known examples include electricity generation. Power stations were built rapidly in many developed countries during the 1960s and 1970s, resulting in large surpluses of capacity. The conventional economic response to such a surplus is to accept that the capital investment, having been made, cannot be recovered; it is a *sunk cost*. The bills must be paid, but this should not influence alternative opportunities for future use of the investment. What is important is to seek a use for the investment that will maximize future benefits to the economy rather than worry about making past expenditures look good.

There are problems with this approach. If the initial decisions were made on grounds of political expediency (as was the case in many power station developments), the result is the deliberate preempting of scarce resources, including capital. This cannot fail to limit opportunities for the future and will in some cases result in one government's selfish or incompetent decisions having effects that last for generations. The argument is not peculiar to energy supply, but since energy resources can be used only once, the results may involve irreparable damage to the opportunities available to future generations. The problem is, at base, that of the workings of a democratic political system. If the tools currently available to politicians are manifestly inadequate for the task (as I argue in this book), good decisions are even more difficult to reach.

Uncertainty and Risk in Economic Evaluation

In practice, most economic forecasts contain large uncertainties over time periods as short as one year. Many countries' recent experiences with large energy-based projects should be a warning not to place reliance on short-term projections of economic benefit. Even more, they focus attention on the need to acknowledge the uncertain basis of many political-economic theories of development and wealth creation.

Nevertheless, uncertainty (a common concern of economics) is not the same as *indeterminacy*, the characteristic of complex systems that are not in equilibrium with their surroundings. All such (dissipative) structures have an evolutionary aspect to their existence, in which periods of stability are followed by irreversible, spontaneous change (see chapter 5). This is entirely different from *uncertainty*, a process characterized by modest (usually reversible) deviations from an equilibrium state. Since social systems are known to be dissipative structures, we should be aware of the likelihood that such behavior is also an inherent characteristic of economies.[22] No theory exists, in physics or in economics, to predict the exact outcome of this type of behavior, hence the use of the term "indeterminate"—the outcome becomes clear only after the event.

ECONOMICS AND ENERGY

In conventional economics, the marketplace is where decisions are made about the uses of energy. Everything of importance about energy is incorporated in its price, and the freer and more competitive the market, the more accurate is the price evaluated by it. Energy is simply a tradable commodity, the demand for which is affected by its price.

It is appropriate to see energy in this context as largely represented by consumer fuels, since that is how energy is traded in the marketplace. Goods are said to be substitutes if an increase in the price of one leads to an increase in the consumption of another whose price is lower. Thus, if an increase in the price of oil leads some consumers to change to natural gas as a heating fuel, these are substitutes. Note, however, the point made in chapter 3 that energy itself has no substitutes. Only fuels, which can be seen as *energy carriers*, can often be substituted for one another.

Energy and Wealth

For decades, energy consumption has been used as an indicator of an economy's wealth. As a broad generalization, it appears that there is a strong relationship between energy consumption and gross national product (GNP). [23] There are problems with the criterion; some countries of very different types have roughly similar energy demands, whereas some of similar types have different demands. Nevertheless, greater energy consumption has long been seen as a necessary prerequisite for economic growth.

The relationship between energy consumption and economic activity, previously thought to reflect some underlying law of economics, has been shown by a number of studies in recent years to be significantly less direct than previously believed. [24] This has arisen because of substantial improvements in the efficiency of energy use in some countries that previously consumed large quantities of oil, following the 1973 and 1979 price increases inspired by the Organization of Petroleum Exporting Countries (OPEC). Many countries have significantly reduced their energy consumption per unit of GNP. In some cases, this increase in efficiency was the result of moving to other fuels, notably natural gas in Europe and the United Kingdom, but the technology of energy use also improved markedly in some sectors.

The ratio E/GNP is commonly known as the energy intensity of GNP. For most countries in the Organization for Economic Cooperation and Development (OECD), energy intensities have fallen steadily over the past decade, after the OPEC oil price increases. [25]

Depletion

Scarce resources are valuable because they are scarce; if they were plentiful, they would not be valuable. Should one use all of a scarce resource quickly, in order to maximize one's present benefit, or slowly, so that others who come later may have a share? These are the types of questions addressed by the area of resource economics that deals with depletion.

There are fossil fuel reserves in the ground that should last hundreds of years, so why is depletion a problem? According to the political-economic viewpoint, it is not. From the biophysical systems viewpoint, however, we come to a very different conclusion, as I discuss in chapter 7. The subject is heavily affected by perceptions of the nature and relevance of humankind's historical record in dealing with past resource shortages. When wood became scarce as a fuel, coal resources were developed. Oil then took over from coal, and gas is now replacing oil in many markets. The conventional economic view is that the global total of resources is effectively infinite and that technology will always be available to secure the energy supplies to enable economic growth in the future, just as it has in the past. Thus, some economists believe that the world's resources are being used too slowly and that the interests of future generations will be better served by leaving them production equipment rather than minerals in the ground.[26]

That view is based on assumptions (especially the assumption of substitutability) within the framework of the market model commonly used by economists. I examine aspects of this model in more detail on the following pages and in chapter 7 and show that in many respects, it is incompatible with modern science. There is, nevertheless, every reason to believe that the physical resources of the earth's crust are indeed greater than current estimates of recoverable deposits. It is therefore reasonable to assume that higher prices will provide incentives for exploration and development of less-accessible areas and as yet undiscovered resources.[27]

Many people, including some economists, criticize this viewpoint as ignoring the fact that the most valuable resources (e.g., easily accessible Middle Eastern oil) are expected to become increasingly scarce toward the middle of the twenty-first century. Others accept the possible existence of long-term limits but claim that for a long time to come, supplies from technologies such as nuclear breeders and fusion reactors will provide all the energy that human economies could possibly need. As a generalization, most who hold to the political-economic viewpoint feel that human adaptability and innovative capability will ensure that such problems will always be overcome. A logical outcome of that argument is that it is positively beneficial to future generations to develop now the capital and other structures to ensure that they inherit wealth directly rather than leave them the resources and opportunities to create it themselves.

It is also worth noting that to the mainstream economic view, everything has a substitute. Thus, there can be no such thing as a limiting factor.[28]

ECONOMICS AS A SCIENCE

Economics is not a homogeneous discipline. "Economics" is a term used to cover an area of activity in the social sciences in which aspects of human behavior are analyzed in such a way as to assist in the understanding and prediction of such behavior. Economics can thus be seen as an attempt to understand activities involved in social life and a means of organizing and controlling those activities in order to achieve social goals.

As in the physical sciences, the study of economic behavior started with the reductionist approach. This involved examining the smallest component of the economic system—namely, the individual person. Using hypotheses about the nature of and reasons for certain types of individual behavior, economists then went on to develop hypotheses about social behavior, all built on the logical foundation of the presumed behavior of the individual.

Nowadays, most social scientists have concluded that the fundamental structures of social systems are groups and communities, not individuals. The behavior of a group is often very different from that of the sum of its individual members.[29] This cultural aspect of humanity is shown in families, in kin and other groups, and in many communities and is often characterized by the gift relationship, not market exchange. Although well known to sociologists and anthropologists, the place of culture in human behavior is largely ignored by economic theorists.

I suspect that neither the atomistic individual perspective nor that of the group is sufficient of itself to describe a society, even at a single stage in its development. Since anything as complex as a human social system is also fluid, ever changing in response to its own internal dynamics and its relationship with the environment, it seems presumptuous to think that any mechanistic theory of behavior could be adequate.

Adding this perspective to our knowledge of the indeterminate way in which dissipative structures behave, it becomes clear that there may be good reasons for believing that economic systems are not predictable at all. Like other dissipative structures, they may be stable for substantial periods of time, then unstable in the face of apparently small disturbances until new, temporarily stable states are reached. This insight may provide a partial explanation for what is seen by some economists as cyclic phenomena, which may in time be seen as evidence of evolutionary behavior.

PROBLEMS IN ECONOMICS

In modern economics, the primary concern is the process by which goods and services are exchanged. This process is usually mediated by money. Activities usually omitted from consideration include those that do not involve money, examples of which are

- inputs and outputs for which no price or markets exist;
- "bads and disservices," as distinct from goods and services;

- effects of economic decisions on the natural world (ecology, climate, ozone layer, etc.);
- the effects of economic decisions on institutions within which human economic behavior occurs (political, social, religious, etc.).

Further problems arise from lack of common ground between *microeconomics*, which deals with the behavior of individuals and firms, and *macroeconomics*, which deals with the behavior of the economy as a whole.[30] I examine some of these problems in later chapters to show why I believe that present-day conventional economics is seriously deficient in its ability to contribute meaningfully to development of a truly sustainable society.

THE PLACE OF ECONOMICS

Economics as a field of study as we know it today arose from, and gained its legitimacy within, goods and services markets in European cultural and social systems. In recent years, some its practitioners' aims have extended far beyond the social and cultural systems within which economics arose. In many ways, economics has now become the reflection of a code. Although its origins, and much of its current practice, lie in the laudable attempt to improve the lot of individuals in society, economics is now widely seen (and often used in practice) as a means of defining how individuals in a society *should* behave. People can be imprisoned by such a code. The norms of rational economic behavior are usually defined in advance by those who espouse a particular political-economic world view.

I believe that instead of attempting to be an objective means of studying human economic behavior, economics has in many areas descended to the level of a political tool, used by governments and power groups to enhance control of people's behavior. To the extent that economics is used openly and with full consultation to assist people to achieve their democratically stated collective goals, this is entirely proper. To the extent that it is used to impose unstated goals or to support social structures about which people have not been adequately consulted, it is gravely undemocratic and is a form of colonization of people's minds, better termed "economic imperialism."[31] As the economist Joan Robinson commented, "The purpose of studying economics is not to acquire a set of ready made answers to economic questions, but to learn how to avoid being deceived by economists."[32]

To be set free, people must be given the means to understand the reality beyond the code that underlies much of standard economics. What is called "choice" in society is not that which exists within the narrow confines of the marketplace. Choice exists within the reality of social life itself and is incapable of codification, for to do so would be to destroy the fragile reality of that which is to be served. For this reason, I believe it is reasonable to claim that although conventional economics has been a tool from which society has obtained many benefits in the past, it is now time to build a new economics that will contribute to creation of sustainable societies in a sustainable world. Ethical contributions, such as those of John Rawls on justice, may well be part of the process.[33]

In this book, I also emphasize that neither free-market nor socialist economies as we know them are sustainable in that biophysical systems issues are virtually ignored by both. What is needed is a new economic synthesis that incorporates humanistic concerns for allocation and distribution with a concern for scale that reflects biophysical systems understandings. Hence, my (perhaps utopian) ideal is that societies seek a synthesis of the best of the neoclassical, neo-Marxist, and neo-Malthusian views, all clarified through the best of democratic participation and aided by the best of modern science.

5

The Systems Approach

In this chapter, I show how valuable the systems approach can be in enlarging perspectives obtained from other viewpoints. It enables us to understand more about reality, and as such, it is not normally in conflict with other viewpoints. Indeed, it can be used to extend them. *Systems thinking* implies thinking about the world outside ourselves in order to improve understanding of how we can initiate and guide our actions as persons, groups, and nations.

SYSTEMS BACKGROUND

The systems approach is one to which lip service is often paid, but it is seldom defined or explained.[1] It involves the use of a set of ideas in trying to understand the world's complexity. The central idea is of a *set of elements* connected and related in order to form a whole, whose properties are not those of the component elements but are properties of the whole itself. As a simple example, the taste of water is a property of water itself, not of the hydrogen and oxygen of which it is formed.

The idea of studying systems *as systems* came about through the realization that some intractable problems that arise from use of the reductionist scientific method can be resolved only by looking at the problems from a wider perspective. In this way, interconnections among the parts can be identified. Thus, the movement of a finger can be fully understood only if its linkages with the hand, the arm, the whole body, and the brain (and, via the brain, with the eyes, and so on) are taken into account.

The systems approach is not a discipline in itself so much as a means of studying what happens within and among systems that "belong" to other disciplines. It concentrates on interactions among the different parts of a whole, and as such it complements and extends the reductionist, positivist approach of conventional science. People brought up with the classical approach can find systems thinking very difficult. For most "ordinary" people, however, everyday life has always involved thinking about the whole.

HARD AND SOFT SYSTEMS

As a generalization, *hard systems* are the everyday concern of technologists. The many successes of engineering and technology over the past hundred or so years, along with the success of early applications of systems ideas in building and operating complex engineering structures (moon-landing craft, jumbo jets, automated chemical plants, robots, computers, and so on), gave rise to the desire to apply these techniques to social systems.

Social systems are *soft systems*, since the goals of human social systems often are not clear and change as people's perceptions and priorities change. The hard systems approach was, perhaps understandably, not successful when applied to soft problems. Soft systems thinking is now seen as *a way of thinking about social systems.* Seen in this light, soft systems thinking goes some way to answer important questions raised by people such as Jacques Ellul who have criticized the expansion of "technique" into all domains of life. Ellul claimed that ours is a civilization committed to "the quest for improved means to carelessly examined ends . . . technique turns means into ends."[2] It is not necessary, however, for a method that aims to understand something of the complexity of human social structures to eliminate all that is human from it. On the contrary, I argue that better understanding holds out the possibility of enabling people to gain more control over their personal and community lives and to work together to create a better world. (Regrettably, I also have to admit that a dictator with good soft systems understanding is likely to be able to stay in power longer than one who does not!)

What Is a System?

A system is a whole that cannot be divided into independent parts. Systems have two very important properties:

- Each part has properties it loses when separated from the system.
- Every system has some essential properties that its parts do not have.[3]

The most important feature of systems is relationships. To define a system, one must specify the relationships among its elements. Another important characteristic of a system is its variety, the number of distinguishable states each part of the system can adopt (and which thereby influence other parts). The greater the variety, the more complex is the system's behavior.

From the systems perspective, the whole of a complex system is always more than the sum of its parts. Thus, "reality" is a collective, not an individual, phenomenon. *The place of a living individual (human, animal, or plant) can be evaluated meaningfully only when it is seen in its integrative, collective, ecological context.*

Systems thinking is founded on two related pairs of ideas, those of emergence and hierarchy and of communication and control.

Emergence and Hierarchy

It has long been known that at certain levels of complexity of systems, properties arise that are *emergent* at that level. In other words, the system has properties that cannot be explained through the understanding obtained at a lower level and that emerge only when the system is studied at the higher level. "Can't see the wood for the trees" is a metaphor that brings out the point very well.

The systems approach is also concerned with *hierarchy,* because parts may be arranged in ways such that each level of increased complexity shows emergent properties. Several hierarchical levels of complexity may be present in any one system, each showing new emergent properties.

Characteristic of the systems approach is the study of organization; in many respects, this is the opposite of the classical reductionist approach. Microscopic examination of plants and living organisms, for example, shows that living things contain a hierarchy of structures that follow a sequence of increasing complexity, with emergent properties at each level. Molecules are combined in organelles (cell components); organelles combine to form cells; cells, to form organs; and organs, to form the whole organism. Many animals form groups or social systems, in turn within ecosystems, with yet more levels at which emergent properties appear.

The fact that the workings of cells and organs can be explainable in terms of the known facts of physics and chemistry (at least in part) does not enable us to explain the behavior of organisms and animals as entities. The entity itself has properties that depend on the way in which its components are organized. Thus, a sheep is patently not the same as a cow, despite the fact that the majority of physical and chemical processes that characterize animal life are common to both. The specific organization of its components is the clearest distinguishing feature between the vital happenings of a real organism and the processes of physics and chemistry that underlie it.

Communication and Control

The second pair of ideas at the root of systems thinking involves communication and control. In any hierarchy of levels (e.g., among the components of an organism), maintenance of the structure involves communication of information, with the aim of regulation or control of the system.

In a car engine, effective working of the system involves communication of the engine speed to the ignition subsystem to ensure that the spark is delivered at precisely the right time for the fuel mixture in the cylinder to fire for the power stroke. If communication is not achieved via the appropriate linkages, the engine will not function properly.

Open and Closed Systems

In open systems such as living organisms, maintenance of life depends on the ability to exchange matter and energy with the environment and on a high degree of communication and control. Animals are highly complex organisms that depend for their survival on the ability of parts of their system to intercommunicate via a central nervous system to achieve coordination and control, for example, of movement. Much of this is completely "automatic" and able to cope with substantial changes in the animal's surroundings. The term for this behavior is *homeostasis*. Communication among organisms or animals in a group regarding the group's survival and health often follows similar principles.

FEEDBACK

Proper functioning of the control and communication component of a system depends on the presence of feedback. *Feedback* is the communication of information about the state of one part of the system to another part so that corrective action can be taken, if necessary, to change that state.

For example, a room's thermostat is usually wired to switch off the heater whenever the room temperature rises above a level chosen to ensure comfort. If the temperature drops below that set level, the thermostat switches the heater on again. Feedback occurs when the measurement of temperature in one part of the system (the air in the room) enables comparison of it with some desired state (a preset "comfortable" room temperature) and, if required, communication of a signal that will alter the condition of another part of the system (the heater switch) to bring the temperature back to the set level. The temperature sensor and the switch are often in the same box, but they have quite separate functions.

Feedback is a fundamental characteristic of natural and social systems. *Negative feedback* corrects an undesirable departure of the system from normality, as in the case of the thermostat that turns off the heater in a room that is too hot. *Positive feedback,* on the other hand, enlarges any departure from normality. Positive feedback would arise if the wiring were reversed; when the room became too hot, the heater would be turned on, and when it became too cold, the heater would be turned off. Thus, the feedback would increase the departure from normality rather than correct it.

The presence of positive feedbacks always indicates the risk of instability in a system.[4] Under such circumstances, small deviations, such as deviations of temperature in a room, for example, can give rise to rapid departures from the desired stable state. Even negative feedbacks, if overpowerful (e.g., when the heater is too large), can cause uncomfortable fluctuations, with the room being alternately too hot or too cold. In more complex systems, feedbacks often cause oscillations and other undesirable behavior.

If the environment changes faster than the system can change itself, the system can never be stable (a slow boxer cannot win over a fast one!). All open systems maintain their characteristics within certain limits specific to each case. If the system exceeds those limits, it is likely to become a new system. All systems can adapt up to a point, but they cannot be pushed too close to their limits without risking collapse. As an example, if global climate change occurs as rapidly as is currently predicted, many organisms (plants especially) will not survive, and ecosystems will change to new ones. This is an example of a situation in which the environment is being changed by one of its components—humanity. Unless we humans learn to control our interventions, we will in all probability destroy a great deal of that which gives us life.

Information

Control is associated with the flow of information, in the form of instructions or constraints. Communication and control are so closely linked in any system that they must be regarded as a pair, not as separate functions.

In any natural system, information exists prior to feedback, and an effective feedback mechanism comprises both a sensor capable of detecting potentially disruptive changes in the environment and the means of initiating appropriate remedial action. Thus, a person's ability to avoid burning a finger on a hot stove depends on the ability of skin (a sensor) to detect high temperature and a nervous system (for information transmission and feedback) connected through the brain (which has the stored information to enable detection of an undesirable situation) to muscles, which will enable the hot finger to be pulled away (corrective action) before burning occurs. Time lags are of critical importance, since any significant delay between sensing and corrective action will increase the intensity of the burn. No one factor will function without all of the others.

Feedbacks and Growth

Although positive feedbacks are absurd in the case of the room thermostat, they are natural in the initial stages of many natural processes. For example, consider the growth of an organism in a place where a food supply flows continuously past it. The initial stages of growth involve positive feedback—an *autocatalytic* process in which new organisms breed yet further organisms. Reproduction is encouraged by the availability of food, and population growth may be very rapid. In later stages, when there is not enough food to go around, a form of negative feedback occurs, with surplus population dying off until only that which can be supported by the food supply is left. If the organism evolves to a form that makes more efficient use of the food supply, greater numbers can be supported, but the overall constraint remains.

Growth is inherently a process involving positive feedbacks (see chapter 7), and unless self-regulatory structures are present within the system, growth will continue until it is constrained by external factors. Such is the case in nature, in which there is a web of communication and control feedbacks working to maintain the stability of the ecosystem.[5] When the population of one species grows too large, negative feedback ensures, for example, that a predator's population also increases in size. If this balance is upset, it is likely that the system will change suddenly. The change may be evolutionary, moving toward a more developed, more complex level of organization, or destructive, moving toward a lower level of organization.

Positive feedbacks are also common in economies, but only relatively recently have they been incorporated in any comprehensive way into economic thinking.[6] The pressures that humans are placing on nature require a much better understanding of her dynamic characteristics. There is a desperate need to modify socioeconomic behavior in order to limit interference to a level that can be sustained in the long term.[7]

CHARACTERISTICS OF COMPLEX SYSTEMS

People are not accustomed to thinking formally in systems ways. In complex systems, however, everything influences everything else; nothing can be done in isolation.[8] Nonlinearity is inherent in feedback system behavior in that an effect may be seriously out of proportion to the cause. In a complex system, cause and effect are distant in time and space, and the points at which control may be applied are often not obvious. The behavior of complex systems is inherently dynamic, with change occurring on many time scales; some parts change quickly as a result of alteration in some important factor, and others may not change at all.

Feedback is often wrongly perceived by people. In real complex systems, time lags between cause and effect may be minutes or years long. How does one modify one's behavior (one's "sociopersonal control system") to take account of unknown outcomes of known present-day actions? How does one recognize trade-offs between the short-term and long-term effects of today's actions?

It can be very difficult for people or governments to respond to change in ways that reflect the needs of the social and ecological structures in which they live. A decision made now can be expected to change the state of the system, thereby altering its behavior. Thus, the outcome may be that today's decisions influence future outcomes—and therefore the nature of, and need for, future decisions. In such situations, many apparently obvious solutions fail or actually worsen the situation. This has been found with many economic policies over recent years. Actions suggested by a systems analysis may appear counterintuitive to people brought up in the simple "presystems" world, yet they are essential if we are to develop sustainably.

OPEN SYSTEMS BEHAVIOR

All systems open to the inflow of energy and/or information, whether they be a worm, a human being, an economy, or a galaxy, have certain characteristics.[9] Open systems (dissipative structures) tend to maintain a metastable state, often called *dynamic instability*. This reflects the fact that they are far from a state of equilibrium with their environment and depend on inflows, especially of energy, to maintain their state.

Self-regulating Systems

Open systems function via two complementary and related processes: self-regulation and self-organization. In *self-regulation,* the system preserves its stability by adapting and adjusting, using the inflow of information to regulate its internal processes. A self-regulating system can adjust to its environment. Thus, the bird that fluffs out its feathers in winter is operating in a self-regulating manner to keep its body temperature stable. Ecologists have developed the concept of *resilience* to describe an ecosystem's ability to maintain its structure and behavior patterns in the face of externally imposed disturbances.[10] In a similar manner, a number of aspects of economic life, e.g., the ideal free market, have self-regulating characteristics.

Self-organizing Systems

Self-organizing systems tend, under certain circumstances, to intensify and accelerate some aspects of the normal functioning of the system, causing fluctuations and instability. This is because a system that is far from equilibrium can reach a point at which it can either dissolve into disorder or evolve to a new, more complex level of organization. It may result from the fact that under conditions of sensitivity or strain, the system may be inordinately sensitive to changes in its environment. This might, for example, be the case for an organism or species in an ecosystem that is changing rapidly, perhaps due to climate change.

At this crucial moment, called a *bifurcation point* by Ilya Prigogine, it is impossible to determine in advance the direction in which change will occur.[11] Before and after the bifurcation point, the system is self-regulating; the powerful mechanisms of self-organization predominate to drive the processes of change. At the bifurcation point, the system might disintegrate into disorder if it has reached a high level of complexity, or it might make a qualitative leap into one of several possible new levels of complexity and organization. Bifurcation changes can go one way or the other, depending on what may at the time be quite tiny changes in a critical factor occurring at the "right" moment.

For example, a forest ecosystem that may have been stable for millennia is still a fragile thing. Careless logging of trees in such systems can expose roots and make soil susceptible to rapid erosion when heavy rains occur, thereby rapidly and irreversibly destroying the ecosystem and replacing it by a much poorer one. In other circumstances, strains of this sort can give rise to richer, more complex systems. Such was probably the case with the replacement of dinosaurs by mammals as the result of a vast cataclysm (possibly the impact of a large meteorite or a volcanic eruption) millions of years ago.

This "order through fluctuation" theory (referred to by Prigogine as "from being to becoming") has been supported by work in chemistry and physics and has strong support from observations of the ecological behavior of natural systems. Recent research in economics suggests that the same process is also present in human activity systems.[12] In such systems, the distinctive feature of humans—our awareness—could be an organizing, or triggering, principle. If so, it could allow human systems, such as societies, to control themselves to develop into higher levels of organization, just as it could enable a drop to lower levels. Circumstantial evidence exists that this sort of thing does indeed happen. Under certain circumstances, the role played by parts (e.g., individuals and groups) could therefore be decisive. This means that the present-day behavior of the system cannot be taken as predetermining its future development. Self-organizing processes in nonequilibrium systems are characterized by a delicate interplay between chance and necessity, between instability and stability.

An example that is directly relevant to our time is the serious risk of disruption of the world's climate system. We do not know whether our continuing to push large quantities of "greenhouse gases" into the atmosphere will create instability and cause the climate system to self-organize or whether it will continue to self-regulate. The likely penalties for misjudgment are great. Regrettably, the worst offenders (the United States, Europe, and Japan) are so blinded by the fear of changing their consumerist ways that even now, they dismiss the probability of global warming. Interestingly, and regrettably, they do so by using the very nineteenth-century reductionist approach of arguing from false foundations and insisting on pre-Popperian requirements of "proof" that encouraged development of the systems approach in the first place.[13]

THERMODYNAMICS AND SYSTEMS THEORY

Dissipative nonequilibrium structures are complex, self-organizing systems existing within an environment from which they obtain negative entropy.[14] Economic and social systems involve groups whose behavior shows emergent properties relative to the sum of individual behaviors. Their properties also depend on structure, linkages, communication, feedbacks, and control mechanisms. Flows of information in systems can be analyzed using entropy as a measure of organization of information, but the similarities between thermophysical systems and information systems are largely analogies.[15] By using both tools together to aid thinking and analysis, a remarkable synthesis may be achieved, resulting in a better understanding of the real world.[16]

THE SYSTEMS APPROACH AND POLICYMAKING

Each system is simultaneously engaged both in maintaining its status quo and in orientation toward change and transformation. To our historically conditioned way of thinking, this is a profoundly disturbing conclusion. It brings into question many of our beliefs, particularly those that depend on confidence in the stability of the world around us. The fact that what we humans look on as stability is in fact metastable, or dynamically unstable, suggests that we can no longer depend on anything.

Although this is correct and can in one sense be seen as threatening, I also believe it is very encouraging. The fact that instability is a prerequisite for evolutionary change suggests that at the "right time," by a very small effort, a system can be altered toward change from which it will emerge at a higher level of organization. At other times, the process may require so much effort that it may be impossible.

The systems perspective can aid understanding in many areas in which humans interact with the physical environment. Its advantage is in the insights one gains from thinking about and analyzing issues in a "systems" manner.[17] Its major disadvantage (in policy matters) is that many perceptions gained from its use are rather general. It is not possible, for example, to determine a unique value for environmental resources, to evaluate an optimum depletion profile for their use, or to estimate the cost of damage to an ecosystem from a waste material. This drawback is inevitable in that it reflects the reality of the world in which we live[18] rather than the well-ordered, nineteenth-century (imaginary) world of neoclassical economics.[19] As the economist Herman Daly pointed out, however, "it is better to deal incompletely with the whole than to deal wholly with the incomplete."[20]

Systems thinking is still at a relatively early stage of development. Its value lies not so much in what it enables us to predict about the world as in the help it gives us in thinking in systematic ways. It can help us gain a metaperspective—a broader vision of the world we live in—that shows more clearly the interrelationships that characterize it. Systems thinking gives us a multiplicity of points of view that could help us build bridges across domains of culture, technology, ethics, and economy. Systems thinking constitutes, in itself, a learning process for those performing it, if it is remembered always that to do so is only a means, not an end in itself.

6

The Biophysical Systems World View

FROM THE BIOPHYSICAL systems perspective, a social system such as an economy is seen in terms of the *physical* activities that take place in it. This is clearly different from the *social* ways in which the activities of society are seen from the political-economic perspective.

THE PHYSICAL BASIS OF ECONOMIC ACTIVITY

Early human societies tapped into stores of potential energy that were available via natural mechanisms, directly or indirectly from the sun. The materials needed for food, clothing, shelter, and so on were obtained from plants and animals by gathering and hunting. Industrial societies developed rapidly because they gained access to additional sources of potential energy, notably the fossil fuels coal, oil, and gas. Technology, via human ingenuity, provided pathways for the utilization of these resources so they could be used to gain access to nonmuscular means of doing work. The increasing availability of "energy slaves" vastly increased humans' ability to control and transform the physical environment—the process of industrialization.

Each stage of industrialization was built on a foundation of previous industrialization. All, without exception, required prior consumption of available energy from the environment. The continuing transformation of available into unavailable energy resources (in accordance with the second law of thermodynamics) is an unavoidable part of the functioning of all economies. There is no process known that did not start off by using some form of raw material (available, "source," energy) and that does not end up somewhere as waste (unavailable, "sink," energy).

The interaction between energy and matter is the basis of life itself; therefore, it is also the basis for human life and culture. That is not to say that life is *only* energy—far from it. It is nevertheless vital to recognize the key role of energy in the physical world; otherwise, it is fatally easy to fall into the trap of thinking that all processes of importance in human decision making are internal to the economy. That view is, unfortunately, typical of both neoclassical and Marxist economic perceptions. This does not leave much room in the political spectrum for other views, but I believe it is essential to do so and thereby add important information to both.

The inclusion of energy in a world view points to the help that the biophysical systems perspective can give in clarifying the relationship between a social system and its environment. It also helps us see where the biophysical viewpoint contrasts with the political-economic and thus indicates areas in which conventional assumptions may need deeper examination.

ENERGY IN SOCIETY

Matter normally enters an economic system as raw resources from the environment (or as imports). Unless temporarily accumulated within the economy (e.g., as capital goods) or recycled within the economic process, it must be disposed of. This gives rise to pollution, known as externalities in economic terminology. Externalities are also seen as feedbacks in systems terminology.

The flow of "useful" matter into and through an economic system can be characterized in terms of the available energy expended in carrying out the transformation processes in which the matter is involved. Thus, energy can be used as a numeraire, or unit of account, enabling a wide variety of goods and services to be accounted for in terms of the quantity of one important characteristic, the energy used in the processes of transforming them into marketable products.[1] From this viewpoint, capital accumulation and stocks of durables are seen as a temporary store for (upgraded) energy resources. In time, these depreciate and wear out, eventually ending up as waste.

In physical terms, as in economic terms, energy is of "value" only by virtue of its ability to cause physical or chemical change, or, in the language of chapter 3, to do work. From the biophysical systems perspective, what is important is the amount (i.e., the physical "cost") of energy used in a process and embodied in a product, not its price in the marketplace.

In this chapter, I use energy as a means of following the way in which an economy works, just as I used energy to follow the way an ecosystem works in chapter 1. As there, the concept of embodied energy is used to follow the use of available energy in the production of goods and services. In contrast to the political-economic perception, I examine only the physical processes of production, not the social valuation of that production in the marketplace.

The use of energy to describe the workings of a social system can also be seen as an attempt to respond to the misgivings held by many physical scientists about the apparent inability of standard economics to take full account of the central position of energy in the physical world. I have deep concern about the assumptions (implicit in much of economics) that humanity will always find new resources when current ones become too costly and that technology is without limits.

The most important attribute of the biophysical systems approach, however, is that it is an entirely different way of thinking—a different world view. In any real system, as I discussed earlier, the ruling state is metastable, reflecting physical disequilibrium. That understanding is, I believe, essential to a proper understanding of economic activity within its physical environment.[2] The use of this concept gives an entirely different viewpoint on "development" in an economy, and of its effect on options for future development, than is gained from the standard economic perspective. Used together, I believe the biophysical systems approach and the standard economic approach help us gain a perspective that is clearer and more powerful than either used alone.

ENERGY AND THE ECONOMIC PROCESS

Although relatively little attention has been paid to their work, in the nineteenth century two people examined energy flows as a consistent means of studying the economic system in a total ecological context. One was Serhii Podolinsky, a Ukrainian; the other was Patrick Geddes, a Scot. At around the same time, Lord Kelvin evaluated the energy requirements for production of the copper wire used for conducting electricity. The scientist Frederick Soddy further developed an understanding of the relationship between energy and economics in the first half of the twentieth century. (See *Ecological Economics* by Juan Martinez-Alier [Oxford: Basil Blackwell] for a fascinating review of their work and its place in modern ecological economics.)

Several other people have described the physical and biological basis of economic activity. Probably the most notable is Nicholas Georgescu-

Roegen, an economist who in a small number of seminal papers described thermophysical limits to economic activity. He felt that economists have not seen the relationship that exists between physics and economic scarcity.

Kenneth Boulding and Herman Daly, other eminent economists, have also written extensively on the physical limits to the use of depletable resources. Like Georgescu-Roegen's, their writings in this area have been largely ignored by conventional economists, who appear not to accept that thermodynamics has anything to say about human action and policy. The two viewpoints are diametrically opposed. One of my purposes in this book (see chapter 11 especially) is to try to clarify the issue to show that the answer is not entirely clear-cut, and also to help people to understand more about it and thereby be given the opportunity to come to their own conclusions about this important subject.

ENERGY ANALYSIS

The branch of physical science that follows economic production and consumption through their energy consequences is known as energy analysis. In its basic form, *energy analysis* involves determination of the amount of primary energy, direct and indirect, that is dissipated in producing a good or service and delivering it to the market.[3]

There are two common techniques for evaluating the embodied energy of goods and services—process analysis and input-output analysis. *Process analysis* involves the systematic study of the inputs to and outputs from a process, with determination of energy requirements for each input. These are then added up to give the total energy requirement of the product.

As an example, a process analysis of running an automobile would first concentrate on gasoline consumption, since this is the most obvious large input. After that, the less important direct inputs would be assessed, such as engine oil consumption. Energy for tire manufacture, a significant indirect input, also needs to be evaluated; that would require determination of the energy involved in making the tire from its raw materials plus the energy to transport, store, and install it on the wheel. If one goes further back still, the energy required to make steel for the car body, engine, and transmission and to manufacture upholstery, paint, and so on would also have to be found, as well as the energy needed to build the machines and factories where these parts were made.

Clearly, the total task is a daunting one, and few process analyses have been carried out beyond the first or second stage. This technique is good at giving an accurate estimate of *direct* energy inputs but not at evaluating the *indirect* inputs, such as the energy required to make the steel for the car body, let alone that to build the car factory itself—or the steel mill, or the mines that provided the iron ore to make the steel.

The second common technique is *input-output energy analysis*, a modification of a standard economic tool.[4] This is obtained from a detailed survey of the operations of an economy. In effect, it addresses the production part of the economy, with explicit accounting for the energy inputs required to keep the economy going. By a straightforward but time-consuming method (usually involving a computer), the *total* (i.e., direct plus indirect) energy requirements of production of goods and services may be evaluated. Thus, all of the energy inputs to the processes that precede the output of a given good or service in the economy are evaluated, right back to the coal mine, oil well, power station, or gas field.[5]

As a generalization, process analysis is appropriate for study of specific processes. Input-output analysis is appropriate when one is examining the effects of changes in technology, resource use, and so on for a whole economy. The difference in quality, or ability to do work, of the various forms of energy is not specifically brought out in either approach, although it is possible to evaluate it.[6]

THE ENERGETIC MODEL OF SOCIETY

In the conventional economic model (see figure 4.2), the main processes of economic activity are seen as *internal* to the economy. A biophysical model proposed by the engineer Martha Gilliland represents the economy as a pathway by which energy resources are used to convert raw materials into the goods and services needed for the economic system's normal functioning.[7] Figure 6.1 is a diagrammatic representation of Gilliland's model (extended from the simple energy transformation pathway model of figure 3.1 and the economic model of figure 4.2), with the economic production and consumption sectors separate from the energy transformation sector.

Money in this physical model flows in the opposite direction to energy. Although some writers have suggested a direct equivalence between the two flows, this is really an analogy. Energy use in the biophysical systems perspective usually represents physical "cost" and is a different concept from monetary flow in the economic perspective, representing market "price." They should not be confused. Thus, I make no suggestion that energy consumption be used as a measure of social value in an economic context, although it can have strong, albeit sometimes indirect, implications for prices, especially in the long term.

In practice, primary resources have to be transformed to make them usable by an economy. The energy transformation system normally starts with a coal mine or an oil or gas well, at which the resource is physically extracted from its geological deposit. This stage can then be followed by, for example, a power station that takes coal, oil, or gas and transforms it into electricity; an oil refinery that takes crude oil and produces refined gasoline, diesel fuel, and other products; or a hydroelectric power station that produces electricity from the potential energy of the water in an elevated lake or river. For convenience in this discussion and to separate out the energy transformation sector as an important factor, figure 6.1 shows that sector as outside the economy. In economic convention, it is usually included as part of the production sector.

One important characteristic of an energy transformation sector is that it

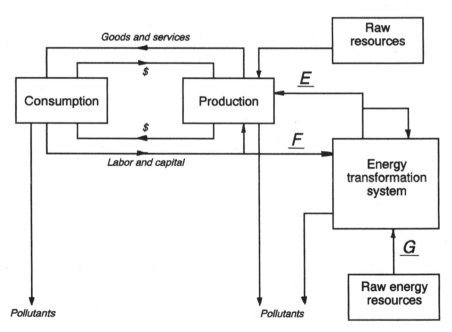

FIGURE 6.1 Energy Supply to an Economy. E, *flow of consumer fuels and electricity to the economy after refining or other processing in the energy transformation system (ETS); F, embodied energy in goods and services (capital, plant, maintenance, operating requirements) supplied from the economy to the ETS; G, flow of raw energy resources (coal, oil, gas) from geological deposits to the ETS (coal mine, oil/gas well, refinery, etc.).*

functions by absorbing capital, operating, maintenance, and other inputs from the economy, represented here by the feedback flows of energy embodied in them. It is only when the flow of "useful" consumer energy E is greater than F, the sum of embodied feedback flows, that there is a supply of *net energy* to the economy. This concept is analogous to one common in economics: revenue or turnover alone is not enough to indicate financial success of a project; net cash flow is what is important.

NET ENERGY AND PHYSICAL ACCESSIBILITY

Different writers use different criteria to measure the net energy performances of processes such as these in delivering a flow of energy E to an economy (refer to figure 6.1) from a gross resource flow G, using a feedback flow F.[8] The net energy criterion, in whatever form, is the means of indicating the *physical accessibility* of a resource. It is the amount of effort, measured in energy terms, required to extract the resource and deliver it in the appropriate form to the consumer.[9]

Over the past century or so in most industrializing countries, economies have gone from an almost complete dependence on biomass-based fuels (mainly wood) to coal, then to oil and natural gas. Each transition was characterized by change to a more accessible energy source, but that change was not possible until technology had developed to the stage at which the greater level of accessibility was achievable.[10] Thus, coal was not accessible in large quantities until the technology of underground mining was developed, and open-cast coal could not be won in quantity until large earth-moving machines were developed. Oil and gas were not accessible until drilling, transportation, and refining technologies had been developed. All of these depended heavily on the development of systems for long-distance transportation of both raw materials and products.

In each case, the accessibility of the new resource (measured by both net energy and economic methods) was better than for the previous one. This meant that costs were lower, so substitution, once started, could proceed rapidly. This outcome is believed by some workers from the political-economic viewpoint to be the result of factors internal to economic systems. To the extent that technological developments were required, that is true. The underlying physical accessibility mechanism is a separate component, however, and should not be excluded from the argument.

There is increasing evidence that energy is becoming more difficult to obtain and process into readily usable forms. Worldwide, oil discoveries per meter of well drilled are declining, and exploration is being done in ever more inhospitable places.[11] Many countries have substantial reserves of fossil fuel (mainly coal), but the majority is usually of low quality. In other words, resources are not homogeneous, and humankind has (quite reasonably) exploited the easily accessible, high-quality resources first. Lower-quality, less-accessible resources are left for future generations, in the expectation that the price mechanism will offset any shortages.

The second law of thermodynamics tells us that as an economy changes its sources over time from high-quality (high-availability) energy sources to low-quality (low-availability) sources, the efficiency with which work may be done by those resources will decline. In addition, the move from resources that are easy to mine to those that are deeper and/or more difficult to mine means that a greater amount of economic (e.g., engineering) effort will have to be expended in order to tap those resources and supply useful net energy to the economy. In our terminology, this means that at the same time, the resources are also becoming less accessible. In both cases (refer to figure 6.1), a greater flow of either G or F or both is needed to maintain a constant flow E. In time, the energy transformation industry will have to grow and absorb a steadily increasing quantity of economic activity just to maintain the system.

If there is a steady increase in the resources that need to be expended from the economy (flow F) in order to obtain a given quantity of energy E, then in the long term, one can envisage a situation in which no *net* energy is supplied. In other words, the energy content (embodied in buildings, machinery, maintenance, and operation) of the economic effort needed to extract energy and deliver it could rise to such a level that as much embodied energy is flowing back into the energy supply industry as is being supplied to the economy. *If F equals E, a point of futility has been reached* at which all that is happening is that a lot of socioeconomic effort is going into a process equivalent (in energy terms) to going around in circles.

When resources are relatively inaccessible, the primary resource flow will be greater than it was for the earlier, high-accessibility case. Thus, the rate of depletion of primary resources will also increase for a given (constant) flow of net energy to the economy. Pollution and other externalities will also be greater due to the increased rejection of unavailable energy.

Net Energy of Resources of Declining Accessibility

As an example of what could happen, consider a simple coal mine. Let us assume that the coal seam is vertical, starting at the surface. (Although this scenario is exaggerated to make a point, it represents very much the sort of thing that will happen in the long term, because coal that is closest to the surface will always be extracted first, leaving deeper seams until later.)

At the start of the mining operation, only simple materials and resources are needed to mine the coal and deliver it to trucks or railway wagons. As the coal face recedes, the total work that has to be done to get the coal to the surface increases because of the increased vertical height up which it has to be lifted. The greater the height, the heavier and more complex the lifting mechanism has to be, and the faster it has to run just to maintain a constant rate of delivery of coal at the surface. At this stage, a substantial proportion of the energy in the coal delivered to the surface will be needed just to build, run, and maintain the machinery needed to get the coal out. This is quite separate from the effort expended in other activities, such as pumping water to keep the mine dry and taking the precautions necessary to ensure safety at the coal face, where the working conditions are becoming ever more inhospitable.

Thus, as the depth of the mine increases, the amount of net energy delivered to the surface declines because more and more of the mine's output is needed just to drive the mining machinery itself. To ensure a constant supply of net energy at the surface (as is normal for economies), the rate of mining will therefore have to increase. It is not difficult to appreciate that the mining rate will accelerate under such circumstances. The faster the miners try to get the coal out, and the greater are the demands placed on the mine by the economy, the faster the process approaches the stage at which the whole operation is energetically pointless. Clearly, the end result is stalemate, in that the mining operation does not actually do anything for the economy other than supply employment. Beyond the point at which the net energy yield is zero, the operation is in fact taking more than it supplies. *This will happen irrespective of the amount of coal left in the mine.* After a certain stage, therefore, further mining is pointless and the resource is economically and energetically useless. [12]

It is possible to predict from dynamic energy analysis the depth at which the work required to lift the coal exactly equals that available from the energy in the coal lifted. The lower the quality of the energy resource, the sooner this will happen. Peat and lignite will be accessible at shallower depths than will bituminous coal and anthracite. The direct and indirect energy requirements of the other parts of the mining activity will ensure that in practice, the depth that is minable will be very much shallower than that calculated from the energy requirements of lifting alone.

Many people who hold the political-economic viewpoint rely on improvements in technology at this stage to ensure that the economy will always get what it wants. Such a view is not supported by physics. It is quite possible that lifting machinery and water pumps will be improved, but there is an absolute minimum energy requirement for lifting a ton of coal to the surface and pumping a liter of water that is absolutely unalterable by technology because it is a consequence of the second law of thermodynamics. The most that can be hoped for from technology is that it will enable mining to go a little deeper; the constraint remains.

NEW ENERGY TECHNOLOGIES

The further question may then be asked of whether we can envisage making more radical changes in technology. For example, would underground gasification enable the coal resource to be made available with a lower expenditure of feedback energy? The answer is not clear because of so many unknowns. However, we know that such methods are unsuitable for many coal seams (e.g., those with geological faulting) and also incur large increases in depletion rate, wastage, and pollution due to the low efficiency with which the coal is converted into gas. The capital structures needed to carry out such operations would also be substantial.

There is a considerable literature relating to the "breeder" type of nuclear reactor, which has been claimed to produce more fuel than it consumes. For some people, this possibility has engendered confidence that humans can continue to treat the world's resources as limitless. In fact, the claims are illusory, resulting from a misunderstanding of some fairly simple facts of physics. The fuel for conventional (fission) nuclear power plants is the uranium isotope U-235. But the most common form of uranium in the world (around 99 percent of known reserves) is the nonfissionable form U-238. To obtain fuel for nuclear plants, the small quantities of U-235 have to be separated out, producing an "enriched" uranium.

It was soon realized that if a neutron from a fission reaction is captured by an atom of U-238, it is converted into plutonium 239, a highly fissionable material. The so-called breeder reactor (of which a few prototypes exist) converts nonfuel U-238 into fuel Pu-239. It does not make fuel out of nothing; it is simply a resource-upgrading plant that embodies energy in one material in order to turn it into a more "useful" one. All that the process does is multiply the known reserves of fissionable material by a factor that is substantial but by no means unlimited. That Pu-239 is an extremely dangerous material, and one that is very suitable for making nuclear weapons, is a further reason for us to be on our guard against sloppily worded claims as to the importance of the breeder option. The further fact that breeder reactors are both costly and troublesome to operate is yet another reason for caution.

The "ultimate," unlimited form of energy is believed to be nuclear fusion. In this, deuterium, a naturally occurring isotope of hydrogen, would serve as fuel for plants that would duplicate the reactions that occur in the interior of the sun—at temperatures of millions of degrees. Although claims of break-throughs in this area have been with us since I left school some thirty-five years ago, fusion reactor programs have so far produced nothing more than the ability to absorb vast amounts of money. They have also absorbed vast amounts of energy in construction and operation of ever more elaborate ex-perimental machines. Whether they will ever show an economic or energetic benefit nobody knows, but even if they do, the results will be available only to a few rich nations; fusion power will almost certainly be too expensive (and too dangerous) for anybody else. This option involves too many unhatched eggs to be part of realistic plans.

DYNAMIC ENERGY SYSTEMS ANALYSIS

The example of the coal mine illustrates stages in the evolution of an econo-my's energy supply. To generalize the analysis, we must acknowledge that in reality, the energy system and the economy itself are changing all the time. It is therefore necessary to look at the way in which the energy supply system and the economy interact over a long period of time in order to understand the nature of net energy effects shown in figure 6.1.

This problem has been studied for real economies by a number of workers, who have confirmed that as an energy system expands into resources of de-creasing accessibility, the energy intensity of economic activity does indeed increase.[13] As a result, under some circumstances, the total primary energy input to the economy can be expected to rise very rapidly for only modest increases in production of goods and services.

Along with the increased energy intensity of economic activity that re-sults from such system growth go increases in the cost of substitute forms of energy. In an economy in which energy costs are rising rapidly in real terms (as is likely in the later life stages of many major natural gas fields, around the beginning of the next century), it can be expected that the cost of plants to manufacture substitutes (e.g., synthetic natural gas [SNG] produced from coal) will also rise.

From our understanding of the behavior of complex systems, we would also have to acknowledge that the future is, in reality, indeterminate anyway. Thus, we cannot even make a realistic forecast of when a gas field will run out, let alone of the costs of substitute gas. The only reliable conclusion we can reach is that current predictions seriously underestimate the current value of gas and encourage wasteful use.

The Importance of Growth Rate

A great deal of energy-intensive capital investment goes into the development and expansion of energy sources, and *under high growth rates,* it is quite possible for energy supply programs to be *net consumers of energy.*[14] A very important factor here is the rate of expansion; the lower the rate, the better the net energy performance.[15] It appears that the rate of growth of energy supply may be a critical factor in evaluating the net energy obtainable from a system, because of the strong positive feedback energy flows required for rapid system growth. Overall, although net energy is not the only resource that an energy technology must supply, one can conclude it is the first and the most important.[16,17]

It is a basic tenet of neoclassical economics that substitution is always possible, which effectively makes scarcity only relative.[18] But from biophysical systems reasoning, substitution of a resource by another of lower accessibility is not a situation in which the two resources can be considered separately—they exist in a systems relationship, in which the one affects the other. The increased energy requirements of access to new energy resources give strong indications that the cost of delivered energy will rise at an accelerating rate in the future and that substitution is by no means automatic.

ENERGY AND SYSTEMS

The universality of the process of consumption of available energy and its rejection as unavailable energy by physical systems makes energy *one* logical means of studying the structure and dynamic behavior of real physical systems. It also provides *one* means of combining concepts from a range of disciplines and thus of assisting in the development of a more unified understanding of the behavior of complex physical systems.

Thermodynamics is concerned with the properties of systems, not of things on their own. In energy analysis, the expenditure of energy and time to do work is a linking mechanism between the natural environment system and the human socioeconomic system. This link may enable a unified, more complete analysis of the combined environment-economy system to be carried out. Some scientists feel that in the long term, the two solutions may come closer together, but in the meantime they are often far apart.

AIMS OF THE BIOPHYSICAL SYSTEMS WORLD VIEW

From the foregoing discussion, it will be clear that the biophysical systems perception has little to contribute to the determination of how people are likely to react in social situations. That is because the biophysical systems approach is based on the physical, not the social, world. With few exceptions, most physical scientists would agree that the perception is applicable to the physical constraints and long-term *limits* to social activities, not to the day-to-day activities of people within those limits.

The picture that comes from the biophysical systems view is that

- *the long-term economic costs of energy resource development are likely to be much higher than currently believed, and*
- *these costs are likely to increase at an accelerating rate over time.*

If these insights alone were to be incorporated into resource economics and the treatment of subjects such as depletion, the economics of sustainable alternatives such as energy demand management ("energy conservation") would be seen as much more favorable.[19] The approach makes it clear that there are strong indications of the existence of limits to growth of economies in any sense involving the production and consumption of material goods and services.

Although the immediate aims of the biophysical systems perception are modest, the effects of acceptance of its findings would be far reaching, at least in the field of the use of energy resources in society.[20]

Part II

LIMITS

The Dark Side

7

The Physics and Morality of Growth

IT IS THE aim of virtually all political systems to promote a growth economy. Growth, in economic terms, means increase in the production (and consumption) of goods and services. Conventional political-economic wisdom is that this is the same thing as increase in human welfare.

By means of growth, the total economic "pie" is made larger, so everyone can, in theory, get a bigger slice. Uniform, sustained growth enables politicians to avoid difficult problems such as equity, the relative size of different slices of the pie. Conventional politics buys off problems and social conflict by promising more things for more people and less for no one, forever and ever.[1] As an environmentalist put it, "Politicians feel pathetically insecure when they cannot promise growth."[2]

THE MEANING OF GROWTH

My aim in this chapter is to argue that the form growth takes has the potential either to improve or to damage the system within which it occurs. In planning for growth, quality is incomparably more important than quantity. To illustrate my point, consider the following claim: "What does Labor want? More." For years, this misquotation of Samuel Gompers, first president of the American Federation of Labor, has been used to justify the idea that everyone wants more of everything. The full text of what he said, at a meeting in Chicago more than ninety years ago, gives a very different story: "What does Labor want? . . . We want more school houses and fewer jails; more books and fewer arsenals; more learning and less vice; more constant work and less crime; more leisure and less greed; more justice and less revenge; in fact, more of the opportunities to cultivate our better natures."[3]

There are parts of the body of society in which growth should be encouraged because they are, economically speaking, underfed. There are others for which I argue that growth has already been more than adequate and a modest amount of slimming (negative growth) would be beneficial to good social health. In some parts of society, growth can be likened to cancers or ulcers on the social body. Measurement of growth by simplistic aggregates such as GNP cannot help but ensure social and moral problems for society in discriminating among the forms of growth and their relative desirability.[4]

ARITHMETIC OF GROWTH

An obvious consequence of growth, often implicitly ignored by its proponents, is that any system that grows increases in size. To illustrate some of the arithmetic of growth, table 7.1 gives values for the change in size of something (e.g., money or population) over a period of years at different rates of compound interest. The starting value of one is chosen for convenience.

The 0 percent column is inserted to provide a no-growth reference with which the other data may be compared. It is clear that compound interest growth increases the size of a system *at an accelerating rate*. This type of growth, in which a quantity increases at a fixed percentage per year, is known as *exponential growth*.

TABLE 7.1 *Growth and Compound Interest*

Years	0%	2%	5%	7%	10%
0	1.00	1.00	1.00	1.00	1.00
10	1.00	1.22	1.63	1.97	2.59
20	1.00	1.49	2.65	3.87	6.73
30	1.00	1.81	4.32	7.61	17.45
40	1.00	2.21	7.04	14.97	45.26
50	1.00	2.69	11.47	29.46	117
60	1.00	3.28	18.68	57.95	304
70	1.00	4.00	30.43	114	790
80	1.00	4.88	49.56	224	2,048
90	1.00	5.94	80.73	441	5,313
100	1.00	7.24	132	868	13,781
150	1.00	19.50	1,508	25,560	1,617,718
200	1.00	52.48	17,293	752,932	189,905,000

NOTE: Percentages above 100 have been rounded.

Exponential Growth

For many purposes, especially those involving money, the figure of 5 percent does not seem excessive. Even after inflation, many economies have achieved such GNP growth rates at times during the past two or three decades, and all governments would dearly love to achieve them again. The basically unstable nature of this type of growth (in that it runs away to infinity after a time, even at low rates) is easy to forget if one looks at the process over only ten or twenty years. Such a time period is too short for the real effects of growth (e.g., on the environment or on depletion of nonrenewable resources) to become clearly visible.

Probably the most important property of exponential growth is that the time needed for a quantity to double in size (grow by 100 percent) is constant. The doubling time t (in years) is approximately related to the growth rate P (as a percentage) by the simple equation $t = 70/P$.[5] Thus, at a rate of 5 percent per year, the growing quantity will double in 14 years. In two doubling times (28 years), the quantity will increase by a factor of 4; in three doubling times (42 years), by 8; in four doubling times (56 years), by 16; and so on. Refer back to the 5 percent column in table 7.1 and note that in 30 years, the size has increased by more than 4 times; in 40 years, by approximately 7 times; in 60 years, by more than 18 times; and so on. *Exponential growth is characterized by doubling,* and a few doublings lead quickly to enormous numbers. After 100 years at 5 percent, the original quantity has increased in size by 132 times and is still increasing at an accelerating rate. At a growth rate of 10 percent, the doubling time is 7 years.

The arithmetic of compound interest is inexorable—growth goes on forever, and *the rate of growth becomes virtually infinite.* As an example, imagine that Captain James Cook or Thomas Jefferson had invested $1, at 10 percent compounded annually, 200 years ago. At compound interest, after 100 years that single dollar would have grown to around $13,800, and after a further 100 years (which brings us close to the present day), to the staggering sum of $190 million, at which time interest would be payable at a rate of $19 million per year, $52,000 per day, or $36 per minute! Of course, the result is absurd, but that is what compound interest leads to *if taken to its logical extreme.* This point is very important, since most financial transactions and economic calculations are based on the assumption that compound interest is indeed the dominant process and will continue indefinitely. (A notable proponent of economic growth was awarded the Nobel Prize for theoretical work that "proved" that an exponentially growing population in an economic system experiencing exponential growth could enjoy an increasing real wage.)[6]

That the increase in size in any doubling time approximately equals the sum of all the preceding growth explains a statement by U.S. president Jimmy Carter in 1977: "In each of these decades (the 1950s and 1960s), more oil was consumed than in all of . . . previous history combined."[7] This apparently remarkable observation is the simple consequence of growth that has a doubling time of ten years. The growth rate with this doubling time is $P = 70/10$, or 7 percent per year. Thus, the consumption in one decade approximately equals the total of all of the previous consumption (see table 7.1 for data on growth at 7 percent).[8]

If such projections are applied to electricity demands, as was done in some serious long-term planning studies in several countries, it means that the planners seriously believed that after twenty-five years, per capita electricity consumption would be about five and a half times current usage; after fifty years, about thirty times current usage; and after seventy-five years, about one hundred and sixty times current usage.[9] What people could possibly do with that amount of electricity—even if it were supplied free—is a question to which no satisfactory answer was ever given. The question of how the electricity could be generated, let alone construction paid for, if the rate of growth meant that a new large-scale power station had to be commissioned every few days or weeks, was never answered. Yet politicians paid enough attention to these absurd "forecasts" to initiate construction programs that created huge surpluses of capacity, wasting billions of dollars and causing massive environmental damage.

Life of a Finite Resource When Growth Is Exponential

Stock resources are finite in size. In time, it is likely that they will be found to be larger (or smaller) than is currently believed, but nevertheless they are not unlimited. This is particularly true of the highest-grade, most easily accessible reserves of coal, oil, and gas that fuel most economies. The question of how long resources will last is one of the most important that can be asked in an industrial society. The answer is dominated by assumptions as to the rate of growth of use of the resources.

When growth in use of a resource is exponential (i.e., accelerating), it is a direct consequence that *the amount remaining in the reserve declines at an accelerating rate.* The coal resources of New Zealand provide an instructive example that could easily be translated for most other countries. The estimated coal reserves in 1985 amounted to some 6,357 million tons. The annual consumption in that year was only about 2.24 million tons, so it is not difficult to estimate that this resource would be good for another 2,838 years.

However, in 1985, consumption of coal was forecast to rise rapidly over the next few years; the projection for 1999 was 5.30 million tons. Even at that rate (some 2.4 times the 1985 consumption), the resource could be expected to last for comfortably more than 1,000 years. Clearly, there was nothing to worry about . . . or was there?

Yes, there was! What the calculations show is the estimated lifetime of the coal resource *at constant consumption rates.* But the forecast of an increase in consumption of 2.4 times over a time period of only fourteen years means that this was definitely not seen to be the case. There was, in fact, an assumed growth in consumption during these fourteen years of around 6.5 percent.

To show by how much even moderate growth rates reduce the life of the resource, it is a straightforward matter to calculate that at a growth rate of 6.5 percent, starting from the 1985 annual consumption figure of 2.24 million tons, the resource of 6,357 million tons would be entirely consumed in just more than eighty years.[10] There would be a low rate of depletion in the first fifty years of use and rapid depletion in the last thirty years. Even if new discoveries resulted in a doubling of the size of the coal resource—say, by another 6,357 million tons—that would still supply only another eleven years of use, to a total lifetime of ninety-one years. A further increase of 6,357 million tons would last less than six more years. The insidious and inexorable arithmetic of compound interest has taken over, showing the lack of common sense of the approach when taken to its logical conclusion.

The fact that compound interest leads to absurdities over quite modest periods of time, and has no basis in physical reality anyway, is realized by almost everyone involved in social and political-economic activities. But it is ignored as "too difficult" to incorporate into the decision-making process. But, as Aldous Huxley once pointed out, "facts do not cease to exist because they are ignored."[11] As in so many things, nature has something to tell us about growth if we will only stop, look, and listen.

GROWTH IN NATURE

In the early stages of biological growth, most of the energy an organism consumes goes into growth. At maturity, however, most inputs are required to maintain the system. This apparently nonproductive growth is needed to renew the fabric of the system and ensure its continuing health. (If we wonder why so much of societies' use of energy goes into maintenance, such as street repair, we have only to look to nature for the answer.)

The maximum power principle (described in chapter 1) helps us understand something of the place of energy in evolution and competition. It states: "Those systems that survive in the competition among alternative choices are those that develop more power inflow and use it best to meet the needs of survival."

The businessperson will readily understand the principle if an analogy is drawn between a business and the natural system, as described in chapter 1. Provided energy is available, maximization of energy flows (of whatever type) enables a business to grow faster than those of competitors who do not maximize their flows. Once the business is larger than its competitors, it commands greater resources, can use yet more power, and can grow even faster. Again by analogy, it is possible to grow too fast in business by forgetting the need to "put down deep roots in case of a drought." Alternatively, by concentrating too much on "roots," one risks being overtaken by a faster-growing competitor. Similar arguments can be applied to the macroeconomic objectives of a nation competing with other nations.

Logistic Growth

As mentioned in chapter 1, a more realistic form of arithmetic than that of compound interest is available to describe this type of growth. It accurately describes many characteristics of growth in nature under conditions in which there is a steady supply of flow energy (e.g., from the sun); such conditions apply to most ecosystems. The method involves the *logistic function,* whose initial growth behavior is close to exponential but which soon "flattens off" with a reduced growth rate, leading to ultimate stability.[12] Figure 1.2 summarized the basic principles of logistic growth. Since the logistic function reflects a stable, "sensible" situation, it must be regarded as a better method of forecasting than the exponential function. But even the logistic function does not adequately describe growth that depends on the use of stock energy resources; it applies only to growth from continuous, renewable resources. Since much of the growth in industrialized economies depends on the use of stored fossil fuels, it is necessary to look at the extent to which growth is possible from resources that are inherently limited, albeit large in comparison with current use.

THE POLITICAL-ECONOMIC PERSPECTIVE OF GROWTH

Whether one believes that continued growth is possible (or desirable) depends to a considerable extent on one's world view and value system. Standard economists believe not only in the possibility of continuous material growth but also in its axiomatic necessity. This belief ("growthmania," according to some economists) has given rise to an enormous literature in which exponential growth is taken as the normal state of affairs.[13]

According to the conventional political-economic world view, growth can continue forever because humanity is believed not to be subject to the physical limitations of lower orders of life. Central to this view is that increases in productivity of use of raw materials, and substitution of scarce resources by more abundant resources, will ensure that economic growth continues indefinitely (see also chapter 11).

Unlimited Wants

Most economists and politicians and many technologists remain convinced that people have unlimited wants.[14] Since the satisfaction of some wants is always assumed to stimulate others, wants are seen as infinite and growth as always justified. Even if this were true, however, in most industrially advanced countries, growth has in practice come to mean satisfaction of more and more trivial wants. Beyond a point at which the essentials of life are met, wants are artificially created by manipulation of people's preferences.[15] By subtle psychological methods, advertising overstimulates people's normal instincts for physical gratification and generates abnormal pressures to buy new goods and services. Television and radio advertisements endlessly extol the unlimited acquisition of everything as a way of life. That many of the wants are manufactured along with the product indicates that they are not inherent in human nature. An American marketing consultant put it bluntly: "Our enormously productive economy . . . demands that we make consumption a way of life, that we convert the buying and use of goods into rituals, that we seek our spiritual satisfactions in consumption. . . . We need things consumed, burned-up, worn out, replaced and discarded at an ever-growing rate."[16]

A cartoonist expressed the same thing even more succinctly with the following caption: "Buy! Consume! Waste! Let's get our economy moving again, with conventional economics."[17]

Growth feeds on itself. To achieve economic growth, capital investment in new productive capacity is needed. As soon as the productive capacity is ready, consumption must also increase to use it up, which in turn will justify further production and yet more consumption. Since wants are assumed infinite from this viewpoint, growth is a self-justifying and self-reinforcing process without apparent end. Industrial society thus has a built-in bias toward excessive production and consumption of economic goods. Its social messages and responses are those of a positive feedback system. Society's institutions are better adapted to promote growth than to control or direct it, but they have not absorbed what we know about the inherent instabilities of positive feedbacks. Ideological commitments to growth by governments, capitalist and socialist alike, have prevented the problem from being addressed properly.[18] Herman Daly makes a telling point:

> But in a finite world continual growth is impossible. Given finite stomachs, finite lifetimes, and the kind of [person] who does not live by bread alone, growth becomes undesirable long before it becomes impossible. But the tacit, and sometimes explicit, assumption of the Keynesian-neoclassical growthmania synthesis is that aggregate wants are infinite and should be served by trying to make aggregate production infinite, and that technology is an omnipotent deus ex machina who will get us out of any growth-induced problems.[19]

In some affluent countries, significant numbers of people are rejecting the idea of continued growth in consumption. Jorgen Norgard and Bente Christensen have shown in their surveys in Scandinavia that a majority of people in those countries find their material standard of living sufficient.[20] This attitude of material satiation appears primarily as a preference for more leisure time over more income. The less affluent the country, the less support there is for the idea of satiation. Surveys in other countries have shown similar results.

Growth in Externalities

At the same time as wants are both created and satisfied, the ecosystem services on which they ultimately depend are depleted by ever more powerful and toxic externalities, so that only poorer resources remain. Growth in the economic system and associated depletion of resources and production of wastes are the central causes of such effects. To defend ourselves against these externalities, we produce more, in the vain hope that new products will fix the old problems or that we will at least create the wealth that will enable us to fix them. In addition, instead of subtracting these *defensive expenditures* from GNP, we add them.[21] As a friend of mine pointed out, cheese making results in benefits to society, whose value is added to GNP. The cost of cleaning up the effluent from the cheese factory should be subtracted from GNP but again is added to it. If we make alcohol from the effluent and use it in vodka, we detract from people's health; if we use it as a motor fuel, we benefit transportation, with costs and benefits for society. These are all added to GNP indiscriminately.[22]

Hospital expenses and other costs of cigarette-induced cancer and bronchitis, carnage on the roads due to drunk driving, and costs of pollution control and toxic waste cleanup are all added to GNP. If these were seen clearly for what they are—damaging negative effects on the quality and duration of life—they would be subtracted. To add their transaction costs while promoting indiscriminate growth in GNP as a good thing in itself is equivalent to encouraging misery, death, and pollution. Growth of this sort should, according to Daly, be labeled "swelling," since it is of real harm to the society within which it occurs. One of the best comments of this type comes from Marilyn Waring in a scathing examination of the United Nations System of National Accounts (UNSNA), the accounting structure used to measure GDP (gross domestic product):

> When it dawns on you that militarism and the destruction of the environment are recorded as growth, it is the UNSNA that has made it so. When you are seeking out the most vicious tools of colonisation, those that can obliterate a culture and a nation, a tribe or a people's value system, then rank the UNSNA among those tools. When you yearn for a breath of nature's fresh air or a glass of radioactive-free water, remember that the UNSNA says that both are worthless. [23]

Common to socialist and capitalist ideologies alike is the belief that improvement in the material basis of society is the precondition of all social progress. Although this is probably valid in early stages of economic development, I believe it is certain that the process cannot be extrapolated indefinitely. Quite apart from physical factors, there is a strong economic case that at higher general levels of education and material fulfillment, the marginal returns to people of further material consumption appear to diminish. This seems to be partly due to some form of satiation and partly due to the undesirable side effects of growth. There is a great deal of doubt among many economists as to the validity of the growth assumption in the long term. [24]

Public consciousness of damage to ecosystem services has increased over the past ten to twenty years, but ways of dealing with the problems have not. Technologists and engineers strive to build bigger and better end-of-pipe pollution control systems while seldom examining the justification for the processes that produce the pollution in the first place. [25] Economists are concerned more with searching for an allocation of property rights that will ensure an "efficient" set of product prices than with helping to develop social instruments that will enable a collective resource (e.g., air or water) to be kept clean for all, for all time. It is uncommon for engineers or economists (or the politicians whom they advise) to recognize that their answers are, in the main, addressed to the wrong questions. The very fabric of our socioeconomic system must be questioned, and this is why I believe we must examine the foundations of our value system, not spend time and wealth on tinkering at its periphery.

The idea that the future will take care of itself it deeply embedded in Western growth ideologies, which see the interests of the present as overwhelmingly more important than those of the future. Acid rain, global warming, damage to the ozone layer, and toxic and radioactive wastes have such great potential for affecting options for future generations, however, that we can no longer ignore them or treat them as of low priority. Production of wastes changes everything in an irreversible way.[26]

Leaving severe externalities for our children and grandchildren to clean up is characteristic of the immorality that characterizes growth. Leaving only the poorer-quality, less-accessible resources of energy and materials is another. Neither is defensible in the light of modern scientific understanding. As David Brower observed, "The promotion of growth is simply a sophisticated way to steal from our children."[27]

Growth and Satiety

Growth has been considered in a moral context by many writers, including economists, over the past two centuries.[28] The economist Richard Tawney (1880–1962) strongly criticized the idea of continuous growth. He saw Western society as acquisitive, based on competition, individualism and the divine right of self-aggrandizement, and the assumption that what is good for one is in the long run good for all.[29] Despite these and many other attempts by people of eminence in their time to draw attention to the consequences of growth, moral arguments still fall on deaf ears. The theologian John Taylor pointed out: "Excess is . . . the enemy which I . . . invite you to fight year in and year out . . . ruthless, unbridled, unthinking excess. We are being made to expect too much. We are taking too much. We are scrapping too much. We are paying, and compelling others to pay, far too high a price."[30]

Many social (and physical) scientists regard morality as irrational, unscientific, or even emotive. They try to construct their logical systems without any reference to "nonrational" influences. But the foundations of science are firmly grounded in cultural and social history and cannot be seen as value free or independent of the activities of society.

If there is an element of choice in the activities of people and societies, how can it be exercised unless ethical or moral standards are agreed on and goals are set in accordance with them? Surely it is only after this is done that it is possible to use the tools of economics and technology to achieve the specified goals? This process has not been carried out in most Western societies in the twentieth century. Ethical or moral questions are put aside; they are either trivialized or seen as too difficult. Now, when seventeenth-, eighteenth,- and nineteenth-century perceptions are known to be inadequate for twentieth-century science, it is time that questions such as the meaning of growth are addressed by societies, using the best of modern systems understanding.

DESIRABLE AND UNDESIRABLE GROWTH

Food production provides a useful illustration of the illogic of much of the ideology of growth. Already, enough food is produced to provide the entire population of the world with an adequate diet, and food production has (approximately) kept pace with population increases. But two-thirds of the world's population survives on little more than a subsistence diet, and many millions are literally starving. At the same time, one-third of the world promotes an economic system that gives rise to growth while resolutely refusing to accept the logical consequences. Surpluses in one economic system go on increasing to the extent that food is often destroyed (e.g., in the European Community) while people in other economies starve (often at the same time as good land in their countries is turned over to the production of cash crops, which enable the rich countries to grow even richer). Humans have finite stomachs, yet food production in and for the rich countries increases. Clearly, the rich nations' economic and political pursuit of their own growth has reached the stage at which it can only be regarded as immoral. Since food production in these countries depends on large quantities of nonrenewable resources and chemicals, it also causes immense damage to soils, aquifers, and ecosystems. In short, it is not sustainable. In this context, Taylor is of the opinion that growth "is maintained by creating discontent in the rich countries and inescapable poverty in the poor countries."[31]

When one also looks at the disproportionate consumption of nonrenewable resources, one must agree with the economist E. F. Schumacher's comment:

> It is obvious that the world cannot afford the USA. Nor can it afford Western Europe or Japan. In fact, we might come to the conclusion that the earth cannot afford the "Modern World." It requires too much and accomplishes too little. It is too uneconomic. . . . The poor don't do much damage; the modest people don't do much damage. Virtually all the damage is done by, say, 15%. . . . The problem passengers on Space-Ship Earth are the first-class passengers and no-one else.[32]

To promote increases in the size of the economic pie while steadfastly ignoring the way in which it is cut up, whether locally or globally, is one of the major social and ethical scandals of present-day political economy. To increase consumption of a medicine because a modest quantity does one good is known to be dangerous, but this argument is never extended to economic growth, despite its known addictive and damaging consequences when taken to excess. Growth itself has become the goal of human activity, not a means to the achievement of some higher goal. As the economist John Hobson (1858–1940) wrote, "Getting and spending, we lay waste our powers."[33]

That comment was a lament over the philosophy of materialism that seems to be the inevitable consequence of an economy in which narrow-minded and tunnel-visioned economists, technologists, and politicians never take off their blinkers long enough to see the whole picture. The important questions, left unanswered by those in power, keep recurring: Who benefits and who loses? What is the purpose of production? In what way does production minister to the dignity and happiness of humanity? What is the ultimate goal of economic activity?

Taylor's comment, "I am not concerned with numbers but with disproportion. I am not worried by the many but by the mania," is a poignant reminder that the idea of "enough" does not enter into conventional economic, technological, or political decision making.[34] The pursuit of growth as an end in itself has resulted in our being seduced by an artificial code of behavior. Unless this is recognized and the socioeconomic value system altered, we will soon lose our humanity forever. We will also lose that part of our environment that sustains us in the style to which we have become accustomed. The latter process has already come to the poor; it can be expected to arrive at the doorsteps of the rich before long.

Who Benefits and Who Loses?

It will be evident that I do not see either the costs or the benefits of growth as falling uniformly or equitably on people or countries or on generations. The rich and powerful seldom starve or put up with acrid air or revolting rivers; they move to a more pleasant environment. The poor and powerless are trapped.

Historically, the commons in Britain were owned by the "common people," but at the time of the Land Clearances of the eighteenth and nineteenth centuries, most of these lands were forcibly alienated into private hands. The benefits of the change did not, of course, accrue to the commoners, although many of their great-grandchildren did eventually have some benefit.[35] Nowadays, the major beneficiaries of environmental protection measures for forests, rivers, and wilderness areas are those of reasonable means and readily accessible transportation (usually private cars or tour buses) rather than those who live in dirty, run-down, polluted urban areas.

The same argument applies to the overall consequences of economic growth. Whether in the affluent, industrialized countries or in the poor, underdeveloped countries, the benefits of growth accrue mainly to a small elite. In other words, growth usually occurs without development (see chapter 15). Morality must be the spring from which flows economic policy. Growth of itself, pursued as an end in itself, is always amoral and has results that are often highly immoral.

The legacies of the past remain in the industrialized, affluent one-third of the world, but environmental pressure groups are gradually ensuring that new developments are not undertaken as easily and carelessly as they used to be. No such protection is available for the developing two-thirds of the world. As controls tighten in the developed countries, corporate interests turn toward places where governments are so deeply in debt to international moneylenders that they are providing transnational corporations what may be the world's final, grim commons. Only a change in morality can alter this process, which is directly encouraged by conventional political, economic, and technological perspectives.[36]

THE BIOPHYSICAL SYSTEMS PERSPECTIVE OF GROWTH

Economics centers its attention on the value of a good or service, not on physical units such as its mass or the energy required to make it. Economic value could conceivably grow forever, but the physical mass of goods and services to which the global total economic value is attached must decline if the planet is not to be irreversibly damaged. The constraints of physics on the growth in value are important and must be respected.[37]

It is a salutory reminder of the reality of growth that according to current estimates, around 40 percent of the net photosynthetic production (i.e., of biomass) on the world's land surface is already appropriated by humans. Since the remaining 60 percent provides ecosystem services for the millions of species of other life forms, it is clear that there is not much opportunity for further human appropriation.[38]

In the longer term, economic growth will be possible only in those areas where needs for material, energy, and ecosystem services are much lower (per unit of economic output) than for current activity. By this means, a substantial reduction will occur in the demand for resources.[39]

Unless growth at the margin eventually becomes effectively nonmaterial, however, even that phase of growth cannot last for long. Economics has no theory demonstrably applicable to an economy in which the majority of production and consumption is of nonmaterial commodities. The very idea of producing commodities of this nature raises problems of identification and measurement as well as of property rights.

The fundamental point of my arguments in this book is that the only reliable long-term prediction that can be made about growth in a sustainable society is that *in the physical sense,* there are real limits to growth. Material economic activity must tend toward a more or less steady state. Growth will then occur for maintenance and replacement, not to increase the absolute physical size of the flows of material in the economy. In the long term, such an economy will be sustained by flow energy from the sun, with contributions from carefully husbanded resources of stock energy and raw materials.[40] In a material sense, it should be smaller than at the present time, but in quality of outcomes it could be very much better.

According to some writers, the process of moving away from resource-intensive production has already begun in some industrialized nations.[41] I doubt whether this effect is universal, however. There is a lingering suspicion in my mind that what has happened reflects a shift of resource- and pollution-intensive activities to poor countries, which continue to supply commodities directly (and ecosystem services indirectly) to the rich countries.

Population Growth

Population growth is another issue that must be squarely faced. In general, the poorest countries have the greatest population growth rates and the most severe food and welfare problems. That these problems are to a significant extent the result of political, economic, and military interference (past and present) by the rich, developed countries is no reason to ignore the issue. Already, the world population is almost certainly greater than can be sustained in the long term. It is possible now only because nonrenewable resources are being used in vast quantities. The rich nations, especially the United States, European countries, and Japan, use far more than their fair share, but even if resources were shared fairly, the dependence on nonrenewables means that global population still has to be drastically reduced over the next decades. Ideally, that will be achieved by giving every person and family the opportunity to control their own futures. That Mohandas Gandhi understood the reality of physical and moral constraints on economic activity is shown in his famous observation, "The earth has enough for everyone's need, but not for everyone's greed."

Herman Daly tells the story of an economist who, when asked, "What is it that economists economize?" gave a repulsive but illuminating answer: "Love, the scarcest and most precious of all resources."[42] If one asks how this is achieved, the answer is that it is done by maximizing growth in production and consumption of goods and services. If growth continues, unequal distribution can be justified as necessary, because if everyone has the same, there is no incentive for the individual effort that creates further growth. If growth does not continue, the burden of sharing places too great a strain on the precious store of love, which should never be used because it is so scarce.

It has been cynically claimed that one purpose of economic theory is to make those who *are* comfortable *feel* comfortable.[43] I would comment that increased profits (e.g., tax breaks) are widely used by governments as inducements for the rich to work harder, whereas greater poverty (e.g., benefit cuts) is the accepted inducement for the poor to do likewise.

DIRECTIONS FOR THE FUTURE

If the global system is seen in systems terms, with everything influencing everything else and with inherent capacity for change, we can see the risks of destabilizing the system. The foundations underlying a new morality must include acknowledgment of these factors; otherwise, the factual basis for moral judgments will be inherently faulty. Again, John Taylor provides salutary words: "My concern is with diagnosis more than prognosis, and I believe that what is wrong is not so much what we are doing as the frame of reference within which we are doing it. . . . My object is not to calculate where we shall be by the end of the century, but to disclose what manner of civilization we have become and what kind of spirit it is that possesses us and drives us."[44]

At present, we have both opportunity and responsibility to take off the spectacles we use to view the world and regrind the lenses to a new prescription. We need to look at things differently, as individuals and as fellow travelers on Spaceship Earth. The economist Brian Easton put it well: "The pursuit of narrow self-interest (as encouraged by our economic system) is not a moral imperative, rather it is a rule to enable the economic system to operate. Normally, we expect individuals to pursue the much richer morality that we have within us."[45]

8

Feedbacks and Externalities

THE STANDARD POLITICAL-ECONOMIC perception is that consumption is a void into which all goods and services eventually disappear. Only capital and labor are returned from the consumption sector to the production sector. The biophysical systems perception, on the other hand, tells us that although "used" (unavailable) energy (as heat) does indeed eventually disappear (into the cosmic void of outer space), in the meantime both it and the discarded matter associated with it, which remains on earth, can cause substantial damage to the physical, and hence the economic, environment. There are real limits to the ability of ecosystems to absorb undesirable waste products of any economic activity, and in many parts of the world these limits have been exceeded.

ENERGY AND ECOLOGY

Figure 8.1 illustrates the relationship between human economies and their surrounding environment. Globally, there is extinction of species and depletion of both plant nutrients (soil and water) and easily accessible mineral and fuel resources. Accompanying these are siltation of rivers and estuaries and growing mountains of waste, some biodegradable, some toxic, some disease carrying. Cycles of nature have been interfered with, and toxic wastes have the potential to create enormous problems over long time periods.

Not included in conventional thinking is the fact that nature provides humanity with a wide range of *ecosystem services*. Even if we include only those of importance in the economic sense, they include such essentials as purification services for air and water and gene bank services for crops. Aesthetic services could also be included, since for most of us there is inherent beauty in nature. None of these is paid for in any economic sense, although ecologically the cost of their loss is often very high.

Feedbacks affect nature in many ways. The most common result of sustained felling of forests, especially tropical and subtropical rain forests, is massive damage to their ecosystems and silting and flooding of river valleys and plains. The accelerated rate of global warming produced by increased emissions of carbon dioxide and other gases is mainly the result of burning of large quantities of fossil fuels. These are typical examples of the dynamic feedback effects produced when the amount of waste from an economic activity becomes important enough to put that economic system, or another one, at risk.

Some "pollutants" occur in nature; ecosystems have evolved to cope with such factors. The damaging effects of industrial pollution arise from the generally higher concentrations of pollutants and the presence of many chemical species not found in nature. Urban air pollution, wastewater streams, and toxic metal contamination of soils are examples of outcomes of economic activity that may go beyond the natural absorptive capacity of ecosystems and can give rise to rapid, irreversible changes in the balance of nature.

When the amount or nature of a waste exceeds the absorptive capacity of the local environment, feedback becomes important. The fact that pollution feedbacks often do not directly affect the producer (as in the case of a waste discharge that pollutes a river for all downstream users) is an ethical matter of no small importance for society.

Since neither matter nor energy can be destroyed, all available energy and all matter used in the economic process eventually end up as waste returned to the environment in one form or another. Most pollution and waste in industrial countries is, directly or indirectly, associated with the extraction, production, and use of fossil fuels. The Swedish scientist Svante Arrhenius

FIGURE 8.1 The Economy, Resources, and Feedbacks

pointed out a hundred years ago that we are "evaporating our coal mines into the air."[1] Extraction and refining of minerals and production of chemicals are also highly polluting. High-intensity (mechanized) agriculture pollutes water and soil.

To illustrate some relationships between ecosystem services and the use of fuels and economic practices, I now discuss the issue of human-induced accelerated global climate change.

GLOBAL WARMING AND THE GREENHOUSE EFFECT

The *greenhouse effect,* apparently first speculated on almost two centuries ago by the French mathematician Jean-Baptiste-Joseph Fourier[2] and the subject of detailed predictions a century ago by Arrhenius,[3] relates to an expected accelerated rate of change in global atmospheric temperature due to the buildup of gases.[4] The main culprit is carbon dioxide (CO_2), with methane (CH_4) and chlorofluorocarbons (CFCs) major future problems due to their rapid rate of increase and their very high solar energy absorption. Nitrous oxide (N_2O) accounts for a small amount of greenhouse gases (GHGs) but is increasing. Burning of fossil fuels is the main source of carbon dioxide and nitrous oxide, and methane results from certain types of farming, especially those involving ruminant animals.

The greenhouse effect (GHE) is, of itself, perfectly natural. Without it, there would not be life on earth as we know it, since the planet would be a great deal colder. The problem arises because the greenhouse gases, which increase the heat storage capacity of the atmosphere, interfere with the transmission of heat to outer space. The result is that the atmosphere will heat up, analogous to the inside of a greenhouse. Over geological time periods, the earth's climate has entirely naturally gone through several temperature fluctuations, probably due mainly to small changes in the sun's activity. The concern about global warming reflects the probability that emissions of greenhouse gases are now sufficient to cause a speedup in the *rate of change* of global temperature—by as much as five or ten times. Such an increase in what is naturally a slow rate of warming will have serious effects on climate and ecosystems. The likely long-term consequences of accelerated global warming are still far from clear, but they almost certainly involve changes in climate, especially in extremes of weather (cyclones, etc.), and possible raising of sea levels. None of these is desirable, and they are likely to be ecologically and socially disastrous.

Atmospheric CO_2 levels are estimated to have risen about 25 percent since early in the past century, when industrialization was just starting.[5] Fossil fuel burning has contributed a large proportion of this, but desertification, deforestation, and expanding agriculture have also made large contributions. As well as the burning of large quantities of woody material, these actions also result in the removal of large quantities of biomass from the global ecosystem and thereby less fixation of CO_2 by photosynthesis in plants.

From the biophysical systems viewpoint, since the atmosphere is a complex, nonlinear feedback system, it is entirely to be expected that the outcomes of changing its chemical composition cannot be accurately predicted. Even if we knew much more about the atmosphere's past and present behavior, we would still have to acknowledge that its future behavior is, and always will be, indeterminate; only broad-brush projections of future behavior are possible. That is all that modern science can do.[6]

Some projections suggest that changes in average global climatic temperatures of the order of 1.5 to 4.5 degrees Celsius could occur over the next few decades. Such temperature rises could cause a rise in sea levels of 20 to 140 centimeters. Current theories suggest that trends will be clear by about the year 2000, but the likely longer-term consequences are still not clear—they could be disastrous or they could be mild, as one would expect of a complex system like the global atmosphere. Of one thing we can be sure: change will occur. It is better to take action now than to wait until it is too late. It is worth remembering that humanity's entire social and cultural infrastructure, developed over the past 7,000 years, evolved within a climate that deviated by only about 1 degree Celsius from today's climate.[7]

TECHNICAL CONTROL OF POLLUTION

Many technologies exist for reducing the effects of polluting discharges from technologies. The simplest is to change the process itself so that only smaller quantities, or less harmful wastes, are produced. In extreme cases, the appropriate action is simply to shut down the process altogether. In many cases, only small changes are needed for substantial reductions in pollution.

Emissions of sulfur and nitrogen oxides from electrical power stations are conventionally taken care of not by their removal but by the use of tall chimneys that simply disperse the pollution far and wide. The fact that such emissions contribute to the global total, and thereby to the acid rain problem, is generally ignored by the major polluters, especially in the United States and

Britain. Major industrial groups in these countries spend a great deal of money lobbying against measures that could affect their "freedom" of operation and their "competitive advantage."[8]

No matter how good control technologies may be, the fact remains that no technology exists that has no waste products; this is ensured by the second law of thermodynamics. In addition, even the manufacture and operation of pollution control equipment involves production of materials such as steel, together with the associated engineering work to fabricate, transport, erect, and maintain the equipment. All of these processes involve production of wastes, directly or indirectly.

Because of the complexity of interrelating the many parts of both the economic and the environmental systems, it is not possible to determine in a total environmental sense whether the overall effect of introducing a specific control technology is better or worse than if it had not been used. Although the effects at the plant itself may be improved, we have no way of determining whether the totality of the many small effects produced elsewhere in the system is greater or smaller; thus, we cannot tell whether the overall result is good or bad. As one writer put it, "The fouling of the nest which has been typical of [human] activity in the past on a local scale now seems to be extending to the whole system."[9]

DYNAMIC FEEDBACKS

The examples of the greenhouse effect and acid rain highlight the dynamic feedback effects shown in figure 8.1. Acid rain results from the burning of a fuel to produce energy in one place, but it may have the consequence, in combination with a myriad of other emissions from other places, of destroying a forest somewhere else. That forest could have provided the biomass resource for other energy developments.

The existence of dynamic feedbacks outside the economic system suggests that for the long-term health of human societies, it is essential to move from a perception in which all processes internal to the economy are assumed to be controllable by economic agents (the political-economic viewpoint) to a perception in which it is clear that the economic agents exercise only partial control (the biophysical systems viewpoint). That change would acknowledge that the global environment system evolves in ways that are to a considerable extent independent of direct human control. It would also serve as a stern messages to humanity to beware of the risks of overconfidence.

In *Ecologist* magazine's "Blueprint for Survival," published in 1972, the tragic dislocation between humanity and nature was pointed out: "To suppose that we can ensure the functioning of the ecosystem ourselves, with the sole aid of technological devices, thereby dispensing with the elaborate set of self-regulating mechanisms that has taken thousands of years to evolve, is an absurd piece of anthropomorphic presumption that belongs to the realm of pure fantasy."[10]

THE ECONOMICS OF POLLUTION

Pollution can be seen in economic terms if its effects are expressed as costs to those who have to put up with it. In economic jargon, *externalities* arise when one person is affected by another's actions but receives no payment or compensation.[11] If the action is beneficial, it is an *external benefit*; if the effect is adverse, it is an *external cost*. The greater the size of the externality, the greater is the divergence between public and private costs or benefits. In practice, market prices for goods and services ignore the damage associated with their production. Consumers are therefore led to an erroneous idea of the cheapness of things they buy, because resources from the environment (and ecosystem services) are given no value.

Consider a decision to mine for minerals in a known beauty spot. Before mining, the area had been a source of benefit to residents and visitors; afterward, its aesthetic benefit is lost or reduced. Often, the environmental loss to the community is not given adequate prior consideration because land-owners are not paid to maintain aesthetic values. In deciding to allocate land to mining, landowners will consider only their own costs and benefits, not the external costs and benefits of the destruction of a community amenity. The problem is that since social efficiency (in a market sense) will be achieved only if social costs (private plus external) are taken into account, we can conclude that the market system will not achieve efficiency on its own; some means of imposing the requirement to internalize externalities must be introduced. Recent economic history is full of examples in which it has been found necessary to restructure private markets by publicly invoked constraints.[12]

It is widely believed by economists that creating markets in externalities by assigning people property rights to pollute the environment will result in individual polluters' being held accountable for at least some of their actions. But because of the inevitable delays between cause and effect, such as in transmission of effects and time for results to become clear, it can never be *socially* optimal to leave the settlement of disputes over external effects in private hands.[13] Private free markets in environmental situations seldom, if ever, work in the real world. In reality, little or no attempt is made to take account of the costs of environmental damage.[14]

As Richard Benedick puts it, in the context of damage to the ozone layer:

> Unfortunately the current state of economics is not helpful in analyzing such a situation. Its traditional methods of measuring income and growth appear increasingly irrelevant in the modern world; the more CFCs a country produces, for example, the greater is the growth in its gross national product. And the economist's prescription for coping with future monetary flows is inadequate for responding to large but distant dangers. . . . The application by policymakers and investors of the tools of conventional economics may result in ecologically very misleading decisions.[15]

THE TRAGEDY OF THE COMMONS

In an essay published some twenty years ago, Garrett Hardin pointed out that there is no *technical* solution to the problem of pollution; the problem is an *ethical* one.[16] He explained his point by using a simple story of people grazing cattle on common pastureland where there are no (social or other) constraints on the number of animals. Since each grazier receives the whole price gained by selling an animal but shares only the loss in average animal weight that results from overgrazing, there is every incentive for each grazier to keep adding cattle to the pasture.

This parable is relevant to the issue of pollution, whereby each polluter gains an advantage from being able to get rid of waste without significant cost yet shares only in the average deterioration in environmental quality. The invisible hand does not operate where that which is polluted is owned by all and where it is usually not possible to evaluate external costs to a person or group. Air, for example, is owned by everyone and cannot be parceled up or fenced off, with "property rights" assigned to those willing to bid highest to gain control over its use.[17]

Society recognizes such situations under the concept of *common property*. In some cases, the government holds land or resources (e.g., national parks), ostensibly for the people. Government property is not normally the same as common property, however, in that its use and ownership can be assigned to individuals through legal instruments such as mining rights. No such possibility arises with the air we breathe. Whereas individually owned property places a responsibility on the owner not to destroy it or render it unproductive (since it would then be of reduced or no value), common property apparently imposes no direct responsibility on the individuals who use it. One person may foul the air, confident in the knowledge that the wind will normally take the foulness away and deliver fresh air for further fouling. For each individual polluter, therefore, there is always a greater advantage in using the air as a "sink" for pollution than there is in taking action to reduce or contain it. The person who controls his or her pollution may thus deliver a benefit to everyone else but receives only a fraction of that benefit personally. Hence Hardin's use of the term "tragedy," in the sense that "the essence of dramatic tragedy is not unhappiness. It resides in the solemnity of the remorseless working of things."[18]

Since it appears on the surface to be in everyone's individual interest to use the common to the maximum extent, each person is locked into a system that compels continual increase in demand for the common and the inevitability of its eventual destruction. Since the world is limited, so is the common. Air has an enormous capacity for self-cleaning. Even so, some forms of pollution create others (e.g., acid rain) when the air cleans itself, whereas other pollutants concentrate in the atmosphere, damaging the protective ozone layer or changing world climate. Everyone who pursues personal interest contributes to the destruction of the commons. Freedom in a commons eventually, and inevitably, brings ruin to all.

Since there is no economic reason for the polluter to stop polluting, the only alternative is to seek other possibilities for control. When society as a whole, or a local community as a group, imposes control on the polluter, protection of common property is possible. Any such imposition implicitly acknowledges the absence of a generally accepted individual sense of ethical responsibility.

That Hardin's case has been shown to be in some respects oversimplified does not detract from its value in concentrating attention on the issues of individual versus community responsibility and individual versus community ownership of resources. I must point out, however, that there is good historical evidence that the commons in Europe operated sustainably (e.g., with the manorial system) for upward of a thousand years, and had strong social controls on activities such as grazing,[19] before being alienated (often forcibly) from their communities of occupiers and owners in the eighteenth and nineteenth centuries.[20] Thus, tragedy is not inevitable.

VALUATION OF THE ENVIRONMENT

There are examples of "commons" in any country: air, water, soil, national parks, wild and scenic rivers, mountain ranges, natural forests, wild animals in indigenous ecosystems, and so on. Standard economics recognizes the value of these resources only in the sense of the functioning of the market-place. When that process is not applicable, as in the case of the commons, it is regarded as *market failure* and requires nonmarket valuation. In order to allocate resources in an economy, a value for each and every thing must be measured or imputed.

By concentrating on the idea of market failure or nonmarket valuation in too narrow a sense, however, we risk diverting attention from the fact that much of what humankind regards as important has nothing whatever to do with the operation of any kind of market. Marilyn Waring writes:

> I turn . . . to the mountains. If minerals were found there, the hills would still be worthless until a mining operation commenced. And then as cliffs were gouged, as roads were cut, and smoke rose, the hills would be of value—their value would be the price the minerals would fetch on the world market. No price would be put on the violation of the earth, or the loss of beauty, or the depletion of mineral resources. That is what value means, according to economic theory. [21]

To impose market valuation mechanisms on what are in many cases reflections of deep human social, cultural, or spiritual needs is to debase and risk destroying that which is being measured. The same goes for attempts at *nonmarket valuation* of the environment, in which some conventional research on valuation aims to find out what people are willing to pay to kill an animal, fish, or bird in a wilderness area or to travel to and stay in a national park. [22] I have considerable difficulties with the approach, which appears to involve the tail wagging the dog. Does a climber actually value the view from the top of a mountain peak in monetary terms? Is the money spent on boots and jacket, or on transportation to the base of the mountain, a measure of the value of getting to the top? Is the value of a rare species of bird in any way related to the price that could be obtained for timber from its forest home? [23] To me, the idea not only is offensive but also has similarities to gangsters' protection rackets. It also has nothing to do with what to most people is the value of the environment.

The nub of the matter is that where economic valuation mechanisms can be shown both to be meaningful and to work in practice, they should be used as a component of the overall process of management. Where they are not demonstrably meaningful to people or clearly do not work, they should be rejected. To call such situations "market failure" is absurd; so far as the environment is concerned, *the market does not fail; it simply does not exist in any economically meaningful way.* Nor should it be expected to. *Homo sapiens* is far more complex than *Homo oeconomicus* and always will be.

Jeremy Rifkin suggests that the concept of externalities "is just a convenient dodge to try and avoid the consequences of the second law of thermodynamics."[24] The disorder created by each new technology is not a side effect, nor is it necessarily lower in social cost than the benefits of using that new technology. Each technology always creates a temporary island of order at the expense of greater disorder in the surroundings. Externalities are ad hoc corrections introduced by economists for the sake of appearances.[25]

Since there are both physical and ethical constraints on human economic development, it is important to hold open the view that noneconomic tools may be of key importance in the social resolution of resource allocation problems. As we know, "economics" is a term derived from the Greek *oikonomia*, "management of the household." Interpreted broadly, it could incorporate a systemwide meaning that encompasses all things in the global household. Interpreted narrowly, as at present, it reduces everything and everyone to economic neuters: items of production, consumption, and exchange in a marketplace that is often imaginary. Again quoting Marilyn Waring, "The current state of the world is the result of a system that attributes little or no 'value' to peace. It pays no heed to the preservation of natural resources or to the labor of the majority of its inhabitants or to the unpaid work of the reproduction of human life itself—as well as its maintenance and care. The system cannot respond to values it refuses to recognize."[26]

Many tribal communities value resources as treasures, passed down to them from their ancestors and held in trust for their descendants. In such communities, resources may not be sold; they are sacred. Conventional economics is not applicable, since there is no opportunity cost against which the resources may be valued. Such stewardship regimes are totally different from those centered on conventional, individual ownership, as promoted by Western colonial nations and often forced on indigenous peoples.[27]

AGENDAS FOR THE FUTURE

The World Commission on Environment and Development (WCED) recently put forward an alternative agenda for dealing with problems arising from conflicts between environmental and economic pressures.[28] First, they considered the fact that standard agendas tend to focus on the effects of environmental problems rather than their causes. Although awareness of a problem should lead to measures to cure or reverse it, the "react and cure" approach often drives out its less-costly but politically more demanding alternative—that of "anticipate and prevent."

Second, the standard agenda encourages people to see complex issues as exclusively environmental rather than as developmental or joint environmental-developmental issues. Masking the interconnections perpetuates the idea that environmental issues are in some way the special responsibility of ministers of the environment or federal environmental officials. In fact, the roots of many problems lie across the spectrum of bureaus of energy, trade, industry, agriculture, finance, transportation, and so on. Only if this interrelationship is recognized can a total system viewpoint be attained.

Third, for a long time, "environment" has been regarded as an "add-on," or "retrofit," field to "more important" areas. Fuel and energy use, however, is a key determinant of environmental quality, and most major pollution issues have a common source in energy policy. Environmental factors must therefore be incorporated at the very start of policymaking, not left until problems arise. All things are linked, and a study of energy flows in the context of a biophysical systems world view provides a valuable means of concentrating on the physical mechanisms, linkages, and feedbacks that underlie social possibilities, options, and responsibilities on planet Earth.

An essential part of all this is that nature is at risk. If humanity continues with its past ways, even if they are modified to reduce some of the worst outcomes, the questions remain: Is nature to be the servant of "man," or the reverse? Are we to pursue the goal of some utilitarian utopia or accept a higher, perhaps transcendent, perception of our place in nature? If the first, then life itself will lose most of its meaning. Humans will still exist, but part of humanity will have gone, probably forever. However, in the words of Bill McKibben, "should we choose, we could exercise our reason to do what no other animal can do; we could limit ourselves voluntarily, choose to remain God's creatures instead of making ourselves gods."[29]

9

Myths of the Political-Economic World View

A MYTH IS a traditional story that offers an explanation of some fact or phenomenon. Myths are neither wholly true nor wholly untrue. They may have been more true in the past than now, but people act as if they are still true, even when they no longer really believe in them. Some modern usages of the word have connotations that suggest that myths are irrelevant or wrong, but this is not necessarily so. Myths are of considerable importance to people, and for some, they may reflect ultimate personal truth. The critical need is for people to be given the opportunity to find out which myths are meaningful and which are not.

THE MEANING OF MYTHS

A myth is a mental model with which people try to interpret reality and respond to it. Myths have value in enabling us to organize the way we perceive facts and see ourselves and the world. Myths speak through rich symbols, helping to bring order into what may otherwise be a chaos of personal experience. Whether true or not, myths help us make sense of what is going on around us. Myths can provide a valuable doorway into the value structure of a society or culture and may give insights that are difficult to achieve by more conventional means.

Some myths, like belief in fairies, are probably harmless. Others may be dangerous if they distort the way we see the world and the ways we deal with problems. How does one tell the difference? How does one help people recognize the existence of other perspectives of reality without offending deeply held beliefs? One good way to start examining a myth is to find out what it meant to those who created it (the process of exegesis). Many social and scientific myths of the twentieth century originated in the seventeenth and eighteenth centuries, so this is not difficult to do. The next task is to find out what the present-day followers of the tradition of a myth mean by it (the process of hermeneutics). The final task is to compare the myth with the reality it seeks to represent. This stage often runs into trouble with adherents because to them, a myth cannot be questioned without challenging the believer's self.

Most myths present themselves as authoritative and able to account for facts, no matter how completely at variance they may be with the real world. A myth gains its authority not by *proving* itself but by *presenting* itself. And the greater the political authority that lies behind the myth and the more often it is presented, the less likely it is to be challenged. Such is the case with many political and scientific myths of the twentieth century.

Over the past two hundred years, Western societies have cast aside many of the myths and institutions that had served them for hundreds of years. The great belief systems—the idea of a divine lawgiver; the sanctity of the family, kin group, or tribe; the rituals, customs, conventions, ceremonies, and festivals that gave meaning and purpose to the smaller communities of earlier times—are mostly in ruins. But in the haste to throw off apparently outmoded burdens, people also lost the valuable side of those myths and institutions. The feelings created by people's confidence in their place in nature and in the stability of the social systems that supported them have been vandalized. Many people are left with nothing but the despair engendered by new myths that they do not understand, often because the myths have been imposed on them without explanation.[1]

MYTHS OF THE WORLD VIEW

Throughout history, people have felt it necessary to organize life's activities by constructing a frame of reference within which to fit them: a world view that explains the hows and whys of daily existence. Such processes have been the essential ingredient of many cultures' responses to the world they perceived. A world view is usually so internalized, from childhood on, that it is seldom challenged.

In the Western world, the belief that neutral and impersonal laws govern what can be done in society and the world is deeply embedded in technology and economics.[2] But if that sort of belief is dominant, things are taken out of the political arena that properly belong there. Such is the outcome of taking seriously many assumptions of mainstream political economics. In reality, most of the assumptions are myths: partly true and partly false. They must therefore be treated with considerable caution.

The Myth of Unlimited Resources

Perspectives on the use of resources and on technology's ability to achieve anything we might want are clouded with scientific and political-economic myths. Consider, for example, the following statement: "Through technological advance we [will] seek to simulate and redesign to our liking all biological processes, so that we may achieve ever more control over the conditions of life."[3] Myths such as these are widely held, but their foundations are so weak that they need to be replaced with others to guide our thinking as we set our course toward the twenty-first century.

The Prime Myth

The *prime myth* in the context of this book claims that *lower-grade resources will always be available to humankind in a continuing and virtually endless sequence.*[4]

Since exploitation of resources always, and without exception, requires expenditure of available and accessible energy, as I pointed out in chapter 3, this myth is critically dependent on the continuing availability of energy resources. For that reason, I will reword it into a more specific form: *Lower grade **energy** resources will always be available to humankind in a continuing and virtually endless sequence.*

Nicholas Georgescu-Roegen, a trenchant critic of the myth, states: "The favorite thesis of standard and Marxist economists alike . . . is that the power of technology is without limits. We will always be able not only to find a substitute for a resource which has become scarce, but also to increase the productivity of any kind of energy and material."[5] William Catton exposes further flaws in this "favorite thesis":

Two non-repeatable achievements had made possible four centuries of magnificent progress. Those two achievements were (1) the discovery of a second hemisphere, and (2) development of technology that could unearth and exploit the planet's energy savings, its fossil fuel deposits. [Hu]mankind's increasingly relentless search for new sources of energy and for more costly energy technologies expresses our wish to deny that achievements like those two were uniquely resultant from bygone circumstances.[6]

Part of the problem of evaluating the prime myth is that economists usually think of resources in monetary terms—in other words, as homogeneous. The inadequate information supplied by market prices for resources means that conventional (neoclassical) economics is largely incapable of according resources—especially nonhomogeneous, nonrenewable fossil energy resources—the meaning they actually possess.[7]

In order to give the prime myth the attention it deserves, we need to examine some of the myths on which it depends or that are used to derive policies stemming from it. These myths are deeply ingrained in the Western cultural tradition and are central to many areas of decision making. The reader is invited not to reject those that may be ill founded (and I strongly emphasize this point) but to treat them always as partial truths and partial perceptions of reality. They may be useful under certain limited circumstances, but they should never be used outside those narrow confines.

I would also make the point that by the term "resources," I include ecosystem services along with the conventional meaning of extractable resources.

The Myth of Divine Authority

According to some writers,[8] Western culture, shaped by interpretations of the Bible, particularly the early books of the Old Testament, pictured humans as separate from all other creatures and dominating them.[9] Many still feel what is almost a divine imperative to "master" nature. It stems from a linear, hierarchical, authoritarian world view in which God is above, nature is below, and man is in between, set above everything but God (not forgetting that woman is set hierarchically below man).[10] The British theologian C. S. Lewis suggested that the truth is rather more prosaic: "What we call Man's power over Nature turns out to be a power exercised by some men over other men with Nature as its instrument."[11]

Recent theological studies have shown that the belief of God giving man authority over nature is not necessarily supported by the Bible.[12] The *dominant themes* go far beyond what is gained from literal interpretation of specific verses (e.g., Genesis 1). In reality, there are two creation myths in Genesis: the "Yahwistic" (Genesis 2:4, in which man was created out of dust) and the "priestly" (Genesis 1:24, in which man was "given dominion," etc.). The Yahwistic version, dating from around 1000 B.C., is closer to a holistic, "systems" view, but it was apparently superseded by the priestly version, dating from around 600 B.C. The latter clearly reflects dominance of political structures, which may have been as strong in the relationships between priests and kings in ancient Hebrew society as they are today between economists and politicians.

A full analysis must also combine major themes from both the Old Testament and the New Testament. These do not support the view that humans are above nature but suggest the contrary—that they are part of it. In Genesis 1, God declared plants and animals good independently of humans; they are therefore *inter*dependent.[13] In a sense, God, humanity, and nature exist in a systems relationship. From a biblical viewpoint, stewardship is the primary function of humanity, whose function is to take care of God's creation, giving special (but not exclusive) attention to itself, including future generations. Stewardship requires extending brotherhood and sisterhood not only to all existing people but also to future and past people, and to all other life forms, in appropriate degrees.[14]

MYTHS OF ECONOMIC BEHAVIOR

It is part of the belief structures of most Western peoples that the world is proceeding toward a more "valuable" state as a result of the accumulation of knowledge and technology. Most also believe that the individual exists as a separate, autonomous entity, that people have always desired private property, and that competition has always existed. They believe that scientific observation is objective, that the natural world has a mechanistic order to it, and so on.

All of these beliefs are considered to be part of human nature and therefore basic and unchangeable. When looked at from other viewpoints, however, they are seen to be only partly true and therefore are validly described as myths. Beliefs of individuals and small groups should always be respected. Myths of social systems should not, because they can be a means of oppression and control of the weak by the powerful.

The Myth of Primacy of the Individual

The conventional political-economic viewpoint depends on two crucial assumptions about the individual: that the individual is the best judge of his or her own interests and that over time, tastes (i.e., preferences) do not change—or, if they do, they change as a result of better information. These are often summarized as "the independence of individual preferences."

Although these assumptions apparently have the status of received wisdom when seen from one viewpoint, they are at best half-truths. It may be politically expedient to declare that everyone is the best judge of his or her own interest, but few people would not want to undo many of their past mistakes. The fact that many apparently normal people subject themselves voluntarily to various forms of psychoanalysis, or indulge in the search for truth through religion, or follow the forecasts of astrologers, means that in respect to the larger questions that govern their lives, they are far from certain where their true interests lie. [15]

The modern liberal view of the place of the individual in the marketplace, expressed by such philosophers as Friedrich von Hayek, is interesting in this context. As described by Bruce Jesson, their view is that

> "true individualism . . . is a social individualism. It requires a society with a stable family structure, voluntary community associations, and conformity to tradition and convention . . . true individualism requires a rigid moral code and a sense of social responsibility. It bears little resemblance to the acquisitive, self-indulgent and amoral spirit of modern individualism . . . (which) is deficient in its lack of ethics." [16]

This model reflects cultural factors coming from groups rather than individuals. By breaking down group behavior into "socially responsible" individual behavior, one may pave the way for authoritarian controls on group action, nominally to increase individual freedom. Even though this may be done in the name of freedom, in reality it reduces the power of those with whom individuals are associated and on whom they may depend. Trade unions, under threat in many countries, are an example.

The assumption that the individual is in some sense supreme in the marketplace axiomatically leads to the conclusion that reliance on individual self-interest is the only requirement of the economic (and indeed the political) system. [17] But a free market assumes that people have equal access to information about what is taking place and that they are all sufficiently self-reliant to exist without buying or selling. This reflects a utopian situation, found only in some small communities (in which group cohesion is a central element of community structure). It has long been known by anthropologists, sociologists, and psychologists that in most societies, group behavior is markedly different from that of individuals. Long-term goals of families and communities take into account factors that seldom enter into the decision making of isolated individuals, and this is nowhere more important than in the context of relationships with the environment. [18]

From the systems perspective, the view of economist Lester Thurow is helpful: "Societies are not merely statistical aggregations of individuals engaged in voluntary exchange but something much more subtle and complicated. A group or a community cannot be understood if the unit of analysis is the individual taken by himself. A society is clearly something greater than the sum of its parts despite what the price-auction model would maintain." [19]

Conventional economics is mainly built on simplistic and outmoded concepts drawn from nineteenth-century behavioral psychology. When economists talk about "economic man"—*Homo oeconomicus*—they make assumptions about rational behavior, human needs, goals, and values that have been largely demolished by workers in the social sciences.[20] The demolition occurred mainly in sociology and adult education, by empirical testing (using the Popperian criterion of falsifiability)[21] and by use of more modern ideas of behavior, such as humanistic psychology[22] and the human potential movements.[23]

The idea that the individual is the central (and sole) unit of decision making in society is rejected by many cultures. Indeed, the idea is in many respects deeply offensive, and it goes against centuries of their history. For settlers of (usually) European cultures to *impose* that ideology on people is yet another example of the long history of insensitivity and brutality that has characterized colonization. The idea also must be recognized as relatively new in human history, gaining its main strength from political theories of the seventeenth and eighteenth centuries in Britain and Europe. To many Europeans, the more cooperative social structures of the past may now be too far distant to be clearly remembered, but such is not the case in most other cultures. The dominance of European-based cultures enabled the ideology of individualism to be spread far and wide, but the historical fact of its acceptance does not prove it is "right"; the reality is that its supporting political, economic, and military structures were more powerful than those they supplanted.

The phenomenal successes of advertising, the vast amounts of money spent on it, and the involvement of psychologists supply evidence that up to a point, it is quite possible (and certainly very lucrative) to change people's preferences.[24] The methods used owe more to psychological manipulation than to any inherent law of human nature in that planning is extended to the consumer to ensure that he or she will "want" what is produced.

The Myth of Rational Behavior

It is widely believed that some form of the "rational behavior" observed of particles in classical physics must also be present in human behavior. The idea of rationality in human behavior was in the eighteenth century, however, and still is, only an analogy with classical physics. Since the nineteenth century, the idea has been shown to be a very weak one. It is more a political theory, a code of human behavior, than a reflection of natural laws. Nevertheless, rational behavior is at the core of neoclassical economics and its modern offshoots. The approach is reductionist, looking at the individual in order to try to understand the economy. It relies on the assumption that a whole is the sum of its parts.

There are actually two quite different meanings of the term "rationality." According to Karl Popper, the *rationality principle* means that "having constructed our model, our situation, we assume no more than that the actors act within the terms of the model, or that they 'work out' what was *implicit* in the situation." Popper makes it clear that the rationality principle "has little or nothing to do with the empirical or psychological assertion that [people] always, or in the main, or in most cases, act rationally." [25]

In other words, the rationality principle applies to the *a priori* domain of development of models. It has nothing to do with the *empirical* domain of observed human behavior. Popper goes on:

> Rationality as a personal attitude is the attitude of readiness to correct one's beliefs. In its intellectually most highly developed form it is the readiness to discuss one's beliefs critically, and to correct them in the light of critical discussions with other people. [26]

> I am a rationalist. By a rationalist I mean a [person] who wishes to understand the world, and to learn by arguing with others. (*Note that I do not say a rationalist holds the mistaken theory that [people] are wholly or mainly rational.*) [27]

The difference between the two meanings is vitally important, but they are commonly confused. In the general sense, rationality is an a priori concept, but when the word is applied carelessly to the empirical world, the result is the expectation of *rational behavior* (i.e., actions performed according to a model of behavior) rather than acknowledgment of the richly human, creative, intellectual behavior of a *rational person,* who takes a critical attitude to his or her beliefs.

From careful consideration of the emphasized sentence in the latter quotation from Popper, I am led inescapably to the conclusion that *a rationalist should never believe in rational behavior!* To do so is to accept a model as a standard for behavior rather than to observe critically the empirical reality of actual behavior. The two meanings are inherently in conflict, and Popper exposes the point very effectively: *a belief in rational behavior is in itself irrational!*

At the empirical level, the underlying assumptions of rational behavior are largely untested and probably untestable. Despite this, many economics textbooks still promote the model of rational *Homo oeconomicus.* That many economists recognize its inadequacies but continue to teach (and preach) the concepts gives me cause for concern about the scientific basis of political-

economic theories. (The economist Mark Blaug suggests that some economists play tennis with the net down!)[28]

The imposition (e.g., through fiscal policies) of the *requirement* that
people act in conformity with a model of behavior in order to gain access to
some privileges of citizenship (employment, education, health care, welfare,
etc.) is inherently authoritarian and violent. It induces—and often forces—
people into individualistic behavior against their natural instincts. Nor does
the rational behavior model give adequate attention to changes in value over
time, that is, to intergenerational equity. Deeply human ideas, such as leaving resources for one's grandchildren or planning allocation by need rather
than greed, have no clear place in its calculus; that sort of behavior is labeled
as irrational. (Proponents of economic rationality commonly apply this label
to those who disagree with them, especially to those who value the environment highly.)

In this context, it is worth noting that in law, there is the concept of the
reasonable person, who (in contrast to the rational person) is: "a person who
is not only protective of his/her own rights, but also has a fair regard for the
welfare of others."[29] The reasonable person is concerned with justice
and fairness, with equity rather than efficiency. Justice and fairness are
absent in much of conventional economics, yet they are central to most people's ideas about how society should be run. Humanistic economics is all
about replacing the model of the rational person with that of the reasonable
person.

The Myth of Bounded Rationality

More recently, concepts of rationality have been extended to include ideas
such as *bounded rationality*, in which people make decisions without perfect
knowledge. In some respects, the approach is an alternative world view to
that of neoclassical economics, and it reflects the fact that human behavior
consistently violates economic principles of rationality.

Basically, the bounded rationality approach acknowledges that people
have limited cognitive capabilities.[30] This implies limitations in attention,
perception, memory, and abilities to process information and communicate.
Use of bounded rationality criteria results in simpler problem-solving approaches and attention to subgoals rather than overall goals. Altruism and
opportunism are incorporated in some theories of bounded rationality.[31]

From a systems point of view, the approach appears to be limited in application. It works only when a system can be broken down into its parts and
each part studied separately (in systems terminology, such a system is *loosely
coupled*). In real systems, feedbacks and nonlinearities are usually strong,

and one cannot change one part without affecting another. The result is that application of the ideas of bounded rationality can result in suboptimization and system dysfunction. Thus, these developments appear not to have much relevance to practical aspects of policymaking. Rather than testable hypotheses (in a scientific sense), I see them as sincere attempts to correct the logic of rational behavior for obvious deficiencies. (Blaug, using Popperian arguments, warns against the use of "ad-hoc auxiliary assumptions," or "immunizing stratagems," when working toward verification of theories.)[32]

The Myth of Freedom

It is a central belief of those of the mainstream market liberal political-economic viewpoint that freedom of the individual is the most important characteristic of a society. For these people, freedom is entirely an economic construct. Freedom exists in the unfettered market and ceases to exist if market processes are hedged about by regulation.[33] Freedom thus has a meaning akin to choice, the availability of alternatives in a marketplace.

For most people in society, freedom has entirely different meanings, few of them capable of codification. Freedom from hunger and want? Freedom of speech and of association? Freedom from arbitrary constraints? Freedom to be creative and artistic? These are not the same as freedom of choice.

Free-marketers hold to a negative freedom. "Freedom *from.* . . . " What is important is freedom from restrictions that prevent them from getting on with whatever they want to do (mainly the accumulation of wealth). Positive freedom, on the other hand, is the more creative "freedom *to* . . . ," such as the freedom to live within a context that encourages the pursuit of things spiritual and creative. The assiduous promotion of ideas of negative freedom, especially in the market liberal context beloved of Treasury officials and business roundtables, is yet another step in the attempt to mold *Homo sapiens* into *Homo oeconomicus*—"the human as consumer"—the manipulated market cipher who will always behave as markets require. "Freedom" in this context has many characteristics of a myth. It also involves the hijacking of a word with an old and honorable meaning into a new and dishonorable service.

The Myth of Universal Property Rights

A basic requirement of the market model is that anything individually owned is tradable. It is a small step to believe that in order to make full use of the "efficiency" of the marketplace, everything that possibly can be, *must* be in private ownership.[34]

For many people, the idea that natural resources can be regarded as private property, let alone as tradable, is bizarre. When the first English settlers "bought" land from the Maori in Aotearoa–New Zealand, they believed that they were carrying out a simple transaction giving them ownership rights.[35] To many of the Maori (at least in the early years), the transaction had no such meaning; it was the exchange of the gift of the temporary use of land for other gifts, some of them monetary.[36] When the full weight of the colonists' laws (and military forces) was used to enforce exclusive occupation, the Maori found out what had happened; it was then too late. North American Indians had comparable experiences, as did many of the indigenous peoples of Africa, India, and Asia.

Some extreme free-market proponents argue that "scarce resources" such as elephants would be better safeguarded by assigning people ownership of the animals than by collective action (e.g., cessation of the ivory trade). The idea is that if someone "owned" and "farmed" the elephants, and earned the resources needed to head off poachers, the elephants would survive.[37]

I note that such suggestions usually come from people who live in societies in which the levels of wealth are such as to be the prime causes of stress on less-developed countries and their ecosystems, through their excessive consumption habits.[38] As a further, nontrivial point, in practice, the initial assignment of property rights in such situations tends to be associated more with local power ploys and corruption than with equity and long-term environmental factors. This outcome seems to be common to developed and developing countries and to political systems of both left and right.

In the systems context, hierarchies and nonlinearities indicate that all things are not equal and some take precedence over others. For social system stability, the rights of the collective must always take precedence over those of individuals; individual rights can never be paramount. To be more specific, the rights of *some* individuals must never be allowed to take automatic precedence over those of the collective.

The Myth of the Free Market

In practice, free markets do not exist.[39] What commonly happens is that some organizations and corporations become large enough to dominate production of their particular commodity (e.g., automobiles or soaps and detergents), in which case theirs is termed an *oligopoly*. In an oligopoly, all participants have a degree of common interest and none is willing to rock the boat; competition is polite, not predatory.

Nevertheless, most economists still see the market in the sense of the equilibrium price auction, in which the individual is a utility-maximizing consumer or producer within free markets that establish equilibrium prices for goods and services. Because so much of standard economic theory depends on this erroneous assumption, one must be careful not to ascribe power to the market that it does not possess, while acknowledging that there are indeed many socioeconomic functions that the market appears to carry out effectively and well.

As an example, in many countries, centralized planning has produced major blunders when governments became involved in projects in which the private sector declined to take part. This is usually taken as evidence that planning is inherently inefficient and that a market will do better. The first statement is probably correct (although planners are so subject to interference from politicians that one cannot claim the planning process itself was to blame). It is not axiomatic, however, that the conclusion is also valid; the world is full of stories of corporate blunders and cruelties. Real-life decision making is not the sole preserve of caricatures such as the individual on the one hand or the state on the other.[40]

Further, according to some eminent economists, free markets do not work—indeed, they cannot work—in situations in which externalities are important.[41] As I have pointed out in several places in this book, externalities are everywhere, albeit seldom acknowledged.

According to the economist Lester Thurow, who is critical of aspects of the market philosophy, free-market theory also extends far beyond the realm of conventional economics: "It is, in short . . . also a political philosophy, often becoming something approaching a religion."[42]

Free-market theory can also be expressed in mathematical form, which lends it the appearance of scientific truth and renders it incomprehensible to all but the initiated. This book is not the place to review these criticisms. Suffice it to record that the fundamental assumptions of market theory are considered by some economists to be so weak that it fails as a predictive tool or as a scientifically based theory. In short, it has many characteristics of a myth. This is not to say that the underlying qualitative model is not useful or important; the point is that it is not a reliable indicator of social behavior. It remains a means for gaining insight into some of what goes on in part of society, and it is a useful microeconomic tool.

The Myth of Utility

The core problem in economics is that of measurement of *utility*, the satisfaction obtained by an individual from the use of goods and services. The theories of economics depend on the assumption that each individual seeks to maximize his or her utility from a limited income. Since the utility an individual supposedly seeks to maximize cannot be observed or measured directly, and since the assumption therefore cannot be tested, the argument is tautological. The presumed existence of utility is rooted in political-economic beliefs and ideologies rather than empirical science. The fact that the problem is acknowledged by economists and then circumvented (or fudged) by *imputing* utility maximization from subsequent actions does not detract from this conclusion.[43] Lester Thurow writes:

> No other discipline attempts to make the world act as it thinks the world should act. But of course what Homo sapiens does and what Homo oeconomicus should do are often quite different. That, however, does not make the basic model wrong, as it would in every other discipline. It just means that actions must be taken to bend Homo sapiens into conformity with Homo oeconomicus. So, instead of adjusting theory to reality, reality is adjusted to theory.[44]

As an example, in modern economies, governments actually account for a substantial proportion of all transactions. Economic theories that attempt to describe the behavior of economies on the basis of individuals, each assumed to be maximizing his or her own utility, thus provide limited insight. The conventional response of free-market economists is, of course, to get governments out of supplying services so that the market can do the job. Thus, the economy is modified to fit the theory.

The Myth of Value

To most of us, some things or people in our lives or in nature are priceless. That does not mean that they have no value, nor does it mean that their value is infinite; it just means what it says—that they have no price! The idea that some things may not be capable of valuation in terms of cash seems to me entirely sensible, but it is inadmissible to conventional economists. It is central to mainstream economics that the price a good or service fetches in a marketplace is a measure of that item's value to the buyer in his or her personal life. As the lawyer Richard Posner put it, "Value . . . is defined by willingness to pay."[45]

This sort of economics largely sidesteps the issues of ethics and equity involved with the *ability* to pay, which is of course related to the potential buyer's level of wealth. In other words, it assumes a dollar is worth exactly the same to a billionaire as to a beggar.

Money Fetishism

It is a short step further to the associated assumption that the sum total (in dollars) of production or consumption in an economy (e.g., expressed as GNP) is a measure of the value of life—or of general welfare—in that society.

That view has been described as money fetishism, in which the abstract symbol becomes indistinguishable from the reality.[46] For example, since abstract exchange value flows in a circle in the neoclassical economic model, so must real goods and services. Or, since money can grow forever at compound interest, so too can real wealth. What is true for the token of wealth is held to be true for the artifacts of concrete wealth itself.

Since the "paper economy" offers more scope for "growth" than the real economy, monetary activity (in the form of mergers, takeovers, junk bonds, and tax avoidance) has in many instances become more profitable than production of the very goods and services that are essential for life in society.

Insofar as economics concerns itself with (and, in its application, depends on measurements of) monetary value measured in the marketplace and manipulated as abstract symbols or tokens in the paper economy, it concerns itself with only a tiny part of life's value. This is not to say that market value is not important or useful, only that it is an inadequate measure of total value. The fact that such total value (or total welfare) cannot be measured is no excuse for not acknowledging its existence, nor, on the other hand, for claiming more for gross economic measures than they deserve.

The economist E. F. Schumacher put the problem into focus thus:

> To press non-economic values into the framework of the economic calculus, economists use the method of cost benefit analysis. This is generally thought to be an enlightened and progressive development as it is at least an attempt to take account of costs and benefits which might otherwise be disregarded altogether. In fact, however, it is a procedure by which the higher is reduced to the level of the lower and the priceless is given a price. It can therefore never serve to clarify the situation and lead to an enlightened decision. All it can do is lead to self deception or to the deception of others; for to undertake to measure the immeasurable

is absurd. . . . The logical absurdity, however, is not the greatest fault of the undertaking; what is worse and destructive of civilisation is the pretence that everything has a price or, in other words, that money is the highest of all values.[47]

The Myth of Discounting

As we saw in chapter 4, a dollar in the hand today is worth more than a dollar in a year's time, and a dollar in the future is worth less than a dollar today. This arises from the fact that money can be invested to produce a return and thus can increase in value over time. It is when this arithmetic is applied to real things that problems arise.

For example, it can be logically argued that if different people's lives are of equal "value," at a 10 percent discount rate, an action that would save 1 person's life today is effectively of the same value as a similar action that would save 117 people's lives in fifty years' time (see table 7.1). Thus, it would be better, for example (if funds are scarce), to spend one's money on saving 2 people today than 117 in fifty years.[48] Similar logic tells us that risks left to future generations, such as toxic waste dumps, are of insignificant importance to today's decision makers. It can be highly "economic" (in cost-benefit analysis terms) to save money today by leaving major problems for future generations to solve.

This arithmetic arises from the use of CBA in an area in which it has no validity. To discount physical and social things and people in the same careless way as is done for money in a bank account is absurd and immoral. It is yet another example of money fetishism and the fallacy of misplaced concreteness. This is a good illustration of why major issues, such as ozone layer depletion or accelerated global warming, must not be left in the hands of free-market economists.

The Myth of the Invisible Hand

Adam Smith's doctrine of the invisible hand that guides each individual who acts in his or her self-interest to promote the interests of the society in which he or she lives is strongly supported by many people today.[49] Followers of the doctrine forget, however, that the society within which Smith developed his theories was very different from today's. In Smith's time, there were strong social and community constraints on individual behavior, derived from shared morals, religion, custom, and education.[50] These are not present to the same extent today, and indeed there are strong forces opposing them. In Smith's time, however, these social mores were so pervasive and so obvious that he would have felt it unnecessary to include them in his argument.[51] Two hundred years ago, for example, there was no question but that God was an all-powerful Being with the ability to affect the lives of each and every individual. It was a society in which self-interest included the responsibility before God to answer for life's actions and transgressions on the Day of Judgment. To change Smith's argument into a license for limitless self-gratification distorts his writings beyond recognition.

The invisible hand must be acknowledged as a partial truth—in other words, a myth. Some form of invisible-hand model is probably valid to describe some of what happens in a village marketplace of the type Smith described. But the belief that the sum total of market actions, each derived from individual self-interest (in practice massively influenced by advertising and distorted by externalities), in some way adds up to a guarantee of the best interests of society as a whole stretches the imagination to the breaking point. Group identity, collective responsibility, and respect for common property are also known to be critically important cultural components of any stable society. Important areas of human social activity (concern about the distant future; respect for land, resources, and environment; spirituality; etc.) have little to do with independent individual preferences.[52]

Markets must always be held accountable to the greater social interest, something that may be forgotten by those caught up in the excitement of economic reform.[53] The greater *environmental* interest is no less important.

The Myth of Competition

According to the political-economic world view, competition is the normal way in which people and animals interact. Economists are beginning to acknowledge, however, and social scientists have known for a long time, that a more basic mode of interaction among people is *cooperation*, within small and large groups. This is especially true in the context of people's attitudes toward their environment.[54]

It is even more true in ecological systems, in which competition among animals or plants may be obvious to the onlooker but cooperation is the dominant process in ecosystem stability. In many cases, cooperation is far more efficient than competition in terms of the output gained from a given set of inputs. The motives behind cooperative behavior may in some cases still be those of a form of self-interest; group cooperation may be a better and more efficient way than individual competition of achieving species advantage.[55] However, that is not the same as atomistic self-interest in free-market economics.

For powerful groups in society, the whole point of competition is to create an *unfair* market. According to some economists, many important markets are oligopolies anyway.[56] To the extent that the "free" market exists, it does so in villages or in situations in which production is a function of large numbers of small producers such as farmers, motor repair shops, and small businesses.

The Myth of Efficiency

According to lawyer Richard Posner, "Efficiency means exploiting economic resources in such a way that human satisfaction measured by aggregated consumer willingness to pay for goods and services is maximized."[57] Efficiency is defined in economics with respect to the presumed existence of an optimum allocation of resources, normally best achieved through the actions of a marketplace. It is known, however, that even in the limited context of economic theory, optimum allocation depends on the initial distribution of resources among members of society. As an example, a Pareto optimal distribution is achieved when resources cannot be reallocated to make at least one person better off without making someone else worse off. But the prices that are determined in the free market, and that determine the final allocation, are themselves preempted by the initial allocation. In a market in which there are a few rich people and a lot of poor people when trading starts, the final allocation of wealth will be very different from that in a market in which everyone had the same resources at the start. As an economist put it, "A Pareto-optimum is said to obtain when nothing more can be given to the hungry, the cold, the ragged and the homeless without incommoding the glutton, the miser, the usurer and the play-boy."[58] A similar situation arises in the context of ownership and use of natural resources, including ecosystem services.

Imperfect markets are the norm; free markets are figments of the theoretician's imagination. Anything like a free market usually results in large, powerful firms taking over or putting out of business smaller, weaker ones. Although this is often claimed to be the result of "efficiency," other arguments suggest that it has more to do with the economic muscle of large organizations. The idea of economic efficiency has so many unknowns that it remains unvalidated in practice, although undisputed in theory. The term is also used widely by politicians but in most cases as an almost meaningless buzzword.

None of this is to suggest that markets have no place. On the contrary, no matter how imperfect, markets often have an extremely useful function in allocation of resources. The point is that any such achievement of the market has to be acknowledged as being, at best, one of obtaining an improvement in allocation, not of achieving an optimum. Determination of whether an improvement has actually taken place involves empirical political and social measurements, not a priori arguments.

The systems approach cautions us against falling into the trap of suboptimization. The whole of a system is always more than the sum of its parts. If links among parts of the system are ignored or oversimplified, it is easy to optimize only one or more subunits, to the detriment of the whole. The function of most optimization studies in economics is to seek an improvement (e.g., in allocation), on the assumption that all other things remain unchanged. This assumption is more often than not heroic in practice.

The Myth of Stability

It is assumed in much of conventional economic theory that the world is an unchanging, static system, or else it is only slowly changing. In discussions of growth, for example, it is believed that steady growth is a natural state of economies. Nonlinearities, time delays, and the distinction between stocks and flows are seldom taken into account in these models. From systems considerations, it is clear that these assumptions may be very misleading in practice. The historical record of social and natural systems is actually one of change. Change has sometimes been slow, but it has often been sudden and unpredictable. Wars, floods, famines; the changing habits of consumers, producers, and investors; stock market crashes; technological and business innovation; and political follies of every description are factors external to economic models that influence them in countless ways. Human history is more turbulent than is commonly acknowledged, and static and other simple models are rendered less real because of it.

The Myth of Substitution

Most economists have sufficient faith in the free-market price mechanism to assert that it will prevent any resource scarcity. They believe that as the price of one resource rises due to scarcity, another will step in when the price is right and take over the market. In the short term—say, until the early years of the twenty-first century—they are probably right. In the longer term, I believe there is increasing evidence that they are badly wrong.[59] I showed in chapter 6 that the theory of the free market has serious deficiencies in the field of energy resources. There is also some empirical evidence to support a lack of faith in the theory.

The proposed substitution of crude oil by shale oil has been investigated in some detail in North America over many years, and the conclusions are highly relevant to this discussion. The fallacy in the traditional economic substitution argument arises from a problem of logic, which has been clarified by the engineer Malcolm Slesser.[60] It was asserted in the early 1970s that shale oil production would be economically viable when the price of conventional oil reached $6 per barrel. The assertion was made on the implicit assumption that the shale oil facility could be built with the cheap oil. In other words, it assumed the same energy base for industries in the economy and the same price structure as at the time of the assertion. Obviously, while conventional oil at $2 was available, no one would build a shale oil facility producing at $6. Unfortunately, when conventional oil rose in price above $6, it was no longer possible to build a shale oil facility that could deliver product at $6. When reevaluated, the new shale oil price was found to be $5 above the new crude price.

This behavior is consistent with the biophysical systems perception of the world but not with the political-economic approach. It is worth noting that conventional economic theory has been unable to explain many effects of the oil price rises of the 1970s. According to economists at Resources for the Future: "Neither energy's share of GNP nor the slow rate at which energy consumption patterns change accounts for the sharp changes in production, productivity, unemployment, or inflation that occurred in 1974 and 1979. It appears that something amplifies the effect of oil price swings."[61]

The substitution argument is questionable in the context of accessibility of primary energy resources. It has even less validity in the context of such global problems as destruction of the ozone layer, global warming, and buildup of toxic wastes. Prices in the marketplace are relevant to short- and perhaps medium-term decisions, within a static context. They are crude but useful means for allocating a given resource flow from nature among alternative uses in the service of a given population of already existing people with a given distribution of wealth and income.[62] Market prices should not be allowed to decide how fast a resource is used or how to distribute resources among different people or generations. William Rees suggests that "Perhaps most important in the long run are the philosophical arguments against market approaches.[63] 'Commoditizing' the ecosphere is a technical solution that merely extends the materialist world view without questioning society's fundamental values and assumptions. If the world is to be salvaged the motivation will flow more from changing attitudes than it will from improved economic incentives."[64]

MYTHS OF MARKET FAILURE

Much of what humankind regards as important has nothing to do with any kind of market. Mark Sagoff comments that in many situations, there are no relevant markets to have failed—these include situations involving "matters of knowledge, wisdom, morality and taste that admit of better or worse, right or wrong, true or false, and not mere economic optimality. Surely environmental questions—the protection of wilderness, habitats, water, land, and air as well as policy toward environmental safety and health—involve moral and aesthetic principles and not just economic ones."[65]

The term "market failure" presupposes that whenever market forces do not produce the best possible allocation, it is an exception to the rule. Since the existence of the market is questionable in the first place, this presupposition makes use of a circular argument in which exceptions to a rule are explained in terms of the rule itself. Even if we accept the presupposition, we should still, to be logical, describe what the market is aiming to achieve—efficiency, equity, sustainability, and so forth. Although seldom specified, the market, and therefore its failure, means something different in each case.[66]

THE MYTH OF ENERGY AS COMMODITY

To many mainstream economists, energy is simply a commodity whose attributes, although unique and important, do not distinguish it in any significant way from other commodities, such as water, steel, butter, or carrots. Thus, energy should not be singled out for individual care and attention.[67]

This view reflects a basic misunderstanding of the science of energy in that it does not distinguish between two markedly different meanings of the word "energy." The everyday meaning relates to the fuels wood, coal, oil, and gas. These are often referred to as energy, but they are more correctly termed sources of potential energy, or energy carriers. The scientifically important meaning relates to energy as *the generalized attribute of physical transformation and change.*

Specific fuels can be treated as (substitutable) commodities in many situations, but energy itself cannot. The laws of thermodynamics apply not only to heat and work processes in machines but also to the heat and "work" associated with chemical and biochemical transformations of all types. Thus, the laws apply to the processes of photosynthesis, growth, decomposition, and decay in the natural world; to the processes of circulation and precipitation in the global atmosphere; and to the processes of production and consumption in an economy every bit as much as to the processes in the mechanical worlds of physics and engineering.

THE MYTH OF ENVIRONMENT AS COMMODITY

My government's philosophy was given in the following statement: "To give the environment a fair hearing, and represent it across the entire alignment with development, you have to communicate in economic terms."[68] Conventional economics asserts that if the environment and its resources can be seen as similar to other goods or services (like cheese, toothpaste, or carrots), the market is the appropriate place for valuation to be carried out. This approach has a number of fatal flaws.[69]

The first is that the "prices" of widespread child abuse, or of losing the Amazon forests, for example, are not available; there are no markets in which they may be "valued." Economists then have to invent a "shadow price" to take them into account. But these shadow prices are only estimates of *transactions associated with the events*—for example, hospital and/or psychiatric counseling costs (in dollars) of treatment of a physically or psychologically abused child.[70] They in no sense evaluate the misery and hurt experienced by the child. Nor do shadow prices evaluate the long-term loss of social income or ecosystem services from the absent forest, let alone the cost of restoring something whose loss may be intolerable and/or irreversible.

The second flaw comes about by virtue of the fact that no numerical value can possibly take account of people's spiritual relations with their environment or with one another. To attempt to reduce emotions and spirituality to numbers leads to the debasement of everything.

PROBLEMS IN ECONOMICS

It will be apparent that there is a great deal of concern about the validity of much of standard economic theory.[71] This comes mainly from within the economics profession itself; in these pages, I have only reported a few of the criticisms that economists have been making of their own discipline, since 1970 at least.[72] The critic Irving Kristol recently commented, in reviewing a book by Lester Thurow, an economist who is critical of many current theories, that "on the one side, he shows that much of what passes for 'scientific methodology' in economics is pretentious pseudoscience. On the other, he reveals to what extent economists propel themselves into a muddle by a simple-minded identification of *homo oeconomicus* with *homo sapiens*."[73]

Much of theoretical economics has ceased to be related to real human societies.[74] This is part of the reason why mainstream market liberal economics on the one hand and anthropology, sociology, and psychology on the other have drifted so far apart. The latter are based largely on empirical observation; the former, largely on a nineteenth-century logical-mathematical approach. The economist Peter Wiles has commented, "The main thing that is wrong with economics is its disrespect for fact."[75] That same economist also commented that "it is perfectly possible for a science to be sick, and ours is now."[76]

Marilyn Waring has pointed out that since early this century, the standard economic approach has been first, to observe facts in order to gain an insight into economic relations; second, to deduce the general laws of political economy from premises drawn from the prior observations; and third, to test the laws by inductive verification.[77] This method is contrary to the requirements of modern science. The ultimate empirical test of a hypothesis is whether its propositions correspond to reality (using the criterion of falsifiability). In a priori science, all that is required is that the deductions from a given set of axioms are logically correct.[78] So long as the axioms of mainstream economics remain divorced from the reality they claim to represent, their results will be unacceptable to those who study, let alone those who suffer from, their outcomes.

The Myth of Objectivity in Economics

Economics is so closely related to political theories that many of its practitioners fail to remember the ideological underpinnings of their studies.[79] The economist Mark Blaug suggests, for example, that the scope of positive economics is smaller, and that of normative economics larger, than is frequently claimed by economists.[80] It is also common, as Mark Lutz and Kenneth Lux write, for the positive "is" analysis to be carried on, perhaps unconsciously, to the normative "ought to be" conclusion.[81]

Robert Kuttner points out:

> The study of who gets what and why, unlike the study of plants or planets, cannot help being an ideologically charged undertaking. Despite the laborious techniques

and scientific pretensions, most brands of economics are covertly ideological. Marxian economics, with its labor theory of value, assumes the inevitability of class conflict, and hence the necessity of class struggle. Keynesianism, with its conviction that industrial capitalism is systemically unstable, offers an equally "scientific" rationale for government intervention. Neoclassical economics, with its reliance on the efficiency of markets, is an embroidered brief for laissez-faire.[82]

As D. Paarlberg puts it, "It is impossible to give the right answer to the wrong question; the tragedy is that we spend so much of our time asking the wrong question and trying to answer it."[83]

THE PLACE OF ECONOMICS

It does not in any way follow from these arguments that I believe conventional economics has nothing interesting, useful, or important to say about socioeconomic policy. *I cannot emphasize that point too highly.* But what conventional economics has to say—according to many critics from within the profession itself—is of a general nature and is not easily translatable into the specifics of policy. This is why, when it comes to policy matters, economists are often in disagreement. Interpreting information about what is happening in the economy is an art, not a science.

Let us not forget that economics as a discipline is very young. In many respects, it is conceptually at the stage physics was in the Middle Ages, before Galileo showed that the sun, not the earth, was at the center of the known universe.[84] Economic laws are mainly generalizations, perceptions of regularities of economic behavior that are in reality conditioned by cultural and social relations and institutional settings.[85] If we realize this, we will see the predictive capabilities of economics in a more realistic and modest context than that engendered by computers and stock markets.

The main purpose of economics is to gain insight into the workings of economies, not to develop theories for every action and reaction.[86] In such matters, a mixture of intuition, imagination, worldly experience, a good sense of history, and plain common sense is more important than any sophisticated acquaintance with theory, mathematics, or computers.[87]

In practice, many elaborate models of politics and economics are inherently and deeply flawed in their basic structures.[88] They are incapable of giving other than a rough indication of what might happen in the future, and then only with the proviso that other things remain equal. Given the known indeterminacy of socioeconomic systems, that proviso cannot be valid in practice. It is therefore not possible to set a specific question to a model and expect a demonstrably valid answer.

There is one exception, however, and that is where legal and/or fiscal mechanisms are set in place to require or induce people to behave "rationally." In other words, a model will "predict" accurately if people are required to modify their behavior to satisfy the requirements of the model. I suspect that many current policies are being prepared in the expectation that they will be backed by legislative and fiscal powers to achieve their end result. The resultant (and inevitable) social conformity will be the logical consequence of following policies built on assumptions that elevate the idea of "freedom of the individual" to its peak. This outcome is described as "economic imperialism" by some authors.[89]

This discussion exposes a fundamental problem relating to the place of markets. Democracy is usually defined in terms of freedom, but in practice, the "free" market is inherently incapable of achieving what I (and many others) believe democracy is all about.

A WIDER PERSPECTIVE FOR ECONOMICS

It has been suggested that mainstream economists ought to be less reductionist and more alert to the sociological, political, or even aesthetic dimensions of the human condition than they are. A clearer understanding of the relatively modest potentialities of their discipline alone will make them better economists. To quote Thurow again, "If economists are to be charged with any crime, it is not that of knowing too little relative to what they *can* know, but with the crime of being too certain about what they think they do know."[90]

Since there are real physical and ethical constraints on the options available for human economic development, it is also important for politicians to embrace the view that noneconomic scientific tools may be of comparable importance (and may even be the most important) in areas where they seek advice on the social resolution of resource allocation problems. As the economist Charles Perrings points out:

> Once we begin to conceptualize the behaviour of economy-environment systems over time, unprotected by the assumption that the price system contains all the information we need to know, we find not the comfortable order of stable or relatively stable equilibria but a seemingly chaotic drive to change, paralleled only in the recent findings of physicists investigating the time behaviour of structures far

from equilibrium. More important, we observe little warrant for the simple Smithian faith in the invisible hand that underpins the market solution, and no warrant at all for the argument that forward markets will compel private interests to secure the information that renders the price system complete.[91]

"Economics" has the same linguistic root as "ecology." Interpreted narrowly—as the currently dominant viewpoint requires—economics reduces everything and everyone to economic neuters: items of production, consumption, and exchange in an imaginary marketplace. Interpreted broadly and humanistically in its equally valid meaning of "loving care of the household," it could incorporate a systemwide meaning that encompasses the stewardship role of humans in our relationship with all things in the global household. It is my fervent hope that the profession of economics will rapidly move in the latter direction. In the words of Boris Pasternak, "What is laid down, ordered, factual, is never enough to embrace the whole truth; life always spills over the rim of every cup."

10

Myths of Science and Energy

THE PHILOSOPHER OF science Karl Popper once said, "Science must begin with myths, and with the criticism of myths."[1] With the passing of many old myths, a new set has emerged. Trust in science ("scientism") is one. In this myth, science has the last word in establishing answers to questions; ultimate truth is revealed by science instead of by, say, the Bible. The accounts of Genesis were the ultimate truth of creation until a century ago; they still are for many people, for whom biological evolution is a myth.

There are many other myths in science and technology. In order not to be overimpressed by so-called scientific views and opinions, it is necessary to review some of them to obtain a more balanced view of the strengths and weaknesses of science, especially as applied to human affairs and policymaking. That some of these myths are more often held by nonscientists does not invalidate their discussion here, because they are commonly associated with science and technology.

THE MYTH OF LINEARITY

Much of what is known in science has been built around simple models in which cause and effect are related through what are called "linear" mechanisms. In other words, if whatever causes an effect is changed by a given amount, the effect changes by a proportional amount. If an electric heater is switched from half to full power, for example, twice as much heat is given out.

This sort of relationship—that of direct proportionality—is in fact very common, but only up to a point. Beyond that point, the effect may be quite out of proportion to the cause. Take the biblical story of the straw that broke the camel's back. Every individual straw added until that point added an equal amount to the load, with steadily increasing (but reversible) stress on the animal's back. But then another factor came in—the camel's back, unable to take any more weight, broke. The linear relationship that had been valid up to that point suddenly failed; the relationship became nonlinear (actually, discontinuous) and irreversible.

In nature, this sort of thing is normal. Up to a point, which usually cannot be predicted in advance, the system may respond in a way that is repeatable and even reversible. Beyond that point, it does not—its behavior is unpredictable and irreversible. This is a normal characteristic of complex systems such as dissipative structures; it is also a characteristic of virtually all structures and processes known to humanity. As the threshold of nonlinear behavior is approached, much of classical science (and most of standard economics) becomes inapplicable. The claim made in the nineteenth century that "nature does not make jumps" has been shown time and time again to be erroneous.[2] For example, the cost to a person of taking just one more step may be to fall over a cliff or be hit by a truck!

For these reasons, it is important not to extrapolate. That something has happened reliably up to a certain point is no reason to suppose that going beyond that point will give rise to the same effect. It may do so, but it may not. Without a detailed study of what happens beyond the point at which one's existing knowledge runs out, extrapolation is dangerous; it may break the camel's back, or it may not. Only by doing several (presumably fatal) experiments to determine the breaking load of camels' backs is it possible to know how heavy a load other camels are likely to be able to carry—and then only approximately. Extrapolation is inherently a risky business. Many disasters have occurred because scientists and technologists pushed components and systems beyond the point at which their knowledge was reasonably certain. Less well known, but nonetheless real, are the social disasters produced by application of political-economic theories of human behavior to societies and economies beyond the point at which knowledge was reasonably reliable.

THE MYTH OF SCIENTIFIC OBJECTIVITY

One would hope that all scientists are indeed experts who attempt to be objective in their pronouncements. Alas, the evidence is clearly to the contrary. There is a long history of gullibility, ignorance, and stupidity among scientists.[3] It usually results from their taking on responsibility for pronouncements in areas beyond their expertise. This in turn is a consequence of many of them having an inflated opinion of their ability to determine the truth of a situation from what is often nothing more than a cursory study.[4] The ability of many experts to ignore anything but their own world view may not be readily apparent,[5] but when a scientist takes on the role of advocate and makes authoritative-sounding claims without presenting clear supporting evidence for them, one should beware.[6]

Science is supposed to be objective. That means that when applied meticulously, the scientific method is a step-by-step approach to the study of something, with testing of hypotheses at every stage. In practice, science is carried out not by robots but by people. It is thus less than perfect and more than just a method. It is a creative, and intensely human, activity.

Scientists and technologists like to picture themselves as rational, pragmatic beings who are unswayed by emotion or dreams. Paradoxically, they have also been responsible for large numbers of technological fantasies: moon landings, aircraft powered by nuclear reactors, spaceships powered by atomic bombs, biological weapons, psychosurgery to cure undesirable behavior, feeding the poor of the world by using more fertilizers and hydroponics, "Star Wars" defense systems, and so on. Some of these dreams have been achieved—at a price. Others are so flawed in their views of the real world that they may never succeed.[7] Engineers and economists are perhaps more to blame than most in this context. Narrowness of vision and understanding and arrogance in dealing with others are not peculiar to them, however; such failings are commonly found in all of the professions and show up the dangers inherent in specialization.

THE MYTH OF THE TECHNICAL FIX

In the book *The Next Hundred Years*, prepared in 1957 by several eminent technologists with the assistance of executives of some of the United States's largest corporations, the authors provided the following vision of what they called an emerging "technical-industrial civilization":

> If we are able in the decades ahead to avoid thermonuclear war, and if the present underdeveloped areas of the world are able to carry out successful industrialization programs, we shall approach the time when the world will be completely industrialized. And as we continue along this path we shall process ores of continually lower grade, until we finally sustain ourselves with materials obtained from the rocks of the earth's crust, the gases of the air, and the waters of the seas.

By that time the mining industry as such will long since have disappeared and will have been replaced by vast, integrated multipurpose chemical plants supplied by rock, air, and sea water, from which will flow a multiplicity of products, ranging from fresh water to electric power, liquid fuels, and metals.[8]

It was believed that the main obstacle to attainment of this resource El Dorado was not a shortage of resources (nor the threat of overpopulation) but a lack of enough trained scientists and engineers to build and maintain the technical wonderworks needed by the developing countries. It was a time when there were "no problems, only solutions." Many scientists and engineers would now assert, however, that in reality there is no complete technical or economic solution to the resource problems that face us. I have discussed several aspects of this in previous chapters. There is also no simple solution to problems such as the tragedy of the commons. The solution can come only from an ethical or moral base.

Jacques Ellul, a trenchant critic of unthinking use of technology, suggests, "History shows that every technical application from its beginning presents certain unforeseeable secondary effects which are more disastrous than the lack of the technology."[9] He also suggests that "every successive technique has appeared because the ones which preceded it rendered necessary the ones which followed."[10] Although these claims might seem somewhat overstated, it is true that neither the full extent nor the nature, let alone the approximate sum of external costs, of major developments is known. No method exists to give more than a rough estimate of the cost of even the direct, short-term external consequences of new technologies. When indirect effects are concerned (good examples being accelerated global warming and destruction of the ozone layer), conventional methods are powerless. Thus, no possibility exists for Ellul's claim to be validated. It remains a somber warning, for which there is significant circumstantial evidence and which should not be ignored.

THE MYTH OF CHEAP ENERGY

Countries with large reserves of fossil fuels or hydroelectric poetential are often encouraged to use their "cheap energy" as a means of encouraging rapid economic development. Although such countries may indeed have cheaper resources than many others, it is a fact that no country incorporates the environmental or social externalities of fuel use in the price of its resources, and thus all of them distort the economics of fuel supply. Thus, consistent undervaluing of resources becomes part of economic policy and prevents decisions being made that have the potential both to improve overall economic efficiency and to protect local and global environments. In reality, there is no such thing as cheap energy; it is the social and environmental costs of its supply that are artificially cheapened in many economies.

THE MYTH OF RENEWABILITY

Many people believe that some forms of energy (the renewable ones) are more environmentally benign than others. This is generally true, since hydroelectricity and wood fuel can usually be produced with lower pollution and environmental damage than can coal-fired electricity and oil fuels. Nevertheless, the assumption that resources such as these are entirely benign is more than a little naive.

Hydroelectric dams create substantial damage to local soil and vegetation systems and to river ecology, both before and after construction. The indirect effects of production of the cement, steel, and machinery used in their construction create other problems further back in the economic system. Hydroelectric dams also have a limited life. Depending on the characteristics of the river that supplies them, they can be expected to silt up, perhaps as soon as a decade after construction. The electricity produced from them may be renewable for a while, but the river itself is irreversibly changed.

Fuel production from trees is another example. Wood production from a forest appears, on the surface, to be possible in perpetuity. After all, if the forests have been in existence for millions of years, can this situation not continue forever? The answer lies in the fact that in its natural state, a forest is approximately a closed system, in that mineral matter and soil remain within it (water, oxygen, and carbon dioxide obviously enter and leave the forest system via air movement). When a tree dies, it decomposes and in doing so provides food for a myriad of bacteria, fungi and other organisms, and small animals, which in turn provide food for higher animals. The end result is that the minerals, the trace elements, and a great deal of organic matter are recycled back into what is a complex ecosystem for use by the next generation of plants, organisms, and animals. When timber is removed from the ecosystem for use in an economy, via sawmills or pulp mills, the recycling process stops. Unless the timber that is removed is only a small proportion of the total biomass of the forest ecosystem, the system can suffer severe, possibly devastating, damage. Thus, extractive wood production is not normally renewable in the long term, although it may appear so within the limited lifetime of individual decision makers. The ecosystem itself seldom survives regular timber extraction.

THE MYTH OF SUSTAINABILITY OF INDUSTRIALIZED SOCIETY

If we cannot rely forever on stock fossil and other energy resources, only the sun is left (together with wind, rain, and other solar-related flows). Can one conceive of a developed, industrialized society that takes all the energy it needs, directly or indirectly, from the sun? This question is at the center of a great deal of current research work in many countries. No unequivocal answer can yet be given.

The biggest problem we face is that it is not clear whether it is possible, using purely solar energies, to carry out many of the energy-intensive activities that we now depend on. Smelting of iron and manufacture of liquid fuels are obvious examples. At present, it is only by using fossil fuel to construct plant and machinery that these processes are carried out. In other words, we cannot yet see how it is possible for a society to make everything from solar-derived energy flows if that society continues along the industrial path. No matter what directions are chosen, for some time to come societies will have to use stock resources, if only to make the equipment that will enable solar sources to be harnessed (using steel, copper, glass, etc.). Provided this use is at a modest level, there should be no significant problems either of supply or of pollution.

In short, the use of solar energy as the sole primary energy source for a technologically advanced consumerist society has not yet been shown to be viable. It is therefore vital that we start to move toward making careful use of the valuable stock resources we now have, to ensure that at least some will be available for future generations for as long as possible. In this way, breathing space will be available to examine options for future social and technological developments. Regrettably, the standard political-economic world view denies the possibility that humankind will not be able to achieve any technological feat that may be needed, and in the meantime, resources are being used without any thought for the future.

THE PLACE OF SCIENCE

Science is the attempt to be objective about the study of nature. Scientists themselves, however, are only human. For this reason, the process of scientific endeavor has always had, and always will have, a substantial element of human subjectivity. According to the critic Stanislav Andreski, "The natural sciences did not advance in virtue of the universal appeal of rationality. Their theological, classicist and metaphysical opponents were not converted but displaced . . . scientific method has triumphed throughout the world because it bestowed upon those who practiced it power over those who did not."[11]

The place of science in human decision making is to help people understand why things happen. It can also help distinguish what is possible from what is not. I feel this is the most important contribution that thermodynamics and systems theory can provide in the field of resource use. Thermodynamics sets limits to social phenomena through its ability to predict constraints on the use of energy sources and materials in economic processes, now and in the future. Regardless of how economic value is established, the economic process cannot violate natural laws. Nevertheless, thermodynamics does not govern decisions within the economic process; it is a constraint on some important aspects of the social valuation (price) mechanism, not a direct determinant of it.

11

Ecology versus Exemptionalism

ACCORDING TO THE political-economic world view, the earth is a place in which human ingenuity in using science and technology will ensure that resources and food, the ability to control pollution, and so on will keep pace with needs indefinitely. From the biophysical systems viewpoint, the world is a place in which humans are important but are neither exempt from ecological constraints nor guaranteed indefinite survival.[1]

I accept that to express a complex issue such as this as a two-party clash is to oversimplify it. However, I feel its main characteristics are well brought out by comparing the ecological and exemptionalist schools of thought. In a more detailed study, psychological factors, such as personal biases that occur when scientists of different persuasions address a complex issue, would also need to be incorporated into the discussion.[2]

WORLD VIEWS

The exemptionalist world view is generally supported and promoted by politicians and businesspeople and by many economists and technologists. The ecological world view is also widely held, mainly by natural and physical scientists. The differences of opinion of these two schools are so fundamental as to ensure that the argument between them is as yet unresolved.

Since they are interested mainly in immediate or short-term growth and development opportunities, politicians of both capitalist and socialist persuasions are usually exemptionalists. Human nature being what it is, politicians always claim things will get better during their time in power. Anything that smacks of pessimism is political suicide.[3] If there are limits, they are such a long way off that they have little, if any, relevance to today's practical political decisions.

In contrast, those from the ecological viewpoint dispute the idea that humans are so different from other animals as to be exempt from the normal limits set by nature. They thus present a challenge to humanity's view of its place and role in the universe.

To explain why I believe both views are in some senses correct and in others wrong, I will review a relatively recent and often acrimonious debate between proponents of the two views. Both are Americans; the exemptionalist view is promoted by Julian Simon, a professor of economics at the University of Illinois; the ecological, by Paul Ehrlich, a professor of biology at Stanford University.

The distinction between the world views is not absolute; many economists hold to the ecological position, and many scientists are exemptionalists. That people from within disciplines disagree indicates that the roots of the conflict go deeper than simple disciplinary barriers.[4]

THE EXEMPTIONALIST ARGUMENTS

In 1980, Simon published an article titled "Resources, Population, Environment: An Oversupply of False Bad News." As the title suggests, Simon argued against what he felt was the generally held view that things were getting worse. He claimed that arable land was increasing, that food production was not declining in less-developed countries, and that environmental quality was improving. Natural resources and raw materials such as fuels were not running out, and if they ever did, technology would soon enable other planets and, indeed, the universe as a whole to be used as a source. His main points were that "cost . . . is the only meaningful measure of scarcity in peacetime" and that the cost of most resources was going down.[5] Because of the power of the marketplace, there would always be a substitute when the price of one resource rose, ensuring a continuous supply for humanity forever. Simon claimed:

> In summary, because we find new lodes, invent better production methods and discover new substitutes, the ultimate constraint upon our capacity to enjoy un-

limited raw materials at acceptable prices is knowledge. And the source of knowledge is the human mind. Ultimately, then, the key constraint is human imagination and the exercise of educated skills. Hence, an increase of human beings constitutes an addition to the crucial stock of resources, along with causing additional consumption of resources.[6]

Other economists have put the same argument slightly differently: "The only nonrenewable and nonsubstitutable resource is the set of institutions known as a market order, which eliminates crises with respect to physical resources."[7]

Simon's arguments are based on two main assumptions, both of which have some support from historical evidence. These are that the past contains lessons that can be extrapolated into the future and that humanity will always adapt smoothly and in time to avert the possibility of catastrophe. Thus, more humans and more consumption are good and should be encouraged. Humans always come first.

Other writers in the exemptionalist school of thought have written similarly. Many draw attention to the arguments of the economist William Jevons, who in the nineteenth century predicted the inevitability of a shortage of coal. That his predictions were soon shown to be incorrect by discovery of reserves unknown to him at the time seems to support the exemptionalist viewpoint. Oil discoveries (until recently) also supported the view. Why should this process not continue forever?

According to these writers, resources have always increased to meet demand.[8] All that is needed to ensure that they always will is incentives, and the principal incentive is profit available to the entrepreneur in the marketplace. Seawater, for example, is known to be an enormous resource. Despite the minute concentration of many minerals in seawater, the sheer size of the oceans means that the total quantities are colossal. Exemptionalists believe that technology will come up with methods to enable resources to be extracted from the sea once the price is right. In the context of growth, Simon makes the startling claim that "there is no meaningful physical limit—even the . . . weight of the Earth—to our capacity to keep growing forever."[9]

In summary, the exemptionalist world view holds that the resources problem, whether of fuels or of raw materials, is a relatively minor problem for society as a whole and does not require any government intervention for its solution. Reduction of the most common forms of pollution to insignificant levels is also believed to be relatively simple and cheap.[10]

THE ECOLOGICAL ARGUMENTS

In response to Simon, Ehrlich made a number of counterclaims about resources and pollution, many directly contradicting Simon's arguments (one article had the title "An Economist in Wonderland").[11]

Ehrlich criticized Simon for using a limited number of indicators for assessing environmental improvement. As well as the airborne sulfur oxides and particulates mentioned by Simon, it is also necessary to take into account sulfates, nitrates, carbon dioxide, and acid rain. Toxic wastes in the environment and the suitability of water for aquatic life are matters of deep concern, and in many such areas there is no evidence of improvement. Bringing more arable land into cultivation usually results in more deforestation and erosion, and much of the land brought into cultivation is marginal, less productive, and subject to more rapid degradation than the land it is substituting for.

Resources have a value that goes beyond that given by the marketplace. The loss of species of animal life (e.g., whales) has a meaning that goes beyond the availability of substitutes (e.g., for their meat and oil). The driving of species to extinction may be perfectly rational in a market economic context, in which substitution is always possible, but it is incomprehensible to someone familiar with the real world.

Simon was also criticized for the view that humans must come first. The rights of nonhuman species to exist and the aesthetic poverty of a world with no room for unmanaged environments were pointed out as factors that conventional economics ignores.

Ehrlich's arguments concentrate mainly on ecosystems, but he makes the point that the environment also provides free resources of materials and energy and free cleanup facilities (ecosystem services) that are known to be inherently limited in capacity and are subject to human control only up to a point. The idea of continuity in the exemptionalist world view is invalid in the ecological world view, at least insofar as ecosystem services are concerned.

Ehrlich's general points are that since there is a limit to what the environment can supply and absorb, discontinuity is a basic characteristic of the relationship between economic activity and the system that sustains it. Although his earlier predictions of catastrophe were in some cases premature, Ehrlich holds to the opinion that catastrophe is an inevitable consequence of the exemptionalist world view and there is not much time left if survival of human and many other species is to be ensured. He points out that the rate of cultural evolution of social systems far exceeds the rate of genetic evolution in nature. In other words, economies are changing faster than nature's ability to supply and absorb the consequences of economic activity. In Ehrlich's words, "Most ecologists see the growth-oriented economic system and the economists who promote that system as the gravest threat faced by humanity today."[12]

Other contributors to the Simon-Ehrlich debate made further points. Simon's claim that "cost . . . is the only meaningful measure of scarcity in peacetime" has been criticized on the grounds that two-thirds of the world's population was expected to remain so poor that they would be able to consume few raw materials and would have to sell what they had to the industrial one-third. That expresses what is regarded as a realistic, sociopolitical attitude to resource scarcity rather than an idealistic, market economic solution.

Ehrlich suggests that both ecologists and social scientists share many problems in common, such as the need to understand systems of incredible complexity. Both must avoid the temptation to allow their "physics envy" to direct them into problems that are solvable in terms of mathematical equations but are utterly irrelevant to any understanding of the real world. In that context, it is worth noting that Ehrlich has made the point that there are three things of importance that his profession can offer to decision makers: "specific predictions on certain limited problems, a description of human dependence on the public service functions of the ecological system, [and] the lesson that humanity should be extremely conservative in its treatment of earth's ecosystem."[13]

PARADIGM CONFLICT

The often bitter debate between Simon and his critics, particularly Ehrlich, needs to be explained further. Simply to attempt to summarize the points made by these writers is not enough; it is necessary to try to show where their world views come from and where they conflict.

In the conclusion of his reply to the criticisms of his first paper, Simon makes a telling point when he suggests that although his critics seem to assume resources to be finite, he tends to assume otherwise. He hints at the fundamental nature of the debate by noting that the choice of which assumption one makes "is not subject to scientific test . . . [but] . . . profoundly affects our thinking."[14]

The sociologist Riley Dunlap, in commenting on the debate, feels that this point not only clarifies the specific nature of the debate between Simon and his critics but also provides insight into the larger debate over the probable future of humankind.[15] Dunlap suggests that the two views of resources reflect the ways scientists view the subject matter of their investigations.[16] Because adherents to different world views see the world quite differently, they often give opposing interpretations of the same facts and may even disagree on what constitutes relevant information.

The political-economic and biophysical systems world views (which broadly correspond to the exemptionalist and ecological camps) result from differing perceptions of the relative importance of historical, cultural, political, and physical factors in a nation's development. Simon points out that the assumptions behind the views are not scientifically testable.

I do not think Simon's claim is strictly correct. Even if a resource (such as a coal field) were so large as to be effectively infinite, the energy accessibility problem would ensure that only a finite amount of the coal would ever be delivered as net energy to an economy. If the system boundary were extended to include the energy required for the technology to deal with externalities (e.g., acid rain) that would result from use of the coal, the net accessible quantity of the resource would be even further reduced. These ideas are relatively easy to test, and it has been done.

The exemptionalist viewpoint is largely based on extrapolation from the past. Data on prices of energy and materials, for example, appear to be largely consistent with the views of Simon. But if the energy accessibility argument is correct, as I believe it is, the future must be, and will be, different. As an example, data from several studies relating to the energy requirements of ore refining show that after initially following a reducing energy requirement curve, requirements subsequently increased exponentially, for a linear reduction in ore quality.[17] From the point of view of accessibility, Simon's notion that once resources are exhausted, other planets or star systems will be minable are sheer fantasy.

Many of Simon's arguments have also been shown to be based on inadequate scientific foundations and on misleading logic.[18]

However, it is interesting to note that in the midst of their debate in 1980, Simon suggested, and Ehrlich accepted, a bet on the price in ten years' time of any natural resource. If it increased, Simon would pay Ehrlich the difference; if it decreased, Ehrlich would pay Simon. They agreed to base their bet on the combined price of a quantity of five metals: chrome, copper, nickel, tin, and tungsten. The idea was that this bet would serve as a test of their respective world views. In 1990, Simon won the bet.[19]

Not surprisingly, the outcome has not resolved the differences between the two. Nor, in my opinion, should it have been expected to. The complexity of their difference in world views cannot be simplified into a test based on price movements within markets for natural resources. Prices of metals are in practice determined in highly imperfect markets, many of which depend on the economic exploitation of debt-ridden Third World countries. A test of the two world views requires a complex, systemwide consideration of outcomes over long time periods. The biophysical systems world view cannot be used to determine short-term price movements; its predictions are of a much longer time scale and will be testable generally only over periods longer than ten years.

The ecological viewpoint is that everything in the world is finite and that in many instances, humanity is close to the limits either of the supply of some critical resources or of the pollution absorption capacity of the environment. The uniqueness of stock energy and mineral resources and ecosystem services is clear to ecological adherents but is not important to exemptionalists. The dependence on capital and other direct and embodied energy flows for extraction, refining, and delivery of lower-quality resources to an economy is not explicit in either viewpoint. As a concept, however, it is much closer to the ideas of ecologists than of exemptionalists.

PROSPECTS FOR THE FUTURE

The exemptionalist world view was built primarily on evidence from the industrialized, affluent one-third of the world's population. There is no evidence that the generalizations made about past events are valid for the other two-thirds. It is fair to say, however, that the exemptionalist position is lived by the rich one-third and the ecological is lived by the poor two-thirds. Since most of the poor understandably want a slice of the cake made by the rich, this implies they should put their ecological past behind them and set out on the path of exemptionalism. Many governments and businesses support them in that notion. The fact that some ecologically minded people from rich nations suggest another course of action is often seen as evidence of the collective hypocrisy of the rich.

China and India are good examples of poor countries that seem set on traveling the growth paths of the "advanced" nations but lack all of the resources to do so. The Scandinavian countries are examples of rich ones that have begun to see their past patterns of development as unsustainable and are making efforts to change direction.

Exemptionalists explicitly hold to the idea that growth is good. They assume that everyone in the world aims to achieve a standard of living typical of the middle class in developed countries. Many economists and virtually all ecologists now believe, however, that anything like that scenario would put great pressure on resources and generate huge amounts of pollution. Fossil fuel prices would skyrocket, and forests and ecosystems would disappear even more rapidly than at present.

Political policymaking in the rich nations depends on the world views of those in power. Exemptionalists believe that human ingenuity will eventually triumph and therefore no action is needed by the rich, other than to ensure the smooth working of the marketplace. Ecologists believe that catastrophe can be averted only by concerted action of people and governments to preserve ecosystem services from further degradation. Thus, the fate of the poor as well as that of the environment depends on the way people in positions of power see the place of *Homo sapiens* in the world. For these reasons, the debate between the exemptionalists and the ecologists reflects some of the most important issues facing societies today. That the debate is in many ways a "dialogue of the deaf" makes its resolution even more important, before it tears us apart.

In this context, the naturalist Gerald Durrell comments:

To halt and reverse the deterioration of the ecospheree, to let Gaia refresh and renew herself, to stop the rot that is weakening the Ark and help repair the timbers—this is the single most urgent task challenging our species in today's uneasy, but on the whole still peaceful world. Should we ever suffer global war, I am convinced that the root cause will be environmental, not religious, cultural or even social, although the immense pressure of human numbers and their immense demands on natural resources will most likely spark it off. If global war comes, the result will not be as it was after the last two; much suffering and destruction, but afterwards a new age of technological advance and a mood of optimism. No. It will bring devastation, regression and despair, maybe forever, or at least for a very long time. And the unsolved issues of human development and the conservation of natural resources which caused it will be regarded in what's left of human memory as no more than a feather carried away on the wind.[20]

A NEW WORLD VIEW

Clifford Harvey, another commentator on the debate, suggests:

Experience has shown that in a purely economic analysis, the human race has become better off as the population has grown. We are making more money, driving more cars, consuming more goods, seemingly ad infinitum. And, true to statistical positivism, Simon deduces that since things have been getting better as population has risen, things must get even better still as population rises even higher still. To fight that sort of logic in kind may be fine in the laboratory, but in this instance, where the fate of the global ecosystem may be at stake, a new paradigm is in order.[21]

Harvey suggests that the ecological world view needs to be extended by going beyond asking whether the world is finite and humans are constrained by that finiteness to ask instead how much we really need. "The new ecological world view sees the world not as economically finite or infinite, but as a Place for Being. The processes of nature have been around at least as long as the processes of the marketplace, and they seem to hold more promise for the longevity of mankind if they are heeded and adapted to—rather than conquered and subordinated to human economic whims."[22]

Harvey also makes the point that many possibilities for development of new perspectives and world views are being overlooked by the failure of most people in positions of political and economic power to recognize the validity of nonscientific criticisms of their findings. There are more ways than one to criticize a world view, and a firm moral or ethical base provides a good starting point for all of them. What could be seen as "the truth" is much closer to the ecological than to the exemptionalist view, but the debate must be extended by taking account of the systems perspective (which includes energy accessibility) and the ethics and morality of growth.[23]

We must also acknowledge that many who adhere to the ecological world view are not scientists at all but "ordinary" people. They hold to ethical and moral values that are widely shared. But it is important that these values be founded on as complete an understanding as possible of the physical constraints on directions in which society may develop in the future. From arguments given in earlier chapters, I believe it is clear that the way of material growth cannot continue without putting life on earth in danger.

Although neither the exemptionalist nor the ecological paradigm is sufficient as a world view for the future, I believe the ecological view has a great deal more to recommend it than the exemptionalist. The new paradigm that must be developed will go beyond both of them, taking into account even broader perspectives. Identification of solutions to our global problems is critically dependent on our understanding more about the ecosystems in which we all live and more about the ways people function collectively in societies. The first is the domain of the natural and physical sciences; the second is the domain of the social sciences. Application of the solutions that come from that understanding is the place of the democratic political process.

12

Humanity Separated from Nature

IN THE EIGHTEENTH and nineteenth centuries, it was widely believed that application of the methods of science was all that was needed to understand humanity's place in the world. As we have seen, developments in the physical sciences over the past hundred years have shown this idea to be seriously in error. The world is not a machine; it is an incredibly complex, energetically open, dissipative biophysical system with a vast number of complex, interrelated ecological subsystems. These have a considerable ability to regulate their own functions, but they can also react to changing circumstances by rapidly altering their internal structure and organization. No matter how much is known about their past behavior, their future can never be predicted with any certainty.

SCIENCE AND HUMANKIND

The natural and physical sciences have long recognized that the reductionist scientific method has significant weaknesses as well as undoubted strengths. Some social sciences, on the other hand, have found it much more difficult to give up the idea that somewhere there might be a mechanistic, individual-based explanation for social behavior. More particularly, the belief that social systems have the power to control their destinies is still at the center of most political and economic theories. The fact that generalization from the past has long been known to be an inadequate scientific tool is widely ignored in the search for more and more elaborate mechanisms to explain the past and attempt to predict the future behavior of systems that other scientists see as indeterminate.[1]

The difference of opinion between the natural and physical sciences on the one hand and some social sciences (mainly economics) on the other is still a massive gulf, as I brought out in the previous chapter. In this chapter, I explain why I believe the dominant political-economic thinking of so-called developed societies (whether of the political left or right) is largely based on illusion. This way of thinking is similar to a house of cards: apparently stable at present but due for collapse as soon as the door to the real world is opened to let the winds of change come in. The structure can be shored up for a while, but it is still nothing but cards.

THE ENLIGHTENMENT

The main project in the life of Francis Bacon (1561–1626) was the conquest of the universe by man. To do this, it was first necessary to find out how nature worked, for "Nature to be Commanded must be Obeyed."[2]

The separation of humanity from nature is a relatively recent event in human history.[3] The process gained strength in the eighteenth century, after two centuries of intellectual ferment, during which time Bacon, Sir Isaac Newton, and René Descartes published their theories about the way the universe functioned. Historians give the name the Age of Enlightenment to the time when this set of beliefs took hold in Europe.

When the wise men of that time looked at the well-ordered world of classical (Newtonian) science, they could hardly fail to compare it with the real world of the activities of people in society. The erratic behavior of people and the imperfect workings of government simply did not square with the reliable, predictable mechanical world. Their dilemma was quickly resolved: if society was not behaving in the same way as the universe, the only explanation was that it was not keeping to the natural laws that govern the universe.[4] The obvious next stage was to figure out how these natural laws related to humans and societies and to apply them. The mechanical laws of Newton were used as guides to the ultimate natural laws that were believed to govern everything everywhere. Humanity now had a new goal—the search for perfection in this world rather than salvation in the next.

Three men led the attempt to discover these universal laws and to determine how they influenced the workings of society. Thomas Hobbes (1588–1679) and John Locke (1632–1704) examined the workings of government and society, generally in line with the vision of the world as a machine, and

Adam Smith (1723–1790) did similarly with the workings of people in the economy. Their theories were developed further by Jeremy Bentham (1748–1832) and John Stuart Mill (1806–1873) in their theories of utilitarianism.

The central ideas of Hobbes and Locke concentrated on the individual. The ideals of seventeenth-century liberal democracy have come down to us from these men, in many respects changed only in detail. The concepts of freedom, rights, obligation, and justice in liberal democratic societies were powerfully shaped by their ideas. The essentially *economic* nature of these *political* theories of Hobbes and Locke is made clear by C. B. Macpherson: "Society consists of relations of exchange between proprietors. Political society becomes a calculated device for the protection of this property and for the maintenance of an orderly relation of exchange."[5]

John Locke

Using "reason," Locke set out to determine the "natural" basis of society. He soon decided to exclude religion, since God was by definition unknowable and therefore could not be incorporated in a mechanical model. Human beings existed as physical entities in a mechanical universe. Once useless custom and superstition were removed, society could be seen as comprised solely of individuals creating their own meanings. Society as a whole had only one purpose: to protect and allow for the increase of the property of its individual members. Personal liberty, expressed as self-interest, was the proper basis for activities of people in a society, which could then be described as materialistic and individualistic. Reason led Locke to believe that this was the natural order of things. Natural laws called each individual to follow the goal of amassing personal wealth; self-interest was the only reasonable basis for society.

For Locke, government's purpose was to allow people freedom to exert their power over nature to acquire material prosperity. "The negation of nature is the way toward happiness," he wrote. People must become "effectively emancipated from the bonds of nature."[6] Because at that time there appeared to be enormous quantities of resources in nature, people had complete freedom of action in using them. Locke thus became the philosopher of unlimited expansion based on material abundance.

Locke went further. He pointed out that the ownership of property was also a social duty. Land left to nature was "waste." Nature was of value only when humans combined their labor with it to make it productive. One who appropriated land for personal use to produce more benefited society more than one who left the land alone. This was probably the first statement of what is nowadays known as the trickle-down theory, in which it is believed that the more wealth one person generates, the more society collectively benefits.

Many of Locke's ideas touched sympathetic nerves in the new, frontier societies. The U.S. Constitution reflects many of his theories, and parts of the Constitution are taken from his writings. Locke's views, and those of his disciples, can (in this context) be seen as encouraging production and consumption as activities with inherent meaning in themselves. Everything comes down to the pursuit of material self-interest.

Adam Smith

Adam Smith, similarly convinced of the validity of the mechanical world view, set out to formulate a theory of economics that would reflect the universal truths of economic behavior. He took Locke's ideas further in developing the relationship between natural resources and human economic production: "The earth furnishes the means of wealth; but wealth cannot have any existence, unless through industry and labour which modifies, divides, connects, and combines the various production of the soil, so as to render them fit for human consumption."[7] Just as the planets conform to the laws of nature, so too did the economic behavior of individuals in society. If these laws were obeyed, economic growth would be ensured. Government interference in the economy violated natural laws and therefore stifled the activities of individuals in markets.

The market—the interaction of atomistic individuals in a freely operating exchange of goods and services—was the natural expression of material self-interest. It was a simple step further to conclude that anything that departed from the market ideal was bad for society. Like Locke, Smith believed that the pursuit of individual self-interest ensured the health and well-being of society as a whole.

To Smith, the universal laws of human behavior provided a ready-made value system. So long as each individual was as free as possible, the invisible hand would ensure that socioeconomic activities (i.e., those of the marketplace) would be as efficient as possible and society would be as perfect as possible.[8] Thus, egoism was reconciled with the common good, and privilege became rationalized. This doctrine, coming when it did, could only be welcomed by the rich and powerful. What the poor and powerless thought of it is not known but may be guessed at, since they at least had direct experience of the dark side of its effects.

Utilitarianism—Bentham and Mill

The philosophers of the utilitarian school attempted to lay down an objective principle for determining when a given action was right or wrong. They called this the principle of utility: "An action is right insofar as it tends to produce the greatest happiness for the greatest number."[9]

In essence, the utilitarian philosophy concentrated on the effects of an action. If the action produced more good effects than bad, it was right; otherwise, it was not. It was the consequences of an action that were important in determining whether it was right or wrong, not the motives.

There are many criticisms of this philosophy, among which are that it emphasized the sheer number of good outcomes against the number of bad ones. The nature of the outcomes, in terms of the happiness or unhappiness they gave rise to, was not relevant. In addition, if an evil action gave rise to some good outcomes, the evil action could be seen as good. This philosophy was tailor-made for the new economics, since it was a justification for determining the value of a policy in terms of the dollar sum of the costs and benefits arising from it. Complex systems feedback relations, ethical and moral values, and the different effects of costs and benefits on different people in different situations could all be comfortably ignored.

Subsequent Developments

On the surface, it appears that between them, Locke and Smith could completely dispense with morality and ethics. To an extent, that was true. However, the society in which those men lived differed markedly from that of today. To extrapolate their writings by two centuries without fully considering their historical and cultural context (i.e., without a proper exegesis) is to do them a great disservice. It is unlikely that they foresaw their words taking on the status of holy writ among "born-again" politicians and economists in the later years of the twentieth century. Nevertheless, whatever Locke and Smith meant, their ideas were soon expropriated by people with neither scruples nor responsibility.

Smith apparently believed that control of an economy via the invisible hand would ensure that individuals would not exploit one another and that their pursuit of personal self-interest would automatically lead to the common good. But he was referring to the village or town market, where simple items were exchanged among people of roughly similar levels of wealth, each of whom generally knew what was going on in the district. To extend his model to the operations of transnational corporations, or to elevate them into a definition of "freedom," is a bizarre extrapolation.

I would also draw attention to the misery of the working class in the eighteenth and nineteenth centuries. Perpetuated in most developing countries to this day, that misery gives the lie to any claim that the invisible hand has power to prevent exploitation in a context larger than that of a village, in which blood and cultural relationships took care of many of the basic requirements of life. The even more desperate conditions of people in colonies, which supplied a great deal of wealth to the affluent British (mainly English, actually) in those times when slavery was the norm, confirms that Smith was really writing in the context of his own country (and race) and his own socioeconomic class. We cannot blame him for that, but we can avoid applying his philosophy literally in a world where the moral imperatives are markedly different.

In Europe, Britain, and North America, the classical economic world view of Smith and his followers evolved in the late nineteenth century into the neoclassical world view, with a similar emphasis on the importance of the individual as the center of economic and social activity. Over time, the neoclassical world view gave rise to the widespread use of sophisticated analytical and mathematical tools.

Thus, the basic assumptions of the mechanical world view and the philosophical legacies of Locke and Smith are with us today.[10] The dominant idea remains that one of the main purposes of human activity is to rearrange the raw materials of nature into a more "ordered" form so that the sphere of human activity reflects the order that is believed to exist in the universe. The more material wealth we amass, the more ordered the world must become. And the more ordered it is, the closer it approaches some form of "perfection." "Progress" (often misnamed "development") means amassing greater quantities of material wealth on the way to perfection. Science and technology are the means whereby this is carried out. The free market is where the myriad of small decisions in a society ensure that the whole operation is efficient, that is, that it follows the laws of nature.

In the nineteenth century, Karl Marx (1818–1883) published theories claiming that the real interaction in society was the conflict between powerful and powerless groups, the owners and nonowners of the means of production, not that of equal individuals in the marketplace. As did the capitalist theoreticians, Marx saw nature in a utilitarian way, as a source of resources for human use. All that was of real importance was social organization, and the main problems were those of ownership and control of capital.

THE PROTESTANT WORK ETHIC

To some, it appears that the cultural values on which Western societies have been built are rooted in the Protestant work ethic. These values are described by Alvin Toffler as an emphasis on unremitting toil and deferral of gratification—traits that channeled enormous social energies into the tasks of economic development.[11] Neil Smelser describes different but complementary values, including freedom to exploit the natural environment; hard work for its own sake; achievement and personal ambition as desirable human characteristics; and the use of scientific rationality in the organization of economic and social life.[12]

Theologically, it is arguable that the so-called Protestant work ethic should not be considered as a religious ethic at all, since in many respects it is a distortion of the broader teachings of the Christian religion. These teachings include the view that humankind is the steward of God's creation, but they also place humanity's power over nature in the context of a responsibility to answer to God for any such actions. When humans reject responsibility to God, what was a nonviolent rule becomes, in practice, domination.[13]

Because of an overliteral interpretation of certain passages of scripture, some religious teachings of the Bible have been taken out of context, magnified, and secularized. The result has been the justification of behavior such as alienation of people from one another by competition and envy, through encouragement of individual material rewards for achievement or service; the perpetuation of this alienation through an uneven distribution of wealth; and the use of physical, economic, or military force to protect or extend commercial interests. All of these are, I believe, directly contrary to the teachings of the Founder of the Faith.

THE SEPARATION OF HUMANITY FROM NATURE

René Descartes (1596–1650) had suggested (following Greek tradition) that people and nature are separate. This way of thinking was continued by Hobbes, Locke, Smith, and their disciples. From this viewpoint, since nature is separate from humanity, its resources are therefore available to advance the material interests of humankind. The result was two centuries of industrial expansion in Britain, Europe, and North America, based on what was then a cornucopia of resources. As soon as one resource (e.g., fuelwood) appeared to be running out, another (e.g., coal) was found. When one country ran short of resources or space, new countries (e.g., Africa) and a new hemisphere (e.g., South America) were "discovered." No problem arose that could not be overcome by technology, courtesy of the marketplace.

That this perception of the way things worked was largely limited to the powerful and the wealthy should be no surprise to anyone. The poor and the powerless, as always, were buffeted by forces they neither understood nor controlled. But since history is usually written by, and for, the powerful and wealthy, it was a long time before the sense of exhilaration brought on by headlong expansion began to be dampened seriously. The questions Who benefits? and Who loses? were not asked before governments, landowners, and industrialists unleashed social and economic forces that were, at best, only partly understood.

The "success" of these two centuries and the fact that until recently, there was no reliable evidence that resources would not be available in unlimited quantities forever combined to prevent any real examination of the fundamental basis of political-economic theories that have come down to us from Locke and Smith virtually unchanged. Even Marx's theories depend on the belief that humans will always be able to use technology to overcome "problems" of shortages of resources. Thus, Marx's theories suffer from some of the same scientific defects as those of the capitalist camp.

As we know, physical and natural sciences have moved on since then. The universe is known not to obey simple mechanical laws but to comprise highly complex systems with their own internal structures, each different from the others. The systems obey general laws such as the second law of thermodynamics, but these set constraints within which systems operate rather than being mechanisms by which every cause can be clearly related to its effect.

HUMANITY AND HYPER-REALITY

Modern life for many people in industrialized societies has, in a sense, become a process in which people tend to follow the imperatives of their programming.[14] Things and people are measured, evaluated, and judged according to the models that define the "reality" within which they live. Models of the marketplace, of consumerism, and so on are held up to us as the ideal basis for existence. Insofar as people submit to (or are induced or compelled to submit by advertising or the closing off of other options), they enter a "hyper-real" existence in which reality appears to be "more real than real." Real life becomes a simulation of itself. "Life-style" may be modern or traditional, but it is still a simulation. People are encouraged to behave as statistical aggregates, economic neuters, items of production, consumption, and exchange. All that matters is that they keep on playing the game and conforming to the hyper-reality. Freedom is not a meaningful concept when for so many, choice is limited by those who provide the goods and services that add up to the "necessities" of life.

Even though the picture I have painted here is clearly not valid for the majority of the world's population, it is valid for many who live in urban centers in industrialized countries. Since these countries control (directly or indirectly) most of the world's resources and virtually all of the world's military might, their behavior is of greatest concern to those concerned about the way the world is going. Institutional and structural rigidities within these countries are such that although it will not readily be admitted, the probable end result of their activities is the engineering of *Homo sapiens* into its simplistic political-economic subset, *Homo oeconomicus*. This change would produce people who are less than fully human, albeit most of the time conforming perfectly to the mechanistic theories of standard market liberal political economics.[15] The disease, unease, confusion, and mindless violence that characterize much of life in these societies confirm that people are not happy with it either but feel they have lost control of their own lives. That is not what freedom is about.

COLLAPSE OF THE ILLUSION

To put it bluntly, we now know that the classical, pre-twentieth-century scientific perception is inadequate for other than simple systems. It therefore cannot be applied to people and societies, whose complex behavior is now known to be, always has been, and to the best of our knowledge always will be, indeterminate.

From these arguments, it will be clear that many conventional theories of politics and economics are symbolic abstractions largely based on myths, not established knowledge. They have validity within limited situations but cannot be generalized and should not be used for prediction or policymaking. To do so is to impose on people the views of those in positions of power, elected or otherwise.

Only in some simple systems is prediction possible; in real, complex systems and societies, one can only suggest possibilities for the future.[16] The facts of discontinuity and unpredictability in the real world are what distinguish modern science from classical science. Unless political and economic theories take these facts into account, they will be forever limited to function as tools of social control along lines set by the past, not of social liberation for the future. Many of the theories must change; many will be thrown into the dustbin of history. Politics and economics will not be the same afterward, but they will be ready to serve their broader function, which, I argue, is to help people adapt to, control, and invent (up to a point) their futures. They must not be used in vain attempts to repeat the successes (and excesses) of the past, in spite of determined efforts by followers of the teachings of Locke and Smith to do just that.

LESSONS FOR THE FUTURE

Protestant work ethic values may have been appropriate (in an evolutionary sense) in the developing, "frontier" societies in which they were forged. Continued adherence to them at a time when resources are no longer there for the taking may constitute a large part of the reason why we now face the probability of rapid deterioration in the health of ecosystems and reduction in accessibility of environmental resources.

The illusion is collapsing as the three assumptions on which it is founded become less and less certain: cheap energy sources cannot be relied on indefinitely; global externalities are rapidly becoming ever more serious; and people's confidence that the economic system actually meets their real needs is declining. A new reality is urgently needed.[17] Ironically, after two centuries of struggle and at the point of apparent mastery of the universe, the foundations of our Western value system appear to have become at least questionable and perhaps even irrelevant. The questions then arise: What are we living for, if not for more material achievement? In what directions can we turn if we can no longer trust the guidelines of the past?

Commonsense recognition of the place of the second law of thermodynamics and of the energy accessibility problem means that we must learn to perform our productive tasks, whatever they may be, in ways that minimize waste and maximize efficiency in the use of physical resources. Self-interest as a guideline for individual action is not enough when the commons are overloaded. This means, among other things, a collective concentration on improving the physical efficiency of processes throughout every economy, in the expectation that such improvement will in time also ensure economic efficiency. Bill McKibben sums it up:

> The problem, in other words, is not simply that burning oil releases carbon dioxide, which happens, by virtue of its molecular structure, to trap the sun's heat.

The problem is that nature, the independent force that has surrounded us since our earliest days, cannot coexist with our numbers and our habits. We may well be able to create a world that can support our numbers and our habits, but it will be an artificial world—a space station.[18]

The basic messages of our time are now crystal clear:

- Look at the *whole* system.
- Use only what you need from it.
- Avoid waste.

These messages have a number of consequences for a country's energy policy as well as for its social policies.

Part III

CHOICES

Toward the World as It Could Be

13

Values for a Sustainable Future

I START THIS chapter with a statement of belief: *The future is for people to invent.* It is not for political-economic ideologies to do on their behalf. Invention implies creation of alternatives that would enable people and societies to evolve within the envelope of constraints set by physical reality while regularly checking that they remain true to their principles and values. The values base of a society is the foundation on which options and policies for the future can be built.

A VISION

For a number of reasons, no doubt obvious to anyone who has read this far, I also want to affirm and promote a particular type and direction of change. This is not to say that I know where we should be going. I believe, nevertheless, that there is a limited (but still wide) range of directions in which we can go. Once we know these, it is then up to people, as individuals and as groups, to decide what sort of future they want, within the bounds of what is realistic and possible. Thus, it is how we travel into the future that is important, not the identification of any particular destination.

An economy in which the use of energy and materials is kept to a very modest level and efficiency in use and reduction of waste are given much greater importance will be built only on a new morality. Self-interest may have been a valid starting point in the time of Locke and Smith, but the commons of this planet will not survive if the unending material growth to which that individual self-interest leads us continues unabated. Clearly, the virtues of conscious cooperation, implicitly rejected by followers of these men in favor of the pursuit of individual self-interest, need to be brought to the forefront again. Only if this is done can the global commons be safeguarded. I have already argued that this sort of cooperation is entirely natural and normal human behavior.

The Context

Planet Earth is physically isolated. All living things live their lives entirely within its global ecosystem. Life exists only within a physical environment and is constrained by the physical characteristics of that environment. Life is fragile in comparison with the great forces of nature, as earthquakes, hurricanes, floods, and droughts frequently confirm. The sad story of the animals and birds that are now extinct or reduced to tiny populations is familiar to everyone. As William Rees points out, "Since we cannot separate the economy from the biosphere, we must restructure the relationship that binds them." [1]

The Reality

My understanding of the reality that could exist in the future is that it depends on invention of a social system that enables us to live our lives, participating justly and peacefully with one another, sustainably with the rest of life on earth. I also know that if we do not very soon invent that system, we will have destroyed many more options for the future and many other life forms as well. Humans have power to destroy life on earth, but no corresponding power to recreate that which has gone. There is no substitute for the environment. It is the field on which all other games are played. The responsibility that faces us is awesome.

GLOBAL NEEDS

The basis of society, and of life itself, is and always will be physical. Without good-quality air to breathe, water to drink, food to eat, protection from the elements, and so on, cultural, social, economic, and artistic activities are not possible or at best are severely stunted. Physical needs are critical for the billions of people who currently live lives of unrelieved poverty and deprivation. Even in the affluent world, physical needs come first. The econ-mist Nicholas Georgescu-Roegen put the physical perspective compelingly:

> The maximum of life quantity requires the minimum rate of natural resources depletion. By using these resources too quickly, [humans] throw away that part of solar energy that will still be reaching the earth for a long time after they have departed. And everything that [humans] have done in the last two hundred years or so puts them in the position of a fantastic spendthrift. There can be no doubt about it: any use of natural resources for the satisfaction of non-vital needs means a smaller quantity of life in the future. If we understand well the problem, the best use of our iron resources is to produce ploughs and harrows as they are needed, not Rolls Royces, not even agricultural tractors.[2]

Yet the demands of the affluent for easily accessible and "cheap" resources are so large that little is left for the poor, even if they could afford to buy. In this context, it is worth noting Adam Smith's claim that

> the rich only select from the heap what is most precious and agreeable. They consume little more than the poor, and in spite of their natural selfishness and rapacity . . . they divide with the poor the produce of all their improvements. They are led by an invisible hand to make nearly the same distribution of the necessaries of life which would have been made, had the earth been divided into equal portions among all its inhabitants.[3]

One would not wish to hold Smith responsible for what was at the time probably little more than ivory-tower speculation. Nevertheless, after two centuries of colonization and exploitation of the world's poor (a process carried on to this day by transnational corporations and international bankers), there is still not a scrap of evidence that the rich nations have to any significant extent divided with the poor "the produce of all their improvements," by an invisible hand or otherwise. A similar argument applies to the perpetuation of privilege within countries; one seldom hears of significant levels of unemployment among aristocratic or financial dynasties. Quite simply, Smith's hypothesis is nonsense. A modern version, the trickle-down theory, is even worse—a political confidence trick intended to protect the privileges of the affluent.

CONSTRAINTS

There are real constraints to human achievement. These arise primarily from the existence of impossibilities in nature. The most basic laws of science are statements of impossibility:

- it is impossible to create or destroy matter-energy;
- it is impossible to convert a given amount of heat into an equal amount of useful work;
- it is impossible to have perpetual motion;
- it is impossible to travel faster than the speed of light;
- it is impossible for an organism to live in a medium consisting only of its own waste products; and so on.[4]

If scientists wish to solve problems, it is important for them first to try to demonstrate that a solution to the problem exists; if it does not, they will save an enormous amount of futile effort trying to find it. The idea that perpetual growth in the use of resources and in production and consumption of material goods and services in a perpetually growing population is not only possible but also desirable is a central assumption of conventional economics. A careful analysis of the assumption using modern biophysical systems understanding shows it to be neither.

Science has moved on since the time when unending economic growth and unlimited resources were regarded as the normal state of affairs, to be questioned only by heretics. Modern science makes it clear that if we continue to accelerate the rate at which we use up our environmental capital and destroy the environment within which we have our existence, we not only bring forward the day when we must learn to live again on renewable sources of energy but also put at risk everything that we have created in the meantime.

Social and ideological pressures to expand must be relieved. Economic activity and economic growth need to be redefined to discriminate between that which has meaning and that which has only number; between that which feeds the body and enriches the spirit and that which enslaves both.

PROBLEMS OF THE MARKETPLACE

The free market acting alone is not capable of liberating people to invent their own futures. As Herman Daly points out: "There is a widespread belief among economists that market prices determine everything. . . . In other words, as long as we base all our decisions on free market prices, resource constraints disappear as a long-run concern."[5] He goes on to say:

> Prices are important but are not all-powerful. Market prices are relevant only to temporally and ecologically parochial decisions, whose major consequences lie wholly within the human economy of commodity exchange and within the pres-

ent generation. Market prices are excellent means for efficiently allocating a given resource flow from nature among alternative uses in the service of a given population of already existing people with a given distribution of wealth and income. Market prices should not be allowed to decide the rates of flow of matter-energy across the economy-ecosystem boundary or to decide the distribution of resources among different people (or among different generations, which, of course, are different people). The first must be an ecological decision, the second an ethical decision.[6]

Individual and Collective Behavior

The biggest problems we face are related to human behavior. The problems have been created largely as a result of mainstream political-economic theories, built on ideological instead of empirical models of humanity. Nowadays, most sociologists observe that the main social, ecological, and global issues that protect and create people's social condition (e.g., health) do not reflect individual behavior. Life-styles, for example, are a crucial determinant of health, but they are collective phenomena; they are socially and culturally constructed and are the property of groups and whole societies, not simple characteristics of individuals.[7]

Even within conventional economics, the distinction between the private rate of time preference (authorized by private property) and the social rate (authorized by common property) is recognized as critical.[8] Advocates of the market response to environmental and resource problems assume the prime position of private property and the individual perspective on time. With the need to move to a form of steady state society (in the material sense), policies must change to reflect the social rate, not the private. That the social rate is not adequately measured by current techniques is a serious problem.

Animals are restricted in the damage they can inflict on others and on their environment by abilities that are not extensively modified by culture and technology. We humans invented tools that enabled us to escape the mediation imposed by evolutionary forces, but we have not yet agreed on limitation of behavioral options. Effective controls are readily available through cooperation within and among groups, but first it is essential for us to acknowledge that only by accepting our interdependence, and creating policies that reflect that fact, will we be reempowered to view others positively and not as potential enemies.[9]

Individual and Collective Property

Primary title to environmental resources must rest with the collectivity. Private exploitation will then be on terms that reflect the collective interest.[10]

This view is central to the deeper feelings of many people. It is time for people to assert their claim to common property and take back its steward-ship from those who remain wedded to the theories of Locke and Smith. As the lawyer Joseph Sax points out: "The use of land, or at least of much land, will be shaped increasingly by its role in the global ecosystem rather than by its capacity to produce a return to its owner. . . . The innovativeness that has been used so boldly over the last two centuries to subdue natural systems should be equally available to utilize those systems more efficiently and less disruptively."[11]

Nonmarket Values

Most politicians, economists, and technologists agree that there is more to life than consumption of goods and services. Resources, nature, and ecosys-tems do not fit comfortably into the political-economic calculus that drives policymaking. Market economic models are powerless to describe the rich-ness that is human life, let alone that of the ecosystem within which it exists. Insistence on numbers requires what is important to be reduced to what can be measured. The complex systems interactions and feedbacks that charac-terize the activities of real humans in a real society are reduced to mechanis-tic reflections of an artificial code of behavior that, if adhered to, promises pleasure and goodies without limit, forever. Promotion of such a code by governments and businesses owes more to the desire for social control than to any idea of liberating people to control their own lives and invent their own futures.

RESOURCES FOR FUTURE GENERATIONS

Three arguments are commonly put forward on the subject of resource use and future generations. These are at best highly debatable and at worst plain wrong.[12] They are as follows:

- *What the future needs is not resources but productive capacity.* The idea is that by using resources now, we create capital stock and a healthy economy, which future generations will find more useful than raw resources.

There is strong empirical evidence to the contrary from many countries. In many cases, high-quality resources are being used for higher consumption today rather than being invested for the future. In any case, in one situation, future generations have the choice of what to do; in the other, the choice is made for them. I argue that we increase the options of future generations more by leaving them high-quality resources to be used in a myriad of ways than by leaving capital stock built for today, which will be obsolete by tomorrow.

* *If we leave resources for future generations, we deprive the present generation of wealth.*

This idea comes from the use of economic models that inadequately reflect the future value of high-quality resources. In any case, the careful, efficient use of resources in a way that reflects a high value for future options need not reduce present wealth and would probably increase it.

* *Private property rights for resources will encourage protection more than public ownership would.* If a resource is being sold below its (discounted) future value, it will be bought by someone prepared to conserve it for greater future reward.

The contrary arguments revolve around the certainty that such resources are not adequately valued by present markets;[13] that future values will probably be much higher than presently believed; and that current perceptions encourage most business ventures to maximize present extraction rates in order to make profits quickly. The additional point—that there is no evidence that the market actually works in the way suggested—is no doubt obvious to the reader.

These three arguments spring from the mainstream political-economic world view. If the policymakers' world view were to be broadened to include the biophysical systems world view of indeterminacy and exponentially increasing costs (both of supply and of ecosystem services), policies would be very different.[14] We badly need an approach to resource stewardship that acknowledges both world views—and more besides.[15]

THE NEED FOR RESTRAINT

Since it is people in the powerful, affluent, and articulate upper and middle classes in society who set standards of consumption and generate patterns of expectation—just as it is the affluent countries that set international comparisons of wealth—it is with them that restraint must begin. It is the ultimate hypocrisy, in national and international contexts, for the rich to preach the virtues of poverty to the poor. The rich must give up power and (at least) some of their wealth; otherwise, the poor will be forever trapped and the environment plundered and poisoned until it collapses under the burden. The rich can expect to isolate themselves for some time to come, so they feel no compelling reason to change their habits of consumption. For many of the poor, however, no such choice exists. Future generations, whether of rich or of poor, take no part at all in current decision making where it matters—in the houses and councils of the rich and powerful.

Where resources are concerned, especially nonrenewable deposits of fossil fuels and ecosystem services, the standard perspective is inadequate. These resources are in a moral sense the inheritance of all people, present and future, not just of the government or the "owner" of the land that covers them. For most of human time on earth, people lived off nature's interest, but over the past two thousand years, and especially the past hundred, we have been drawing more heavily on her capital. This cannot continue.

There is a powerful economic counterargument to all of these problems: *Asset stripping should be done only for a business in liquidation. Planet Earth is not in that category!*

STEWARDSHIP OF THE TOTAL SYSTEM

Economic and physical perspectives should be used in parallel, together with ethics and morality, to give complementary views as to what is and is not possible and desirable. In the current climate, the Treasury is the center of political-economic wisdom and power in most countries. It is vital that governments' understanding be expanded to take account of factors that cannot be reduced to monetary values. This means, among other things, ministries for the environment that have the power and resources to interpret data according to models fundamentally different from those of conventional economics. Such ministries could then take up the stewardship role on behalf of people living now and in the future. To do so, however, they would need to be taken seriously by government as a primary source of information (i.e., ahead of the Treasury) in matters relating to stewardship issues. In the future, I hope we will develop a value system that acknowledges nature and the environment as important of themselves, not just in the context of the uses to which we put them.[16]

INVENTING THE FUTURE

In the biophysical systems world view, not only do complex systems show emergent properties not present at lower levels of organization but also there is the opportunity for components to contribute to self-organizing changes in the structure of the whole system. If this general concept is taken into account, groups and organizations may realize they have properties and powers not available to individuals. The power of small groups to initiate far-reaching changes in societies that are going through periods of instability has been known for millennia. Real systems (including social systems and economies) exist at all times in a (metastable) steady state, not one of long-term stability. This characteristic can be cause of revitalization as well as of disaster. If ignored, out of resistance or fear, action for change can be left until too late. If anticipated and planned for, change can result in achievement of a higher level of evolutionary organization.

If change is unexpected or sudden, however, it can result in a system's moving to an undesirable, possibly chaotic, new state. Such is, I believe, a reasonable explanation (from a systems viewpoint) of many political and economic events of the past few years, such as those that followed the OPEC price jumps of 1975 and 1979 and the Iraq confrontation of 1990–1991. Transformation and change are central to the political process, but they are still inconsistent with standard political-economic models. Assumptions of continued growth in the production and consumption of material goods and services are seen from the systems viewpoint as inherently destabilizing, but they remain central to many conventional political-economic theories. [17]

Planning

Planning will always be needed in society. But the function of planners is, I suggest, first to recognize the existence of the physical constraints on society and then, in democratic partnership with people, to help determine limits to individual and collective behavior where necessary. It is not the function of planners to tell people what to do or to design the future.

Following Herman Daly, I argue that the market has a proper place in allocating resources within the envelope of constraints but not in setting the constraints themselves. [18] These must be set according to ecological and ethical criteria. To a free-marketer, however, the most efficient allocation of resources is always (and only) obtained in a free market. My response is that to someone with a hammer, everything looks like a nail! But to build even a simple shelter also requires something like an axe, to cut timber into appropriate lengths before nailing. To build anything with doors and windows, the builder needs saws, chisels, screwdrivers, and other tools.

The market hammer and the technological axe have vitally important parts to play in constructing social shelters for people. If they are used alone, however, a lot of things get bashed or hacked that should be gently and carefully shaped. The carpenter has a responsibility to learn skills in the use of all tools, not just the simple and powerful hammer and axe. (Of course, the wielding of hammers and axes is a "macho" activity that gives most men a great feeling of achievement and of "doing something," never mind the consequences!)

More important than the tools, however, are the materials and the specification of the end product to be constructed. By concentrating on tools, we forget that the important questions of our time relate to the availability of resources and the specification for shelters. Once the right questions are asked, it is usually possible to obtain a technically or economically competent technician (engineer or economist) to work out possible answers.

Nonmarket Factors

Rates of resource extraction and waste production are biophysical systems problems. Responses to the problems are constrained by what can be extracted from a given resource and what the ecosystem can absorb of the wastes. Neither is directly answered by the marketplace. The market can allocate only some resources into some processes, not achieve efficient allocation in a system whose deeper characteristics it cannot measure. Contrary to many economists' views, these do not reflect "market failure"; that is a loaded term.

ENDS AND MEANS

The critical value questions of our age relate to the ultimate means of low-entropy matter-energy and the ultimate ends for which they are used. Technology provides intermediate means and economic consumption provides intermediate ends, but the ultimate means and ends remain unexamined in conventional economics and technology. Gerald Smith claims: "'Doing' becomes its own justification. We no longer ask 'Doing what?', even less do we explore 'Doing what for what?' or analyze the consequences of 'Doing what for what and with what?' "[19]

Daly suggests that a consideration of the ultimate means and ends forces us to ask two questions: "What, precisely, are our ultimate means, and are they limited in ways that cannot be overcome by technology?" and "What is the nature of the Ultimate End, and is it such that, beyond a certain point, further accumulation of intermediate means (bodies and artifacts) not only fails to serve the Ultimate End but actually renders a disservice?"[20]

The biophysical systems viewpoint gives us important information on the nature and size of the ultimate means of low-entropy matter-energy and on the ability of the environment to supply the ecosystem services affected by the use of those resources. It tells us clearly that the means are ultimately limited in ways that cannot be overcome by technology.

There is also support for the idea that further accumulation of capital and other goods and services can actually detract from our average quality of life. This is not only because we cannot spend all our waking hours consuming but also because production and consumption cause serious deterioration in the environment within which we live. Macroeconomic growth now involves more bads than goods for a lot of people.

The only question no individual can adequately answer is that of the nature of the ultimate end. I believe it is a spiritual and religious question, notwithstanding utilitarian opinions to the contrary. That being so, a model of it probably has to be created by each community and each generation, and at best it can only be seen dimly by a social system, never actually reached. Personally, however, I feel closer to the Ultimate among community groups and among trees and mountains than in the forest of temples to Mammon that fills central business districts of big cities today.

TOWARD SUSTAINABILITY

Three pointers are important in developing a framework of decision making for a sustainable future:

• Ignorance is no excuse.
• Keep options open by biasing decisions against irreversible choices.
• Modify economics toward sustainability, with a longer time frame.[21]

The first pointer means that politicians must examine the whole of any problem before deciding what are the "best" or "most efficient" courses of action open to them. In a context such as this, politicians' and economists' ignorance of the tools and insights of ecology, thermodynamics, and energy analysis is no more acceptable than biologists', engineers', and physicists' ignorance of the tools and insights of political economics.

The second pointer accepts that we do not know and can never predict what will happen in the future because it is indeterminate, within the envelope of physical possibilities. But we do know the ultimate limits to technologies, and we can make good—albeit often rough—estimates of their likely practical limits. We can therefore bias our decisions toward preserving resource options and preventing irreversible damage to ecosystems. The economists' idea of policies that "minimize regrets" has a lot to recommend it in this context.

The third pointer makes clear that it is overdue for policymakers to acknowledge the long term as a social and physical reality. If we can no longer trust technology to get us out of trouble, we cannot discount the future in the bland expectation that it will take care of itself. We have an ethical responsibility to leave as many resources as possible, of both raw materials and ecosystem services, for future generations.

Collective well-being, inclusive of future generations, must be at the forefront of our minds. Humanistic economics can be the base for our view of the person in society.[22] This view is in stark contrast to the market approach, which puts present-day individual sovereignty on a pedestal.[23] Sustainability implies not leaving "time bombs" for the future in the form of greenhouse gases, ozone-depleting chemicals, or toxic waste dumps whose likely future effects are much greater than their known effects today.

STEADY STATE

Policies of the type I have been discussing would encourage a society to move toward a "steady state" life-style with substantially reduced waste in the use and disposal of resources. For some time to come, technological advances could permit modest growth in the production of some types of goods and services, but the material flow component of this growth must decline. Societies would then have within them many opportunities for evolutionary change. Decision making in such societies would mainly reflect "the moral commonsense of the ecologically informed person."[24] Environmental strategies associated with the steady state have as their primary concern the well-being of the collectivity and secondarily that of specific individuals in it.[25]

Aldo Leopold illuminated the paradoxes that are repeated everywhere in developed societies: "man the conqueror versus man the biotic citizen; science the sharpener of his sword versus science the searchlight on his universe; land the slave and servant versus land the collective organism."[26]

AN ETHICAL POINT OF DEPARTURE

The economist Johannes Opschoor suggests that we seek to identify institutions that promote the value criteria of the continuity of human life, or perhaps of life in general.[27] Standard economics, being shortsighted and human centered, is fundamentally and structurally at odds with environmental imperatives. To overcome these deficiencies, we could set explicit social objectives that relate to the use of natural resources and processes. The objectives would be specific to each society and to each stage in its history. They would relate to and be consistent with the ability of that society's local environment to supply resources and ecosystem services sustainably. To maintain ecosystem integrity, management of that process would be based as far as possible on prudence and avoidance of risks. To achieve these aims, new economic policy instruments are needed.

But new policy instruments will not be enough. Opschoor also points out that the fundamental issues facing us are not those that techniques such as economics or technology can address directly in a meaningful way:

> More is needed . . . one cannot escape the need to specify an ethical point of departure. If "sustainability" of resource utilization, "justice" in the distribution of the fruits thereof and partial "responsibility" for the continued evolution of all life forms including *Homo sapiens* are ethically defendable human values and objectives, then (i) *prudence* in our dealings with nature, from (ii) a basic attitude of *partnership* in a coevolutionary sense between humankind and the other life forms, and even (iii) an *extended moral community* including other species, are called for.[28]

He concludes: "From this position a restricted human influence within the biosphere is asked for. This is a question not so much of social ethics [as] of life ethics."[29]

14

Energy for a Sustainable Future

IVAN ILLICH SUGGESTED some years ago that "the energy policies adopted during the current decade will determine the range of social relationships a society will be able to enjoy by the year 2000."[1] In this chapter, I look at the general question of a country's energy future. While addressing the topic directly, I make no suggestion that it is more important than the issue of pollution of the environment. On the contrary, the two are inextricably related. It is by making drastic changes and improvements in the way we use energy and its carriers (fuels) that we will make the largest and the cheapest reductions in pollution. Just as energy is an unsubstitutable means to achievement of socioeconomic aims, our energy policies for the future are central to reducing the insults we visit on our biosphere and its inhabitants, including ourselves.[2]

But it is essential that our energy policies move rapidly toward reflecting this reality. Leaving things as they are for much longer runs the risk of requiring panic reactions in a few years' time that may eventually achieve what common sense would have done earlier and much more cheaply.

THE GLOBAL CONTEXT OF ENERGY PLANNING

In the years since the first OPEC oil shock, energy has become a major concern for most countries.[3] Long-term prospects for health of any economy cannot be expected to improve substantially unless productivity in the use of all types of resources improves markedly. An important part of a response to this problem is that the severe pressures placed on an economy by the expectation of relentless increases in demand for energy (electricity and transport fuels especially) must be reduced so that scarce social and physical resources (such as capital) can be allocated to more productive areas.

Supply-obsessed energy strategies have dominated policymaking in most countries. The strategies are full of optimism and are imaginative in respect to technical fixes, but they all assume "business as usual" in the future and ignore problems of resource accessibility. By putting priority on additional energy supply rather than on improved efficiency of use, proponents of economic growth are making precisely the wrong choices, for both short-term and long-term health of society.

Regrettably, I have to point out that worldwide, energy research and development spending by the industrialized countries still emphasizes the use of nuclear and nonrenewable technologies. International Energy Agency (IEA) research and development spending data for 1989 indicate that 47 percent went toward nuclear fission, 15 percent went toward fossil fuels, and 12 percent went toward nuclear fusion, for a total of 74 percent. Only 7 percent of spending was for renewables, and only 5 percent was for energy conservation.[4] By contrast, developing countries currently get 40 percent of their energy from renewables and less than 1 percent from nuclear fission. The IEA levels of spending clearly show active government promotion of centralized, high-technology options depending on nonrenewables, at the expense (and often with deliberate exclusion) of small-scale, more appropriate renewable options.[5]

The supply approach to energy planning is not an effective strategy for meeting the needs of humanity as a whole, nor is it sensitive to a broad range of global issues related to the energy problem. Such issues include poverty in more than half of the countries of the world, inadequate distribution of essentials such as food supplies, global insecurity, the danger of nuclear war, and environmental degradation on a massive scale. These problems are interrelated, and all have energy components.

The well-known famine in northern Africa is intimately related to energy. The primary requirements for life in many of those countries are, in order of importance, clean water, cooking fuel, and food. The supply of food is closely linked to the accessibility of cooking fuel, since without readily available fuel, low-grade (but nutritionally adequate) foods often cannot be cooked enough to be digestible. Without adequate fuel, high-grade foods must be obtained, but these are not available to communities at starvation level; they must be supplied (usually at vast expense) by other countries.

Any strategy to deal with the energy problem must be sensitive to a broad range of concerns and to the complexity of interactions among them. To use the famous quotation, "Think globally, act locally" is a more appropriate guiding principle for any country than concentration on narrowly conceived economic growth. Jorgen Norgard and Niels Meyer point out:

> By the year 2030 the world population is estimated to have at least doubled, compared to today's 4 billion people. If these 8 billion people were to have the same per capita energy consumption as in the richest countries today, the global energy consumption would increase by more than a factor of 10. This is an absurd assumption. . . . Nevertheless all official energy plans for the industrial countries are still based on increasing energy consumption. . . . If the industrial countries expect the developing countries to follow a different energy path, then they must give a credible example. They must demonstrate the potential of alternative energy solutions in their own countries. They have the technical expertise and the resources to do so. One way to influence the authorities is the presentation of realistic and well-documented low-energy scenarios.[6]

In this chapter, I look at energy futures along lines suggested by Norgard and Meyer and by other workers. I have been inspired by the conviction that there are answers to the so-called energy problem that are compatible with answers to many other major problems of the world, a world no country can pretend not to be a part of.[7]

In doing so, I think it is worth remembering that although our fossil fuel resources are almost unimaginably large, they were accumulated over more than 100 million years. They are still miniscule compared with the solar energy that washes over us. We should see such a slow-to-accumulate resource as a catalyst, or a bridge, that enables us to learn to live sustainably in the long term from solar energy.[8]

THE END USES OF ENERGY IN AN ECONOMY

The strategy that I and many others want to promote is based on an analysis of how energy is used and for what purposes; on an appreciation of the interactions between energy use and other activities in society; and on a shift in technological focus from the supply of energy to its end uses. This end-use focus enables us to look at energy as an instrument for achieving a sustainable, better world rather than for perpetuating social, economic, and engineering structures. Peter Steen and co-workers comment:

> Social activities are determined by value judgments and objectives with regard to present and future living standards in the widest sense. Production, consumption,

accommodation and transport require energy. The level of necessary use of energy, and consequently the demand for a certain energy supply, depends not only on the existing activities, but also to a high degree on the choice of technology. It is thus not energy as such, but the way in which it is used, that determines whether we succeed in shaping society to suit our needs and expectations.[9]

Because energy use is not a goal in itself but rather a means of maintaining and improving the quality of life, we also need to relate these end uses to human needs. Meyer and Norgard point out that it is necessary to look at the energy system as a whole.[10] Jose Goldemberg and co-workers suggest that the appropriate response is to bring energy costs under control in a manner consistent with solutions to related global problems:

> Our most important finding is that it *is* possible to formulate energy strategies which are not only compatible with, but even contribute to, the solution of the other major global problems—including North-South disparities, the poverty of the majorities in the developing countries and of minorities in the industrialized countries, food scarcities and undernutrition, environmental degradation in both the industrialized and developing countries, the threat of global climatic change, the pressure from population growth, and global insecurity and risks of nuclear weapons proliferation and thus the threat of nuclear war. Thus it appears that the energy problem can be turned into a powerful and positive force for improving the human condition on this globe. Instead of being the destabilizing force that it is today, energy can become an instrument for contributing to the achievement of a sustainable world.
>
> The formulation of such energy strategies is made possible by shifting the focus of energy analysis from the traditional preoccupation with energy supplies to the end-uses of energy. In this end-use approach much closer attention is paid to present and future human needs served by energy, the technical and economic details of how energy is being used, and alternative technological options for providing the energy services that are needed.[11]

Whether such efforts end up actually reducing total primary energy demands or whether they only lower the rate of growth in demand matters little in the short term; in both cases, demands on the economy will be substantially reduced. The main point is very clear, however: *improving the efficiency of fuel utilization will allow significant improvement in the physical quality of life, with a decrease in the amount of primary energy that has to be supplied.*

This conclusion has been in the past, and will be in the future, entirely missed if supply of primary energy is the preoccupation of governments. Only end-use energy, the service energy carriers supply, is important. The separate technical efficiencies with which primary energy is converted successively into secondary, consumer, and end-use energy are critical in determining how much primary energy is needed to supply a given service to the consumer. Unnecessary waste detracts from the consumer's quality of life by increasing costs and by depleting resources, especially of ecosystem services.

I am aware that current attitudes to energy-planning mistakes of the past will ensure that they are unlikely to be repeated. Nevertheless, the moral vacuum that characterizes present attitudes is, by default, allowing the marketplace to determine future policies. This option is equally deficient.

INCREASING END-USE EFFICIENCY

It has been known for most of the twentieth century that a myriad of opportunities exist for improving the efficiency with which energy is used in machines and appliances.[12] Over recent years, many studies have shown the technical possibilities of options as varied as engine-tuning checks on motor vehicles and better sizing and operation of boilers in industry to minimize the use of fuel. Many technically attractive options also show the promise of being highly economical, as has been shown over many years by Amory Lovins and co-workers[13] and by others.[14] Regrettably, this point still evades many of those who advise politicians.[15]

The conclusion drawn by all of these workers is that conservation is a much cheaper source of "supply" than, for example, electricity from new power stations. It will also provide more overall employment in the economy than construction of new capacity.[16] Many studies have shown that improvements in the use of energy and materials, decentralization of employment, and encouragement of local self-sufficiency and self-reliance can be expected to create more employment[17] and a happier and more equitable society.[18]

INSTITUTIONAL BLOCKS TO ENERGY CONSERVATION

In many situations, energy efficiency measures would save electricity at an average cost that is half that of constructing new stations. If the aim is to enable people to stay warmer in winter, for example, good house insulation saves a lot of money and fuel relative to the cost of supplying electricity from new power stations. So why should not a generation utility spend money on insulating customers' buildings rather than putting up more supply capacity? The answer lies in a combination of market failure, institutional blocks, and political inertia, not any lack of appropriate technology. In several areas, it is clear that entrenched power structures such as the nuclear lobby have managed to sabotage more benign (and more economical) alternative technologies. [19]

Market Failure: Electricity and Conservation

Many economic options in energy conservation are not taken up. Coal and wood in open fires were long ago shown to be very costly for room heating; large sections of industry and commerce have consistently ignored options with rapid payback; motorists drive cars that are grossly mistuned; and so on. Virtually all studies have shown that the market has not responded in the way that would be expected. Consumers have not responded "rationally" to clear market messages unless they were so large that they could not be ignored. Left to themselves, markets have failed to deliver. It is a logical consequence that they should be helped to do so. [20] As an economist pointed out, "Something has to give a kick-restart to improved energy efficiency, before [hu]mankind burns itself off the planet." [21]

Equity

If electricity were charged for at a rate that reflected the cost of power from new power stations (commonly around double the average rate charged to the consumer), there would be plenty of incentive for conservation. But the political consequences would be severe if the cost of such an essential service were increased to a substantial extent. One obvious response is that there could be an immediate compensating increase in income for households so that they would end up neither worse off nor better off. The net effect, however, would be that the costs of consumption would be clear to the consumer, and the advantages of conservation would be real, not largely imaginary as they are at present.

A different way of achieving the same result could be to change the way electricity is charged for to reflect better the long-term costs of increasing supply. Instead of everyone paying the same basic rate and heavy users getting concession rates, the tariff structure would be turned upside down. In the "lifeline" tariff, every household gets a basic allowance at below-average price. Consumption beyond this level is charged for at higher rates. This is already done in some countries, and in some cases there may even be two or more steps in the tariff. Modest increases in consumption over the basic level are not penalized too severely, but beyond it, the cost increases enough to hurt.

The major problem with any policy to reflect the cost of new power stations in consumers' electricity bills is that of equity. Large new pulp mills should pay the full cost of the new generating capacity they will use. High-rise office buildings often have demands comparable with those of a small town and could similarly afford to pay the full cost of power. Unless the price realistically reflects the actual costs of increasing the capacity of the system, however, users who put in central heating, air conditioning, spa pools, and saunas have their electricity effectively subsidized by everyone else.[22] That too is manifestly unjust. The political problems involved in this area are not trivial, and they will not go away.

In California (which no one could accuse of being a socialist utopia), markets have long been known to be inadequate, and policies have been introduced to ensure the success of conservation options that are in the general interest.[23] Insulation and appliance efficiency improvements are brought about by the use of building and other construction standards. Energy utilities have been legally empowered to become involved in selling end-use "energy services" rather than just electricity or gas. Thus, installation of, say, attic insulation is paid for by the consumer as part of the regular energy bill, which makes financing easy and also puts the economic messages directly before the consumer. Savings are shared by consumer and producer alike. Everyone benefits.

CHOOSING OUR FUTURE ENERGY DEMAND—INVENTING OUR FUTURE

The demand for energy is a matter in which we, as individuals, nations, and a global community, have considerable freedom of choice. Within the limits of physical, social, and global reality, we also have the freedom to invent our own future. This is an even more creative activity than choosing among alternatives, because it acknowledges that we can tread paths that have not been prepared for us.

Future energy demand involves our making three types of choice:

- choice of material standard of living;
- choice of social (including economic) structure to achieve that standard of living;
- choice of technology to provide the standard of living.[24]

In the past, these three areas have often been dealt with in reverse order, with choice of technology made first, usually by central government. As we now know, technology is a matter of choice, since many options are available within the overall physical constraints of resource accessibility. What is vitally important is that we determine our collective social goals and moral values first, and only then decide on how to achieve them.

The New Zealand Commission for the Future, as part of a project to assist people to clarify their values and aspirations, used "Contexts for Development" as a means of clarifying available options:

> In imagining an energy future, for example, many people these days see an energy self-sufficient New Zealand. Some want to use our gas, coal and all available development capital to achieve this goal as quickly as possible. They believe that resources exist to be used for our benefit. Shortages of resources in the future will be overcome. Others dislike this version of an energy self-sufficient New Zealand. They want to use renewable resources such as solar energy or liquid fuels produced from trees to achieve self-sufficiency. Since gas and coal are not renewable resources, they should be conserved and used carefully over a number of generations. In this example different values and perceptions have led to different chains of logic and different pictures of an energy self-sufficient New Zealand. Each chain of logic can become part of a context for development. A society which seeks to develop the art of anticipation is one which considers many contexts before making decisions.[25]

People in many other countries would recognize the perceptions expressed in that quotation.

SOFT AND HARD OPTIONS

It is a common misconception that the "soft," conservation-based alternatives are quite unrealistic (they have been dismissed as "freezing in the dark in caves"), whereas the "hard," high-demand options are in some sense inevitable ("you can't stop progress"). In reality, it is the hard options that are unrealistic, since few have ever been tried. The soft options, on the other hand, have already been tried and proved; the technical requirements for much better energy utilization are mostly well known, and the social and environmental structures needed for them are already available. Their effects on current living habits are likely to be favorable, and British, American, and Scandinavian studies give evidence that further improvements in material life-style could be possible for some time to come with no increase in demand for fossil fuel energy and materials. Recent information suggests that much less energy intensive consumption patterns could be in prospect, perhaps to only one-third of current levels, for a standard of living higher than that currently enjoyed in Scandinavian countries.[26]

But the "hard" attitude has been typical of many politicians and their advisers for many years. Recently, for example, leaders of the United States and Britain have claimed that measures to constrain emissions of greenhouse gases and acid rain precursors will be "unbelievably expensive" or even involve "draconian sacrifice." This is arrant nonsense. It is a fact that highly economic options have been available for years and are improving in economic benefit every day (even before internalization of what are in many cases very large external costs).[27] It is the current policies that are too costly! Regrettably, those who advise politicians either are not up to date or are so blinded by ideology that they cannot see what is beneath their noses. The influence of large oil companies, car manufacturers, and road construction contractors appears to have been more palatable than the scientific advice of those who know what they are talking about.

SUSTAINABILITY

The question of sustainability is also of importance in the general context of this discussion. We know that *sustained growth* in the production of material goods and services is not possible; it must stop sometime, and the sooner the better. But what about *sustainable energy*? The answer depends on the purposes for which the energy is needed and where it would come from. A society that depends on only solar and natural energies can obviously exist almost indefinitely. But industrialized societies that meet their energy requirements from fossil fuel sources clearly cannot expect these supplies to be available indefinitely, nor can they expect to make a transition overnight. So the term "sustainable energy" has to be explained further.

Stock Resources and Sustainable Development—A Contradiction?

On the surface, as James Baines points out, there would appear to be a contradiction between the use of nonrenewable resources (a process that is in the long term obviously unsustainable) and the goal of sustainable development for society as a whole (implicitly a long-term process).[28] Two arguments tend to dispel this contradiction.

The first is that people are primarily concerned with sustaining a level of utility or end-use service rather than with sustaining consumption of a particular resource. The end-use service can therefore be sustained while resource consumption shifts from stocks to renewables. Sustainable development would be compromised only if rates of resource consumption reached while using stocks were to lead to demands that overloaded the substitute renewable resource systems.[29]

The second argument derives from giving policy priority to the avoidance of substantial or irreversible harms. These are exemplified in a general way with reference to the natural environment. By and large, people now see the threat of ecological damage with greater certainty than the threat of scarcity of resources, although the two are obviously related. The environment is thus central to the energy dilemma, and ultimate limits on energy use are more likely to be imposed by rising environmental and sociopolitical costs than by simple resource exhaustion.[30]

Establishing decision rules for sharing the once-only "goods" of resource stocks across the many generations who might claim interests in the resource base is an extremely difficult policy issue to resolve. By contrast, establishing decision rules to try to avoid creating permanent "bads" is a straightforward task, already supported by current evidence and perceptions. This approach has several potential policy advantages:

- the policy initiatives are called for in terms of environmental protection anyway;
- it does not distinguish between stock and renewable resources;
- many of the initiatives would be as beneficial now as in the future.

Incentives for technological innovation arise if either resource scarcity or environmental damage is seen as threatening. Both would encourage greater efforts at conservation and substitution. Whichever is the cause hardly matters if unsustainable outcomes are avoided. As Baines writes: "Thus, the use of stock resources *need* not lead to any contradiction or dilemma for policy prescription. However, this is not the same as saying that it *will* not."[31]

THE FUTURE

Robert Costanza asks: "Will fusion energy or solar energy or conservation or some as yet unthought of energy source step in to save the day and keep economies growing? The technological optimists say yes and the technological pessimists say no. Ultimately, no one knows. Both sides argue as if they were certain but the most insidious form of ignorance is misplaced certainty."[32]

What is the prudent path for public policy on the management of stock resources? Uncertainty about future technological developments means that the general thrust of sustainable development policy must be avoidance of unsustainable outcomes, with the emphasis on avoiding irreversible and costly impacts on environmental systems and the resource base.[33] Three arguments have been advanced in support of this type of policy stance:

- there is greater certainty about the effects of "bads";
- it gets away from the "language of sacrifice";
- it is what might be termed a "reversible" policy stance.

The risks of unsustainable environmental outcomes that are seen with most certainty are, I believe, the risks of irreversible impacts and long-lived wastes; climatic instability; species and ecosystem extinction; resource contamination; and damage to ecosystem resources. Some management of the use of nonrenewable stocks can thus be implemented by policy instruments aimed primarily at pollution abatement and reduction of ecological risk. These will affect the relative economics of stock use without necessarily prohibiting them outright.

Energy stocks, in the form of fossil fuels and fissionable uranium, are critical contributors of environmental bads. In this case, substitution by renewable energy sources and a concerted drive to improve energy efficiency provide prudent and strategic medium-term options. Compared with further advances in nuclear technology, these have the advantage of virtually certain technical outcome and, in many cases, competitive economics as well.[34] They do not involve sacrifice on the part of the present generation; they simply make good economic sense and keep options open. Glaring inconsistencies between this view and the realities of research and development spending by International Energy Agency countries show, however, that realism and vision are not in the forefront of current decision making in the industrialized one-third of the world.

Indicators of sustainable energy development will be needed in any future policy context. Although they are not easy to formulate, clearly the main requirement is that societies follow the path of low-impact energy development in the future, involving increases in the physical efficiency of fuel use, greater security of supply, a transition to renewables, and a reduction in the environmental costs associated with fuel use.[35]

MAKING SHORT-TERM OBJECTIVES CONSISTENT WITH LONG-TERM GOALS

To put sustainability goals into practice, we need institutional arrangements to influence the ways in which people and societies use natural resources. These arrangements will, of necessity, be in the nature of "control procedures." Wherever possible, it may be appropriate for them to take the form of microeconomic instruments, which, once set in place, ensure that people act in their best interests to achieve the best interests of society as a whole. *Market methods should be used wherever they can be shown to be both socially and environmentally appropriate.* The first and most important step toward doing so is to start the process of bringing market prices in line with the "full" costs of using fuels, by incorporating as much as possible of the environmental and social burdens associated with their use into prices.[36]

However, in many situations, markets have functioned in such a way as to create the very (macroenvironmental) problems we are trying to overcome; they may be economically efficient, but they do not serve the whole system properly. Thus, in a context such as that of sustainable development and the use of stock resources of the natural environment, microeconomic tools (based on individual "freedom") must always be subservient to the macroenvironmental requirements of sustainability. That requirement in turn comes from moral and ethical imperatives, including responsibility to future generations and to those millions who, in this age, do not have the power to avoid development paths that are clearly unsustainable.

15

Sustainable Development

WE KNOW THAT much of the resource-intensive technology that underpins present-day consumerist life-styles is not environmentally sustainable. It is therefore not economically sustainable by any reasonable interpretation of the meaning of economics. Interestingly, a number of studies show that the ancient societies of Mesopotamia, the eastern Mediterranean region, and Central America collapsed because they developed life-styles that made excessive demands on their environments.[1]

Herman Daly suggests that the real problem facing humanity is how to use *ultimate means*—the useful stuff of the world, or environmental resources—wisely in the service of the *ultimate end*—that which is intrinsically good.[2]

The How to? question is, I believe, well addressed by some of the scientific tools I have described in previous chapters. The complementary question, Why?, is much more difficult but is probably the most important question that faces us, not least because of the need to address it wisely. I believe we should face the question squarely, using ethics, morality, and theology to help us. If we do not do so, we imply willingness to drift into the future, with no attempt to choose our paths and little or no interest in possible destinations.

ENVIRONMENT AND DEVELOPMENT

What we call development is a dynamic environment-society process involving transformation (in both physical and social senses) as part of its meaning.[3] Social and economic development can result from managing the natural environment, but the environment itself is not under social control. It has a dynamic of its own, and manipulation of it involves risks of damaging it, perhaps irreversibly. If we are to exploit natural resources in a sustainable way, we need a better understanding of the environmental repercussions of our activities. This is especially so in the case of agriculture, which provides the food on which our lives depend.[4] It is an obvious consequence that we must also recognize ecological principles more forcefully in our institutions and policies. The context within which we interpret these relationships should be one in which we see society as *part of* the biosphere, not *apart from* it.

It is therefore heartening to come across similar statements by eminent politicians such as Geoffrey Palmer, former prime minister of New Zealand:

> Now as never before our developmental activity must be shaped by our need to sustain our environment to meet the needs of future generations. Sustainability must become our keyword. This is not to say that all development must cease. . . . But it does mean that waste and destruction of resources must be checked. Our wasteful use of energy and other scarce or non-renewable resources must be halted. The very survival of our species depends on it.
>
> In the long term, sustainable development is the only way to live within our means without destroying the environment which gives us life. Most people face major changes to our lifestyle, in order to maintain the quality of life. The greenhouse effect and ozone depletion are two symptoms of the deeper malaise which we must learn to cure. And we need strong medicine for a sick planet.[5]

This statement puts our present-day societies into their broader perspective. On an evolutionary, let alone a geological, time scale, humanity is but a tiny speck, and we might be more humble about our place in creation. The need is to fit human activities into nature's patterns.

But the word "development," as used in the everyday sense, has connotations that relate exclusively to human-centered concerns. It comes from the Lockean context of a belief that the environment exists solely to gratify human desires, with no intrinsic value. Those connotations explain why decades of "development" have left the world environment in a far worse state overall than when they started.[6] The World Bank and related organizations have contributed enormously to destruction of the global commons through mindless concentration on a utilitarian ideology quantified by cost-benefit analysis. Many problems of developing countries (especially forest loss, soil erosion, and ecosystem services destruction) can be directly related to such bodies. There has been a change in the past couple of years in their public statements but as yet only circumstantial evidence of change in underlying policies. It is clear that most of these organizations' policymakers have little or no understanding of the physical basis of life or of the ecological imperatives of our age. The attempt to "balance" economic against ecological priorities is a case in point.

IS BALANCE POSSIBLE?

Pluralism, which arose in the 1960s, claimed to be a reform of the rationalist approach.[7] Pluralism held that pursuit of individual interests in a democratic process will promote the common good. With pluralist reform, "the pretense of adversarial debate conceals the absence of questions regarding systemic problems. . . . It interprets society in terms of private or inter-group conflict, when the pivotal conflict is special interests versus the public interest in natural resources and amenity."[8]

Pluralism perpetuates myths not based on reality, such as the myths that power cannot be monopolized; there is real freedom to choose; the system is sound; and government is neutral. Pluralism balances values but does not judge them.

In the heyday of the rationalists, resources were considered unlimited and conservation was not an issue. Most environmental legislation in recent years has been based on the idea of "balancing of interests" between conservation and development. What this amounts to is that laws now attempt to mediate in conflicts between the general public (which includes future generations) and powerful special interests. In practice, this sometimes slows resource depletion, but the overall process is still much the same as before. Development (as exploitation) is the "default" option, and other interests have to produce counterarguments. In this day and age, the default option should be conservation, with exploitation having to argue its case in a generally hostile social environment!

From the systems viewpoint, I would also make the point that balance in a hierarchy is seldom possible. The reality of emergent properties in complex nonlinear feedback systems means that the notion of balance has to be replaced by a much more subtle understanding that reflects the whole system and its linkages, not parts selected for their ease of analysis. Thus, as Stephen Viederman puts it: "The environment is not a competing interest with other areas of national or international concern. It is the playing field upon which all other interests compete. Therefore, calling attention to the environmental dimension of development is not special pleading. It is laying the foundation."[9]

SUSTAINABLE DEVELOPMENT AND HICKSIAN INCOME

There are many definitions of the term "sustainable development" and a great deal of confusion about its meaning.[10] What people mean depends critically on their personal, cultural, or institutional standpoints, which often bear little or no relationship to those of scientists who work in the field.[11] For that reason, in this chapter I attempt a broad-brush review of some important points.

In microeconomics (e.g., in business management), it is unreasonable to treat capital consumption as income. The economist J. R. Hicks pointed out many years ago that income is the maximum amount a person or community can consume over some time period and still be as well off at the end as at the beginning.[12] Capital must not be run down in order to keep income constant. Hicksian income is by definition sustainable.

No shareholder would trust a company's profit statement without checking that the balance sheet showed that the company's resources were being maintained or increased, unless the business was in liquidation, with assets being sold off. A nation that determines its income without counting the drawdown of the community's environmental wealth and resources, as is currently the case with measurement of GNP or GDP, is not sustainable.[13] Yet national income is determined by just such a method. The foundation of my discussion of sustainability is, therefore, the conviction that "it is both morally and economically wrong to treat the world as a business in liquidation."[14]

The Brundtland Report

The United Nations' World Commission on Environment and Development (WCED), in its Brundtland report, devoted a lot of attention to sustainable development.[15] The major objective of development, it concluded, is the satisfaction of human needs and aspirations. It was careful to distinguish among different types of need: "Perceived needs are socially and culturally determined, and sustainable development requires the promotion of values that encourage consumption standards that are within the bounds of the ecologically possible and to which all can reasonably aspire."[16]

Many commentators have observed that in this area in particular, the Brundtland report is weak in that it regards human interests as dominating the reasons for global action on the environment. Some policy recommendations in the report (e.g., a new era of growth to benefit developing nations) fail to acknowledge the inadequacies of GNP as a measure of development in that many forms of economic growth involve more "bads" than "goods."[17] The WCED recommendations largely evaded the real issue, which is the requirement for the rich nations to consume less so the poor can consume enough, while keeping total global resource and pollution flows at a manageable level.[18]

The best-known and probably most widely used definition of sustainable development was given by the WCED as "development that meets the needs of the present without compromising the ability of future generations to meet their own needs."[19]

Unfortunately, this definition is so general that it can be met via several (probably mutually exclusive) strategies. For that reason, unless we take the matter further, there is a real danger that sustainability as a goal will lose its credibility. In other words, as Janice Wright suggests, the Brundtland definition may be "better than nothing for as long as there is nothing better."[20]

The central point is that when we talk about sustainability, the *physical* attributes of the environment are our prime concern. Physical sustainability is a prerequisite to social or economic sustainability. Without physical sustainability, words are empty. Regrettably, the Brundtland report's failure to make this point clear means that although its analysis of environmental problems was good, its policy synthesis reflected both political-economic myths and what the rich nations felt was politically convenient rather than what was clearly needed.

The Meaning of Sustainable Development

Herman Daly, in a brave attempt at definition, clearly distinguishes between sustainable development and sustainable growth—concepts that are frequently confused.[21] The first is concerned with quality, the second with quantity. As we know, sustainable growth is impossible as well as literally self-contradictory. Sustainable development, on the other hand, is normal, natural, and desirable.

Nevertheless, the criticisms remain that sustainability is too vague, too general; it cannot be defined. One response is to turn the criticisms back on the critics by pointing out that words such as "efficiency" and "equity" are equally hard to define but are used widely by economists and politicians. Another is to point out that people actually appear to be more clear about the things they see as unsustainable than about those that are sustainable.[22]

For the present, I feel sustainability should be seen in relative, rather than absolute, terms. We can move toward more or less sustainable situations. (To know in which direction we are moving, indicators will be needed; that is an issue I do not address here.)[23]

The best statement on sustainability I have come across is that of the scientist Bert de Vries:[24] *"Sustainability is not something to be defined, but to be declared. It is an ethical guiding principle."*[25]

This guiding principle is enough to give us a good start in developing policies for sustainable development. But it is still not a definition. I have skirted the problem of definition by substituting "an ethical guiding principle." I believe it is reasonable to do so, given the discussion in previous chapters and the lack of a generally acceptable precise definition.

The American economist Hazel Henderson pointed out in a related context that running an economy on indicators such as GNP is like trying to fly a jumbo jet with only one gauge on the instrument panel![26] It is a sad reflection on the prevalence of nineteenth-century mind-sets and the lack of twentieth-century scientific understanding that many politicians and economists still insist on a definition of sustainable development that can be codified or evaluated as a number. They do so on the grounds that otherwise, they will find it very difficult to make policies. An obvious reply is to point out that a jumbo jet, despite its complexity, is nevertheless a much simpler system than a modern economy, yet no pilot would consider taking off without a fully operational instrument panel. Pilots have the training and experience to interpret a mass of information from different instruments and to integrate it into an understanding of how well they are progressing toward their destination. They do this at the same time as they are analyzing a myriad of other inputs relating to the safety and integrity of the aircraft in its surrounding airspace at all points in the journey. To expect an economy to be managed in a purposeful manner on any small set of simplistic criteria is simply absurd. Of course, if one is happy to let the economy drift, there is no problem. I believe we humans are more purposeful and that we expect our governments to reflect community purposes in their policies as guidelines within which economics and technology operate.

A HIERARCHY OF POLICY OPTIONS

The Brundtland Commission emphasized that economy and natural environment are closely linked in the physical world and urged far better integration of environmental considerations into all aspects of economic and development policy. This is not an unreasonable expectation. Indeed, it already exists in many countries and in many societies. From my own country, for example, there is a Maori[27] proverb: *Tukino ao tukino koe,* "destroy nature, destroy yourself."[28]

This suggests the adoption of a hierarchy built on sustaining the integrity of the natural environment. As James Baines puts it, the need is to accept that

- ecological sustainability is an underlying principle for
- sustainable resource use and waste management, which is, in turn, the basis for
- a sustainable society.[29]

Ecological sustainability involves not interfering with major cycles in the biosphere to an extent that makes them hazardous for life. It involves maintaining genetic and ecosystem diversity as the basis for biological resilience. This is a biophysical imperative.

Sustainable resource use should not threaten ecological sustainability. It means harvesting resources within the capacity of the renewable resource systems involved. It means linking stock depletion with resource conservation and recycling, to avoid fueling unsustainable resource demands that would jeopardize an orderly transition to renewable substitutes.

Sustainable waste management also should not threaten ecological sustainability. It involves minimizing waste production and managing waste disposal within the receiving capacities of environmental sinks, and it includes avoiding the production of hazardous substances.

These two policies are ethically and morally driven in that they involve societies determining priorities based on the biophysical imperative. These priorities may well be expressed in the form of standards for performance of processes and perhaps for human behavior.

A *sustainable society* involves accepting the physics of ecological sustainability, sustainable resource use, and waste management. It also requires elimination of material poverty, integration of ecological, social, and economic considerations into resource management policies and decision making, and development of ecological and integrative sciences. This option is predominantly political-economic in its form and structure.

Sustainability and Unsustainability

There are many sustainable futures. A policy of sustainable development is rather like one that seeks to promote efficiency. In economics, there is no single efficient use of resources and no single optimal level of efficiency. In practice, we usually increase efficiency in our use of resources by reducing the incidence and level of inefficiency. Similarly, *sustainable development is given practical effect by minimizing the incidence of unsustainable outcomes, by aiming to avoid such risks if at all possible.* It is therefore both anticipatory (proactive) and adaptive. This meaning is, I believe, consistent with the ethical principle of de Vries.

In its proactive mode, sustainable development policy is built on research to provide good baseline information. We need to know how ecosystems behave and what makes them vulnerable to breakdown. We need to know about thresholds for irreversible damage, about critical limiting factors and indicators of environmental health, and about the state of particular resources within these systems. All of these are biophysical criteria, and they reflect the physical policy imperative discussed earlier.

STRATEGIES FOR INTEGRATING ECONOMICS AND ECOLOGY

Consistent with these arguments, Daly has suggested that there are three reasonably well-known strategies for integrating economics and ecology in the context of policymaking for sustainable development.[30] Figure 15.1 illustrates these strategies for an economy existing within its surrounding ecosys-

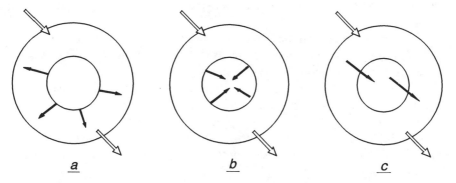

FIGURE 15.1 Three Common Strategies for Integrating an Economy and Its Surrounding Ecosystem. a, *economic imperialism;* b, *ecological reductionism;* c, *the economy as a steady state subsystem. White arrows represent energy flows through the surrounding ecosystem. Flows in are of solar energy; flows out are of heat.*

tem, into which available energy flows and from which low-grade waste energy is dissipated.

Economic imperialism is the conventional approach used in most capitalist and socialist countries. The boundaries of the economic subsystem expand until they coincide with those of the total ecosystem, thus bringing all flows under the regulating influence of prices or central planning. In capitalist societies, tradable property rights usually must be established for environmental goods; markets for environmental services then ensure efficient allocation.

Ecological reductionism is a popular alternative. Often associated with environmental movements, this strategy aims to contract and weaken the boundaries of the economic subsystem to ensure that humans obey the same rules as does the rest of the ecosystem. The economy will then cause minimal disruption to its environment.

The economy as a steady state subsystem contains elements of both of the other approaches but is, I believe, a more realistic approach than either. It reflects the biophysical systems view of ecosystems as self-contained closed systems needing only energy from the sun to produce the material requirements of the economy. In contrast, economies are open systems that take resources from, and reject wastes to, their surrounding ecosystems.[31] Recognizing this dependence of economy on environment, the approach concentrates on defining and maintaining clear boundaries. The flow of matter-energy across the ecosystem-economy boundary (the *throughput*) is then seen clearly as the metabolic flow by which the economy lives off its environment. Constraints on that flow—especially on its growth—will always be needed to ensure that the economy and its ecosystem jointly remain healthy and stable.

The third approach implies that a sustainable economy-environment system must exist in a quasi-steady state. If the economic system is growing in size, it is not sustainable. The two systems, economy and environment, are connected by the flows that cross the boundary; the inflow of physical raw materials (minerals, energy, etc.) and the outflow of physical waste (heat, pollution, greenhouse gases, etc.).[32] The outflow is at all times a direct and unavoidable consequence of the inflow. As a direct consequence of this argument, *no significant reduction in outflow is possible without a comparable reduction in inflow.*

Both flows are influenced, directly or indirectly, by decisions made within the human economy. Historically, most economists and politicians have tended to emphasize policies that increase inflows. They have largely ignored the outflows by relegating them to the status of externalities when they are, in fact, inescapable consequences of economic activity. When we are faced by sustainability issues (e.g., accelerated global climate change or damage to the ozone layer), the biophysical systems viewpoint helps us understand that *the throughput of matter-energy across the environment-economy boundary is the prime issue to be addressed in our policies.*[33]

Unless we plan to limit the scale of throughput when we develop a political-economic context for sustainable development, our policies will never be workable. Sustainable development is predominantly a matter of scale of the quantity of matter and energy processed by an economy. Once we start thinking in this way, it soon becomes clear that market instruments may be entirely appropriate *within* the economic subsystem but must never be extended *beyond* it. There are several reasons why this is so.

The standard economic approach is to seek to allocate the throughput of resources to alternative uses—for example, by means of prices.[34] But microeconomic allocative efficiency is an irrelevance in this context, since conventional macroeconomics ignores the question of the optimum size of the throughput. Endlessly continued growth in the macroeconomy is the sine qua non of conventional economics; the more the better. This uncritical pursuit of growth ignores the fact that the size of the throughput (e.g., the outflow of greenhouse gases from the economy) is the principal cause of environmental damage. Continued *material* growth (especially involving the use of fossil fuels) is now known to be highly undesirable. The biophysical systems approach (the steady state subsystem) makes this quite clear, whereas the standard economic approach hides it.

Steady State Economies

It is an inevitable consequence of these arguments that in order to ensure long-term sustainability of an economy-environment system, flows across their boundary must be kept below some threshold level at which damage will be avoided. This threshold level is where the term "steady state" comes in; it refers to a throughput of matter and energy at which the economy is physically sustainable within its ecosystem. At the global scale, and in most countries, it is virtually certain that the threshold has already been crossed and that the scale of human-induced flows of matter and energy is enough to disrupt natural cycles severely. This in no way implies that the *value* of economic activity—a measure of its *quality*—need be so constrained, only that the quantity of energy and materials used in that activity must not rise above a threshold level and should preferably be reduced.

POLICY ISSUES

Over the past two centuries, the principal limiting factor in economic development has been the rate of accumulation of (human-created) capital. We have entered an era in which the limiting factor is the declining "natural capital" of the environment. To ensure that human society is sustainable, natural capital must be at least maintained and preferably increased—for example, by conserving nonrenewable fossil fuel resources and preserving and expanding carbon sinks such as forests.[35]

In neoclassical economic theory, human-made capital is an almost perfect substitute for natural resources—one can substitute one item for another and then substitute back again. Modern science has shown that natural and human-made capital are in fact more often complements than substitutes.[36] A sawmill is useless without a forest to supply logs, and fishing boats are useless if no fish are left in the ocean. Natural capital is rapidly replacing human-made capital as the limiting factor in economic development.[37] One can substitute concrete for timber in a house, but one cannot substitute more power saws for less timber. If natural resources and human-made capital were indeed perfect substitutes, the converse would also be true. In that case, one wonders why societies bothered to build their own capital structures if they could do everything with the natural ones!

One suspects that many economists stick to the notion of substitutability because it avoids the need to revise most of the development policies of the past and enables them to retain a comfortable, albeit false, sense of security.

Strong and Weak Sustainability

Maintaining total capital intact has been referred to by Daly as "weak sustainability" in that it is based on generous assumptions about the substitutability of capital and labor and of human-made capital for natural resources.[38] "Strong sustainability," on the other hand, requires that we maintain both human-made and natural capital intact, quite independently, acknowledging their complementarity.

If we concentrate on strong sustainability, our policy efforts need to be directed toward whichever type of capital—human-made or natural—is currently the limiting factor on development. Economic logic tells us that we should maximize the productivity of the scarcer limiting factor as well as increase its supply wherever possible.[39] Standard national accounting ignores natural capital completely and thus misses the point that at the margin in many developing countries, natural resources are the main limiting factor on their development. It also ignores the fact that natural resources always have to be used to create the very human-made capital that is supposed to substitute for natural resources anyway!

Enhancement of natural capital is investment in resources that are commonly owned and generally unmarketed. These investments need to be seen in the same light as investment in infrastructures such as education and health, investment that makes other, complementary investments possible. It is difficult to calculate a rate of return on many forms of natural capital, but that should not deter us from making the investment in faith.

Sustainable Resource Use

Where flow (renewable) resources are involved, no great analytical ability is needed to determine that the rate of use must not exceed the rate of flow and that where one use competes with another (e.g., a human use competing with a natural use, such as the need of an ecosystem for water), the human rate of abstraction must not exceed that which the ecosystem can afford to do without. Similarly, disposal of waste must not exceed the receiving ecosystem's ability to assimilate it.

Where stock (nonrenewable) resources are involved, it is not such an easy issue. Clearly, any use of that resource is unsustainable, but that is no reason for giving it up entirely. One solution is to use some of the income created by its exploitation to invest in a complementary renewable resource that can (in the long term) substitute for it, so that by the time the stock resource is gone, the new, renewable one is ready to fill the gap.[40] This approach tells us not what is the optimal rate of depletion of the stock resource but how much we can consume and how much we should invest from the income we gain from its use to finance its replacement over time. It sets guidelines for exploiting nonrenewable resources within the requirements of sustainable development. Once these criteria are met, choices among alternative ways of meeting them could well be made according to conventional economic criteria.

Policies for Sustainability

Referring back to Baines's hierarchy of policy options discussed earlier, the primary policy issue—the principle that underlies everything—is that of ecological sustainability. Using this (declared, not defined) principle, we can then address the following question: Will maintenance of current behavior cause unsustainable outcomes (e.g., in world climate) in the near future? I believe the answer to this question is clear, with the conclusion that among other things, pollution emissions must be substantially reduced. That, in turn, is closely associated with the point I made earlier, that resource flows must be reduced.

We then have to determine by how much to reduce resource flows, as the basis for social-environmental policy. This is the secondary policy issue, that of sustainable resource use and waste management. The optimum quantity of throughput cannot be determined by prices, however. It must be determined by ecological and ethical considerations, including sustainability and inter-generational justice. As Daly has pointed out, *ethical and ecological principles are price determining, not price determined.* [41,42]

The critical questions are not how much of the environment's matter-energy *can* be converted into people and artifacts but how much *should* be so converted, and at what rates, in a sustainable world.

Once these questions are resolved, and not before, we can address the tertiary policy issue, which predominantly involves the construction of legal, economic, and other policy tools to help us go forward in directions that serve the goal of a sustainable society. As I see it, economic instruments are in most cases necessary, but they are not sufficient components of the insti-tutional arrangements needed for sustainable development policy. I address that topic in the next chapter.

"Bolt-on" Environmentalism?

The arguments I have summarized in this chapter do not support the notion that all that is needed is to bolt cleanup facilities onto the current dirty pro-cesses. The need is to ensure that total resource throughput is substantially reduced, and for that reason, end-of-pipe technological improvements are not adequate. It is much more sensible to cut down on "beginning-of-pipe" inputs to processes. Similarly, political-economic messages that encourage increased supply rather than demand management need to be seen as "end-of-pipe economics." For a political economy of sustainability, we need "begin-ning-of-pipe economics," which uses the best of our understanding of both science and human behavior to help develop policies that will reduce mate-rial throughputs and risks to future generations.

ENVIRONMENT, EQUITY, AND GENERALIZABILITY

The World Commission on Environment and Development has highlighted equity as a central issue: "Sustainable development requires meeting the basic needs of all and extending to all the opportunity to fulfil their aspirations for a better life."[43] One of the main criticisms made of the WCED report is that it proposes to achieve equity by raising everyone's living standards. But to raise living standards of the rich, who already have so much, while making only a pittance available to the poor, would be obscene.[44]

If we are serious about "extending to all the opportunity," what are the physical implications of this for resources and the environment? After all, we know that most people in the world consume very few resources; it is the rich who consume the majority. Daly has done some simple calculations to estimate that the annual extraction of nonrenewable resources would have to increase by roughly seven times if the entire global population were to consume resources at current U.S. per capita rates.[45] An analysis by the U.S. Geological Survey comes to a similar conclusion.[46]

Any such estimates are obviously highly speculative. However, even if they overstate the case by, say, 100 to 200 percent, the implications for global pollution are horrifying. In the opinion of several eminent economists, the pressing need is for the rich to curb their appetite for resources while transferring the best of appropriate high-efficiency technology to the poor. That would enable the standards of living of the poor to be raised without excessive increases in global resource consumption and pollution. Both parties would benefit by that process. "Lifting up the bottom" is essential, but if at the same time "lowering the top" is not done, the demands for resources and ecosystem services will almost certainly prove more than nature can deliver sustainably.

In past discussions, most attention has been given to what might be possible in terms of resource availability and technical innovation. The more pressing issue nowadays is the global risk associated with generalizing trends in environmental degradation and pollution.

POPULATION, RESOURCES, AND ENVIRONMENT

Sustainable development requires that the ingredients of development, and the physical standards of human well-being that development brings, be maintained indefinitely. To achieve that development for human benefit, it is necessary to use resources and environmental services. But if population rises as fast as development proceeds, there is no improvement in per capita living standards, only a larger number of people at the same level. In many countries, despite significant overall economic development, the standard of living of those least able to protect themselves has in fact been dropping.[47]

Until relatively recent times, when population increased, new lands and new technologies could always be brought into use to provide for the new people. There was always "room for one more." Nowadays, the tragedy of the commons is painfully obvious in many countries in that "one more" has turned into millions more, all looking for sustenance from a fixed land area. The result is an inexorable trend toward destruction of the biophysical (and therefore the economic) base for all.

In the future, increased food production will have to come from land already under cultivation, from marginal land currently used for grazing, or from clearing of the remnants of land that still retain forest cover. That will have immense consequences for soils and on demand for fertilizers, tractors, water supply, and so on. Even then, the process cannot proceed indefinitely. There are limits to the ability of land to grow food, and they are only temporarily avoided by the use of artificial fertilizers, chemicals, machinery, and so on. The ultimate constraint, a fixed physical resource base, remains. The historical reality of enhanced production often causing long-term deterioration or destruction of the agricultural resource base is confirmed by the experience of virtually all countries, developed and developing.

Unless all countries face up to the issues honestly, it is likely that the current phase of human expansion will end in catastrophe.[48] There is not much time left in which to take decisive action. The links among population, resources, and the environment must be examined in an integrated manner. To look at them separately is to miss the essential and unavoidable, albeit complex, relationships among them. Biophysical systems–based thinking and tools can help us understand more about the links. They may help the human race develop meaningful policies for sustainable development for the many countries that are rapidly running out of options.

Biophysical systems–based approaches may also help those in the affluent, developed countries to understand that their own position is by no means secure. Most of these countries built their affluence by using poor countries as sources of cheap raw materials and sinks for surplus goods and services (often military). The rich are keeping many of the poor in a state of perpetual poverty by loading them with appalling levels of debt, which they are encouraged to take on in order to buy those same goods and services. The rich nations' manipulation of terms of trade such that the poor are unable to build up their resources to a state that will allow them to service their debt assures permanent poverty for the poor nations and, effectively, perpetual servitude to the rich. That is an ethical and moral issue. Unless it is addressed soon, and seriously, the world community will be left with a menu of a small number of very costly options for future development.[49]

16

Ecological Economics

WE ARE CREATING "bads" at a greater rate than "goods," at a time when natural capital must be at least maintained and preferably increased. How do we make the transition from life-threatening economics to life-maintaining economics?

Sustainable development is development without material growth. How can we alleviate poverty by development if we do not allow flows of material and energy to grow? If we do not create more wealth, how will we alleviate poverty and protect the environment?[1] (Perhaps we need some form of "birthday party economics," in which competition for resources among developed and developing nations is resolved by the "one cuts, the other chooses" method!)

THE NEW POLITICAL-ECONOMIC IMPERATIVE

According to the market liberal economic view, sustainability is the automatic outcome of decisions that achieve the highest-value use of resources. In other words, if the market is left to its own devices, it will achieve sustainability. In reality, this attitude comes from economic theory and depends on assumptions such as the prime myth; substitutability between natural and human-made capital; value adequately defined by "willingness to pay"; discounting; and so on, all of which are questionable. They do not provide us with an adequate base for the future; a new political-economic imperative must be enunciated.[2]

The first thing we have to do is find out how to ensure a long-term, stable physical relationship with our environment. We then need to develop social decision-making procedures to ensure that environmental factors are properly taken into account when political-economic policies are developed. This means a political economy of sustainability in which the best of biophysical systems thinking and economic thinking are brought together, working cooperatively.[3] In a systems context such as this, actions to promote sustainability will introduce negative feedbacks into social signals to bring under control the destabilizing positive feedbacks of indiscriminate growth and competition.

THE POLICY HIERARCHY

In the previous chapter, I discussed the need to consider some important policy issues in order according to a hierarchy.

The first-priority policy question is a scientific one. It derives from examining the question of whether current human behavior patterns will cause unsustainable outcomes in the near future. We now know clearly that the answer is yes, meaning that resource use and pollution emissions must be substantially reduced. We therefore need to change from the "cowboy" economy, in which production and consumption are free from environmental constraints and market economics sets its own goals, toward seeing the economy as a steady state subsystem of its surrounding environment. In that economy, society as a whole consciously sets its goals, acknowledging the interdependence of the biophysical factors that govern life and economic activity.[4]

We then have to determine by how much we must reduce resource use and pollution emissions as the basis for a sustainable relationship with the environment. This is the second-priority question, and its answer depends on the values base of people in society. The optimum quantity of throughput cannot be determined by prices; it must be determined by ethical and moral considerations, based on the physical and ecological understandings shown by addressing the primary question. These will include issues of intergenerational justice.

Without standards of some sort, the thrust of market capitalism will always result in investment being directed toward areas in which costs are lowest. Only if environmental costs are internalized will investment decisions be favorable to societies and their environments. Even then, all countries and regions must adopt similar standards to ensure that capital does not rush to those places where "costs" are apparently lowest.

The critical questions are, therefore, not how much of the matter-energy of the environment *can* be converted into people and artifacts but how much of it *should* be so converted, and at what rates, in a sustainable world. Thus, one can say again, with Daly, that ethical and ecological principles are the true determinants of price, not the reverse.

In the sociopolitical context, we have to think about sustainable development as concerned primarily with material sufficiency. Sufficiency is an ethical and moral matter, which relates to questions such as How much is enough? and Do we have responsibilities toward our brothers, sisters, grandchildren, and so on?

Once the ecological and ethical questions are resolved (and not before), we can address the third-priority question, which is how to construct legal, economic, and technological tools or instruments to respond to the prior questions and create policies for their implementation. These will require the efficient use of material resources to be a central component of sustainable development policies.[5] Efficiency is a technical matter, and it relates to the extent to which societies can do more with less resource use (or, better, do the same with a lot less!).

ECOLOGICAL ECONOMICS

Ecological economics is a good general name for the new ways of thinking that are needed to help build a new future. Ecological economics is concerned with extending and integrating the study and management of "nature's household" (ecology) and "humanity's household" (economics). Integration is necessary because conceptual and professional isolation has led to economic and environmental policies that are mutually destructive rather than mutually reinforcing in the long term.[6] We must stop thinking of ecological and economic goals as being in conflict. Economic systems depend totally on their ecological life support systems, and that fact needs to be incorporated into our thoughts, actions, and policy developments.[7]

Ecological economics is based on strong sustainability, with natural and human-made capital maintained separately and effort going into whichever is the greatest limitation on development—usually natural capital.

Ecological economics also tells us that we need one or more socioeconomic institutions with functions analogous to that of the Plimsoll line on a ship.[8] These would help us know by how much we can load the system before running the risk of its capsizing in rough weather. It is pointless to argue about the distribution of passenger load when the boat is awash, although it is entirely reasonable to do so if one has plenty of freeboard. By analogy, one can say that economic efficiency is an important goal in a sustainable society, but it must yield its policy position when the primary imperative is the physical one of staying afloat.

Only when the permissible scale of our resource use is explicitly limited will we make maximum use of technologies that increase efficiency of use rather than quantity of resource throughput. The central point is that of separating the questions of allocation and scale, that is, of development and growth, and of explicitly including consideration of ethical values in collectively setting the environmental Plimsoll line.[9]

Ecological economics will involve us in using old tools in new ways and in creating new tools for new functions.

For example, cost-benefit analysis (CBA) is no longer seen as an appropriate methodology, since it does not furnish information about the means to achieve ends determined by means other than economics (e.g., ecology and ethics).[10] What we need is cost-effectiveness analysis instead of CBA. Discount rates that reflect long-term factors, including the possibility of negative rates, may be part of the new methods.

Other tools of ecological economics could take the form of regulatory controls on depletion rates, perhaps in the form of maximum permissible mining of coal (e.g., in terms of maximum tonnage), to drive up the price and encourage everyone to increase efficiency of use. They could take the form of substantial taxes on such primary resources, which would also affect prices. Tax revenues could be spent to counter poverty arising from increased prices and to improve the technology of resource use, thereby looking after the future. Some workers have suggested that the entire taxation system could be replaced by a single large tax (a "Unitax") levied on primary energy resource extraction, thereby enormously simplifying the bureaucracy of taxation and ensuring that attention is concentrated on the use of resources rather than on the use of labor or human-made capital.[11]

To introduce the subject, let us look at ways in which the mainstream economic model can be modified to take account of some aspects of modern biophysical systems understanding, remembering the need to change from looking at the "end of the pipe" to starting with "beginning-of-the-pipe" views on resource use.[12]

BROADER PERSPECTIVES ON SUSTAINABILITY

As we saw in figure 6.1, the neoclassical model can be made scientifically and ecologically more realistic by embedding it in a broader biophysical systems perspective, using the model of Martha Gilliland.[13] In this model, the energy transformation sector is clearly identified as the physical "engine" of the economic subsystem. If we see the social economic subsystem as dependent on the physical economy and that, in turn, dependent on its surrounding ecological system, we gain an understanding of the ways in which biophysics constrains economics.

Gilliland's model—and much of ecological economics—focuses attention on energy. This is for three good reasons. First is the well-known fact that the interaction of energy with matter is fundamental to all of physics; the laws of thermodynamics can never be ignored. The second reason is that since available energy is always expended in the production of goods and services, it is a convenient indicator of flows in the economy, as it is in ecosystems. Third, energy use (especially fossil fuel use) is directly and indirectly associated with most of the pollution and waste that accompany economic activities in industrial societies and thus provides a convenient means of evaluating pollution effects of fuel use.

To use understandings such as these to aid ecological economic decision making for sustainable development, two main lines of study have been developed:

1. *Modifications to conventional economics.* These require that prices be adjusted to account for resource and environmental factors—for example, by internalizing estimates of the value of externalities. Alternatively, promoters of new developments can post a large bond with government as a guarantee of good behavior. Both of these usually mean that prices of resources will increase; thus, they transmit messages to consumers about the effects of consumption.
2. *Incorporation of physics into economic methods.* There are two common ways of doing this:
    a. By *modifying conventional economic tools* to show up some of the consequences and dependencies of economics on physics. As an example, energy analysis can evaluate many primary energy demands and pollution consequences of economic activity.
    b. By *dynamic biophysical systems analysis.* This involves studying the biophysical economy in its surrounding environment to help determine the nature and extent of physical limits to development—for example, with system dynamics models, using energy as a numeraire.

I now briefly discuss each of these lines of study to show the ways in which they can be used and their respective strengths and weaknesses. All are at relatively early stages of development, and all have a great deal of potential, which we will not understand fully until more research has been done.

MODIFICATIONS TO CONVENTIONAL ECONOMICS

The protection of nature from damage is from the outset a matter of essential economic concern to us all. Gerhard Maier-Rigaud asks: "Which kind of wealth do we prefer? The sort of unsustainable wealth generated by markets and directed only and systematically to meet the demands for private goods? Or would we prefer wealth encompassing the sectors of private and public goods, like a sound and sustainable environment? The economy can provide both kinds."[14]

Economic tools will be vitally important in developing policies for transition to a sustainable future. Herman Daly suggests that the institutions we already have must be bent and stretched but not abolished, since we are as yet unable to replace them. We should

> seek to combine micro freedom and variability with macro stability and control. This means, in practice, relying on market allocation for an aggregate resource throughput whose total is not set by the market, but rather fixed collectively on the basis of ecological criteria of sustainability and ethical criteria of stewardship. This approach aims to avoid both . . . centralized planning and . . . the tragedy of the commons.[15]

Macroeconomic Indicators

Conventional economic indicators such as GNP or GDP are based on aggregate production or consumption in an economy. Drawing down of capital stocks (nonrenewable resources, ecosystem services) is not included. Worse still, in most countries, the proceeds of resource depletion are used to finance current consumption.

Robert Repetto and co-workers point out that failure to extend the concept of depreciation to the capital stock embodied in natural resources seriously distorts economic evaluations.[16] These resources are a significant source of income and consumption for many countries, especially developing ones. In their study, they applied a correction to the GDP calculation for Indonesia. In recent years, that country has apparently shown remarkable economic growth, averaging 7.1 percent between 1971 and 1984. But these data fail to take into account massive depletion of tropical hardwood forests, petroleum resources, and soil. When estimates of these three factors alone were incorporated into the accounts, the "true" GDP was very much lower.

A number of economists have addressed this issue in general terms over recent years, with the aim of developing an index that counts such losses as negative contributions to income.[17] No clear consensus has yet been reached as to the most appropriate methodology. However, there is an urgent need to inform decision makers that the environment, on which our economies depend, is in most cases suffering a massive reduction in asset value while we remain under the impression that our total wealth is increasing.

It is becoming abundantly clear, however, that GDP and GNP are obsolete measures of progress for any society striving to meet people's needs as efficiently as possible and with the least damage to the environment.[18] What counts is not growth in output but quality of services rendered. As Garrett Hardin puts it, "For a statesman to try to maximize the GNP is about as sensible as for a composer of music to try to maximize the number of notes in a symphony."[19]

We still have the problem of distinguishing among changes needed to achieve strong sustainability, a more meaningful and more stringent requirement than that of weak sustainability. This requires us to distinguish between those natural resources that are genuinely substitutable by human-made resources and those that are complements. It is at the macro level that collective intervention is needed to ensure sustainability of the total system. The global context of sustainability also means that one (rich) country must not export its sustainability problems to another (poor) country.

Microeconomic Tools

Daly has pointed out that in standard economics, resource problems of the type we are addressing have to be addressed in ad hoc and unintegrated ways, outside the structure of formal models.[20] Thus, they are incorporated (if at all) as externalities: a means of bringing as many aspects of economy-environment interaction as possible within the control of prices and markets. The interest in market-based tools reflects a general lack of confidence in the performance of laws and regulations in many countries. It has been noticed that either many laws are not enforced or the cost of enforcement is too high for enforcement to be achieved. Most Western economists believe the market can do the job more efficiently.[21]

Many economists assert that if a market does not exist for something like clean water, a market must be created. This means that everything must have an "owner" who has "property rights" and can make others pay to use it.

Owners may be individuals, corporations, or the state. It is then necessary to put a "price" on environmental resources and ensure that users pay for them. For example, industries and communities that take water from aquifers or rivers have to pay the owner of the water or the appropriate government agency for what they take. If many groups all want access to a limited supply, competition will cause the price to rise, thereby ensuring that only those users for which the water has the highest value will be able to afford to pay for it.[22] The higher the purity of the water, the higher the price. The high price also encourages users to be very careful in using the water.

Where nonrenewable resources are concerned, the price to be paid should also reflect the fact that once used, that resource is no longer available for the future. Coal, oil, and natural gas are obvious examples in which use today prevents use in the future. Therefore, today's use has a social cost that must be acknowledged, although it is very difficult to evaluate.[23] We know, however, that the cost is substantial. (In biophysical systems terms, a tax on fossil fuel can be seen as a positioning, or set-point, adjustment in a complex feedback system to encourage it to adjust to new goals.)[24]

Damage to the environment from pollution is also associated with a cost to ensure that polluters pay a penalty for causing damage. Thus, wastewater flows are accepted into a waterway only if they are of an acceptable purity standard; if not, a penalty is charged. A penalty high enough to hurt will encourage users to install treatment plants. This is known as the "polluter pays principle." The idea is that estimates of the values and costs of environmental goods and services that have always been external to the economy (and thus treated as "free") are now included in the everyday costs of using them, and for the first time they are included in economic calculations and decision making. This approach can give rise to more forward-thinking ideas, such as the concept that "pollution prevention pays."[25]

Problems with Market Economic Methods

Market-based economic tools operate on the assumption that people act in their self-interest. Nothing happens that does not reflect the sum of individual desires and priorities, expressed in terms of willingness to pay for goods and services in markets. But price is nothing more than a tool for helping a society find the optimal allocation of a resource. The optimal scale of use of that resource is something altogether different, and the market has no criteria by which to limit scale.[26]

Market-based tools also require that property rights or other forms of exclusive ownership be established over the environmental domain. This raises many problems of ethics and of power and is a source of deep concern for many people.[27]

Ecological economics requires that the scale of use be set first, according to criteria of sustainability and collective ethical requirements; only then can it be decided whether and to what extent the market has a part to play in a resource's allocation. In most real situations, it is not possible to obtain a realistic value for the external economic cost. The more sensible policy is first to decide the physical requirement (e.g., the scale of use) and then to create or adjust economic instruments (e.g., incentives or disincentives) to achieve the required outcome. In this situation, economics is the servant of policy; when the attempt is made to evaluate cost first, one risks letting the market tail wag the policy dog.

Market economic methods have value in many situations, but their use is also subject to substantial doubt about the validity and relevance of the market model itself and of many of its ways of evaluating externalities.[28] In particular, application of the market model to situations involving higher human values than those of individual self-interest creates many problems.[29] It is common for economic tools of the types described here to be rejected by the people involved.[30] It is also well known that the market cannot take account of things like equity and fairness or the needs of future generations. Even though poor people need clean water, for example, they are unlikely to get it in a free market. Allocative efficiency can be bought, but at a high cost to society.

Despite these problems, I readily acknowledge that socioeconomic decisions would be much more environmentally favorable than they are at present if prices were to include even crude measures of external costs.

Market Mechanisms and Public Goods

Market mechanisms also cannot be expected to "self-start" in dealing with problems such as global warming, because the resource—the global atmosphere—is a nonmarketed public good; there is no chance of privatization of the air to enable it to be traded.[31] Thus, one can only consider whether artificial marketlike mechanisms can be created to assist people and societies to act for the common good. This assumes first, the will to do so and second, the ability to enforce global interests over national interests. I cannot be sanguine about the possibilities of collective action, but at the same time, I believe the time is not far off when the nations of the world will have to implement joint courses of action of some sort.

Policy options in this area include one or more of the following:

- impersonal market mechanisms, with individuals buying rights to pollute at prices rising high enough to reduce emissions to the desired level;
- direct legal restrictions on individual emission sources;
- carbon taxes or similar levies on fossil fuels to encourage their efficient use and/or substitution by less-polluting alternatives;
- government responsibility for territorial net emissions, with international accountability (probably with sanctions for noncompliance), in which each country is responsible for deciding its own means of meeting the standards.[32]

According to economists, the most effective, simple, self-enforcing, and politically acceptable methods would be based on the use of markets wherever possible. As an example, Denmark has in recent years adopted a policy of maintaining high taxes on energy use, especially oil and coal, to the extent that it currently has the highest energy taxes in the European Community. The result has been much more careful use of energy. In 1989, some 6 percent of public revenue came from energy taxes; they have been used to keep retail prices approximately constant (and high) in real terms, despite the drop in oil prices during the 1980s. Some of the tax revenue has been used to subsidize home insulation and promote wind energy projects. Results have been very favorable: a 30 percent drop in total energy consumption for space heating at the same time as a 20 percent increase in total heated building area.[33]

Similar favorable outcomes have been observed with water pollution control in Holland.[34] There is no doubt that where appropriately and sensitively applied, economic instruments have the potential to improve social-environmental decision making considerably.[35]

Microeconomic and Macroeconomic Policy Conflicts

Economic efficiency and sustainable development (and the policy goals that go with them) will both be goals of economic management in the future.[36] Sustainable development is sometimes criticized by economists because it does not maximize the net present value possible from resource extraction and use. (Similar reasoning could, of course, be used by ecologists to assert that economic efficiency is invalid simply because it does not ensure long-term sustainable development.) Talbot Page responds to this by pointing out: "The reasoning is surely wrong. . . . One cannot use one criterion to bludgeon another. They are on the same logical level. The most one can say at this point is that the two criteria conflict; they imply different states of the world."[37]

A number of economists[38] have commented on the inconsistency between microeconomic goals applied in the microeconomic context and microeconomic goals applied in the macroeconomic context. According to Robert Goodland and George Ledec:

> In microeconomics, growth in production (or consumption) is possible or is considered desirable only to the point where the marginal benefit (e.g., revenue) equals the marginal cost. In macroeconomic theory, there is usually no concept of the optimum size of an economy over the long term; rather bigger is always better. This approach neglects the often severe environmental and other social costs associated with high and growing rates of per-capita natural resource consumption.[39]

Society as a whole is encouraged to do what no firm would contemplate rationally: to maximize resource throughputs irrespective of the associated costs.[40] In reality, however, the two goals are not in conflict. Economic efficiency is a microeconomic goal concerned with short-run individual behavior, particularly with present-day allocation of economic resources. Sustainable development goals are macroeconomic and macroecological and are concerned with long-term aggregate behavior. Clear establishment of sustainable development policy objectives is needed to help set conditions within which markets will be able to do what they do best. Page suggests, "By modifying the flows across the boundary between the environment and the economy, myopic markets can be encouraged to be consistent with long-range social goals."[41]

Economic instruments are usually necessary, but they may not normally be sufficient components of the institutional arrangements we need to put in place to implement sustainable development policy.[42]

Market Biases

Imposition of some macroecological policy on markets does not in itself invalidate the efficiency criterion. But it can change the resulting balance between depletion and conservation, disposal and durability, and so on. Exclusion of environmental and disposal costs has maintained a bias against efficient use and material recycling in virtually all economies.

Among market distortions, taxation measures can influence the balance either way, as can regulatory measures. Tax write-offs for exploration and preferential status for mining activities in land-use planning (both commonly applied in many countries) penalize the search for more efficient extraction from existing operations and more efficient use of the product. Severance taxes, bounties for scrap materials, and more stringent standards for emissions will move the balance the other way.

Competitive market behavior has an inherent bias toward current beneficiaries in that cost-benefit analysis centers on present-value maximization.[43] This is ethically understandable only if one believes future generations will inevitably be better off than the present generation. In reality, long-lived wastes, material depletion, and damage to ecosystem services may impose a legacy of shared risk rather than shared benefits and thus may invalidate the approach.

Ultimately, the need for corrective policy action is influenced by unfolding outcomes. For example, if pollution is judged to be excessive, measures (such as standards of performance) can be put in place to encourage increased efficiency of material and energy use or increased recycling effort. Thus, the physical requirement to reduce pollution is the driving force behind the policy decision.[44] Economic (and/or legal) instruments are then used as tools to achieve the policy aims. There is no direct attempt to measure the cost of the problem in economic terms, since economics cannot do so in any consistent manner. In this context, economics and the law are used (separately) as instruments to achieve physical and ethical imperatives; the dog wags the tail!

Demythologizing Property Rights

Individual property rights are usually considered to be inviolable in the conventional market liberal political-economic world view. The only exception is when property is needed for the collective good. In state redistributive economies, all property is owned by the state. Neither provides a valid base for an ecological economics of sustainability. Since the basis of every economy is physical, land must regain a meaning that is consistent with stewardship of the physical base of a complex, nonlinear-feedback biophysical system. Economic and other nineteenth-century theories based on analogies with classical physics must be superseded.[45]

I see the need to shift from an absolute concept of property rights (no matter whether based on the individual or on the state) to one that reflects the requirements of sustainability in biophysical systems. In that approach, system dynamics and stewardship of resources are mutually reinforcing concepts. By deliberating on what this implies, we are then, of course, faced with important questions related to the meaning of democracy and development and also with the place of social cooperation and mechanisms for resolving conflicts.[46]

INCORPORATION OF PHYSICS INTO ECONOMIC METHODS

Environmental accounting[47] and natural resource accounting[48] are different names for the same general attempt to expand conventional economic information by including data on the use of flow and stock resources from the environment and on pollutants to the environment.[49] The long-term aim is to identify changes in the sustainability of national economies and economic sectors and, where appropriate, to take corrective action. Accounts of this type can take a wide variety of forms, from detailed information on every sector of resource use (e.g., types of fish caught, breeding stocks, etc.) to broad-based monetary estimates (e.g., of the value of trees cut down and not replanted). At present, the field is undergoing substantial evolutionary change, and no clear basis for accounting has yet emerged. However, the need for improving simple economic accounts is now widely accepted.[50]

As indicated previously, energy provides the most important means of describing and characterizing physical activities within an economy. Although they contain only part of the information needed to expand economic indicators for sustainability, energy-based tools are nevertheless further developed than most other (nonmonetary) techniques, and they can contribute important information. For that reason, tools of energy analysis have for some time been central to the attempt to incorporate a physical dimension into economic decision making.[51] These tools are also of value in providing essential data for dynamic systems models using biophysical systems analysis (see the following section). Since I have discussed energy analysis tools in some detail in chapter 6, I will not reiterate them. Suffice it to say that they expose some severe, and probably fatal, flaws in the prime myth (of infinite resource substitution), which is central to current economic thinking, and therefore they force us to rethink a number of policy assumptions.

DYNAMIC BIOPHYSICAL SYSTEMS APPROACHES

In the dynamic biophysical systems approaches, links are made explicitly between processes in the economy and between those processes and their effects on the environment, in terms of both resource extraction and pollution emission. Economies are socially organized, but the underlying processes of production and consumption are always physical. The main purpose of this type of study is to clarify the extent to which physical factors constrain a society—for example, in its attempt to determine the options for feeding a growing population or improving the per capita standard of living.

The literature in this topic area has been dominated over the past decade by two important schools of thought, which nevertheless have significant areas in common.

Resource Accounting

The school led by Malcolm Slesser has been developed to clarify options for increasing the carrying capacity of developing countries.[52] In this approach, the economy is seen as an interlocking set of actions quantified in physical resource terms in such a way that feedback between cause and effect is taken into account. It draws on Gilliland's model for its basic principle, but its goal orientation is based on determining the physical feasibility of alternative actions. Thus, it can be seen in one sense as consistent with a neoclassical economic growth model, but with substantial modifications to ensure that it obeys the laws of thermodynamics that govern physical reality. As described by Slesser:

> Energy analysis offers a means of making a precise statement of what is implied in the sustainability of an economy. Economic growth depends on the growth of capital stock (= embodied energy) to enable labour to provide enhanced output (= dissipation of energy). If this is to be sustainable, then the rate of energy flow (more precisely, flux) must always be maintained (up to a point, it can be compensated for by technical progress). This in turn means that part of the energy flow must, through capital and operating energy, be recycled to drive the energy transformation system by which resources in the ground become economically useful fuel. As energy resources become less accessible, the energy that must be dissipated in the process of acquiring fuel rises, that is the energy requirement for energy rises. In money terms they become more expensive to extract. . . . Economic sustainability may thus be defined as a state where the rate of growth of energy flow into the economy is sufficient to liberate and harness the resources needed to maintain indefinitely or enhance the material standard of living of the people living within that economy.[53]

A resource-accounting model[54] thus informs one about the physically feasible set of outcomes from a given set of policies in the context of a specific economy (world, country, or region). It is thus capable of measuring many of the critically important determinants of physical sustainability, in the context of a set of realistically chosen policy options. When individual economies are modeled in this way, a delicate balance is often found between demand for physical capital and the ability of the appropriate sectors to produce it. In developed, industrialized countries, there is a considerable ability to produce; in many developing countries, especially those with fast-growing populations, there may be little ability to produce.

Systems Ecology

The school led by Howard Odum originated in systems ecology and was soon extended to economic systems.[55] As well as reflecting the laws of thermodynamics, Odum's approach uses the maximum power principle: "Those systems that survive in the competition among alternative choices are those that develop more power inflow and use it best to meet the needs of survival."

This principle supplies the main goal definition in systems dynamic-feedback models of this type—namely, that the goal is maximization of power flows among competing alternatives for the available energy supply. The approach also requires the evaluation of *transformities,* which are a quantitative indication of the solar energy equivalent of each form of energy as it is embodied in higher levels of an energy chain. All forms of energy are thereby linked by relating them to the fundamental form of terrestrial energy, that of the sun. The approach implicitly relies on the use of embodied energy (in the sense of transformities) as a measure of the value of a flow of resources. In general, the higher the value, the better the user will be able to compete with alternative users of the energy flow.

Odum's approach has shown marked successes when applied to ecological systems and is the basis of an important branch of ecology. Some critics are less confident of the application of this approach to human economies because of some far-reaching assumptions inherent in the causal linkages assumed to exist between socioeconomic behavior and that of organisms in ecological systems. Both are believed to follow the maximum power principle.

In some situations, examination of otherwise similar situations by this approach and others has given rise to significantly different numerical results, and the reasons for these differences have not yet been clarified to the satisfaction of all concerned. However, the qualitative conclusions reached using Odum's approach are generally in tune with those reached by using other systems-based approaches.

CONFLICTS BETWEEN ECONOMICS AND PHYSICS

To incorporate aspects of natural resource accounting into a nation's economic accounts is a difficult task. It is made more difficult by many economists' resistance to the explicit suggestion that conventional economic tools cannot incorporate all of the information needed for policymaking for sustainable development.

Since economics and physics are based on foundations that are scientifically incompatible, in that one depends on physical absolutes and the other depends on social relativities, it is likely that they can never be merged into a "super-tool." It is the hope of many people working in this area that economics and physics will be used side by side to inform people and governments and guide their decision making. In that way, the best of both approaches can be brought to bear on problems that will, if not solved, damage the earth and its inhabitants for generations to come.

As part of our response, it is essential that we all accept physics and ecology as clarifying the ultimate constraints on human development and that many of these constraints can already be clearly identified. The constraints are not so severe as to prevent humans from achieving full potential, but they will prevent all people's reaching standards of material consumption currently found in some affluent countries.

The policy issues that face the affluent, developed countries are therefore mainly of an ethical and moral nature. Money and power will usually enable one to get a place in an overcrowded lifeboat or ensure that the lifeboat is owned by those with money and power and is not available to those with neither. Only after ethical issues such as these have been answered is it appropriate to use socially based decision tools such as economics.

Using the image of an old forest, Jorgen Norgard and Bente Christensen have demonstrated that a steady state economy could be both humanly stimulating and environmentally benign.[56] Like a climax ecosystem, with plenty of dynamics, competition, and development but without growth in total biomass, such an economy would not involve stagnation. Indeed, it could be much more diverse and richer in opportunities than a madly growing economy, in which the urge to outsmart others masks everything of human importance.

17

With People's Wisdom: Stewardship and Sufficiency

AT THE UNESCO Spring Session 1988, the following statement was made: "On the threshold of the twenty-first century, humankind is faced with three major issues—peace, development, and the environment."[1]

Not only are we humans socially embedded within communities, we are also physically embedded within natural environments. To maintain the integrity of both structures, societies have to accept environmental goals as primary. Only if that is done can they ensure the sustainability of the systems that give them both physical and social life. The goals have been illuminated by physics and ecology and interpreted by ethics and morality. How the goals are worked within is a cultural and political question, specific to each society, in which I see representative democratic processes and adult education as the keys to development of social tools for sustainability.[2]

In some respects, the new social structures will be more complex, in terms of their variety, than the simplistic structures of neoclassical or centrally planned economies. Trying to understand them, and to design them for stability, will require advanced systems thinking applied to social goals as well as an improved understanding of the ecological systems within which we live. New forms of economics will be vital components of societies' tool kits for the future. Rita Bladt asks: "Where do we stand? With the 'realists,' who simply acquiesce in a world which has programmed its own destruction? Or with those who are still daring enough to dream of, and work at bringing about, a better future?"[3]

There are at least three major sectors within society.[4] Conventional political economy recognizes the individual and the state, with market and government institutions, respectively, arising from them. For most people, there is also a third sector that is neither commercial nor statutory in its structure and activities. That sector—and it has substantial influence—reflects the collective-community side of people's behavior, referred to by Neva Goodwin as the "human commons."[5] It is the sector of society from which people (often in environmental and community organizations) express concerns about the inhumanity and destructiveness of commercial and statutory structures, especially where resources and the environment are concerned. This chapter concentrates on that third sector.[6]

PREREQUISITES FOR A SUSTAINABLE FUTURE

Several changes are required to bring everyday behavior more into line with the requirements of sustainable development.[7] The primary need is not for new technologies or even new laws, although both will be useful. The crucial needs are for recognition of the biophysical realities of the world we live in and development of patterns of collective (especially economic) behavior that reflect long time horizons and sophisticated understanding of the long-term dynamics of complex systems. To achieve these, societies need to improve their understanding, procedures, and tools and use them to design paths to the future that reflect concern for people in other lands, for future generations, and for the planet as a whole.[8]

Seeing people as caricatures whose interests revolve around the accumulation of as much personal wealth and power as possible for a minimum of actual work is a singularly unhelpful starting point for the design of social control systems in contexts as complex as that of the natural environment.[9]

Each society will need to decide the value of the whole of its activities rather than rely on market-based determination of the prices of some of its parts. Economists cannot stand back from this process, since all economic theories come from politically normative standpoints. Each of us has to decide which side we are on. Not to do so is to support the status quo and maintain the political economy of greed and destruction rather than creating a new political economy of sustainability and justice.

Planning for the Future

The process of transition to a sustainable society and a sustainable world will require major—and sometimes painful—changes in many countries. It is therefore essential that societies plan for their future—and, so far as possible, for a "soft landing." This does not mean setting up think tanks and telling them to design a perfect future; that fantasy belongs in the past. But it does mean that if societies do not plan, it will be done for them. The powerful logic of the marketplace governs planning by large corporations and cannot help but affect us all unless we constrain those organizations to conform to the aims of society as a whole. The most vociferous opposition to planning commonly comes from corporate giants (usually acting through business roundtables and chambers of commerce), for whom planning is essential to their own survival. Their protestations should be seen as no more than special pleading on behalf of the already privileged.

Russell Ackoff points out that planning in practice is "a participative way of dealing with a set of interrelated problems when it is believed that unless something is done, a desirable future is not likely to occur; and that if appropriate action is taken, the likelihood of such a future can be increased."[10]

Planning is a central and essential part of life for those who have the power to choose their futures. Those who have no power depend on it being used wisely by those who have. For us in the developed nations of the world, the future for everyone else depends on the ways in which we, a small proportion of the human race, plan our own paths to sustainable development. If we get it wrong, others will suffer more than we do. If we get it right, we will all benefit. That, surely, is a noble goal to pursue.

The Context of Education

The first question of importance when developing policy for sustainability is to determine where people are. It is a short step further to ask: Are all people's views of equal value? Is a democratic vote a good way to understand a society's views?

I think not! The idea that one person's vote should have the same electoral power as another's is central to a democratic political system, and I support it. To go on to suggest that people's views are not equally valid could be taken to imply that I believe I am possessed of superior understanding, but the issue is not that simple. As the homespun philosopher Artemus Ward put it, "It ain't so much the things we don't know that get us in trouble. It's the things we know that ain't so."[11]

"The things we know that ain't so" about policy making worry me a lot. As an empirical scientist, my training leads me to test the hypothesis that people's views ("the things we know") are of equal value. If they are not, all that is likely to be achieved by votes, referenda, or opinion polls is the pooling of ignorance—hardly a sound foundation for policy. Science has helped us understand a number of fundamental things about ourselves and the world that are not open to debate and cannot be decided by a democratic vote. Whether the earth is flat or round is one; whether evolution takes place is another. The second law of thermodynamics places absolute bounds on what can be done with energy resources; it also defines the direction of time. Yet most people in positions of power and influence have had little or no exposure to modern scientific understanding. Few know of the insights thermodynamics and systems theory can give into the way ecological and social systems function and into their limitations.

The social sciences, especially sociology, have valuable tools for testing the hypothesis that one person's view is as good as another's. They confirm that even where definable issues are involved, a superficial process of inquiry seldom brings out the fullness of a society's knowledge or the richness of the potential response. That knowledge and that response reflect to a considerable extent the collective dimension of people's social lives, which includes spiritual matters. The collective dimension is nowhere better shown than in the context of attitudes toward the environment, the use of resources, and future generations. The social sciences also help us understand why and how a well-resourced program of adult learning can contribute to the participatory democratic process. The views that come from such programs go far beyond the sum of votes of individuals.

Like most physical and natural scientists, my position is that in sustainable development policy, we have an issue that involves societies and governments trying to create social structures to ensure that we use the resources of the environment for the common good. If the views of people and the aims of government in this context can be clarified and tested according to the methods of science—and I believe many of them can—we can determine which are valid and which are not. That there will often be a grey area in between does not affect this overall argument, although it will often introduce the requirement for a degree of expertise in interpretation.

As I have also indicated at several points in this book, there is no single tool that we can use to help us shape our policies. Like any good craftsperson, we need a kit of several good (and sharp) tools, to be used with care and sensitivity where appropriate. In practice, we do not confuse the separate functions of a chisel and a screwdriver, in spite of their superficial similarity. In the same way, we cannot depend on economics, ecology, or engineering, used alone, for policymaking in the area of complex nonlinear-feedback systems. As Richard Norgaard points out: "The use of a single framework, without modification for regional differences, facilitates control from a single center of analysis. Thus the use of a single framework disenfranchises or disqualifies the majority, facilitates the tyranny of technocrats, and encourages centralization. Openness to multiple frames of analysis is a prerequisite to democracy and decentralization."[12]

It is not for scientists to specify the form of sustainable development policy. But it is most certainly their place to help society identify the bottom line of what may or may not be done to ensure long-term health of the fragile ecosystems and resources that sustain us. Within the constraints set by scientific understanding, there is still a great deal of freedom of action for human societies. That a bottom line may be identifiable is not to say that humans cannot go beyond it and destroy their environment; that they have done so and still do is painfully clear. So we also need to examine why many people and groups feel impelled to follow behavior patterns that threaten everyone's ecosystem.

ADULT LEARNING

In spite of my belief that participatory democracy is the proper way to make decisions, I accept that in many respects it does not work at present. There is a "them and us" reality for most people in which government and power structures are seen to be (and often are) in conflict with people. In such situations, public participation exercises can be a false form of democracy in which people take part in severely prescribed discussions that turn out, not surprisingly, to confirm what the decision makers want them to. In these situations, passivity (often wrongly described as apathy) is the logical and subtle response, and information transfer is thereby constrained.

Modern adult education movements concentrate on developing people's understanding of the context within which they live and their own power to take action to control it. The Brazilian educator Paolo Freire is a seminal contributor in this field. Skill development ("training") is often an important component of that overall process, engaged in as a result of decisions made after careful consideration of goals. Rather than concentrating on the realm of supposedly rational and objective knowledge (the traditional process of education), modern approaches stress the importance of including the whole person and the whole social-environmental context. The aim is to get away from the straitjacket of (classical) positivism by emphasizing the importance of studying values as well as facts and realizing that they are often intimately related, contrary to conventional mythology. Not surprisingly, this approach is under threat because it often challenges the status quo, especially entrenched political-economic power structures.

Education does not consist of filling up empty vessels. Learning is a creative and interactive process in which teacher and learner participate and often exchange places. In many situations, people learn better in groups than on their own. Group activity also has the advantage that learners benefit from several points of view, with each person assisting others to get away from the narrowness of the single-discipline approach and move toward a multidisciplinary synthesis.

It is not only politicians and their advisers who should be environmentally aware and educated. Citizens who have the knowledge, skills, and motives to cope with environmental needs will support the call for a healthier, cleaner earth.[13] Environmental adult education works to achieve the transformation that is essential if we are collectively to achieve sustainable development.[14]

One of my aims in this chapter is briefly to expose some working educational models to help us design structures to bring out the wisdom that I am convinced is there in our societies, ready and waiting to be used. I see social tools, especially adult education, as central to the successful application of such models.[15]

Gaming as a Tool for Designing Sustainable Development Paths

Dennis Meadows, in analyzing the changes required to bring society's behavior more into line with the needs of sustainable development, has suggested that "the need is for new patterns of behavior that reflect longer time horizons, more sophistication about the dynamics of complex systems, and greater mastery of communication skills involved in analysis, negotiation, compromise and planning."[16]

Well-designed operational games can be extremely helpful in this respect. Such games range from simple pencil-and-paper exercises to computer-simulated economies and can take from a few minutes to hours or days.[17] Most are relatively inexpensive, especially for educational institutions. All need competent facilitators.

Science and Folk Knowledge

Science has come to be the province of the expert and is usually seen as closed to "ordinary" people. Yet it has often been noted that in practice, the observations of ordinary people are just as tenable, factual, and testable as those of the scientist.[18] Folk knowledge, although seldom formal, in practice uses processes of testing and search that often differ little from those used by the scholarly community. Often taking a long time to develop, folk knowledge can encompass a whole system understanding that may be denied to scientists who come in and sample what they see but do not take time to understand fully.

The Environmental Reality of Indigenous Peoples

Cultural anthropologists and human ecologists have long known that among indigenous societies, cultural and religious rituals are often interwoven with the natural cycles of the environment and contain embedded understandings that come out of generations of experience in the local ecosystems. Indigenous peoples often have an enormous, irreplaceable fund of knowledge about their environment and what they can and cannot do in it.[19] As an example, the Maori of Aotearoa–New Zealand[20] have a world view and an understanding about their origins and relationship with the natural world that differs markedly from that of more recent settlers in that country.[21] Indigenous peoples of many other countries have related wisdom.[22]

For the Maori, belief in *mauri*, the life force of the natural world, and the need for its protection exerted a real influence over economic affairs. Mauri fostered an atmosphere of respect and fear obviating deliberate destruction of essential resources. Through these and other concepts, such as the treatment of resources as *taonga*, or treasures, regulation of people's conduct toward their natural environment was achieved. Included in Maori views are the familiar notion of the wise use of resources and the maintenance of the health of a resource. Sustainability and the need to preserve options for future generations are also recognized. A treasure is of value not just because of its usefulness to humankind but also for its own sake. Incorporating a spiritual component extends the concept of a resource beyond that encompassed by conventional Western economic understanding. The term is consistent with intrinsic values—values inherent within the environment but outside the human condition.

The social structures of the Maori are built on a network of shared responsibilities and group (tribal or subtribal) ownership of resources such as land. They owe little to behavior patterns, such as individual ownership of land, of the type promoted by settler colonial structures. Many settlers now regard the Maori perspective as exposing valuable options for twenty-first-century policies, especially in the context of stewardship of environmental resources.[23]

Resources are gifts from the past with both physical and spiritual significance.[24] The present generation has a responsibility to preserve them and

pass them on to the future unharmed. *One may not sell them; they are sacred.*
This is because all treasures possess the ethos of the Creator Being. This
concept does not exist meaningfully outside a collective context.[25, 26] Tribal
stewardship is totally different from conventional individualistic ownership,
especially land tenure, which is nevertheless the keystone of the dominant
Western legal and economic systems.

Where the environment is concerned, nature's laws are paramount. But in
the Western cultural tradition of the past century or two, nature has been
relegated to a back seat. In Western societies, it is one of the signs of our
times that men (strongly led, in many cases, by women) are now beginning
to see the need for a new way of thinking about our place in the global ecosystem. Society as a whole, working in a *participatory* manner, is the place to
do it. The group context and the concept of gifting[27, 28] also allow consideration of environmental and intergenerational issues, largely excluded or trivialized by the individualistic approach.

ADULT EDUCATION MODELS

Thomas Jefferson (1743–1826) had some useful comments in the context of
adult education: "I know of no safe depository of the ultimate power of society but the people themselves; and if we think them not enlightened enough
to exercise their control with a wholesome discretion, the remedy is not to
take it from them but to inform their discretion by education."[29] But adult
education of this type ("informing their discretion") does not mean top-down
instruction! To understand this point, we need to distinguish among the formal education system (schools and institutions); the informal education system (e.g., commercial advertising); and the nonformal system, in which
people (mainly adults) set their own agendas and learn with others, inviting
experts to participate as guests.[30]

The latter is clearly a "bottom-up" process. Many environmental and citizens' organizations belong in this category. A process of learning involving
development of personal understanding in people's economic, political, cultural, and social lives, such as is promoted by nonformal education, enables
people to perceive needs that are closer to their deeper selves.[31] Such a process is, I argue, more likely to contribute to social harmony, justice, and stability.

In 1985, at UNESCO's Fourth International Conference on Adult Education in Paris, a "Right to Learn" statement was agreed on. This statement
starts:

The right to learn is:
* the right to read and write;
* the right to question and analyze;
* the right to imagine and create;
* the right to read one's own world and to write history;
* the right to have access to educational resources;
* the right to develop individual and collective skills.

But the right to learn is not only an instrument of economic development; it must be recognized as one of the fundamental rights. The act of learning, lying as it does at the heart of all educational activity, changes human beings from objects at the mercy of events to subjects who create their own history.[32]

Participation in policy development therefore involves much more than conducting stage-managed, government-controlled exercises. It means devolving power to people, individually and collectively, to think and question and make decisions on matters that affect them and theirs. For that reason, what is commonly termed adult education may be better called "adult transformation," in that its aim is commitment and action.[33] The place of experts in such situations is that of partners who gift their knowledge and information to support people and groups who have set their own priorities. That is not a naive, unrealistic idea—it happens everywhere already, and many models are available. The main problems in its development are institutional and political.[34]

People and groups must insist on reclaiming some of their power and information and must demand the responsibility for creating their own futures, jointly with others. Abilities to see models for what they are and critically examine their logical bases are the key skills to be learned by people who wish to take an active part in building policies in a participatory democracy. Without such a sociopolitical structure, ideologies will remain in control. Only a broadly conceived program of adult education, especially nonformal education, seems capable of achieving such skills.

Participatory Research

Rajesh Tandon describes participatory research thus:

> There is a preconceived idea that most people can't think for themselves and analyze a situation. Those who think that way take upon themselves the arbitrary responsibility of thinking for other people. An elite class of people has appropriated to itself the role of thinkers for others. It has legitimated certain behavior,

training, qualification and external symbols, to determine whether what you do is research or not. This act has increasingly controlled the definition of knowledge. What is the printed word is equated with knowledge.

We believe people have knowledge, information, analysis, insight, which may not be "legitimated knowledge." One of the important characteristics of participatory research is its recognition and validation of popular knowledge, which has been systematically denied in the interests of the elite class that calls itself the knowledge providers.[35] This is challenging the very basis of what is knowledge, and who has the capability to produce knowledge.

Knowledge is also the most powerful method of control, and as people begin to get involved in their own research, investigation and analysis, they begin to discover themselves, their own collective sense of "we can do it." It has a great mobilizing effect.[36]

Folkeoplysning—Danish General Adult Education

Folkeoplysning is a difficult word to translate into English because it is primarily an attitude of mind. The first part of the word, *folke,* refers to the cultural tradition and national identity of the people. The second part, *oplysning,* meaning "enlightenment or clarification," expands its meaning into the creation of cultural understanding. Folkeoplysning is intimately involved with liberty, in that self-management and responsibility are of vital importance for the Danish democratic system:

> Folkeoplysning demands active participation from everybody. No one can determine the precise content of it. But it appears through communication. It is a common matter with no limits involving and clasping the one who takes an interest in it. The approach is subjective and participatory—not detached and informative. It is characteristic that even the highest ranking civil servants within the educational world speak of folkeoplysning in the first person plural.[37]

In 1983, the Danish Parliament established the Danish Research and Development Centre for Adult Education as a means to strengthen the opportunities of the population to predict, influence, and adjust to social changes. The Centre is funded by government and functions as a private foundation. Its functions include giving advice on new projects in general and adult education, establishing an information center, and collating and analyzing experiences of the projects on a nationwide basis. From this base, the government has access to a great deal of well-researched and well-informed opinion from all in the community who wish to express it.

The Highlander Model of Adult Education in Tennessee

The Highlander Research and Education Center of New Market, Tennessee, was founded in 1932. It provides a resource base for learning and education:

> [The Highlander Center] seeks to create educational experiences that empower people to take a democratic leadership towards fundamental change. . . . We bring people together to learn from each other. By sharing experience, we realize that we are not alone. . . . Through our participatory research and cultural program we seek to affirm and document the knowledge, concerns, and struggles of the people with whom we work. Highlander staff persons also develop and conduct workshops across the region, link communities grappling with common issues and provide other education assistance in the field. . . . The power of the Highlander experience is the strength that grows within the souls of people, working together, as they analyze and confirm their own experiences and draw upon their understanding to contribute to fundamental change. [38]

The Highlander Center's funding comes from a range of philanthropic institutions and from participants, community groups, and unions. Its early activities centered on civil rights and social justice. In recent years, it has been closely associated with people who are involved in, or are victims of, environmental pollution in the southeastern United States. Participants have learned, for example, that environmental issues are also social justice issues. [39]

Instead of relying on conventional, individualistic, expert-based modes of inquiry, approaches based on participatory research have been developed. These range from systematizing and validating people's own knowledge in participatory modes of inquiry to attempting to develop an approach to science that is responsive to people's needs and accountable to their oversight. [40]

The Sarvodaya Shramadana Movement of Sri Lanka

The word "Sarvodaya" combines the words *sarva* ("all") and *udaya* ("awakening") into one word that means "the awakening of all." In the Sarvodaya concept of development, these combine to set in motion a process that leads to the harnessing of human potential and natural resources for individual and collective welfare. In the context of Sarvodaya, spiritual, moral, and cultural awakening in the individual are essential for the spiritual, moral, cultural, social, political, and economic development of the person, family unit, and village or urban community. [41] Sarvodaya has "an uncompromising insistence on a form of development which is wholly indigenous, [and] which comes entirely out of the perceptions of the village community."[42] As A. T. Ariyaratne points out:

> Sarvodaya did not believe in getting people to participate in activities not decided upon by themselves. The kind of solicited participation in programs decided upon by political or bureaucratic elites, may, at best, succeed in mobilizing people by offering them various piecemeal incentives. But, that kind of mobilization does not lead to the organization of people for a more equitable kind of total development. Sarvodaya always aimed at organizing people based on goals and programs which they themselves defined, planned and understood, and of course, with the help of those who had the appropriate technological knowledge. It is a kind of organized and intelligible participation by people.[43]

In the environmental context, "Sarvodaya . . . stands for people oriented development based on people's power to ensure sustainable development for the present generation while conserving non-renewable resources to meet the needs of countless generations yet unborn."[44]

At present, 8,000 rural and urban communities out of 23,000 in Sri Lanka participate in the Sarvodaya program.[45] This, above all, shows both that this is not a small movement and that it has been markedly successful in achieving many of its aims. Funding for Sarvodaya comes mainly from international nongovernment aid agencies, with some funds from the local and community levels.

There are many other models that can give valuable help to societies seeking to move toward sustainable development.[46]

GOVERNMENTS, SUSTAINABILITY, AND GENERAL ADULT EDUCATION

The ecological economics of sustainability demands that structural changes be made in society. Accurate identification of these changes involves nurturing the collective, social dimension of people's lives. Since that dimension is fundamental to the workings of a participatory democracy, the process should have access to government resources. But it is a prerequisite that the process of collective activity is first recognized by government, whose function in a democracy is, after all, to serve the people.

The question then arises, How do we name the collective dimension in an industrial, individualistic, political-economic framework? One way of doing so is to determine people's hopes and aspirations by asking questions such as the following:

- What do you want to pass on to the next generation?
- What sustains you in difficulties?
- Where is the pain for you?[47]

This is an interpretive, not a value-free, exercise. It involves people saying what they want, from a collective position in which they learn from one another. It is a challenge for adult education to help elucidate the answers, since in a context such as this it is not possible to ask a simple question and get a simple answer, directly. The Danish, Highlander, and Sarvodaya models indicate ways in which this might be done, and there are many more. Basically, they require that people in communities be able to gain access to information and resources that will enable them to take an informed part in debates on public issues. In practice, it often means the involvement of research and education centers with technical and other advisory capabilities.

Attitudes toward "experts" and "professionals" are important in these processes. The Danish process of folkeoplysning, for example, can be blocked if people (especially experts) do not share what they know. In trying to develop a participatory democracy, it is often difficult to cope with the egos of experts and politicians and prevent their taking over the learning process. On the other hand, there is also the question of how to ensure that those professionals who share knowledge willingly are given adequate recognition and reward.

Perhaps not surprisingly, the collective-community dimension of people's lives is being steadily, and often deliberately, undermined by agents of the individualist market economic ideology. It is also eroded by totalitarian governments of both left and right. But in a situation such as the present, in which the likely penalties for both people and societies of maintaining present unsustainable structures are very high, another way forward must be identified. I see the only democratic option to be the identification and harnessing of people's wisdom (from all cultures) in addressing the major questions that face us.

It is quite unrealistic to rely on market or similar narrow mechanisms to do the job. The task is complex, requiring a combination of people's wisdom and modern systems science. Many people believe it can be done through a program of participatory adult education. As a first step, what is needed is recognition of the existence of people's wisdom plus a commitment of resources to enable the job to be done.

Conclusion

I START THIS final chapter with salutary words from the naturalist Gerald Durrell:

> Real love and respect for nature—for Gaia, or Mother Earth, or whatever name anyone gives to her spiritual form—can only lead to greater understanding of her, and indeed of ourselves, for we are just as much a part of her as every sparrow, every tree and every waterfall. Gandhi is supposed to have said that some people are so poor that God can only appear to them in the form of bread. If we can understand that bread comes from grain, which comes from plants, which come from soil, water, air, light and people's energies in the fields, then what so desperately needs to be done to save the world and all living things will follow quite naturally.[1]

NEW SCIENTIFIC TOOLS

In rereading what I have written in the previous chapters, I realize that some readers may conclude that all I have done is contribute some new tools to the citizen's and policymaker's tool kits and show how crude and blunt many of the existing tools are. To be honest, that was indeed my main purpose when I started to write. Energy and economic policies cannot stand alone; they must be parts of a country's overall social-political-environmental policy.

Instead of always reacting to effects, we need to start scrutinizing the system in which we live to discover causes and understand linkages and feedbacks. The separate perceptions of ecology, physics, and the marketplace can never incorporate the full complexity of the issues.[2] But, as Lindsay Gow warns: "The integration of economic, social and environmental policy will not be successful if in practice, integration just means assimilation of some perspectives into a dominant one, be it economics or anything else. True integration must be in the nature of a partnership between the perspectives."[3]

But at the same time, I also hope to have placed the tools I describe within a wider context than that within which the old tools were conceived and used. Thermodynamics is the physics of economic value, and it underlies everything that happens in the real world, even if it only imposes constraints. Systems thinking helps us understand the linkages and feedbacks that act within these constraints. What comes out of the view I have exposed is that only when the entire physical system—global environment, local ecosystems, nonrenewable resources, and humanity—is seen as a dynamic whole, now and in the future, can one gain a valid understanding of some of its properties. To look at the energy sector alone, or the economy alone, or the environment alone, is to miss seeing the wood because one is seeing only the trees. (Most markets see only the sawlogs!)

LIMITS

Robert Costanza, in discussing ecological economics, suggests:

> Issues of sustainability are ultimately issues about limits. If economic growth is sustainable indefinitely by technology, then all environmental problems can (in theory at least) be fixed technologically. Issues of equity and distribution (between subgroups and generations of our species and between our species and others) are also issues of limits. We do not have to worry so much about how an expanding pie is divided, but a constant or shrinking pie presents real problems. Finally, dealing with uncertainty about limits is the fundamental issue. If we are unsure about future limits the prudent course is to assume they exist. One does not run blindly through a dark landscape that may contain crevasses. One assumes they are there and goes gingerly and with eyes wide open, at least until one can see a little better.[4]

There are indeed limits to economic growth insofar as the use of material resources from the environment and the ability to dispose of wastes are concerned.

Thus, in thinking about the future, we have the physical imperative of sustainability as an overall economic and ecological goal for humanity. We also must move to a way of thinking about social policymaking that encompasses more than present-day economics, valuable as it is.[5] As I have mentioned before, a useful criterion is that of "the moral commonsense of the ecologically informed person."[6]

CHANGES IN SOCIETY

The dominant language of public discourse today is individualistic and utilitarian, with no acknowledgment of the existence of a social fabric.[7] In accepting the biophysical systems foundations of ecological economics, we face ideas of infrastructures and hierarchies of levels of freedom, each constrained in its power to influence the overall structure. Political freedom is not the same as economic freedom, and property rights are not absolute. Political structures are no more sacrosanct in this new world view than economic ones.

The economist Hazel Henderson points out:

> It is less a matter of whether a country is centrally planned, mixed (as most are) or capitalistic, since the effects of the underlying industrial model are similar, but more a matter of whether societies are . . . designed to incorporate feedback at every level of decision-making, from the family and community to the provincial and national levels, from those people affected by the decisions.[8]

My view of the future is not an easy one in that I have not presented a recipe that can be used to cook up new policies. To do so would go against everything I believe in about a participatory democracy. My part is not to develop policy options but to support people and groups who attempt to do so. I enter the decision-making process not as an expert but as a partner. I hope I have the humility to live up to my ideals!

A STRAW MAN?

Some economists, in particular, may come to the conclusion that all I have done is set up an economic straw man, which I have then knocked down. This is not really true. Economists know full well that many of their theoretical models are based on foundations of little strength. In practice, however, they have often built vast logical structures on those poor foundations, ignoring the weakness of the resultant edifices. Those who use economic tools, or who accept advice originating from economic analyses, are often so far removed from the foundations that they fail to realize their inadequacy.

Nevertheless, I would make the point again, as I have in several places in this book, that conventional economics has generally served human societies well over the past century. But we have new problems that require a new economics. The methods of conventional economics are often very useful, despite their weaknesses, but they should never be used outside the strict confines of their validity. The same goes for all other decision-making tools, whether of the social, natural, or physical sciences. The central point is that many forms of growth cost more than they are worth, and a sustainable economy's optimum size is much less than its (unsustainable) maximum possible size.

NEW SOCIAL TOOLS

We already have a range of new tools of science, and it is time to develop the ecological economics of sustainability. This process will be easier from the technical point of view than from the political. Past ways of thinking are deeply ingrained in our elected (and nonelected) decision makers, and they will take time to disappear. But go they must, or society and nature as we know them will soon cease to exist. Some forms of life will still go on, but unless we develop social structures that acknowledge the reality of our dependence on the physical environment, human life will become nastier and more brutish, in the debris of a civilization of affluence and waste that proved unsustainable.

The world is not a grand machine but a place of incredible complexity in which nature can run her own affairs, as she did for the billions of years before humans appeared on the scene. But we also know that if we push nature too far, she may respond with violence or may suddenly and disastrously collapse.[9] Life on earth is fragile.

In such a context, it is abundantly clear that a degree of pessimism is likely to be the most useful basis for looking at the future. The irreversible outcomes of technologically optimistic policies are likely to be much more severe than the results of a mildly overcautious approach.

My overpowering feeling is that the most important thing for people and communities is to gain the power to understand what is going on so that they can make their own choices as to what they want in the future. It is the *way of thinking* that is paramount. Technicians such as engineers and economists can always be found to make and operate tools, but without a clear image of what is wanted, the tools will be used to construct things that do not meet the needs of the users. People must have the power to invent the future for themselves and for others, living and not yet born, in a way that honors the efforts of those generations who have gone before us and on whose shoulders we stand today.

NEW IMAGES

An educationalist suggested recently:

> Basically, what I am suggesting is that the time has come for human society consciously to shift away from power as force to power as energy; to shift from a society where many individuals gain their sense of self-esteem from their ability to dominate the earth and other people, to a society where self-esteem is seen to be properly centered in the ability to nurture the environment and co-operate with other people; to shift from coercion and control to learning and love as the models of adult behavior to which we aspire. Such a shift is not some sort of idiot idealism, the unrealistic vision of ivory-tower theorists. Increasingly, even self-identified conservatives are perceiving this shift as essential to our survival—in business, in bureaucracies, as nations, as a species. [10]

In such a context, the ideas of Ivan Illich on conviviality [11] or those of Herman Daly and John Cobb, Jr., on the person-in-community [12] deserve serious attention.

VALUES

We need to answer the following questions:

- What are our values?
- What are our roots?
- What sustains us?
- What do we want to pass on to our grandchildren?

When we have answered these questions, we will be able to look with reasonably clear eyes at what faces us. If our value system is good, everything else that stems from it—economics, engineering, law, [13] trade policy, [14] and so on—will also be good.

If our value system is good, we will cease to be part of the problem. We can then be freed to participate in the healing of a suffering biosphere. Our service to nature will be our commitment to life and its enhancement wherever it may be, not just in the purely human sphere of activity. We will love and serve the One who cares about the grasses of the field and the fall of a sparrow. That view goes far beyond the view that nature is merely a stage on which the human drama is acted out.[15]

The philosophies, sciences, and biblical understandings of the past three centuries are all potentially enemies of the future. They can, if we let them, blind us to our real oneness with the natural world and to our obligations to it. They have set us on a course that will lead to catastrophe for humans as well as other creatures if we do not see the error of our ways. We are treating the earth as if we had a spare one parked alongside, ready for us to step onto!

Present-day science, especially ecology and thermodynamics, supports the view that the world must be seen as a whole, not as little parts separated from one another. It provides tools that can help us look at the future through new spectacles, if we give them a chance. But we often confuse what science can tell us with what it cannot.

A Maori elder told a story at a gathering in Aotearoa–New Zealand recently. He used a twig from a karaka tree as his example:

> Take a leaf. Look closely. . . . With one set of eyes it has a shiny exterior, known in scientific terms as a waxy cuticle. The cuticle stops water from evaporating too fast and allows transpiration under the waxy cuticle. Underneath is the upper epidermis, the outermost layer of cells where chlorophyll . . . is produced. Looking through a microscope you may see further through to the spongy mesophyll— the inner leaf tissue—and the lower epidermis and eventually the leaf hairs of the plant. The end result of understanding, and remembering the scientific make-up of a leaf may be attaining school certificate, or its . . . equivalent.
> Yet seen through another set of eyes, the leaf of a karaka tree is not just part of a tree, but one of the children of Tane (god of the forest). The sides of a leaf are different, light and dark, signifying life and death. There is no way the two can be differentiated—a leaf cannot be peeled apart revealing two separate entities.[16]

The whole plant has a meaning that is symbolic as well as physical. Many people of Western cultural origins have no difficulty with that image, but our schooling has added the scientific perception to our natural feelings about the wonder and beauty of nature. What often happens is that we allow the scientific viewpoint to overcome our sense of wonder. This is why other cultures can help us reclaim, through metaphor and image, what we may have forgotten.

Some people see their lives as self-made or the product of human society alone. But it is also possible to see life as a gift of the total evolutionary creation process. If we see ourselves in this way, it is appropriate for us to acknowledge the roles of stewardship and servanthood. Perhaps when there is a conflict between the demands of the environment and those of the marketplace, we should give the benefit of the doubt to the Almighty rather than to the almighty dollar. The fitting action in that case is to serve the creation process by helping in its inclusive work.[17]

We could strive to contribute to the progress of growth of life in all its diversity of forms. We might begin with human life, but we must not limit ourselves to it. "Think globally, act locally . . . and analyze regionally" is a good motto.[18] If we think in terms of planet Earth, we get a sense of what is appropriate for us to work for, at our local level,[19] while seeing ourselves clearly in the context of our region. As Lester Brown, Sandra Postel, and Christopher Flavin comment:

> With the ending of the cold war and the fading of ideological barriers, an opportunity has opened to build a new world upon the foundations of peace. A sustainable economy represents nothing less than a higher social order—one as concerned with future generations as with our own, and more focused on the health of the planet and the poor than on material acquisitions and military might. While it is a fundamentally new endeavor, with many uncertainties, it is far less risky than continuing with business as usual.[20]

If reality involves an inclusive world view far beyond the narrow view that some humans have of themselves, there is a real value to the variety of life that we see in the global ecosystem. Our single-minded, callous disregard of the values of the whole of creation for the sake of the price of some of its parts is a modern phenomenon. Many of us feel that it both violates and desecrates creation.

Chief Seattle, a North American Indian, pointed out in 1854 that "to harm the earth is to heap contempt on its Creator." We are all part of the whole of nature, whether we like it or not. It is high time for us to acknowledge our part in the continuing sacrament of creation; we do not exist outside that relationship. Among our other responsibilities is that of using only what we need from nature, and minimizing damage to her, because both she and we are parts of creation.

Appendix

The Venice Declaration

A SYMPOSIUM TITLED "Science and the Boundaries of Knowledge: The Prologue of Our Cultural Past," organized by UNESCO in collaboration with the Giorgio Cini Foundation, was held in Venice March 3–7, 1986. At its conclusion, the participants, "in a spirit of openmindedness and enquiry concerning today's values, . . . agreed on the following points."[1] I reproduce them here because I believe they support my claims about the need to see the world from a much wider perspective than is possible from either the conventional political-economic viewpoint or the classical scientific viewpoint.

1. We are witnessing a very important revolution in the field of science brought about by basic science (in particular by developments in physics and biology), by the upheavals it has wrought in logic, in epistemology and in everyday life through its technological applications. We note at the same time, however, a significant gap between a new world view emerging from the study of natural systems and the values that continue to prevail in philosophy, in the human and social sciences and in the life of modern society, values largely based on mechanistic determinism, positivism, or nihilism. We believe that this discrepancy is harmful and indeed dangerous for the very survival of our species.

2. Scientific knowledge, on its own internal impetus, has reached the point where it can begin a dialogue with other forms of knowledge. In this sense, and while recognizing the fundamental differences between Science and Tradition, we see them as complementary rather than in contradiction. This new and mutually enriching exchange between science and the different

traditions of the world opens the door to a new vision of humanity, and even to a new rationalism, which could lead to a new metaphysical perspective.

3. While not wishing to attempt a global approach, nor to establish a closed system of thought, nor to invent a new utopia, we recognize the pressing need for truly transdisciplinary research through a dynamic exchange between the natural sciences, the social sciences, art and tradition. It could be said that this transdisciplinary mode is inherent in our brain through the dynamic interaction of its two hemispheres. Joint investigation of nature and of the imagination, of the universe and of [humanity], might thus bring us closer to reality and enable us better to meet the various challenges of our time.

4. The conventional way of teaching science by a linear presentation of knowledge masks the divorce between today's science and world views which are outdated. We stress the need for new educational methods to take into account current scientific progress, now coming into harmony with the great cultural traditions, the preservation and in-depth study of which appear essential. UNESCO would be the appropriate organization to promote such ideas.

5. The challenges of our time—the risk of destruction of our species, the impact of data processing, the implications of genetics, etc.—throw a new light on the social responsibilities of the scientific community, both in the initiation and application of research. Although scientists may have no control over the applications of their own discoveries, they must not remain passive when confronted with the haphazard use of what they have discovered. It is our view that the magnitude of today's challenges requires, on the one hand, a reliable and steady flow of information to the public, and, on the other hand, the establishment of multi- and transdisciplinary mechanisms for the guidance and even the carrying out of decision-making.

6. We hope that Unesco will consider this encounter as a starting point and will encourage further reflexion in a spirit of transdisciplinarity and universality.

Notes

CHAPTER 1—ENERGY IN NATURE

1. I use the word "man" deliberately, here and in some other parts of this book, to draw attention to its common use, which reflects a narrow, male, paternalistic viewpoint not shared by at least half of humanity.
2. In this book, the term "billion" indicates the American billion, which is a thousand million.
3. Matter and energy are known to be interconvertible, as shown by Einstein in his famous relationship $E = mc^2$, where E is energy, m is mass, and c is the speed of light.
4. Clark 1989, 135.
5. In the Gaia hypothesis, the atmosphere is seen as a self-regulating "superorganism" that maintains its chemical composition by virtue of the life processes within it.
6. Regrettably, I have to acknowledge that the choices that face us are mainly related to the question of whether to destroy parts of nature. We have no power to recreate her.
7. Baines and Smith 1982, app. 1.
8. The numbers do not add up exactly to 100 percent because of rounding errors.
9. This is a very generalized argument, since some plants (e.g., trees) continue growing throughout most of their life, albeit at a declining rate in later years. Others undergo rapid growth in the later stages of life, when they flower and die. Nevertheless, the general relationship holds, in principle.
10. Leopold 1987, 214, 216.
11. See, for example, Leopold 1987, 214.
12. Humans tend to regard themselves as being at the apex of the pyramid, but given the destructive behavior of many humans, it behooves us to see this position

with a degree of humility and not take it to indicate freedom to abuse the power it gives.

13. See Rifkin 1981, 81.
14. See, for example, Clark 1989.
15. Vitousek et al. 1986; Brown, Postel, and Flavin 1991, 83.
16. See, for example, Odum and Odum 1976, 39.
17. Water is an essential medium for plant and animal life, but it does not supply energy as such. It is, however, the medium in which most life-supporting activities take place.
18. See, for example, Clark 1989.
19. Trace elements appear to be an exception to this energy-based argument, but they too can be assessed in embodied energy terms—for example, via the energy required to supply them by other means.
20. The growth dynamics are described by the general equation $N_t = N_0 e^{rt}[K - N_{t-1}/K]$. r-selectionist behavior is dominated by the rate r, whereas k-selectionist behavior is dominated by the constant k.
21. See, for example, Odum 1988.
22. An exception is minute amounts of meteoritic matter that enter the earth's atmosphere.
23. Lovelock 1979.
24. Gleick 1988, 279; Davies 1989, 131.

CHAPTER 2—THE SCIENTIFIC WORLD VIEW

1. Sir Karl Popper, "Conjectures and Refutations," quoted in Cohen and Cohen 1980, 266, no. 16.
2. I am indebted to D. R. Murdoch for some of this explanation.
3. Ravetz 1990.
4. Rutter and Jones 1983, 7; see also Hammond et al. 1983.
5. Zukav 1982.
6. Sir Karl Popper, *The Logic of Scientific Discovery,* chap. 1, sec. vi, quoted in Cohen and Cohen 1980, no. 18, 266–67.
7. Kuhn 1962.
8. Maxwell and Randall 1989.
9. Whitehead 1929, 11—see Daly 1991, 281.
10. Daly 1991, 280.
11. Ibid., 281.
12. Andreski 1972. See also Hicks 1980.
13. Smith 1980, 215.
14. Gardner 1981.
15. Root-Berstein 1991.
16. Toffler 1985.
17. Quoted in Shallis 1984, 154.
18. Quoted by Waring 1988, on the dedication page.

19. Shallis 1984, 152.
20. Checkland 1981.

CHAPTER 3—ENERGY—A SCIENTIFIC PERSPECTIVE

1. A small amount of matter is also lost, converted by nuclear processes into energy.
2. Add 273 to the Celsius value to get the Kelvin temperature. Thus, 273 degrees Kelvin is 0 degrees Celsius.
3. This point applies to the use of ocean energy for conventional work processes in human society. The contribution of the energy stored in the oceans to the atmospheric "heat engine" that drives climate and weather is, of course, another thing altogether.
4. This terminology avoids the necessity of writing a lot of zeros when dealing with large numbers. Thus, the number 10^3 means 1,000: a one with three zeros following. The superscript gives the number of zeros after the one.
5. Most fuels (coal, oil, gas, wood, and so on) contain hydrogen as well as carbon; therefore, water (H_2O) is one of the products formed when the fuel is burned. The *gross* (or *higher*) calorific value of a fuel is determined by including the energy given up by the gaseous water (i.e., steam) when it condenses to liquid water. The *net* (or *lower*) calorific value assumes that the energy in the water is not recovered. The net calorific value is of more practical use. In general, the difference between net and gross calorific values is of the order of 6 to 8 percent for liquid fuels, 10 percent for gaseous fuels, and (because of the wide variation in hydrogen contents) 2 to 15 percent for coals (see, for example, Baines 1984).
6. Baines 1984.
7. The energy of hot, fast-moving exhaust gas is in fact used in some engines to run auxiliary machinery such as a turbocharger. This process simply intercepts the exhaust flow to squeeze a little more work from it rather than letting it all flow directly out the exhaust pipe.
8. See, for example, Ehrlich, Ehrlich, and Holdren 1977; also Daly 1980a, 44.
9. Rees 1990.
10. One common process that appears to violate the second law is the action of a refrigerator, in which heat clearly flows from the colder body (the inside) to the hotter body (the outside). But this flow of heat does not occur *of itself*. Energy (usually electricity but sometimes gas or kerosene) must be supplied to the refrigerator in order to run it. If this external energy supply is turned off, the colder interior soon heats up to the same temperature as the surroundings; the law has not been contravened.
11. The term "irreversible" means that a process is not perfectly reversible. The fact that a process may be reversed by the use of more energy than was released by the process in the first place does not mean it is *perfectly* reversible. In most thermodynamics, use of the word "reversible" implies perfect reversibility.

12. An exception, mentioned in chapter 1, is a tiny amount of mass in the form of meteoritic debris.
13. Although, of course, all of the sun's radiation is eventually dissipated into deep space.
14. I would make the point, however, that this is really an analogy. The thermodynamics of order and disorder are strictly applicable only under equilibrium conditions. In real societies, things are always far from equilibrium, and the relationship between entropy production and changes in structure is complex and situation specific (see, for example, O'Connor 1991a).
15. Ayres 1988; Rees 1990, 4.
16. England 1990.
17. See, for example, Haavelmo and Hansen 1991, 32.

CHAPTER 4—THE POLITICAL-ECONOMIC WORLD VIEW

1. Perrings 1987, 3.
2. Heilbroner 1980; Galbraith 1977.
3. Colby 1990.
4. "Population, when unchecked, increases in a geometrical ratio. Subsistence only increases in an arithmetical ratio" (Malthus 1798).
5. Heilbroner 1980.
6. Waring 1988.
7. Heilbroner 1980; Galbraith 1977.
8. Friedman and Friedman 1981–82, 1979.
9. Hueting 1990a.
10. I am indebted to John Sterman of Massachusetts Institute of Technology for material on these and related questions. (See Sterman 1990a.)
11. Friedman and Friedman 1981–82.
12. From a presentation by Herman Daly (an informal account of the presentation appears in *Balaton Bulletin*, no. 25:9 [October 1990]). See also Costanza 1991a, 72.
13. Perrings 1987, 152.
14. This a central assumption in conventional (neoclassical) economic theory, but as I explain in later chapters, it is by no means valid in practice.
15. Posner 1973; Turvey 1968.
16. Perrings 1987, xi.
17. The entropy of food-processed mush is greater than that of the components from which it has been produced.
18. Rutherford 1979, 119.
19. For businesses under financial stress, the rate may be closer to 50 to 100 percent, reflecting the requirement for a rapid (one- or two-year) payback for capital investment.
20. Pearce, Markandya, and Barbier 1989, 143.
21. Hueting 1991.

22. O'Connor 1991a.
23. Note that GDP—gross domestic product—is closely related to GNP and is usually within a few percentage points of the value of GNP.
24. See, for example, Goldemberg et al. 1988.
25. Patterson 1989; Bertram 1990.
26. Pearce 1975.
27. Whether the present generation should impose the inevitable burden of higher prices and costly transitions to alternative fuels on future generations sooner rather than later is an ethical question.
28. Herman Daly, in Goodland, Daly, and El Serafy 1991, 23.
29. Goodwin 1991.
30. Daly and Cobb 1989.
31. Lutz and Lux 1988, chap. 9.
32. Quoted in Galbraith 1973.
33. Pen 1990.

CHAPTER 5—THE SYSTEMS APPROACH

1. Checkland 1981.
2. Ellul 1964. Quoted in Checkland 1981, 145.
3. I am indebted to G. A. Britton for some of the information used here.
4. I would make the point, however, that learning and love involve positive feedbacks with very desirable stabilizing characteristics!
5. These self-regulatory functions are achieved not by the use of sensors and controllers, as in a hard system, but by subtle and powerful links and feedbacks achieving communication and control within the ecosystem.
6. Arthur 1990.
7. Norton 1990.
8. Sterman 1990a.
9. Sandelin 1983.
10. Pearce, Markandya, and Barbier 1989, 40.
11. Prigogine and Stengers 1985, 176.
12. Perrings 1987; England 1990.
13. Ray 1990; Leggett 1990; Block 1990.
14. O'Connor 1991a.
15. Although the mathematics of the two approaches are very similar, there is no evidence that the underlying phenomena themselves are the same. See, for example, O'Connor 1991a.
16. England 1990.
17. Sandelin 1983, 1985.
18. Ravetz 1990.
19. Gowdy 1991.
20. Daly 1980a, 12.

CHAPTER 6—THE BIOPHYSICAL SYSTEMS WORLD VIEW

1. Strictly speaking, we should use energy *availability*, according to the second law of thermodynamics. In practice, we usually use the *enthalpy*, or heat equivalent, as a first-law approximation.
2. O'Connor 1989, 1991a.
3. See, for example, Peet and Baines 1986 and IFIAS 1974.
4. Most of the pioneering work in this area was done by C. W. Bullard, Bruce Hannon, and R. A. Herendeen at the Center for Advanced Computation of the University of Illinois. See, for example, Bullard and Herendeen 1975; Bullard, Penner, and Pilati 1976; Herendeen 1978; and Baines and Peet 1989.
5. Input-output data are usually expressed in terms of the energy requirement of output of an economic sector (e.g., as megajoules per dollar of output).
6. Patterson 1983.
7. Gilliland 1977.
8. Typical criteria are as follows: the gross energy requirement (GER) of the flow E is $(G + F)$; the energy requirement of energy (ERE) is $(G + F)/E$; the net energy yield (NEY) is $(E - F)$; the energy yield ratio (EYR) is (E/F); the energy return on investment (EROI) is (G/F). GER and ERE are discussed in Slesser 1978. NEY and EYR are discussed in Odum and Odum 1976, chap. 6. EROI is used in Cleveland et al. 1984. A more comprehensive treatment is in Hall, Cleveland, and Kaufmann 1986. Further treatment is in Gever et al. 1986, where the term "energy profit ratio" is used, similar to the EYR described here. There are significant differences in what is measured by the different criteria, however. The NEY and EYR evaluate the "economic" energy required to deliver consumer energy to the economy and ignore the primary energy flows and energy losses. The GER, ERE, and EROI criteria, on the other hand, take account of resource use but may be less directly related to conventional economic measures. Clearly, no single criterion is adequate—each measures different characteristics of the energy-economy system.
9. For an early general discussion, see Georgescu-Roegen 1976, 10.
10. Baines and Bodger 1984.
11. Gall 1986.
12. After writing this, I came across the book *Beyond Oil* (Gever et al. 1987), in which essentially the same argument is described in the context of oil.
13. The literature is fairly substantial. For an introduction, see, for example, references in Penner 1981 and Gilliland 1977, 1978.
14. Penner 1981; Price 1974.
15. Slesser 1982.
16. Peet et al. 1987. Note that the calculations in this study treated all forms of energy in terms of their heating value according to the first law of thermodynamics. The greater ability of delivered electricity to do work is thus not given full credit. The general conclusions of the analysis are not affected by this point, however.

17. Probably the most comprehensive study of this type is Hall, Cleveland, and Kaufmann 1986.
18. Underwood and King 1989.
19. Holdren 1990.
20. Daly and Cobb 1989, 406 et seq.

CHAPTER 7—THE PHYSICS AND MORALITY OF GROWTH

1. Daly 1980b, 7.
2. Jonathan Porritt, quoted in Waring 1988, 130.
3. Blaikie 1987.
4. Daly 1991, chap. 5.
5. Bartlett 1978.
6. England 1990, 5; Solow 1956; Daly 1991, 115–18.
7. Quoted in Bartlett 1978, 877. Similarly, one of New Zealand's ministers of electricity stated, "During the next ten years power requirements would double, and double again in the following decade" (McGuigan 1973).
8. The rate required to double in ten years is actually a fraction higher than 7 percent, since the formula $t = 70/P$ is only an approximation, albeit a good one.
9. Bauer 1974; Hitchcock 1975.
10. The equation is given in Bartlett 1978.
11. Bartlett 1978, 1.
12. This is described in Odum and Odum 1976 and in Hall, Cleveland, and Kaufmann 1986. Hall (page 118) gives the logistic equation (in the context of the rate of population increase) as

    $N_{t + dt} = N_t + N_t \times r(1 - N_t/K)$, where r is the intrinsic rate of population increase per dt units of time, N_t is the present population level, K is the population level at the carrying capacity, and t is the time interval.

13. Georgescu-Roegen 1977; Daly 1991, chap. 5.
14. Thurow 1980, 120.
15. Galbraith 1958; Thurow 1980.
16. Lebow, quoted in Seymour and Girardet 1987, 77.
17. Trainer, *So You Want to Save the Environment?*, 1990, 19.
18. Trainer, "Environmental Significance of Development Theory," 1990.
19. Daly 1980b, 5.
20. Norgard and Christensen 1984.
21. Tinbergen and Heuting 1991.
22. Wright 1989b.
23. Waring 1988, 40.
24. Galbraith and Salinger 1981, 153; see also several essays in Daly 1980a and Hirsch 1977.
25. There are significant exceptions in that new processes are often designed at the outset to minimize pollution. But the reason for existence of the process in the first place is seldom examined other than via the simple criterion of profit. I

have a recurring nightmare of an environmentally friendly nuclear warhead factory or nerve gas production unit!

26. Perrings 1987, 8.
27. David Brower, quoted in Bartlett 1978.
28. For a good survey, see Smith 1980, 215.
29. Ibid., 231.
30. Taylor 1975, 21.
31. Ibid., 18.
32. E. F. Schumacher, quoted in Taylor 1975, 20.
33. Smith 1980, 227.
34. Taylor 1975, 27.
35. Galbraith 1958, 27.
36. England and Bluestone 1973, 190.
37. Daly 1987b.
38. Vitousek et al. 1986.
39. See, for example, Meadows 1977.
40. Watt et al. 1977.
41. Drucker 1987.
42. Daly 1980c, 349.
43. Lord Thomas Balough, quoted in Daly 1980c, 349.
44. Taylor 1975, 40.
45. Easton 1984.

CHAPTER 8—FEEDBACKS AND EXTERNALITIES

1. Quoted in McKibben 1989, 50.
2. McKibben 1989, 50.
3. Brundtland 1986. So far as I know, the first estimates were made by Arrhenius and published in *Philosophical Transactions of the Royal Society of London* around 1895.
4. The most important atmospheric gas contributing to the greenhouse effect is water vapor. Its concentration is strongly influenced by solar radiation, sea and land surface properties, and so forth, and is one of the most powerful determinants of weather and climate. But the concentration of water vapor arises from other influences, such as solar radiation and the presence of greenhouse gases, and is not *directly* the result of human economic activity, although it is powerfully affected indirectly.
5. Early data have been obtained from analysis of air pockets trapped in glaciers— the air has been reliably analyzed only for the past forty or so years.
6. Sagan 1990a.
7. Goodland, Daly, and El Serafy 1991, 11.
8. *Ecologist* 1990.
9. Kenneth Boulding, quoted in Royal Society of New Zealand, 1986, iv.
10. *Ecologist* 1972, 25.

11. I am grateful for Neville Bennett's assistance in clarifying this argument for me.
12. Haavelmo and Hansen 1991, 34.
13. Perrings 1987, 164.
14. Waring 1988, 126–30.
15. Benedick 1991, 20.
16. Hardin 1968.
17. But see my little story, Peet 1990.
18. Whitehead 1948, 17.
19. Levine 1986.
20. This occurred in such events as the Land Clearances in Britain.
21. Waring 1988, 20.
22. Kerr and Sharp 1987.
23. In this context, I would comment that a rare bird or animal whose survival is at risk should not be seen in isolation as a problem on its own. Often, such *indicator species* are used by ecologists to clarify questions about the general ecological situation in which they live. They should not be seen as separate from their environment.
24. Rifkin 1981, 81.
25. Daly 1987a, 84.
26. Waring 1988, prologue.
27. See, for example, Clark 1990, 19, 21.
28. Brundtland 1986.
29. McKibben 1989, 105.

CHAPTER 9—MYTHS OF THE POLITICAL-ECONOMIC WORLD VIEW

1. Mishan 1980, 279.
2. These ideas apparently originated in some of the writings of Marx in the nineteenth century and have been strongly supported by both Marxist and right-wing economists for a long time. Their roots, however, are still deeply in the "frontier" stage of industrial development, in which new, undiscovered resources were always available. See, for example, Opschoor 1985.
3. W. Leiss, "Instrumental Rationality; the Domination of Nature and Why We Do Not Need an Environmental Ethic," in *Environmental Ethics: Philosophical and Policy Perspectives*, ed. P. Hansen (Burnaby, British Columbia: Simon Fraser University Publications), 178. Quoted in Rees 1990, 1.
4. Weinberg and Goeller 1976 (see also Daly 1985); Simon 1980, 1981, 1982; Beckerman 1975.
5. Georgescu-Roegen 1976, 16.
6. Catton 1980, 188.
7. Hall 1990.
8. Cobb 1980, 162.
9. Genesis 1 and 2.

10. Again, I use the term "man" here to indicate the male, patriarchal, hierarchical tradition that stems from a literal adherence to the texts of the Bible.
11. Lewis 1980, 178.
12. Taylor 1975; Morton 1986.
13. Cobb 1980.
14. Daly 1980a, 371; see also Daly and Cobb 1989, chap. 20.
15. Mishan 1980, 268.
16. Jesson 1987.
17. Galbraith and Salinger 1981, 162.
18. Goodwin 1991.
19. Thurow 1984, 222–23.
20. Wiles 1984, 317; Bensusan-Butt 1978, 151.
21. Cant 1984.
22. Lutz and Lux 1988.
23. De la Cour 1990; Maslow 1954.
24. Andreski 1972.
25. Popper 1985, 359.
26. Ibid., 365.
27. Popper 1983, 6 (emphasis added). I have replaced gender-specific terms with more inclusive ones in these quotations.
28. Blaug 1980, 256.
29. Lutz and Lux 1988, 198.
30. I am grateful to John Sterman for information on this topic (see Sterman 1990b).
31. Frank 1990.
32. Blaug 1980.
33. Hay 1990.
34. See, for example, Martino 1980.
35. Aotearoa is a name commonly used nowadays by the Maori for the country named New Zealand by the seventeenth-century Dutch explorer Abel Tasman.
36. O'Connor 1991b. See also Hyde 1983.
37. Smith 1989; Barbier et al. 1990.
38. Block 1990.
39. Galbraith and Salinger 1978.
40. Here, I would note that in the sense of political theories of society, individualism requires the whole to be seen as simply the sum of its parts, whereas collectivism requires the whole to have no parts. Both models are absurd caricatures of human social behavior, but they are the basis of the two dominant world political ideologies. Much of modern social science passed these simple models by long ago. The systems approach helps us understand that although the truth may have some elements of both models, it also has a great deal more besides, including emergent properties not visible from either perspective.
41. Haavelmo and Hansen 1991, 33.

42. Thurow 1984, xviii.
43. Eichner 1985.
44. Thurow 1984, 21.
45. Richard Posner, *Economic Analysis of Law* (Boston: Little, Brown, 1984), quoted in Sagoff 1984, 147; Lutz and Lux 1988, 187.
46. Daly 1991, 186.
47. Schumacher 1974, 37.
48. Lutz and Lux 1988, 145.
49. Friedman and Friedman 1979.
50. Daly 1987b, 333.
51. Daly and Cobb 1989, 215.
52. Lutz and Lux 1988.
53. Bromley 1988, 16.
54. Goodwin 1991.
55. Hirsch 1977.
56. Galbraith and Salinger 1978; Galbraith 1977.
57. Richard Posner, quoted in Sagoff 1984, 147.
58. Wiles 1984, 313.
59. Hall 1990.
60. Slesser 1982, T1/39.
61. Fri 1987, 40, quoted in Christensen 1989, 33.
62. Daly 1980a, 365.
63. See, for example, Ehrenfeld 1978.
64. Rees 1990, 9.
65. Sagoff 1981, 1296.
66. I am indebted to Jeanette Fitzsimons for parts of this analysis.
67. This view was expressed a short time ago in a ministerial briefing paper by the New Zealand Treasury.
68. Philip Woollaston, in Kerr and Sharp 1987, 6.
69. Goodland and Ledec 1987; Sagoff 1988; Gray 1990.
70. Clark 1990, 12.
71. I am grateful to Evelyn Entwistle for resource material for this and related sections.
72. Schumacher 1974, especially chap. 3; Kristol 1981; Thurow 1984; Arnoux 1982; Eichner 1985; Kuttner 1986; Kuttner 1984; Leontief 1971, 1982; Hall 1990; Lutz and Lux 1988.
73. Kristol 1984.
74. Hall 1990; Levins 1991.
75. Wiles 1984, 293.
76. Ibid., 296.
77. Waring 1988, 59.
78. Perrings 1987, 154.
79. Wiles 1984, 294.

80. Blaug 1980.
81. Lutz and Lux 1988—for example, page 193.
82. Kuttner 1986, 70.
83. Paarlberg 1968, 29.
84. I am indebted to Paul Dalziel for aspects of this argument.
85. Zsolnai 1991.
86. Abouchar 1989.
87. Kristol 1981, 1984.
88. See, for example, Leamer 1983; Leontief 1971; Phelps-Brown 1972; Sterman 1988.
89. Lutz and Lux 1988, chap. 9; Daly 1984.
90. Thurow 1984, 20.
91. Perrings 1987, 7.

CHAPTER 10—MYTHS OF SCIENCE AND ENERGY

1. Cohen 1980, 267.
2. Attributed to Alfred Marshall.
3. Gardner 1981.
4. Westrum 1976–77.
5. Miller 1984–85.
6. I hope the research and documentation I provide in this book is sufficient to protect me from the extremes of my own criticisms!
7. M. Diesendorf, in Diesendorf 1979, 5.
8. Stewart L. Udall, in foreword to Catton 1980, xii.
9. Ellul 1964, 105.
10. Ibid., 116.
11. Andreski 1972, 92.

CHAPTER 11—ECOLOGY VERSUS EXEMPTIONALISM

1. Dunlap 1983b.
2. Miller 1984–85.
3. Gregory 1985.
4. According to some commentators, academic disciplines are a major source of competing world views. See Cook 1981.
5. Simon 1980, 1435. See also Simon 1981, 1982.
6. Simon 1980, 1436.
7. Anders, Gramm, and Maurice 1978, 42.
8. Beckerman 1975.
9. Quoted by Bartlett 1985, referring to Simon 1980, 1436.
10. Beckerman 1975.
11. Holdren et al. 1980; Ehrlich 1981a, 1981b.
12. Ehrlich 1981b, 12.

13. Quoted in Viederman 1990a, 9; see also Robin 1991.
14. Dunlap 1983a.
15. Ibid.
16. Kuhn 1962.
17. Hall, Cleveland, and Kaufmann 1986; Kellog 1976.
18. See, for example, Daly 1985; Bartlett 1985; and Trainer 1986.
19. Tierney 1991.
20. Durrell 1986.
21. Harvey 1984.
22. Ibid.
23. I believe Ehrlich does in fact hold to this position, but some of his papers give the impression of a somewhat narrower viewpoint.

CHAPTER 12—HUMANITY SEPARATED FROM NATURE

1. England 1990.
2. Crowther 1976, 84.
3. It is, incidentally, also a reflection of the patriarchal, male-dominated cultural background from which the philosophy emerged.
4. I am indebted to Rifkin 1981, 23, for some of this argument.
5. Macpherson 1962, 3.
6. Rifkin 1981, 24.
7. Adam Smith, from *Inquiry into the Nature and Causes of the Wealth of Nations*, in Friend and Rapport 1991, 61.
8. Smith acknowledged that justice, defense, and some public services do not fit inside the market model.
9. Popkin and Stroll 1956, 36.
10. England 1990.
11. Toffler 1981.
12. Smelser 1979.
13. Taylor 1975, 56.
14. Arnoux 1982 and unpublished material communicated privately.
15. Jones 1990.
16. Deterministic chaos exists even in some simple nonlinear systems, as described in Gleick 1988 and Davies 1989.
17. Arnoux 1982; Watt et al. 1977.
18. McKibben 1989, 100.

CHAPTER 13—VALUES FOR A SUSTAINABLE FUTURE

1. Rees 1990, 2.
2. Georgescu-Roegen 1971, 21 (gender-specific language changed).
3. Smith 1979.
4. See, for example, Daly 1991, 6.

5. Daly 1980a, 365.
6. Ibid.
7. World Health Organization 1986.
8. Perrings 1987, 12.
9. McLean 1987.
10. Perrings 1987, 161.
11. Sax 1989, 7, 10.
12. I am grateful for Jeanette Fitzsimons's assistance in this discussion.
13. Perrings 1987, 7.
14. O'Connor 1991c.
15. See, for example, Sax 1989.
16. Scott 1986, 169.
17. Henderson 1984.
18. Daly 1980a.
19. Smith 1980, 232.
20. Daly 1980a, 10.
21. Howell 1986, 5.
22. Lutz and Lux 1988; Daly and Cobb 1989.
23. Perrings 1987, 152; Sax 1989.
24. Scott 1986, 172.
25. Sax 1989.
26. Leopold 1987, 223.
27. Opschoor 1988, 18.
28. Ibid, 20.
29. Ibid.

CHAPTER 14—ENERGY FOR A SUSTAINABLE FUTURE

1. Illich 1974, 16.
2. Zelby and Groten 1991.
3. Much of the material in the early parts of this chapter was inspired by Goldemberg et al. 1988.
4. Droste and Dogse 1991, 65. The remaining 14 percent of spending was categorized as "other."
5. Jeffery 1990.
6. Norgard and Meyer 1979, 264.
7. Steen et al. 1981; Goldemberg et al. 1988; Norgard 1979a; Sorensen 1981, 1982.
8. Ragland 1991.
9. Steen et al. 1981, 1.
10. Meyer and Norgard 1989.
11. Goldemberg et al. 1988, 5.
12. See, for example, Lyle 1944, 1947.
13. See, for example, Lovins 1990.

14. See, for example, Wright and Baines 1986.
15. See, for example, Ray 1990.
16. See, for example, several up-to-date and authoritative reports in Leggett 1990; also Bleviss and Walzer 1990.
17. See, for example, Hannon 1977; Daly and Cobb 1989.
18. See, for example, publications by writers such as James Robertson and Hazel Henderson.
19. See, for example, Jeffery 1990.
20. See, for example, Fitzsimons 1990.
21. *Energy Economist* 1991, 18.
22. That is one reason why we often hear the rich loudly proclaiming the desperate plight of the poor when prices go up; economic self-interest is well developed in some sectors of the population!
23. Train, Ignelzi, and Kumm 1985; Brown, Postel, and Flavin 1991, 83.
24. Norgard 1979a.
25. Zepke et al. 1981, 14.
26. Johansson, Bodlund, and Williams 1989; Bodlund et al. 1990; *Balaton Bulletin,* no. 28:2 (August 1991).
27. See, for example, many publications by Amory Lovins—for example, Lovins 1989.
28. This section leans heavily on a similarly titled paper by Baines and Peet (1990).
29. Baines 1989.
30. Holdren et al. 1980; Holdren 1990.
31. Baines 1989, ii.
32. Costanza 1989.
33. Baines 1989, 19–20.
34. Lovins et al. 1981 and many other publications by Amory Lovins and co-workers.
35. Wright 1991.
36. Hubbard 1991.

CHAPTER 15—SUSTAINABLE DEVELOPMENT

1. Ponting 1990; Clark 1989.
2. Daly 1980a.
3. I am indebted to my colleagues Janice Wright and James Baines for significant inputs to this chapter.
4. Wilken 1991.
5. Palmer 1989.
6. Trainer, "Environmental Significance of Development Theory," 1990.
7. I am indebted to Molly Melhuish (1989) for this material.
8. Melhuish 1989, 6.
9. Viederman 1990b, 1.

10. Brown et al. 1987; de Vries 1989; Pearce, Markandya, and Barbier 1989; Bartelmus 1989; Hare 1990; El Serafy 1991.
11. Cocklin 1988.
12. Hicks 1948, 172.
13. Hueting 1990a; Daly 1989a; Waring 1988.
14. Daly 1989b.
15. WCED 1987.
16. Ibid., 43, 44.
17. Hueting 1990a.
18. *Nature* 1987; Lohmann 1990.
19. WCED 1987, 43.
20. Wright 1989b.
21. Daly 1989b.
22. Costanza 1991a, 75.
23. Redclift 1987; de Vries 1989; Liverman et al. 1988.
24. de Vries 1989 (emphasis added).
25. Ibid., 68.
26. Henderson 1990.
27. The Maori, a Polynesian people, are indigenous to Aotearoa–New Zealand.
28. Palmer 1989, 14.
29. Baines 1989.
30. Daly 1984.
31. Rees 1990, 5.
32. Of course, I realize that since the economy is strictly a subsystem of the total system, the distinction is a little forced. Nevertheless, I believe this model is useful for the purposes of the discussion.
33. Daly 1984.
34. Daly 1987b.
35. Pearce 1988a.
36. Georgescu-Roegen 1971, 224–44; Daly 1991, 23.
37. Daly 1989a, 22.
38. Ibid.
39. Daly 1991, 22.
40. El Serafy 1989, 1991.
41. Herman Daly, various papers.
42. I recognize that in practice, prices are often determined according to power relationships and the (often unethical) imperatives of competitive advantage.
43. WCED 1987, 8.
44. Haavelmo and Hansen 1991, 31.
45. Daly 1988, 43.
46. Trainer 1986, 23.
47. King 1987, 4.
48. Tudge 1989.
49. Haavelmo and Hansen 1991, 37.

CHAPTER 16—ECOLOGICAL ECONOMICS

1. Wright 1989b.
2. Costanza 1991b.
3. See, for example, Faber and Proops 1985; Daly and Cobb 1989; Gray 1990.
4. Christensen 1989.
5. In this context, I mean technical (e.g., thermodynamic) efficiency, not economic (e.g., Pareto) efficiency of resource allocation.
6. *Ecological Economics* 1989, "Aims and Scope" (on back of title page).
7. Costanza 1991a, 72.
8. This is a suggestion by Herman Daly. Such criteria will probably be related to an entropic measure of throughput of energy and materials.
9. Daly 1984, 19–29.
10. Sagoff 1988.
11. Slesser 1989b; *Energy Economist* 1991.
12. Some of the material in this chapter was first presented to the Commission for Integrated Survey of Natural Resources of the Chinese Academy of Sciences, Beijing, 1990.
13. Gilliland 1977.
14. Maier-Rigaud 1990, 3.
15. Daly 1987c, 7. Also reprinted in Daly 1991, 191.
16. Repetto et al. 1989; Repetto 1990.
17. See, for example, the treatment in Daly and Cobb (1989), especially in the appendix; Opschoor 1989; Norgaard 1989b; Daly 1988, 41; Hueting 1990b; and Repetto et al. 1989. The German government is working on a measurement of gross ecological product (Hinrichsen 1991). Daly and Cobb's index of sustainable economic welfare (ISEW) has been tested for the U.S. economy in their book.
18. Brown, Postel, and Flavin 1991, 84; Tinbergen and Hueting 1991; Daly 1991, chap. 5.
19. Quoted in Brown, Postel, and Flavin 1991, 84.
20. Daly 1989a.
21. Pearce et al. 1989; Pearce 1988b; Pearce and Maler 1991.
22. Need and ability to pay are not the same thing; equity has no place in the logic of marketplace efficiency.
23. Pearce et al. 1989, chap. 7.
24. Albauer 1990.
25. Meister 1991.
26. Daly 1987c, 7.
27. O'Connor 1991c.
28. Sagoff 1988; Young 1991; O'Connor 1991b, 11–12, 34–35.
29. Daly and Cobb 1989.
30. Peet and Peet 1990.
31. But see Peet 1990.

32. Bertram, Wallace, and Stephens 1989.
33. Meyer 1990.
34. Meister 1991, referring to Bressers 1988.
35. See, for example, Andreasson 1990.
36. I am indebted to James Baines for some of the material in the following section, reported in Baines et al. 1988 and Baines 1989.
37. Page 1978, 188.
38. Page 1978; Goodland and Ledec 1987; Saeed 1985.
39. Goodland and Ledec 1987, 39.
40. Daly 1989a.
41. Page 1978, 204.
42. Schuller 1991.
43. Goodland and Ledec 1987, 21.
44. Tinbergen and Hueting 1991.
45. Faber and Proops 1985.
46. Harris 1990.
47. See, for example, papers in Ahmad, El Serafy, and Lutz 1989.
48. Wright 1989a.
49. Stigliani 1990; Friend and Rapport 1991.
50. El Serafy 1991.
51. See, for example, Slesser 1978; Slesser and King 1988; Peet and Baines 1986; and Gilliland 1978.
52. King 1987.
53. Slesser 1989a, 423.
54. Comprehensive software resources, under the title of ECCO, are available from Malcolm Slesser at the Resource Use Institute, 12 Findhorn Place, Edinburgh EH9, Scotland.
55. See, for example, Odum and Odum 1976; Odum 1983, 1988.
56. Norgard and Christensen 1991, 15.

CHAPTER 17—WITH PEOPLE'S WISDOM: STEWARDSHIP AND SUFFICIENCY

1. Yarmol-Franko 1989, 1.
2. I am grateful to Katherine Peet for many of the insights I share in this chapter.
3. Bladt 1985.
4. Here, I refer only to Western society, with which I am familiar. Other cultures have different models. See, for example, the Indian example given in Prakash, Revi, and Khosla 1986.
5. Goodwin 1991. See also other papers in the same issue of *World Development*.
6. For some writers (e.g., Goodwin 1991), the third sector may be subdivided further into community and family components.
7. Meadows 1990.

8. Probably the most advanced model of this type is Beer's viable system model (VSM). See, for example, Espejo and Harnden 1989.
9. Harris 1990.
10. Ackoff 1981, 51–52.
11. Artemus Ward (1834–1867), from the *Oxford Dictionary of Quotations*.
12. Norgaard 1989a.
13. Yarmol-Franko 1989.
14. Finger 1989; Sutton 1989; Hurst 1989; Chaudhary 1989.
15. For some other models, see Clark 1989.
16. Meadows 1990.
17. Meadows 1989; Meadows and Van der Waals 1990; Moorhead Kennedy Institute 1990; Slesser 1990; Sterman 1990; Johnson 1990.
18. Heerdegen 1990.
19. Clark 1989.
20. Gray 1988; Gray et al. 1988; Gray 1990. I am most grateful to Maurice Gray for helping me in this area.
21. Here, I would contrast the Maori model of humans in their environment (in which God, people, and nature are intimately linked in a complex, integrated systems relationship) with that of the classical Western hierarchical, linear tradition, derived from Greek origins (in which God stands above people ["man"], who in turn have dominion over nature) (Taylor 1975; Morton 1986).
22. Hyde 1983; Clark 1989.
23. See also Sax 1989, 4.
24. See also Hyde 1983.
25. See, for example, Williams 1988.
26. Gray 1988.
27. The (sociological-anthropological) idea of the Gift reflects some very complex aspects of human group behavior. It should not be confused with the economist's idea of altruism (Pearce, Markandya, and Barbier 1989, 76), which relates to individuals in a neoclassical behavioral model.
28. Titmuss 1971; Hyde 1983.
29. Clark 1989, 237.
30. Much of this section came from Peet and Peet 1990.
31. Lifelong Learning Task Force 1985.
32. UNESCO 1985, 1.
33. Finger 1989.
34. Ravetz 1990.
35. "Popular knowledge" should not be confused with "popular culture," a term used by sociologists in the United States. The latter term applies to the most visible level of culture, found between the extremes of elite and folk cultures. Its application outside the United States and perhaps some European countries is questionable. See, for example, Sarachchandra 1989.
36. Tandon n.d.

37. Danish Research and Development Centre for Adult Education 1988.
38. Highlander Research and Education Center 1989.
39. Highlander Research and Education Center 1990.
40. Merrifield 1989.
41. Ariyaratne 1988, 2.
42. Sarvodaya Shramadana 1987, 3.
43. Ariyaratne 1988.
44. Ibid.
45. Ibid.
46. See, for example, Clark 1989.
47. I am indebted to the late Fr. John Curnow for these insights.

CHAPTER 18—CONCLUSION

1. Durrell 1986.
2. Binswanger, Faber, and Manstetten 1990.
3. Gow 1991, 8.
4. Costanza 1989.
5. Norgaard 1988; Costanza 1991a.
6. Scott 1986, 172.
7. Harris 1990.
8. Henderson 1990.
9. Brown and Postel 1987.
10. Pountney 1986.
11. Jones 1990.
12. Daly and Cobb 1989.
13. Weiss 1989; Sax 1989.
14. Shrybman 1990.
15. Taylor 1975.
16. Tauroa 1986.
17. Sagan 1990b.
18. J. B. Opschoor, IVM, Free University, Amsterdam, private communication.
19. See, for example, Gould 1990.
20. Brown, Postel, and Flavin 1991, 85.

APPENDIX—THE VENICE DECLARATION

1. UNESCO 1986.

References

Abouchar, Alan. 1989. "Through the (Economics) Glass Darkly." *Challenge* (May–June): 41–47.

Ackoff, Russell. 1981. "Our Changing Concept of Planning." Chap. 3 in *Creating the Corporate Future*. New York: Wiley.

Ahmad, Y., Salah El Serafy, and Ernst Lutz, eds. 1989. *Environmental Accounting for Sustainable Development*. Washington, DC: World Bank.

Albauer, Hans-Peter. 1990. Institut fur Festkorperphysik, Vienna, Austria. Talk given at ninth annual Balaton Group meeting, August–September, Csopak, Hungary.

Anders, G., W. P. Gramm, and S. C. Maurice. 1978. "Does Resource Conservation Pay?" Original Paper no. 14. Los Angeles: International Institute of Economic research.

Andreasson, Ing-Marie. 1990. "Costs for Reducing Farmers' Use of Nitrogen in Gotland, Sweden." *Ecological Economics* 2 (4): 287–99.

Andreski, Stanislav. 1972. *Social Sciences as Sorcery*. New York: St. Martin's Press.

Ariyaratne, A. T. 1988. "The Challenge of Continuity in Community Awakening: The Realization of Sarvodaya Objectives in the Present Context of Sri Lanka." Talk given at NOVIB headquarters, Den Haag, Netherlands, 4 February.

Arnoux, Louis. 1982. *Energy Within Without*. New Zealand Energy Research and Development Committee draft report. Auckland, New Zealand: University of Auckland.

Arthur, W. Brian. 1990. "Positive Feedbacks in the Economy." *Scientific American*, February, 92–99.

Ayres, Robert U. 1978. *Resources, Environment, and Economics: Applications of the Materials/Energy Balance Principle*. New York: Wiley.

———. 1988. *Self-Organization in Biology and Economics*. IIASA Research Report no. RR-88-1. Laxenberg, Austria: International Institute for Applied Systems Analysis.

Ayres, Robert U., and Steven M. Miller. 1980. "The Role of Technological Change." *Journal of Environmental Economics and Management* 7:353–71 (December).

Ayres, Robert U., and Indira Nair. 1984. "Thermodynamics and Economics." *Physics Today* 37 (November): 62–71.

Baines, James, and John Peet. 1989. *Direct and Indirect Energy Requirements of the New Zealand Economy: An Energy Analysis of the 1981–82 Inter-Industry Survey.* Market Analysis Report no. 89/1008. Wellington, New Zealand: Ministry of Energy.

———. 1990. "Sustainable Development and Stock Resources: Is There a Contradiction?" Paper presented at conference, The Ecological Economics of Sustainability, 21–23 May, at World Bank headquarters, Washington, DC.

Baines, J. T. ed. 1984. *Energy Data and Conversion Factors: A New Zealand Handbook.* 1st ed. Report no. 100. Auckland, New Zealand: University of Auckland, New Zealand Energy Research and Development Committee.

Baines, J. T. 1989. "An Integrated Framework for Interpreting Sustainable Development: Ecological Principles and Institutional Arrangements for the Sustainable Development of Natural and Physical Resources." Report submitted to the Ministry for the Environment, Wellington, New Zealand. Christchurch, New Zealand: University of Canterbury, Centre for Resource Management.

Baines, J. T., and P. A. Bodger. 1984. "Further Issues in Primary Energy Substitution." *Technological Forecasting and Social Change* 26 (3): 267 (November).

Baines, J. T., and D. J. Smith. 1982. *Environmental Energy Flows in the Ne Zealand Economic System.* Lincoln Papers in Resource Management no. 10. Canterbury, New Zealand: Lincoln College, Centre for Resource Management.

Baines, J. T., J. C. Wright, C. N. Taylor, K. L. Leathers, and C. O'Fallon. 1988. *The Sustainability of Natural and Physical Resources—Interpreting the Concept.* Studies in Resource Management no. 5. Christchurch, New Zealand: University of Canterbury, Centre for Resource Management.

Balaton Bulletin, Available from International Network of Resource Information Centers, Box 58, Plainfield, NH 03781.

Barbier, Edward B., Joanne C. Burgess, Timothy M. Swanson, and David W. Pearce. 1990. *Elephants, Economics and Ivory.* London: Earthscan.

Bartelmus, Peter. 1989. *Sustainable Development: A Conceptual Framework.* Working Paper no. 13. United Nations Department of International Economic and Social Affairs, DC 2 Room 2108, United Nations, New York, NY 10017.

Bartlett, Albert A. 1978. "Forgotten Fundamentals of the Energy Crisis." *American Journal of Physics* 46 (1): 878 (January).

———. 1985. Review of *The Ultimate Resource,* by Julian Simon. *American Journal of Physics* 53 (3): 282 (March).

Bauer, H. E. 1974. "Projections of Electrical Energy Demand and Ultimate Resource." *New Zealand Engineering* 29 (12): 340.

Beckerman, Wilfrid. 1975. "The Fallacy of Finite Resources." *Bank of New South Wales Review,* no. 14: 10 (April).

Benedick, Richard Elliot. 1991. *Ozone Diplomacy.* Cambridge, MA: Harvard University Press. Reviewed in *Balaton Bulletin,* no. 28 (August 1991): 18–20.

Bensusan-Butt, D. M. 1978. *On Economic Man.* Canberra, Australia: Australian National University Press.

Bertram, Geoff. 1990. *Energy Intensity in New Zealand: A Working Paper.* Wellington,New Zealand: Victoria University of Wellington, Department of Economics.

Bertram, I. G., C. C. Wallace, and R. J. Stephens. 1989. *Economic Instruments and the Greenhouse Effect.* Wellington, New Zealand: Victoria University of Wellington, Department of Economics.

Binswanger, Hans-Christian, Malte Faber, and Reiner Manstetten. 1990. "The Dilemma of Modern Man and Nature: An Exploration of the Faustian Imperative." *Ecological Economics* 2 (3): 197–223.

Bladt, Rita. 1985. International Federation of Workers' Educational Associations executive. Talk given to IFWEA conference.

Blaikie, Jane. 1987. *National Business Review* (Wellington, New Zealand), 23 June.

Blaug, Mark. 1980. *The Methodology of Economics.* New York: Cambridge University Press.

Bleviss, Deborah L., and Peter Walzer. 1990. "Energy for Motor Vehicles." *Scientific American,* September, 103–9.

Block, Walter E. 1990. *Economics and the Environment: A Reconciliation.* Vancouver, British Columbia: The Fraser Institute. Reviewed by Doug Bandow in *Economic Impact,* no. 71 (1990): 78.

Bodlund, Birgit, Evan Mills, Tomas Karlsson, and Thomas B. Johansson. 1990. "The Challenge of Choices: Technology Options for the Swedish Electricity Sector." In *Global Warming: The Greenpeace Report. See* Leggett 1990.

Boston, Jonathan. 1987. "Buying and Selling Education: The Merits of Education Vouchers." Christchurch, New Zealand: University of Canterbury, Political Science Department.

Bressers, Hans Th. A. 1988. "A Comparison of the Effectiveness of Incentives and Directives: The Case of Dutch Water Quality Policy." *Policy Studies Review* 7 (3): 500–518 (Spring).

Bromley, Daniel. 1988. *Property Rights and the Environment: Natural Resource Policy in Transition.* Wellington, New Zealand: Ministry for the Environment.

Brown, Becky J., Mark E. Hanson, Diana M. Liverman, and Robert W. Merideth, Jr. 1987. "Global Sustainability: Toward Definition." *Environmental Management* 11 (6): 713–19.

Brown, Lester R., and Sandra L. Postel. 1987. "Thresholds of Change." *The Futurist,* September–October, 9–14.

Brown, Lester R., Sandra L. Postel, and Christopher Flavin. 1991. Chap. 8 in *Environmentally Sustainable Economic Development: Building on Brundtland. See* Goodland, Daly, and El Serafy 1991.

Brundtland, G. H. 1986. Essay in *Journal '86* (annual report of the World Resources Institute, Washington, DC), 25.

Bullard, C. W., and R. A. Herendeen. 1975. "The Energy Cost of Goods and Services." *Energy Policy* 3 (4): 268 (December).

Bullard, C. W., P. S. Penner, and D. A. Pilati. 1976. *Net Energy Analysis: Handbook for Combining Process and Input-Output Analysis.* CAC Document no. 214. Urbana: University of Illinois, Center for Advanced Computation.

Cant, Garth. 1984. "Towards the Third Millennium: The Geography of Information and the World of Work." In *Geography for the 1980s: Proceedings of the Twelfth New Zealand Geography Conference,* edited by I. F. Owens and A. P. Sturman. New Zealand Geographical Society Conference Proceedings Series no. 12, 1–16. Christchurch, New Zealand: University of Canterbury, Department of Geography.

Catton, William R. 1980. *Overshoot: The Ecological Basis of Revolutionary Change.* Champaign: University of Illinois Press.

Chaudhary, Anil K. 1989. "Environmentally Sound Alternatives: Setting the Context." *Convergence* 22 (4): 73–77.

Checkland, Peter. 1981. *Systems Thinking, Systems Practice.* New York: Wiley.

Christensen, Paul P. 1989. "Historical Roots for Ecological Economics—Biophysical versus Allocative Approaches." *Ecological Economics* 1 (1): 17–36.

Clark, Mary E. 1989. *Ariadne's Thread—The Search for New Modes of Thinking.* New York: St. Martin's Press.

———. 1990. "Rethinking Ecological and Economic Education: A Gestalt Shift." Paper presented at conference, The Ecological Economics of Sustainability, 21–23 May, at World Bank headquarters, Washington, DC.

Cleveland, Cutler J., Robert Costanza, Charles A. S. Hall, and Robert Kaufmann. 1984. "Energy and the U.S. Economy: A Biophysical Perspective." *Science* 225 (31 August): 890.

Cobb, John. 1980. "Ecology, Ethics, and Theology." In *Economics, Ecology, Ethics: Essays Toward a Steady-State Economy. See* Daly 1980a.

Cocklin, C. 1988. "Environmental Values, Conflicts and Issues in Evaluation." *Environmentalist* 8 (2): 93–105.

Cohen, J. M., and M. J. Cohen, eds. 1980. *Penguin Dictionary of Modern Quotations.* 2d ed. New York: Viking Penguin.

Colby, Michael E. 1990. *Environmental Management in Development: The Evolution of Paradigms.* World Bank Discussion Paper no. 80. Washington, DC: World Bank.

Collard, D., David Pearce, and D. Ulph, eds. 1988. *Economics, Growth and Sustainable Development.* New York: Macmillan.

Cook, Earl. 1981. "The Tragedy of Turfdom." *Social Science Quarterly* 62 (1): 23 (March).

Costanza, Robert. 1989. "What Is Ecological Economics?" *Ecological Economics* 1 (1): 3.

———. 1991a. "The Ecological Economics of Sustainability: Investing in Natural

Capital." Chap. 7 in *Environmentally Sustainable Economic Development: Building on Brundtland. See* Goodland, Daly, and El Serafy 1991.

―――, ed. 1991b. *Ecological Economics: The Science and Management of Sustainability.* New York: Columbia University Press.

Crowther, J. G. 1976. "Nature to Be Commanded Must Be Obeyed." *New Scientist*, 8 April, 84–85.

Daly, Herman E., ed. 1973. *Toward a Steady State Economy.* San Francisco: W. H. Freeman.

―――. 1980a. *Economics, Ecology, Ethics: Essays Toward a Steady-State Economy.* San Francisco: W. H. Freeman.

Daly, Herman E. 1980b. "Introduction to the Steady-State Economy." In *Economics, Ecology, Ethics: Essays Toward a Steady-State Economy. See* Daly 1980a.

―――. 1980c. "The Steady-State Economy: Toward a Political Economy of Biophysical Equilibrium and Moral Growth." Chap. 21 in *Economics, Ecology, Ethics: Essays Toward a Steady-State Economy. See* Daly 1980a.

―――. 1984. "Alternative Strategies for Integrating Economics and Ecology." In *Integration of Economy and Ecology—An Outlook for the Eighties. See* Jansson 1984.

―――. 1985. "Ultimate Confusion: The Economics of Julian Simon." *Futures*, October, 446–50.

―――. 1987a. "A. N. Whitehead's Fallacy of Misplaced Concreteness: Examples from Economics." *Journal of Interdisciplinary Economics* 2:83–89.

―――. 1987b. "The Economic Growth Debate: What Some Economists Have Learned But Many Have Not." *Journal of Environmental Economics and Management* 14:323–36. (Also published in Daly 1991, 224–40.)

―――. 1987c. *The Steady-State Economy: Alternative to Growthmania.* Population-Environment Balance monograph. (Also published in Daly 1991, 180–94).

―――. 1988. "On Sustainable Development and National Accounts." In *Economics, Growth and Sustainable Development. See* Collard, Pearce, and Ulph 1988.

―――. 1989a. "Sustainable Development: From Concept and Theory Towards Operational Principles." Paper presented at Hoover Institution conference, Population and Development Review. (Also published in Daly 1991, 241–60).

―――. 1989b. "Sustainable Development: Towards an Operational Definition." Unpublished draft. Washington, DC: World Bank.

―――. 1991. *Steady State Economics.* 2d ed. Washington, DC: Island Press.

Daly, Herman E., and John B. Cobb, Jr. 1989. *For the Common Good: Redirecting the Economy Toward Community, the Environment, and a Sustainable Future.* Boston: Beacon Press.

Danish Research and Development Centre for Adult Education. 1988. *New Approaches to Adult Education in Denmark.* Copenhagen: Danish Research and Development Centre for Adult Education.

Davies, Paul. 1989. *The Cosmic Blueprint.* London: Unwin Hyman, Flamingo.

Davis, W. H. 1980. Letter to the editor. *Science* 210 (19 December): 1304.

De la Cour, Peter. 1990. Material from The Green College, 17 Western Road, Oxford, United Kingdom.

de Vries, H. J. M. 1989. "Sustainable Resource Use: An Inquiry into Modelling and Planning." Ph.D. diss., University of Groningen, Netherlands.

Diesendorf, M., ed. 1979. *Energy and People.* Canberra, Australia: Society for Social Responsibility in Science (ACT).

Droste, Bernd von, and Peter Dogse. 1991. "Sustainable Development: The Role of Investment." Chap. 6 in *Environmentally Sustainable Economic Development: Building on Brundtland. See* Goodland, Daly, and El Serafy 1991.

Drucker, Peter. 1987. "Dramatic Shifts in the Global Economy." *Dialogue,* no. 75:2.

Dunlap, Riley E. 1983a. "Ecological 'News' and Competing Paradigms." *Technological Forecasting and Social Change* 23:203.

———. 1983b. "Ecologist Versus Exemptionalist: The Ehrlich-Simon Debate." *Social Science Quarterly* 64 (1): 200–203 (March).

Durrell, Gerald. 1986. In Durrell, Lee *The State of the Ark.* London: Bodley Head.

Easton, Brian. 1984. "Seven Days." *New Zealand Listener.*

Ecologist. 1972. "Blueprint for Survival." *Ecologist* 2 (1) (January–February).

———. 1990. Editorial, "The End of Industrialism," *Ecologist* 20 (5): 162–64 (September–October).

Ehrenfeld, D. 1978. "The Conservation Dilemma." In *The Arrogance of Humanism.* New York: Oxford University Press.

Ehrlich, Paul. 1981a. "An Economist in Wonderland." *Social Science Quarterly* 62 (1): (March).

———. 1981b. "Environmental Disruption: Implications for the Social Sciences." *Social Science Quarterly* 62 (1): (March).

Ehrlich, Paul R., Anne H. Ehrlich, and John P. Holdren. 1977. "Availability, Entropy and the Laws of Thermodynamics." In *Ecoscience.* San Francisco: W. H. Freeman. Also published in Daly 1980a, 44.

Eichner, A. S. 1985. "The Lack of Progress in Economics." *Nature* 313 (7): 427 (February).

Ellul, Jacques. 1964. *Technological Society.* New York: Random House, Vintage Books.

El Serafy, Salah. 1989. "The Proper Calculation of Income from Depletable Natural Resources." In *Environment and Resource Accounting and Their Relevance to the Measurement of Sustainable Income. See* Lutz and El Serafy 1989.

———. 1991. "Sustainability, Income Measurement and Growth." Chap. 5 in *Environmentally Sustainable Economic Development: Building on Brundtland. See* Goodland, Daly, and El Serafy 1991.

Energy Economist. 1991. "So Back to the Carbon Tax." *Energy Economist,* no. 18:13–18 (August).

England, Richard W. 1990. "Mechanical, Thermodynamic and Dissipative Phenomena: On the Relationship Between Economics and Physics." Paper presented at ninth annual Balaton Group meeting, August–September, Csopak, Hungary.

England, Richard W., and Barry Bluestone. 1973. "Ecology and Social Conflict." In *Toward a Steady State Economy. See* Daly 1973.

Espejo, Raul, and Roger Harnden. 1989. *The Viable System Model: Interpretations and Applications of Stafford Beer's VSM*. New York: Wiley.

Faber, Malte, and John L. R. Proops. 1985. "Interdisciplinary Research Between Economists and Physical Scientists: Retrospect and Prospect." *Kyklos* 38 (4): 599–616.

Feather, Frank, ed. 1980. *Through the '80s: Thinking Globally, Acting Locally*. Bethesda, MD: World Future Society.

Finger, Matthias. 1989. "Environmental Adult Education from the Perspective of the Adult Learner." *Convergence* 22 (4): 25–31.

Fitzsimons, Jeanette. 1990. "Energy Efficiency: Ten Reasons Why the Market Will Not Deliver." *New Zealand Engineering* 45 (10): 28–31 (November).

Frank, Robert H. 1990. "Beyond Self-Interest." *Dialogue*, no. 88:66.

Fri, R. W. 1987. "New Directions for Oil Policy." *Environment* 29 (5): 17–42 (June).

Friedman, Milton, and Rose Friedman. 1979. *Free to Choose*. San Diego: Harcourt Brace Jovanovich.

———. 1981–82. "Freedom to Choose." *Economic Impact*, no. 34:12.

Friend, Anthony M., and David J. Rapport. 1991. "Evolution of Macro-information Systems for Sustainable Development." *Ecological Economics* 3 (1): 59–76.

Galbraith, John Kenneth. 1958. *The Affluent Society*. Boston: Houghton Mifflin.

———. 1973. *Economics and the Public Purpose*. Boston: Houghton Mifflin.

———. 1977. *The Age of Uncertainty*. Boston: Houghton Mifflin.

Galbraith, John Kenneth, and Nicole Salinger. 1978. *Almost Everyone's Guide to Economics*. New York: Viking Penguin.

Gall, Norman. 1986. "Shock Looms as Oil Consumption Exceeds Discovery." *National Business Review* (Wellington, New Zealand), 19 September, 35. (Reprinted from *Forbes* magazine.)

Gardner, Martin. 1981. *Science: Good, Bad and Bogus*. Oxford: Oxford University Press.

Georgescu-Roegen, Nicholas. 1971. *The Entropy Law and the Economic Process*. Cambridge, MA: Harvard University Press.

———. 1976. *Energy and Economic Myths*. New York: Pergamon Press.

———. 1977. "The Steady State and Ecological Salvation: A Thermodynamic Analysis." *BioScience* 27 (4): 266 (April).

———. 1979. "Energy Analysis and Economic Valuation." *Southern Economic Journal* 45 (4): 1023.

Gever, John, Robert Kaufmann, David Skole, and Charles Vorosmarty. 1987. *Beyond Oil: The Threat to Food and Fuel in the Coming Decades*. New York: Harper & Row, Ballinger.

Gilliland, M. W. 1977. "Energy analysis: A Tool for Evaluating the Impact of End Use Management Strategies on Economic Growth." Paper presented at international conference, Energy Use Management, Tucson, AZ.

———, ed. 1978. *Energy Analysis: A New Public Policy Tool.* American Association for the Advancement of Science Selected Symposium no. 9. Washington, DC: American Association for the Advancement of Science.

Gleick, James. 1988. *Chaos: Making a New Science.* London: Sphere Books, Cardinal.

Goldemberg, Jose, Thomas B. Johansson, Amulya K. N. Reddy, and Robert H. Williams. 1988. *Energy for a Sustainable World.* New York: Wiley; New Delhi: Wiley Eastern Ltd.

Goodland, Robert, Herman E. Daly, and Salah El Serafy, eds. 1991. *Environmentally Sustainable Economic Development: Building on Brundtland.* Washington, DC: World Bank. (Page references refer to the draft version.)

Goodland, Robert, and George Ledec. 1987. "Neoclassical Economics and Principles of Sustainable Development." *Ecological Modelling* 38:19–46.

Goodwin, Neva R. 1991. Introduction to *Global Commons: Site of Peril, Source of Hope.* Special issue of *World Development* 19 (1): 1–15.

Gould, Stephen Jay. 1990. "The Golden Rule—A Proper Scale for Our Environmental Crisis." *Natural History,* September, 24–30.

Gow, Lindsay J. A. 1991. "Integrating Economic, Social and Environmental Policies." Talk given to Pacific Institute of Resource Management seminar at Turbull House, Wellington, New Zealand, 5 July. Wellington, New Zealand: Ministry for the Environment.

Gowdy, John M. 1991. "Bioeconomics and Post-Keynesian Economics: A Search for Common Ground." *Ecological Economics* 3 (1): 77–87.

Gray, Maurice Manawaroa. 1988. "Conservation in Contemporary Maori Tradition." Summary statement presented to the Centre for Resource Management at University of Canterbury and Lincoln College, Christchurch, New Zealand.

———. 1990. *Ka Taoka Tapu Maori O Te Ao Kohatu: Prized Treasures from the Traditional World of the Maori.* Canterbury, New Zealand: Lincoln University, Centre for Maori Studies and Research.

Gray, Maurice Manawaroa, J. A. Hayward, B. D. M. de Ronde, and D. J. Shearer. 1988. *The Treaty of Waitangi and Its Significance for the Resource Management Law Reform.* Christchurch, New Zealand: Ministry for the Environment, Centre for Resource Management, University of Canterbury and Lincoln College.

Gray, Rob. 1990. "Accounting and Economics: The Psychopathic Siblings. A Review Essay." *British Accounting Review* 22:373–88.

Gregory, Geoff. 1985. "Performance Indicators and Goals in Environmental Research." *New Zealand Environment,* no. 47:18.

Grubb, Peter J., and John B. Whittaker, eds. 1989. *Toward a More Exact Ecology. 30th Symposium of the British Ecological Society.* Oxford: Blackwell.

Haavelmo, Trygve, and Stein Hansen. 1991. "On the Strategy of Trying to Reduce Economic Inequality by Expanding the Scale of Human Activity." Chap. 3 in *Environmentally Sustainable Economic Development: Building on Brundtland. See* Goodland, Daly, and El Serafy 1991.

Hall, Charles A. S. 1990. "Sanctioning Resource Depletion: Economic Development and Neo-Classical Economics." *Ecologist* 20 (3): 99–104 (May–June).

Hall, Charles A. S., and Cutler J. Cleveland. 1981. "Petroleum Drilling and Production in the United States: Yield per Effort and Net Energy Analysis." *Science* 211 (6 February): 576.

Hall, Charles A., Cutler J. Cleveland, and Robert Kaufmann. 1986. *Energy and Resource Quality: The Ecology of the Economic Process.* New York: Wiley.

Hammond, K. R., J. Mumpower, R. L. Dennis. S. Fitch, and W. Crumpacker. 1983. "Fundamental Obstacles to the Use of Scientific Information in Public Policy Making." *Technological Forecasting and Social Change* 24:287–97.

Hannon, Bruce. 1977. "Energy, Labor, and the Conserver Society." *Technology Review,* March–April, 47–53.

Hardin, Garrett. 1968. "The Tragedy of the Commons." *Science* 162 (13 December): 1243–48. Reprinted in Daly 1980a.

Hare, W. L., ed. 1990. *Ecologically Sustainable Development.* Australian Conservation Foundation, 340 Gore Street, Fitzroy, VIC 3065, Australia.

Harris, Chris. 1990. University of Auckland, New Zealand. Personal communication.

Harvey, Clifford. 1984. Letter in *Technological Forecasting and Social Change* 25:361–62.

Hay, Peter R. 1990. "The Triumph of Market Liberalism: A Threat to the Environmentalist Agenda." *New Zealand Environment,* no. 65:17.

Heerdegen, Richard. 1990. *New Directions in Environmental Decision-Making: Scientific Perspectives on the Legal System.* Palmerston North, New Zealand: Massey University, Department of Geography.

Heilbroner, Robert L. 1980. *The Worldly Philosophers.* New York: Simon & Schuster, Touchstone Books.

Henderson, Hazel. 1984. "Post-Economic Policies for Post-Industrial Societies." *Revision* 7 (2): 19 (Winter 1984–Spring 1985).

———. 1990. "From Economism to Systems Theory and New Indicators of Development." *Technological Forecasting and Social Change* 37:2 (May). See also quote in *Balaton Bulletin,* no. 24 (June 1990):4–5.

Herendeen, R. A. 1978. "Input-Output Techniques and Energy Cost of Commodities." *Energy Policy* 6(2): 162 (June).

Hicks, John R. 1948. *Value & Capital.* 2d ed. Oxford: Oxford University Press, Clarendon.

———. 1980. *Causality in Economics.* Canberra, Australia: Australian National University Press.

Highlander Research and Education Center. 1989. *An Approach to Education Presented Through a Collection of Writings.* Highlander Research and Education Center, Route 3, Box 370, New Market, TN 37820.

———. 1990. *Highlander Reports,* Fall, 1.

Hinrichsen, Don. 1991. "Economists' Shining Lie." *Amicus Journal,* Spring, 3–5.

Hirsch, Fred. 1977. *Social Limits to Growth*. London: Routledge & Kegan Paul.

Hitchcock, H. C. 1975. *Proceedings of the Second New Zealand Energy Conference*, 80.

Hoare, Anthony G. 1988. "Energy for the Asking: Public Participation in Resource Development in New Zealand." *Applied Geography* 8:207–28.

Holdren, John P. 1990. "Energy in Transition." *Scientific American*, September, 157–63.

Holdren, John P., Paul R. Ehrlich, Anne H. Ehrlich, and John Harte. 1980. Letter in *Science* 210 (19 December): 1296.

Holdren, John P., et al. 1980. "Environmental Aspects of Renewable Energy Sources." *Annual Review of Energy* 5:241–91.

Howell, John, ed. 1986. *Environment and Ethics: A New Zealand Contribution*. CRM Publication no. 3. Published for New Zealand Environmental Council by Centre for Resource Management, Lincoln College and University of Canterbury, Christchurch, New Zealand.

Hubbard, Harold M. 1991. "The Real Cost of Energy." *Scientific American*, April, 36–42.

Hueting, Roefie. 1990a. "The Brundtland Report: A Matter of Conflicting Goals." *Ecological Economics* 2 (2): 109–17.

———. 1990b. "Correcting of National Income for Environmental Losses: A Practical Solution for a Theoretical Dilemma." Paper presented at the Conference on Ecological Economics, May, Washington, DC. Central Bureau of Statistics, Box 959, 2270 Voorburg, Netherlands.

———. 1991. "The Use of the Discount Rate in a Cost-Benefit Analysis for Different Uses of a Humid Tropical Forest Area." *Ecological Economics* 3 (1): 43–57.

Hurst, John. 1989. "Popular Education and the Fourth Biennial Congress on the Fate and Hope of the Earth." *Convergence* 22 (4): 63–70.

Hyde, Lewis. 1983. *The Gift: Imagination and the Erotic Life of Property*. New York: Random House, Vintage Books.

IFIAS. *See* International Federation of Institutes for Advanced Study.

Illich, Ivan. 1974. *Energy and Equity*. London: Marion Boyars.

International Federation of Institutes for Advanced Study. 1974. *Energy Analysis*. Report no. 6. Solna, Sweden: Ulriksdal Slott.

Jansson, A.-M., ed. 1984. *Integration of Economy and Ecology—An Outlook for the Eighties* (the Wallenberg Symposium). Stockholm, Sweden: University of Stockholm.

Jeffery, Jim. 1990. "Dirty Tricks: How the Nuclear Lobby Stopped the Development of Wave Power in Britain." *Ecologist* 20 (3): 85–90 (May–June).

Jesson, Bruce. 1987. Quoted by Simon Upton in "Realizing the Contradictions in Labour's Capitalism." *National Business Review* (Wellington, New Zealand), 13 February, 11.

Johansson, Thomas B., Birgit Bodlund, and R. H. Williams, eds. 1989. *Electricity, Efficient End-Use and New Generation Technologies and Their Planning Implica-*

tions. Lund, Sweden, and Chartwell-Bratt, Kent, United Kingdom: Lund University Press.

Johnson, R. Curtis. 1990. Emeritus Professor of Chemical Engineering, University of Colorado. Several papers on global modeling in an educational context. Contact address: 1400 Mariposa, Boulder, CO 80302.

Jones, Alwyn K. 1990. "Social Symbiosis: A Gaian Critique of Contemporary Social Theory." *Ecologist* 20 (3): 108–13 (May–June).

Kellog. 1976. Quoted in P. A. Bailey, *Mining Engineering,* January.

Kerr, Geoff N., and Basil M. H. Sharp. 1987. "Valuing the Environment: Economic Theory & Applications." *Studies in Resource Management 2* (Proceedings of workshop on nonmarket valuation). Canterbury, New Zealand: Lincoln University, Centre for Resource Management.

King, Jane. 1987. *Beyond Economic Choice: Population and Sustainable Development.* Edinburgh: University of Edinburgh, Centre for Human Ecology, and UNESCO.

Kristol, Irving. 1981. "The Crisis in Economic Theory." *Dialogue,* no. 52:5.

———. 1984. "The Dubious Science." *Dialogue,* no. 63:74.

Kuhn, T. S. 1962. "The Structure of Scientific Revolutions." Chicago: University of Chicago Press.

Kuttner, Robert. 1984. *The Economic Illusion: False Choices Between Prosperity and Social Justice.* Boston: Houghton Mifflin.

———. 1986. "On the State of Economics." *Dialogue,* no. 73:65–71.

Leamer, E. 1983. "Let's Take the 'Con' out of Econometrics." *American Economic Review* 73:31–43.

Leggett, Jeremy, ed. 1990. *Global Warming: The Greenpeace Report.* Oxford and New York: Oxford University Press.

Leontief, Wassily. 1971. "Theoretical Assumptions and Nonobserved Facts." *American Economic Review* 61:1–7.

———. 1982. "Academic Economics." *Science* 217 (9 July): 104.

Leopold, Aldo. 1987. *A Sand County Almanac.* New York: Oxford University Press.

Levine, Bruce L. 1986. "The Tragedy of the Commons and the Comedy of Community: The Commons in History." *Journal of Community Psychology* 14:81 (January).

Levins, Richard A. 1991. *The Whimsical Science.* Draft paper. St. Paul: University of Minnesota, Department of Agricultural and Applied Economics.

Lewis, C. S. 1980. "The Abolition of Man." *Economics, Ecology, Ethics: Essays Toward a Steady-State Economy. See* Daly 1980a.

Lifelong Learning Task Force. 1985. "Action for Learning and Equity: Opportunity for Change." Report submitted to the Minister of Education, National Council for Adult Education, Wellington, New Zealand.

Liverman, Diana M., Mark E. Hanson, Becky J. Brown, and Robert W. Merideth, Jr. 1988. "Global Sustainability: Toward Measurement." *Environmental Management* 12 (2): 133–43.

Lohmann, Larry. 1990. Editorial, "Whose Common Future?" *Ecologist* 20 (3): 82–84 (May–June).

Lovelock, James E. 1979. *Gaia: A New Look at Life on Earth.* Oxford: Oxford University Press.

Lovins, Amory B. 1989. "Abating Global Warming—At a Profit." *Rocky Mountain Institute* 5 (3): 1–2 (Fall).

———. 1990. "The Role of Energy Efficiency." Chap. 10 in *Global Warming: The Greenpeace Report. See* Leggett 1990.

Lovins, Amory B., L. H. Lovins, F. Krause, and W. Bach. 1981. *Least-Cost Energy: Solving the CO₂ Problem.* Snowmass, CO: Rocky Mountain Institute. Reprinted 1989.

Lutz, Ernst, and Salah El Serafy, eds. 1989. *Environment and Resource Accounting and Their Relevance to the Measurement of Sustainable Income.* Washington, DC: World Bank.

Lutz, Mark A., and Kenneth Lux. 1988. *Humanistic Economics: The New Challenge.* New York: Bootstrap Press.

Lyle, Oliver. 1944. *The Efficient Use of Fuel.* London: Her Majesty's Stationery Office.

———. 1947. *The Efficient Use of Steam.* London: Her Majesty's Stationery Office.

McGuigan, T. 1973. Quoted in *The Press* (Christchurch, New Zealand). 25 August, 16.

McKibben, Bill. 1989. "The End of Nature." *New Yorker,* 11 September, 47–103.

McLean, I. 1987. In *The Nuclear Predicament: Problems and Solutions,* edited by Colin J. Burrows, Peacewriters, University of Canterbury. Christchurch, New Zealand: Ilam Booksellers.

Macpherson, C. B. 1962. "The Political Theory of Possessive Individualism." Oxford: Oxford University Press.

Maier-Rigaud, Gerhard. 1990. Institute for European Environmental Policy, Bonn, Germany. "Interventions in Nature or Economy?—On the Scientific Background of a Conflict." Paper presented at conference, The Ecological Economics of Sustainability, 21–23 May, at World Bank headquarters, Washington, DC.

Malthus, Thomas. 1798. "The Principle of Population." In *Oxford Dictionary of Quotations,* 328. 3d ed. Oxford: Oxford University Press, 1979.

Martinez-Alier, Juan. 1987. *Ecological Economics.* Oxford: Basil Blackwell.

Martino, Joseph P. 1980. "Freedom and the Future of Local Action." In *Through the '80s: Thinking Globally, Acting Locally. See* Feather 1980.

Maslow, A. H. 1954. *Motivation and Personality.* New York: Harper & Brothers.

Maxwell, Judith A., and Alan Randall. 1989. "Ecological Economic Modeling in a Pluralistic, Participatory Society." *Ecological Economics* 1 (3): 233–49.

Meadows, Dennis L., ed. 1977. *Alternatives to Growth: A Search for Sustainable Futures.* New York: Harper & Row, Ballinger.

Meadows, Dennis L. 1989. Fish Banks Ltd. software package. Available from The Laboratory for Interactive Learning, Institute for Policy and Social Science

Research, Hood House, University of New Hampshire, Durham, NH 03824-3577.

————. 1990. "Gaming as a Tool for Designing Sustainable Development Paths." Notes presented at ninth annual Balaton Group meeting, August–September, Csopak, Hungary.

Meadows, Dennis L., and Barbara Van der Waals. 1990. *Games on Issue of Sustainable Development*. The Laboratory for Interactive Learning, Institute for Policy and Social Science Research, Hood House, University of New Hampshire, Durham, NH 03824-3577.

Meister, Anton D. 1991. "Overview of Economic Policies and Instruments." Paper presented at PIRM conference, 5–6 July, Wellington, New Zealand. Palmerston North, New Zealand: Massey University, Department of Agricultural Economics.

Melhuish, Molly. 1989. *Energywatch* (Wellington, New Zealand), no. 1:6–7. Review of article by J. Birkland-Corro, "Redefining the Environmental Problem," *Environment and Planning Law Journal* (July 1988); 109–33.

————. 1990. "Global Issues in Resource Management Bill." Draft copy of Occasional Bulletin, 1 February, 2. Wellington, New Zealand: Pacific Institute for Resource Management.

Merrifield, Juliet. 1989. "Putting the Scientists in Their Place: Participatory Research in Environmental and Occupational Health." In *An Approach to Education Presented Through a Collection of Writings. See* Highlander Research and Education Center 1989.

Meyer, Niels I. 1990. "Policy Measures in Implementing Energy Conservation and Renewable Energy: The Nordic Case." Talk given at ninth annual Balaton Group meeting, August–September, Csopak, Hungary.

Meyer, Niels I., and J. S. Norgard. 1989. "Planning Implications of Electricity Conservation: The Case of Denmark." In *Electricity, Efficient End-Use and New Generation Technologies and Their Planning Implications. See* Johansson, Bodlund, and Williams 1989.

Miller, Alan. 1984–85. "Psychosocial Origins of Conflict over Pest Control Strategies." *Agriculture, Ecosystems and Environment* 12:235–51.

Ministry for the Environment. 1988b. *Resource Management Law Reform. Directions for Change: A Discussion Paper*. Wellington, New Zealand: Ministry for the Environment.

————. 1988a. *People, Environment and Decision Making: The Government's Proposals for Resource Management Law Reform*. Wellington, New Zealand: Ministry for the Environment.

————. 1989. *Introducing the Resource Management Bill*. Wellington, New Zealand: Ministry for the Environment.

Mishan, E. J. 1980. "The Growth of Affluence and the Decline of Welfare." Chap. 18 in *Economics, Ecology, Ethics: Essays Toward a Steady-State Economy. See* Daly 1980a.

Moorhead Kennedy Institute. 1990. *Fire in the Forest*. The American Forum for

Global Education, Moorhead Kennedy Institute, 45 John Street, Suite 1200, New York, NY 10038.

Morton, John. 1986. "Dominion over Nature? The Christian Understanding of the Environment." *New Zealand Environment,* no. 49:9.

Nature. 1987. "Defining Half a Global Problem." Editorial in *Nature* 327 (7): 1–2 (May).

Norgaard, Richard B. 1988. "Sustainable Development: A Co-Evolutionary View." *Futures,* December, 606–20.

———. 1989a. "The Case for Methodological Pluralism." *Ecological Economics* 1 (1): 52.

———. 1989b. "Issues Related to the Linkage of Environmental and National Income Accounts." In *Environment and Resource Accounting and Their Relevance to the Measurement of Sustainable Income. See* Lutz and El Serafy 1989.

Norgard, J. S. 1979a. "The Gentle Path of Conservation." Paper presented at international conference, Energia Dolce per L'Europa, 17–20 May, Rome.

———. 1979b. "National Energy System Analysis for Denmark Up to Year 2030." Paper presented at International Conference on Energy System Analysis, 9–11 October, Dublin, Ireland.

Norgard, J. S., and B. L. Christensen. 1984. "Individual Attitudes in Scandinavia Point Towards a Low-Energy, Saturated Society." Paper presented at conference, 1984 Summer Study on Energy Efficiency in Buildings, 14–22 August, in Santa Cruz, CA. *Proceedings of the American Council for an Energy-Efficient Economy.* Vol. F.

———. 1991. *Balaton Bulletin,* no. 27 (April).

Norgard, J. S., and Niels I. Meyer. 1979. "The Industrialized Nations Must Give a Credible Energy Example." In *Changing Energy Use Futures,* edited by Rocco A. Fazzolare and Craig B. Smith. Vol. 1. Elmsford, NY: Pergamon Press.

Norton, Bryan G. 1990. "Context and Hierarchy in Aldo Leopold's Theory of Environmental Management." *Ecological Economics* 2 (2): 119–27.

O'Connor, Martin. 1989. "Codependency and Indeterminacy: A Critique of the Theory of Production." *Capitalism, Nature, Socialism,* no. 3:33–57 (November).

———. 1991a. "Entropy, Structure and Organizational Change." *Ecological Economics* 3 (2): 95–122.

———. 1991b. *Honour the Treaty? Property Right and Symbolic Exchange.* Policy Discussion Paper no. 11. Auckland, New Zealand: University of Auckland, Department of Economics.

———. 1991c. *Value System Contests and the Appropriation of Ecological Capital.* Working Paper in Economics no. 84. Auckland, New Zealand: University of Auckland, Department of Economics.

Odum, Howard T. 1983. *Systems Ecology.* New York: Wiley.

———. 1988. "Self-Organization, Transformity, and Information." *Science* 242 (25 November): 1132–39.

Odum, Howard T., and E. C. Odum. 1976. *Energy Basis for Man and Nature.* New York: McGraw-Hill.

Opschoor, J. B. 1985. "Church, Society and Change." In *Policies and Strategies Towards a Just, Participatory and Sustainable Society*, edited by Dideri Mattijsen. ERE Discussion Paper no. 330. Amsterdam, Netherlands: Ecumenical Research Exchange. (Paper obtained from the author at the Institute for Environmental Studies, Free University of Amsterdam [IVM/VU], Amsterdam, Netherlands.)

———. 1986. "Ecologizing Social-Economic and Scientific Progress." Paper presented at Ecoforum for Peace, 25–28 August, Varna, Bulgaria. (Paper obtained from the author at the Institute for Environmental Studies, Free University of Amsterdam [IVM/VU], Amsterdam, Netherlands.)

———. 1988. "Myopia versus Survival: Economic Decision-making and Ecological Sustainability." Unpublished paper by the director of the Institute for Environmental Studies (IVM). Amsterdam, Netherlands: Free University of Amsterdam.

———. 1989. *Towards Sustainable Development: Environmental Change and Macro Indicators*. Amsterdam, Netherlands: Free University of Amsterdam, Institute for Environmental Studies (IVM).

Paarlberg, D. 1968. *Great Myths of Economics*. New York: New American Library.

Page, Talbot. 1978. *Conservation and Economic Efficiency*. Baltimore: Johns Hopkins University Press, Resources for the Future.

Palmer, Geoffrey. 1989. Prime Minister and Minister for the Environment, New Zealand. Talk given to New Zealand Institute of Landscape Architects and New Zealand Institute of Town Planners, 6 June, Wellington, New Zealand.

Patterson, M. G. 1983. "Estimation of the Quality of Energy Sources and Uses." *Energy Policy* 11 (4): 346–59 (December).

———. 1989. *Energy, Productivity and Economic Growth: An Analysis of New Zealand and Overseas Trends*. Market Analysis Report no. 89/1006. Wellington, New Zealand: Ministry of Commerce.

Pearce, David, ed. 1975. *The Economics of Natural Resource Depletion*. London: Macmillan.

Pearce, David. 1988a. "Economics, Equity and Sustainable Development." *Futures*, December, 598.

———. 1988b. "Economists Befriend the Earth." *New Scientist*, 19 November, 34–39.

Pearce, David, and Karl-Goran Maler. 1991. "Environmental Economics and the Developing World." *Ambio* 20 (2): 52–54 (April).

Pearce, David, Anil Markandya, and Edward B. Barbier. 1989. *Blueprint for a Green Economy*. London: Earthscan.

Peet, John. 1987. "A Human Problem." Letter in *National Business Review* (Wellington, New Zealand), 31 July, regarding an article on the achievements of Gerard Debreu in the same journal, 10 July.

———. 1988. *Natural Resource Policy*. Occasional paper. Christchurch, New Zealand: University of Canterbury, Department of Chemical and Process Engineering.

———. 1990. "A Fable." *New Zealand Environment*, no. 64: 23–24.

Peet, John, and Katherine Peet. 1990. "With People's Wisdom: Community-Based

Perspectives on Sustainable Development." Paper presented at conference, The Ecological Economics of Sustainability, 21–23 May, at World Bank headquarters, Washington, DC. (Available from the author.)

Peet, N. J., and James T. Baines. 1986. *Energy Analysis: A Review of Theory and Applications*. New Zealand Energy Research and Development Committee Report no. 126. Auckland, New Zealand: University of Auckland.

Peet, N. J., James T. Baines, M. G. Macdonald, J. C. Tohill, and R. M. Bassett. 1987. "Energy Supply and Net Energy in New Zealand." *Energy Policy* 15 (3): 239–48 (June).

Peet, Katherine. 1989. "Mapping the Connections: Workers' Education in the 1990s." *Convergence* 22 (2/3): 7–11.

Peet, Katherine, Julie Colhoun, Kevin FitzGerald, Sandra Mechen, and Alma Russell. 1983. "Survey of Adult Learning Activities and Interests in South-East Christchurch and Lyttelton." South-East Workers' Educational Association, c/o Katherine Peet, 87 Soleares Avenue, Christchurch 8, Aotearoa–New Zealand.

Pen, James. 1990. "Towards an Ecologically Based Society: A Rawlsian Perspective." *Ecological Economics* 2 (3): 225–42.

Penner, P. S. 1981. "A Dynamic Input-Output Analysis of Net Energy Effects in Single-Fuel Economies." *Energy Systems and Policy* 5 (2): 89–116.

Perrings, Charles. 1987. *Economy and Environment*. Cambridge: Cambridge University Press.

Phelps-Brown, E. H. 1972. "The Underdevelopment of Economics." *Economic Journal* 82 (325): 1–10.

Ponting, Clive. 1990. "Historical Perspectives on Sustainable Development." *Environment* 32 (9): 4–9, 31–33 (November).

Popkin, Richard H., and Avrum Stroll. 1956. *Philosophy Made Simple*. New York: Made Simple Books.

Popper, K. R. 1983. *Realism and the Aim of Science*. London: Hutchinson.

———. 1985. "The Rationality Principle." In *Popper Selections*, edited by D. Miller, 359. Princeton, NJ: Princeton University Press.

Posner, Michael V. 1973. *Fuel Policy: A Study in Applied Economics*. London: Macmillan.

Pountney, Charmaine. 1986. Notes for speech, "Equity and Excellence."

Prakash, Sanjay, Aromar Revi, and Ashok Khosla. 1986. *A Transcultural View of Sustainable Development: The Landscape of Design*. Development Alternatives, 22 Palam Marg, New Delhi 110 057, India.

Price, J. H. 1974. *Dynamic Energy Analysis and Nuclear Power*. London: Friends of the Earth.

Prigogine, Ilya, and Isabelle Stengers. 1985. *Order Out of Chaos*. London: Flamingo.

Ragland, John. 1991. "Sustainable Agriculture as a Tool for International Development." *Sustainable Agriculture Information Exchange* 2 (1): 1–12.

Ravetz, Jerry. 1990. "Knowledge in an Uncertain World." *New Scientist*, 22 September, 2.

Ray, Dixy Lee. 1990. "Keeping Cool About Global Warming." *Economic Impact,* no. 70:64–67.

Redclift, Michael. 1987. *Sustainable Development: Exploring the Contradictions.* London: Methuen.

Rees, William E. 1990. "W/.y Economics Won't Save the World." Paper presented at conference, The Ecological Economics of Sustainability, 21–23 May, at World Bank headquarters, Washington, DC.

Regan, T., ed. 1984. *Earthbound: New Introductory Essays in Environmental Ethics.* New York: Random House.

Repetto, Robert. 1990. "The Case for Natural Resource Accounting." *Economic Impact,* no. 71:41–46.

Repetto, Robert, William Magrathy, Michael Wells, Christine Beer, and Fabrizio Rossini. 1989. *Wasting Assets: Natural Resources in the National Income Accounts.* New York and Washington, DC: World Resources Institute.

Rifkin, Jeremy. 1981. *Entropy: A New World View.* New York: Bantam Books.

Robin, Jacques. 1991. "The Ecological Choice: Inventing the Future of Our Planet." *International Society for Ecological Economics Newsletter,* no. 3, 4–5 (May). International Society for Ecological Economics, University of Maryland, Box 38, Solomons, MD 20688-0038.

Root-Berstein, Robert S. 1991. "Discovering the Art in Science." *Sciences* (New York), September–October. Reprinted in *Dialogue,* no. 92 (1991): 44–47.

Royal Society of New Zealand. 1986. *Lead in the Environment.* Miscellaneous Series no. 14. Royal Society of New Zealand, Private Bag, Wellington, New Zealand.

Rutherford, R. P. 1979. "Energy Policy and the Optimal Depletion of our Fossil Fuels." In *Energy and People. See* Diesendorf 1979.

Rutter, Michael, and Russell Jones. 1983. *Lead versus Health.* New York: Wiley. Quoted in Royal Society of New Zealand 1986, 7.

Saeed, Khalid. 1985. "Neoclassical Economics and Principles for Sustainable Development." *Ecological Modelling* 38:19–46. See also, by the same author, "An Attempt to Determine Criteria for Sensible Rates of Use of Material Resources." *Technological Forecasting and Social Change* 28:311–23 (1985).

Sagan, Carl. 1990a. "Croesus and Cassandra: Policy Response to Global Warming." *American Journal of Physics* 58 (8): 721–30 (August).

———. 1990b. "Guest Comment: Preserving and Cherishing the Earth—An Appeal for Joint Commitment in Science and Religion." *American Journal of Physics* 58 (7): 615 (July).

Sagasti, Francisco R. 1988. "National Development Planning in Turbulent Times: New Approaches and Criteria for Institutional Design." *World Development* 16 (4): 431–48, esp. 438, 442–43.

Sagoff, Mark. 1981. "At the Shrine of Our Lady of Fatima, Or Why Political Questions Are Not All Economic." *Arizona Law Review* 23:1286.

———. 1984. "Ethics and Economics in Environmental Law." Chap. 5 in *Earthbound: New Introductory Essays in Environmental Ethics. See* Regan 1984.

————. 1988. *The Economy of the Earth: Philosophy, Law and the Environment.* Cambridge: Cambridge University Press. Reviewed by Clive Potter in *Ecologist* 20 (3): 117 (May–June).

Sandelin, Singa. 1983. "Nationwide Planning as a Motivating Factor: Reflections on Images of Future and the Processes of Planning Systems." Paper presented to the European Conference on Motivation for Adult Education, 28 February–4 March, Hamburg.

————. 1985. "Intervention to Commission II." Paper presented at 4th UNESCO Conference on Adult Education, April, Paris.

Sarachchandra, Ediriwira. 1989. "Development and Traditional Values: Moral and Aesthetic." *Dana* (international journal of the Sarvodaya Shramadana movement, Sarvodaya Vishva Samadhi, Moratuwa, Sri Lanka) 14 (12): 9 (December).

Sarvodaya Shramadana. 1987. *Sarvodaya Shramadana Movement—A Mid Term Review.* Condensed version. Moratuwa, Sri Lanka: Sarvodaya Vishva Samadhi.

Sax, Joseph L. 1989. "The Law of a Liveable Planet." Paper presented at International Conference on Environmental Law, 15 June, Sydney, Australia.

Schuller, Phillip D. 1991. "Public Policy Issues for Sustainable Commerce." *International Society for Ecological Economics Newsletter*, no. 3: 6–7. International Society for Ecological Economics, University of Maryland, Box 38, Solomons, MD 20688-0038.

Schumacher, E. F. 1974. *Small Is Beautiful: A Study of Economics as if People Mattered.* London: Sphere Books.

Schwartz, Walter. 1989. *The New Dissenters: The Nonconformist Conscience in the Age of Thatcher.* London: Bedford Square Press.

Scott, Graeme. 1986. "An Ethic for Nature." In *Environment and Ethics: A New Zealand Contribution. See* Howell 1986.

Seymour, John, and Herbert Girardet. 1987. *Blueprint for a Green Planet.* New York:Prentice Hall.

Shallis, Michael. 1984. *The Silicon Idol: The Micro Revolution and Its Social Implications.* New York: Schocken Books.

Shrybman, Steven. 1990. "International Trade and the Environment: An Environmental Assessment of the General Agreement on Tariffs and Trade." *Ecologist* 20 (1) (January–February). Reprinted in *New Zealand Environment*, no. 65 (1990): 27–31.

Simon, Julian L. 1980. "Resources, Population, Environment: An Oversupply of False Bad News." *Science* 208 (27 June): 1431.

————. 1981. "Environmental Disruption or Environmental Improvement?" *Social Science Quarterly* 62 (1): 30 (March).

————. 1982. "Paul Ehrlich Saying It Is So Doesn't Make It So." *Social Science Quarterly* 63 (2): 381 (June).

Slesser, Malcolm. 1978. *Energy in the Economy.* London: Macmillan.

————. 1982. *A Thermodynamic Constraint on the Rate of Global Development.* Institute of Chemical Engineers Symposium Series no. 78. London: Institute of Chemical Engineers.

———. 1989a. "Toward an Exact Human Ecology." Chap. 18 in *Toward a More Exact Ecology. See* Grubb and Whittaker 1989.

———. 1989b. *UNITAX: Taxing Resources, not Labour. Protecting the Environment.* Hydatum/The Resource Use Institute, 12 Findhorn Place, Edinburgh EH9, Scotland.

———. 1990. ECCO simulation software. The Resource Use Institute, 12 Findhorn Place, Edinburgh EH9, Scotland.

Slesser, Malcolm, and Jane King. 1988. "Resource Accounting: An Application to Development Planning." *World Development* 16(2): 293–303.

Smelser, N. J. 1979. *Energy Restriction, Consumption and Social Stratification.* Committee on Nuclear Alternative Energy Strategies Supporting Paper no. 5. National Research Council. Washington, DC: National Academy Press.

Smith, Adam. 1979. "The Theory of Moral Sentiments." In *Oxford Dictionary of Quotations,* 509. 3d ed. Oxford: Oxford University Press.

Smith, Fred. 1989. Competitive Enterprise Institute. Quoted in *The Press* (Christchurch, New Zealand), 2 December.

Smith, Gerald Alonzo. 1980. "The Teleological View of Wealth: A Historical Perspective." Chap. 14 in *Economics, Ecology, Ethics: Essays Toward a Steady-State Economy. See* Daly 1980a.

Solow, Robert M. 1956. "A Contribution to the Theory of Economic Growth." *Quarterly Journal of Economics* 70 (February): 65–94.

Sorensen, B. 1981. "Renewable Energy Planning for Denmark and Other Countries." *Energy* 6:291–303.

———. 1982. "An American Energy Future." *Energy* 7:783–99.

Steen, P., Thomas B. Johansson, R. Fredriksson, and E. Bogren. 1981. *Energy—For What and How Much?* Lund, Sweden: University of Lund, Swedish Defense Research Institute and Environmental Studies Program. (Manuscript of translation of Swedish book published in 1981.)

Sterman, John D. 1988. "A Skeptic's Guide to Computer Models." In *Foresight and National Decisions,* edited by L. Grant, 133–69. Lanham, MD: University Press of America.

———. 1990a. Notes presented at ninth annual Balaton Group meeting, August–September, Csopak, Hungary.

———. 1990b. Various simulation games. Sloan School of Management, E52–562, Massachusetts Institute of Technology, 50 Memorial Drive, Cambridge, MA 02139.

Stigliani, William M. 1990. "Chemical Emissions from the Processing and Use of Materials: The Need for an Integrated Emissions Accounting System." *Ecological Economics* 2 (4): 325–41.

Sutton, Peter. 1989. "Environmental Education: What Can We Teach?" *Convergence* 22 (4): 5–11.

Tandon, Rajesh. n.d. *With People's Wisdom.* Videotape on origins of participatory research. Available from Highlander Research and Education Center, Route 3, Box 370, New Market, TN 37820.

Tauroa, Hiwi. 1986. Notes for speech, "Diversity and Education."

Taylor, John V. 1975. *Enough Is Enough.* London: SCM Press.

Temm, Paul. 1989. Talk given to Waitangi Tribunal, as quoted in *The Press* (Christchurch, New Zealand), 15 August.

Thurow, Lester C. 1980. *The Zero-Sum Society: Distribution and the Possibilities for Economic Change.* New York: Viking Penguin.

————. 1984. *Dangerous Currents: The State of Economics.* New York: Random House, Vintage Books.

Tierney, John. 1991. "A Wager on the World's Resources." *Dialogue,* no. 94:60–65.

Tinbergen, Jan, and Roefie Hueting. 1991. "GNP and Market Prices: Wrong Signals for Sustainable Economic Success That Mask Environmental Destruction." Chap. 4 in *Environmentally Sustainable Economic Development: Building on Brundtland. See* Goodland, Daly, and El Serafy 1991.

Titmuss, Richard. 1971. *The Gift Relationship: From Human Blood to Social Policy.* New York: Pantheon Books.

Toffler, Alvin. 1981. "Toward a Third Wave Civilization." *Dialogue,* no. 51:5.

————. 1985. In *Order Out of Chaos. See* Prigogine and Stengers 1985.

Train, Kenneth, Patrice Ignelzi, and Mark Kumm. 1985. "Evaluation of a Conservation Program for Commercial and Industrial Customers." *Energy* 10 (10): 1079–88.

Trainer, F. E. 1986. "A Critical Examination of the Ultimate Resource and the Resourceful Earth." *Technological Forecasting and Social Change* 30:19–37.

————. 1990. "Environmental Significance of Development Theory." *Ecological Economics* 2 (4): 277–86.

Trainer, Ted. 1990. *So You Want to Save the Environment?* Kensington, New South Wales: University of New South Wales, School of Education.

Tudge, C. 1989. "The Rise and Fall of *Homo sapiens sapiens.*" *Philosophical Transactions of the Royal Society of London* B325:479–88.

Turvey, Ralph. 1968. *Optimal Pricing and Investment in Electricity Supply.* London: George Allen and Unwin.

Underwood, D. A., and P. G. King. 1989. "On the Ideological Foundations of Environmental Policy." *Ecological Economics* 1 (4): 315.

UNESCO. *See* United Nations Educational, Scientific, and Cultural Organization.

United Nations Educational, Scientific, and Cultural Organization. 1985. *The Right to Learn.* Declaration from the 4th International Conference on Adult Education, April, Paris.

————. 1986. *Venice Declaration: Final Communiqué of the Symposium, Science and the Boundaries of Knowledge; The Prologue of Our Cultural Past* (7 March 1986). UNESCO, 7 Place de Fontenoy, 75700 Paris, France.

Viederman, Stephen. 1990a. "Changing the Environmental Behavior of Individuals and Institutions: Questions Toward an Agenda for Funders and Others Concerned with the Future." Draft manuscript, 6 December. Jessie Smith Noyes Foundation, 16 East 34th Street, New York, NY 10016.

————. 1990b. "Environment and Development: Lessons from the Past, Questions for the Future." Talk given at Columbia School of International Affairs, 29 November. Jessie Smith Noyes Foundation, 16 East 34th Street, New York, NY 10016.

Vitousek, Peter M., Paul R. Ehrlich, Anne H. Ehrlich, and Pamela A. Matson. "Human Appropriation of the Products of Photosynthesis." *BioScience* 34 (6): 368–73 (June).

Walker, Ranginui. 1988. "The New Whanau." *New Zealand Listener*, 13 February, 69.

Wallace, Cath. 1988. "Key Concepts in Reform Debates" *Eco News*, no. 8: 3 (March). Environment and Conservation Organization, Box 11-057, Wellington, New Zealand.

Waring, Marilyn. 1988. "Counting for Nothing: What Men Value and What Women Are Worth." London: Unwin Hyman.

Watt, Kenneth E. F., Leslie F. Molloy, C. K. Varshney, Dudley Weeks, and Soetjipto Wirosardjono. 1977. *The Unsteady State: Environmental Problems, Growth, and Culture.* Honolulu: East-West Center/University of Hawaii Press.

WCED. *See* World Commission on Environment and Development.

Weinberg, A., and H. Goeller. 1976. "The Age of Substitutability." *Science* 191 (20 February): 167–78.

Weiss, Edith Brown. 1989. *In Fairness to Future Generations: International Law, Common Patrimony and Intergenerational Equity.* Transnational, Box 7282, Ardsley-on-Hudson, New York 10503. Reviewed in *New Scientist*, 28 October 1989, 44–45.

Westrum, Ron. 1976–77. "Scientists as Experts: Observations on 'Objections to Astrology.' *Zetetic* (now *The Skeptical Inquirer*), 34.

Whitehead, A. N. 1929. *Process and Reality.* New York: Harper & Brothers.

———. 1948. *Science and the Modern World.* New York: Mentor.

Wiles, Peter. 1984. "Epilogue: The Role of Theory." In *Economics in Disarray. See* Wiles and Routh 1984.

Wiles, Peter, and G. Routh, 1984. *Economics in Disarray.* Oxford: Basil Blackwell.

Wilken, Gene C. 1991. "Sustainable Agriculture Is the Solution, But What Is the Problem?" Board for International Food and Agricultural Development and Economic Cooperation, Agency for International Development, Washington, DC 20523.

Williams, Betty. 1988. *Climate Change: The New Zealand Response.* Wellington, New Zealand: Ministry for the Environment.

World Commission on Environment and Development. 1987. *Our Common Future.* Oxford: Oxford University Press.

World Health Organization. 1986. "Vienna Dialogue." Reported in *Choices*, May–June 1987, 3. Wellington, New Zealand: New Zealand Department of Health.

Wright, Janice C. 1989a. *Natural Resource Accounting—A Technique for Improving Planning in New Zealand?* Information Paper no. 12. Christchurch, New Zealand: Lincoln University and University of Canterbury, Centre for Resource Management.

————. 1989b. Private communication.

————. 1991. *Indicators of Sustainable Energy Development.* Information Paper no. 28. Christchurch, New Zealand: Lincoln University and University of Canterbury, Centre for Resource Management.

Wright, Janice C., and James T. Baines. 1986. *Supply Curves of Conserved Energy: The Potential for Conservation in New Zealand's Houses.* Christchurch, New Zealand: University of Canterbury, Ministry of Energy and Centre for Resource Management.

Yarmol-Franko, Karen. 1989. Editorial in *Convergence* 22 (4): 1.

Young, Nick. 1991. "Free as Air?" *New Statesman & Society,* 26 July, 39.

Zelby, I. W., and B. Groten. 1991. "The Scope and Limits of Energy Policy." *IEEE Technology and Society Magazine* 10 (Spring): 16–24.

Zepke, N., M. Harpham, M. Barret, M. Niven, and P. Wilkins. 1981. *Contexts for Development: Clarifying Values.* Commission for the Future. Wellington, New Zealand: Government Printer.

Zsolnai, Laszlo. 1991. "Meta-Economic Choices." *Human Economy Newsletter* 12 (2): 6–7. Box 14, Economics Department, Mankato State University, Mankato, MN 56001.

Zukav, Gary. 1982. *The Dancing Wu Li Masters: An Overview of the New Physics.* London: Unwin Hyman, Flamingo.

Index

About the Author

John Peet is a senior staff member in the engineering faculty at the University of Canterbury, Christchurch, New Zealand. He obtained a degree in chemical technology from Edinburgh University, Scotland, in 1960. After working for a time in a paper mill, he moved to New Zealand, where he completed a Ph.D. in chemical engineering at the University of Canterbury. He subsequently worked as a process engineer in an oil refinery in Britain. Since returning to live permanently in New Zealand, his research work has concentrated on clarifying the links between energy policy and the environment, with particular interest in the function of economic tools.

He is committed to working with the insight and tools of engineering and science to help people in communities build a peaceful, just, and sustainable world.

Also Available
from Island Press

Overtapped Oasis: Reform or Revolution for Western Water
By Marc Reisner and Sarah Bates

Plastics: America's Packaging Dilemma
By Nancy Wolf and Ellen Feldman

The Poisoned Well: New Strategies for Groundwater Protection
Edited by Eric Jorgensen

Race to Save the Tropics: Ecology and Economics for a Sustainable Future
Edited by Robert Goodland

Recycling and Incineration: Evaluating the Choices
By Richard A. Denison and John Ruston

The Rising Tide: Global Warming and World Sea Levels
By Lynne T. Edgerton

The Snake River: Window to the West
By Tim Palmer

Steady-State Economics: Second Edition with New Essays
By Herman E. Daly

Trees, Why Do You Wait?
By Richard Critchfield

Turning the Tide: Saving the Chesapeake Bay
By Tom Horton and William M. Eichbaum

War on Waste: Can America Win Its Battle With Garbage?
By Louis Blumberg and Robert Gottlieb

Western Water Made Simple
From *High Country News*

Wetland Creation and Restoration: The Status of the Science
Edited by Mary E. Kentula and Jon A. Kusler

For a complete catalog of Island Press publications, please write:
Island Press, Box 7, Covelo, CA 95428, or call: 1-800-828-1302